Teach Yourself VISUALLY™ Office XP

From
maranGraphics®
&

Wiley Publishing, Inc.

Teach Yourself VISUALLY™ Office XP

Published by
Wiley Publishing, Inc.
909 Third Avenue
New York, NY 10022

Published simultaneously in Canada

Library of Congress Control Number: 2001091967

ISBN: 0-7645-0854-7

Manufactured in the United States of America

10 9 8 7 6 5 4 3

1K/RQ/QX/QS/MG

Trademark Acknowledgments

maranGraphics Inc. has attempted to include trademark information for products, services and companies referred to in this guide. Although maranGraphics Inc. has made reasonable efforts in gathering this information, it cannot guarantee its accuracy.

The maranGraphics logo is a trademark or registered trademark of maranGraphics, Inc.. Wiley, the Wiley Publishing logo, Visual, the Visual logo, Simplified, Master VISUALLY, Teach Yourself VISUALLY, Visual Blueprint, In an Instant, Read Less - Learn More and related trade dress are trademarks or registered trademarks of Wiley Publishing, Inc. in the United States and other countries and may not be used without written permission. All other trademarks are the property of their respective owners. maranGraphics, Inc. and Wiley Publishing, Inc. are not associated with any product or vendor mentioned in this book.

Important Numbers

For U.S. corporate orders, please call maranGraphics at 800-469-6616 or fax 905-890-9434.

For general information on our other products and services or to obtain technical support, please contact our Customer Care Department within the U.S. at 800-762-2974, outside the U.S. at 317-572-3993 or fax 317-572-4002.

Permissions

Expedia

Microsoft

Netscape

Netscape and Netscape Navigator are trademarks of Netscape Communications Corp.

Wiley Publishing, Inc. is a trademark of Wiley Publishing, Inc.

U.S. Corporate Sales

Contact maranGraphics at (800) 469-6616 or fax (905) 890-9434.

U.S. Trade Sales

Contact Wiley at (800) 762-2974 or fax (317) 572-4002.

Some comments from our readers...

"I have to praise you and your company on the fine products you turn out. I have twelve of the *Teach Yourself VISUALLY* and *Simplified* books in my house. They were instrumental in helping me pass a difficult computer course. Thank you for creating books that are easy to follow."

–Gordon Justin (Brielle, NJ)

"I commend your efforts and your success. I teach in an outreach program for the Dr. Eugene Clark Library in Lockhart, TX. Your *Teach Yourself VISUALLY* books are incredible and I use them in my computer classes. All my students love them!"

–Michele Schalin (Lockhart, TX)

"Thank you so much for helping people like me learn about computers. The Maran family is just what the doctor ordered. Thank you, thank you, thank you."

–Carol Moten (New Kensington, PA)

"I would like to take this time to compliment maranGraphics on creating such great books. Thank you for making it clear. Keep up the good work."

–Kirk Santoro (Burbank, CA)

"I write to extend my thanks and appreciation for your books. They are clear, easy to follow, and straight to the point. Keep up the good work!"

–Seward Kollie (Dakar, Senegal)

"What fantastic teaching books you have produced! Congratulations to you and your staff. You deserve the Nobel prize in Education in the Software category. Thanks for helping me to understand computers."

–Bruno Tonon (Melbourne, Australia)

"Over time, I have bought a number of your 'Read Less-Learn More' books. For me, they are THE way to learn anything easily."

–José A. Mazón (Cuba, NY)

"I was introduced to maranGraphics about four years ago and YOU ARE THE GREATEST THING THAT EVER HAPPENED TO INTRODUCTORY COMPUTER BOOKS!"

–Glenn Nettleton (Huntsville, AL)

"Compliments To The Chef!! Your books are extraordinary! Or, simply put, Extra-Ordinary, meaning way above the rest! THANK YOU THANK YOU THANK YOU! for creating these."

–Christine J. Manfrin (Castle Rock, CO)

"I'm a grandma who was pushed by an 11-year-old grandson to join the computer age. I found myself hopelessly confused and frustrated until I discovered the Visual series. I'm no expert by any means now, but I'm a lot further along than I would have been otherwise. Thank you!"

–Carol Louthain (Logansport, IN)

"Thank you, thank you, thank you...for making it so easy for me to break into this high-tech world. I now own four of your books. I recommend them to anyone who is a beginner like myself. Now... if you could just do one for programming VCRs, it would make my day!"

–Gay O'Donnell (Calgary, Alberta, Canada)

"You're marvelous! I am greatly in your debt."

–Patrick Baird (Lacey, WA)

maranGraphics is a family-run business
located near Toronto, Canada.

At **maranGraphics**, we believe in producing great computer books—one book at a time.

Each maranGraphics book uses the award-winning communication process that we have been developing over the last 25 years. Using this process, we organize screen shots, text and illustrations in a way that makes it easy for you to learn new concepts and tasks.

We spend hours deciding the best way to perform each task, so you don't have to! Our clear, easy-to-follow screen shots and instructions walk you through each task from beginning to end.

Our detailed illustrations go hand-in-hand with the text to help reinforce the information. Each illustration is a labor of love—some take up to a week to draw!

We want to thank you for purchasing what we feel are the best computer books money can buy. We hope you enjoy using this book as much as we enjoyed creating it!

Sincerely,

The Maran Family

Please visit us on the Web at:
www.maran.com

CREDITS

Author:
Ruth Maran

Directors of Copy Development:
Wanda Lawrie
Cathy Lo

Copy Editors:
Stacey Morrison
Roderick Anatalio

Technical Consultants:
Paul Whitehead
Joel Desamero

Project Manager:
Judy Maran

Editors:
Norm Schumacher
Faiza Jagot
Luis Lee

Screen Captures and Editing:
Teri Lynn Pinsent

Layout Design and Illustrations:
Treena Lees
Steven Schaerer
Suzana G. Miokovic

Illustrators:
Russ Marini
Paul Baker

Screen Artist and Illustrator:
Darryl Grossi

Indexer:
Teri Lynn Pinsent

Permissions Coordinator:
Jennifer Amaral

Wiley Vice President and Executive Group Publisher:
Richard Swadley

Wiley Vice President and Publisher:
Barry Pruett

Wiley Editorial Support:
Jennifer Dorsey
Sandy Rodrigues
Lindsay Sandman

Post Production:
Robert Maran

ACKNOWLEDGMENTS

Thanks to the dedicated staff of maranGraphics, including Jennifer Amaral, Roderick Anatalio, Paul Baker, Joel Desamero, Darryl Grossi, Faiza Jagot, Kelleigh Johnson, Wanda Lawrie, Treena Lees, Cathy Lo, Jill Maran, Judy Maran, Robert Maran, Ruth Maran, Russ Marini, Suzana G. Miokovic, Stacey Morrison, Hee-Jin Park, Teri Lynn Pinsent, Steven Schaerer, Norm Schumacher, Raquel Scott, Roxanne Van Damme and Paul Whitehead.

Finally, to Richard Maran who originated the easy-to-use graphic format of this guide. Thank you for your inspiration and guidance.

TABLE OF CONTENTS

GETTING STARTED

1) Getting Started

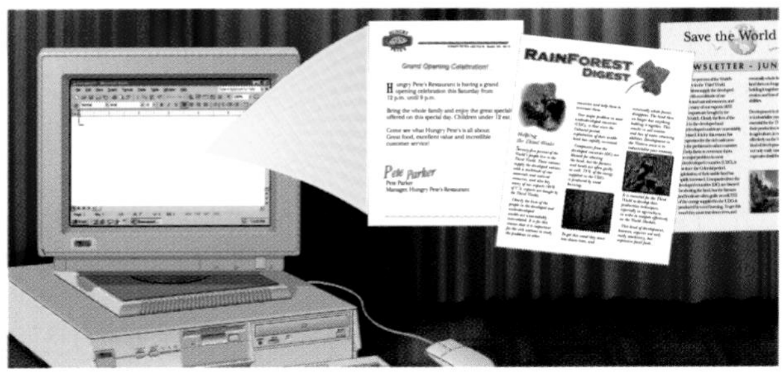

USING WORD

1) Getting Started

2) Save, Open and Print a Document

3) Edit a Document

4) Format Text

5) Format Pages

6) Working With Tables

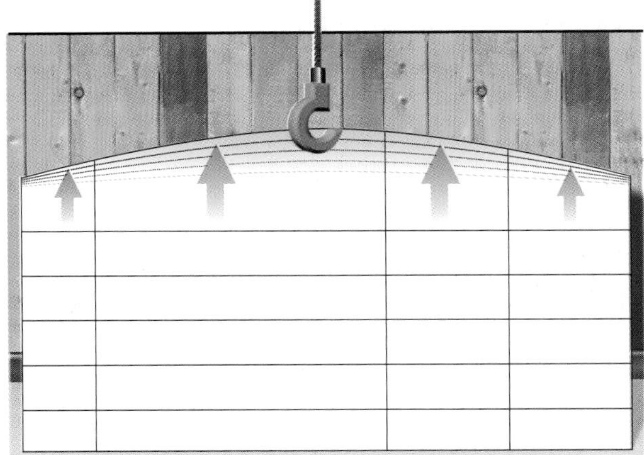

TABLE OF CONTENTS

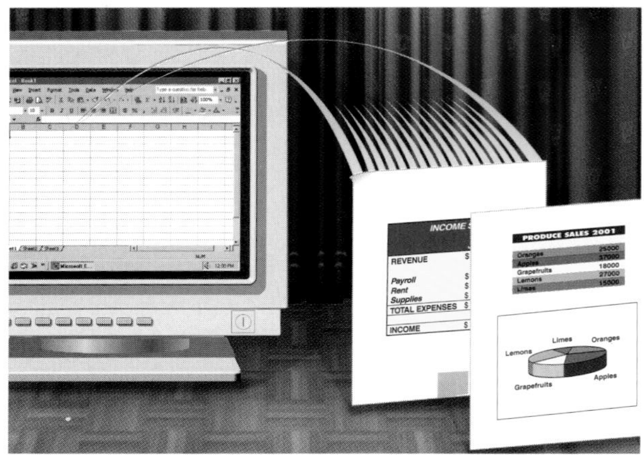

USING EXCEL

1) Getting Started

2) Save and Open a Workbook

3) Edit a Worksheet

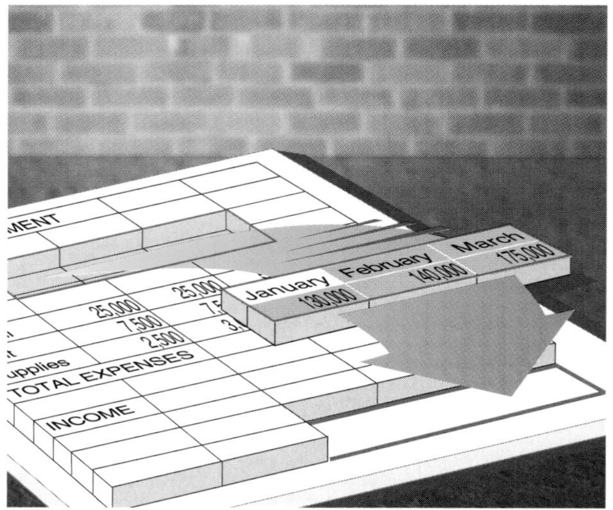

4) Using Formulas and Functions

5) Format a Worksheet

6) Print a Worksheet

7) Working With Charts

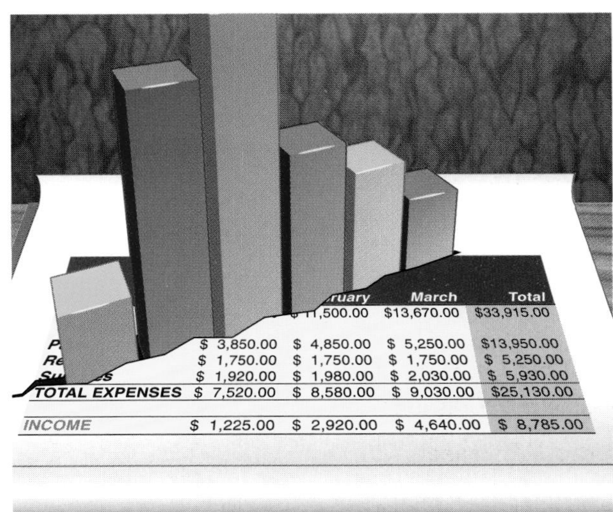

TABLE OF CONTENTS

USING POWERPOINT

1) Getting Started

2) Edit Slides

3) Add Objects to Slides

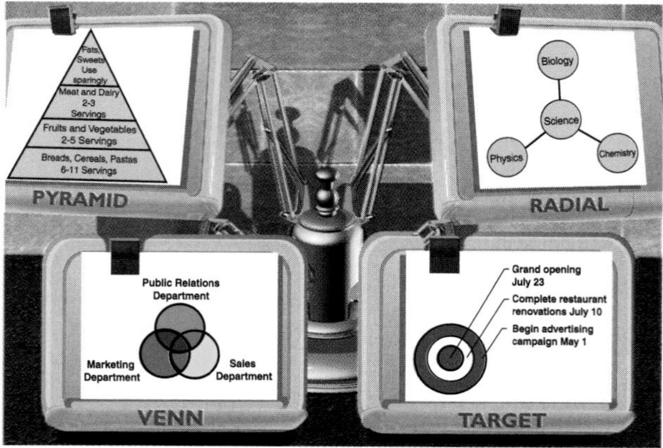

4) Enhance a Presentation

5) Fine-Tune a Presentation

USING ACCESS

1) Getting Started

2) Create Tables

TABLE OF CONTENTS

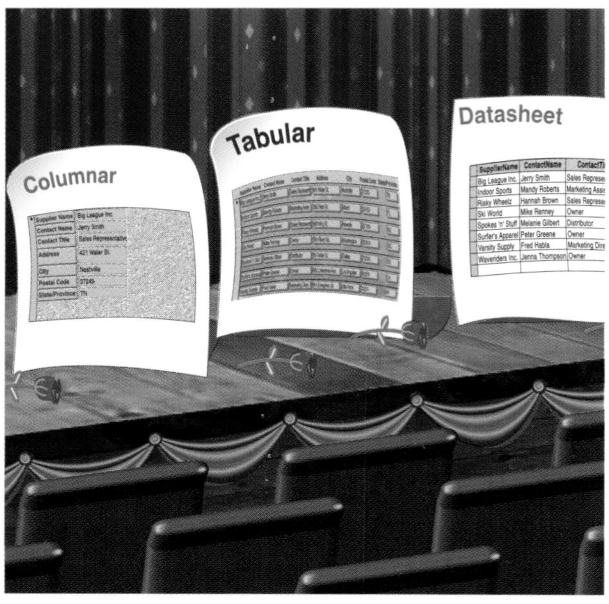

3) Create Forms

4) Sort and Find Data

5) Create Queries

6) Create Reports

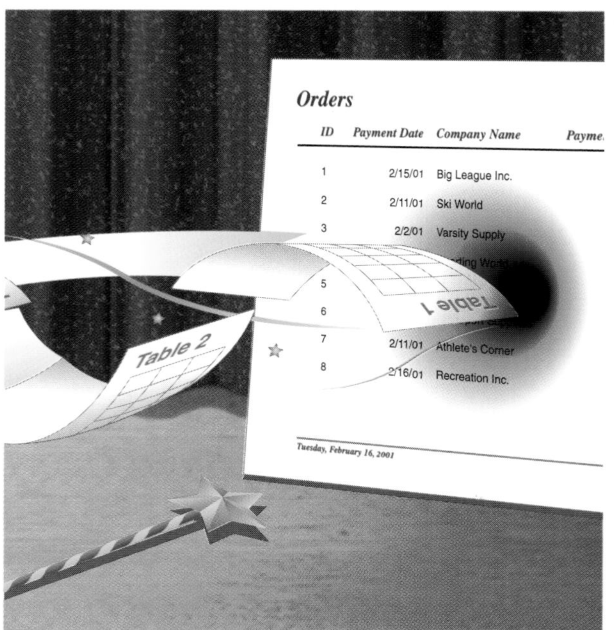

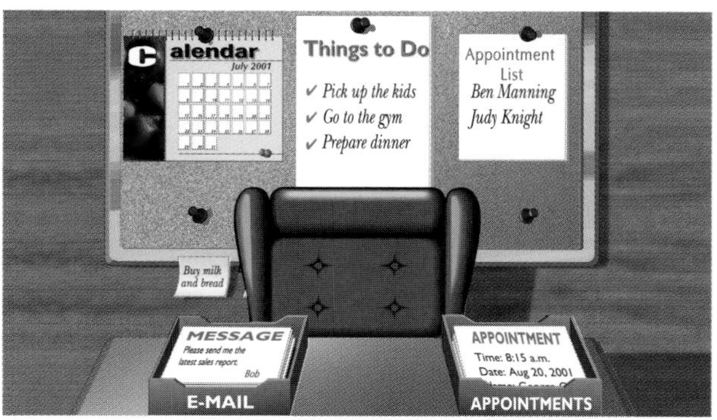

USING OUTLOOK

1) Exchange E-mail

2) Manage Information

USING SPEECH RECOGNITION

1) Using Speech Recognition

MICROSOFT OFFICE AND THE INTERNET

1) Microsoft Office and the Internet

INTRODUCTION TO MICROSOFT OFFICE XP

Microsoft® Office XP is a suite of programs that you can use to accomplish various tasks.

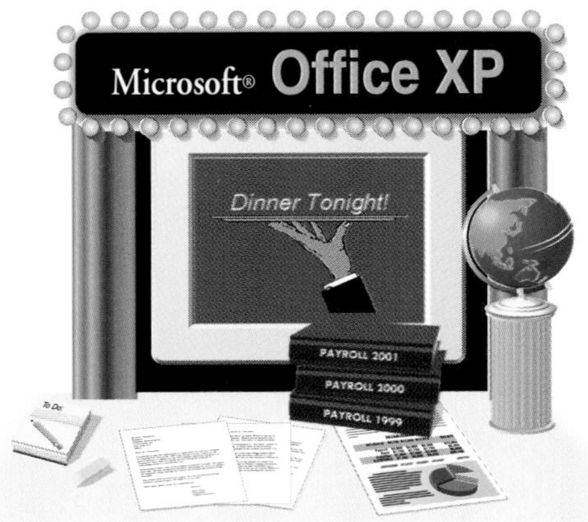

All Microsoft Office XP programs share a common design and work in a similar way. Once you learn one program, you can easily learn the others.

Word

Word is a word processing program that you can use to quickly and efficiently create documents such as letters, memos and reports. Word offers many features that make it easy to edit and format your documents.

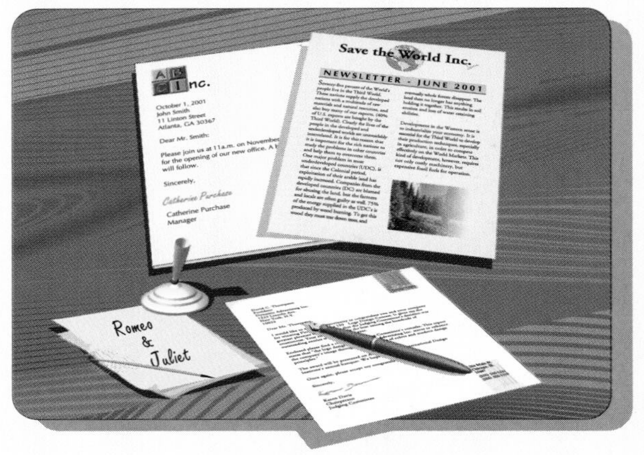

Excel

Excel is a spreadsheet program that allows you to organize and analyze data, such as a budget or sales report. Excel can also help you create colorful charts to attractively present data.

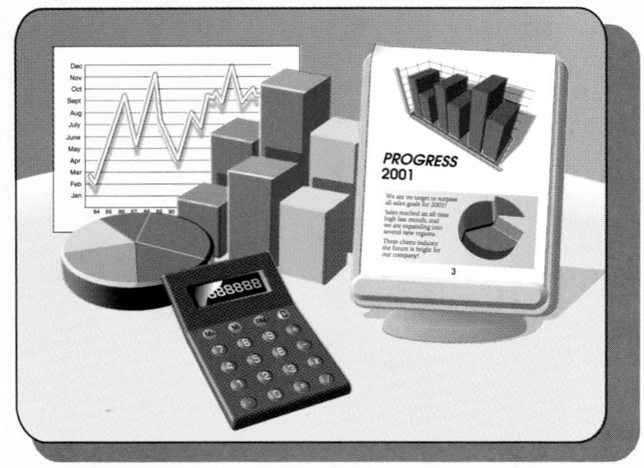

PowerPoint

PowerPoint is a program that helps you plan, organize and design professional presentations. You can add objects such as pictures, charts and diagrams to your presentations to add visual interest to the presentations.

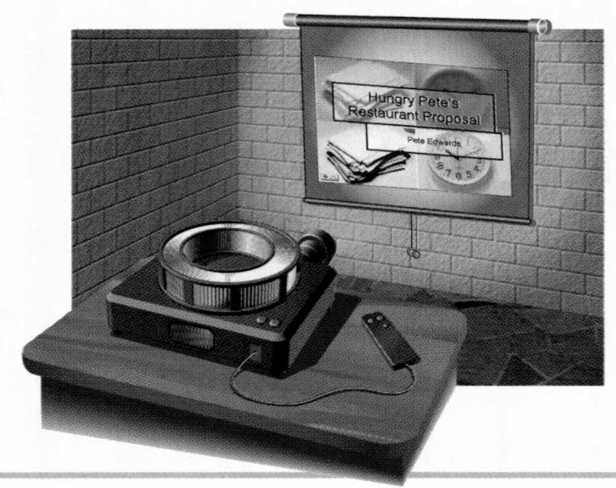

Access

Access is a database program that allows you to store and manage large collections of business or personal information, such as customer orders, expenses or addresses. You can use Access to create database objects such as tables, forms, queries and reports.

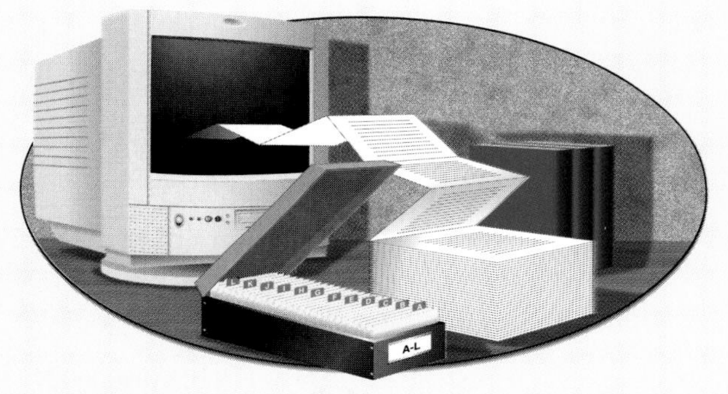

Outlook

Outlook is an information management program that allows you to exchange e-mail messages and manage information, including appointments, contacts, tasks and notes.

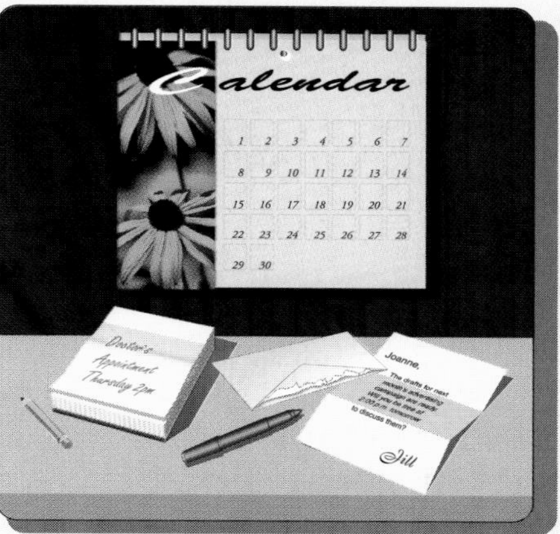

Speech Recognition

The speech recognition feature offered by Microsoft Office XP allows you to use your voice to enter text into an Office program. You can also use your voice to select commands from menus and toolbars.

Microsoft Office and the Internet

Each Office program provides features that allow you to take advantage of the Internet. You can create a hyperlink in an Office file to link the file to a Web page. You can also save Office files as Web pages, which allows you to place your files on the Internet.

There are several editions of Microsoft® Office XP available.

The available Microsoft Office XP editions include Standard, Professional and Developer. Each edition contains a different combination of programs.

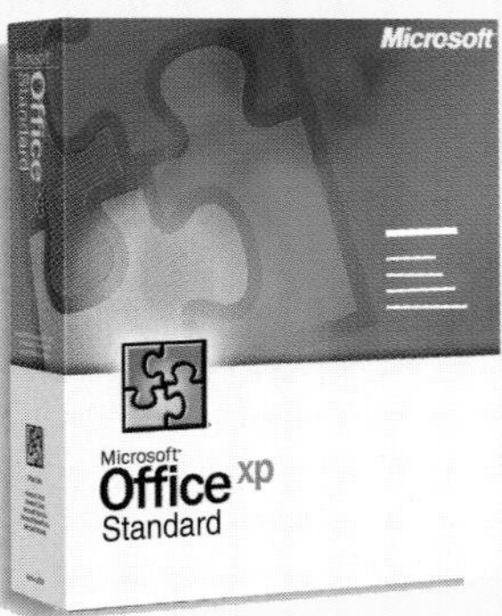

Standard

This edition is useful for home users who require basic Office programs to accomplish day-to-day tasks.

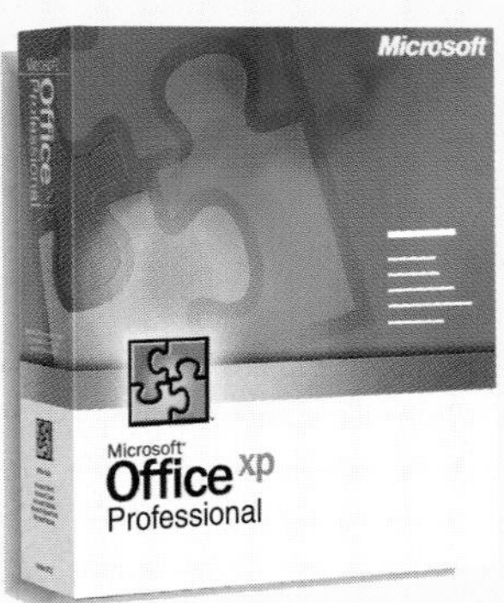

Professional

This edition is suited to users who require a database program in addition to the standard Office programs.

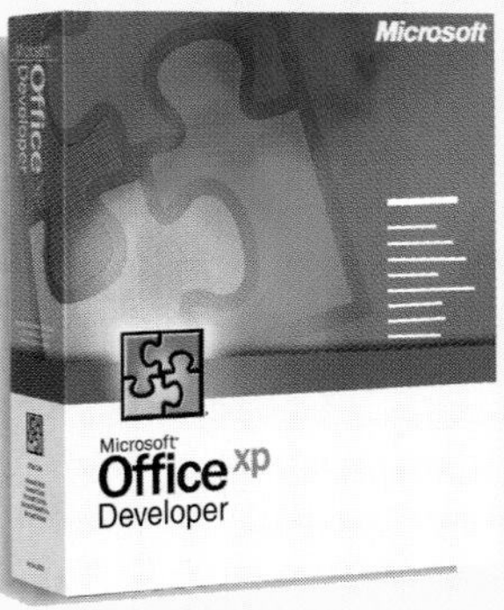

Developer

This edition is designed for professional software developers. Office XP Developer includes tools for building and managing Office-based applications and Web sites.

	MICROSOFT OFFICE XP EDITIONS		
PROGRAMS	Standard	Professional	Developer
Word	✓	✓	✓
Excel	✓	✓	✓
PowerPoint	✓	✓	✓
Access		✓	✓
Outlook	✓	✓	✓
FrontPage			✓
Developer Tools			✓
SharePoint Team Services			✓

FrontPage is a program you can use to create and publish Web pages. Developer Tools are a collection of programs that are useful for software developers. SharePoint Team Services help users share information and work together on projects using a network.

USING THE MOUSE

A mouse is a handheld device that lets you select and move items on your screen.

When you move the mouse on your desk, the mouse pointer on your screen moves in the same direction. The mouse pointer assumes different shapes, such as ↖ or I, depending on its location on your screen and the task you are performing.

Resting your hand on the mouse, use your thumb and two rightmost fingers to move the mouse on your desk. Use your two remaining fingers to press the mouse buttons.

MOUSE ACTIONS

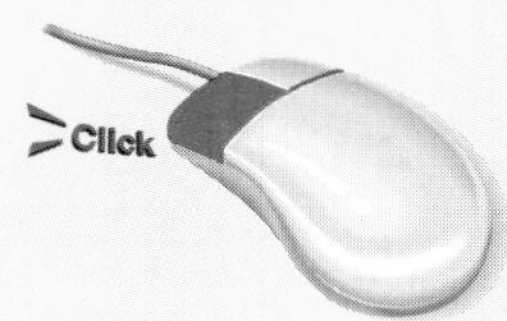

Click

Press and release the left mouse button.

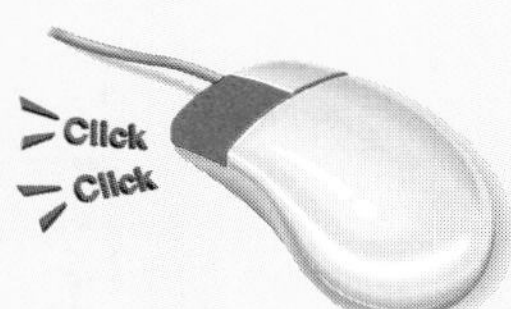

Double-click

Quickly press and release the left mouse button twice.

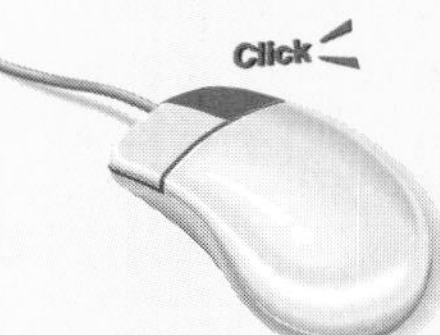

Right-click

Press and release the right mouse button.

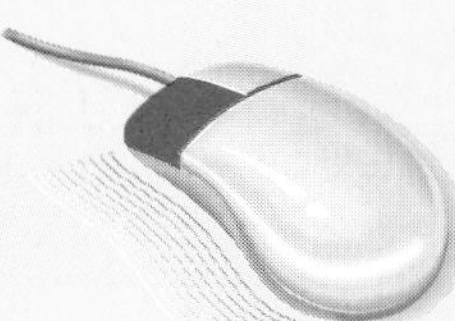

Drag

Position the mouse pointer (↖) over an object on your screen and then press and hold down the left mouse button. Still holding down the button, move the mouse to where you want to place the object and then release the button.

START A PROGRAM

You can start an Office program to perform a task such as creating a letter, analyzing financial data or designing a presentation.

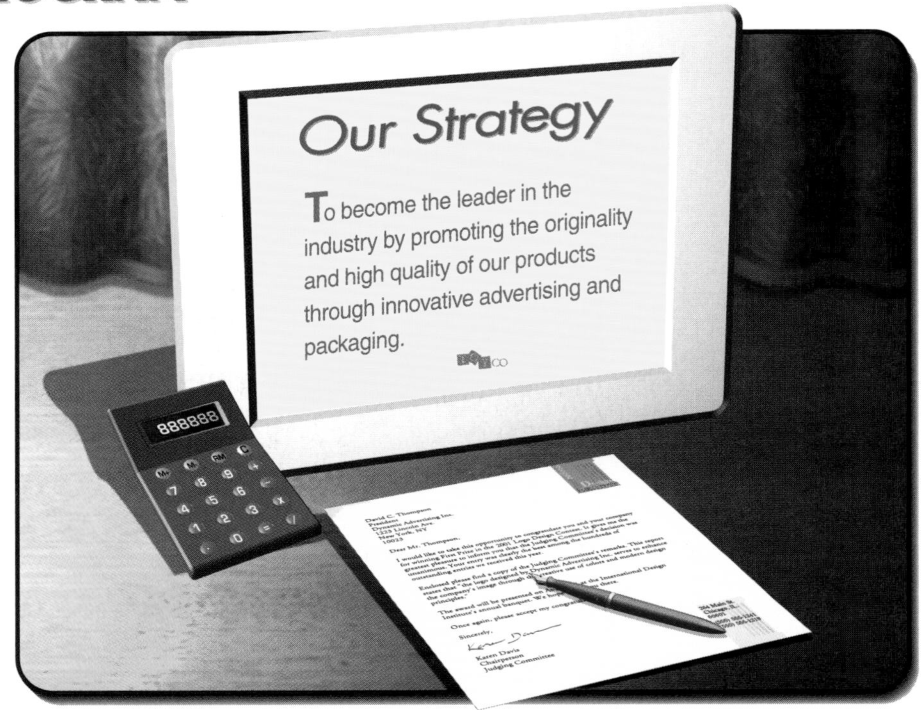

START A PROGRAM

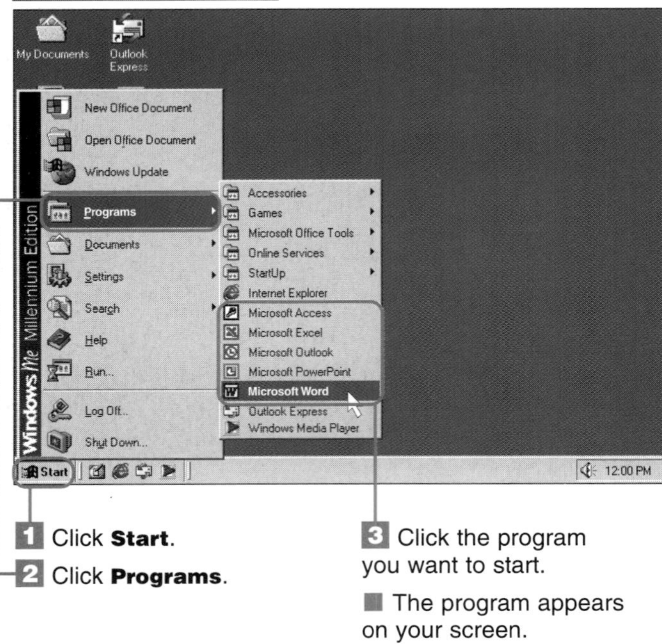

1 Click **Start**.

2 Click **Programs**.

3 Click the program you want to start.

■ The program appears on your screen.

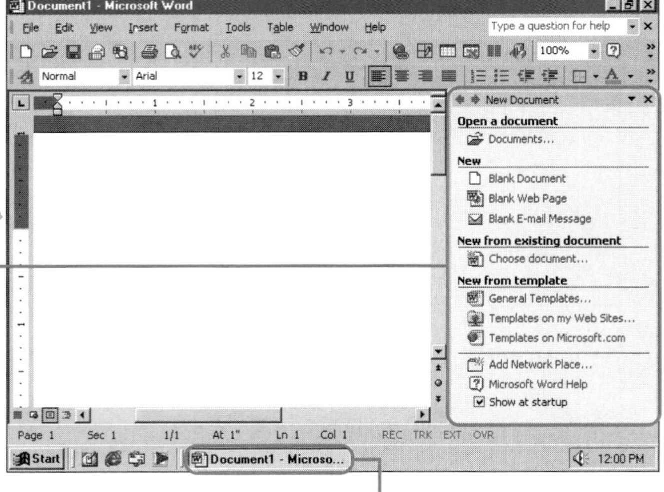

■ A task pane may appear, allowing you to quickly perform common tasks. For information on using the task pane, see page 12.

■ A button for the program appears on the taskbar.

EXIT A PROGRAM

When you finish using a program, you can exit the program.

You should always exit all programs before turning off your computer.

EXIT A PROGRAM

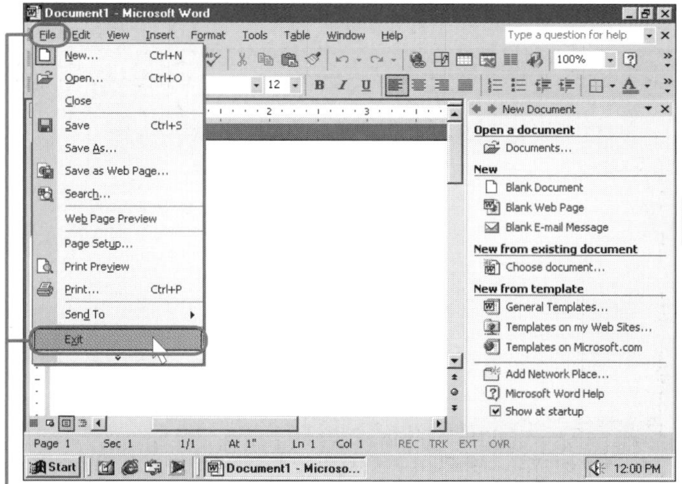

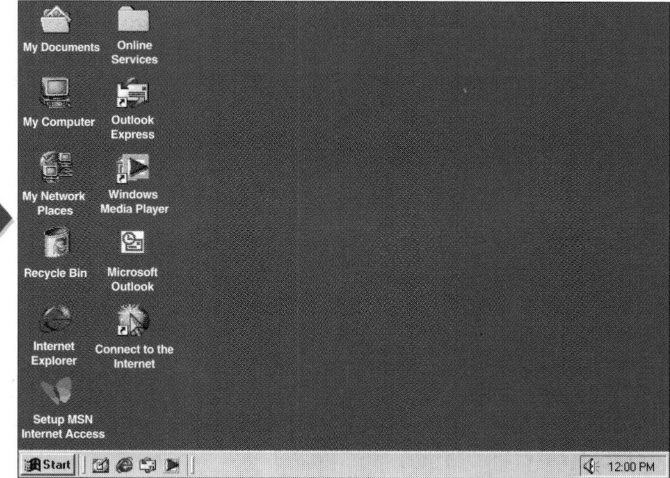

1. Click **File**.
2. Click **Exit** to shut down the program.

Note: If Exit does not appear on the menu, position the mouse over the bottom of the menu to display all the menu options.

■ The program disappears from your screen.

■ The button for the program disappears from the taskbar.

SELECT COMMANDS USING MENUS

You can select a command from a menu to perform a task in an Office program. Each command performs a different task.

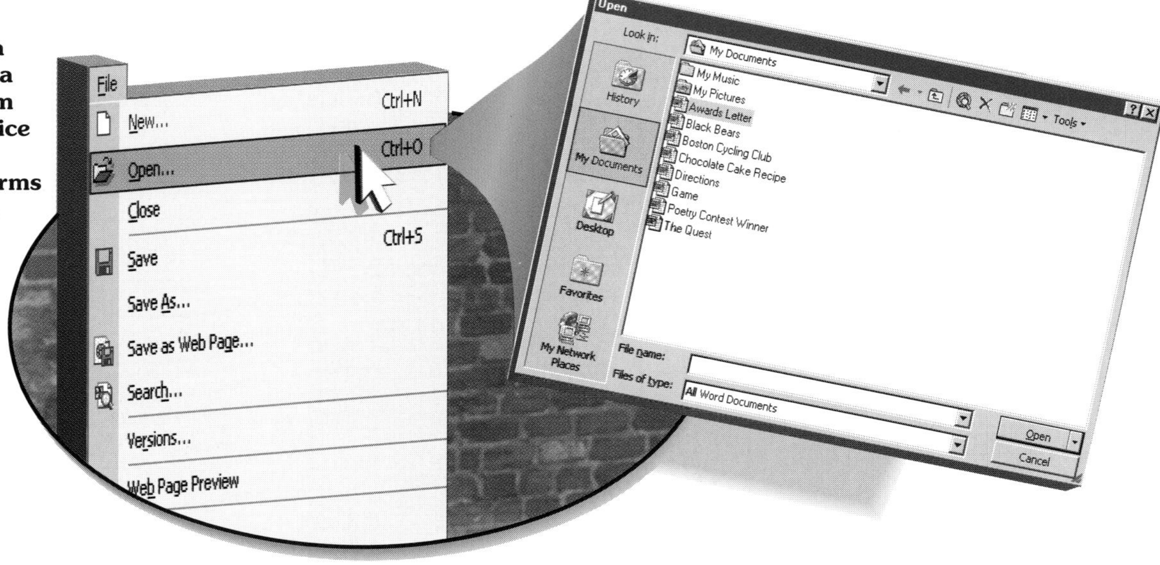

SELECT COMMANDS USING MENUS

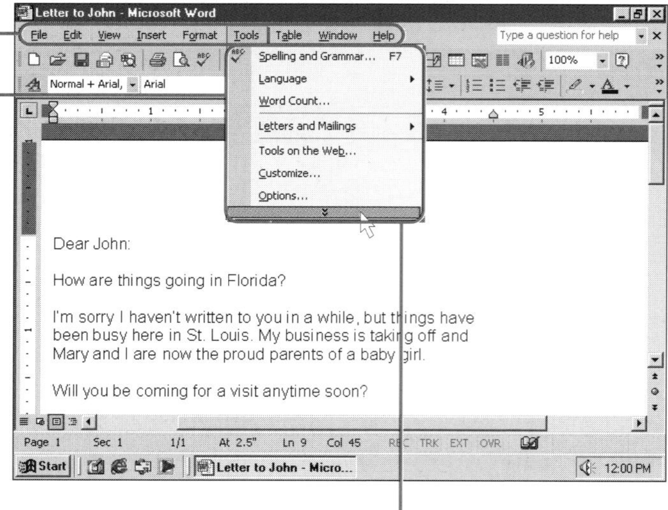

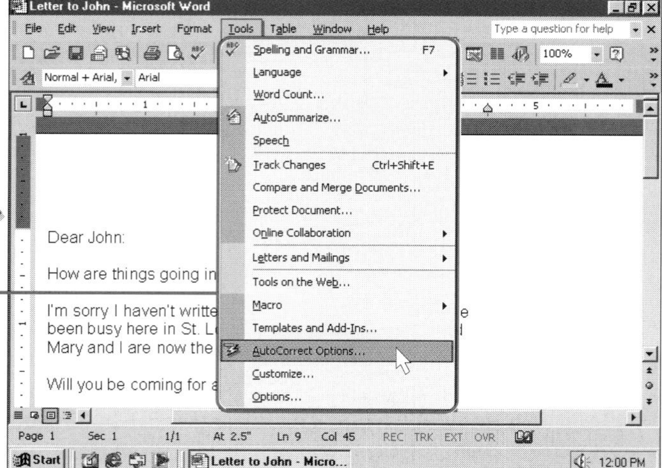

1 Click the name of the menu you want to display.

■ A short version of the menu appears, displaying the most commonly used commands.

2 To expand the menu and display all the commands, position the mouse ⇱ over ⌄.

*Note: If you do not perform step **2**, the expanded menu will automatically appear after a few seconds.*

■ The expanded menu appears, displaying all the commands.

3 Click the command you want to use.

■ To close a menu without selecting a command, click outside the menu.

How can I make a command appear on the short version of a menu?

When you select a command from an expanded menu, the command is automatically added to the short version of the menu. The next time you display the short version of the menu, the command you selected will appear.

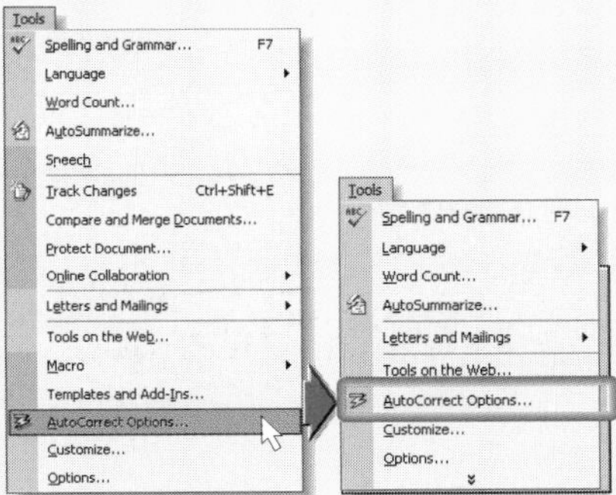

Expanded Menu **Short Menu**

Why do some menu commands have a dimmed appearance?

Commands that have a dimmed appearance are currently not available. You must perform a specific task before you can select the commands. For example, you must select text to make the Cut and Copy commands in the Edit menu available in Word.

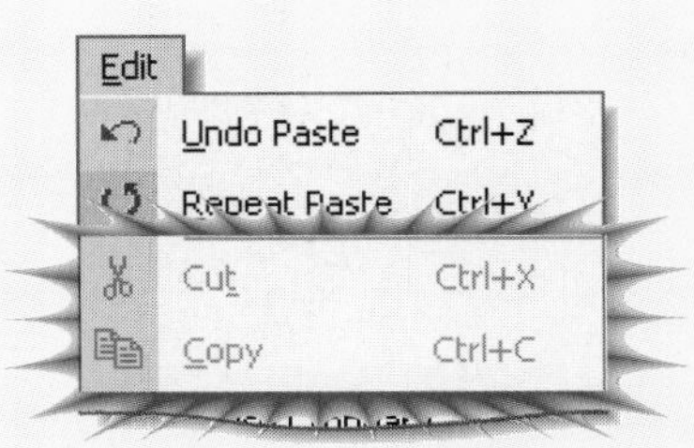

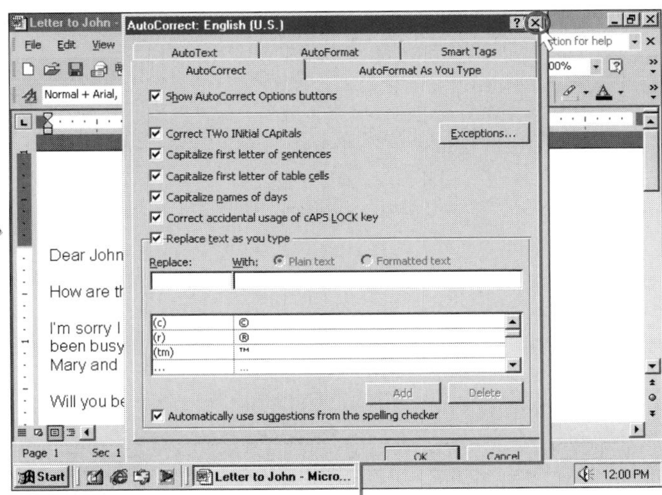

■ A dialog box or task pane appears if the command you selected displays three dots (...).

Note: For information about task panes, see page 12.

4 Select the options you want to use in the dialog box or task pane.

■ To close the dialog box or task pane without selecting any options, click ☒.

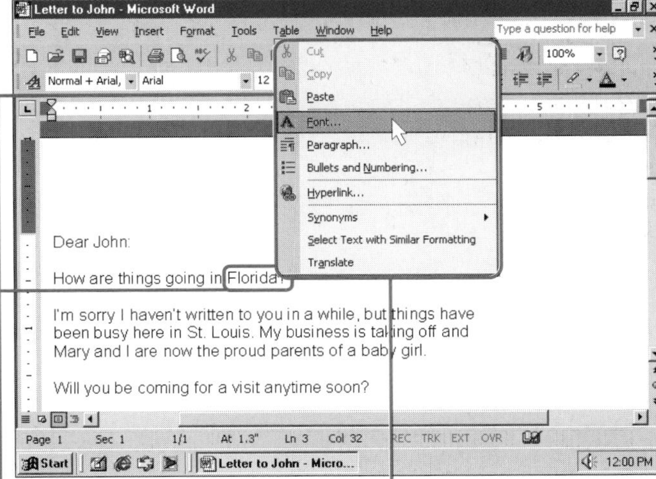

USING SHORTCUT MENUS

1 Right-click an item you want to change.

■ A shortcut menu appears, displaying the most frequently used commands for the item.

2 Click the command you want to use.

■ To close the shortcut menu without selecting a command, click outside the menu.

SELECT COMMANDS USING TOOLBARS

A toolbar contains buttons that you can use to select commands and access commonly used features.

When you first start some Office programs, the most commonly used buttons appear on each toolbar. As you work with a program, the toolbars automatically change to remove buttons you rarely use and display the buttons you use most often.

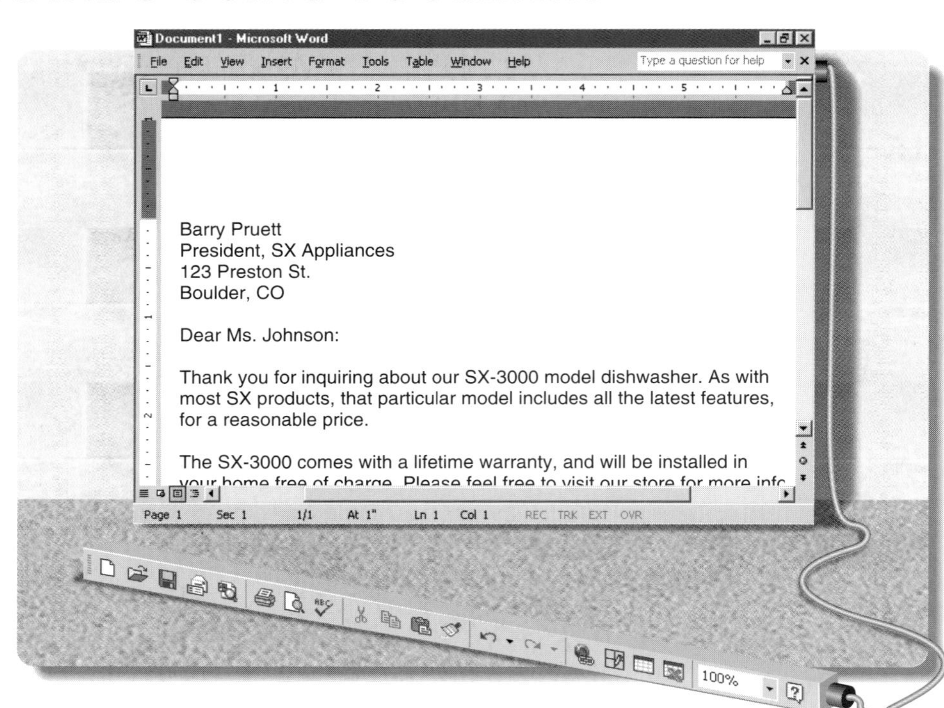

SELECT COMMANDS USING TOOLBARS

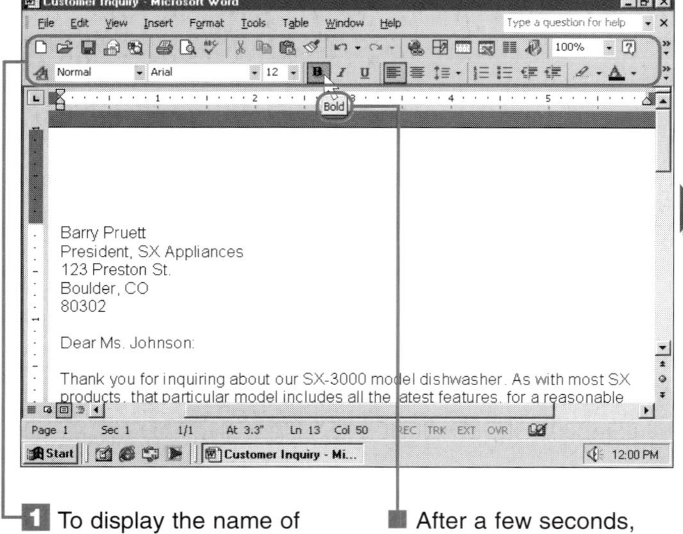

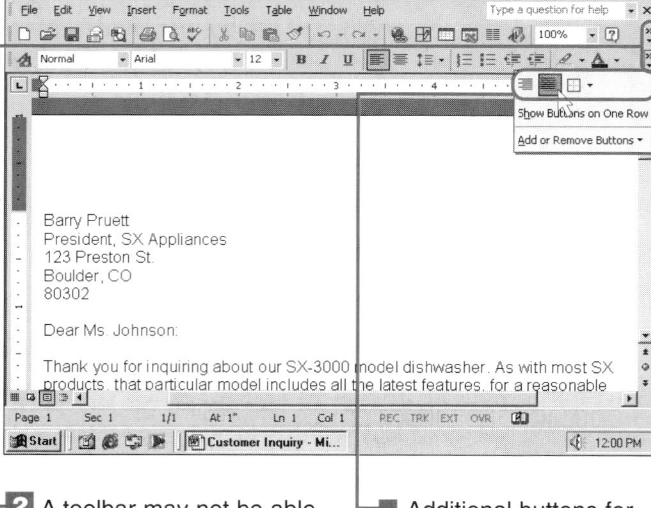

1 To display the name of a toolbar button, position the mouse over the button.

■ After a few seconds, the name of the button appears in a yellow box. The button name can help you determine the task the button performs.

2 A toolbar may not be able to display all of its buttons. Click » to display additional buttons for the toolbar.

■ Additional buttons for the toolbar appear.

3 To use a toolbar button to select a command, click the button.

DISPLAY OR HIDE A TOOLBAR

Each Microsoft Office program offers several toolbars that you can display or hide at any time. Each toolbar contains buttons that help you quickly perform common tasks.

When you first start an Office program, one or more toolbars automatically appear on your screen. You can choose which toolbars to display based on the tasks you perform most often.

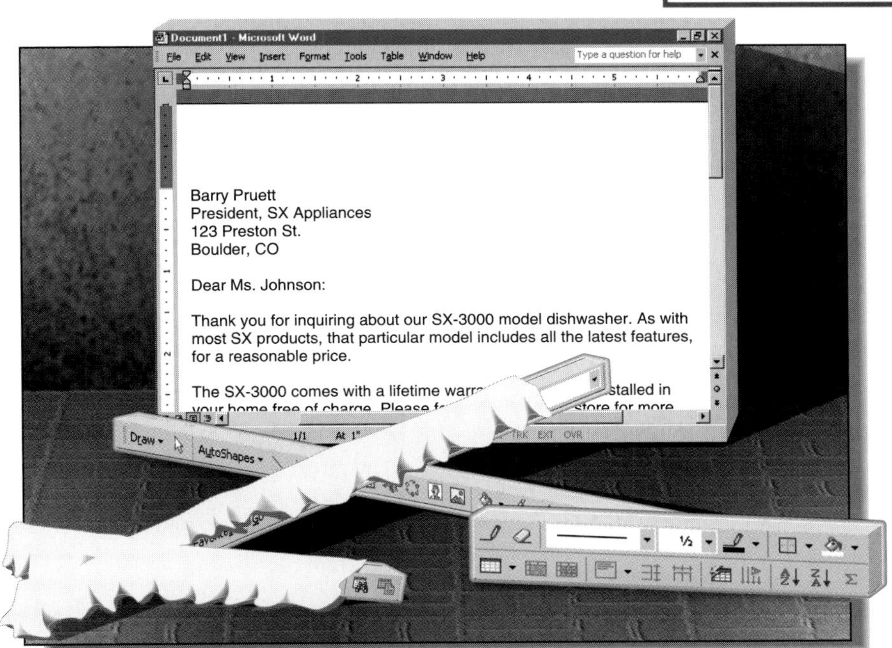

DISPLAY OR HIDE A TOOLBAR

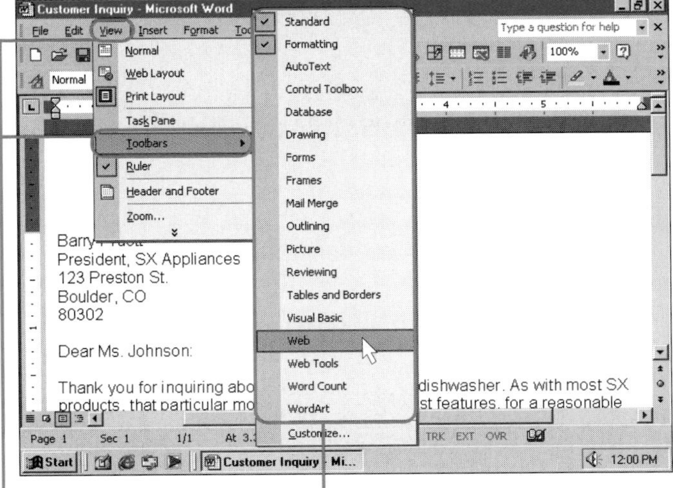

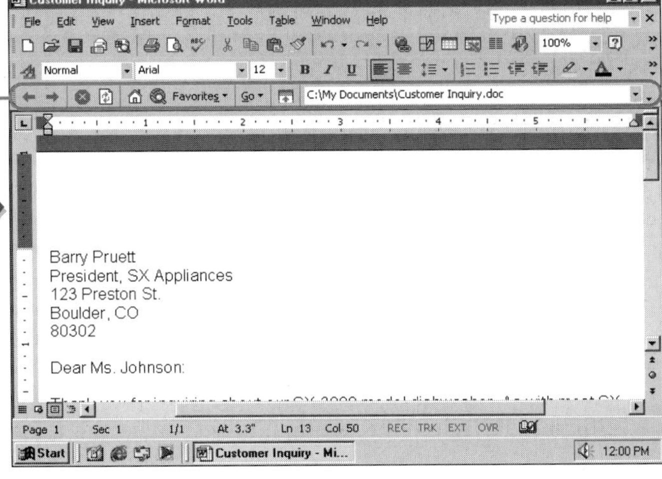

1 To display or hide a toolbar, click **View**.

2 Click **Toolbars**.

■ A list of toolbars appears. A check mark (✓) beside a toolbar name tells you the toolbar is currently displayed.

3 Click the name of the toolbar you want to display or hide.

■ The program displays or hides the toolbar you selected.

USING THE TASK PANE

Many Office programs offer task panes that you can use to perform common tasks.

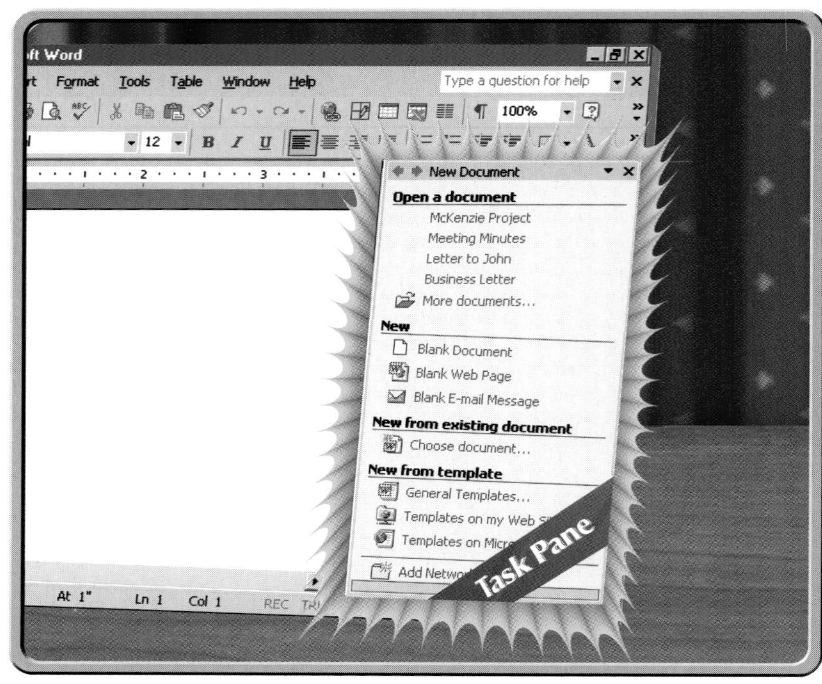

You can display or hide a task pane at any time. When you start an Office program or perform a task, a task pane may automatically appear.

USING THE TASK PANE

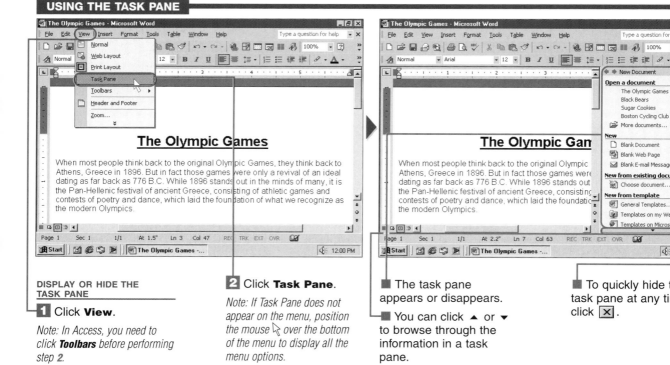

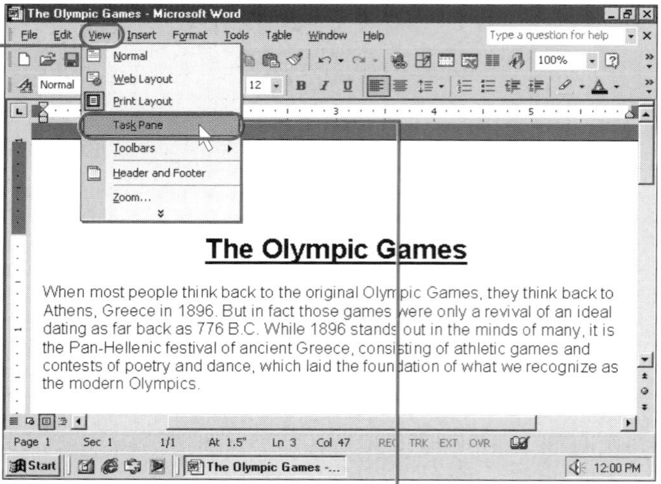

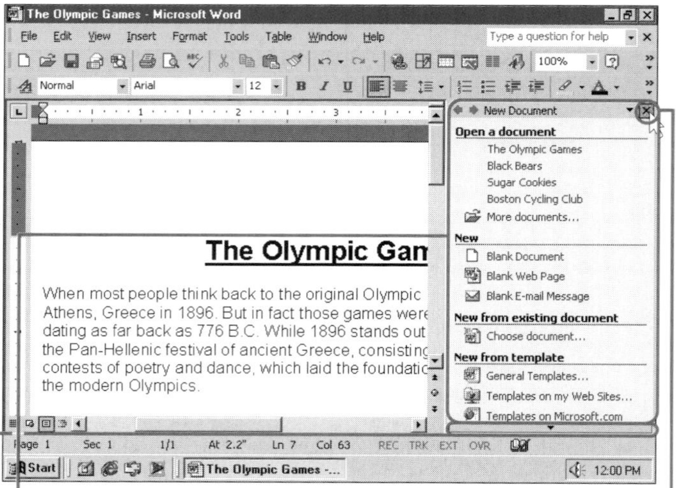

DISPLAY OR HIDE THE TASK PANE

1 Click **View**.

Note: In Access, you need to click ***Toolbars*** *before performing step* ***2****.*

2 Click **Task Pane**.

Note: If Task Pane does not appear on the menu, position the mouse ↖ over the bottom of the menu to display all the menu options.

■ The task pane appears or disappears.

■ You can click ▲ or ▼ to browse through the information in a task pane.

■ To quickly hide the task pane at any time, click ☒.

What task panes are available in Office?

The available task panes depend on the Office program you are working in. Some common task panes are listed below.

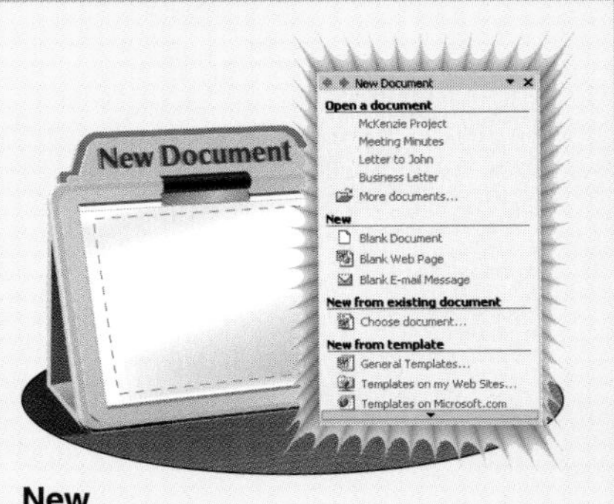

New

Allows you to perform tasks such as creating a new document and opening a file.

Clipboard

Displays each item you have selected to move or copy.

Search

Allows you to search for files on your computer.

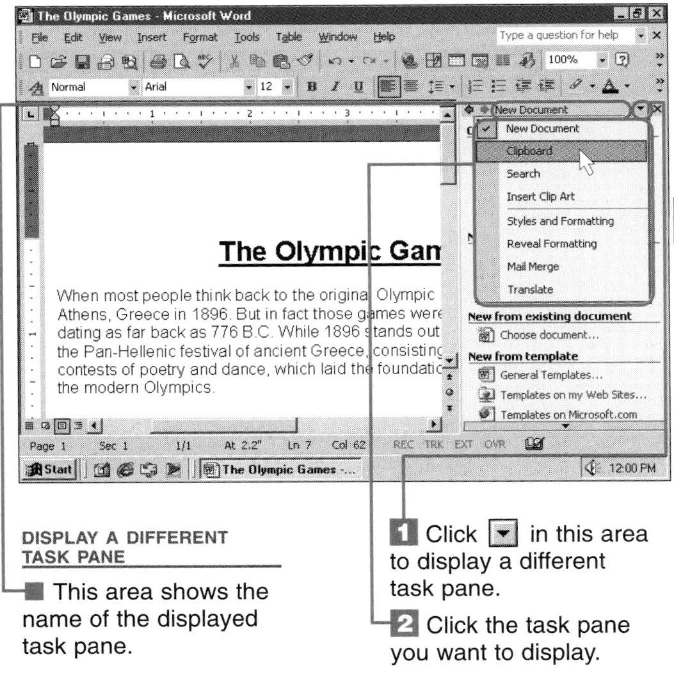

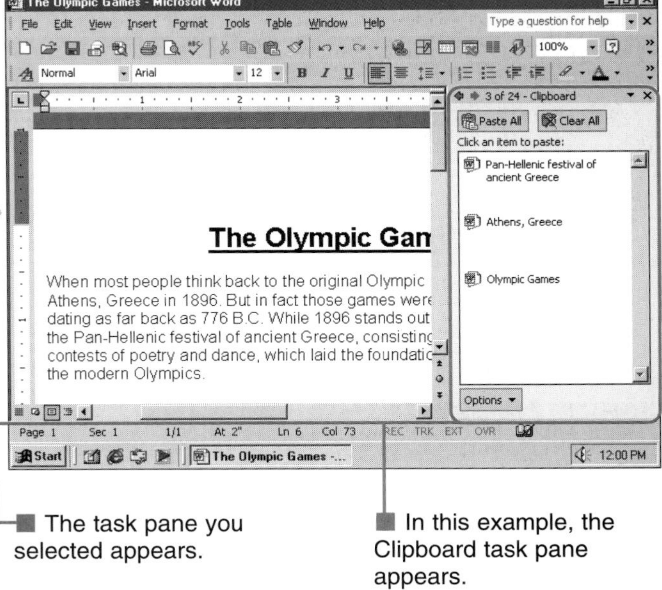

DISPLAY A DIFFERENT TASK PANE

■ This area shows the name of the displayed task pane.

1 Click ▾ in this area to display a different task pane.

2 Click the task pane you want to display.

■ The task pane you selected appears.

■ In this example, the Clipboard task pane appears.

SEARCH FOR A FILE

If you cannot remember the name or location of a file you want to work with, you can search for the file.

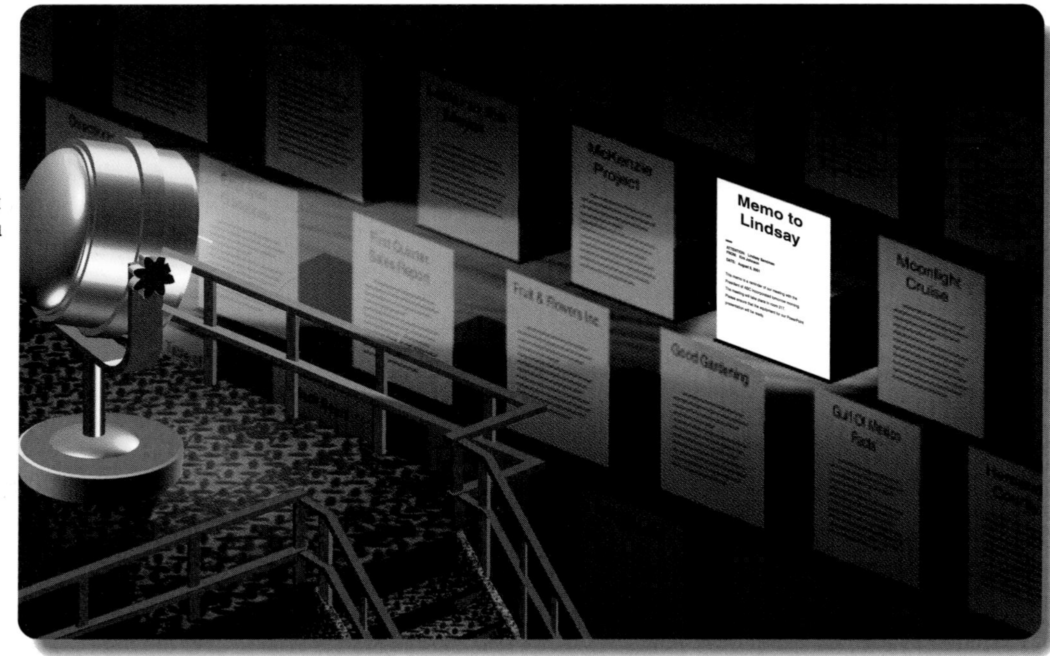

SEARCH FOR A FILE

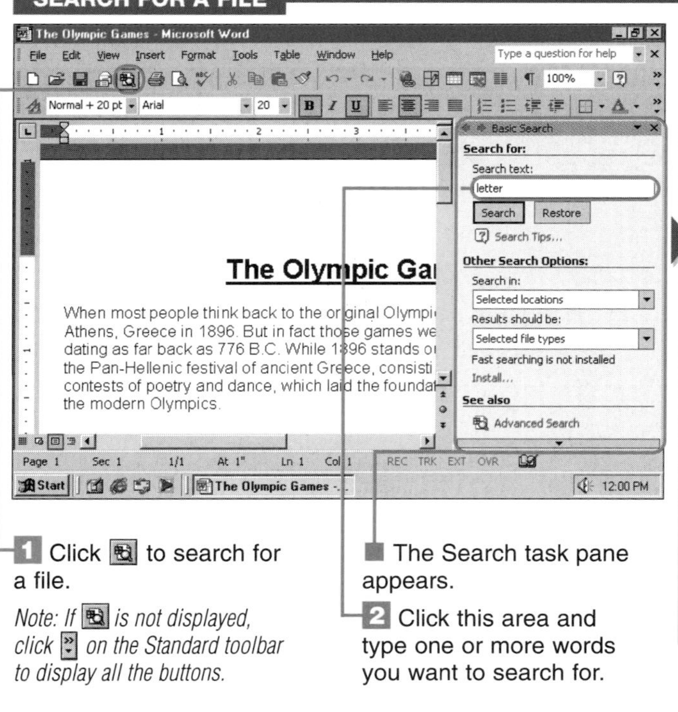

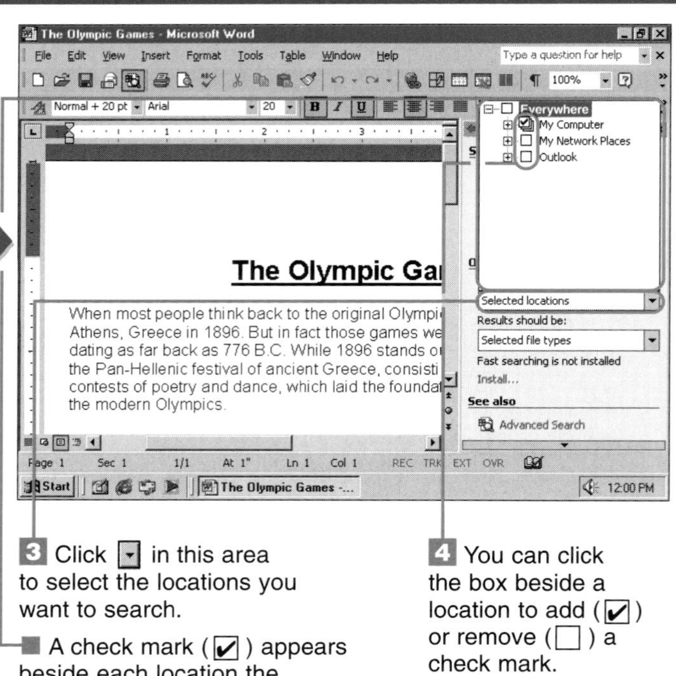

1 Click the Search button to search for a file.

Note: If the Search button is not displayed, click the More Buttons button on the Standard toolbar to display all the buttons.

■ The Search task pane appears.

2 Click this area and type one or more words you want to search for.

3 Click the drop-down arrow in this area to select the locations you want to search.

■ A check mark (☑) appears beside each location the Office program will search.

Note: By default, the Office program will search all the drives and folders on your computer.

4 You can click the box beside a location to add (☑) or remove (☐) a check mark.

5 To close the list of locations, click outside the list.

How will the Office program use the words I specify to search for files?

The Office program will search the contents of files and the names of files for the words you specify. When searching for files, the Office program will search for various forms of the words. For example, searching for "run" will find "run", "running" and "ran".

When selecting the locations and types of files I want to search for, how can I display more items?

Each item that displays a plus sign (⊞) contains hidden items. To display the hidden items, click the plus sign (⊞) beside the item (⊞ changes to ⊟). To once again hide the items, click the minus sign (⊟) beside the item.

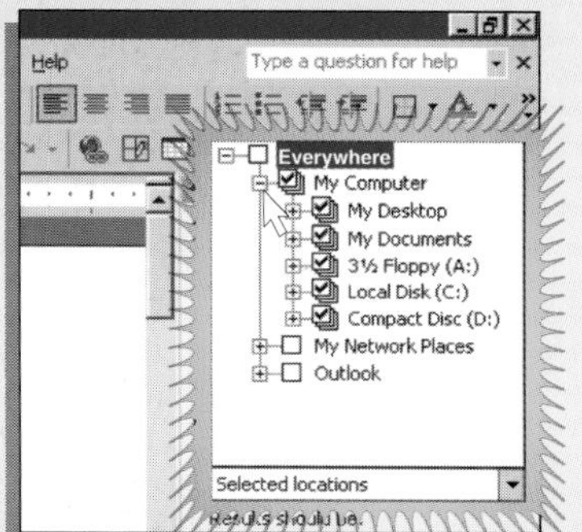

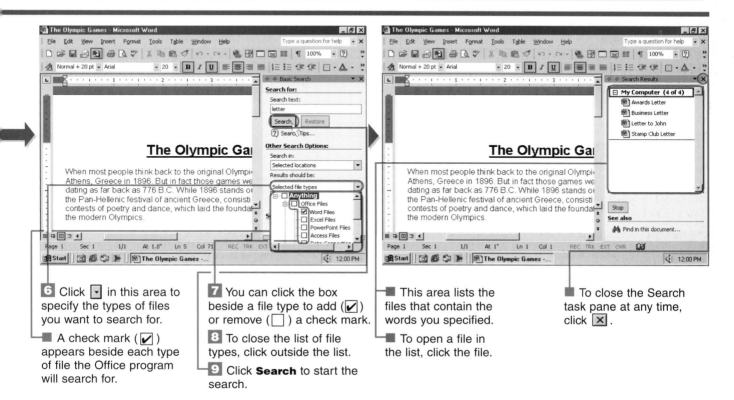

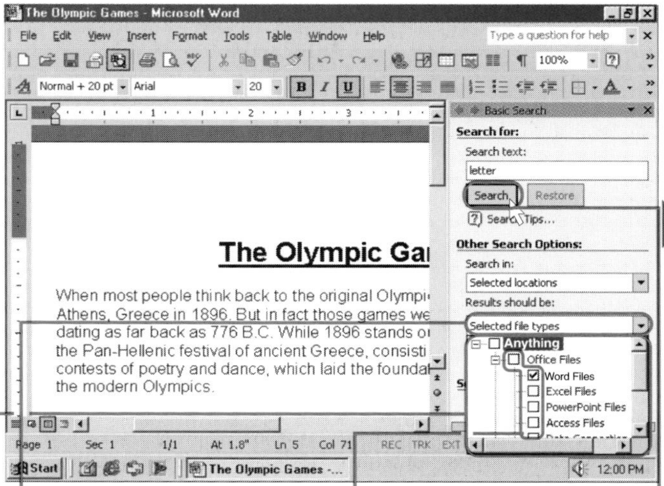

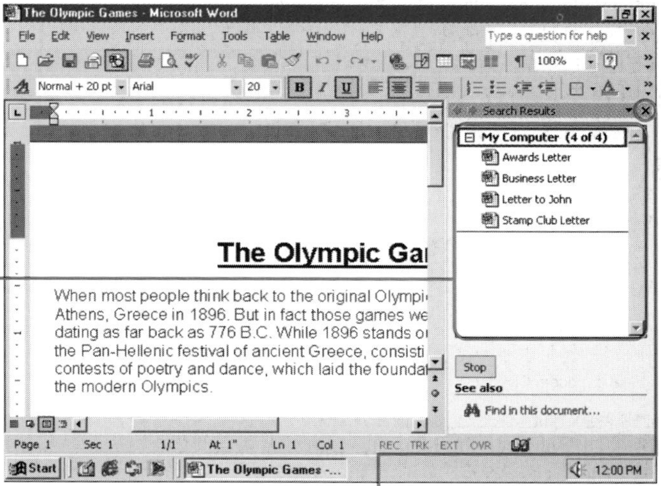

6 Click ▾ in this area to specify the types of files you want to search for.

■ A check mark (☑) appears beside each type of file the Office program will search for.

7 You can click the box beside a file type to add (☑) or remove (☐) a check mark.

8 To close the list of file types, click outside the list.

9 Click **Search** to start the search.

■ This area lists the files that contain the words you specified.

■ To open a file in the list, click the file.

■ To close the Search task pane at any time, click ☒.

If you do not know how to perform a task in a Microsoft Office program, you can search for help information on the task.

GETTING HELP

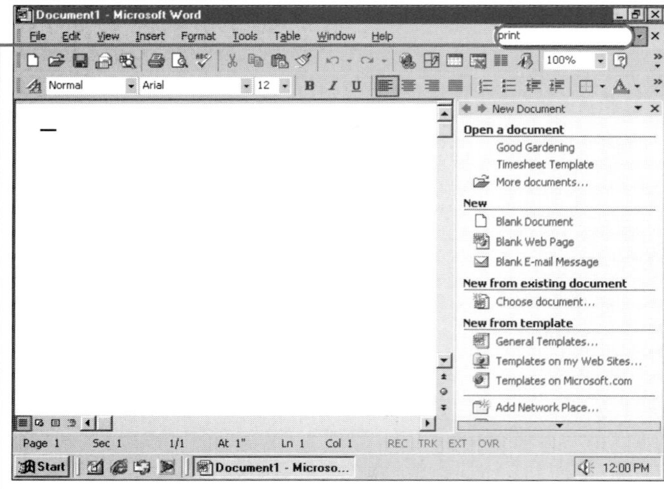

1 Click this area and type the task you want to get help information on. Then press the Enter key.

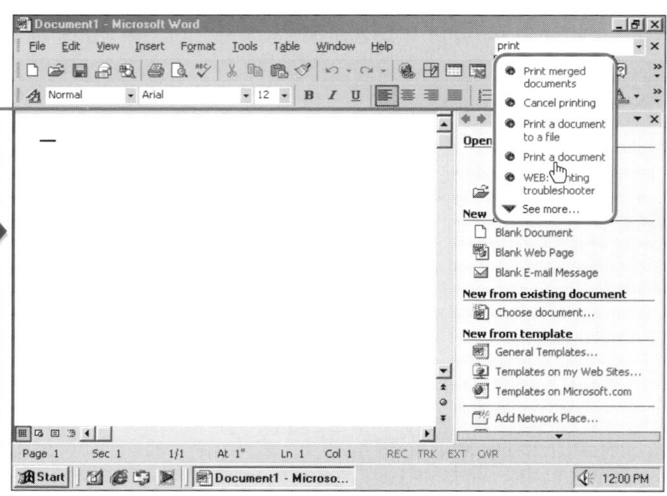

■ A list of related help topics appears.

2 Click a help topic of interest.

Note: If the help topic you want does not appear in the list, you can click ***See more*** *to view additional help topics.*

What other ways can I obtain help?

In the Microsoft Help window, you can use the following tabs to obtain help information.

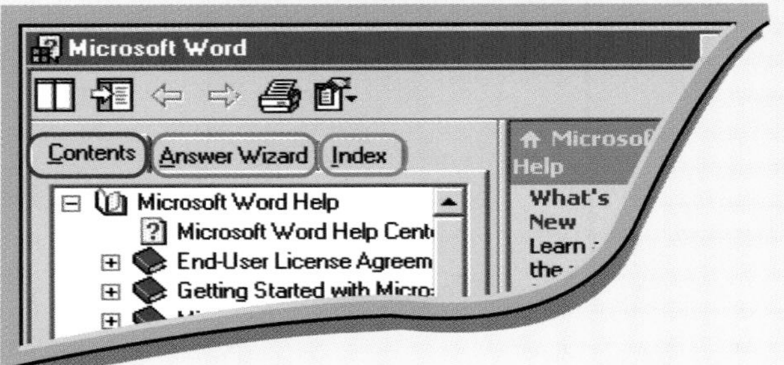

Index

You can type a word of interest or double-click a word in an alphabetical list of help topics. A list of related help topics will appear.

Contents

You can double-click a book icon ( ) or click a page icon ( ) to browse through the contents of Microsoft Help.

Answer Wizard

You can type a question about a topic of interest. A list of help topics related to your question will appear.

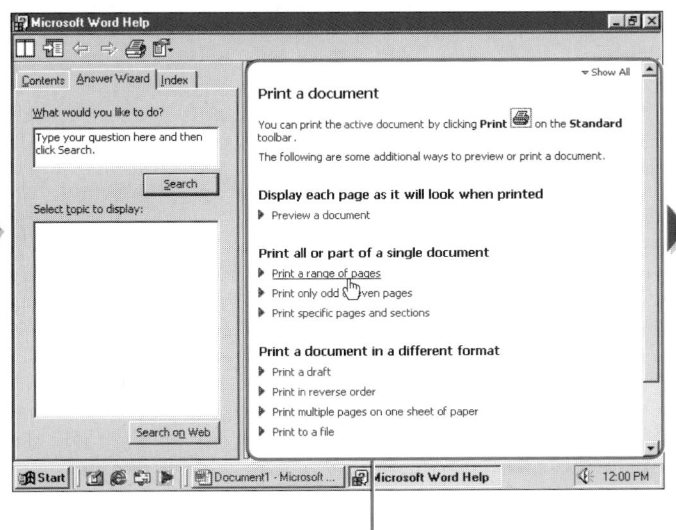

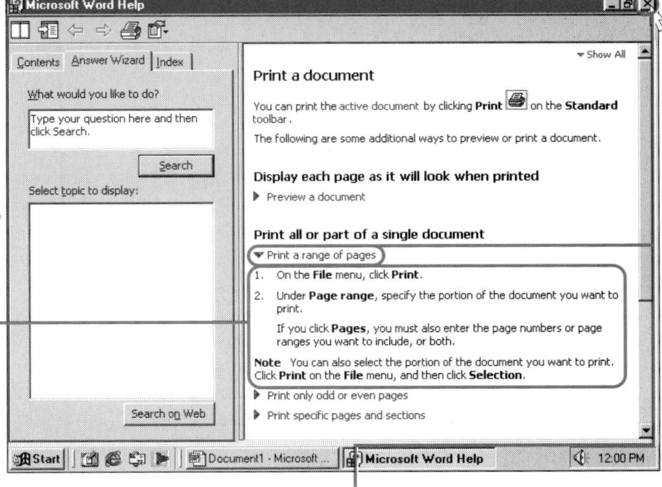

■ The Microsoft Help window appears.

Note: To maximize the Microsoft Help window to fill your screen, click ☐ in the top right corner of the window.

■ This area displays information about the help topic you selected.

■ To display additional information for a word or phrase that appears in color, click the text.

■ The additional information appears.

Note: Selecting a colored word or phrase will display information such as a definition, tips or a list of steps.

■ To once again hide the information, click the colored word or phrase.

3 When you finish reviewing the help information, click ☒ to close the Microsoft Help window.

HUNGRY PETE'S 1328 First St., Seattle, WA., 98119

Grand Opening Celebration!

Hungry Pete's Restaurant is having a grand opening celebration this Saturday from 12 p.m. until 9 p.m.

Bring the whole family and enjoy the great specials offered on this special day.
Children under 12 eat for free!

Come see what Hungry Pete is all about:
Great food, excellent value and incredible customer service!

Pete Parker

Pete Parker
Manager, Hungry Pete's Restaurant

Using Word

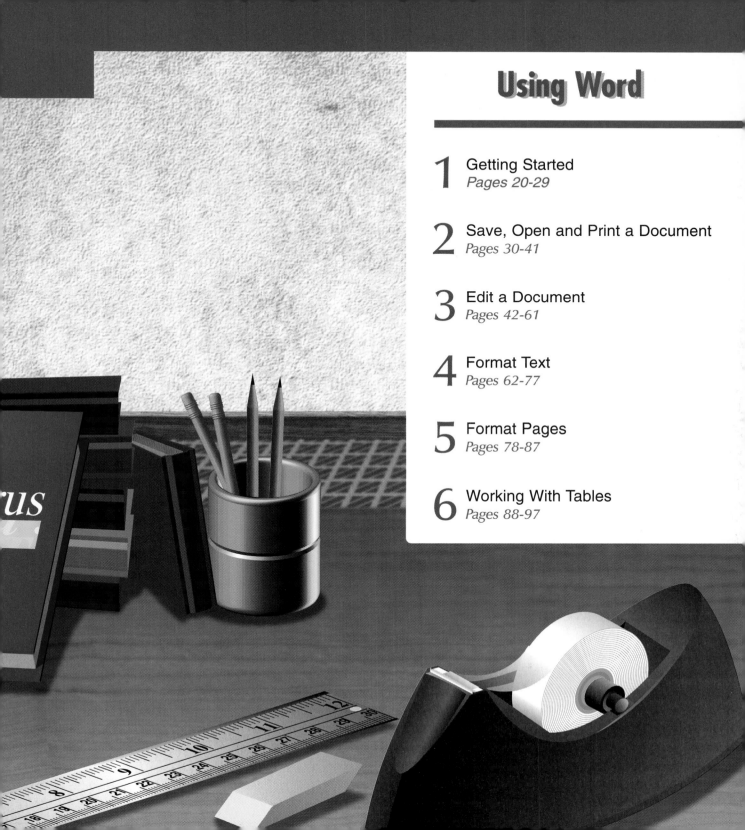

Word is a word processing program you can use to efficiently produce professional-looking documents, such as letters, reports and essays.

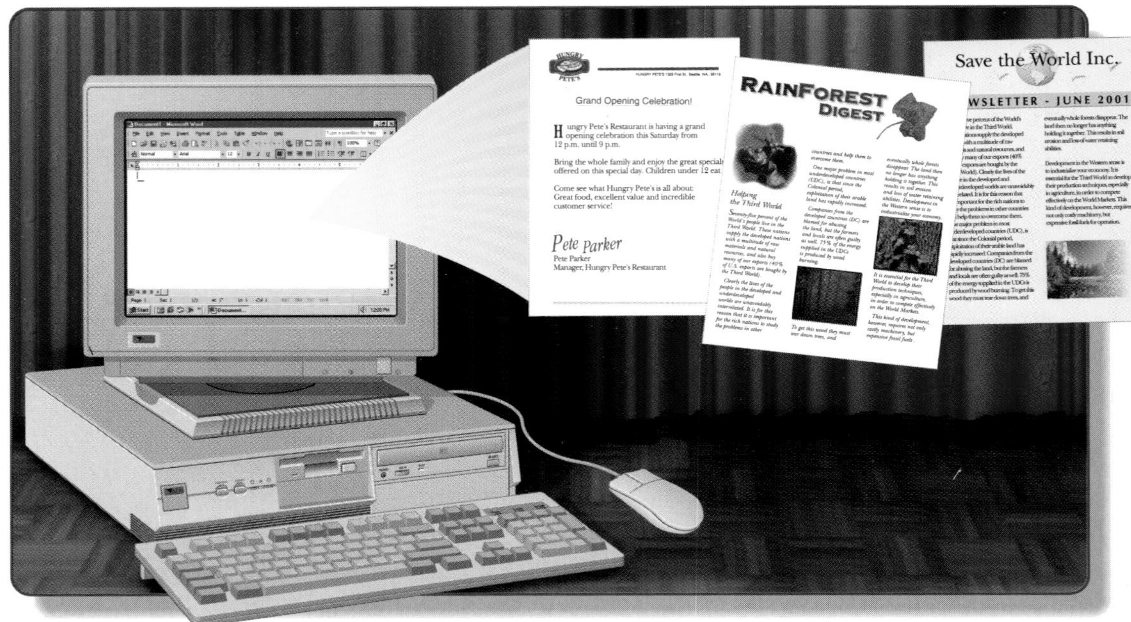

HUNGRY PETE'S
Grand Opening Celebration!
Hungry Pete's Restaurant is having a grand opening celebration this Saturday from 12 p.m. until 9 p.m.
Bring the whole family and enjoy the great specials offered on this special day. Children under 12 eat
Come see what Hungry Pete's is all about: Great food, excellent value and incredible customer service!
Pete Parker
Pete Parker
Manager, Hungry Pete's Restaurant
RAINFOREST DIGEST
Helping the Third World
Save the World Inc.
NEWSLETTER - JUNE 2001

Editing

Word offers many time-saving features to help you edit text in a document. You can add or delete text, re-arrange paragraphs and check for spelling and grammar errors. Word remembers the last changes you made to a document, so you can undo changes you regret.

Formatting

You can format a document to enhance the appearance of the document. You can use various font sizes, styles and colors to make important text stand out. You can also add page numbers, change the margins and use bullets to separate items in a list.

Creating Tables

You can create tables to neatly display information in a document. You can use one of Word's ready-to-use designs to enhance the appearance of a table.

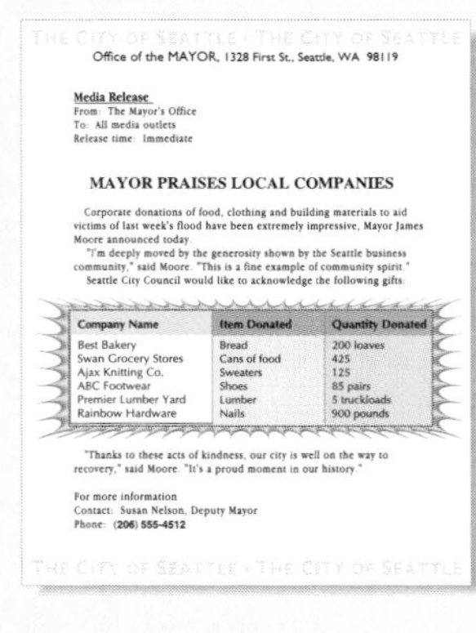

THE CITY OF SEATTLE • THE CITY OF SEATTLE

Office of the MAYOR, 1328 First St., Seattle, WA 98119

Media Release
From: The Mayor's Office
To: All media outlets
Release time: Immediate

MAYOR PRAISES LOCAL COMPANIES

Corporate donations of food, clothing and building materials to aid victims of last week's flood have been extremely impressive, Mayor James Moore announced today.

"I'm deeply moved by the generosity shown by the Seattle business community," said Moore. "This is a fine example of community spirit."

Seattle City Council would like to acknowledge the following gifts:

Company Name	Item Donated	Quantity Donated
Best Bakery	Bread	200 loaves
Swan Grocery Stores	Cans of food	425
Ajax Knitting Co.	Sweaters	125
ABC Footwear	Shoes	85 pairs
Premier Lumber Yard	Lumber	5 truckloads
Rainbow Hardware	Nails	900 pounds

"Thanks to these acts of kindness, our city is well on the way to recovery," said Moore. "It's a proud moment in our history."

For more information
Contact: Susan Nelson, Deputy Mayor
Phone: (206) 555-4512

THE CITY OF SEATTLE • THE CITY OF SEATTLE

THE WORD WINDOW

The Word window displays many items you can use to create and work with your documents.

Title Bar

Shows the name of the displayed document.

Menu Bar

Provides access to lists of commands available in Word and displays an area where you can type a question to get help information.

Standard Toolbar

Contains buttons you can use to select common commands, such as Save and Print.

Formatting Toolbar

Contains buttons you can use to select common formatting commands, such as Bold and Italic.

Ruler

Allows you to change tab and indent settings for your documents.

Task Pane

Contains links you can select to perform common tasks, such as opening or creating a document.

Insertion Point

The flashing line on the screen that indicates where the text you type will appear.

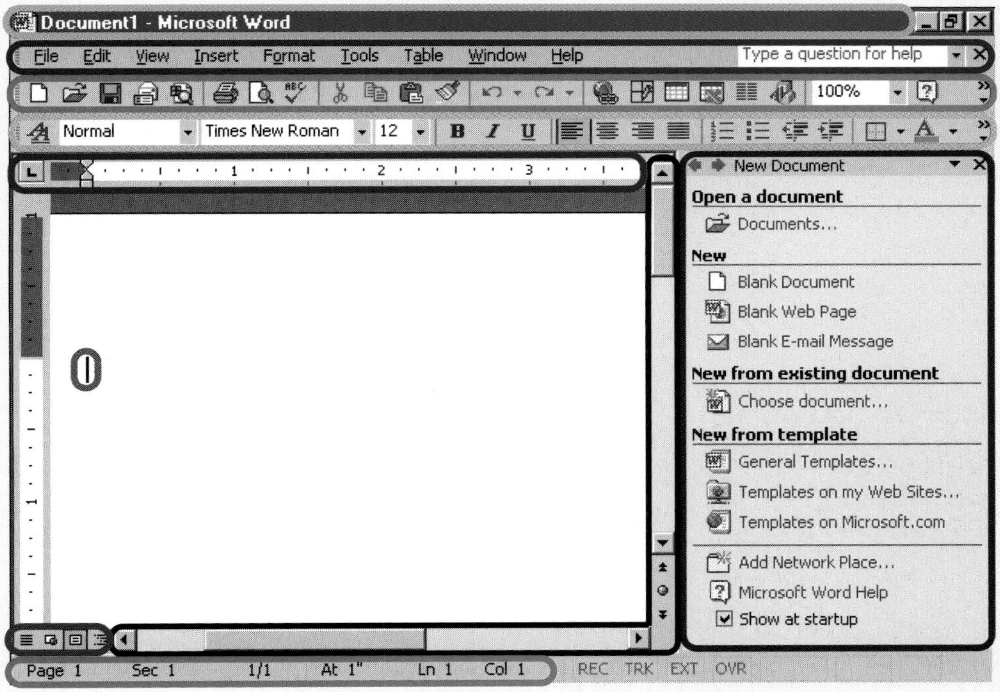

Document Views

Provides access to four different views of your documents.

Scroll Bars

Allow you to browse through a document.

Status Bar

Provides information about the area of the document displayed on the screen and the position of the insertion point.

Page 1

The page displayed on the screen.

Sec 1

The section of the document displayed on the screen.

1/1

The page displayed on the screen and the total number of pages in the document.

At 1"

The distance from the top of the page to the insertion point.

Ln 1

The number of lines from the top margin to the insertion point.

Col 1

The number of characters from the left margin to the insertion point, including spaces.

ENTER TEXT

Word allows you to type text into your document quickly and easily.

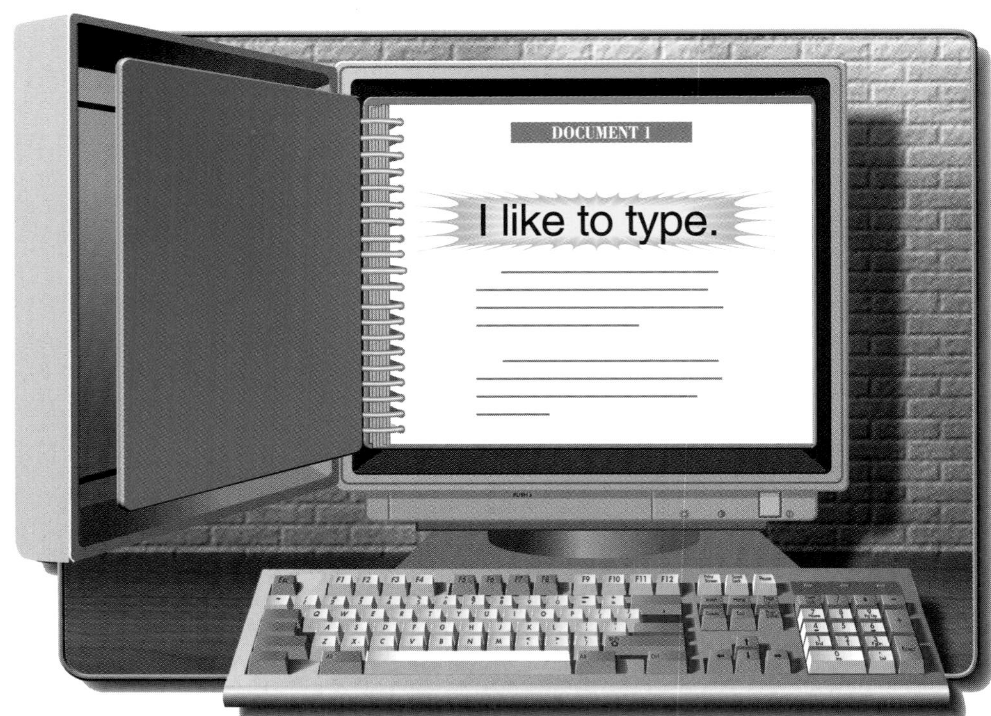

ENTER TEXT

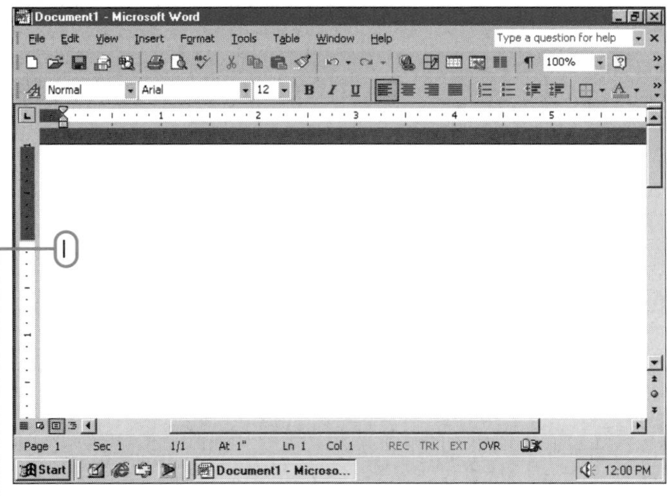

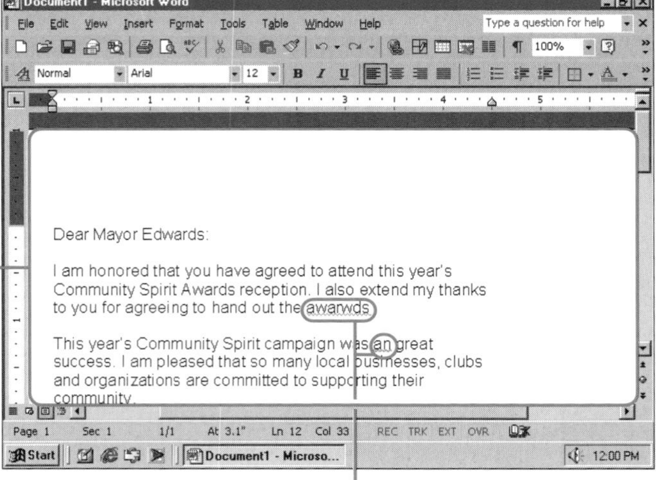

Document1 - Microsoft Word
Dear Mayor Edwards:
I am honored that you have agreed to attend this year's Community Spirit Awards reception. I also extend my thanks to you for agreeing to hand out the awarwds.
This year's Community Spirit campaign was an great success. I am pleased that so many local businesses, clubs and organizations are committed to supporting their community.

■ The text you type will appear where the insertion point flashes on your screen.

1 Type the text for your document.

Note: In this book, the font of text was changed to Arial to make the examples easier to read. To change the font of text, see page 62.

■ When you reach the end of a line, Word automatically wraps the text to the next line. You only need to press the **Enter** key when you want to start a new paragraph.

■ Word automatically underlines misspelled words in red and grammar errors in green. The underlines will not appear when you print your document. To correct misspelled words and grammar errors, see page 50.

Can I enter text anywhere in my document?

Word's Click and Type feature allows you to enter text anywhere in your document. Double-click the location where you want to enter text and then type the text. The Click and Type feature is only available in the Print Layout and Web Layout views. To change the view, see page 28.

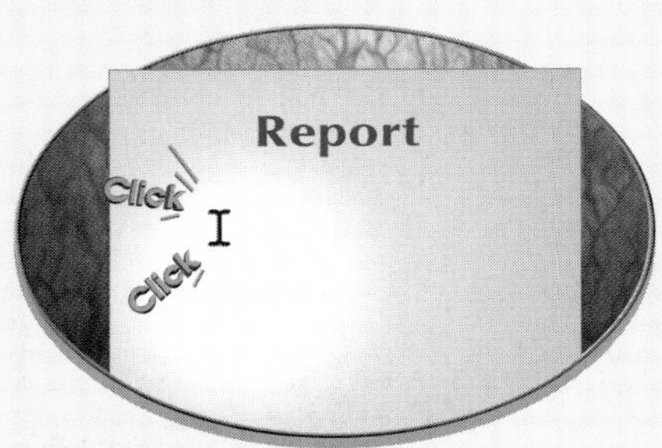

Why does a blue rectangle appear under some of my words?

Word's AutoCorrect feature automatically corrects common spelling errors as you type. A blue rectangle (▭) appears below text that has been corrected, allowing you to change options for the correction.

ent is available for everyone-
's and child alike. We want
ne is **welcome**. Please plan

Change back to "welcom"
Stop Automatically Correcting "welcom"
Control AutoCorrect Options...

1 Position the mouse I over the blue rectangle to display the AutoCorrect Options button ( ).

2 Click the AutoCorrect Options button to display a list of options.

3 Click the option you want to use.

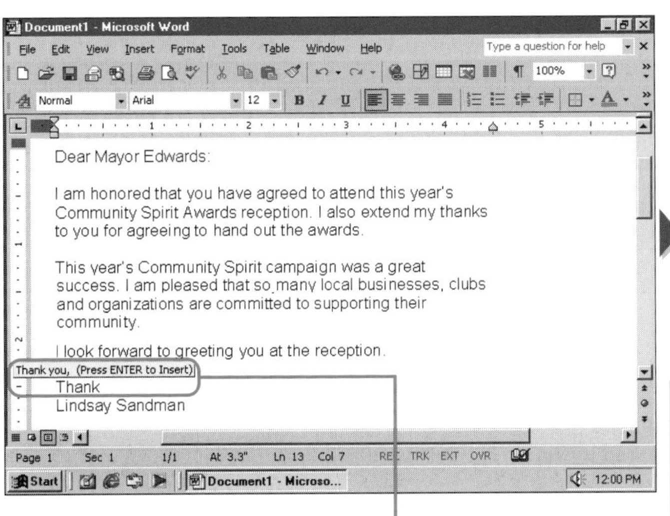

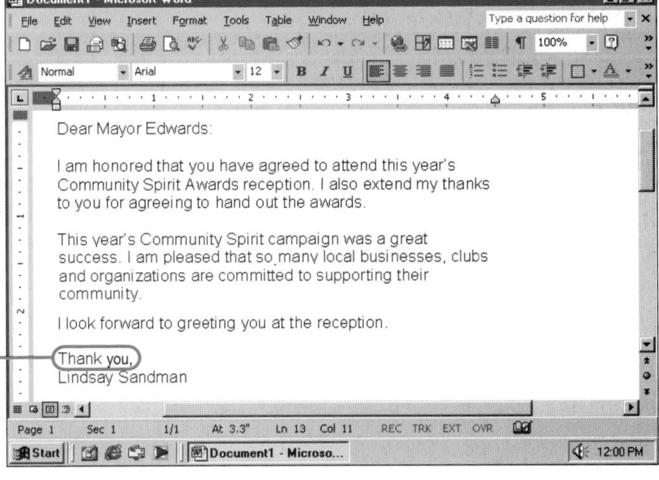

ENTER TEXT AUTOMATICALLY

■ Word's AutoText feature helps you quickly enter common words and phrases.

■ When you type the first few characters of a common word or phrase, a yellow box appears, displaying the text.

1 To insert the text, press the Enter key.

■ To ignore the text, continue typing.

SELECT TEXT

Before performing many tasks in Word, you must select the text you want to work with. Selected text appears highlighted on your screen.

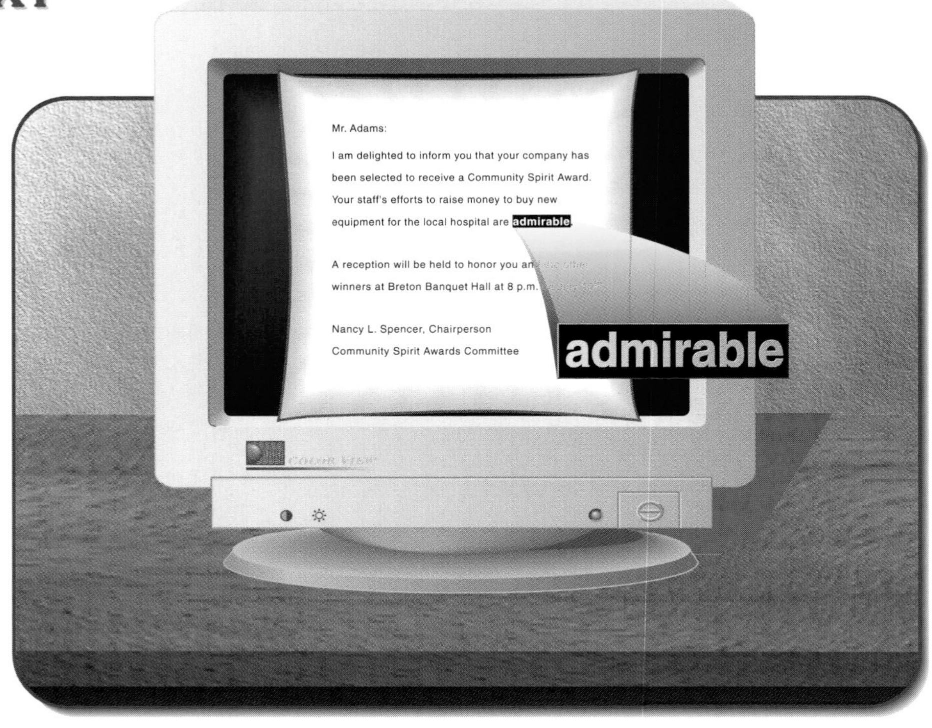

SELECT TEXT

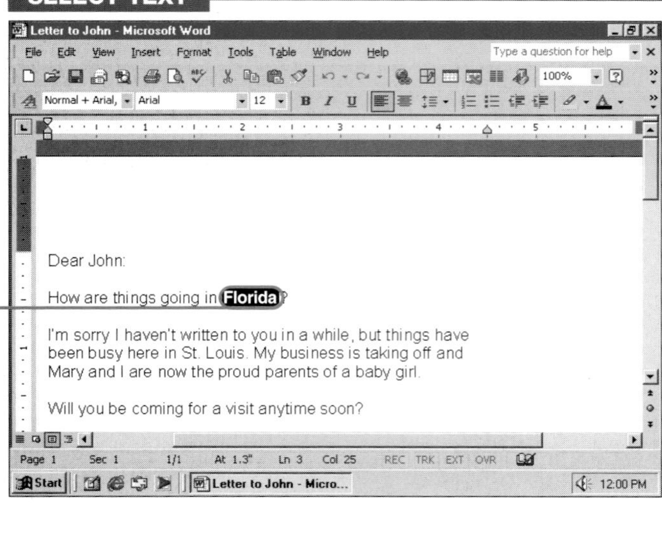

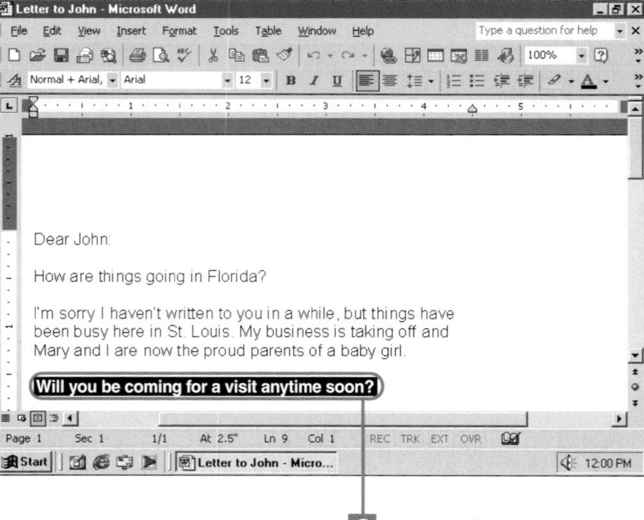

SELECT A WORD

1 Double-click the word you want to select.

■ To deselect text, click outside the selected area.

SELECT A SENTENCE

1 Press and hold down the Ctrl key.

2 Still holding down the Ctrl key, click the sentence you want to select.

How do I select all the text in my document?

To quickly select all the text in your document, press and hold down the Ctrl key as you press the A key.

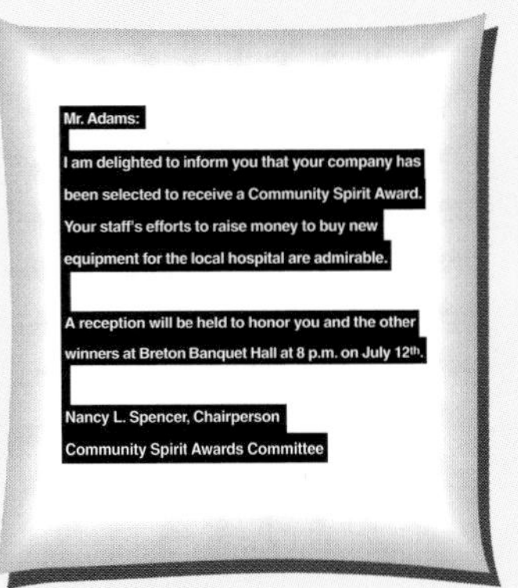

Can I select multiple areas of text in my document at the same time?

Yes. To select multiple areas of text, hold down the Ctrl key as you select each area.

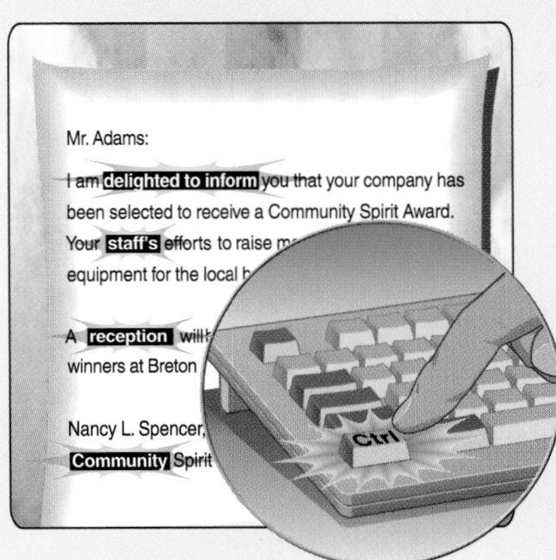

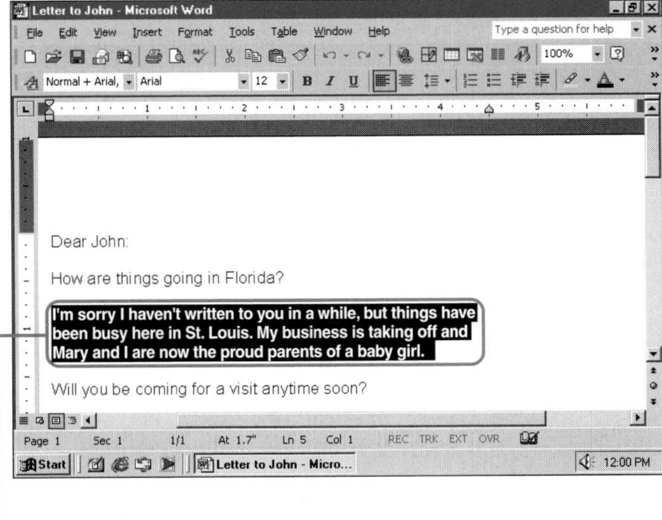

SELECT A PARAGRAPH

1 Position the mouse I over the paragraph you want to select and then quickly click **three** times.

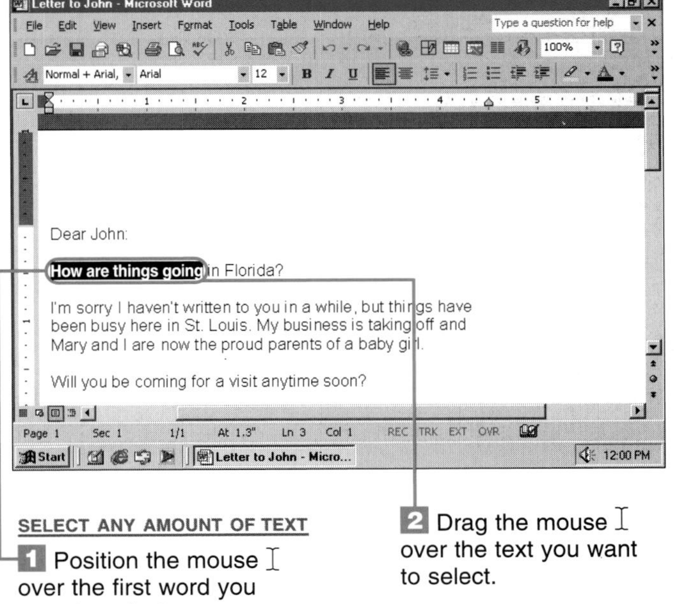

SELECT ANY AMOUNT OF TEXT

1 Position the mouse I over the first word you want to select.

2 Drag the mouse I over the text you want to select.

MOVE THROUGH A DOCUMENT

You can easily move to another location in your document.

If your document contains a lot of text, your computer screen may not be able to display all the text at once. You must scroll through your document to view other parts of the document.

MOVE THROUGH A DOCUMENT

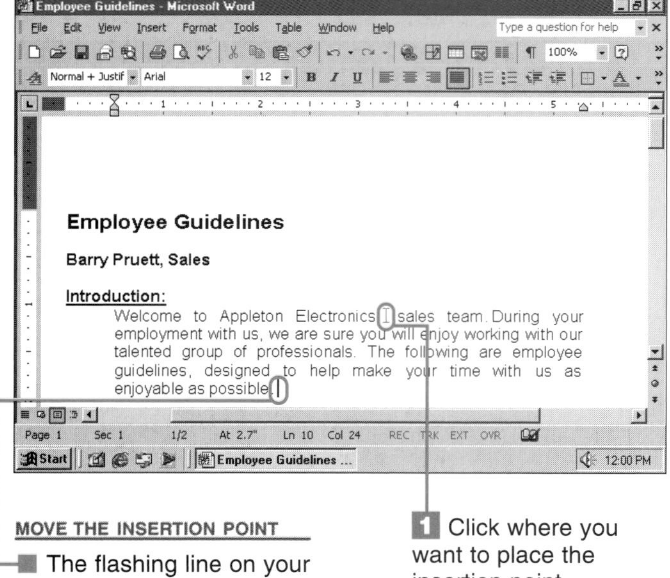

MOVE THE INSERTION POINT

■ The flashing line on your screen, called the insertion point, indicates where the text you type will appear.

1 Click where you want to place the insertion point.

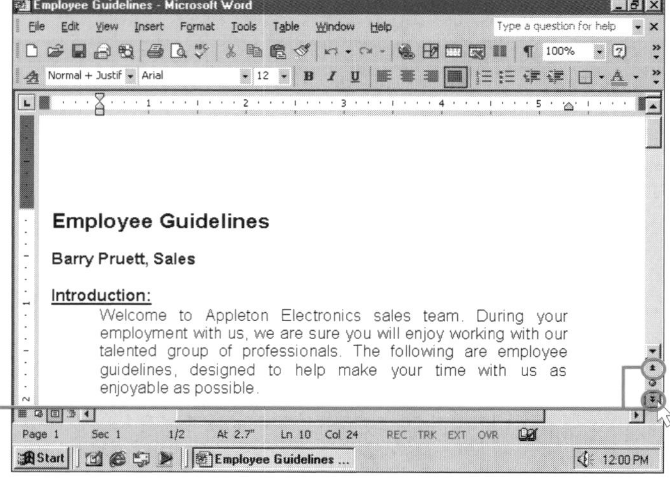

DISPLAY PREVIOUS OR NEXT PAGE

1 Click one of the following buttons.

- Display previous page
- Display next page

How can I use my keyboard to move through a document?

You can press the ←, →, ↑ or ↓ key to move through a document one character or line at a time. You can press the Page Up or Page Down key to move through a document one screen at a time.

How do I use a wheeled mouse to scroll through my document?

A wheeled mouse has a wheel between the left and right mouse buttons. Moving this wheel lets you quickly scroll through your document. The Microsoft IntelliMouse is a popular example of a wheeled mouse.

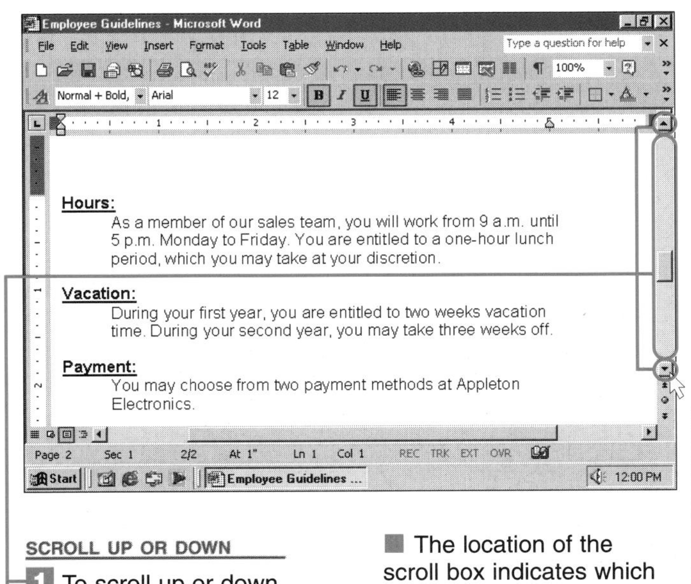

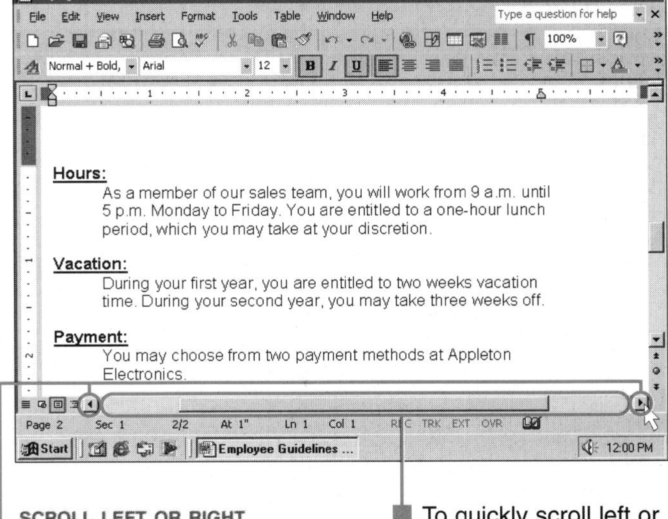

SCROLL UP OR DOWN

1 To scroll up or down, click ▲ or ▼.

■ To quickly scroll up or down, drag the scroll box along the scroll bar.

■ The location of the scroll box indicates which part of the document you are viewing. To view the middle of the document, drag the scroll box halfway down the scroll bar.

SCROLL LEFT OR RIGHT

1 To scroll left or right, click ◄ or ►.

■ To quickly scroll left or right, drag the scroll box along the scroll bar.

CHANGE THE VIEW OF A DOCUMENT

Word offers four different views that you can use to display your document. You can choose the view that best suits your needs.

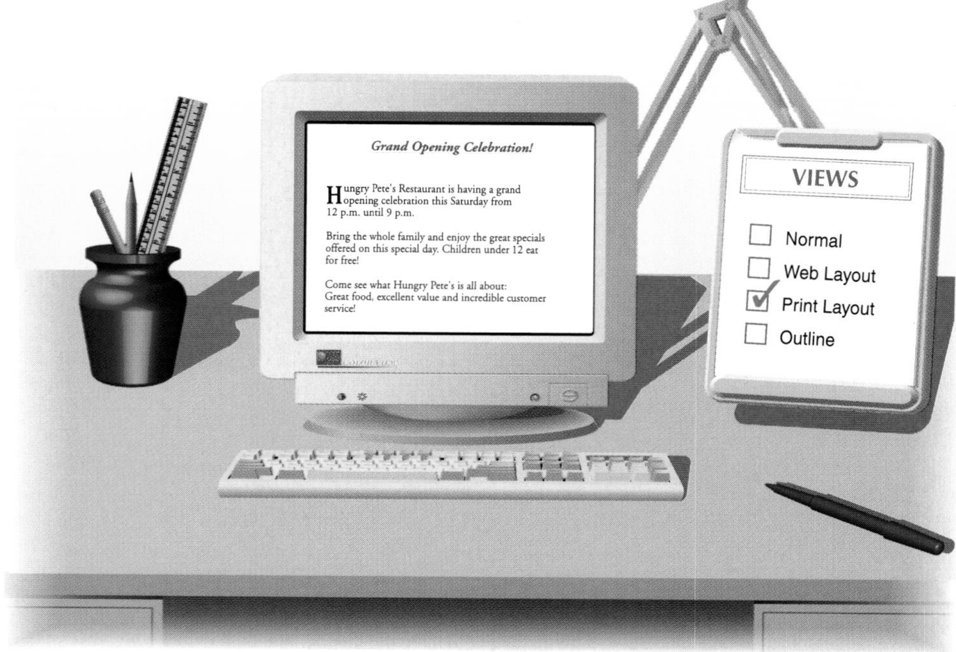

Grand Opening Celebration!
Hungry Pete's Restaurant is having a grand opening celebration this Saturday from 12 p.m. until 9 p.m.
Bring the whole family and enjoy the great specials offered on this special day. Children under 12 eat for free!
Come see what Hungry Pete's is all about: Great food, excellent value and incredible customer service!
VIEWS
Normal
Web Layout
Print Layout
Outline

CHANGE THE VIEW OF A DOCUMENT

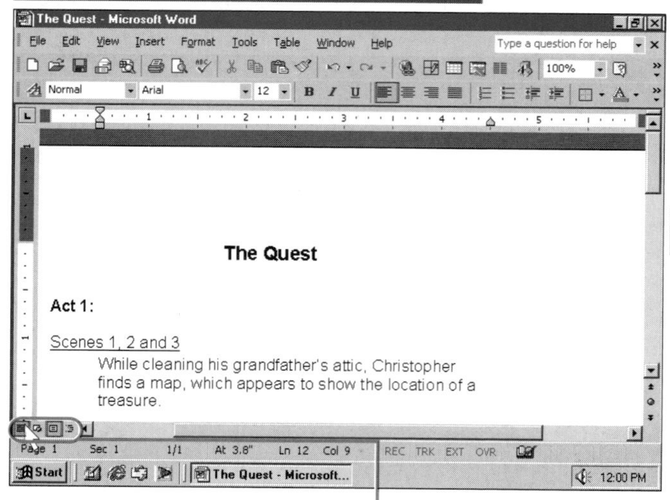

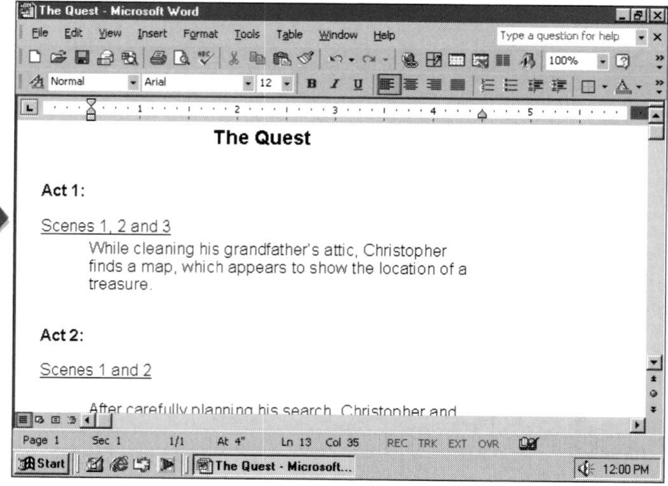

■ When you first start Word, documents appear in the Print Layout view.

1 To change the view of your document, click one of the following buttons.

- Normal
- Web Layout
- Print Layout
- Outline

■ Your document appears in the view you selected.

THE DOCUMENT VIEWS

Normal View

The Normal view simplifies the layout of your document so you can quickly enter, edit and format text. This view does not display certain elements in your document, such as margins and page numbers.

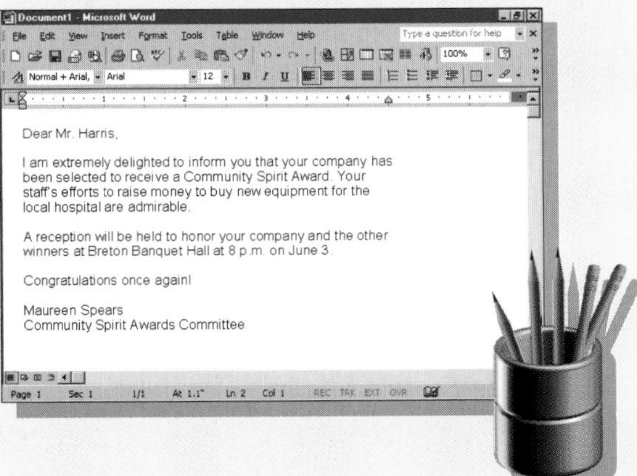

Web Layout View

Working in the Web Layout view is useful when you are creating a Web page or a document that you plan to view only on a computer screen.

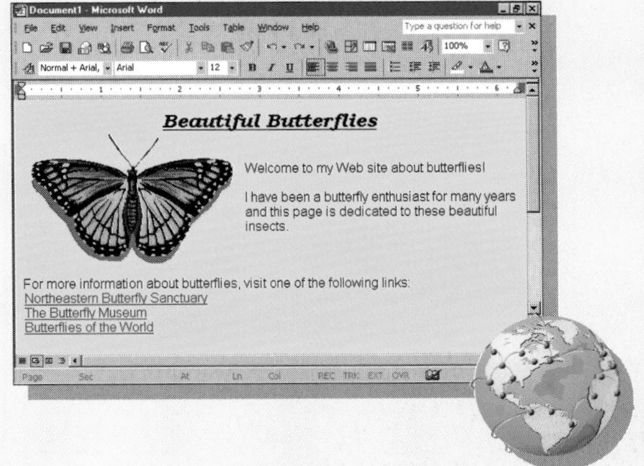

Print Layout View

You can work in the Print Layout view when you want to see how your document will appear on a printed page. This view displays all elements in your document, such as margins and page numbers.

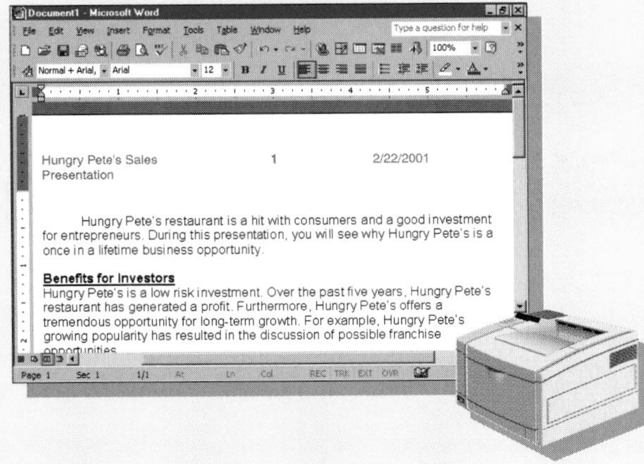

Outline View

The Outline view is useful when you want to review and work with the structure of your document. This view allows you to collapse a document to see only the headings or expand a document to see all the headings and text. The Outline view is useful when working with long documents.

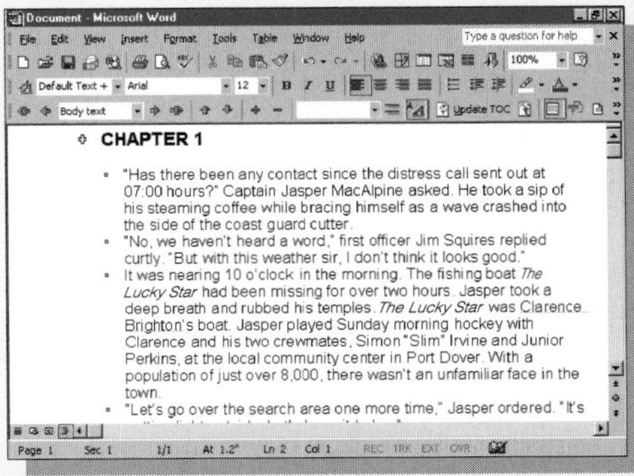

SAVE A DOCUMENT

You can save your document to store it for future use. Saving a document allows you to later review and edit the document.

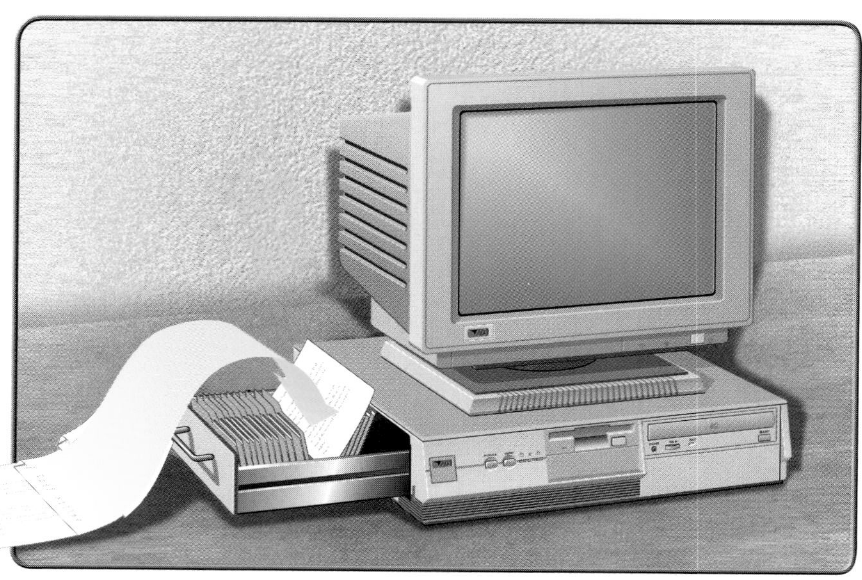

You should regularly save changes you make to a document to avoid losing your work.

SAVE A DOCUMENT

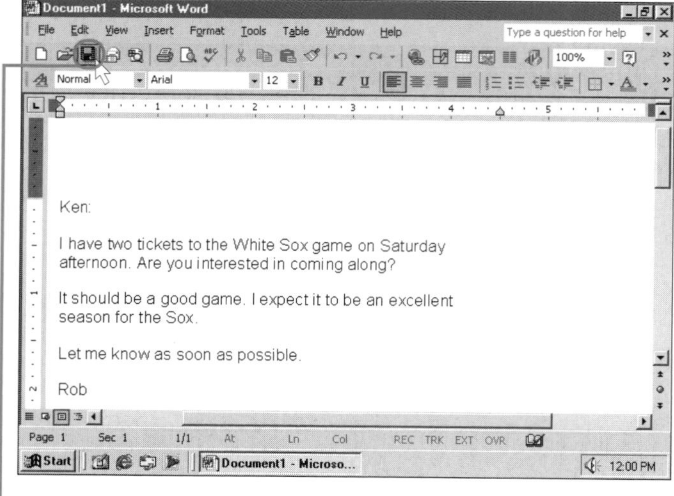

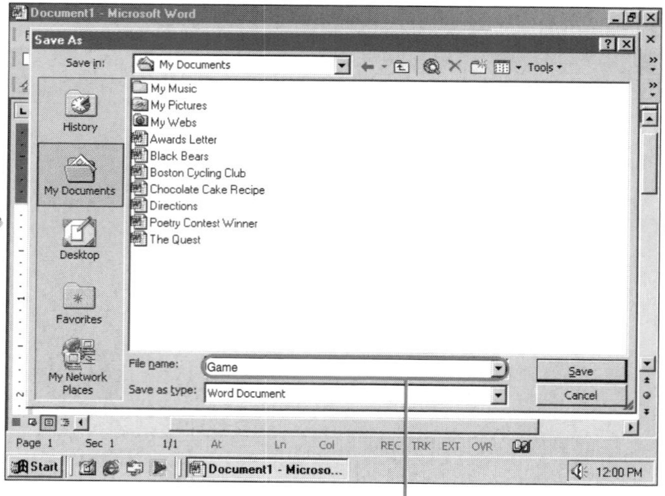

1 Click to save your document.

Note: If is not displayed, click on the Standard toolbar to display all the buttons.

■ The Save As dialog box appears.

Note: If you previously saved your document, the Save As dialog box will not appear since you have already named the document.

2 Type a name for the document.

What are the commonly used locations that I can access?

History

Provides access to folders and documents you recently worked with.

My Documents

Provides a convenient place to store a document.

Desktop

Allows you to store a document on the Windows desktop.

Favorites

Provides a place to store a document you will frequently use.

My Network Places

Allows you to store a document on your network.

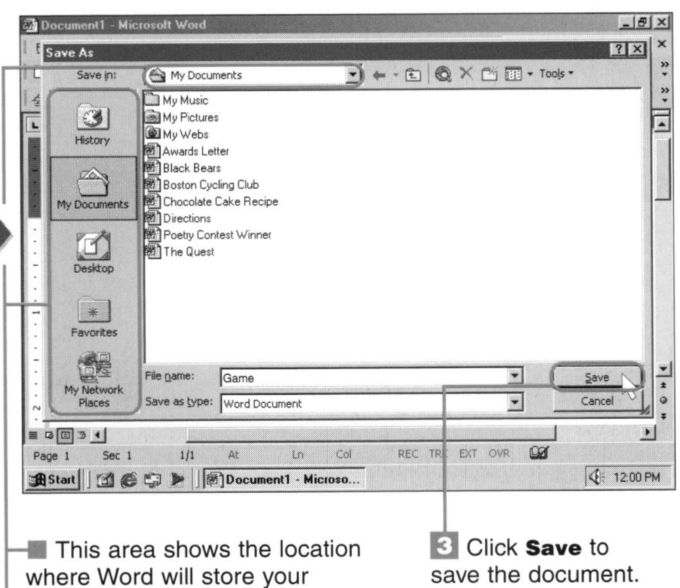

■ This area shows the location where Word will store your document. You can click this area to change the location.

■ This area allows you to access commonly used locations. You can click a location to save your document in the location.

3 Click **Save** to save the document.

■ Word saves your document.

CLOSE A DOCUMENT

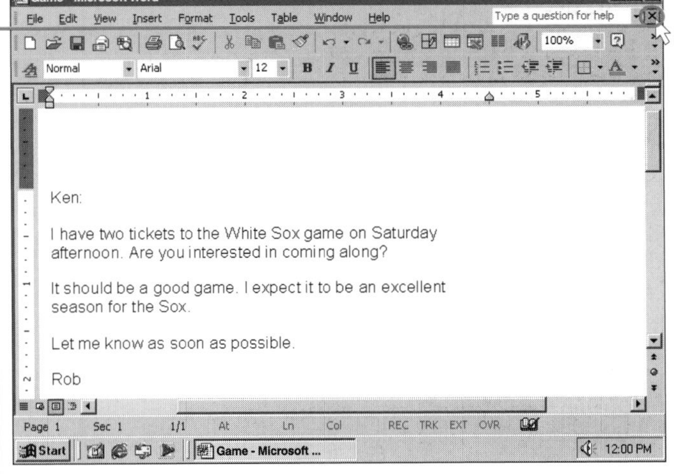

1 When you finish working with a document, click ☒ to close the document.

■ The document disappears from your screen.

OPEN A DOCUMENT

You can open a saved document to view the document on your screen. This allows you to review and make changes to the document.

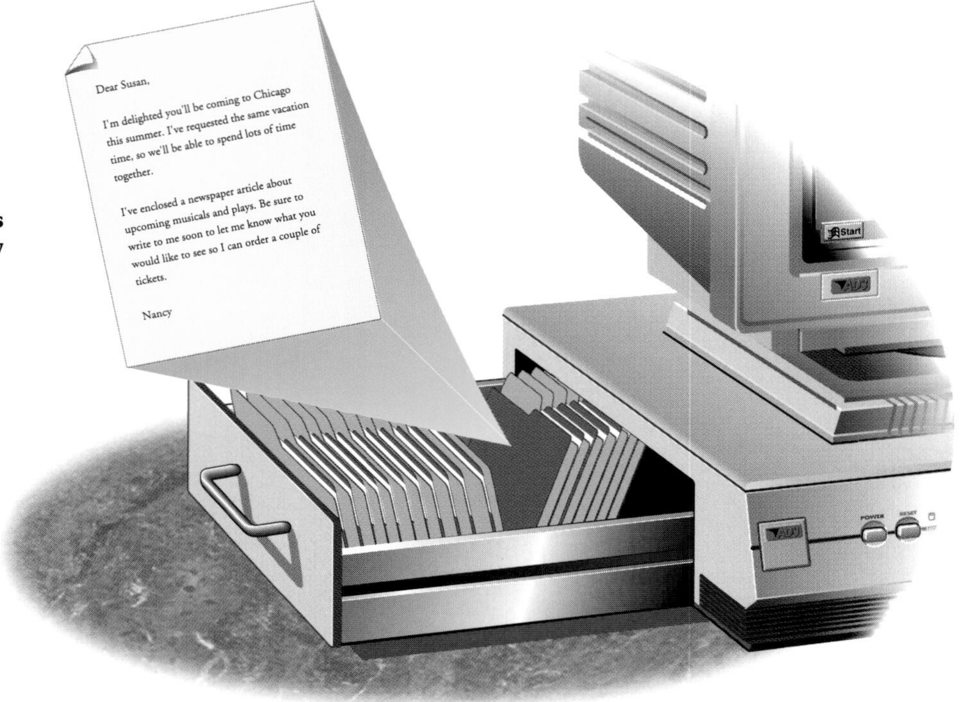

Dear Susan,
I'm delighted you'll be coming to Chicago this summer. I've requested the same vacation time, so we'll be able to spend lots of time together.
I've enclosed a newspaper article about upcoming musicals and plays. Be sure to write to me soon to let me know what you would like to see so I can order a couple of tickets.
Nancy

OPEN A DOCUMENT

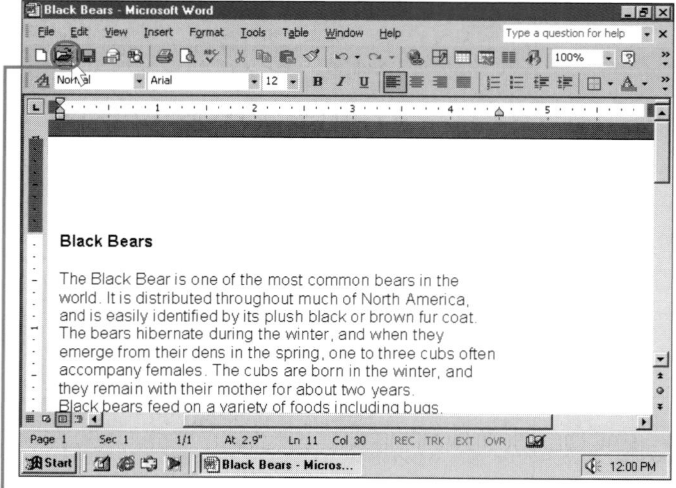

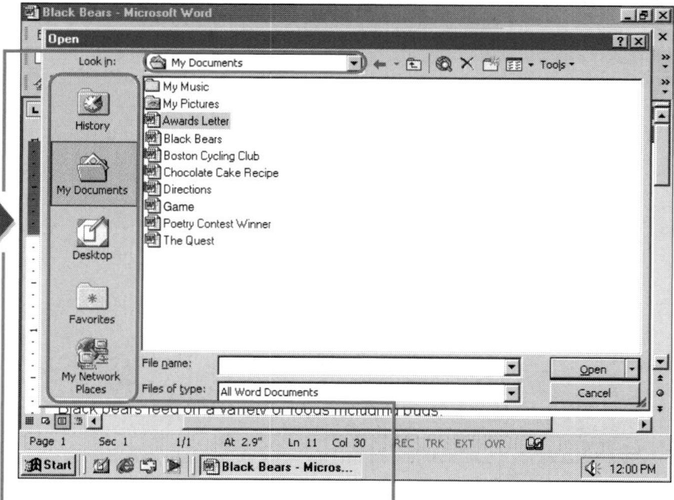

1 Click to open a document.

Note: If does not appear, click on the Standard toolbar to display all the buttons.

■ The Open dialog box appears.

■ This area shows the location of the displayed documents. You can click this area to change the location.

■ This area allows you to access documents in commonly used locations. You can click a location to display the documents stored in the location.

Note: For information on the commonly used locations, see the top of page 31.

How can I quickly open a document I recently worked with?

Word remembers the names of the last four documents you worked with. You can use one of the following methods to quickly open any of these documents.

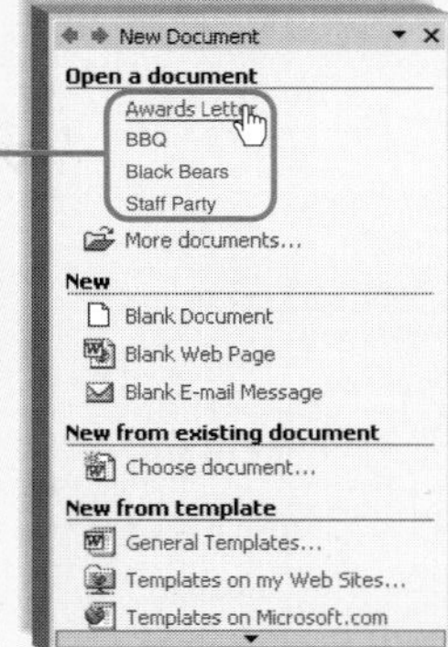

Use the Task Pane

The New Document task pane appears each time you start Word. To display the New Document task pane, see page 12.

1 Click the name of the document you want to open.

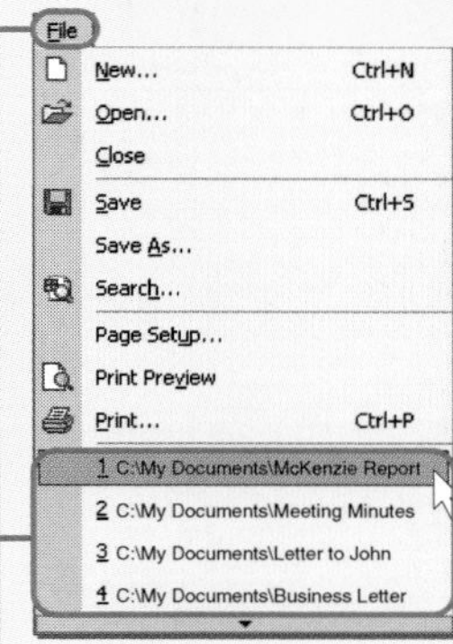

Use the File Menu

1 Click **File**.

2 Click the name of the document you want to open.

Note: If the names of the last four documents you worked with are not all displayed, position the mouse ↖ over the bottom of the menu to display all the names.

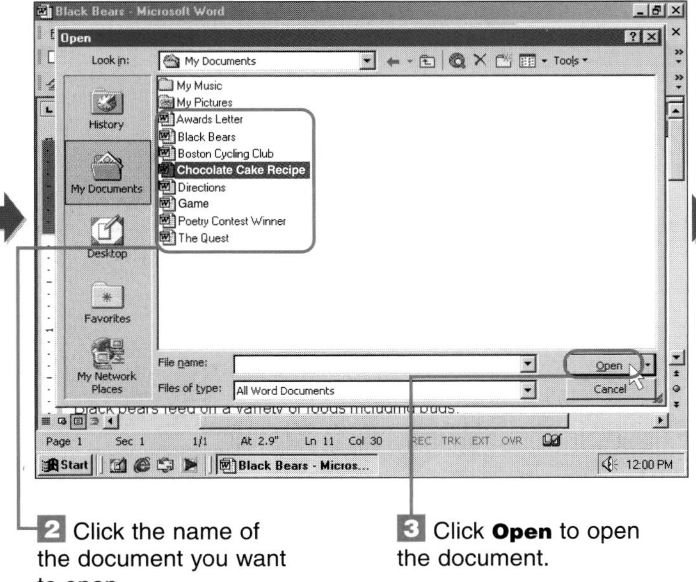

2 Click the name of the document you want to open.

3 Click **Open** to open the document.

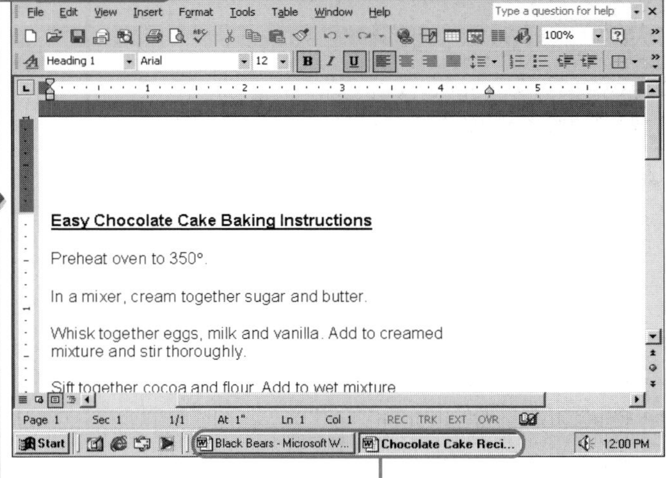

■ The document opens and appears on your screen. You can now review and make changes to the document.

■ This area displays the name of the open document.

■ If you already had a document open, the new document appears in a new Microsoft Word window. You can click the buttons on the taskbar to switch between the open documents.

PREVIEW A DOCUMENT BEFORE PRINTING

You can use the Print Preview feature to see how your document will look when printed.

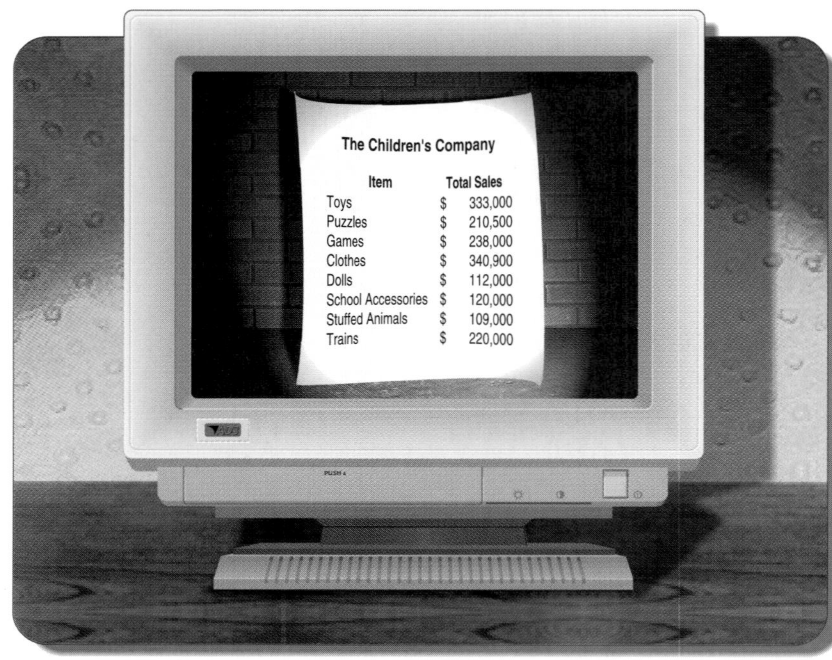

This allows you to confirm that the document will print the way you want.

PREVIEW A DOCUMENT BEFORE PRINTING

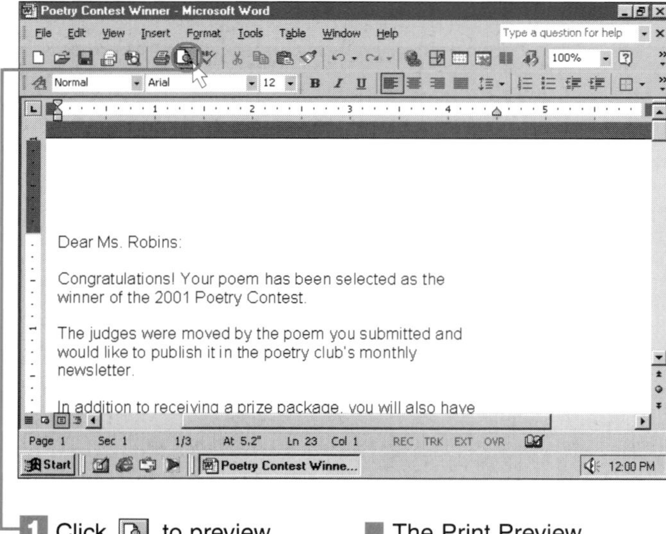

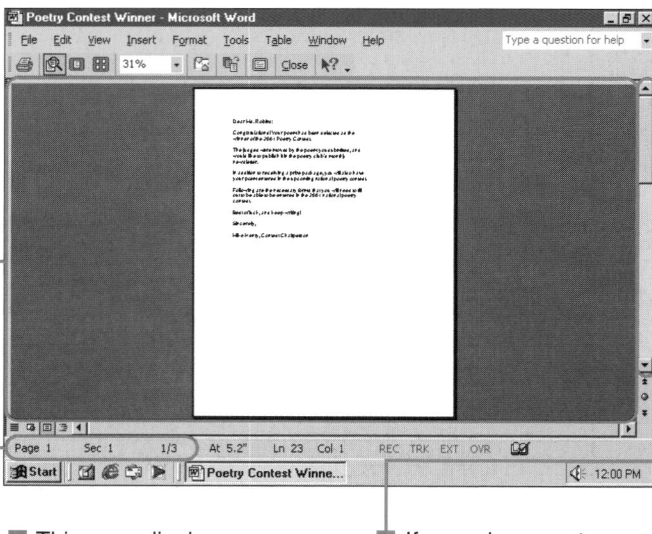

1. Click the Print Preview button to preview your document.

Note: If the Print Preview button is not displayed, click the Toolbar Options button on the Standard toolbar to display all the buttons.

■ The Print Preview window appears.

■ This area displays a page from your document.

■ This area indicates which page is displayed and the total number of pages in your document.

■ If your document contains more than one page, you can use the scroll bar to view the other pages.

Can I edit my document in the Print Preview window?

Yes. If the mouse looks like when over your document, you can edit the document. If the mouse looks like or when over your document, you can enlarge or reduce the size of the page displayed on your screen. To change the appearance of the mouse, click the Magnifier button ( ).

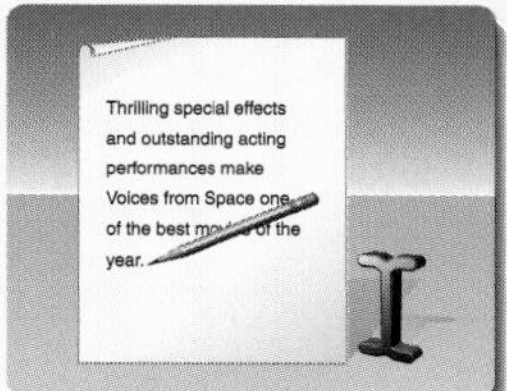

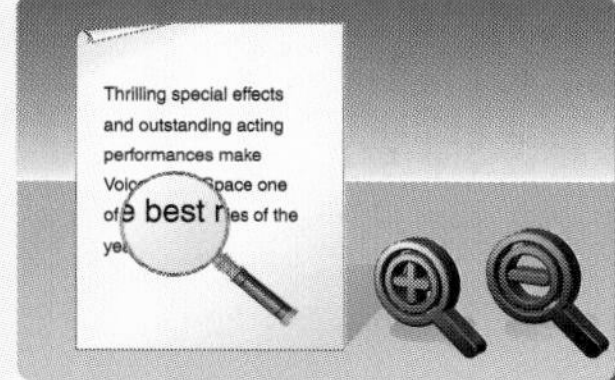

Can I shrink the text in my document to fit on one less page?

If the last page in your document contains only a few lines of text, Word can shrink the text in your document so that the last few lines will fit on the previous page. In the Print Preview window, click the Shrink to Fit button ( ) to shrink the text in your document.

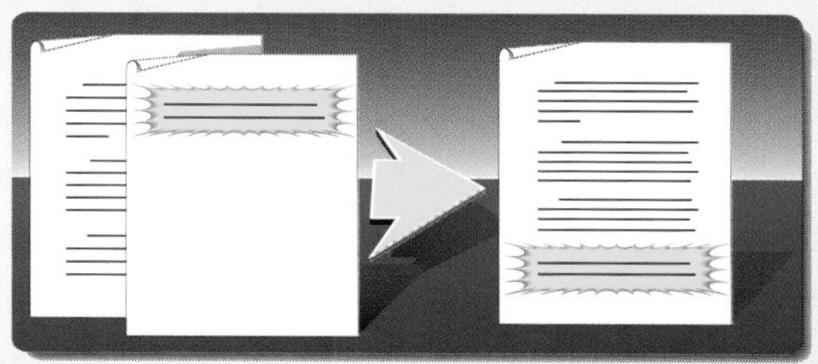

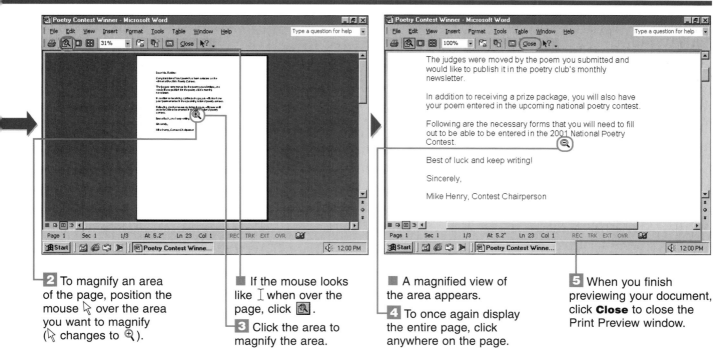

2 To magnify an area of the page, position the mouse over the area you want to magnify (changes to).

■ If the mouse looks like when over the page, click .

3 Click the area to magnify the area.

■ A magnified view of the area appears.

4 To once again display the entire page, click anywhere on the page.

5 When you finish previewing your document, click **Close** to close the Print Preview window.

PRINT A DOCUMENT

You can produce a paper copy of the document displayed on your screen.

Before printing your document, make sure the printer is turned on and contains an adequate supply of paper.

PRINT A DOCUMENT

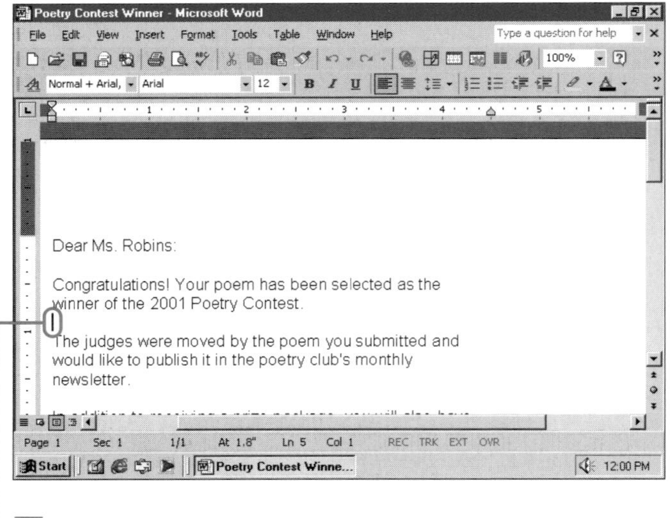

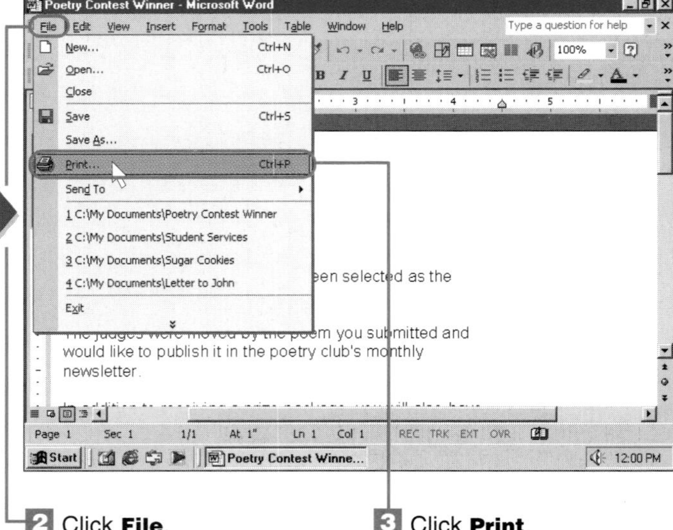

1 Click anywhere in the document or page you want to print.

■ To print only some of the text in the document, select the text you want to print. To select text, see page 24.

2 Click **File**.

3 Click **Print**.

■ The Print dialog box appears.

Which print option should I use?

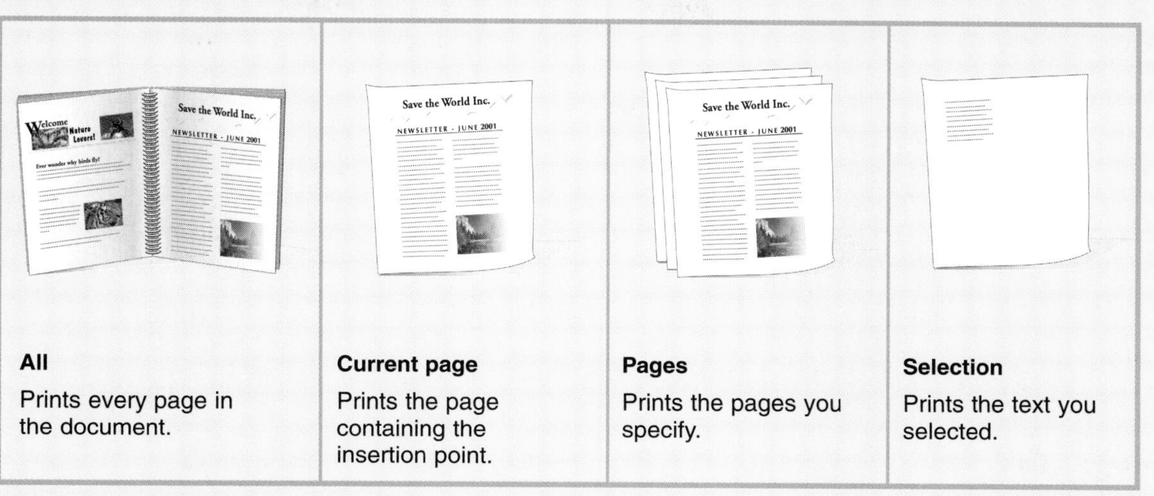

All
Prints every page in the document.

Current page
Prints the page containing the insertion point.

Pages
Prints the pages you specify.

Selection
Prints the text you selected.

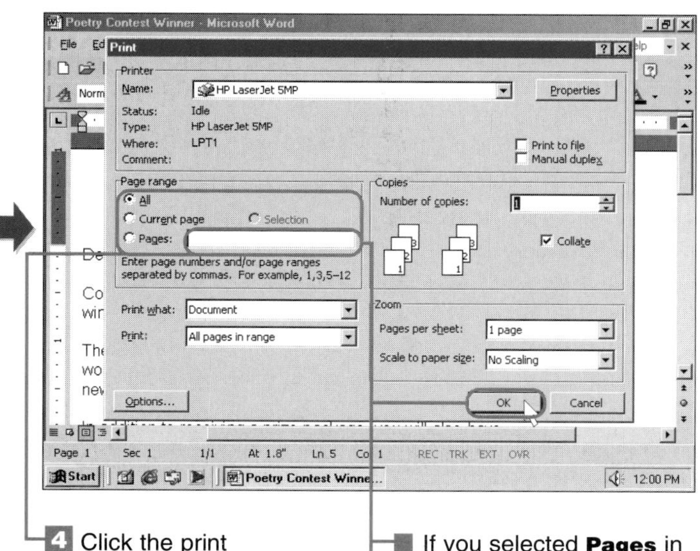

4 Click the print option you want to use (○ changes to ⊙).

Note: For more information on the print options, see the top of this page.

■ If you selected **Pages** in step 4, type the pages you want to print in this area (example: 1,3,5 or 2-4).

5 Click **OK**.

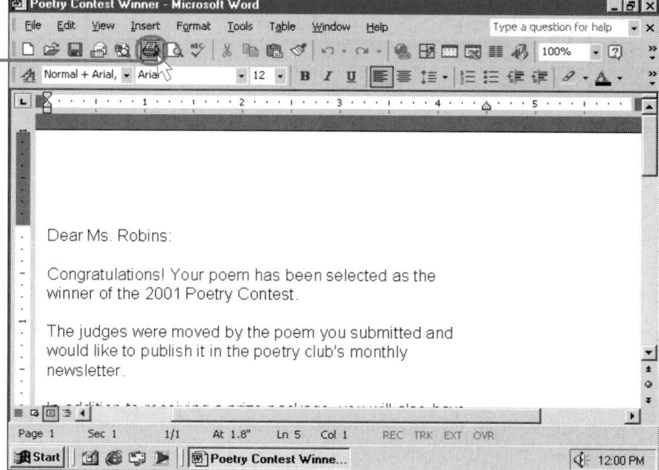

QUICKLY PRINT ENTIRE DOCUMENT

1 Click the print button to quickly print your entire document.

Note: If the print button is not displayed, click » on the Standard toolbar to display all the buttons.

CREATE A NEW DOCUMENT

You can create a new document to start writing a new letter, memo or report.

Each document is like a separate piece of paper. Creating a new document is like placing a new piece of paper on your screen.

CREATE A NEW DOCUMENT

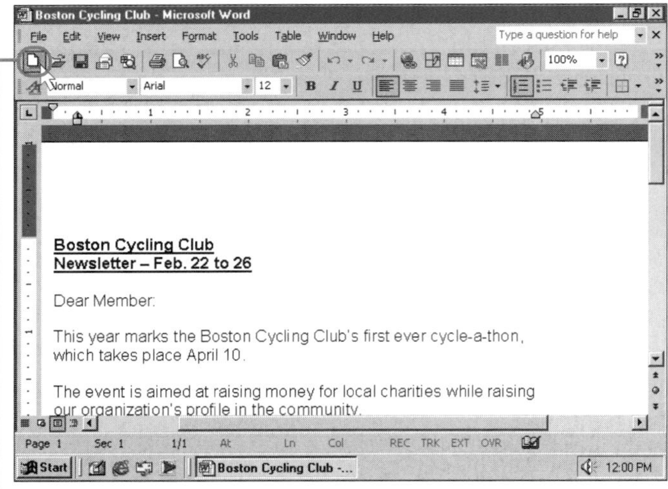

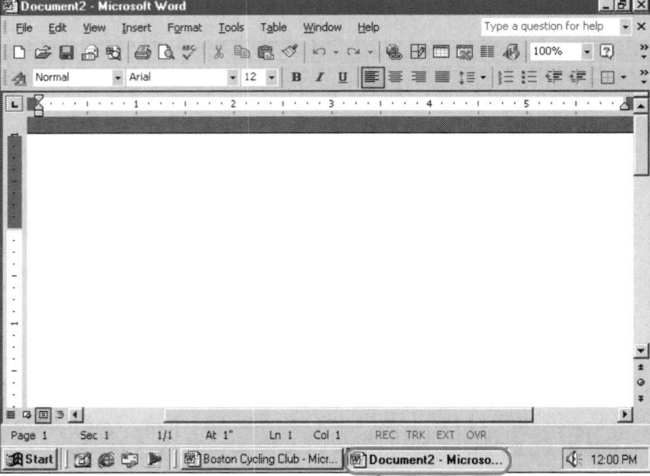

1 Click [new document icon] to create a new document.

Note: If [new document icon] is not displayed, click [» icon] on the Standard toolbar to display all the buttons.

■ The new document appears in a new Microsoft Word window.

■ A button for the new document appears on the taskbar.

SWITCH BETWEEN DOCUMENTS

You can have several documents open at once. Word allows you to easily switch from one open document to another.

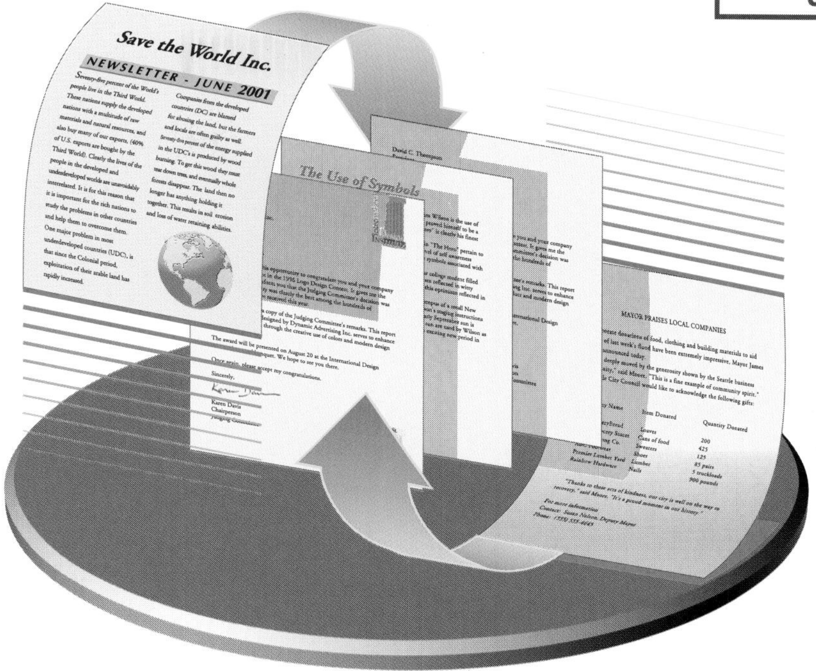

SWITCH BETWEEN DOCUMENTS

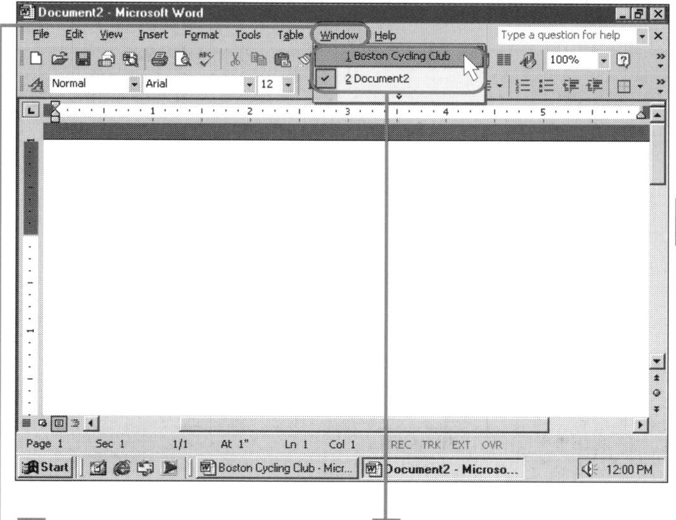

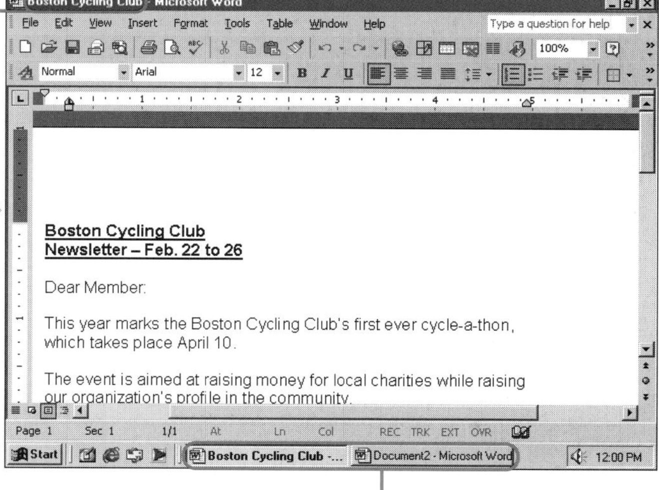

1 Click **Window** to display a list of all the documents you have open.

2 Click the name of the document you want to switch to.

- The document appears.
- This area displays the name of the displayed document.

- The taskbar displays a button for each open document. You can also click the buttons on the taskbar to switch between the open documents.

E-MAIL A DOCUMENT

You can e-mail the document displayed on your screen to a friend, family member or colleague.

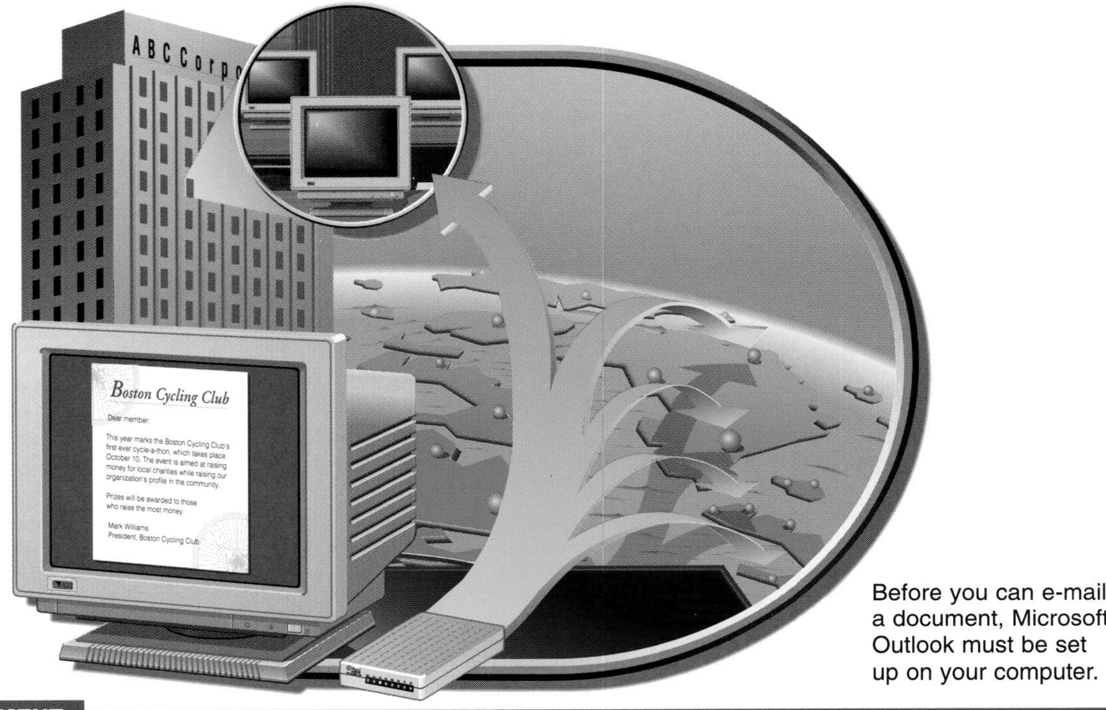

Before you can e-mail a document, Microsoft Outlook must be set up on your computer.

E-MAIL A DOCUMENT

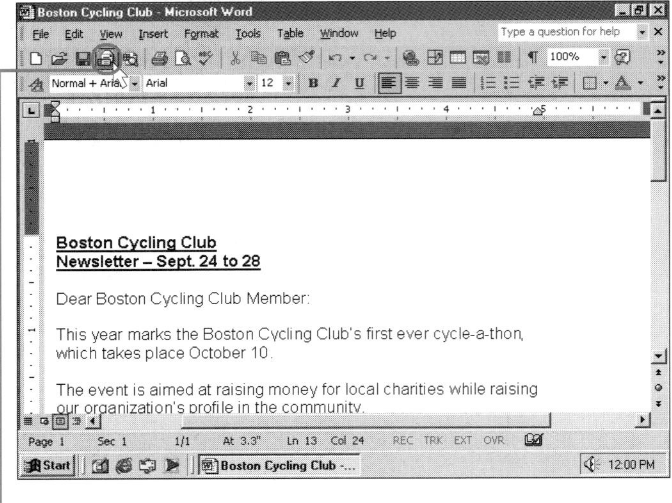

1 Click [icon] to e-mail the displayed document.

Note: If [icon] is not displayed, click [icon] on the Standard toolbar to display all the buttons.

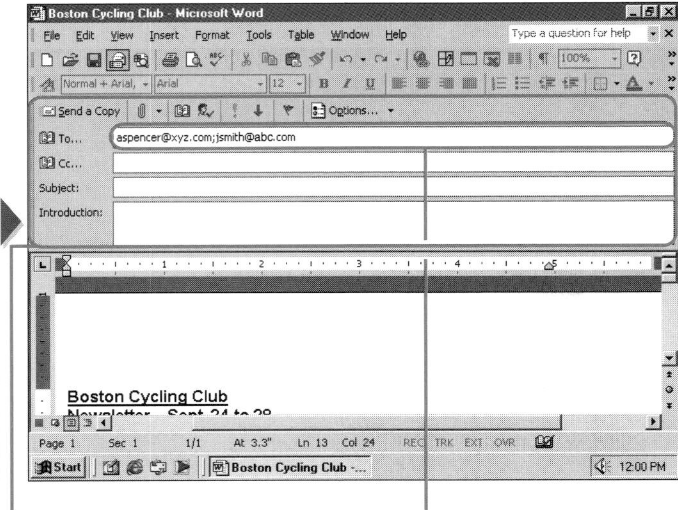

■ An area appears for you to address the message.

2 Click this area and type the e-mail address of each person you want to receive the message. Separate each address with a semicolon (;).

How can I address an e-mail message?

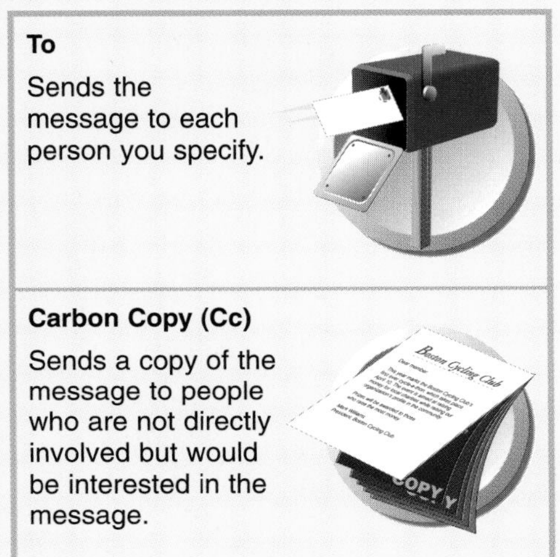

To
Sends the message to each person you specify.
Carbon Copy (Cc)
Sends a copy of the message to people who are not directly involved but would be interested in the message.
COPY

Why would I include an introduction for a document I am sending in an e-mail message?

Including an introduction allows you to provide the recipient of the message with additional information about the document. For example, the recipient may require instructions or an explanation of the content of the document.

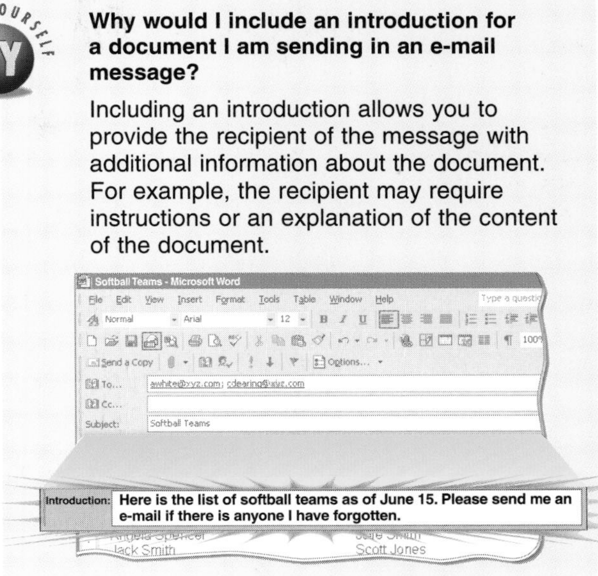

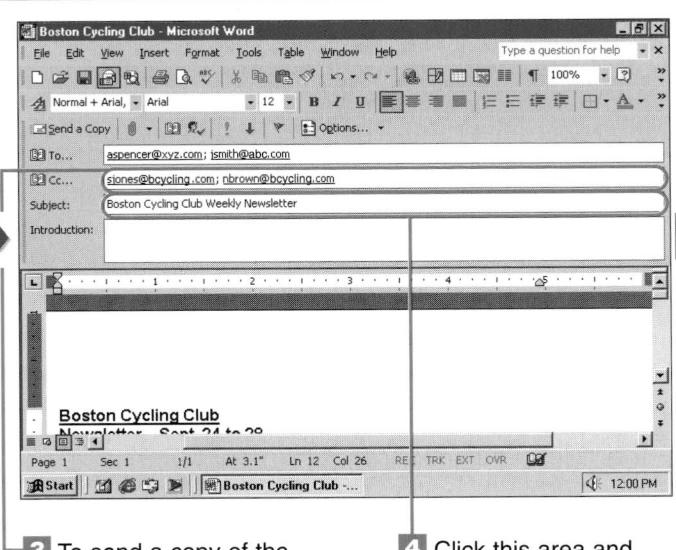

3 To send a copy of the message, click this area and type the e-mail address of each person you want to receive a copy. Separate each address with a semicolon (;).

4 Click this area and type a subject for the message.

Note: If a subject already exists, you can drag the mouse I over the existing subject and then type a new subject.

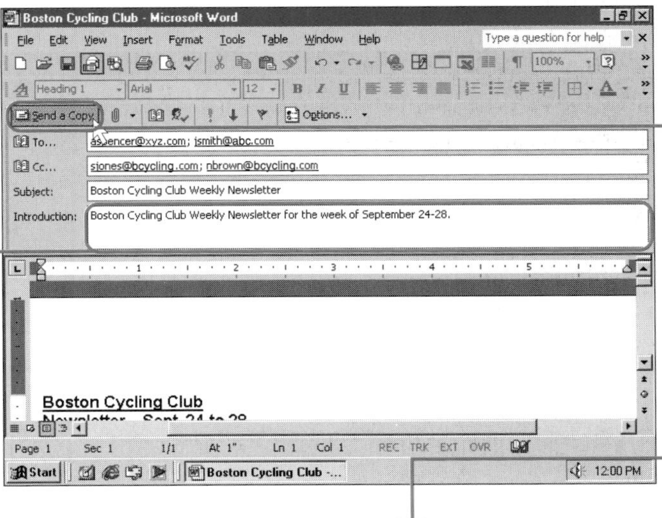

5 To include an introduction for the document you are sending in the message, click this area and type the introduction.

6 Click **Send a Copy** to send the message.

INSERT AND DELETE TEXT

You can easily add new text to your document and remove text you no longer need.

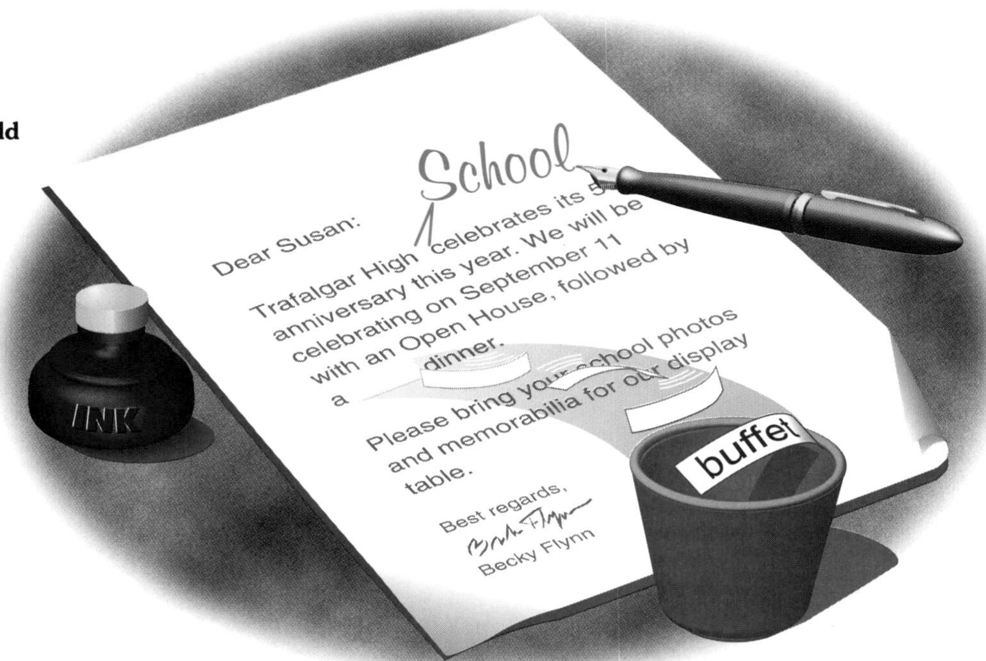

INSERT TEXT

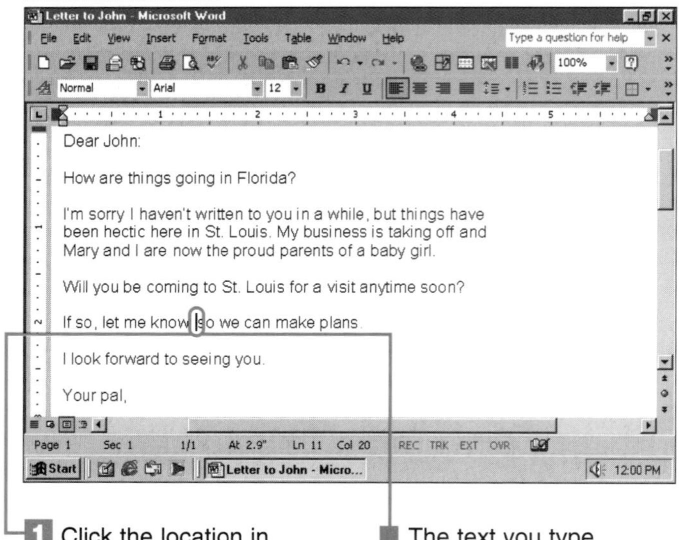

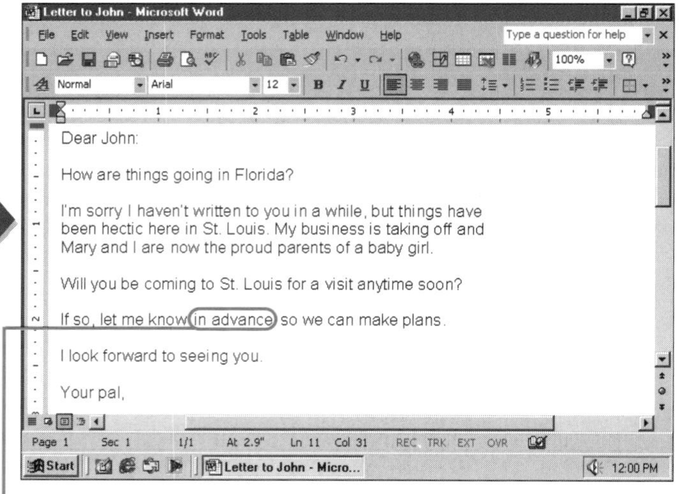

1 Click the location in your document where you want to insert new text.

■ The text you type will appear where the insertion point flashes on the screen.

Note: You can press the ←, →, ↑ or ↓ key to move the insertion point one character or line in any direction.

2 Type the text you want to insert. To insert a blank space, press the **Spacebar**.

■ The words to the right of the new text move forward.

How can I insert symbols that are not available on my keyboard?

When you type one of the following sets of characters, Word automatically replaces the characters with a symbol.

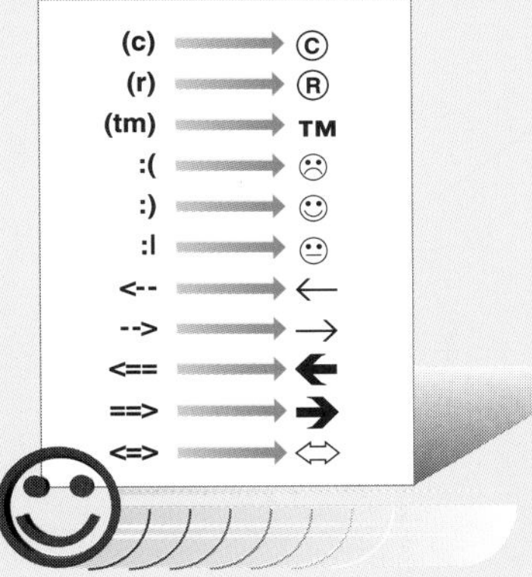

Why does the existing text in my document disappear when I insert new text?

You may have turned on the Overtype feature, which will replace existing text with the text you type. When the Overtype feature is on, the **OVR** status indicator at the bottom of your screen is **bold**. To turn the Overtype feature on or off, press the Insert key.

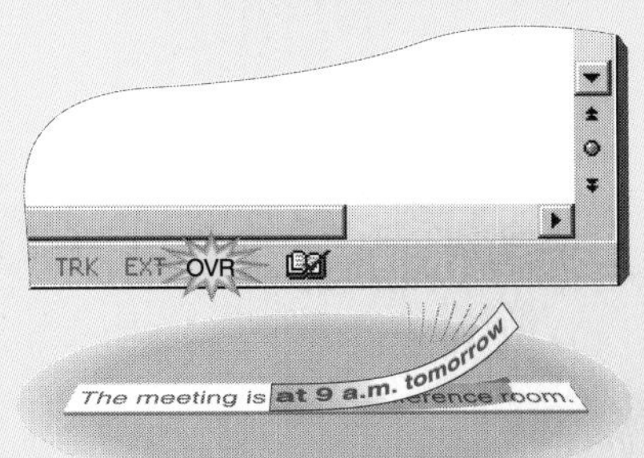

DELETE TEXT

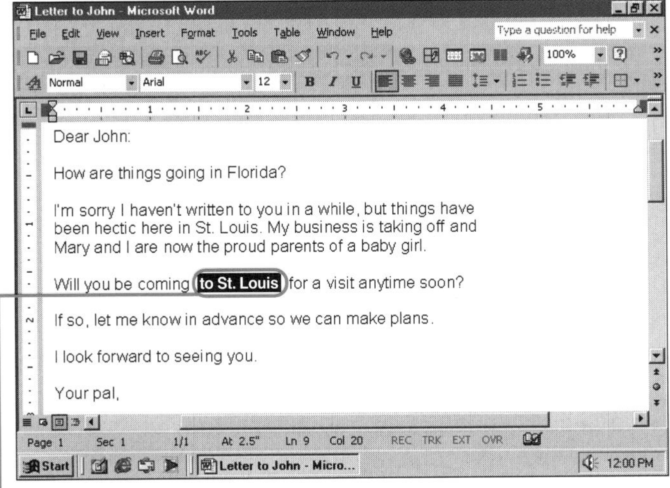

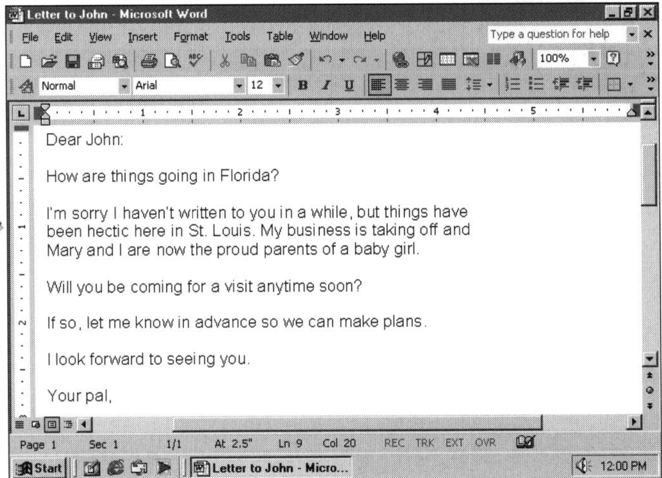

1 Select the text you want to delete. To select text, see page 24.

2 Press the Delete key to remove the text.

■ The text disappears. The remaining text in the line or paragraph moves to fill the empty space.

■ To delete a single character, click to the right of the character you want to delete and then press the ←Backspace key. Word deletes the character to the left of the flashing insertion point.

MOVE OR COPY TEXT

You can move or copy text to a new location in your document.

Moving text allows you to rearrange text in your document. When you move text, the text disappears from its original location.

Copying text allows you to repeat information in your document without having to retype the text. When you copy text, the text appears in both the original and new locations.

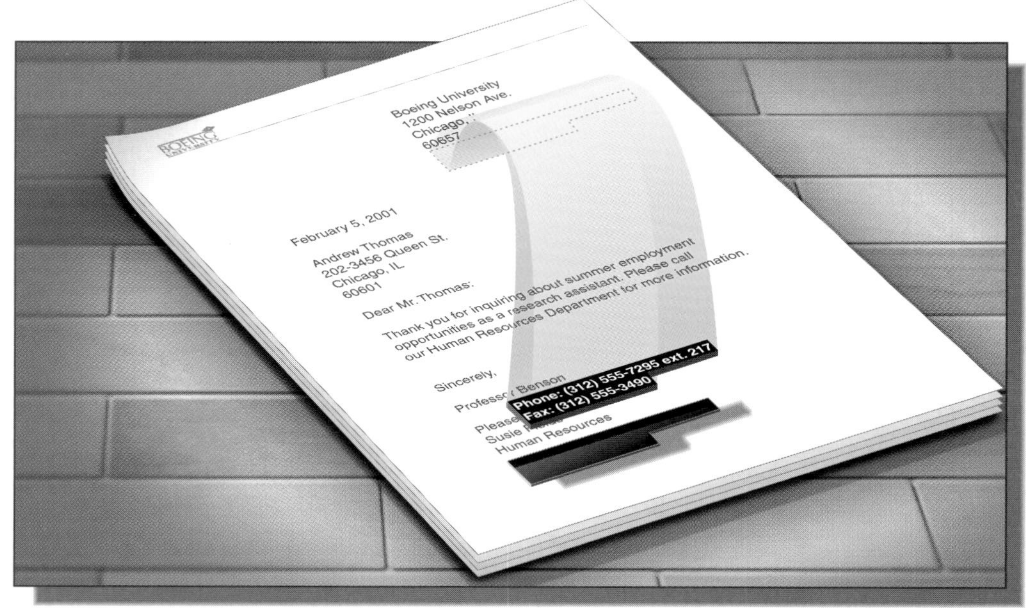

MOVE OR COPY TEXT

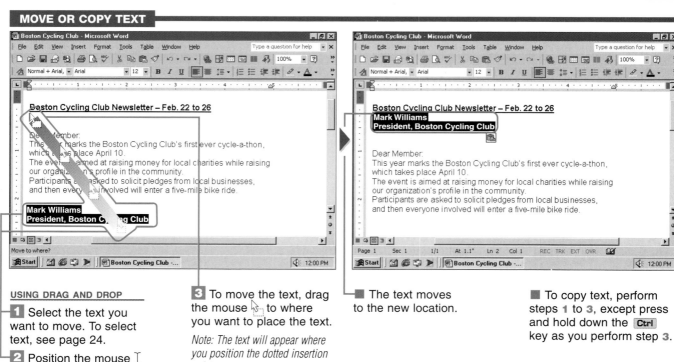

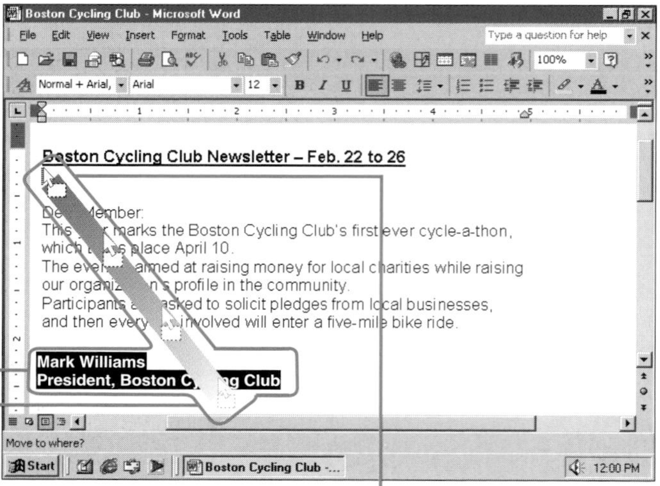

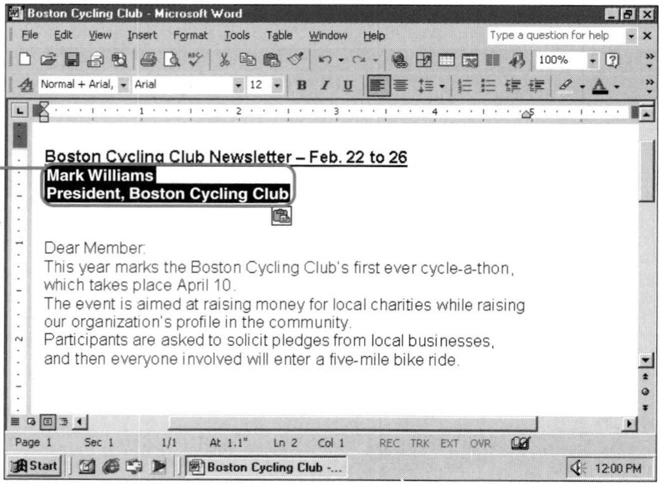

USING DRAG AND DROP

1 Select the text you want to move. To select text, see page 24.

2 Position the mouse I over the selected text (I changes to ↖).

3 To move the text, drag the mouse to where you want to place the text.

Note: The text will appear where you position the dotted insertion point on your screen.

■ The text moves to the new location.

■ To copy text, perform steps 1 to 3, except press and hold down the **Ctrl** key as you perform step 3.

How can I use the Clipboard task pane to move or copy text?

The Clipboard task pane displays the last 24 items you have selected to move or copy. To place a clipboard item in your document, click the location in your document where you want the item to appear and then click the item in the task pane. For information about task panes, see page 12.

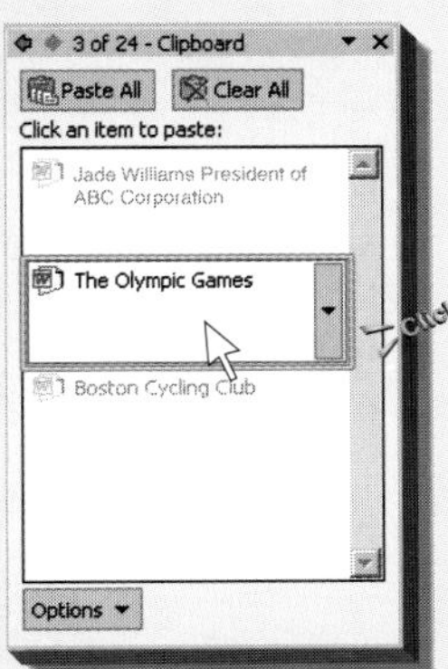

Why does the Paste Options button (📋) appear when I move or copy text?

The Paste Options button (📋) allows you to change the format of text you moved or copied. For example, you can choose to keep the original formatting of the text or change the formatting of the text to match the text in the new destination.

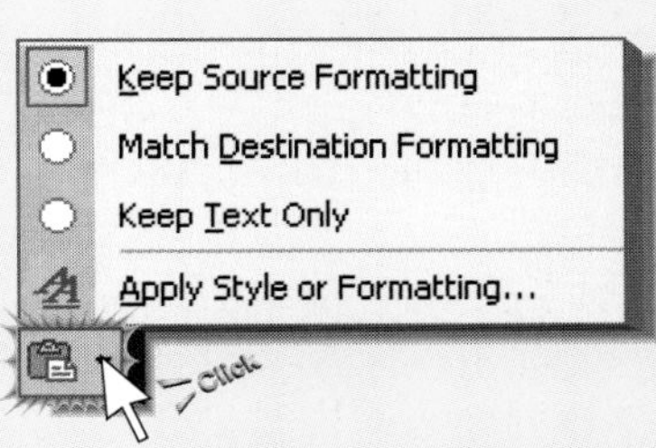

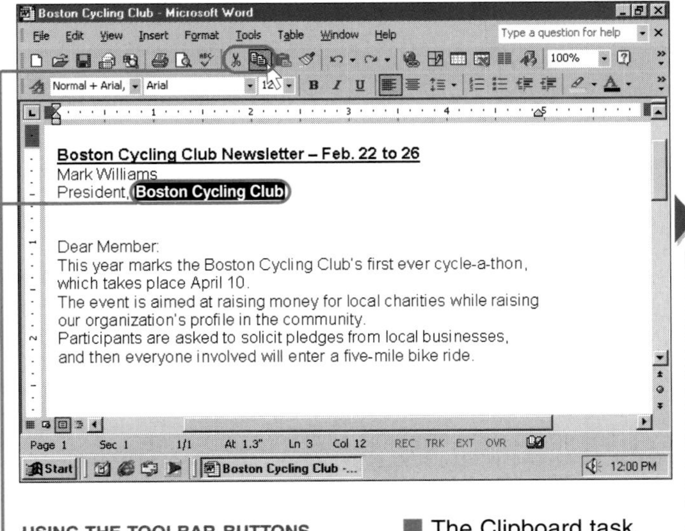

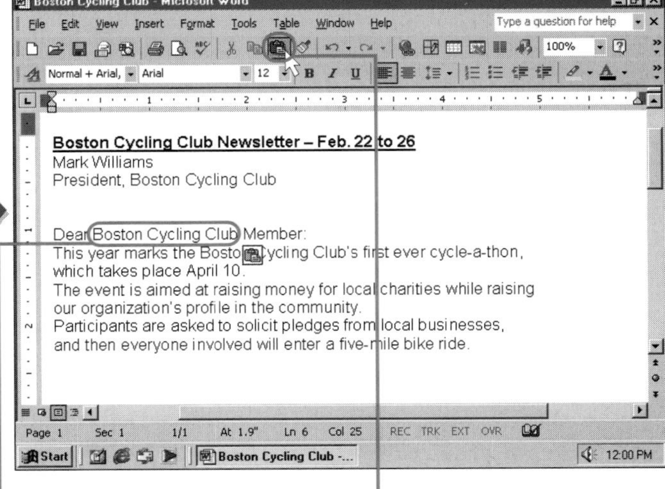

USING THE TOOLBAR BUTTONS

1 Select the text you want to move or copy. To select text, see page 24.

2 Click one of the following buttons.

- ✂ Move text
- 📄 Copy text

■ The Clipboard task pane may appear. To use the Clipboard task pane, see the top of this page.

Note: If the button you want is not displayed, click ⏬ on the Standard toolbar to display all the buttons.

3 Click the location where you want to place the text.

4 Click 📋 to place the text in the new location.

Note: If 📋 is not displayed, click ⏬ on the Standard toolbar to display all the buttons.

■ The text appears in the new location.

UNDO CHANGES

Word remembers the last changes you made to your document. If you regret these changes, you can cancel them by using the Undo feature.

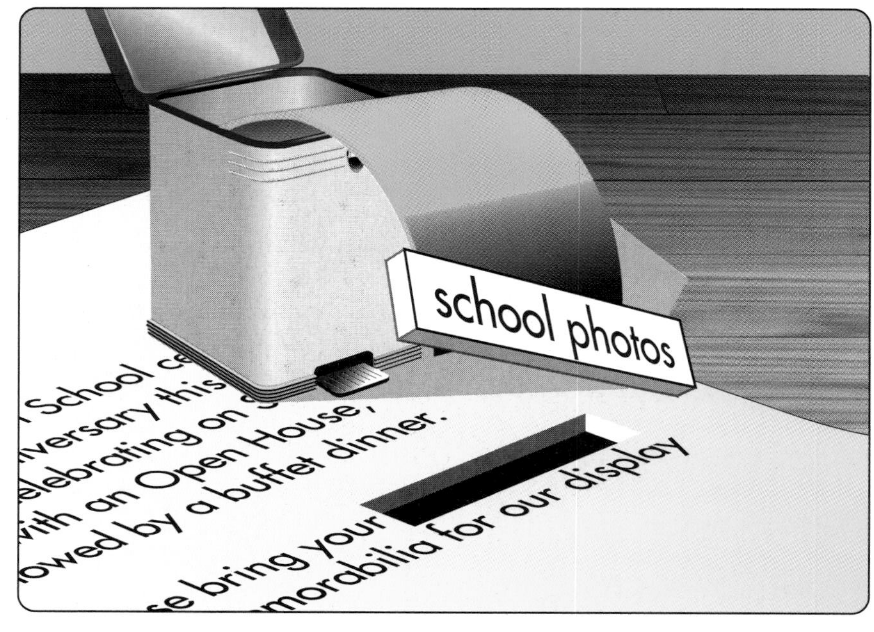

The Undo feature can cancel your last editing and formatting changes.

UNDO CHANGES

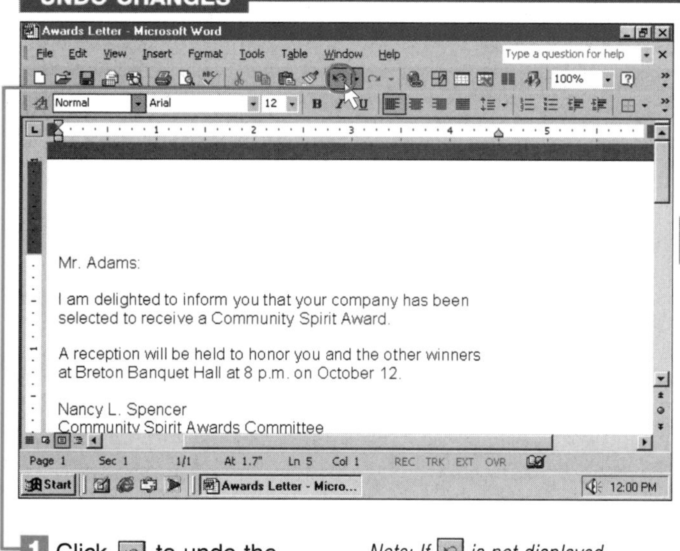

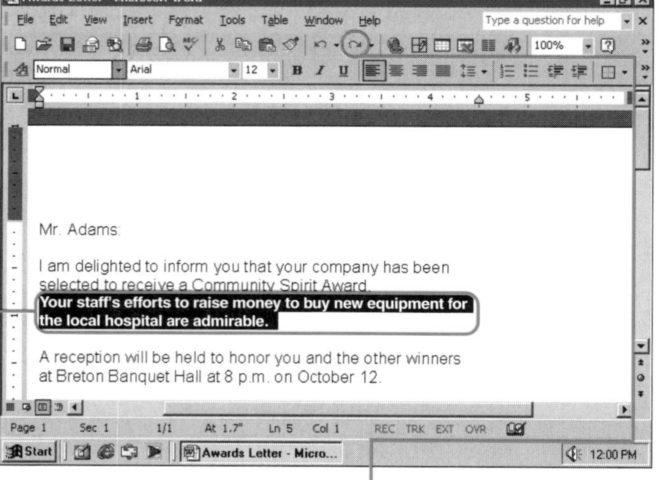

1 Click [undo icon] to undo the last change you made to your document.

Note: If [undo icon] is not displayed, click [»] on the Standard toolbar to display all the buttons.

■ Word cancels the last change you made to your document.

■ You can repeat step **1** to cancel previous changes you made.

■ To reverse the results of using the Undo feature, click [redo icon].

Note: If [redo icon] is not displayed, click [»] on the Standard toolbar to display all the buttons.

COUNT WORDS IN A DOCUMENT

You can have Word count the number of words in your document.

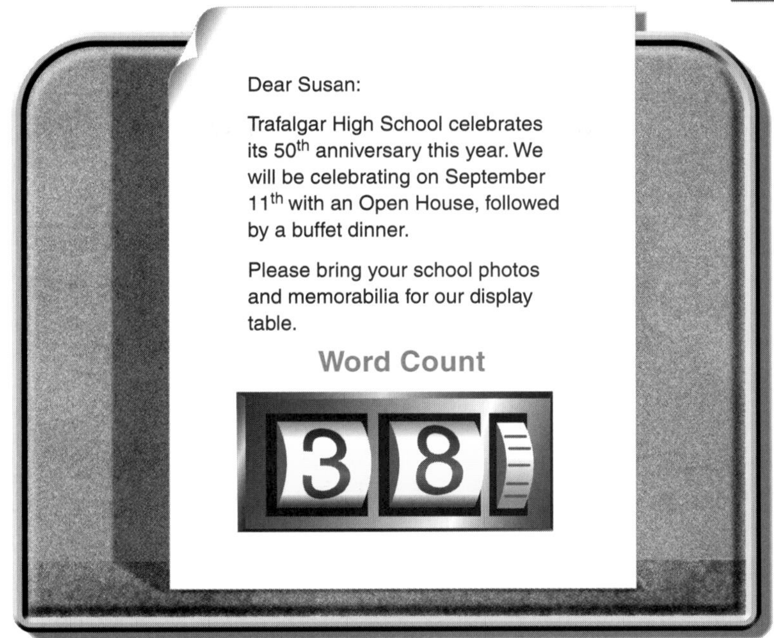

Dear Susan:
Trafalgar High School celebrates its 50th anniversary this year. We will be celebrating on September 11th with an Open House, followed by a buffet dinner.
Please bring your school photos and memorabilia for our display table.
Word Count
3 8

When counting the number of words in your document, Word also counts the number of pages, characters, paragraphs and lines in your document.

COUNT WORDS IN A DOCUMENT

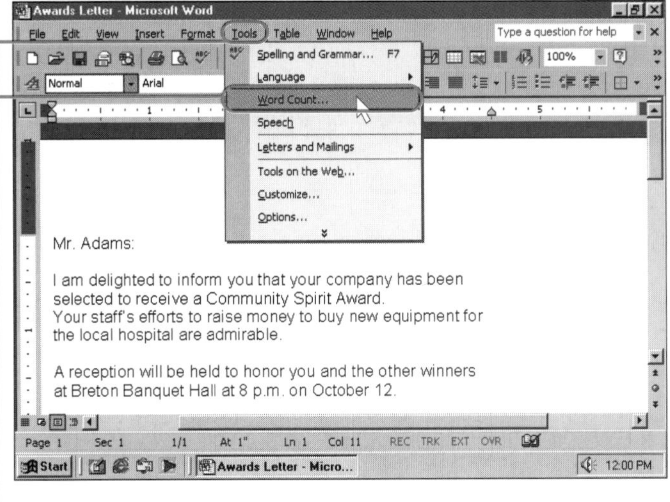

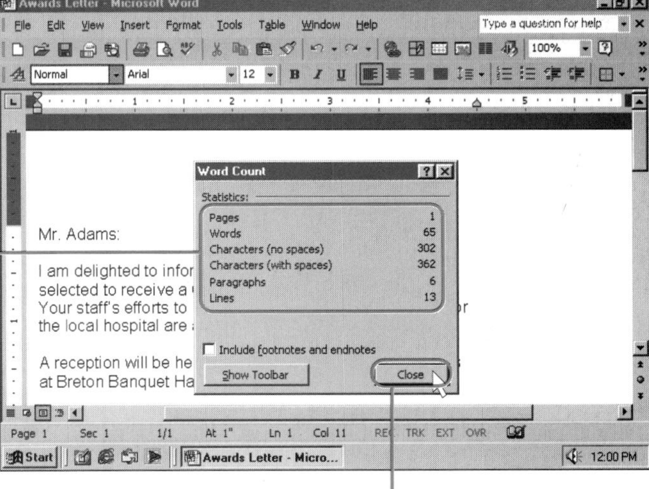

1 Click **Tools**.

2 Click **Word Count**.

Note: To count the number of words in only part of your document, select the text before performing step 1. To select text, see page 24.

■ The Word Count dialog box appears.

■ This area displays the total number of pages, words, characters, paragraphs and lines in your document.

3 When you finish reviewing the information, click **Close** to close the Word Count dialog box.

FIND AND REPLACE TEXT

You can find and replace every occurrence of a word or phrase in your document. This is useful if you have frequently misspelled a name.

FIND AND REPLACE TEXT

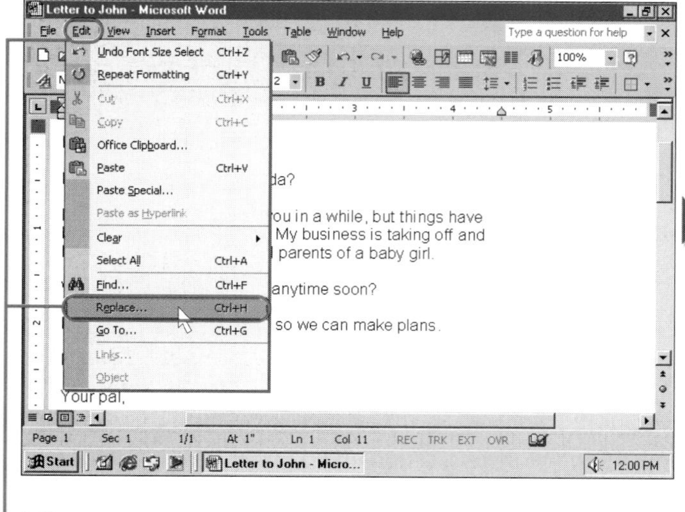

1 Click **Edit**.

2 Click **Replace**.

Note: If Replace does not appear on the menu, position the mouse over the bottom of the menu to display all the menu options.

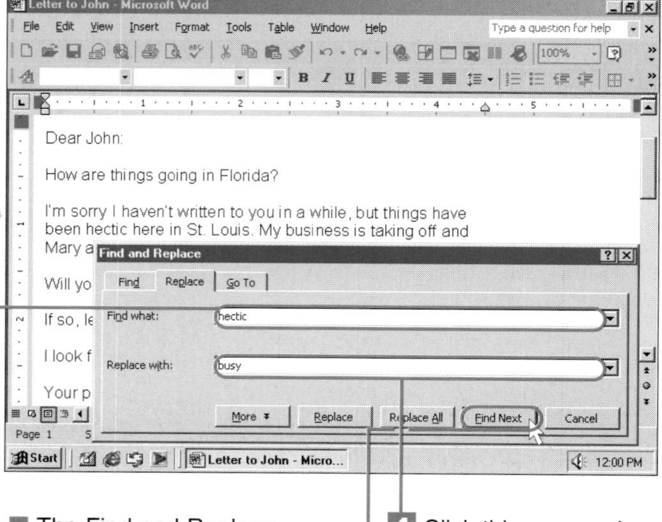

■ The Find and Replace dialog box appears.

3 Type the text you want to find.

4 Click this area and type the text you want to use to replace the text you typed in step 3.

5 Click **Find Next** to start the search.

How can the Find and Replace feature help me quickly enter text?

You can type a short form of a word or phrase, such as UM, throughout a document. You can then use the Find and Replace feature to replace the short form with the full word or phrase, such as University of Massachusetts.

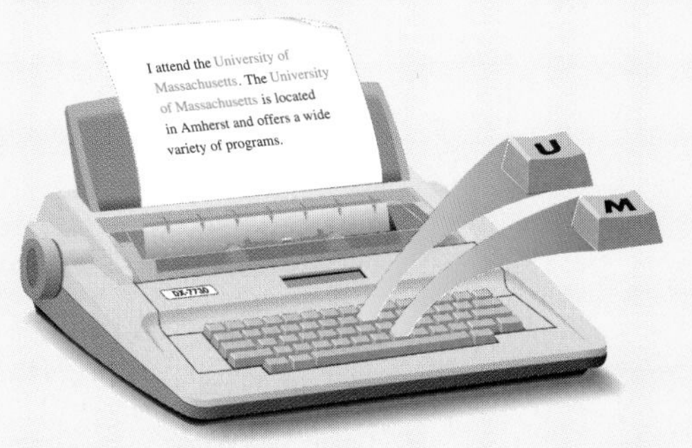

Can I find text in my document without replacing the text?

Yes. You can use the Find and Replace feature to locate a word or phrase in your document. To find text in your document, perform steps 1 to 3 below. Then perform step 5 until you find the text. To close the dialog box, press the Esc key.

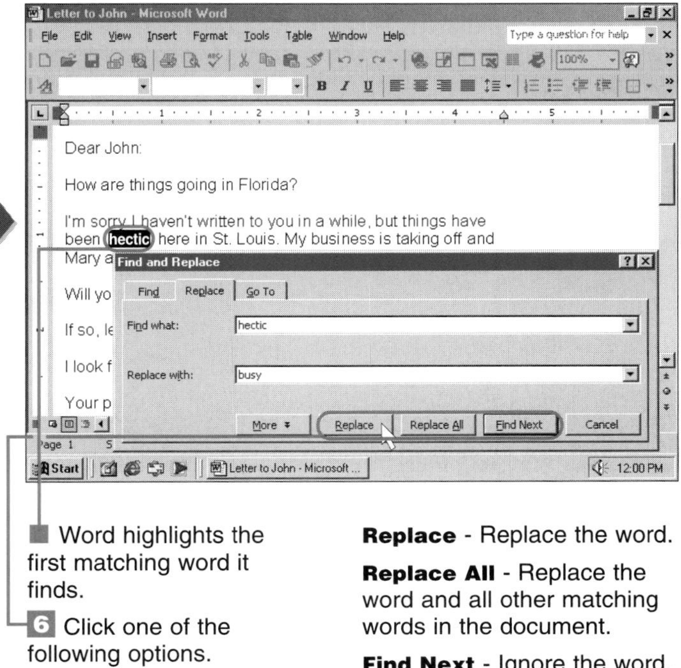

■ Word highlights the first matching word it finds.

6 Click one of the following options.

Replace - Replace the word.

Replace All - Replace the word and all other matching words in the document.

Find Next - Ignore the word.

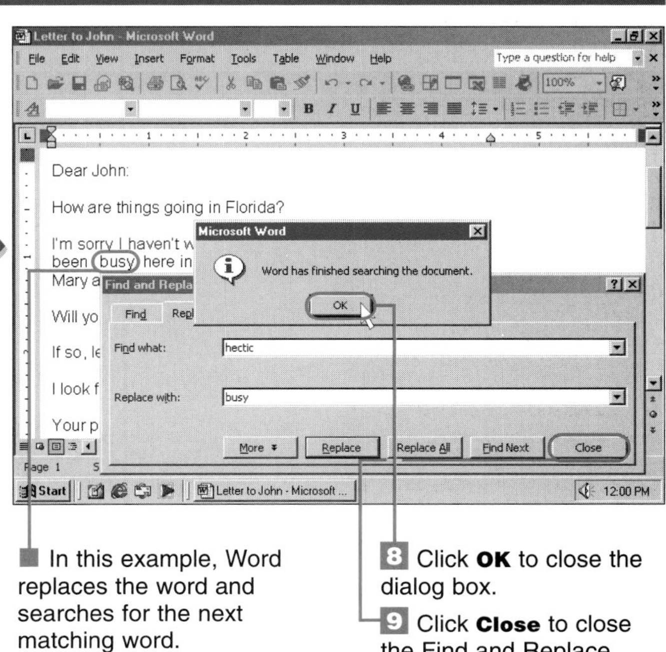

■ In this example, Word replaces the word and searches for the next matching word.

7 Replace or ignore matching words until a dialog box appears, telling you the search is complete.

8 Click **OK** to close the dialog box.

9 Click **Close** to close the Find and Replace dialog box.

CHECK SPELLING AND GRAMMAR

You can find and correct all the spelling and grammar errors in your document.

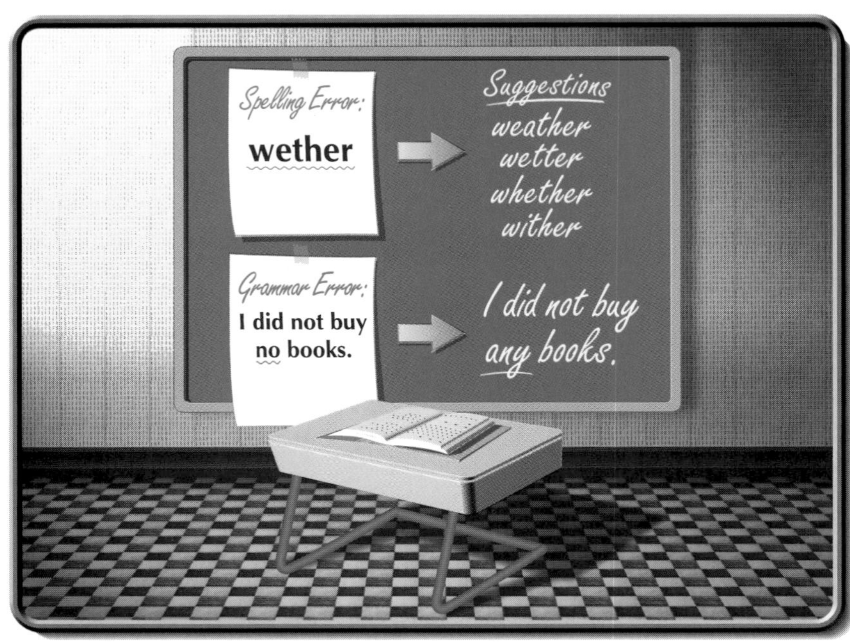

Word compares every word in your document to words in its dictionary. If a word does not exist in the dictionary, the word is considered misspelled.

Word will not find a correctly spelled word used in the wrong context, such as "My niece is **sit** years old." You should carefully review your document to find this type of error.

CHECK SPELLING AND GRAMMAR

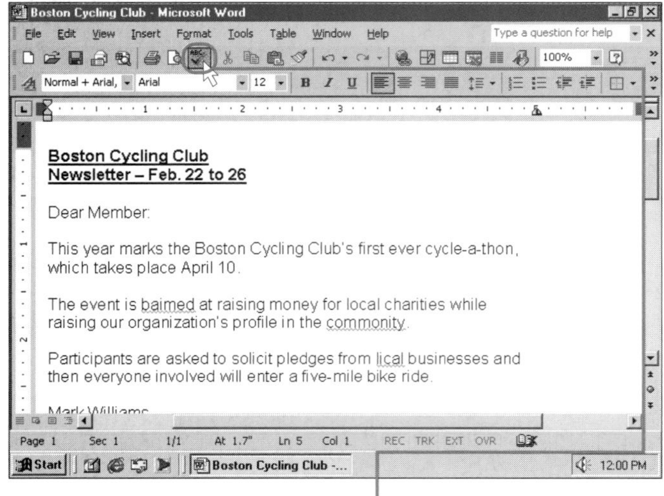

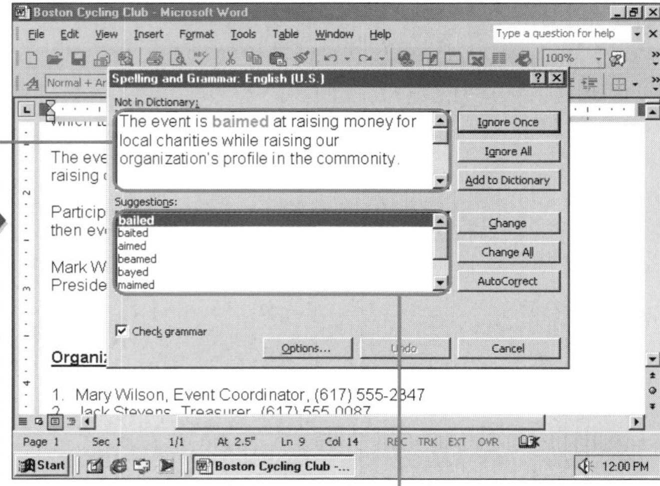

■ Word automatically underlines misspelled words in red and grammar errors in green. The underlines will not appear when you print your document.

1 Click [icon] to start checking your document for spelling and grammar errors.

Note: If [icon] is not displayed, click [icon] on the Standard toolbar to display all the buttons.

■ The Spelling and Grammar dialog box appears if Word finds an error in your document.

■ This area displays the first misspelled word or grammar error.

■ This area displays suggestions for correcting the error.

Can Word automatically correct my typing mistakes?

Yes. Word automatically corrects common spelling errors as you type. Here are a few examples.

adn → and
alot → a lot
comitee → committee
don;t → don't
nwe → new
occurence → occurrence
recieve → receive
seperate → separate
teh → the

How can I quickly correct a single misspelled word or grammar error in my document?

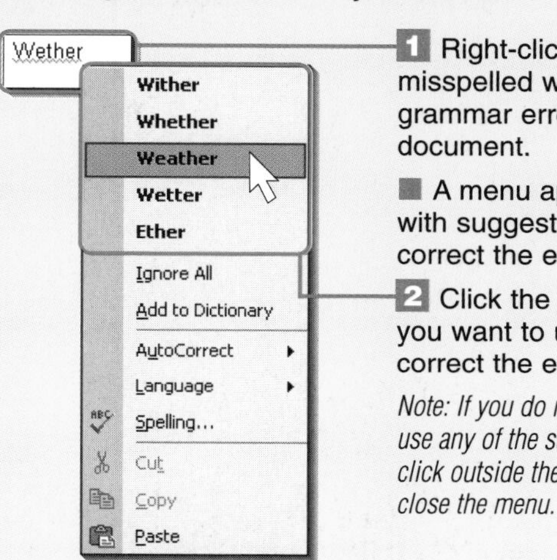

1 Right-click the misspelled word or grammar error in your document.

■ A menu appears with suggestions to correct the error.

2 Click the suggestion you want to use to correct the error.

Note: If you do not want to use any of the suggestions, click outside the menu to close the menu.

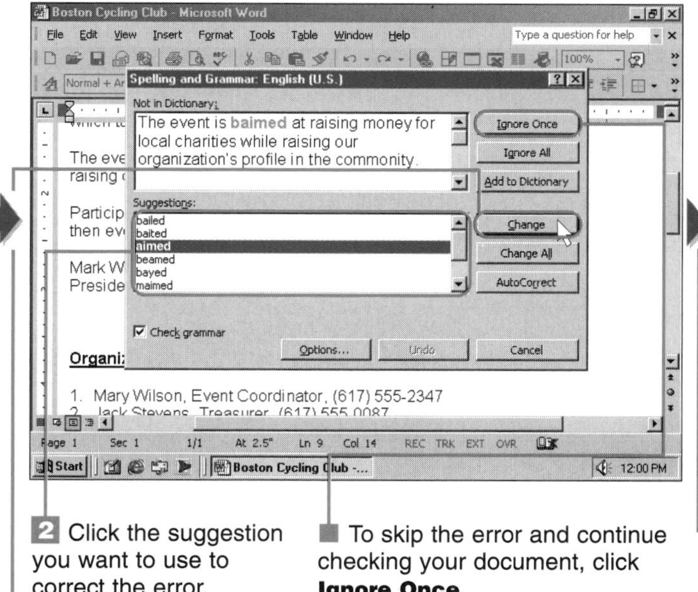

2 Click the suggestion you want to use to correct the error.

3 Click **Change** to correct the error in your document.

■ To skip the error and continue checking your document, click **Ignore Once**.

*Note: To skip the error and all other occurrences of the error in your document, click **Ignore All** or **Ignore Rule**. The name of the button depends on whether the error is a misspelled word or a grammar error.*

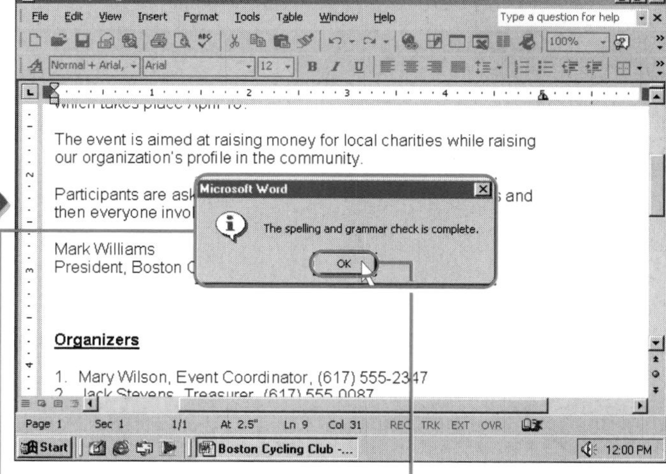

4 Correct or ignore misspelled words and grammar errors until this dialog box appears, telling you the spelling and grammar check is complete.

5 Click **OK** to close the dialog box.

USING THE THESAURUS

You can use the thesaurus to replace a word in your document with a more suitable word.

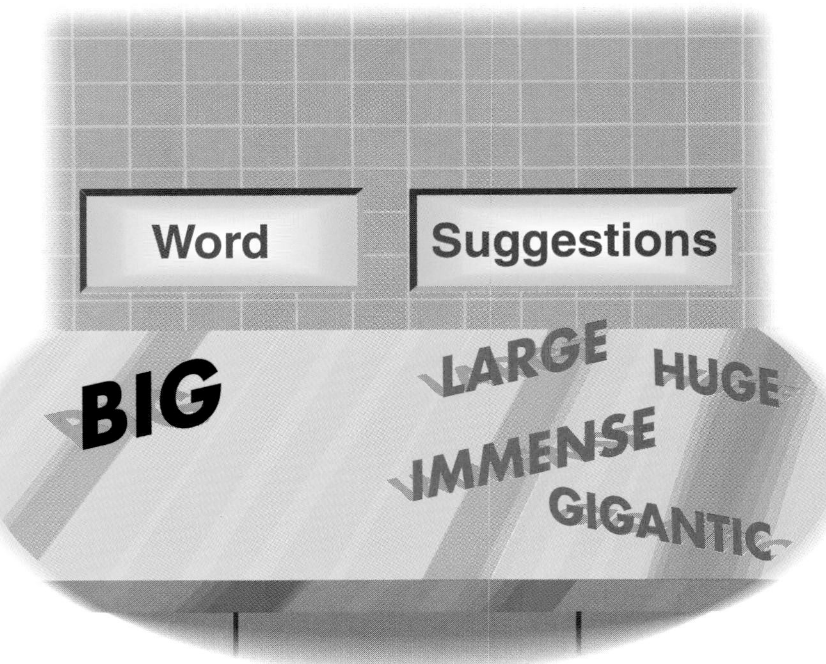

USING THE THESAURUS

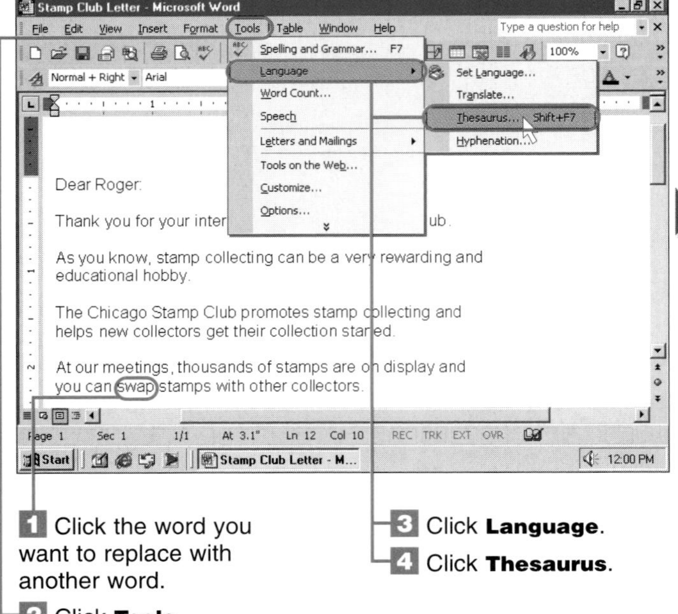

1 Click the word you want to replace with another word.

2 Click **Tools**.

3 Click **Language**.

4 Click **Thesaurus**.

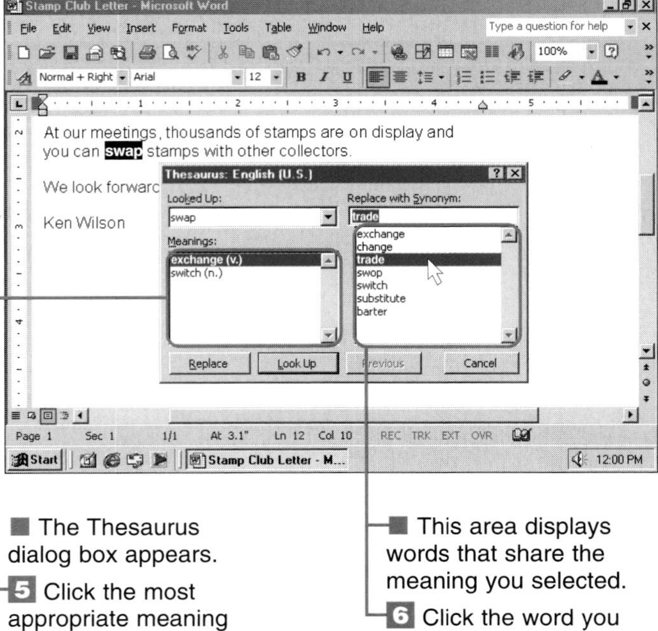

■ The Thesaurus dialog box appears.

5 Click the most appropriate meaning of the word.

■ This area displays words that share the meaning you selected.

6 Click the word you want to use in your document.

Why would I use the Thesaurus?

Many people use the thesaurus to replace a word that appears repeatedly in a document. Replacing repeatedly used words can help add variety to your writing and make your document more professional. You may also want to use the thesaurus to find a word that more clearly explains a concept.

What if the Thesaurus dialog box does not display a word I want to use?

You can look up synonyms for the words displayed in the Thesaurus dialog box to find a more suitable word.

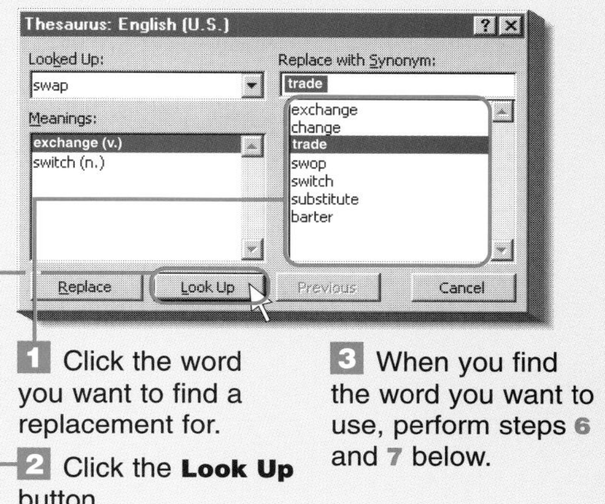

1 Click the word you want to find a replacement for.

2 Click the **Look Up** button.

3 When you find the word you want to use, perform steps 6 and 7 below.

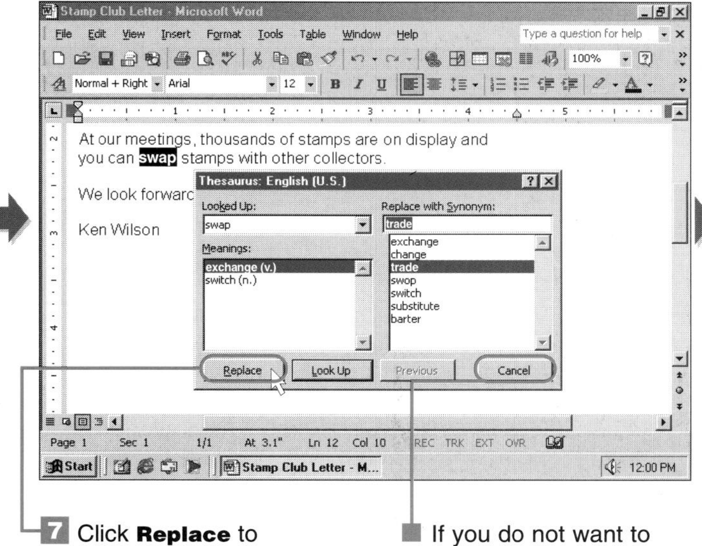

7 Click **Replace** to replace the word in your document with the word you selected.

■ If you do not want to use any of the words the Thesaurus dialog box displays, click **Cancel** to close the dialog box.

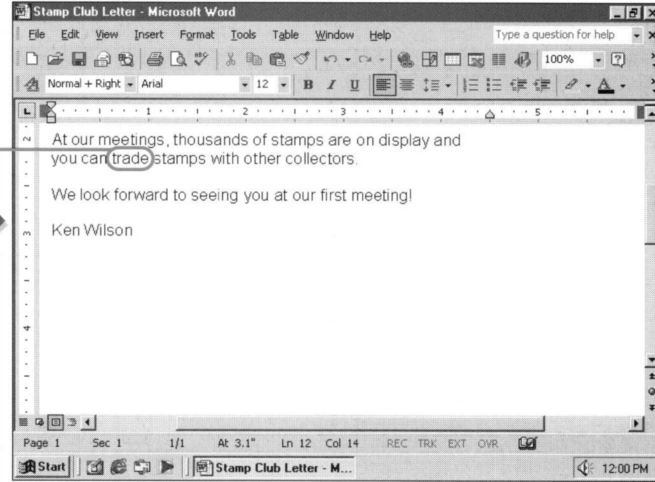

■ The word you selected replaces the word in your document.

USING SMART TAGS

You can use smart tags to quickly perform tasks while working in Word. A smart tag is information, such as a date or address, which Word recognizes and labels.

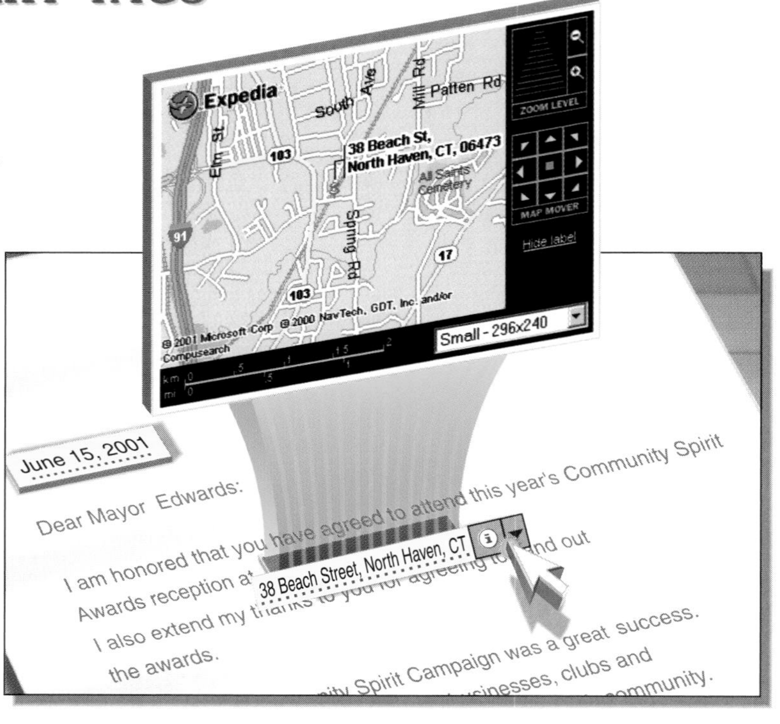

Smart tags allow you to perform actions such as scheduling a meeting for a date or displaying a map for an address.

You can change the options for smart tags to specify the types of information you want Word to recognize and label with a smart tag.

USING SMART TAGS

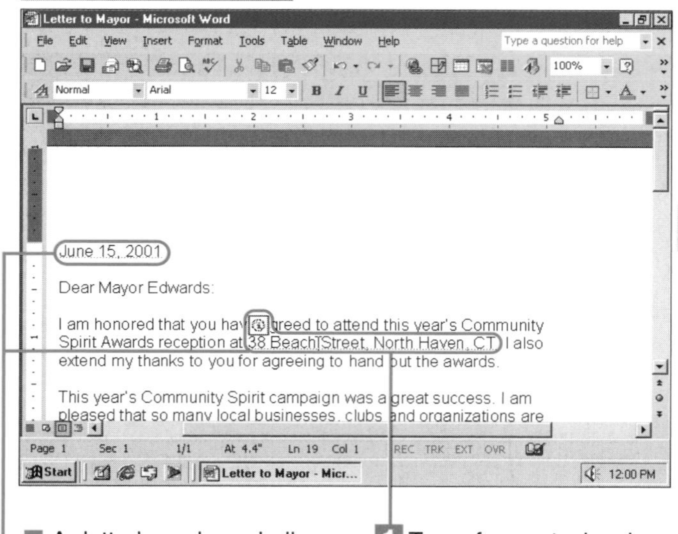

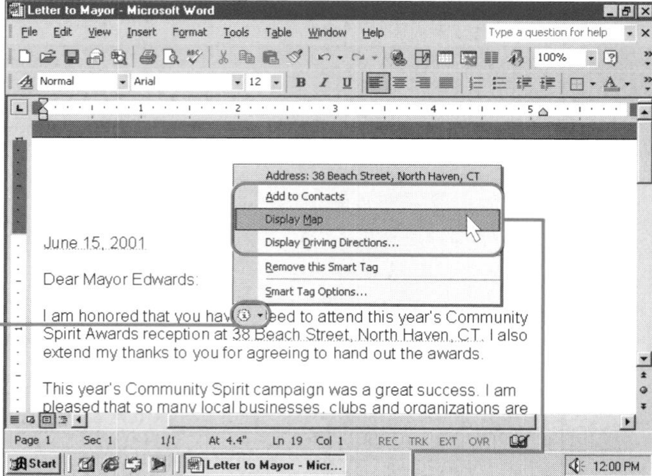

■ A dotted purple underline appears below text Word has labeled as a smart tag.

1 To perform a task using a smart tag, position the mouse I over the text for the smart tag. The Smart Tag Actions button (ⓘ) appears.

2 Click the Smart Tag Actions button to display a list of actions you can perform using the smart tag.

3 Click the action you want to perform.

How can I turn off a smart tag Word assigned to information in my document?

Perform steps 1 and 2 on page 54 to display a list of actions for the smart tag. Then click **Remove this Smart Tag** to turn off the smart tag for the information.

Is there another way to change smart tag options?

While working with a smart tag, you can click **Smart Tag Options** in the list of actions for the smart tag to quickly display the AutoCorrect dialog box. Then perform steps 4 and 5 below to change the smart tag options.

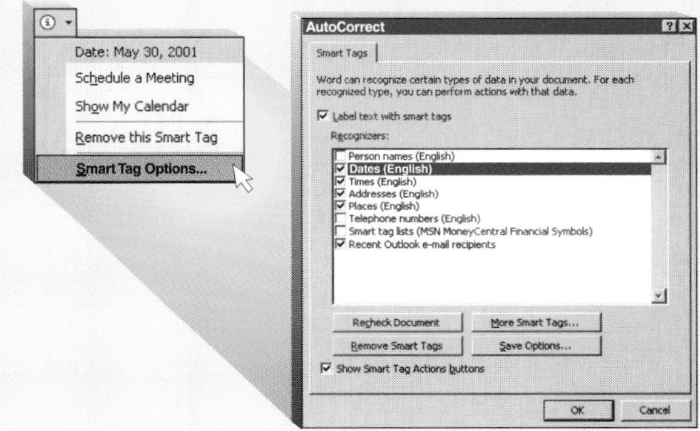

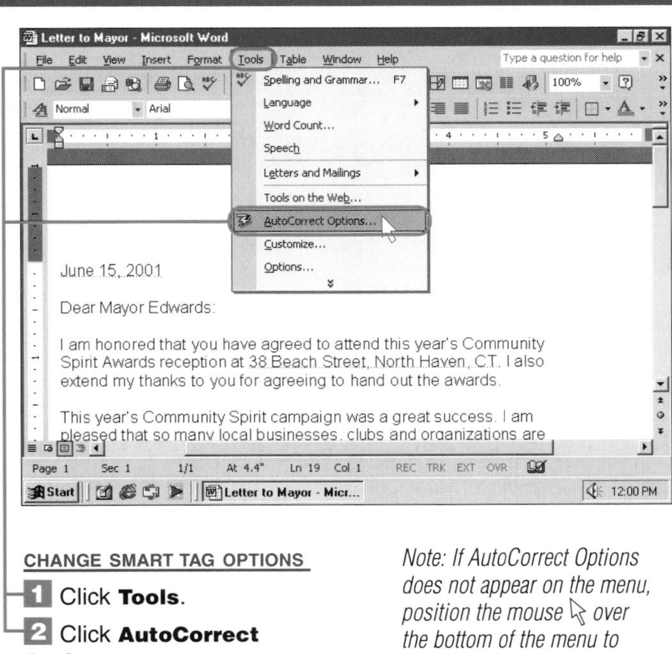

CHANGE SMART TAG OPTIONS

1 Click **Tools**.

2 Click **AutoCorrect Options**.

Note: If AutoCorrect Options does not appear on the menu, position the mouse over the bottom of the menu to display all the menu options.

■ The AutoCorrect dialog box appears.

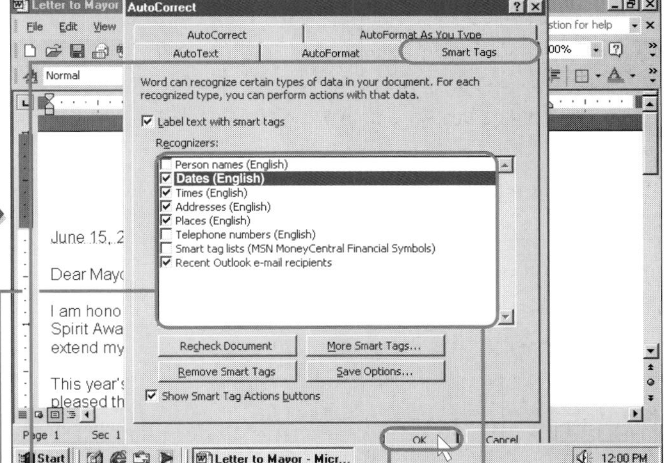

3 Click the **Smart Tags** tab to display the smart tag options.

■ This area displays the types of information Word can label as smart tags. Smart tags are currently turned on for each type of information that displays a check mark (☑).

4 You can click the check box beside a type of information to turn smart tags on (☑) or off (☐) for the information.

5 Click **OK** to confirm your changes.

TRACK CHANGES

Word can keep track of the changes that are made to a document. This is useful when multiple people are working with the same document.

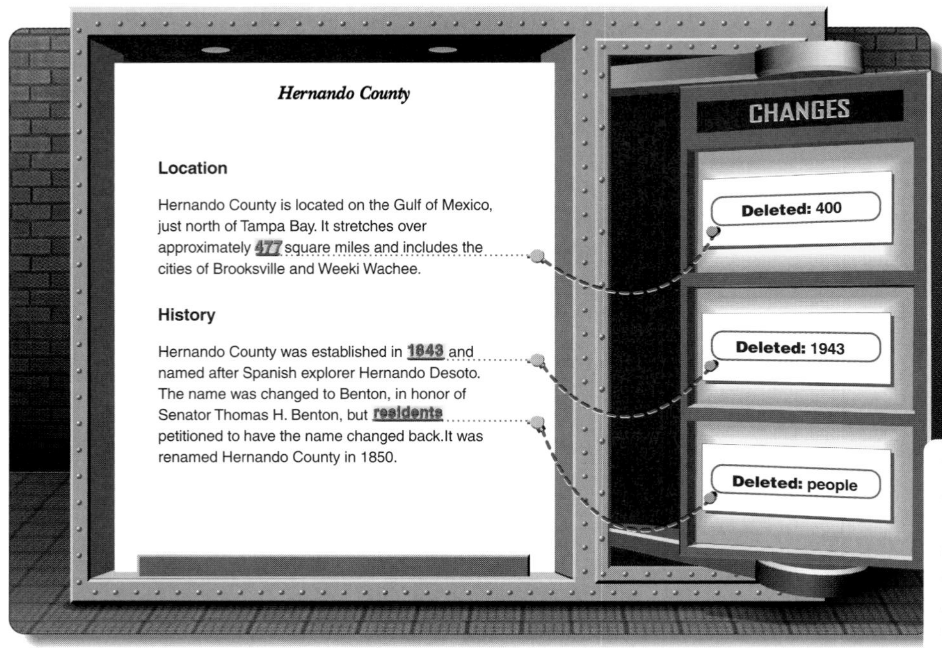

You can review the changes that have been made to a document and choose whether to accept or reject each change.

TRACK CHANGES

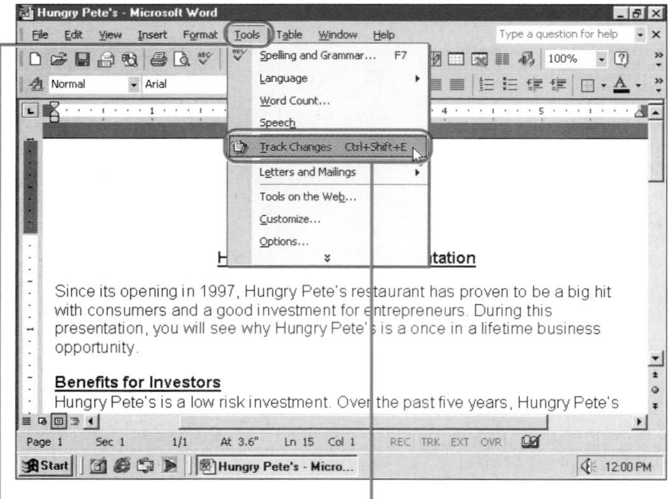

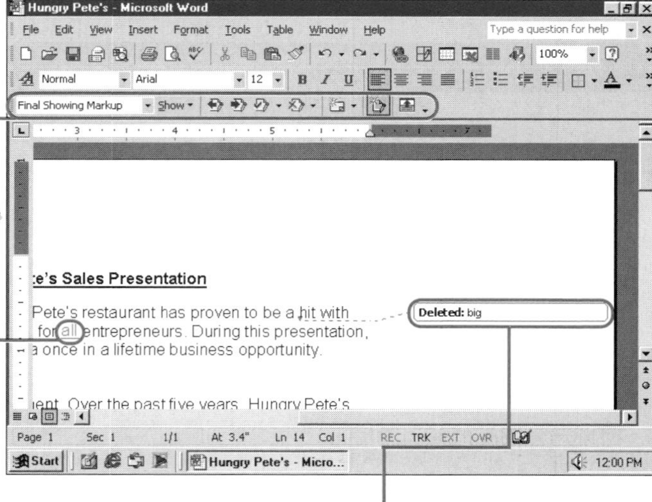

1 To track changes in your document, click **Tools**.

2 Click **Track Changes**.

Note: If Track Changes is not displayed, position the mouse over the bottom of the menu to display all the options.

■ The Reviewing toolbar appears.

3 You can now make changes to the document. Word will track the changes you make.

■ Text you add to the document appears underlined and in color.

■ When you delete text from the document, Word indicates the change using a markup balloon that appears in the margin of the document.

■ You may need to use the scroll bar to view the markup balloon.

The markup balloons do not appear in the margin of my document. What is wrong?

Text you have deleted only appears in markup balloons when your document is displayed in the Print Layout or Web Layout view. When your document is displayed in the Normal or Outline view, text you have deleted appears in the body of the document, crossed out and in color. For information on changing the view of a document, see page 28.

How do I stop tracking changes?

You can click at any time to stop tracking changes in your document.

REVIEW TRACKED CHANGES

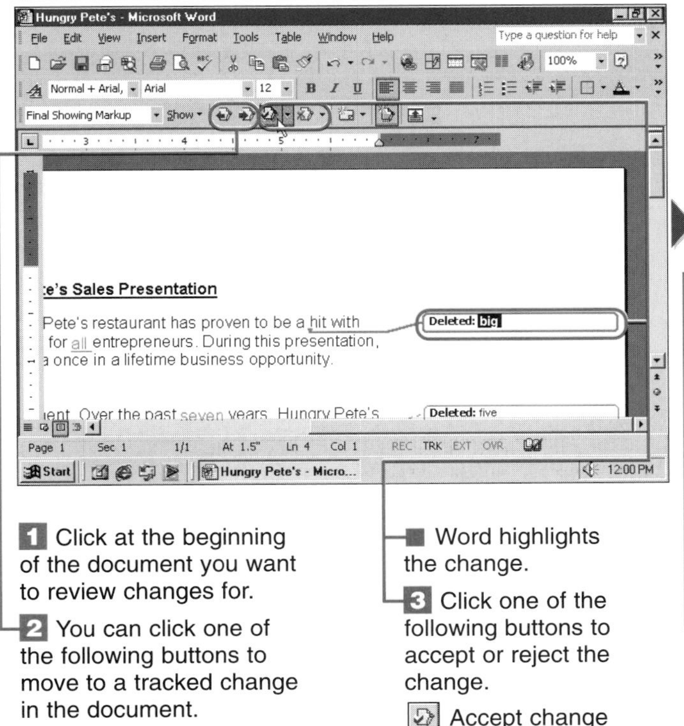

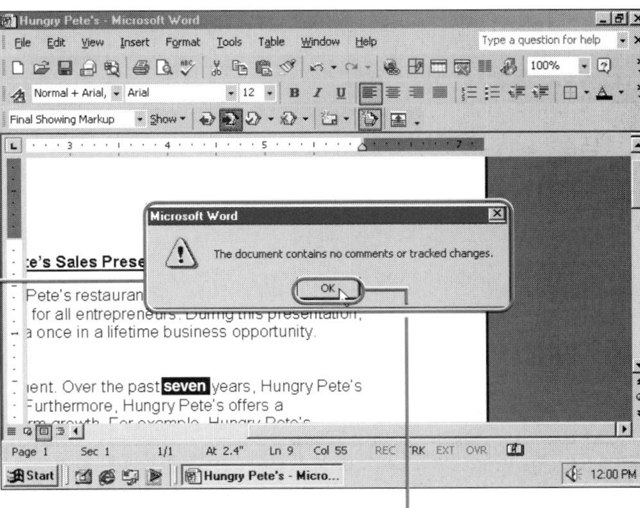

1 Click at the beginning of the document you want to review changes for.

2 You can click one of the following buttons to move to a tracked change in the document.

- Previous
- Next

■ Word highlights the change.

3 Click one of the following buttons to accept or reject the change.

- Accept change
- Reject change

■ Word accepts or rejects the change and stops tracking the change.

4 Repeat steps 2 and 3 until this dialog box appears.

5 Click **OK** to close the dialog box.

ADD A CLIP ART IMAGE

You can add a clip art image to a document. Adding a clip art image can make a document more interesting and entertaining.

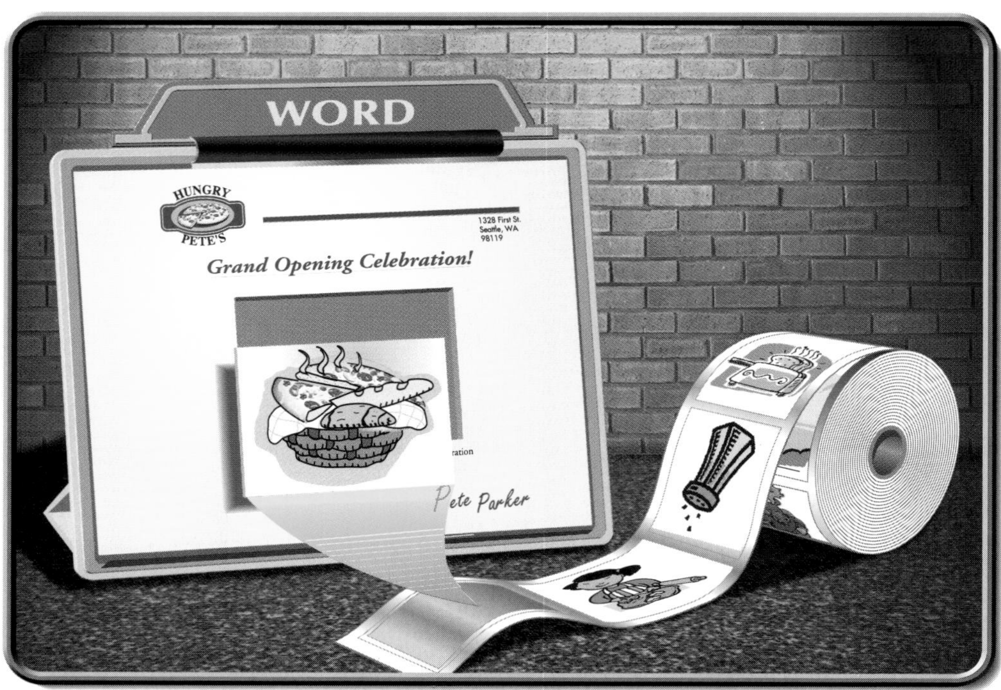

ADD A CLIP ART IMAGE

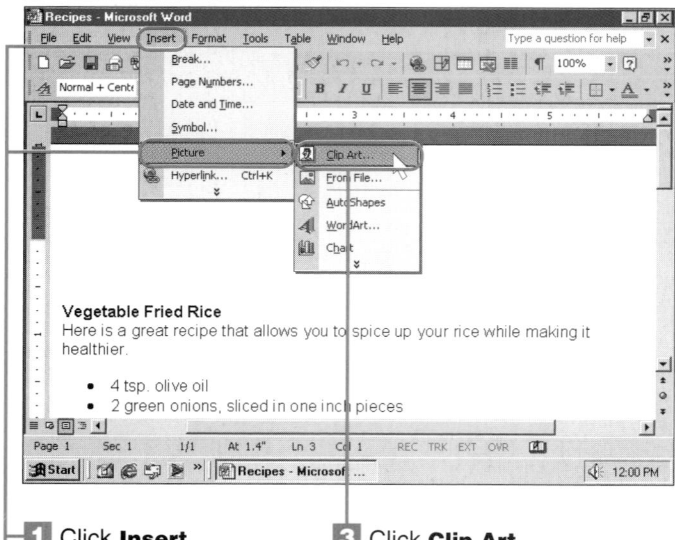

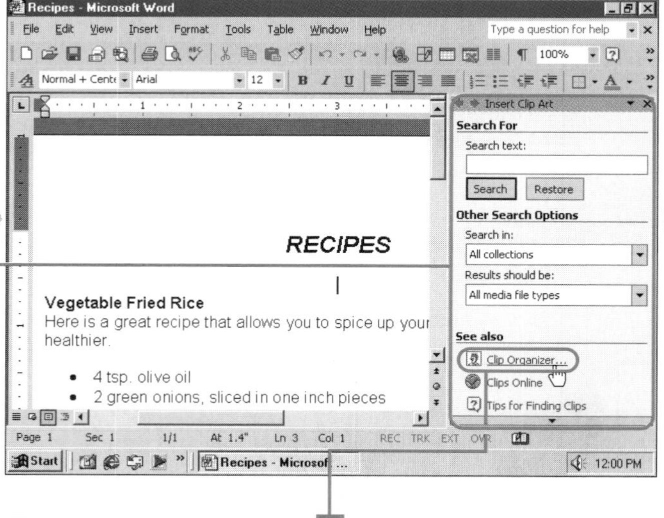

1 Click **Insert**.

2 Click **Picture**.

3 Click **Clip Art**.

*Note: The first time you add a clip art image to a document, the Add Clips to Organizer dialog box appears. Click **Now** in the dialog box to catalog the image, sound and video files on your computer.*

■ The Insert Clip Art task pane appears.

4 Click **Clip Organizer** to view the image, sound and video files in the Clip Organizer.

■ The Microsoft Clip Organizer window appears.

How does the Clip Organizer arrange my image, sound and video files?

The Clip Organizer arranges your media files into three main folders.

My Collections

Displays the media files you have specified as your favorites and media files that came with Microsoft Windows.

Office Collections

Displays the media files that came with Microsoft Office.

Web Collections

Displays the media files that are available at Microsoft's Web site and Web sites in partnership with Microsoft.

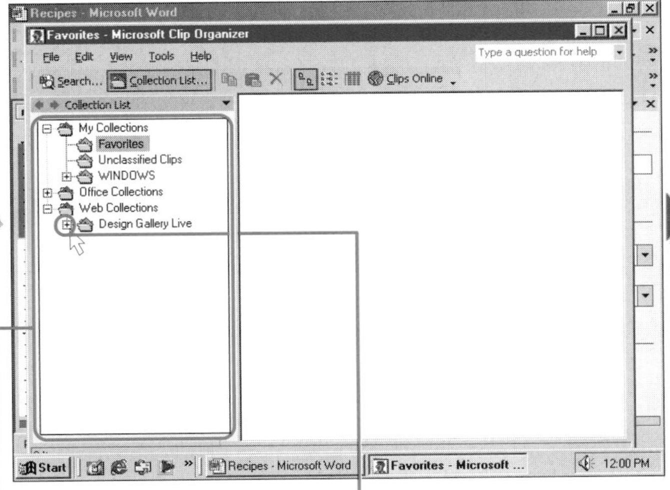

- This area lists the folders that contain image, sound and video files that you can add to your document.
- A folder displaying a plus sign (⊞) contains hidden folders.

5 To display the hidden folders within a folder, click the plus sign (⊞) beside the folder (⊞ changes to ⊟).

Note: You must be connected to the Internet to view the contents of the Web Collections folder.

- The hidden folders appear.

Note: To once again hide the folders within a folder, click the minus sign (⊟) beside the folder.

6 Click a folder of interest.

- This area displays the contents of the folder you selected.

7 Click the image you want to add to your document.

CONTINUED

ADD A CLIP ART IMAGE

After you locate an image you want to add to your document, you can copy the image and then place the image in your document.

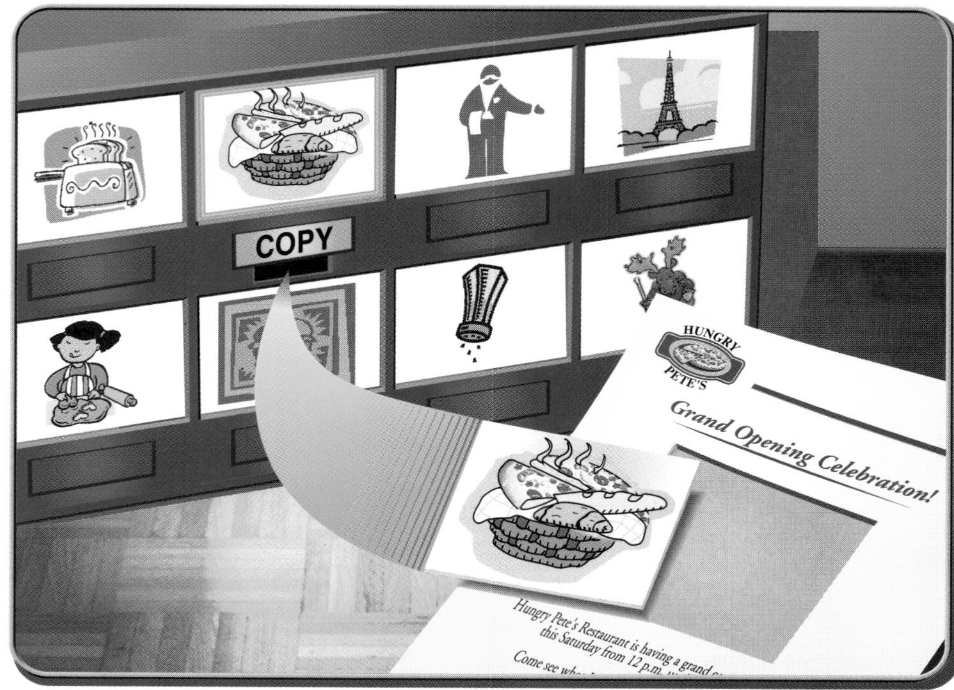

ADD A CLIP ART IMAGE (CONTINUED)

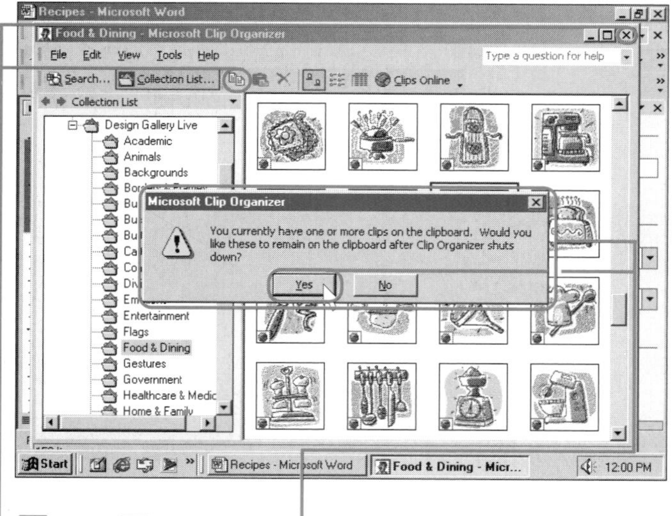

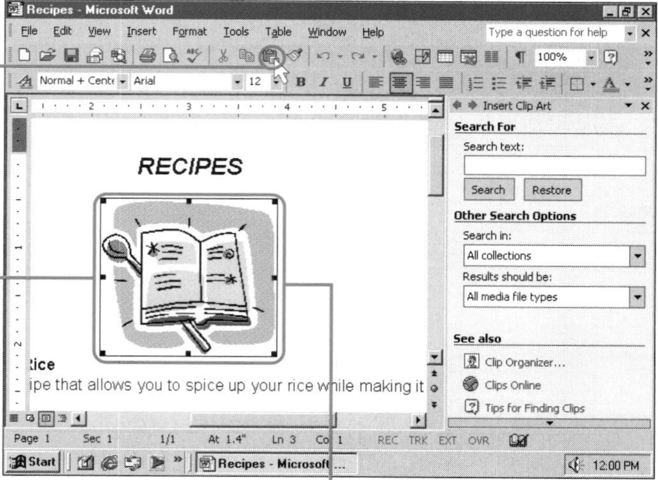

8 Click [copy] to copy the image you selected.

9 Click [close] to close the Microsoft Clip Organizer.

■ A dialog box appears, stating that you have one or more clip art images on the clipboard.

Note: The clipboard temporarily stores information you have selected to move or copy.

10 Click **Yes** to keep the image on the clipboard.

11 Click the location in your document where you want to add the image.

12 Click [paste] to place the image in your document.

■ The image appears in your document.

Note: To resize the image, see the top of page 61.

■ To delete the image, click the image and then press the Delete key.

How do I resize a clip art image?

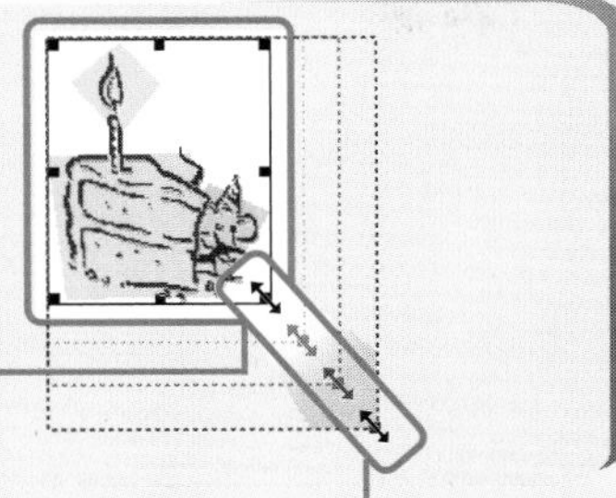

1 Click the image you want to resize. Handles (■) appear around the image.

2 Position the mouse over one of the handles (changes to ↘, ↗, ↕ or ↔).

3 Drag the handle until the image is the size you want.

■ A dashed line shows the new size.

Where can I obtain more clip art images?

You can buy collections of clip art images at computer stores. Many Web sites, such as www.allfree-clipart.com and www.noeticart.com, also offer clip art images you can use in your documents.

SEARCH FOR A CLIP ART IMAGE

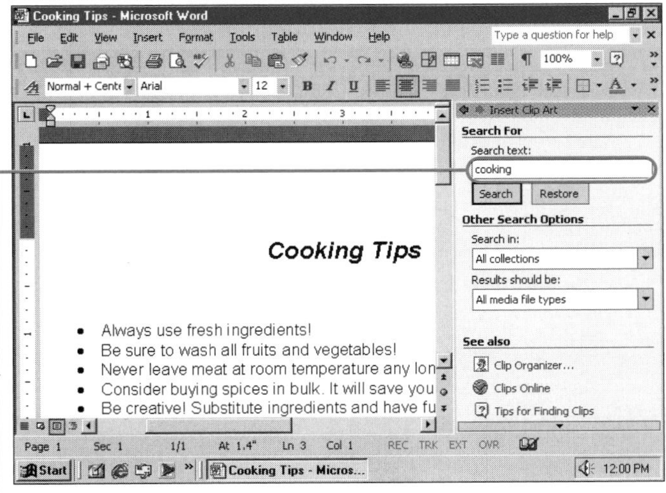

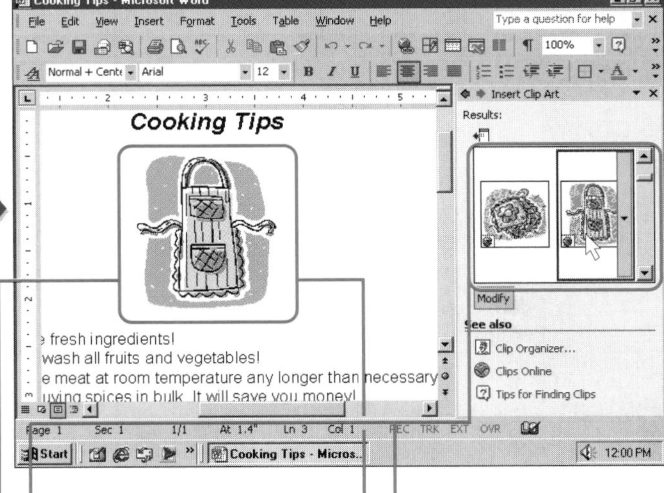

You can search for clip art images by specifying one or more words of interest.

1 Click this area and then type one or more words that describe the clip art image you want to find. Then press the Enter key.

*Note: If the Insert Clip Art task pane is not displayed, perform steps **1** to **3** on page 58 to display the task pane.*

■ This area displays the images that match the words you specified.

2 Click the location in your document where you want to add an image.

3 Click the image you want to add to your document.

■ The image appears in your document.

Note: To resize the image, see the top of this page.

CHANGE FONT OF TEXT

You can change the font of text to enhance the appearance of your document.

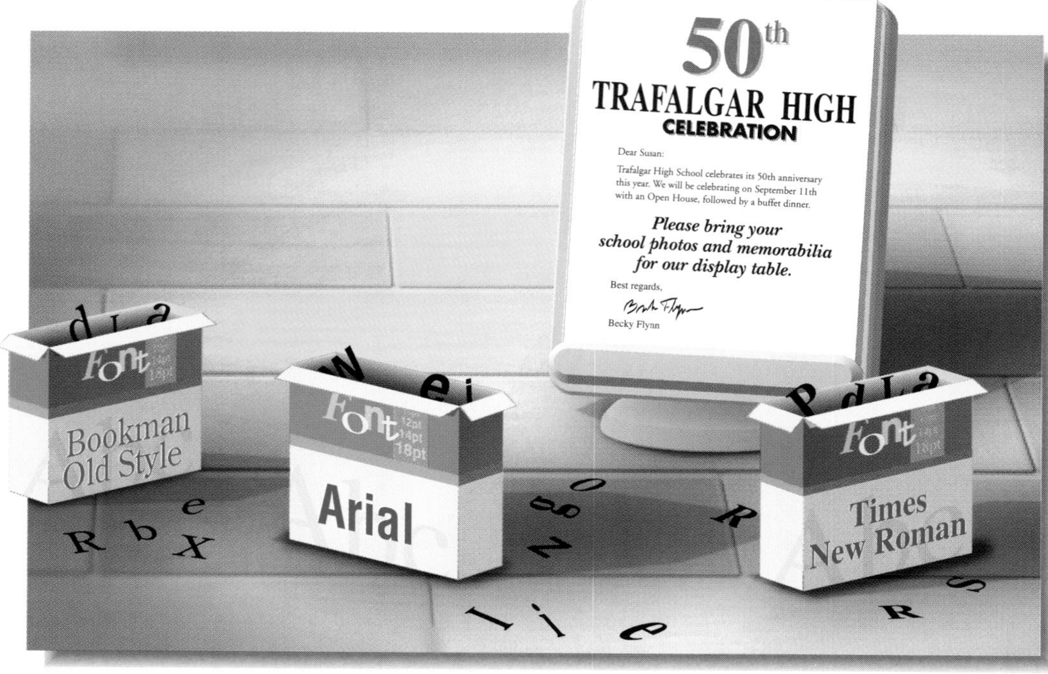

CHANGE FONT OF TEXT

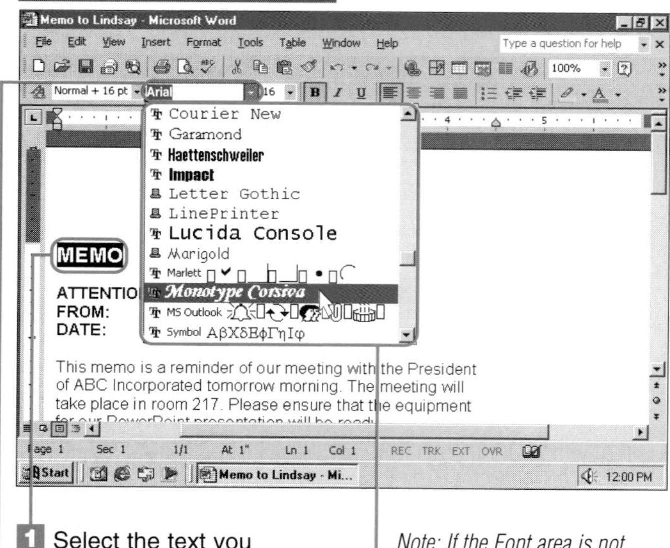

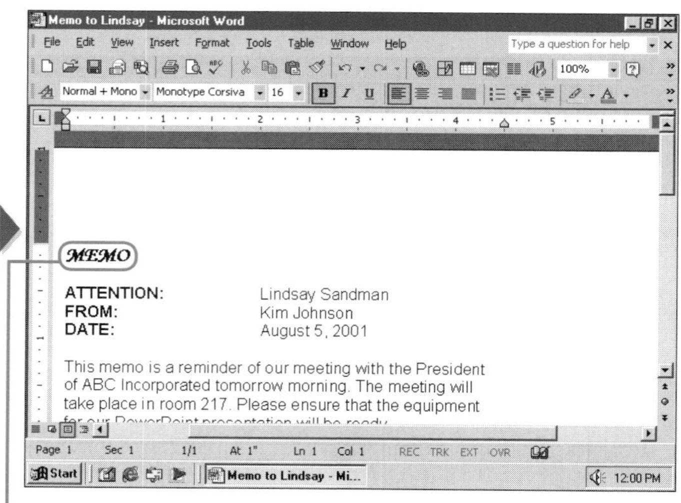

1 Select the text you want to change to a different font. To select text, see page 24.

2 Click ▾ in this area to display a list of the available fonts.

Note: If the Font area is not displayed, click » on the Formatting toolbar to display the area.

3 Click the font you want to use.

Note: Word displays the fonts you have most recently used at the top of the list.

■ The text you selected changes to the new font.

■ To deselect text, click outside the selected area.

CHANGE SIZE OF TEXT

You can increase or decrease the size of text in your document.

8 point
12 point
14 point
18 point
24 point
Word measures the size of text in points. There are approximately 72 points in one inch.

Larger text is easier to read, but smaller text allows you to fit more information on a page.

CHANGE SIZE OF TEXT

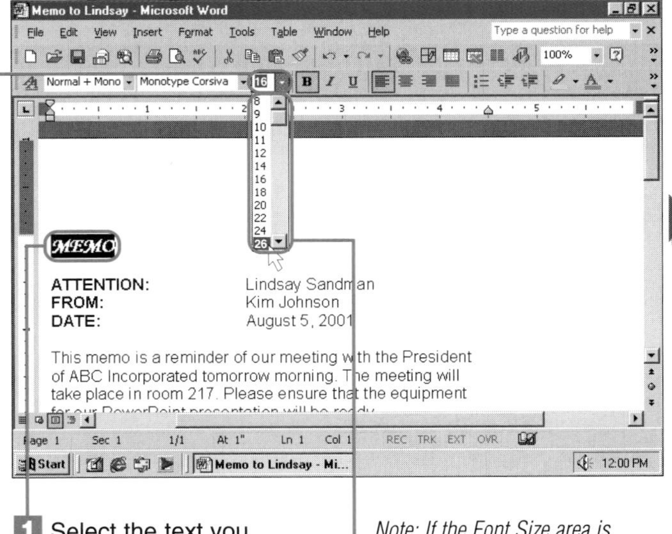

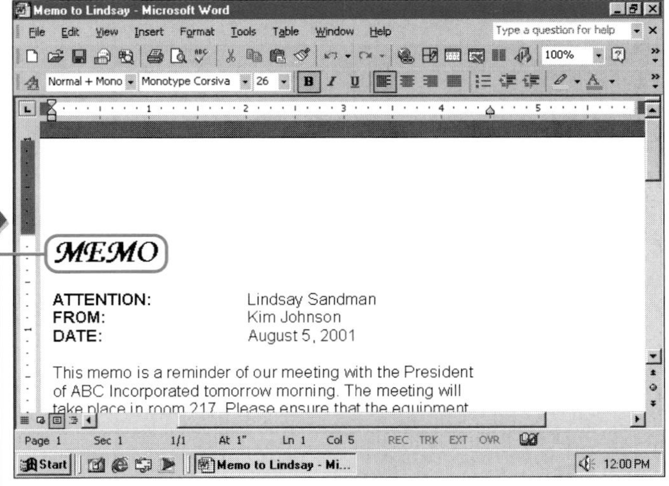

1 Select the text you want to change to a new size. To select text, see page 24.

2 Click ▾ in this area to display a list of the available sizes.

Note: If the Font Size area is not displayed, click » on the Formatting toolbar to display the area.

3 Click the size you want to use.

■ The text you selected changes to the new size.

■ To deselect text, click outside the selected area.

CHANGE TEXT COLOR

You can change the color of text to draw attention to headings or important information in your document.

CHANGE TEXT COLOR

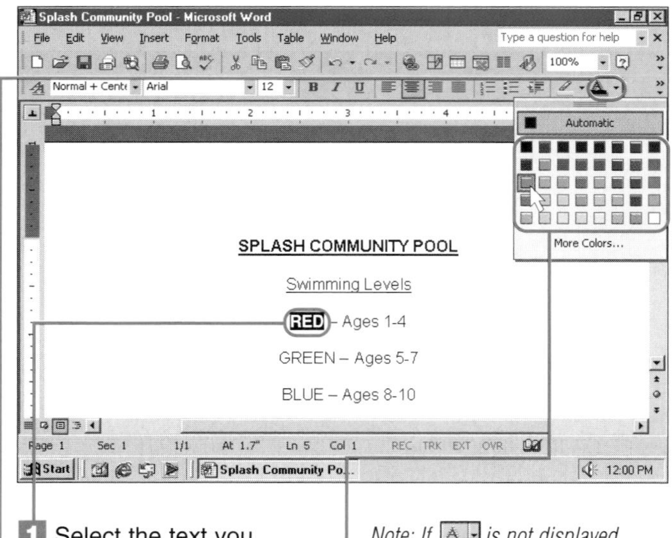

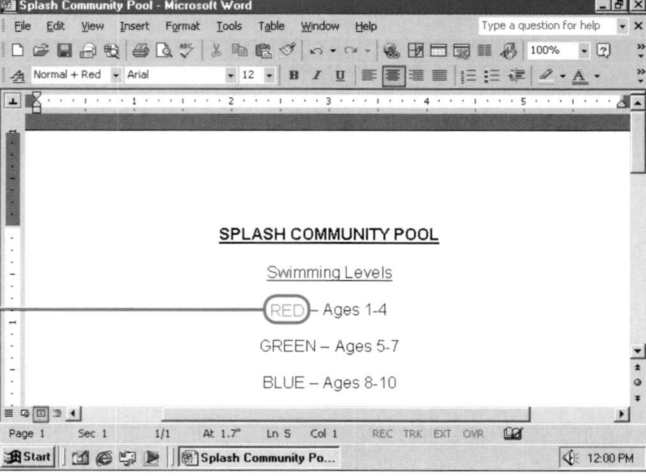

1 Select the text you want to change to a different color. To select text, see page 24.

2 Click ▾ in this area to display the available colors.

Note: If A ▾ is not displayed, click » on the Formatting toolbar to display all the buttons.

3 Click the color you want to use.

■ The text appears in the color you selected.

■ To deselect text, click outside the selected area.

■ To return text to its original color, repeat steps 1 to 3, selecting **Automatic** in step 3.

HIGHLIGHT TEXT

You can highlight text that you want to stand out in your document. Highlighting text is useful for marking information you want to review or verify later.

If you plan to print your document on a black-and-white printer, use a light highlight color so you will be able to easily read the printed text.

HIGHLIGHT TEXT

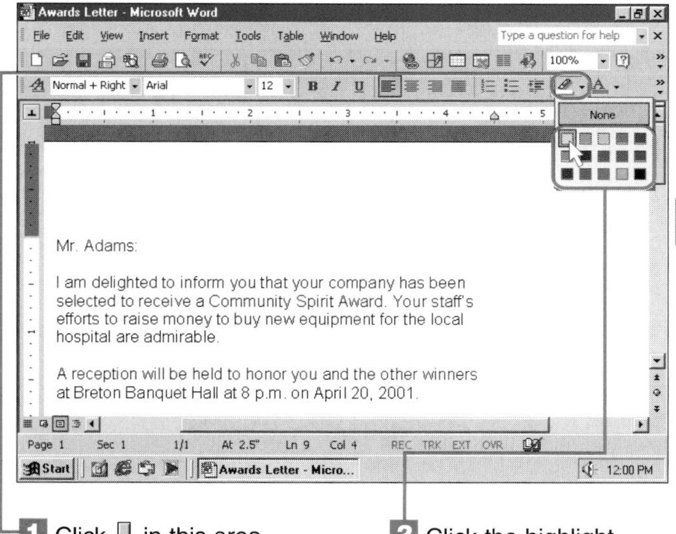

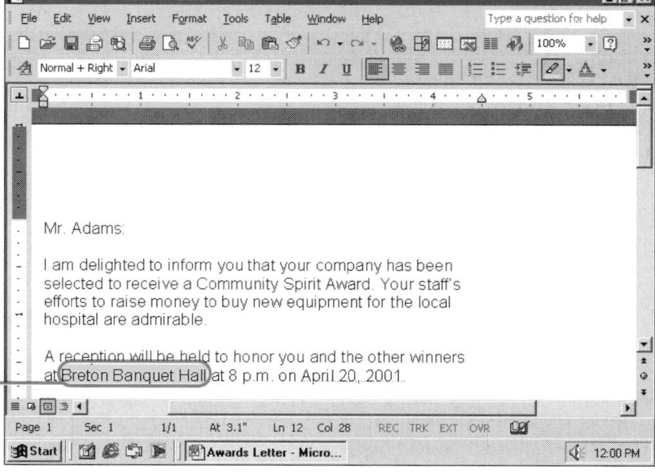

1 Click ▾ in this area to display the available highlight colors.

Note: If ✎ ▾ is not displayed, click » on the Formatting toolbar to display all the buttons.

2 Click the highlight color you want to use.

■ The mouse I changes to ✎ when over your document.

3 Select each area of text you want to highlight. To select text, see page 24.

■ The text you select appears highlighted.

4 When you finish highlighting text, press the Esc key.

■ To remove a highlight from text, repeat steps 1 to 4, selecting **None** in step 2.

BOLD, ITALICIZE OR UNDERLINE TEXT

You can bold, italicize or underline text to emphasize information in your document.

BOLD, ITALICIZE OR UNDERLINE TEXT

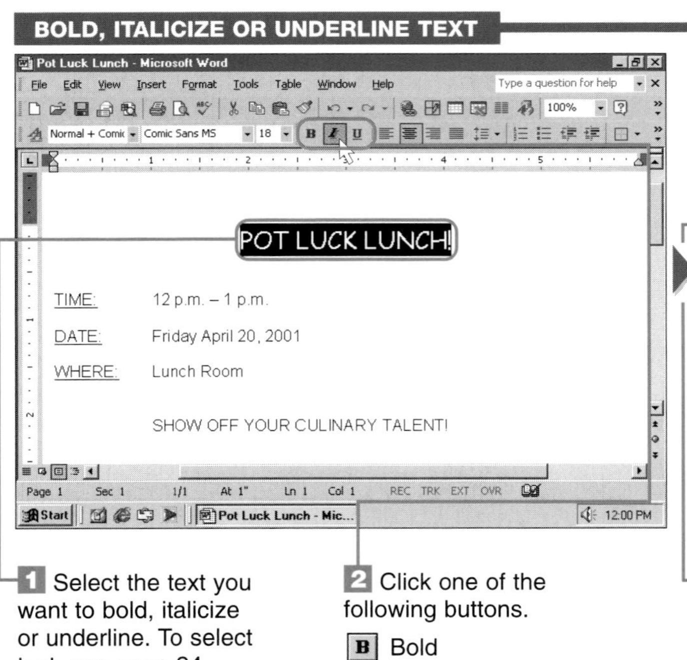

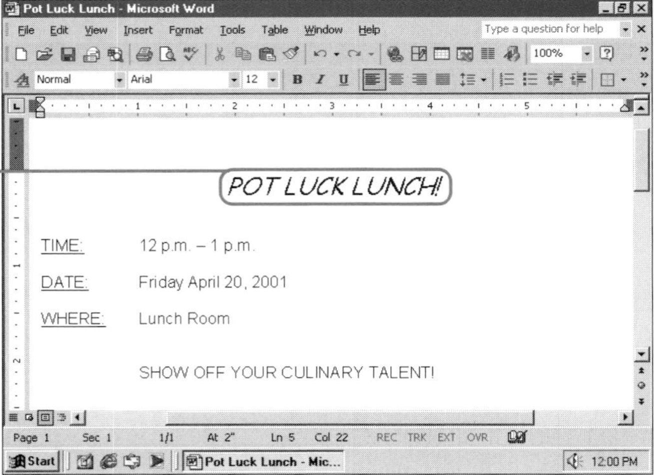

1 Select the text you want to bold, italicize or underline. To select text, see page 24.

2 Click one of the following buttons.

- **B** Bold
- *I* Italic
- U Underline

Note: If the button you want is not displayed, click » on the Formatting toolbar to display all the buttons.

■ The text you selected appears in the new style.

■ To deselect text, click outside the selected area.

■ To remove a bold, italic or underline style, repeat steps 1 and 2.

COPY FORMATTING

You can copy the formatting of text to make one area of text in your document look exactly like another.

You may want to copy the formatting of text to make all the headings or important words in your document look the same. This will give the text in your document a consistent appearance.

COPY FORMATTING

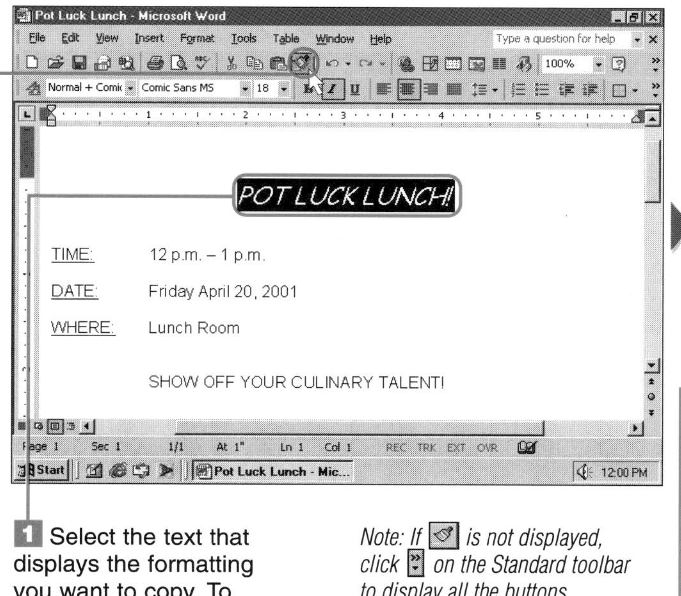

1 Select the text that displays the formatting you want to copy. To select text, see page 24.

2 Click [icon] to copy the formatting of the text.

Note: If [icon] is not displayed, click [icon] on the Standard toolbar to display all the buttons.

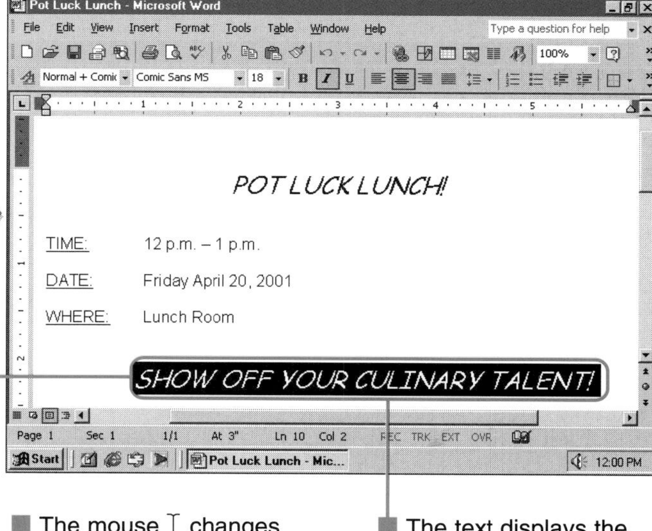

■ The mouse I changes to [icon] when over your document.

3 Select the text you want to display the same formatting.

■ The text displays the formatting.

■ To deselect text, click outside the selected area.

CREATE A BULLETED OR NUMBERED LIST

You can separate items in a list by beginning each item with a bullet or number.

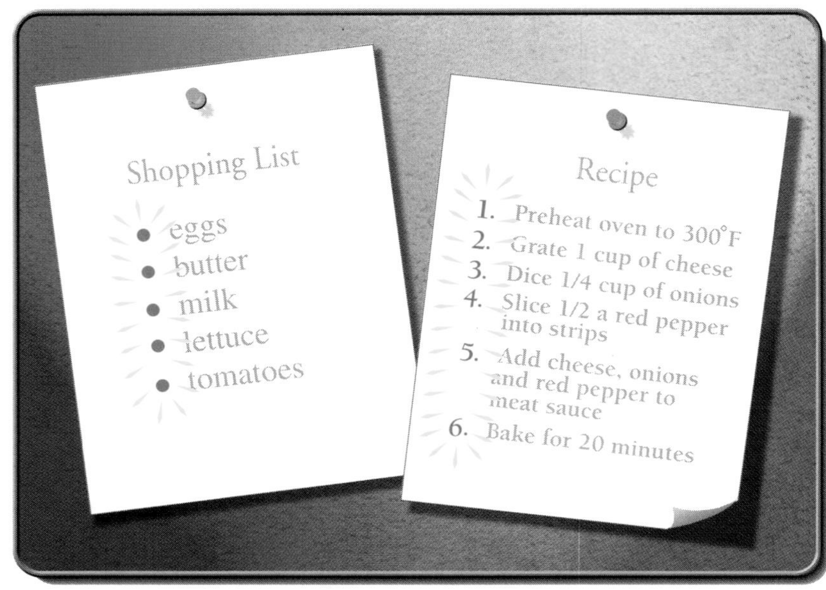

Bulleted lists are useful for items in no particular order, such as items in a shopping list. Numbered lists are useful for items in a specific order, such as instructions in a recipe.

CREATE A BULLETED OR NUMBERED LIST

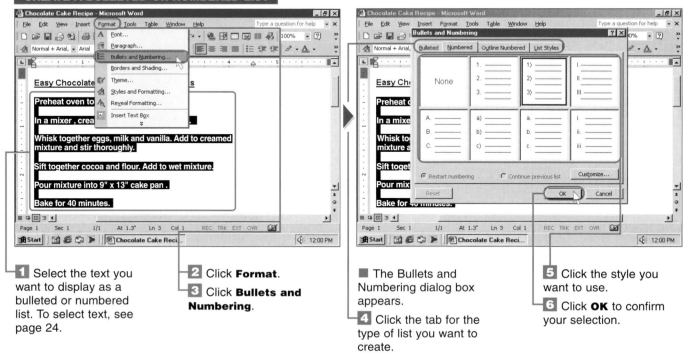

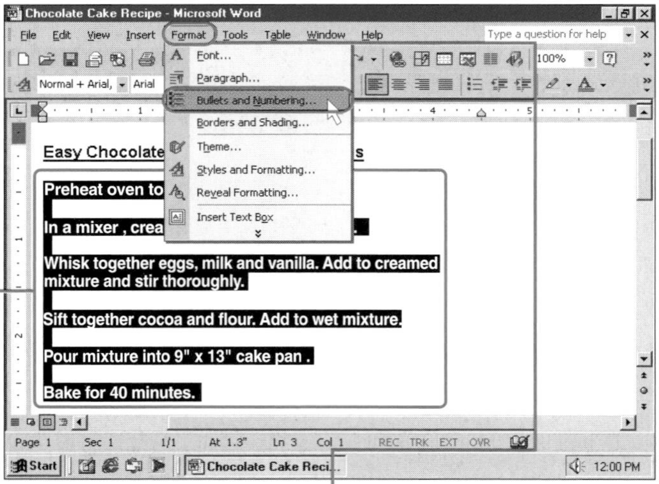

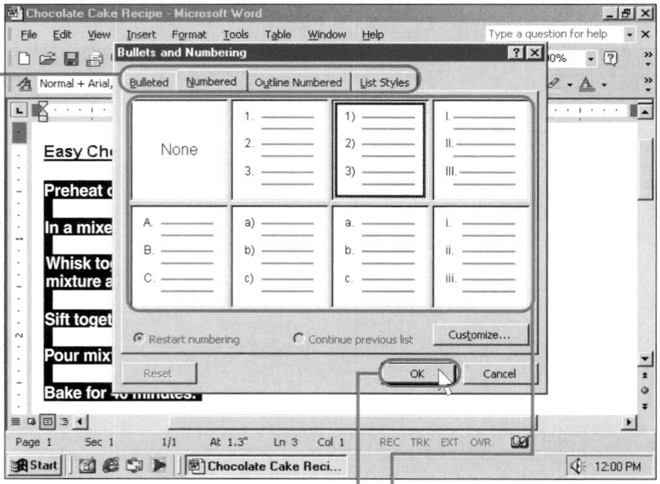

1 Select the text you want to display as a bulleted or numbered list. To select text, see page 24.

2 Click **Format**.

3 Click **Bullets and Numbering**.

■ The Bullets and Numbering dialog box appears.

4 Click the tab for the type of list you want to create.

5 Click the style you want to use.

6 Click **OK** to confirm your selection.

How can I create a bulleted or numbered list as I type?

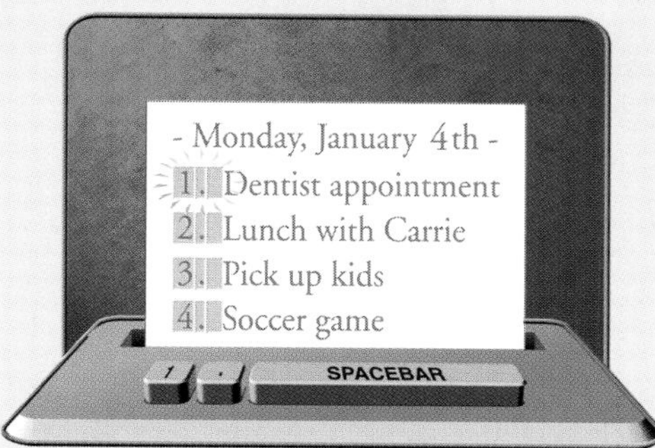

1 Type * to create a bulleted list or type **1.** to create a numbered list. Then press the Spacebar.

2 Type the first item in the list and then press the Enter key.

■ Word automatically adds a bullet or number for the next item.

3 Repeat step 2 for each item in the list.

4 To finish the list, press the Enter key twice.

Note: When you create a bulleted or numbered list as you type, the AutoCorrect Options button ( ) appears. You can click this button to specify that you do not want Word to create bulleted or numbered lists as you type.

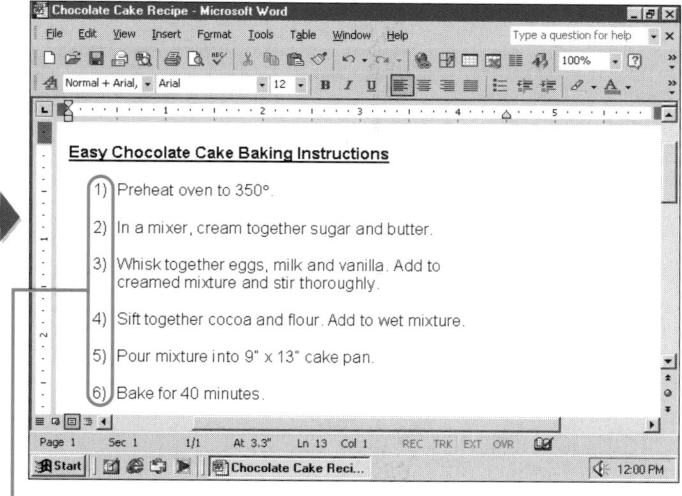

■ A bullet or number appears in front of each item in the list.

■ To deselect the text in the list, click outside the selected area.

■ To remove bullets or numbers from a list, repeat steps 1 to 6, selecting **None** in step 5.

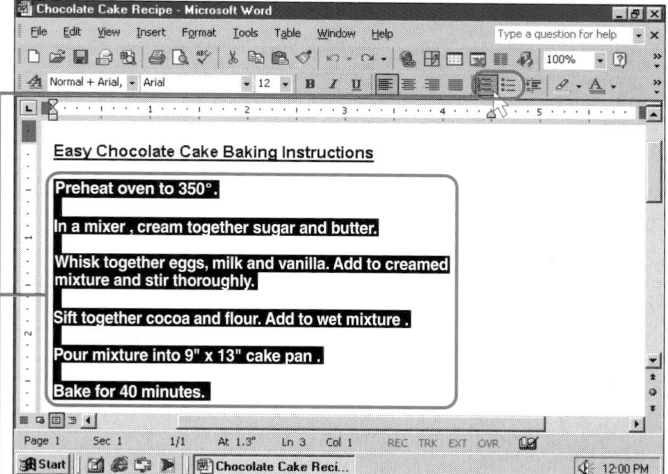

QUICKLY CREATE A LIST

1 Select the text you want to display as a bulleted or numbered list. To select text, see page 24.

2 Click one of the following buttons.

- Add numbers
- Add bullets

Note: If the button you want is not displayed, click on the Formatting toolbar to display all the buttons.

CHANGE ALIGNMENT OF TEXT

You can enhance the appearance of your document by aligning text in different ways.

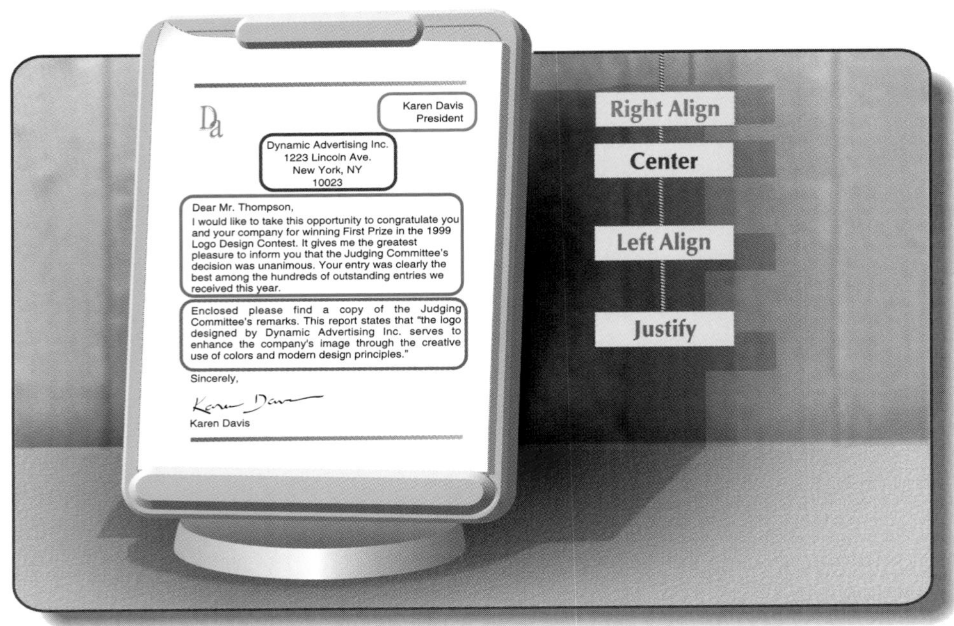

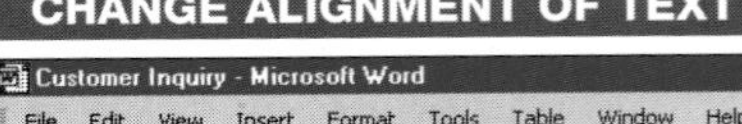

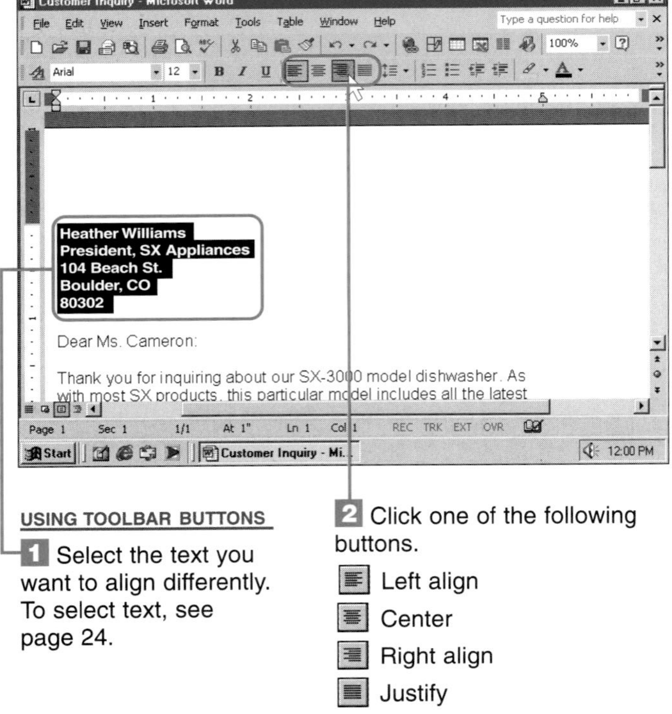

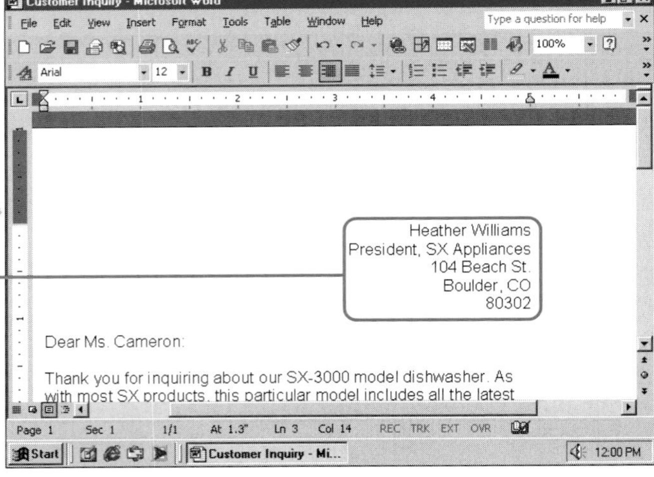

USING TOOLBAR BUTTONS

1 Select the text you want to align differently. To select text, see page 24.

2 Click one of the following buttons.

- Left align
- Center
- Right align
- Justify

Note: If the button you want is not displayed, click on the Formatting toolbar to display all the buttons.

■ The text displays the new alignment.

■ To deselect text, click outside the selected area.

Can I use different alignments within a single line of text?

You can use the Click and Type feature to vary the alignment within a line of text. For example, you can left align your name and right align the date on the same line.

I cannot use the Click and Type feature to align text. What is wrong?

The Click and Type feature is only available in the Print Layout and Web Layout views. To change the view of your document, see page 28.

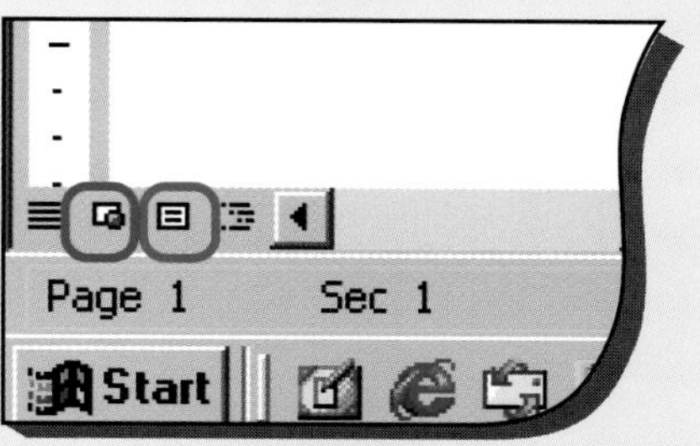

Web Layout

Print Layout

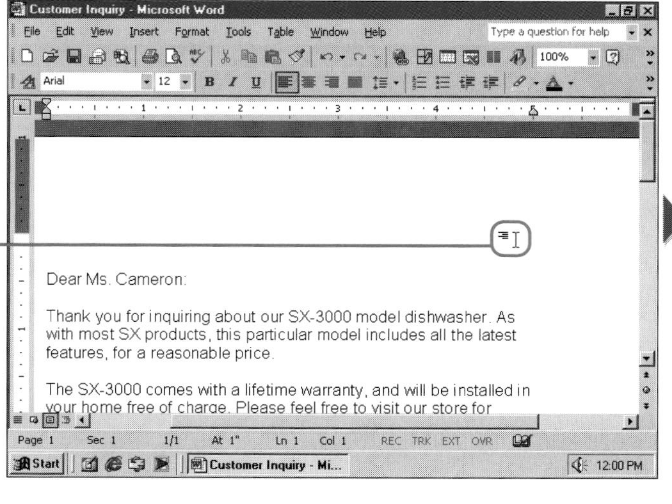

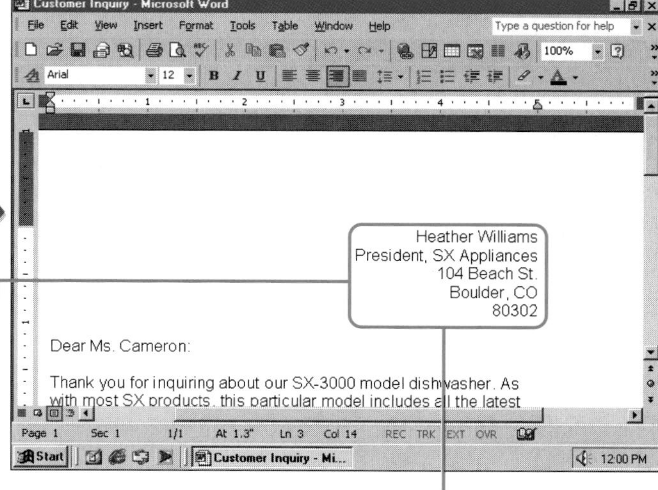

USING CLICK AND TYPE

1 Position the mouse I where you want the text to appear. The appearance of the mouse I indicates how Word will align the text.

I≡ Left align

I Center

≡I Right align

Note: If the appearance of the mouse I does not change, click where you want to add text.

2 Double-click the location to position the insertion point.

3 Type the text you want to add.

You can indent text to make paragraphs in your document stand out.

INDENT PARAGRAPHS

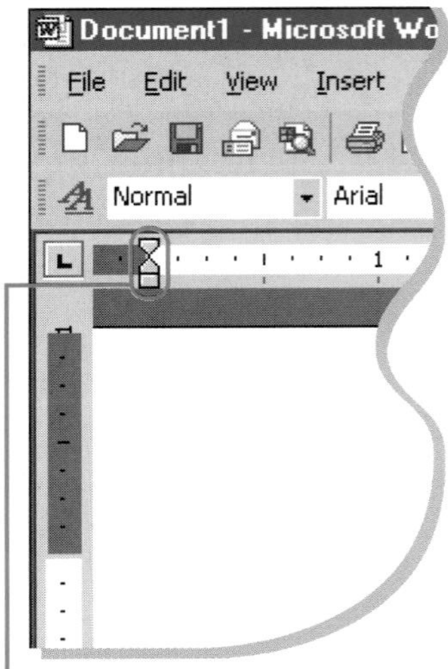

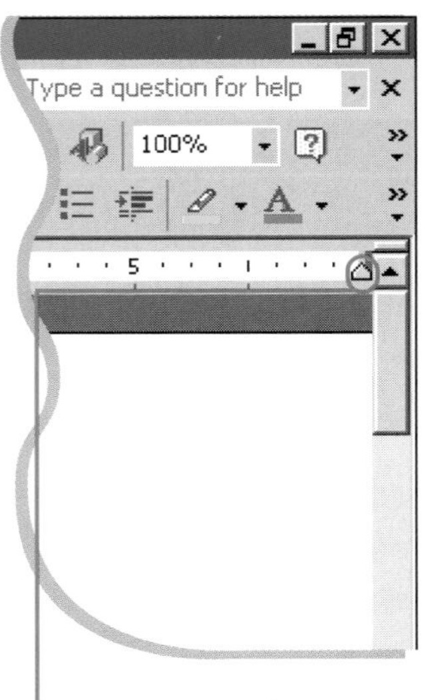

■ These symbols allow you to indent the left edge of a paragraph.

▽ Indent first line

△ Indent all but the first line

▭ Indent all lines

■ This symbol (△) allows you to indent the right edge of a paragraph.

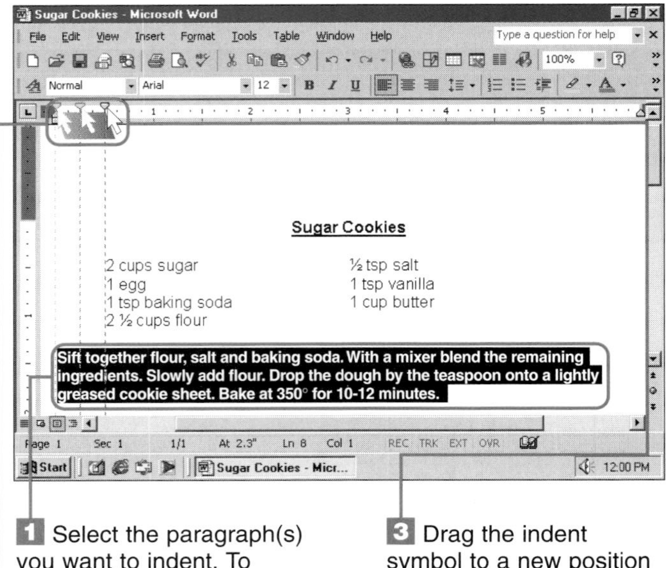

1 Select the paragraph(s) you want to indent. To select text, see page 24.

2 Position the mouse over the indent symbol you want to use.

3 Drag the indent symbol to a new position on the ruler.

■ A dotted line shows the new indent position.

What types of indents can I create?

First Line Indent

Indents only the first line of a paragraph. First line indents are often used to mark the beginning of paragraphs in letters and professional documents.

Hanging Indent

Indents all but the first line of a paragraph. Hanging indents are useful when you are creating a glossary or bibliography.

Indent Both Sides

Indenting both the left and right sides of a paragraph is useful when you want to set text, such as a quotation, apart from the rest of the text in your document.

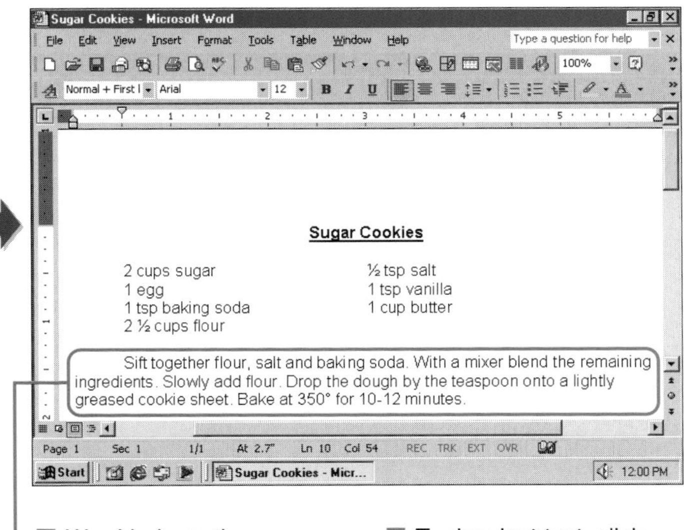

■ Word indents the paragraph(s) you selected.

■ To deselect text, click outside the selected area.

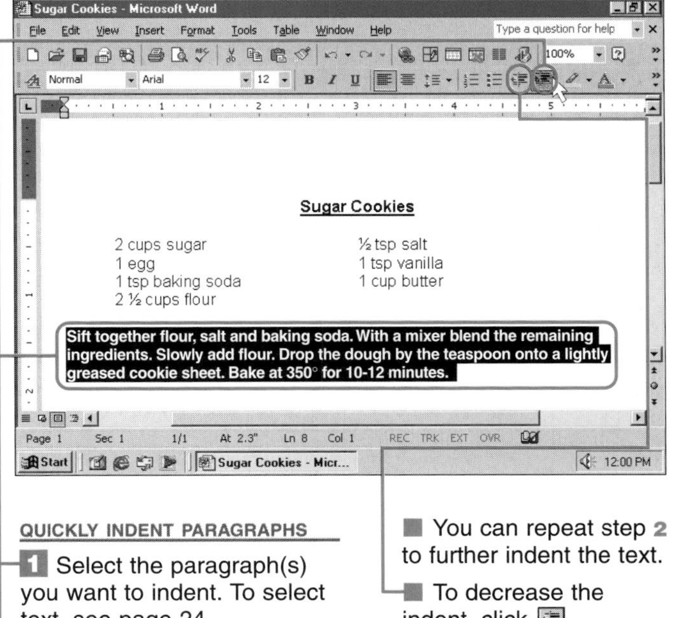

QUICKLY INDENT PARAGRAPHS

1 Select the paragraph(s) you want to indent. To select text, see page 24.

2 Click [icon] to indent the left edge of the paragraph(s).

Note: If [icon] is not displayed, click [icon] on the Formatting toolbar to display all the buttons.

■ You can repeat step 2 to further indent the text.

■ To decrease the indent, click [icon].

CHANGE TAB SETTINGS

You can use tabs to line up information in your document. Word offers several types of tabs that you can choose from.

Word automatically places a tab every 0.5 inches across a page.

CHANGE TAB SETTINGS

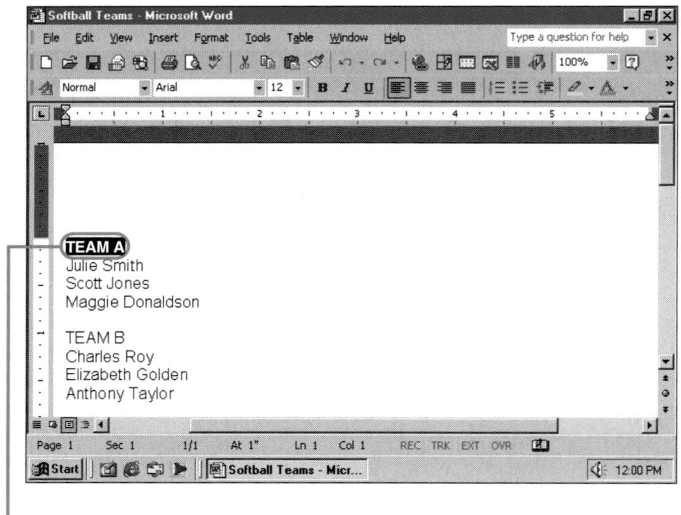

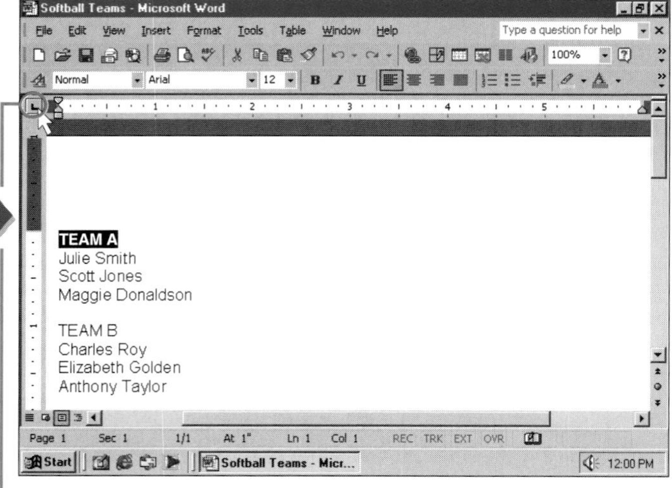

ADD A TAB

1 Select the text you want to use the new tab. To select text, see page 24.

■ To add a tab to text you are about to type, click the location in your document where you want to type the text.

2 Click this area until the type of tab you want to add appears.

- Left tab
- Center tab
- Right tab
- Decimal tab

How can I move a tab?

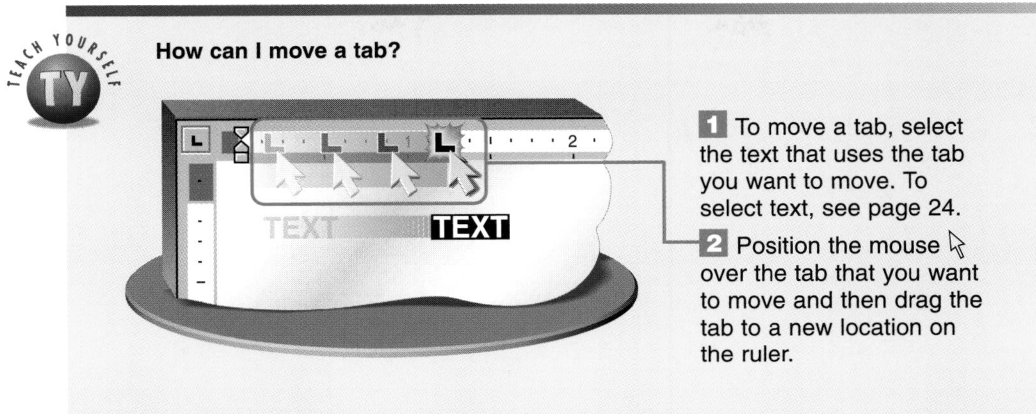

1 To move a tab, select the text that uses the tab you want to move. To select text, see page 24.

2 Position the mouse over the tab that you want to move and then drag the tab to a new location on the ruler.

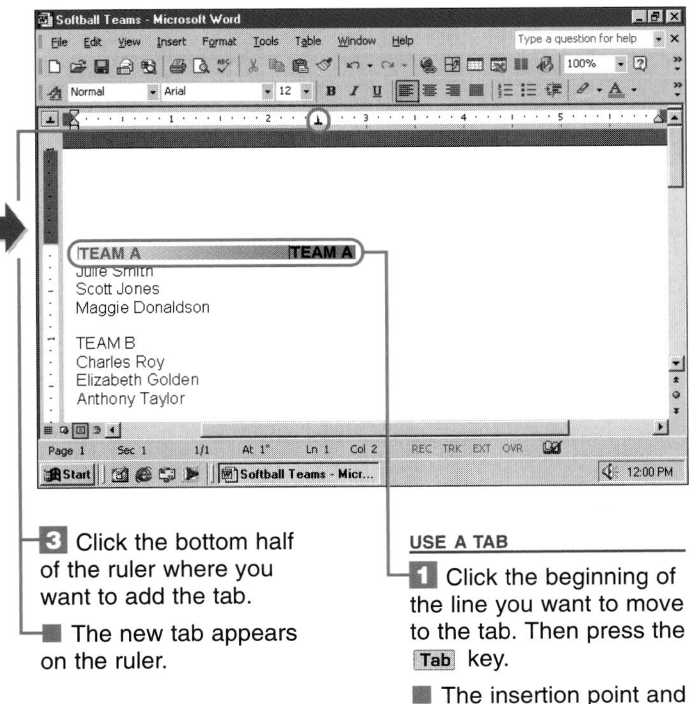

3 Click the bottom half of the ruler where you want to add the tab.

■ The new tab appears on the ruler.

USE A TAB

1 Click the beginning of the line you want to move to the tab. Then press the Tab key.

■ The insertion point and the text that follows move to the tab you set.

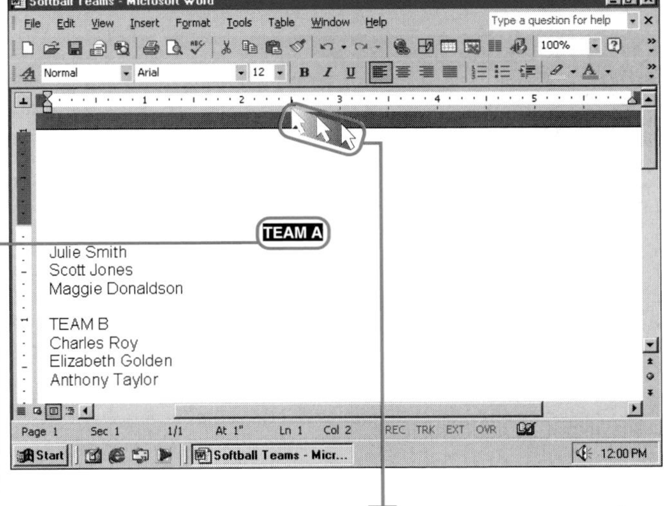

REMOVE A TAB

1 Select the text that uses the tab you want to remove. To select text, see page 24.

2 Position the mouse over the tab and then drag the tab downward off the ruler.

■ The tab disappears from the ruler.

CHANGE LINE SPACING

You can change the amount of space between the lines of text in your document. Changing the line spacing can make a document easier to review and edit.

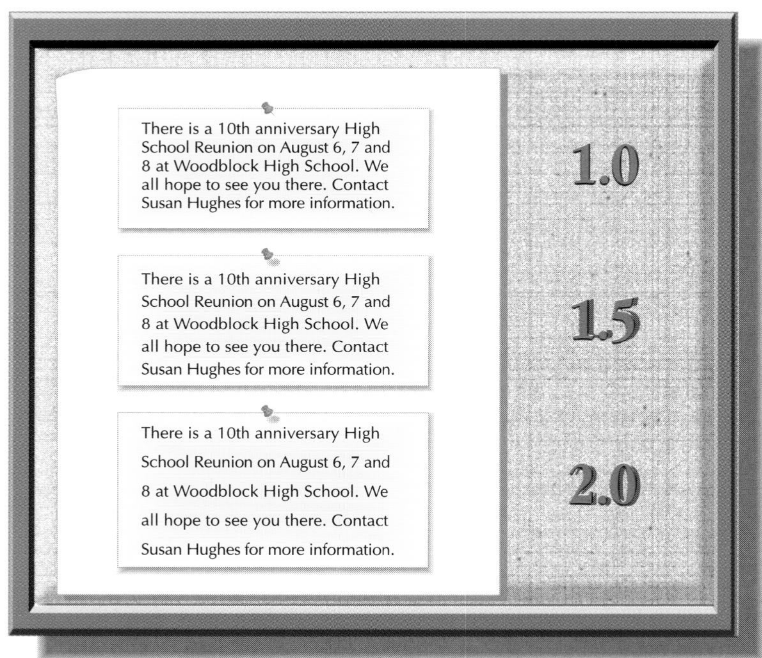

CHANGE LINE SPACING

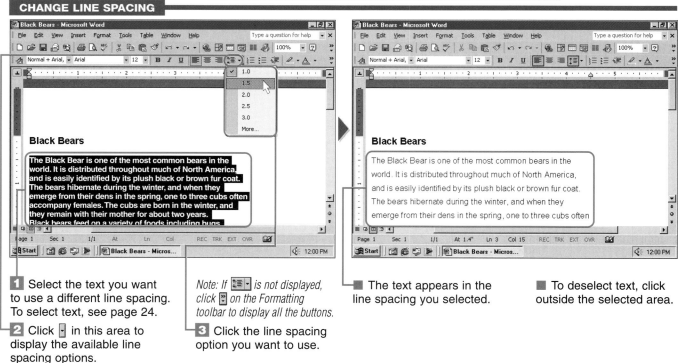

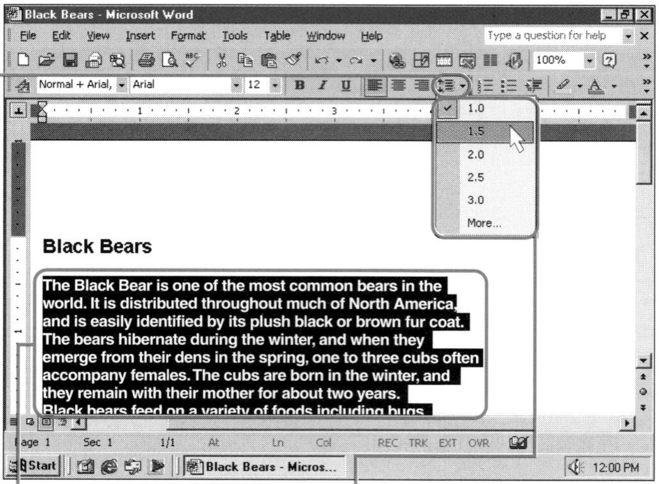

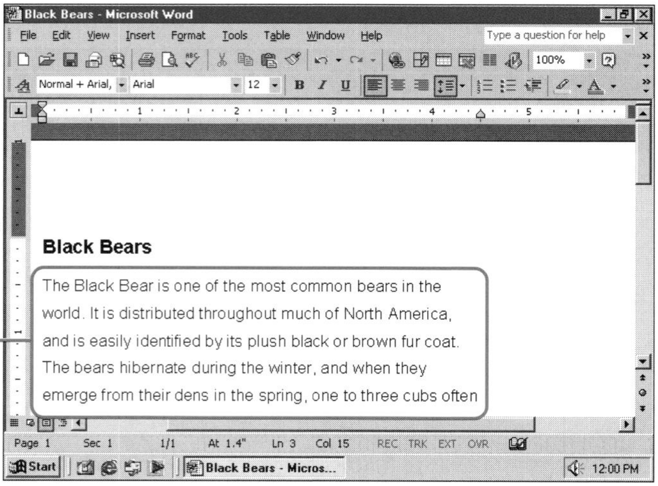

1 Select the text you want to use a different line spacing. To select text, see page 24.

2 Click ▾ in this area to display the available line spacing options.

Note: If ☰▾ is not displayed, click » on the Formatting toolbar to display all the buttons.

3 Click the line spacing option you want to use.

■ The text appears in the line spacing you selected.

■ To deselect text, click outside the selected area.

REMOVE FORMATTING FROM TEXT

You can remove the formatting you applied to text in your document.

REMOVE FORMATTING FROM TEXT

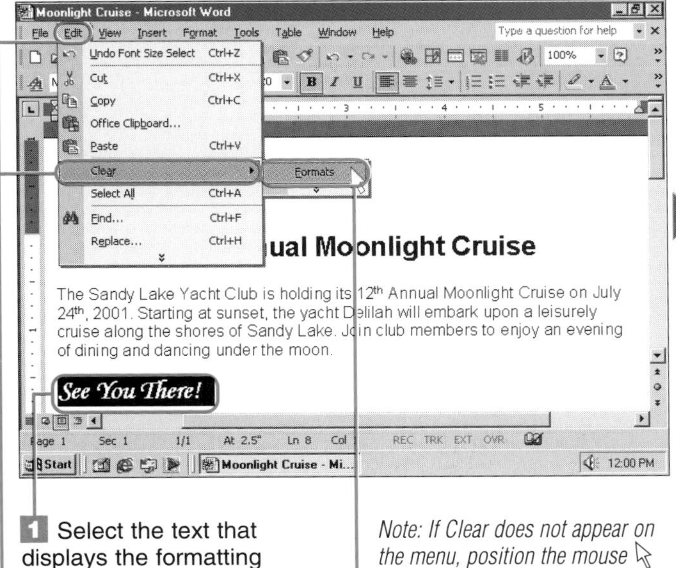

1 Select the text that displays the formatting you want to remove. To select text, see page 24.

2 Click **Edit**.

3 Click **Clear**.

Note: If Clear does not appear on the menu, position the mouse over the bottom of the menu to display all the menu options.

4 Click **Formats**.

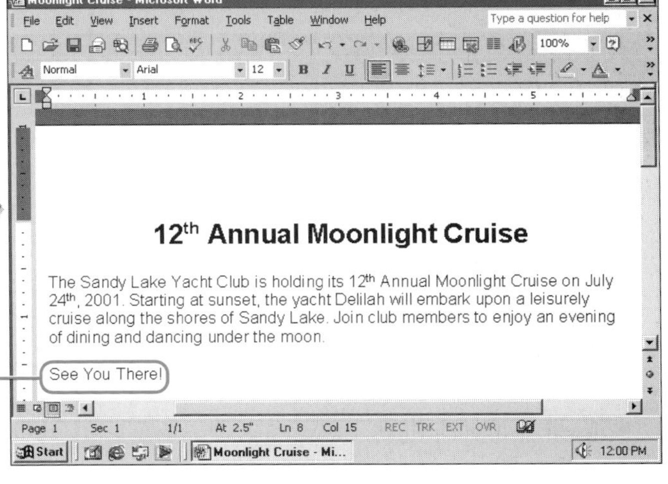

■ The formatting disappears from the text.

■ To deselect text, click outside the selected area.

INSERT A PAGE BREAK

If you want to start a new page at a specific location in your document, you can insert a page break. A page break indicates where one page ends and another begins.

Inserting a page break is useful when you want a heading to appear at the top of a new page.

INSERT A PAGE BREAK

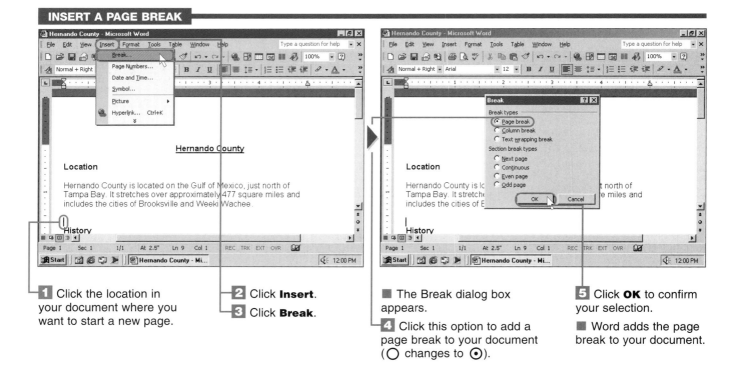

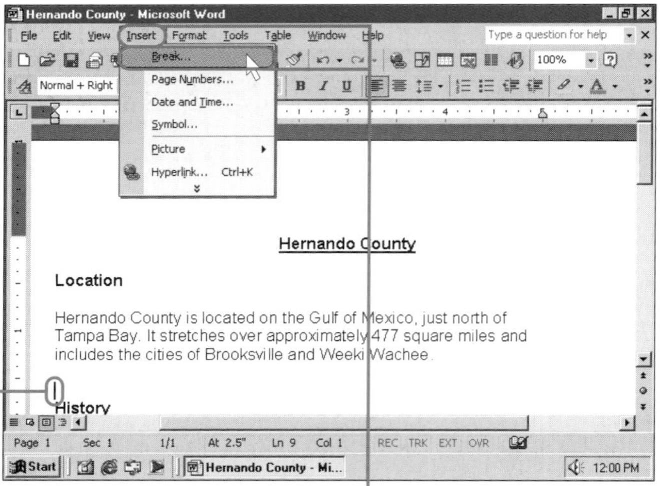

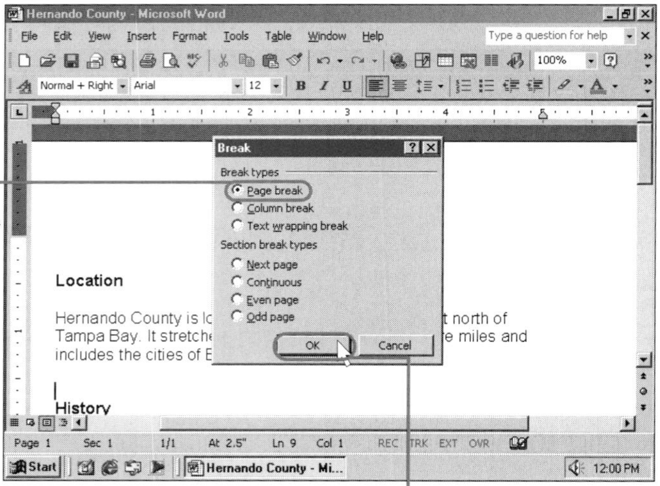

1 Click the location in your document where you want to start a new page.

2 Click **Insert**.

3 Click **Break**.

■ The Break dialog box appears.

4 Click this option to add a page break to your document (○ changes to ⊙).

5 Click **OK** to confirm your selection.

■ Word adds the page break to your document.

Will Word ever insert a page break automatically?

When you fill a page with information, Word automatically starts a new page by inserting a page break for you.

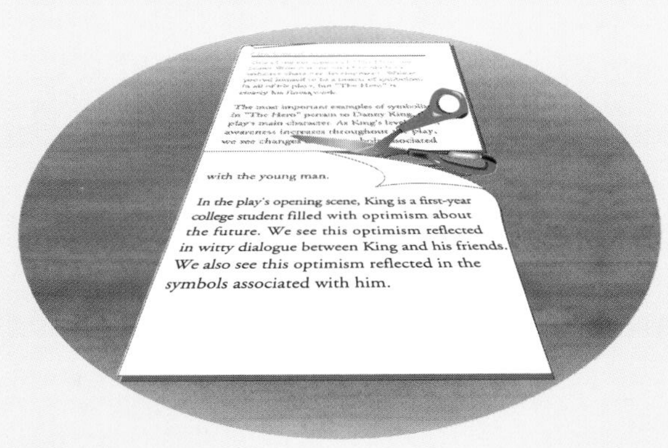

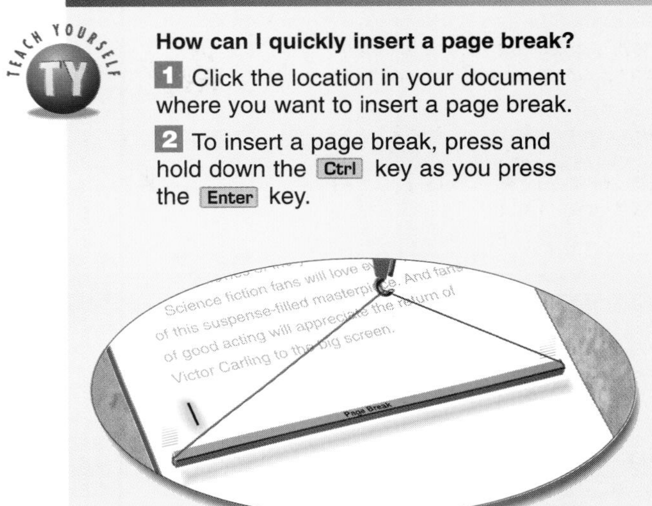

How can I quickly insert a page break?

1 Click the location in your document where you want to insert a page break.

2 To insert a page break, press and hold down the Ctrl key as you press the Enter key.

DELETE A PAGE BREAK

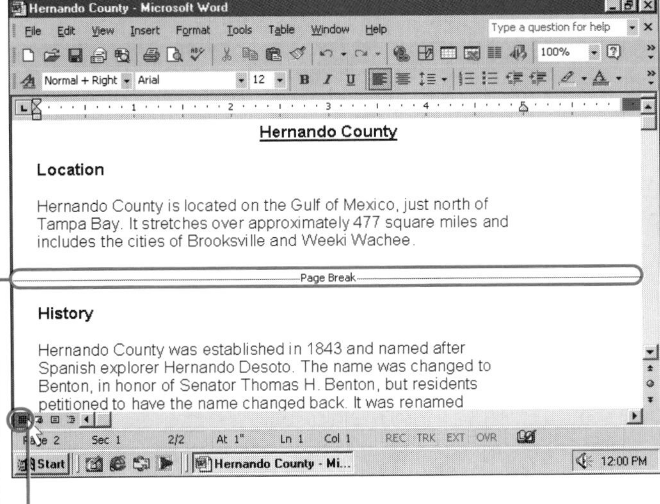

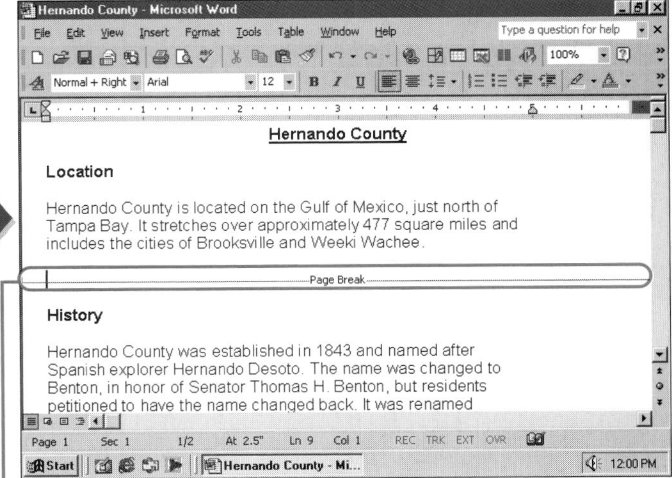

1 Click ≣ to display your document in the Normal view.

■ The **Page Break** line shows where one page ends and another begins. The line will not appear when you print your document.

Note: You may need to scroll through your document to view the line.

2 Click the **Page Break** line.

3 Press the Delete key to remove the page break.

INSERT A SECTION BREAK

You can insert section breaks to divide your document into sections.

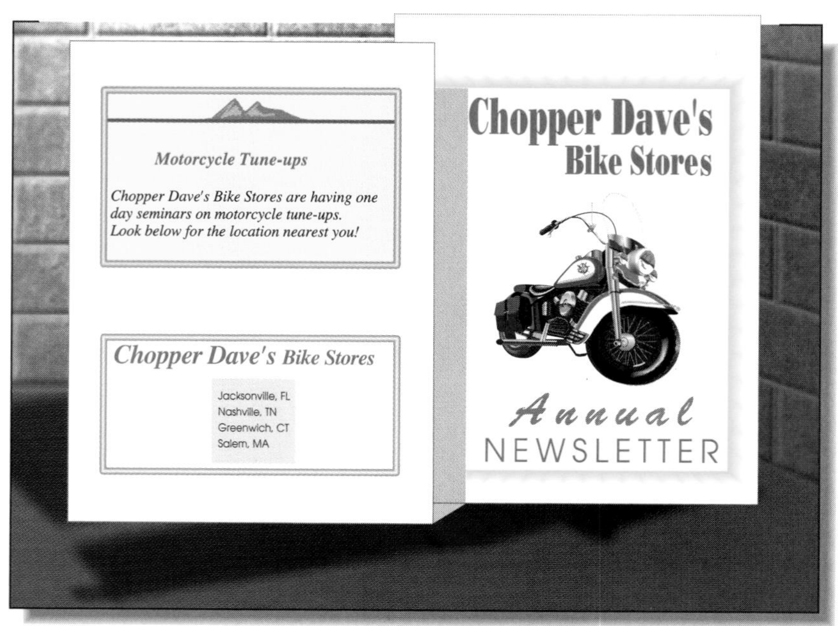

Dividing your document into sections allows you to apply formatting to only part of your document. For example, you may want to vertically center text or change the margins for only part of your document.

INSERT A SECTION BREAK

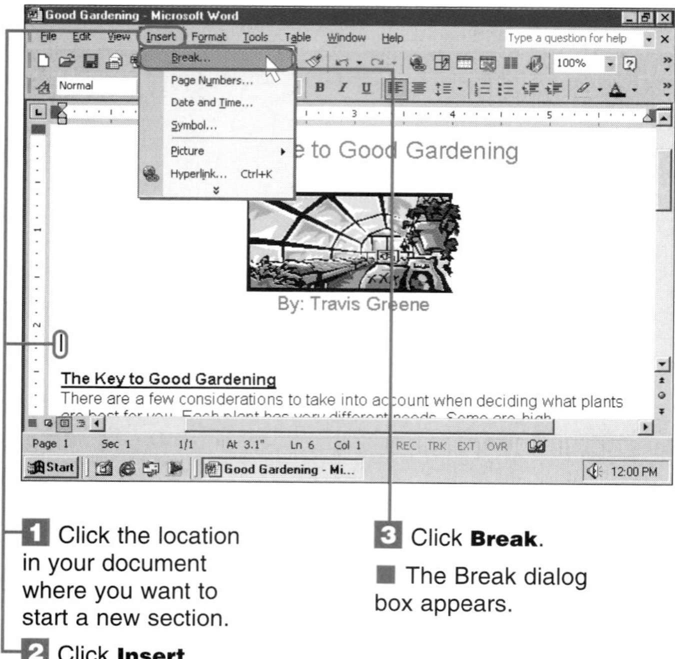

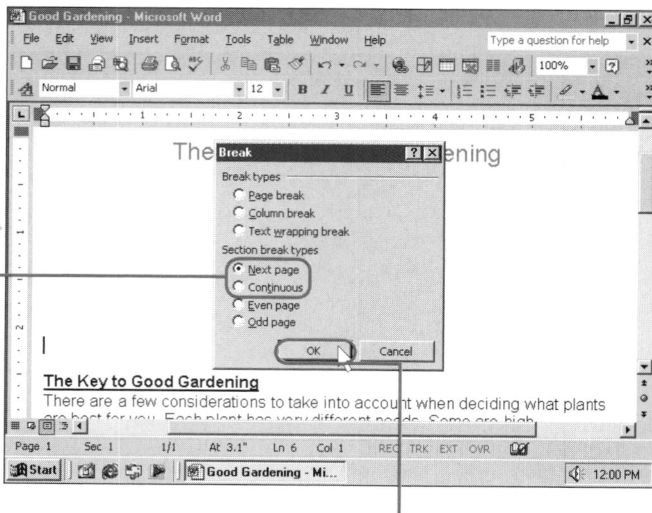

1 Click the location in your document where you want to start a new section.

2 Click **Insert**.

3 Click **Break**.

■ The Break dialog box appears.

4 Click the type of section break you want to add (○ changes to ⊙).

Next page - Starts a new section on a new page.

Continuous - Starts a new section on the current page.

5 Click **OK** to confirm your selection.

■ Word adds the section break to your document.

Will the appearance of my document change when I delete a section break?

When you delete a section break, the text above the break assumes the appearance of the text below the break. For example, if you change the margins for the text below a section break, the text above the break will also display the new margins when you delete the break.

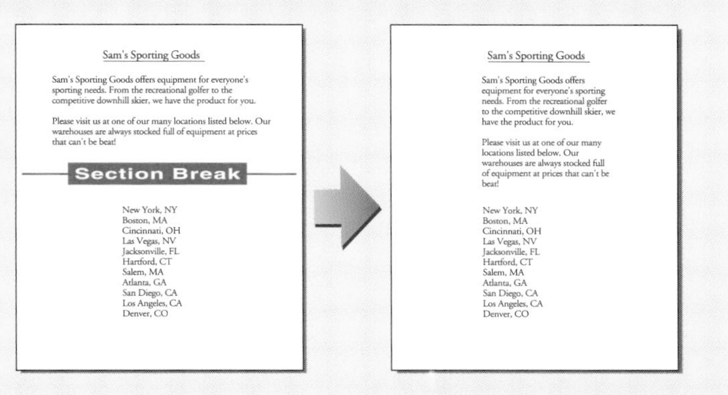

DELETE A SECTION BREAK

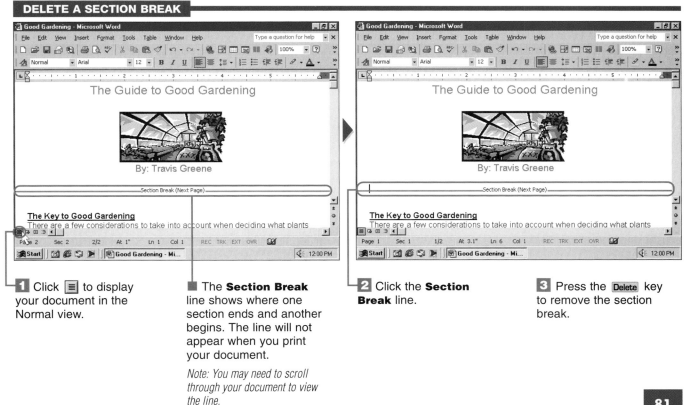

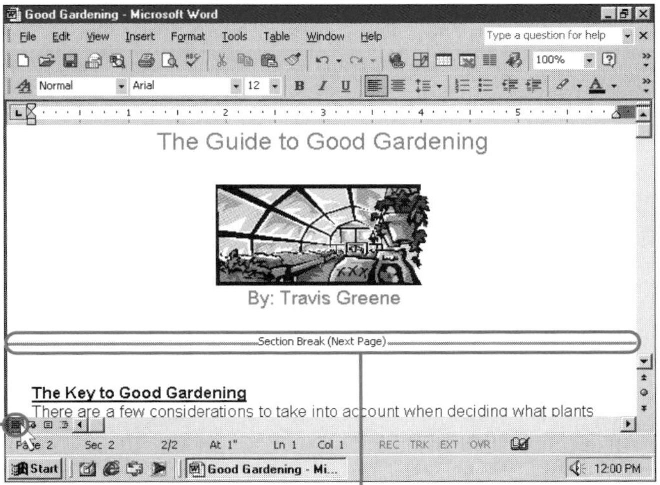

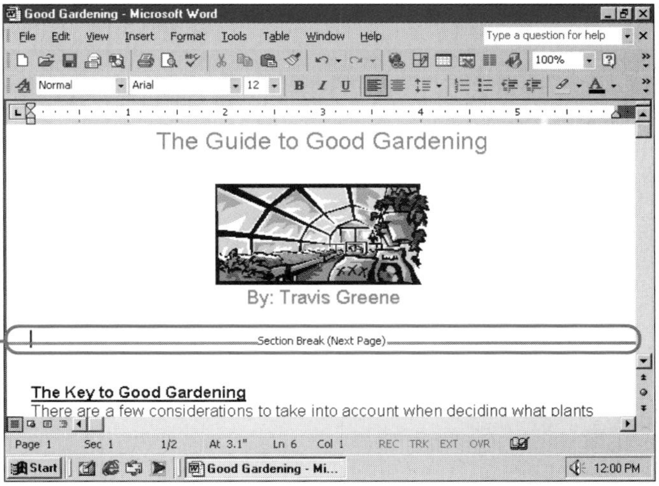

1 Click ▤ to display your document in the Normal view.

■ The **Section Break** line shows where one section ends and another begins. The line will not appear when you print your document.

Note: You may need to scroll through your document to view the line.

2 Click the **Section Break** line.

3 Press the Delete key to remove the section break.

CENTER TEXT ON A PAGE

You can vertically center the text in your document. This is useful when creating title pages and short memos.

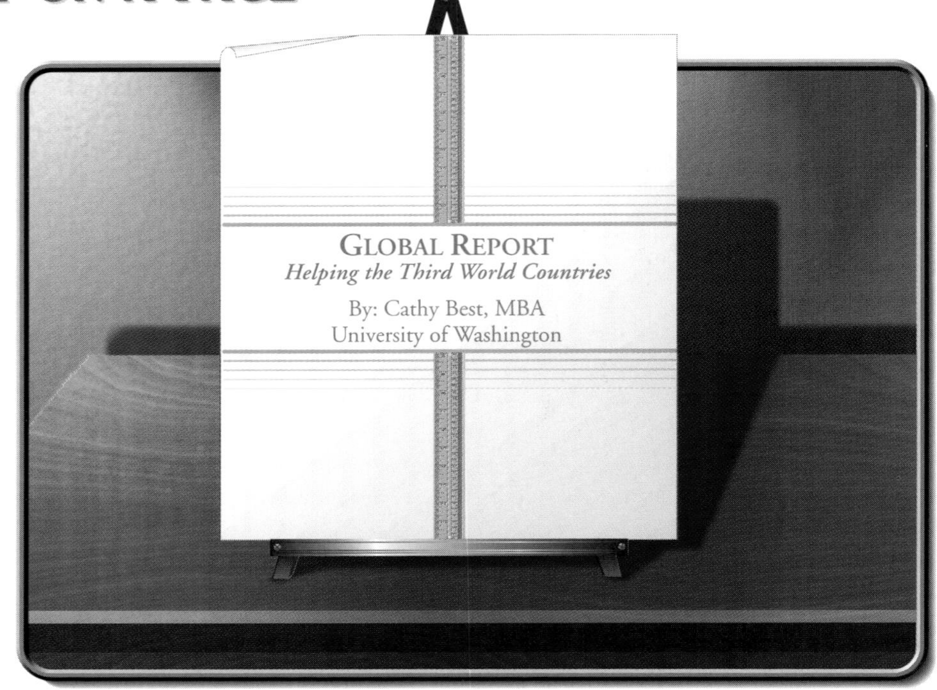

GLOBAL REPORT
Helping the Third World Countries
By: Cathy Best, MBA
University of Washington

After vertically centering text, you can use the Print Preview feature to see how the centered text will appear on a printed page. For information on the Print Preview feature, see page 34.

CENTER TEXT ON A PAGE

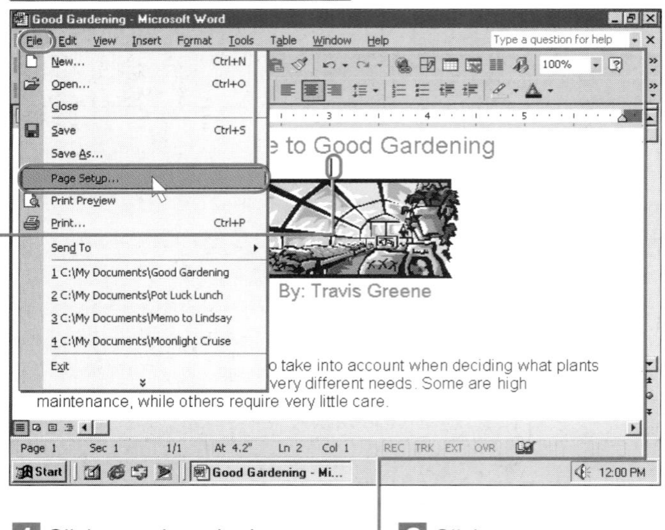

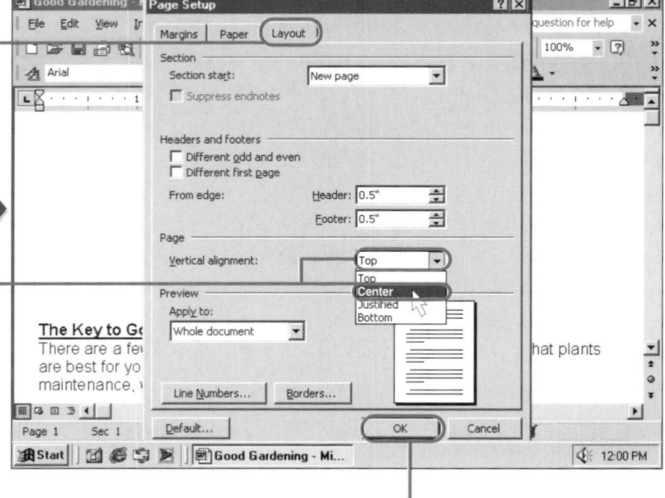

1 Click anywhere in the document or section you want to vertically center.

Note: To vertically center only some of the text in a document, you must divide the document into sections. For more information, see page 80.

2 Click **File**.

3 Click **Page Setup**.

■ The Page Setup dialog box appears.

4 Click the **Layout** tab.

5 Click this area to display the vertical alignment options.

6 Click **Center** to vertically center the text on the page.

7 Click **OK** to confirm the change.

■ To later remove the centering, repeat steps 1 to 7, except select **Top** in step 6.

CHANGE MARGINS

A margin is the amount of space between the text in your document and the edge of your paper. You can change the margins to suit your needs.

Changing margins lets you accommodate letterhead and other specialty paper. Word automatically sets the top and bottom margins to 1 inch and the left and right margins to 1.25 inches.

CHANGE MARGINS

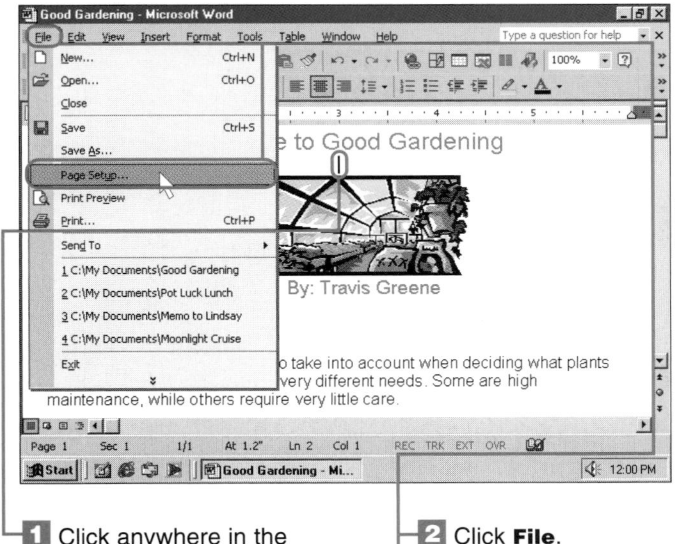

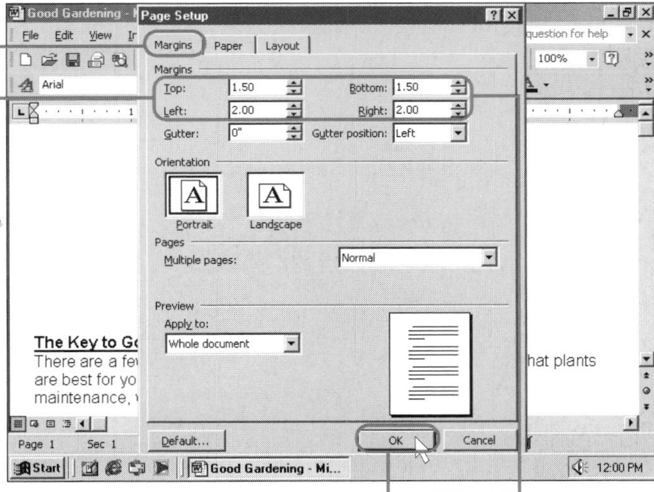

1 Click anywhere in the document or section where you want to change the margins.

Note: To change the margins for part of a document, you must divide the document into sections. For more information, see page 80.

2 Click **File**.

3 Click **Page Setup**.

■ The Page Setup dialog box appears.

4 Click the **Margins** tab.

■ This area displays the margins for the page.

5 Double-click the margin size you want to change and then type a new size.

■ Repeat step 5 for each margin you want to change.

6 Click **OK** to confirm the change.

ADD PAGE NUMBERS

You can have Word number the pages in your document.

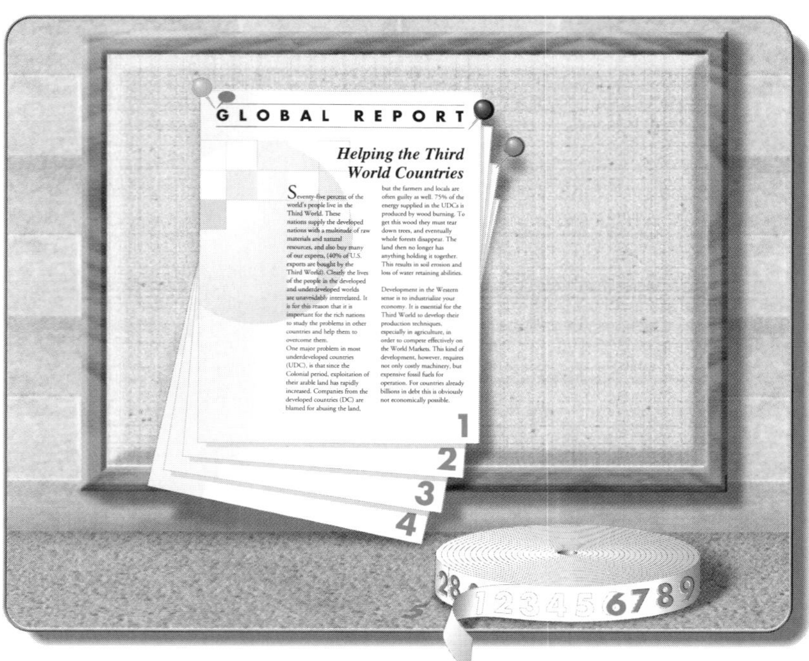

To view the page numbers on your screen, your document must be displayed in the Print Layout view. For information on the different ways you can view a document, see page 28.

ADD PAGE NUMBERS

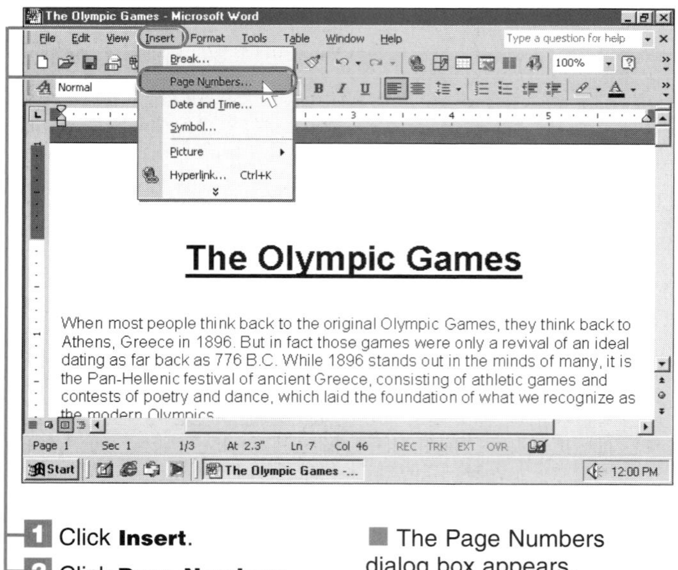

1 Click **Insert**.

2 Click **Page Numbers**.

■ The Page Numbers dialog box appears.

3 Click this area to select a position for the page numbers.

4 Click the position where you want the page numbers to appear.

How do I remove page numbers from my document?

Deleting a page number from your document's header or footer will remove the page numbers from your document.

1 Double-click a page number to display the header or footer area.

2 Drag the mouse over the page number to select the number.

3 Press the **Delete** key to delete the page number.

*Note: To close the header or footer area, click **Close** in the Header and Footer toolbar.*

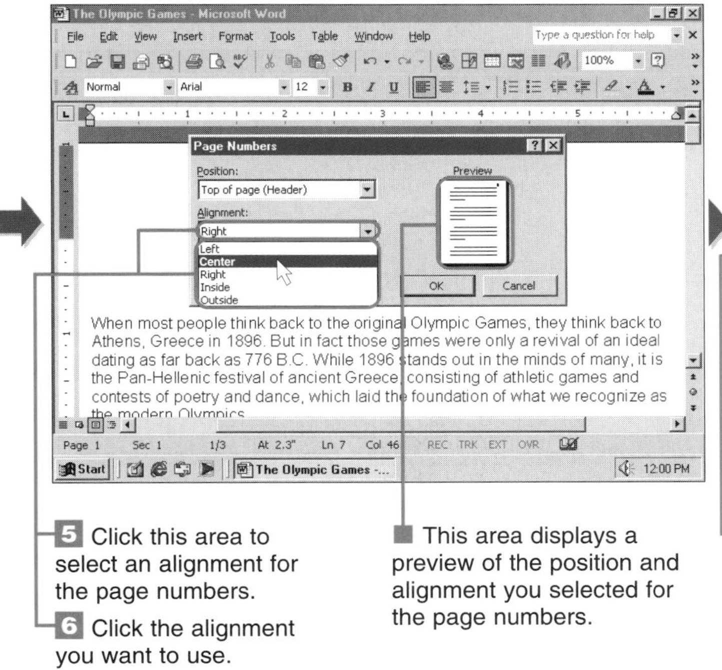

5 Click this area to select an alignment for the page numbers.

6 Click the alignment you want to use.

■ This area displays a preview of the position and alignment you selected for the page numbers.

7 If you want to hide the page number on the first page of your document, click this option (✔ changes to ☐).

Note: This option is useful if the first page in your document is a title page.

8 Click **OK** to add the page numbers to your document.

■ If you later make changes that affect the pages in your document, such as adding, removing or re-arranging text, Word will automatically adjust the page numbers for you.

ADD A WATERMARK

You can display a faint picture or text behind the information in a document. This can add interest to the document and is useful for identifying the status of the document.

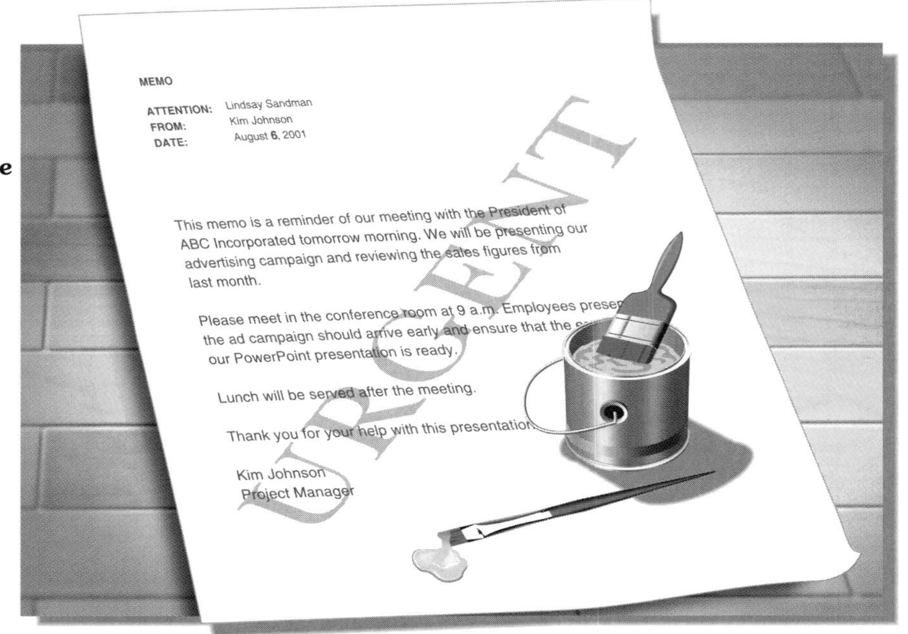

You can add a text watermark such as ASAP, Confidential, Copy, Personal, Sample or Urgent to a document.

Word can only display watermarks in the Print Layout view. For information on changing the view, see page 28.

ADD A WATERMARK

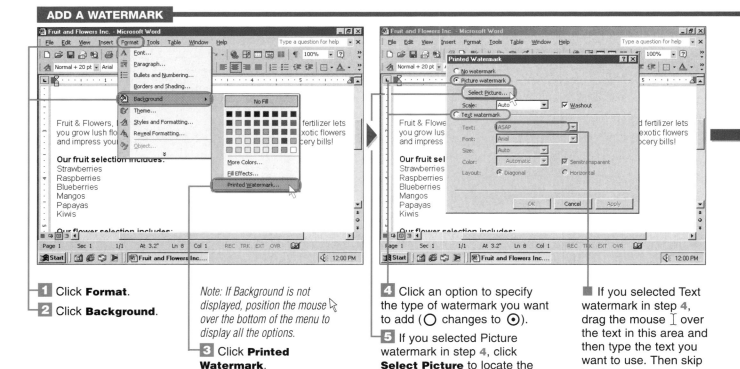

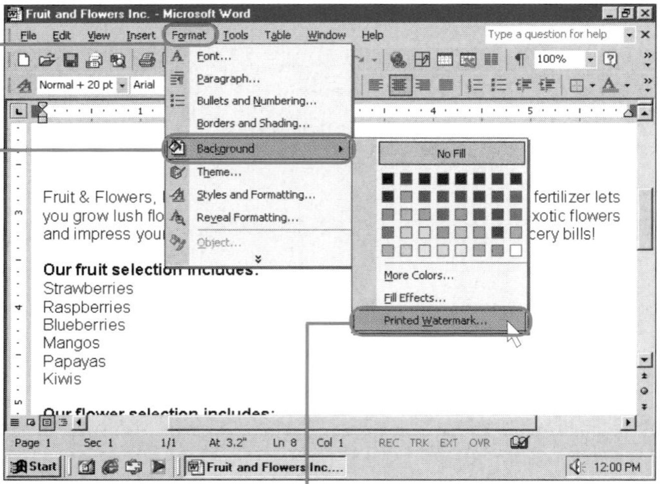

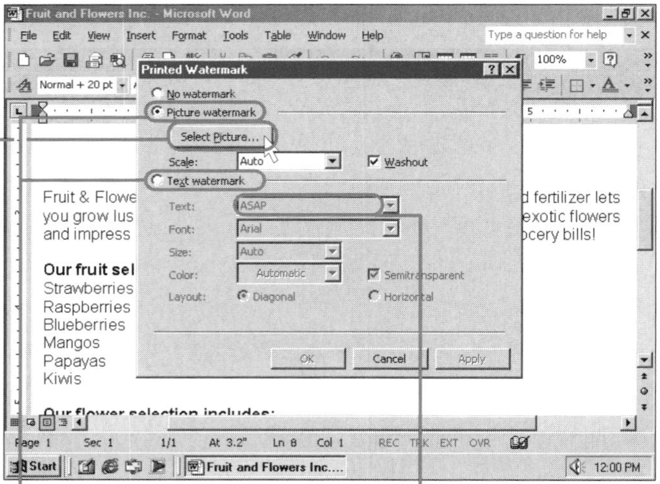

1 Click **Format**.

2 Click **Background**.

Note: If Background is not displayed, position the mouse over the bottom of the menu to display all the options.

3 Click **Printed Watermark**.

■ The Printed Watermark dialog box appears.

4 Click an option to specify the type of watermark you want to add (○ changes to ⦿).

5 If you selected Picture watermark in step 4, click **Select Picture** to locate the picture on your computer that you want to use.

■ If you selected Text watermark in step 4, drag the mouse over the text in this area and then type the text you want to use. Then skip to step 8.

How do I format the text I used as a watermark?

You can change the font, size and color of the text in a watermark.

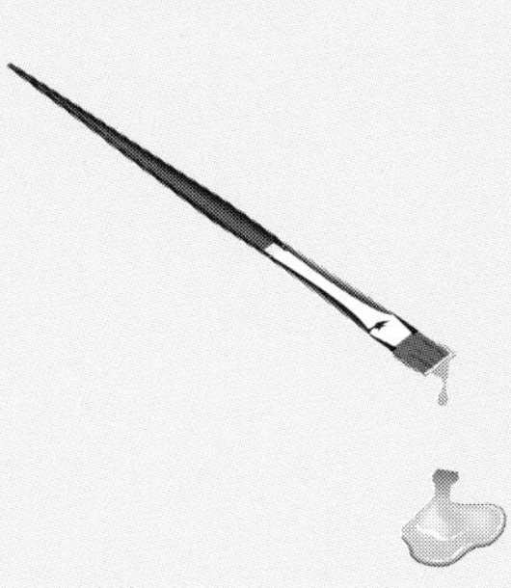

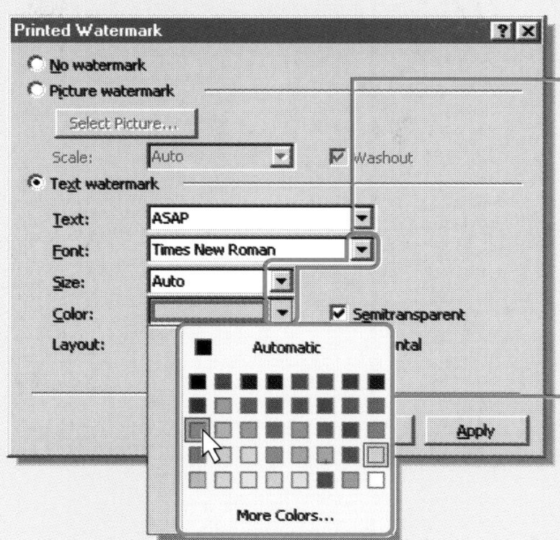

1 In the Printed Watermark dialog box, click ▼ beside the text formatting option you want to change.

2 In the list that appears, select a new formatting option.

■ You can repeat steps **1** and **2** to change another formatting option.

3 Click **OK** to confirm your change.

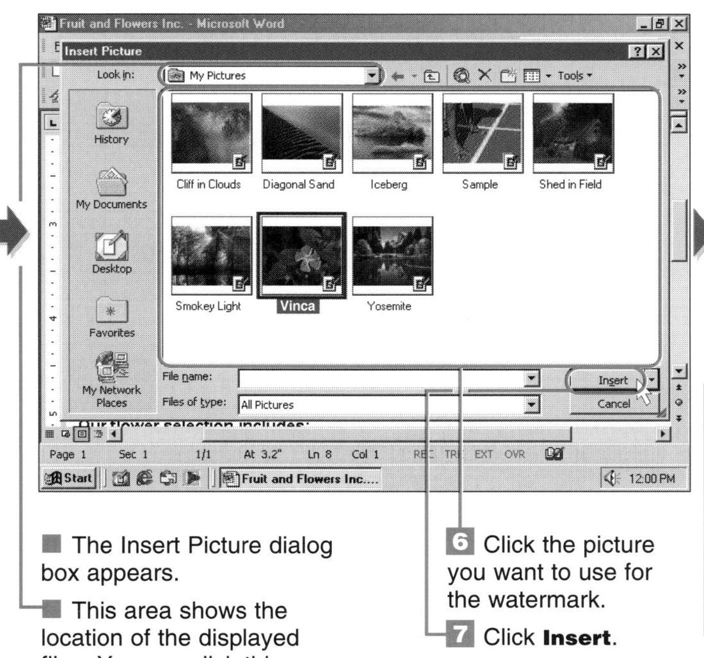

■ The Insert Picture dialog box appears.

■ This area shows the location of the displayed files. You can click this area to change the location.

6 Click the picture you want to use for the watermark.

7 Click **Insert**.

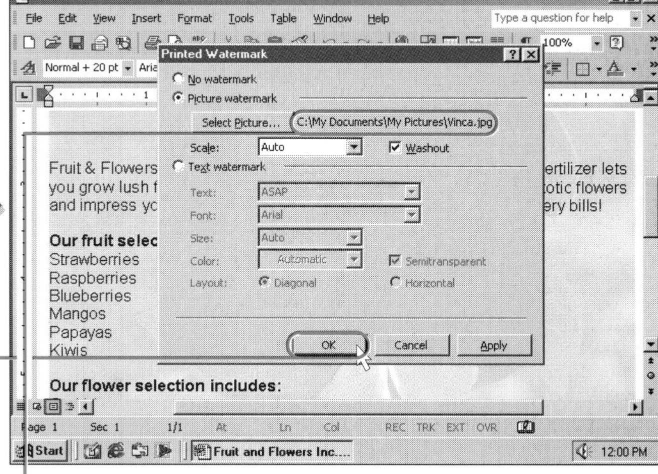

■ This area shows the location and name of the picture you selected.

8 Click **OK** to confirm your change.

■ The watermark appears on your document.

■ To remove a watermark, repeat steps **1** to **4**, selecting **No watermark** in step **4**. Then perform step **8**.

CREATE A TABLE

You can create a table to neatly display information in your document.

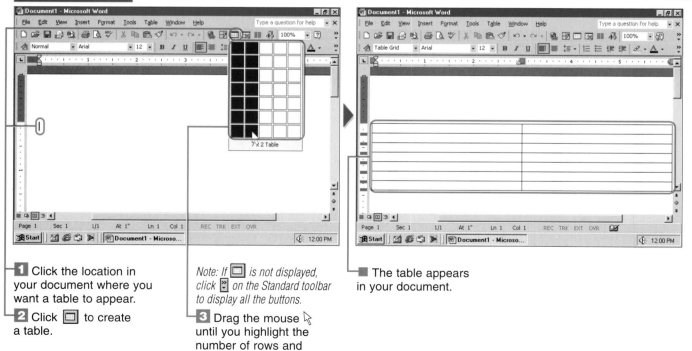

CREATE A TABLE

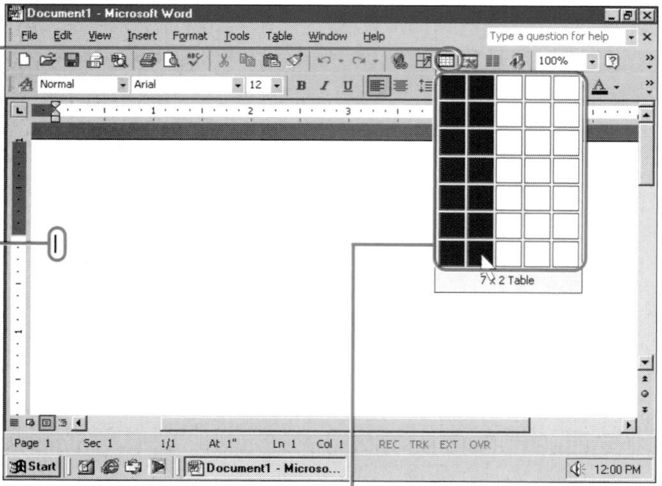

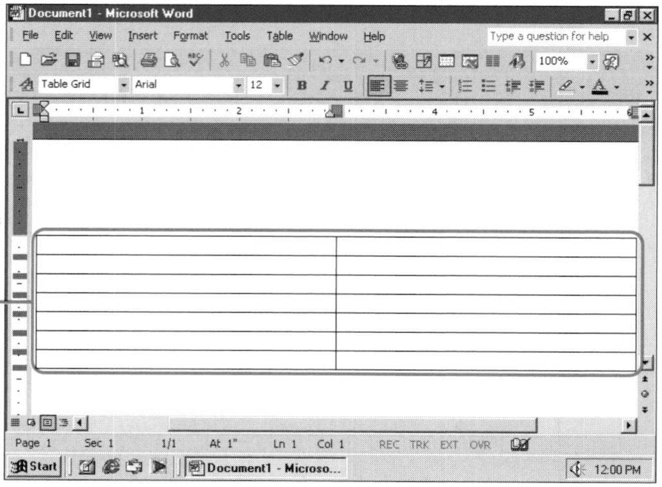

1 Click the location in your document where you want a table to appear.

2 Click ▦ to create a table.

Note: If ▦ is not displayed, click » on the Standard toolbar to display all the buttons.

3 Drag the mouse ↖ until you highlight the number of rows and columns you want the table to contain.

■ The table appears in your document.

TEACH YOURSELF

What are the parts of a table?

A table consists of rows, columns and cells.

Row

Column

Cell

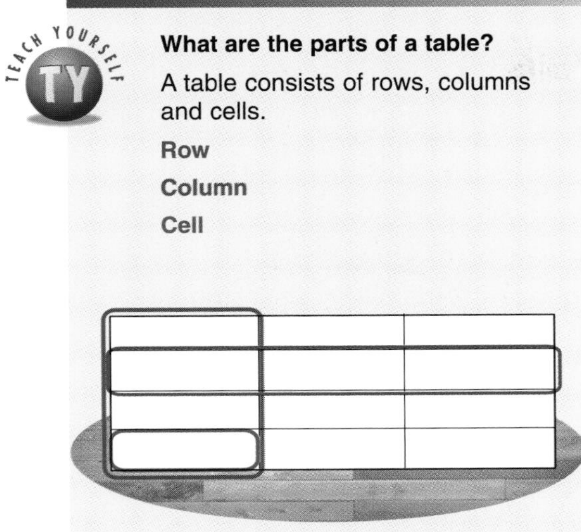

TEACH YOURSELF

Can I change the appearance of text in a table?

Yes. You can format text in a table as you would format any text in your document. For example, you can change the font, size, color and alignment of text in a table. To format text, see pages 62 to 71.

Pianist	Age	Song
Kate Roberts	12	Mary Had a Little Lamb
Morgan Brown	10	Twinkle, Twinkle, Little Star
Patrick O'Reilly	12	On Top of Old Smokey

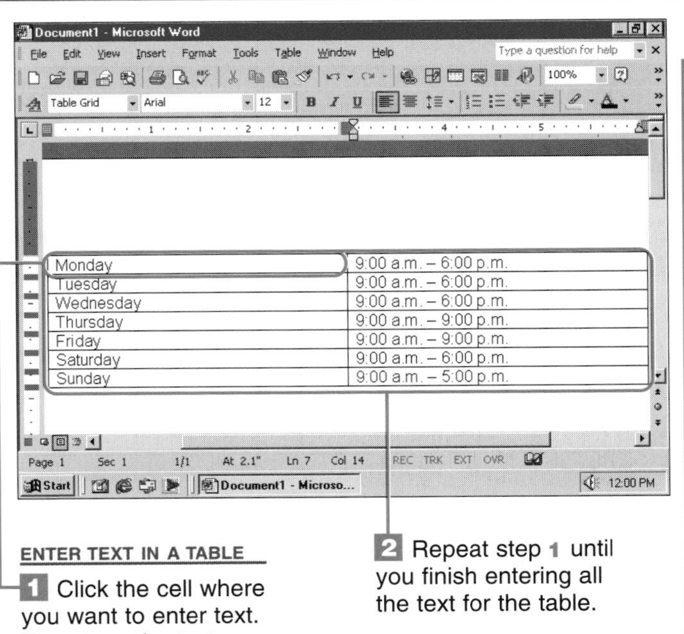

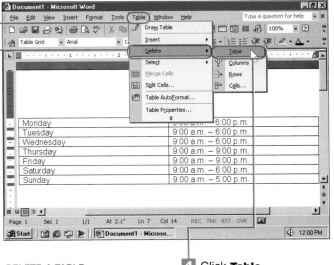

ENTER TEXT IN A TABLE

1 Click the cell where you want to enter text. Then type the text.

2 Repeat step 1 until you finish entering all the text for the table.

DELETE A TABLE

1 Click anywhere in the table you want to delete.

2 Click **Table**.

3 Click **Delete**.

4 Click **Table**.

■ The table disappears from your document.

CHANGE ROW HEIGHT OR COLUMN WIDTH

You can change the height of rows and the width of columns to improve the layout of your table.

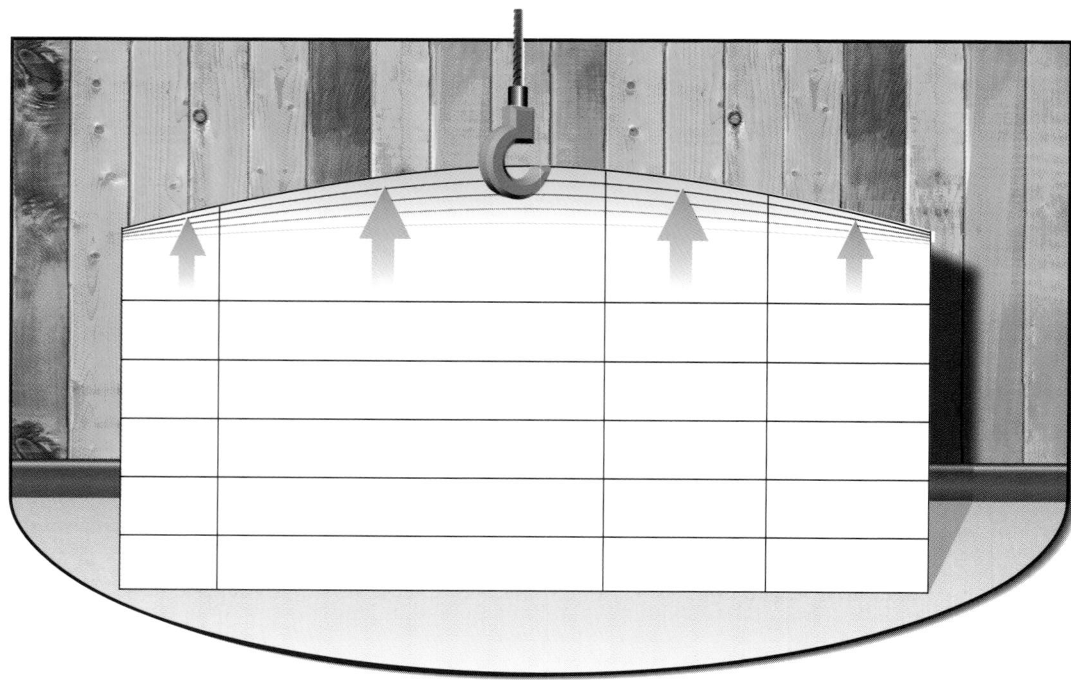

CHANGE ROW HEIGHT

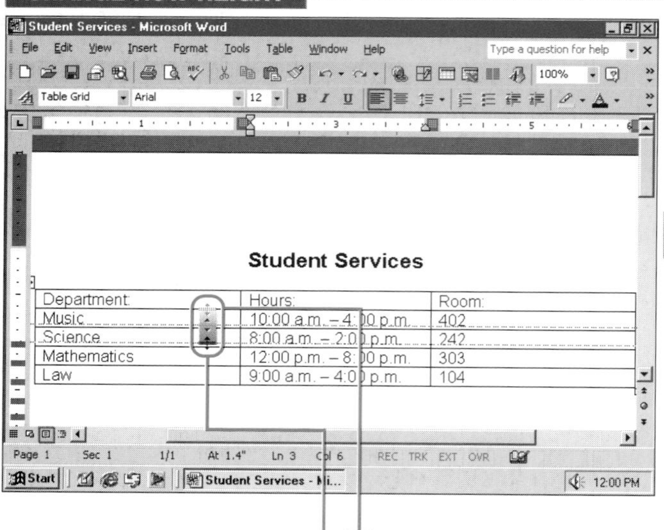

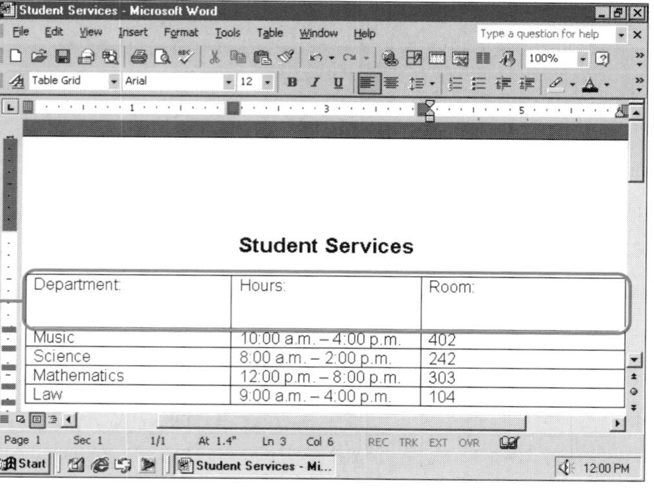

■ You can only change a row height when your document is displayed in the Print Layout or Web Layout view. To change the view of a document, see page 28.

1 Position the mouse I over the bottom edge of the row you want to change to a new height (I changes to ‡).

2 Drag the row edge to a new position.

■ A dotted line shows the new position.

■ The row displays the new height.

Note: When you change the height of a row, the height of the entire table changes.

Can Word automatically adjust a row height or column width?

Yes. When you enter text in a table, Word automatically increases the row height or column width to accommodate the text you type.

I am having trouble making a row height smaller. What is wrong?

The amount of text in one of the cells in the row may be preventing you from resizing the row. Word will not allow you to make a row height or column width too small to display the text in a cell.

CHANGE COLUMN WIDTH

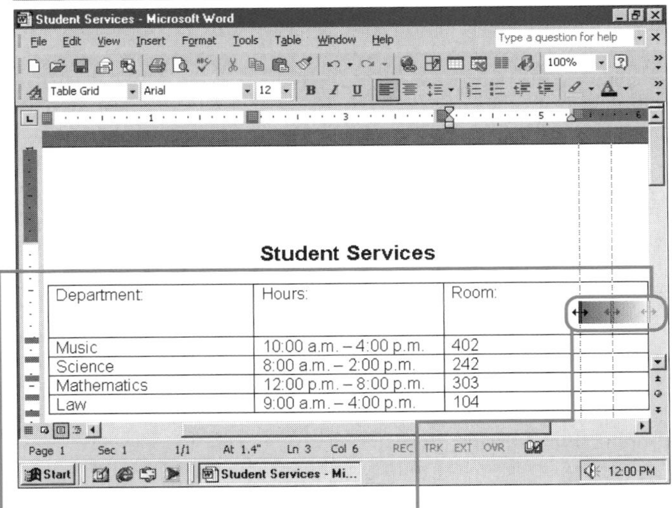

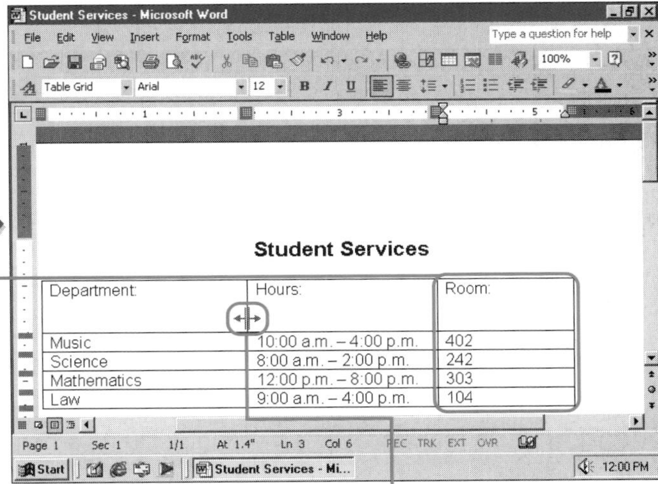

1 Position the mouse I over the right edge of the column you want to change to a new width (I changes to ↔).

2 Drag the column edge to a new position.

■ A dotted line shows the new position.

■ The column displays the new width.

Note: When you change the width of a column, the width of a neighboring column also changes. When you change the width of the last column, the width of the entire table changes.

FIT LONGEST ITEM

1 To quickly change a column width to fit the longest item in the column, double-click the right edge of the column.

ADD A ROW OR COLUMN

You can add a row or column to your table to insert additional information.

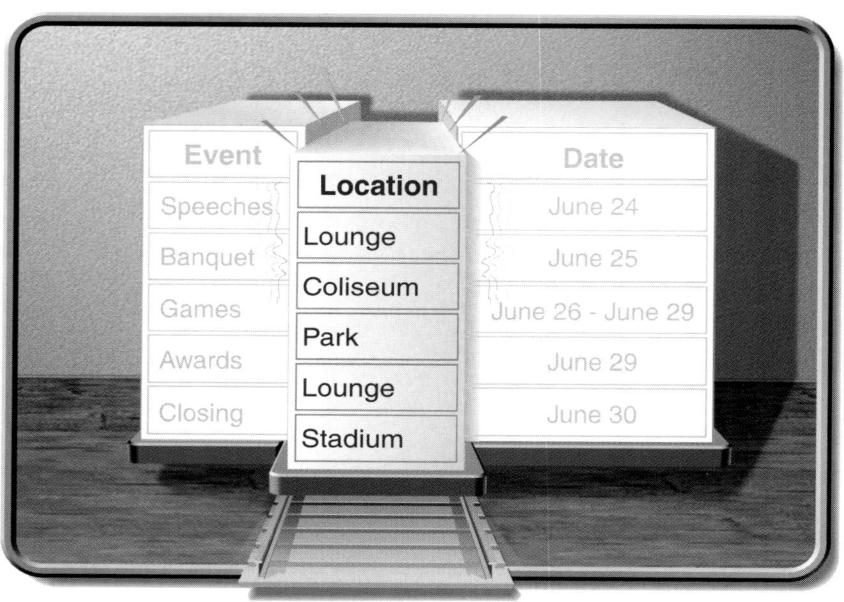

ADD A ROW

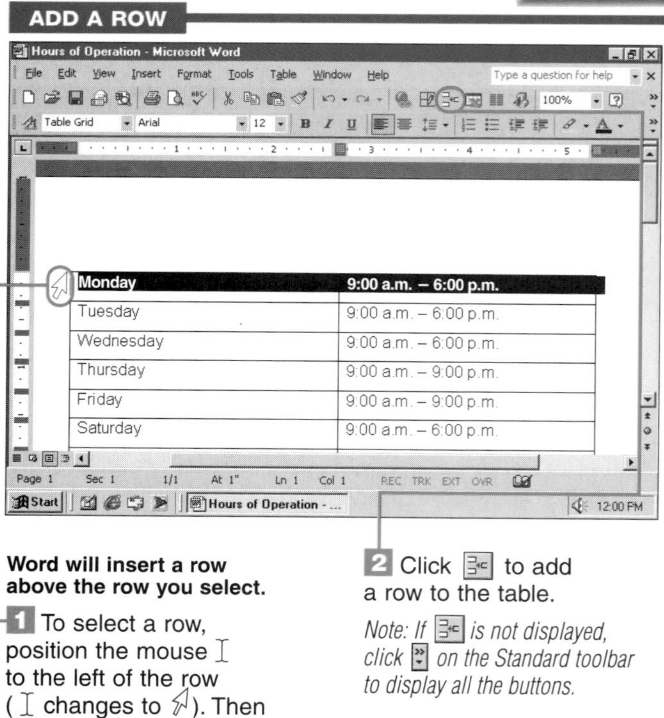

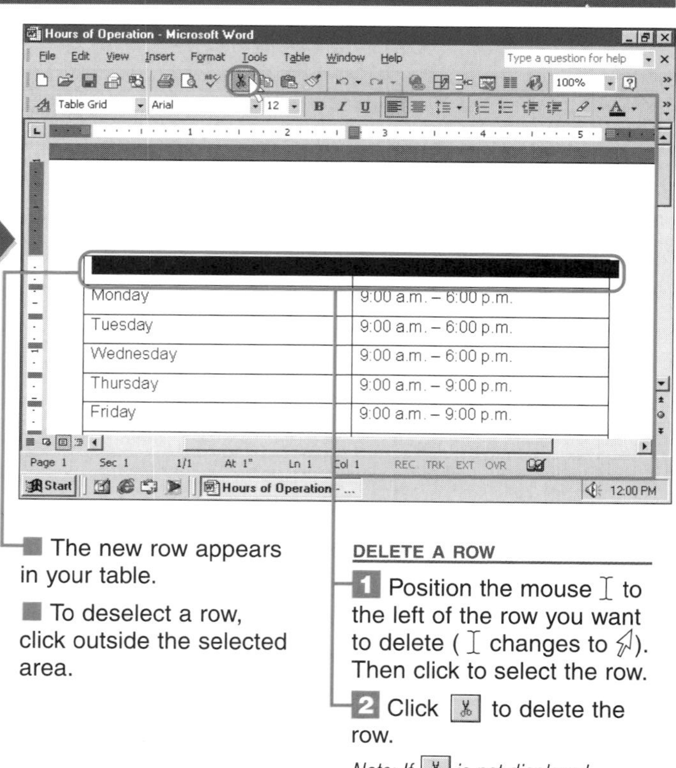

Word will insert a row above the row you select.

1 To select a row, position the mouse I to the left of the row (I changes to ↖). Then click to select the row.

2 Click ⊞ to add a row to the table.

Note: If ⊞ is not displayed, click » on the Standard toolbar to display all the buttons.

■ The new row appears in your table.

■ To deselect a row, click outside the selected area.

DELETE A ROW

1 Position the mouse I to the left of the row you want to delete (I changes to ↖). Then click to select the row.

2 Click ✂ to delete the row.

Note: If ✂ is not displayed, click » on the Standard toolbar to display all the buttons.

How do I add a row to the bottom of a table?

To add a row to the bottom of a table, click the bottom right cell in the table. Then press the Tab key.

Can I delete the information in a row or column without removing the row or column from a table?

Yes. To select the cells in a table that contain the information you want to delete, drag the mouse I over the cells until the cells are highlighted. Press the Delete key to remove the information.

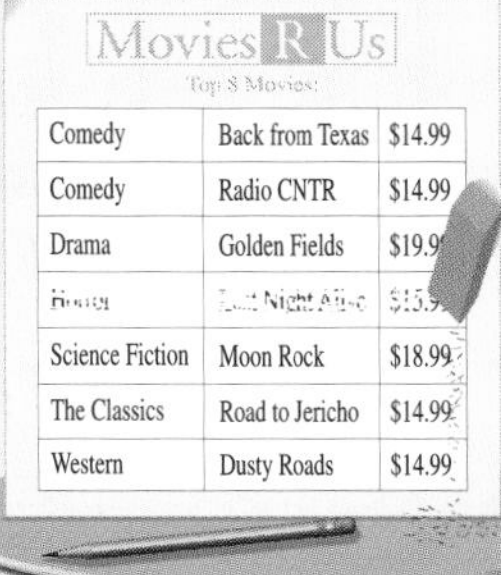

ADD A COLUMN

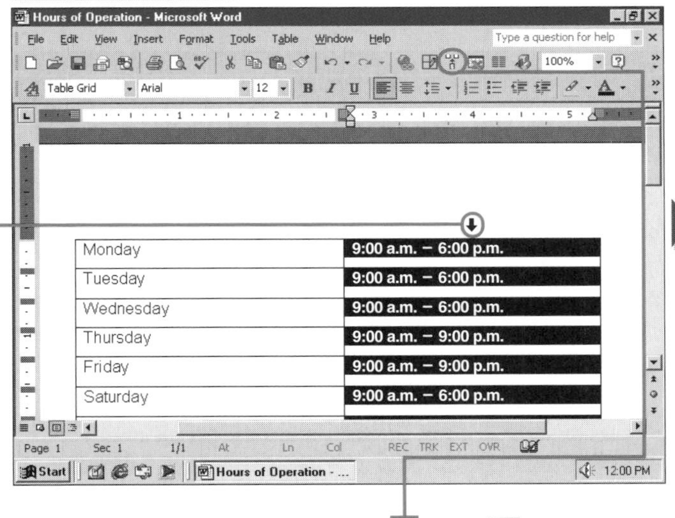

Word will insert a column to the left of the column you select.

1 To select a column, position the mouse I above the column (I changes to ⬇). Then click to select the column.

2 Click [button] to add a column.

Note: If [button] is not displayed, click [»] on the Standard toolbar to display all the buttons.

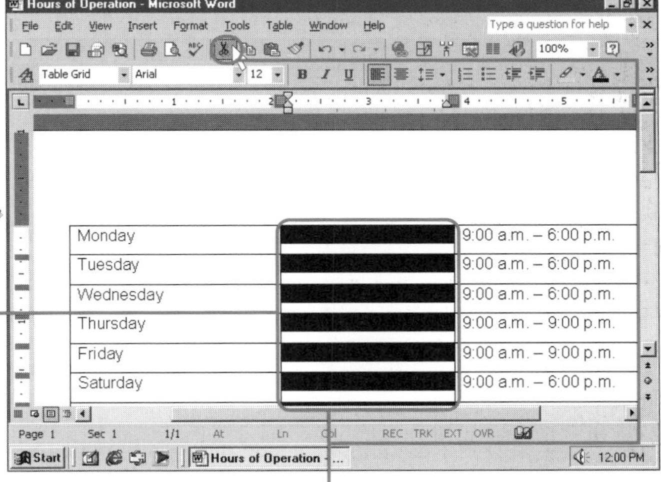

■ The new column appears in your table.

■ To deselect a column, click outside the selected area.

DELETE A COLUMN

1 Position the mouse I above the column you want to delete (I changes to ⬇). Then click to select the column.

2 Click [✂] to delete the column.

Note: If [✂] is not displayed, click [»] on the Standard toolbar to display all the buttons.

COMBINE CELLS

You can combine two or more cells in your table to create one large cell. Combining cells is useful when you want to display a title across the top or down the side of your table.

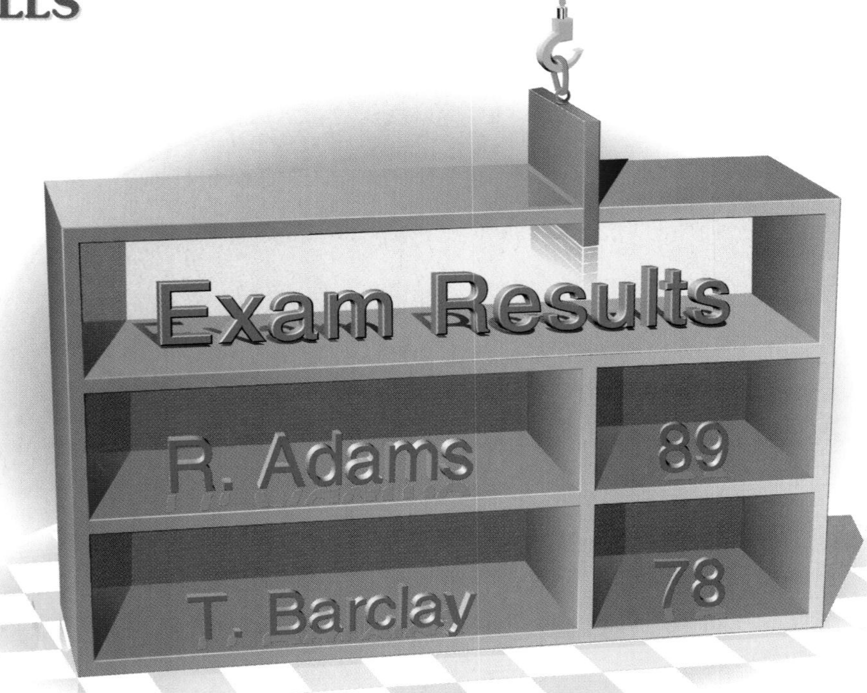

COMBINE CELLS

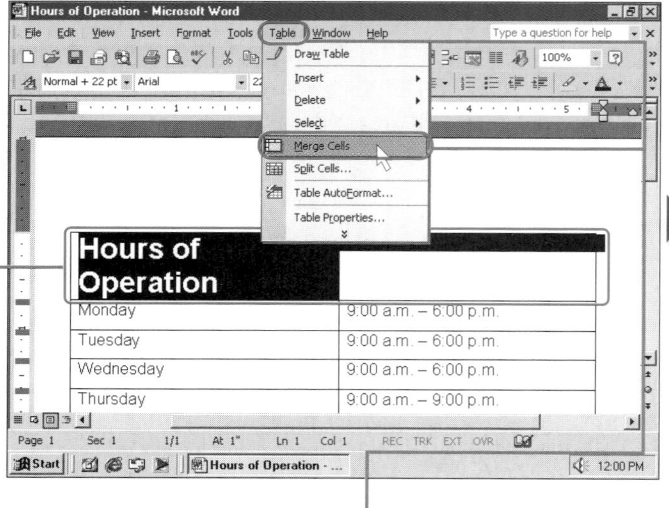

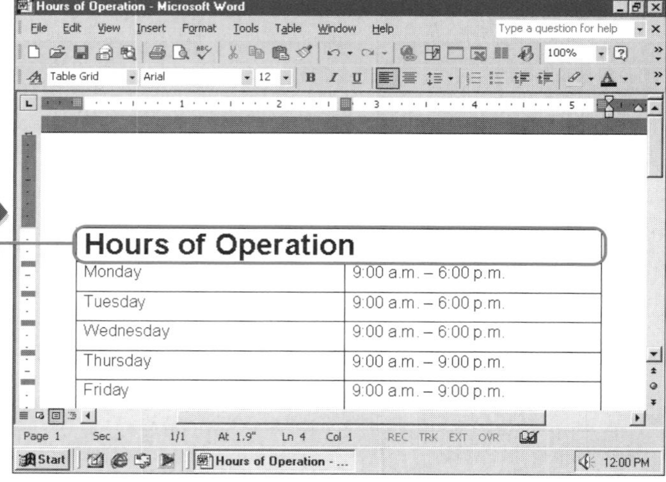

1 Position the mouse I over the first cell you want to combine with other cells.

2 Drag the mouse I until you highlight all the cells you want to combine.

3 Click **Table**.

4 Click **Merge Cells**.

Note: If Merge Cells does not appear on the menu, position the mouse over the bottom of the menu to display all the menu options.

■ The cells combine to create one large cell.

■ To deselect cells in a table, click outside the selected area.

SPLIT CELLS

You can split one cell in your table into two or more cells.

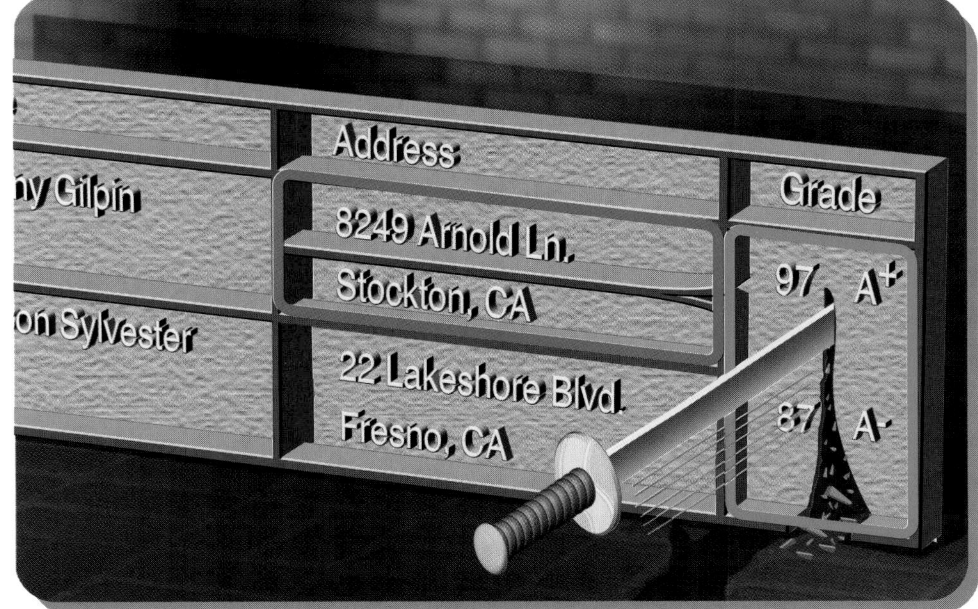

You can split cells into columns or rows.

Split Cell into Columns

Split Cell into Rows

SPLIT CELLS

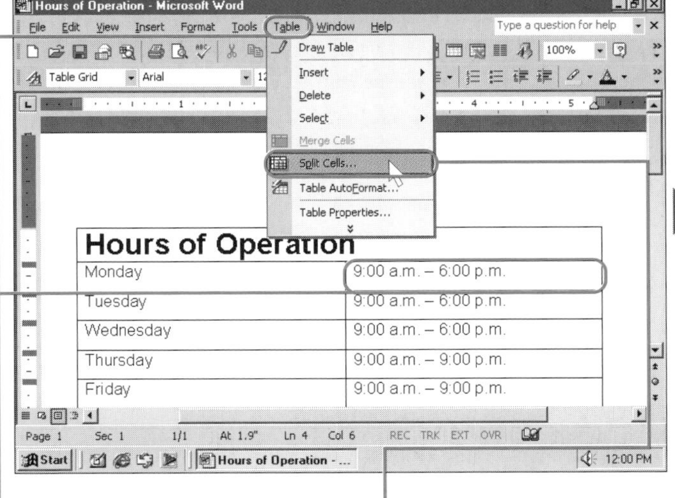

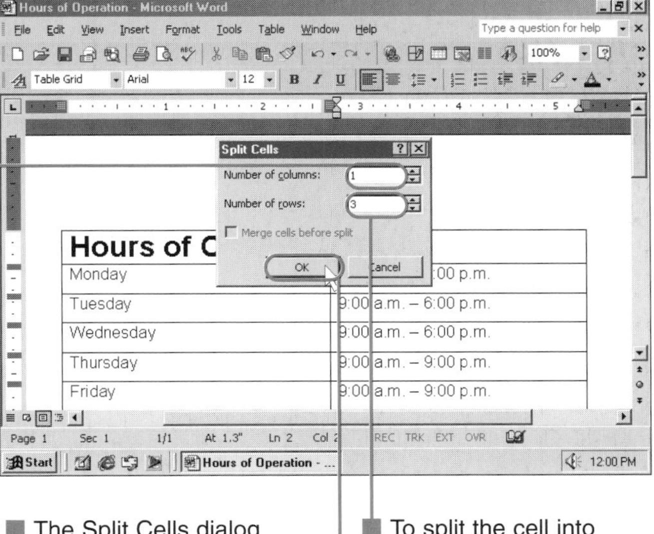

1 Click in the cell you want to split into two or more cells.

2 Click **Table**.

3 Click **Split Cells**.

Note: If Split Cells does not appear on the menu, position the mouse over the bottom of the menu to display all the menu options.

■ The Split Cells dialog box appears.

4 To split the cell into columns, double-click this area and type the number of columns you want to split the cell into.

■ To split the cell into rows, double-click this area and type the number of rows you want to split the cell into.

5 Click **OK** to split the cell.

FORMAT A TABLE

Word offers many ready-to-use designs that you can choose from to give your table a professional appearance.

FORMAT A TABLE

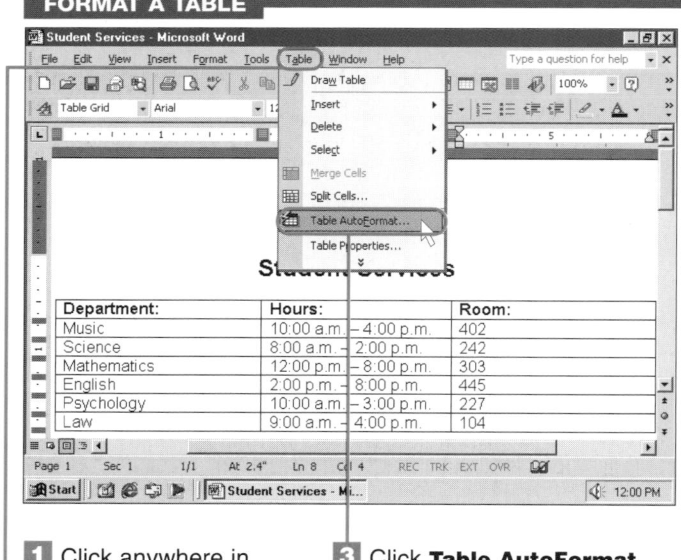

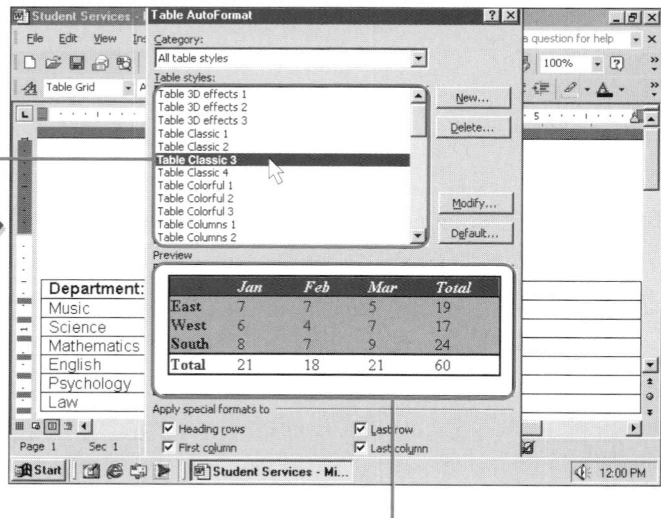

1 Click anywhere in the table you want to format.

2 Click **Table**.

3 Click **Table AutoFormat**.

■ The Table AutoFormat dialog box appears.

■ This area displays a list of the available table designs.

4 Click the table design you want to use.

■ This area displays a sample of the table design you selected.

Note: You can repeat step 4 to view a sample of a different table design.

What parts of a table can I apply special formats to?

The Table AutoFormat dialog box offers options you can use to apply special formats to the heading row, the first column, the last row and the last column in a table. For some table designs, applying special formats to some parts of a table will not change the appearance of the table.

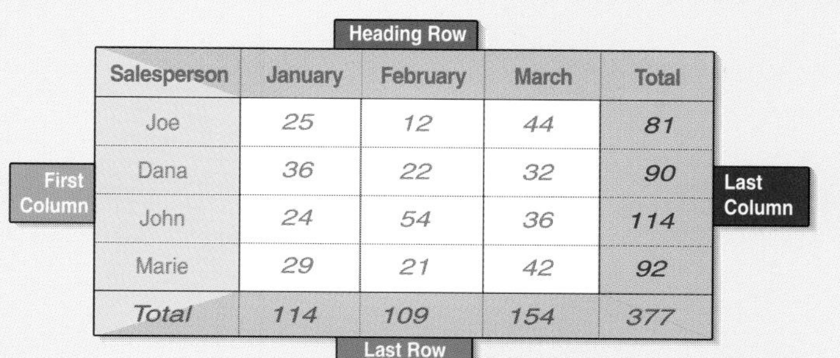

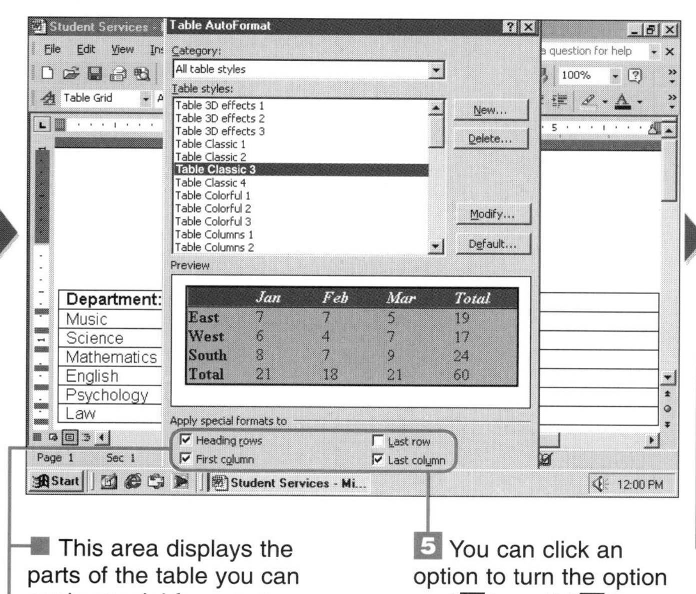

- This area displays the parts of the table you can apply special formats to.
- A check mark (✓) beside an option indicates that Word will apply special formats to that part of the table.

5 You can click an option to turn the option on (✓) or off (☐).

6 Click **Apply** or press the Enter key to apply the design to your table.

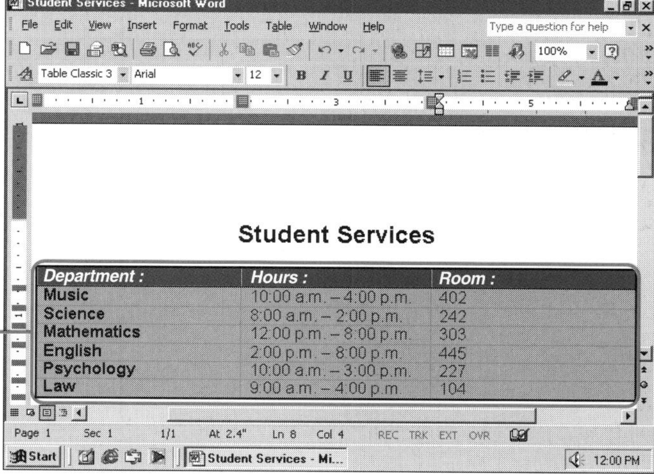

- The table displays the design you selected.

- To remove a table design, repeat steps 1 to 4, selecting **Table Grid** in step 4. Then perform step 6.

Team B
Player Goals Assists Points
B. Laird 5 1 6
A. Tan 2 5 7
P. Phillips 3 2 5
R. Westman 7 1 8
L. Porter 1 4 5
H. Roberts 0 3 3
S. Desert 6 2 8
M. Lee 4 4 8
C. Collins 2 5 7
K. Davids 9 0 9
Team C
Player Goals Assists Points
S. Toner 6 1 7
J. Cane 5 2 7
R. Kinnear
T. Lappen
A. Coster
D. Saire
B. Miller
E. Pelham
G. Cross
Workbook
REVENUE
Payroll
TOTAL EXPENS
Jan

Using Excel

INTRODUCTION TO EXCEL

Excel is a spreadsheet program you can use to organize, analyze and attractively present data, such as a budget or sales report.

Editing and Formatting

Excel allows you to efficiently enter, edit and format data in a worksheet. You can quickly enter a series of numbers, insert new rows or change the width of columns. You can also emphasize data by changing the font, color and style of data.

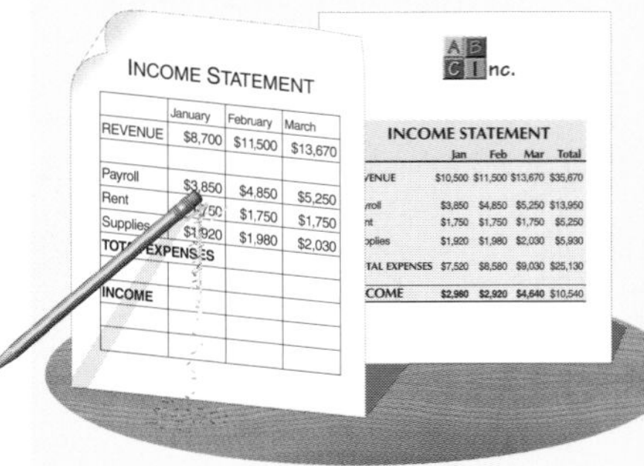

Using Formulas and Functions

Formulas and functions allow you to perform calculations and analyze data in a worksheet. Common calculations include finding the sum, average or total number of values in a list.

Creating Charts

Excel helps you create colorful charts from worksheet data to visually display the data. If you change the data in your worksheet, Excel will automatically update the chart to display the changes. You can move and resize a chart to suit your needs.

THE EXCEL WINDOW

The Excel window displays many items you can use to work with your data.

Title Bar

Shows the name of the displayed workbook.

Menu Bar

Provides access to lists of commands available in Excel and displays an area where you can type a question to get help information.

Standard Toolbar

Contains buttons you can use to select common commands, such as Save and Print.

Formatting Toolbar

Contains buttons you can use to select common formatting commands, such as Bold and Underline.

Formula Bar

Displays the cell reference and the contents of the active cell. A cell reference identifies the location of each cell in a worksheet and consists of a column letter followed by a row number, such as **A1**.

Active Cell

Displays a thick border. You enter data into the active cell.

Cell

The area where a row and column intersect.

Column

A vertical line of cells. A letter identifies each column.

Row

A horizontal line of cells. A number identifies each row.

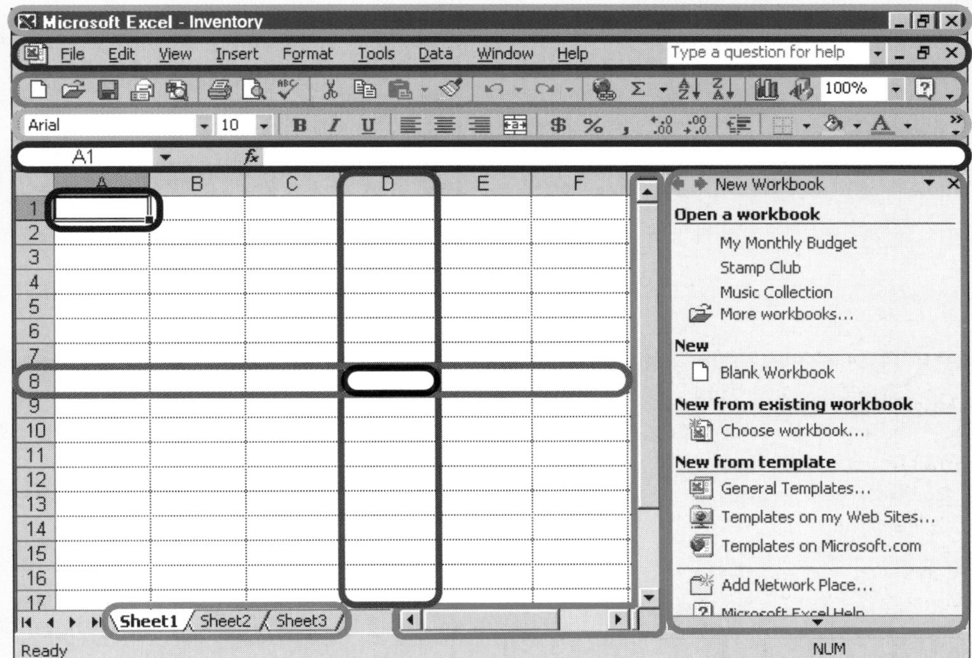

Worksheet Tabs

An Excel file is called a workbook. Each workbook is divided into several worksheets. Excel displays a tab for each worksheet.

Scroll Bars

Allow you to browse through a worksheet.

Task Pane

Contains links you can select to perform common tasks, such as opening or creating a workbook.

CHANGE THE ACTIVE CELL

You can make any cell in your worksheet the active cell. You enter data into the active cell.

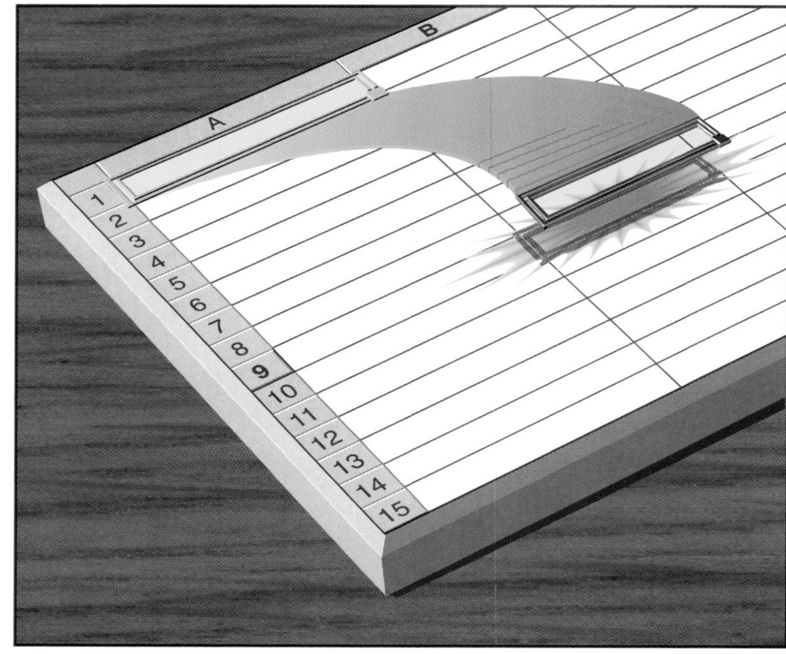

You can only make one cell in your worksheet active at a time.

CHANGE THE ACTIVE CELL

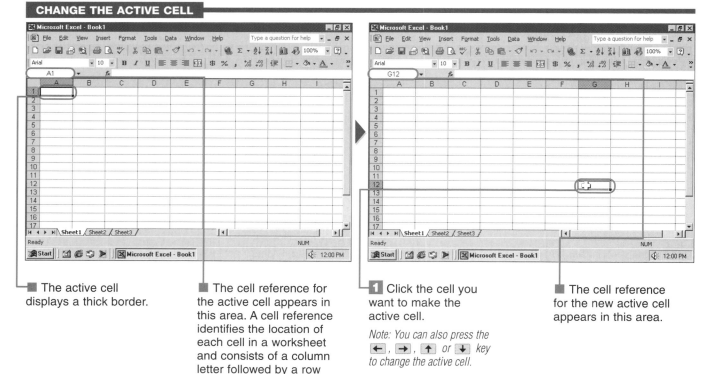

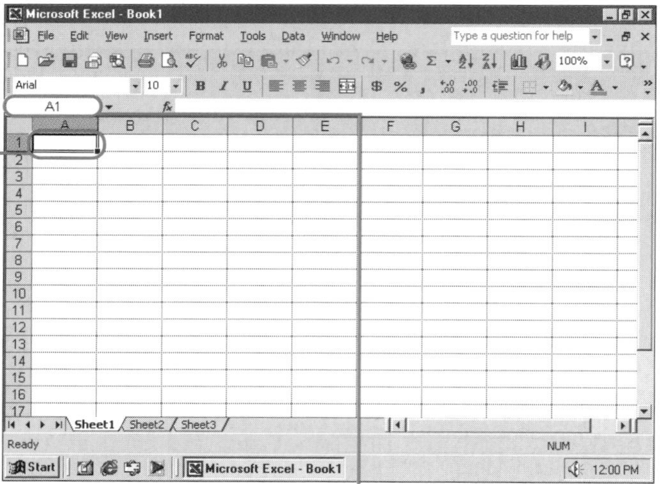

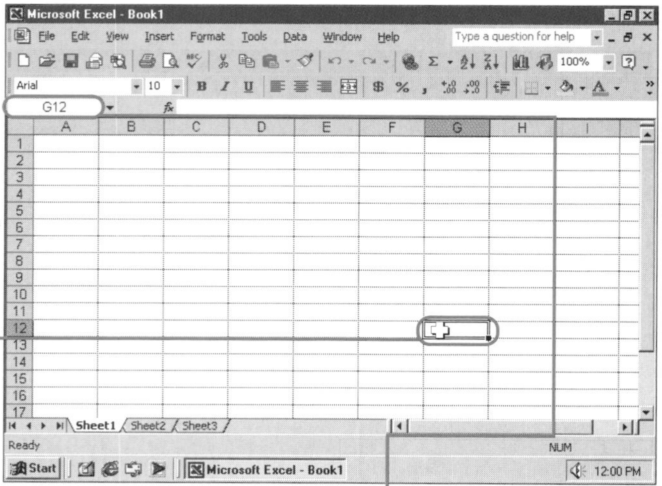

■ The active cell displays a thick border.

■ The cell reference for the active cell appears in this area. A cell reference identifies the location of each cell in a worksheet and consists of a column letter followed by a row number (example: **A1**).

1 Click the cell you want to make the active cell.

Note: You can also press the ←, →, ↑ or ↓ key to change the active cell.

■ The cell reference for the new active cell appears in this area.

SCROLL THROUGH A WORKSHEET

You can scroll through your worksheet to view other areas of the worksheet. This is useful when your worksheet contains a lot of data and your computer screen cannot display all the data at once.

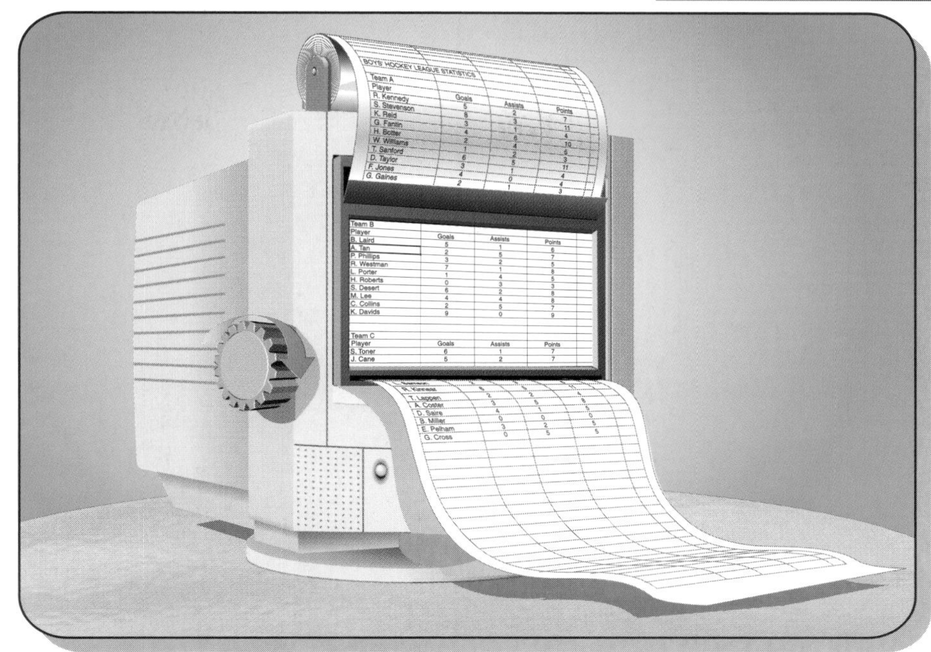

SCROLL THROUGH A WORKSHEET

Microsoft Excel - Soccer Standings

	A	B	C	D	E	F	G
3	Pool A	Games Played	Goals Scored	Wins	Losses	Ties	Points
4	Brian's Boys	6	15	4	1	1	
5	The Good Guys	6	13	3	1	2	
6	Greg'n' Gang	6	12	4	2	0	
7	The Professionals	6	12	3	3	0	
8	All The Way	6	8	1	3	2	
9	Team Spirit	6	4	1	5	0	
10							
11	Pool B	Games Played	Goals Scored	Wins	Losses	Ties	Points
12	We Score	6	16	4	2	0	
13	The Firefighters	6	14	3	2	1	
14	Challengers	6	12	3	3	0	
15	Headers	6	9	2	2	2	
16	The Hurricanes	6	7	1	5	0	

SCROLL UP OR DOWN

1 To scroll up or down one row, click ▲ or ▼.

■ To quickly scroll to any row in your worksheet, drag the scroll box along the scroll bar until the row you want to view appears.

Microsoft Excel - Soccer Standings

	A	B	C	D	E	F	G
3	Pool A	Games Played	Goals Scored	Wins	Losses	Ties	Points
4	Brian's Boys	6	15	4	1	1	
5	The Good Guys	6	13	3	1	2	
6	Greg'n' Gang	6	12	4	2	0	
7	The Professionals	6	12	3	3	0	
8	All The Way	6	8	1	3	2	
9	Team Spirit	6	4	1	5	0	
10							
11	Pool B	Games Played	Goals Scored	Wins	Losses	Ties	Points
12	We Score	6	16	4	2	0	
13	The Firefighters	6	14	3	2	1	
14	Challengers	6	12	3	3	0	
15	Headers	6	9	2	2	2	
16	The Hurricanes	6	7	1	5	0	

SCROLL LEFT OR RIGHT

1 To scroll left or right one column, click ◄ or ►.

■ To quickly scroll to any column in your worksheet, drag the scroll box along the scroll bar until the column you want to view appears.

ENTER DATA

You can enter data into your worksheet quickly and easily.

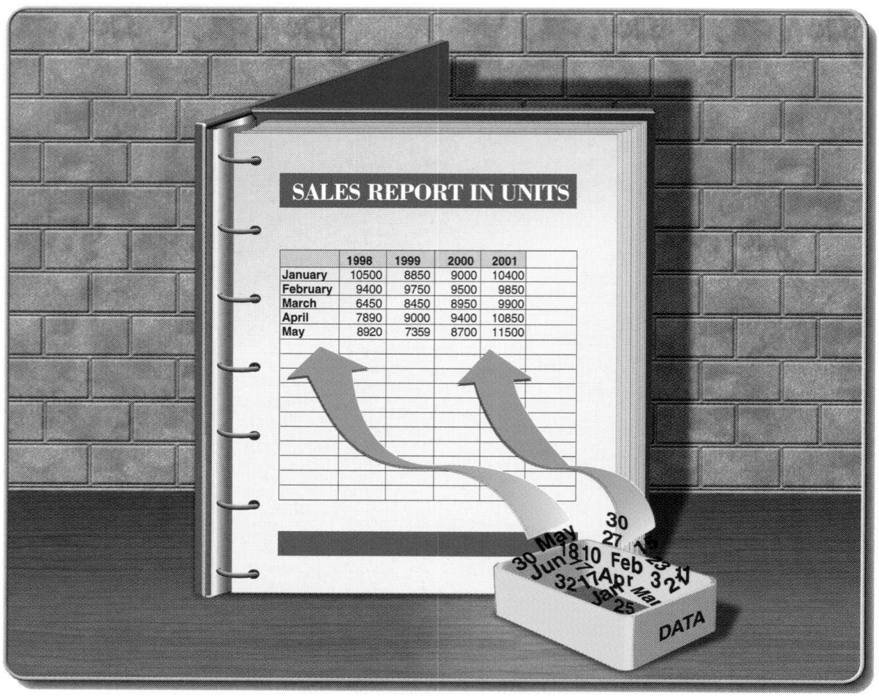

SALES REPORT IN UNITS
	1998	1999	2000	2001
January	10500	8850	9000	10400
February	9400	9750	9500	9850
March	6450	8450	8950	9900
April	7890	9000	9400	10850
May	8920	7359	8700	11500
DATA

ENTER DATA

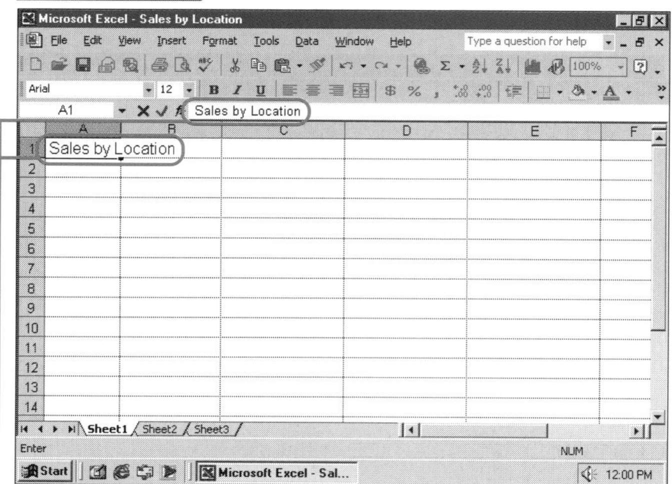

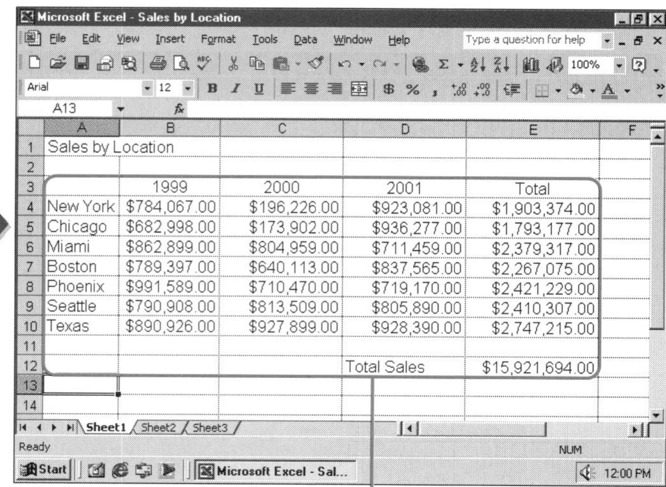

1 Click the cell where you want to enter data. Then type the data.

■ The data you type appears in the active cell and in the formula bar.

■ If you make a typing mistake while entering data, press the **Backspace** key to remove the incorrect data. Then type the correct data.

2 Press the **Enter** key to enter the data and move down one cell.

Note: To enter the data and move one cell in any direction, press the ←, →, ↓ or ↑ key.

3 Repeat steps **1** and **2** until you finish entering all your data.

Note: In this book, the size of data was changed to 12 points to make the data easier to read. To change the size of data, see page 151.

How can I quickly enter numbers?

You can use the number keys on the right side of your keyboard to quickly enter numbers into your worksheet. To be able to use these number keys, **NUM** must be displayed at the bottom of your screen. You can press the Num Lock key to display **NUM** on your screen.

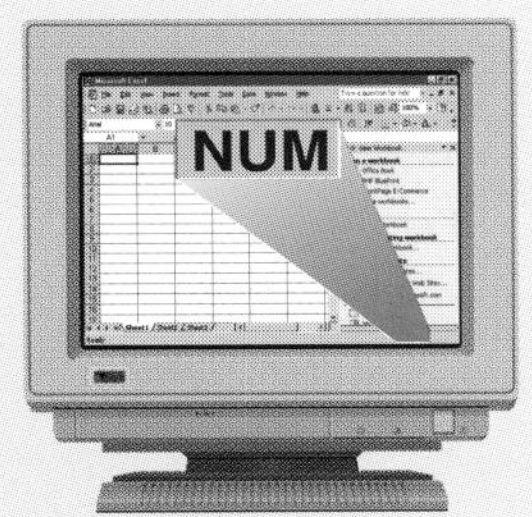

Why did Excel change the appearance of a date I entered?

When you enter a date into your worksheet, Excel may change the format of the date to one of the following date formats: 3/14/2001, 14-Mar or 14-Mar-01. To change the format of dates, see page 152.

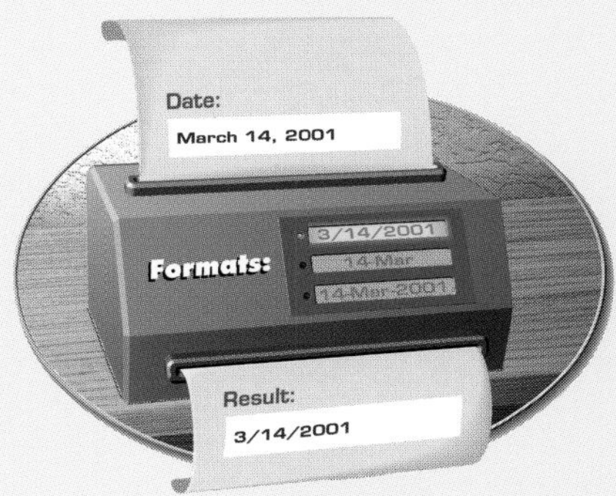

Microsoft Excel - Sales by Location

A11 New York

	A	B	C	D	E
1	Sales by Location				
2					
3		1999	2000	2001	Total
4	New York	$784,067.00	$196,226.00	$923,081.00	$1,903,374.00
5	Chicago	$682,998.00	$173,902.00	$936,277.00	$1,793,177.00
6	Miami	$862,899.00	$804,959.00	$711,459.00	$2,379,317.00
7	Boston	$789,397.00	$640,113.00	$837,565.00	$2,267,075.00
8	Phoenix	$991,589.00	$710,470.00	$719,170.00	$2,421,229.00
9	Seattle	$790,908.00	$813,509.00	$805,890.00	$2,410,307.00
10	Texas	$890,926.00	$927,899.00	$928,390.00	$2,747,215.00
11	New York				
12				Total Sales	$15,921,694.00
13					
14					

AUTOCOMPLETE

■ If the first few letters you type match the text in another cell in the same column, Excel will complete the text for you.

1 To enter the text Excel provides, press the Enter key.

■ To enter different text, continue typing.

4	TOTAL EXPENSES	
5		
6		

4	TOTAL EX	227
5		
6		

LONG WORDS

If text is too long to fit in a cell, the text will spill into the neighboring cell.

If the neighboring cell contains data, Excel will display as much of the text as the column width will allow. To change the column width to display all the text, see page 148.

4	1.22E+10	
5		
6		

4	#####	
5		
6		

LARGE NUMBERS

If a number is too large to fit in a cell, Excel will display the number in scientific notation or as number signs (#). To change the column width to display the number, see page 148.

SELECT CELLS

Before performing many tasks in Excel, you must select the cells you want to work with. Selected cells appear highlighted on your screen.

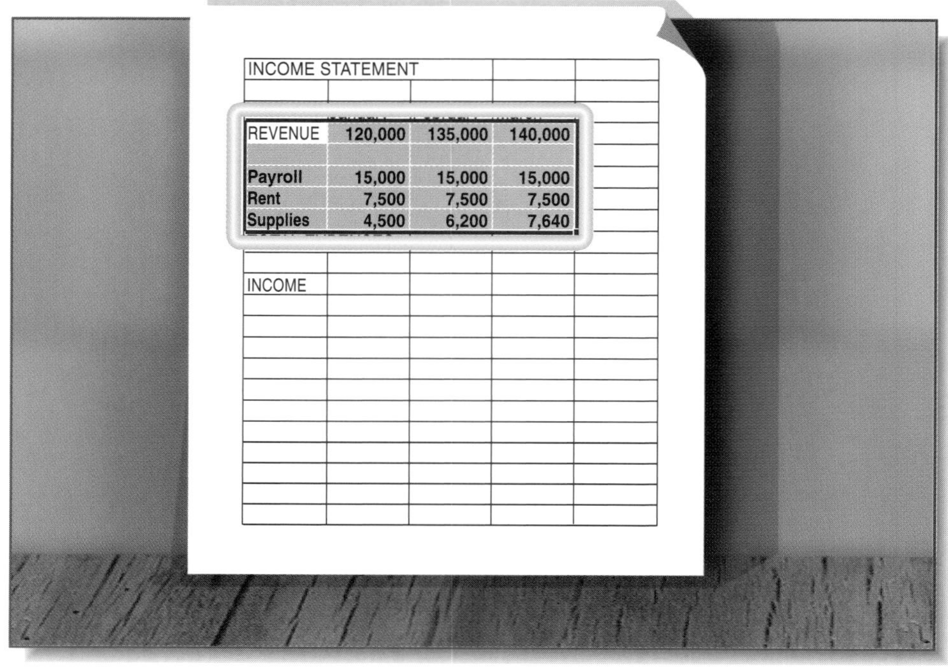

SELECT CELLS

SELECT A CELL

1 Click the cell you want to select.

■ The cell becomes the active cell and displays a thick border.

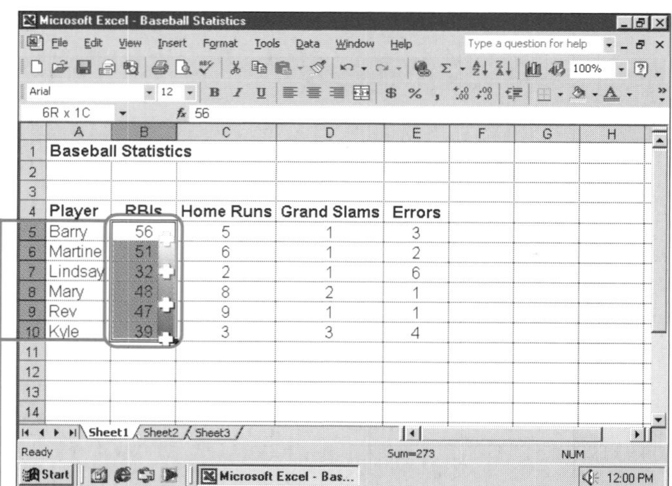

SELECT A GROUP OF CELLS

1 Position the mouse ✥ over the first cell you want to select.

2 Drag the mouse ✥ until you highlight all the cells you want to select.

■ To select multiple groups of cells, press and hold down the **Ctrl** key as you repeat steps 1 and 2 for each group of cells you want to select.

■ To deselect cells, click any cell.

How do I select all the cells in my worksheet?

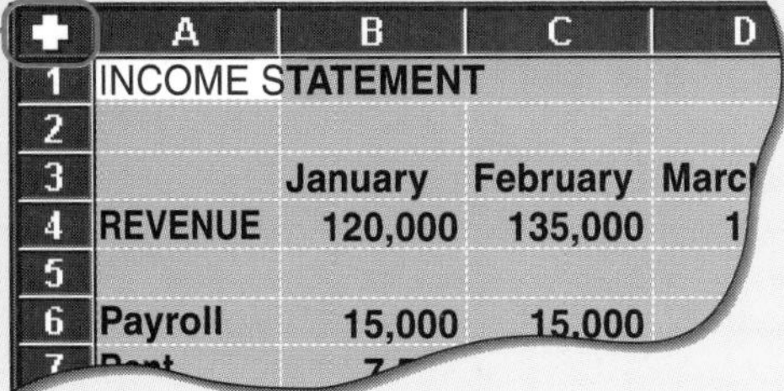

■ To select all the cells in your worksheet, click the box (▭) at the top left corner of your worksheet where the row numbers and column letters meet.

How do I select data in a cell?

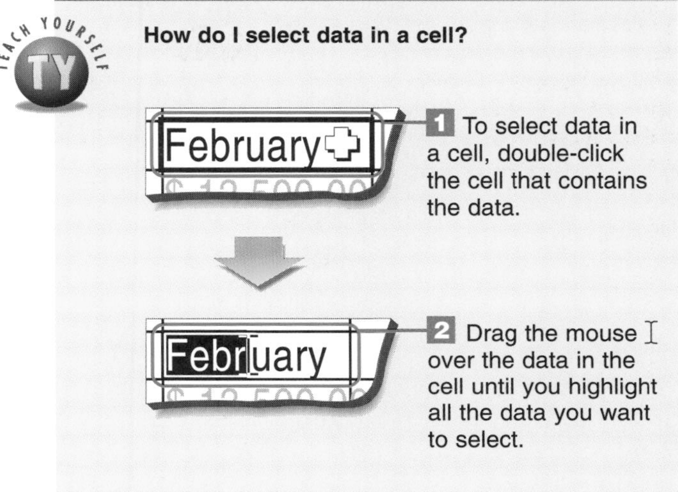

1 To select data in a cell, double-click the cell that contains the data.

2 Drag the mouse I over the data in the cell until you highlight all the data you want to select.

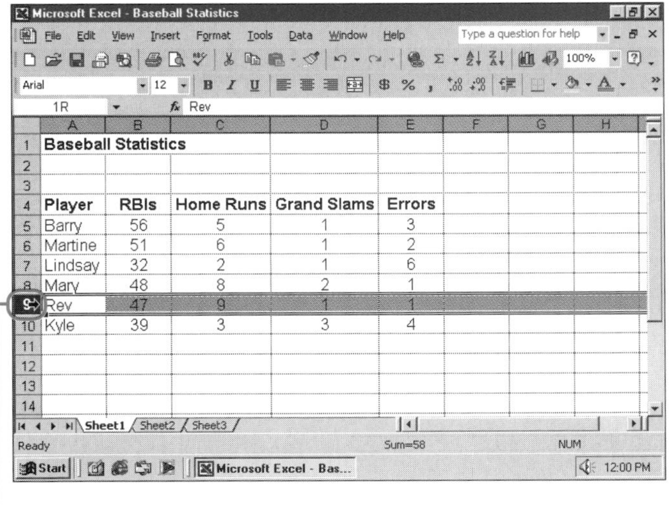

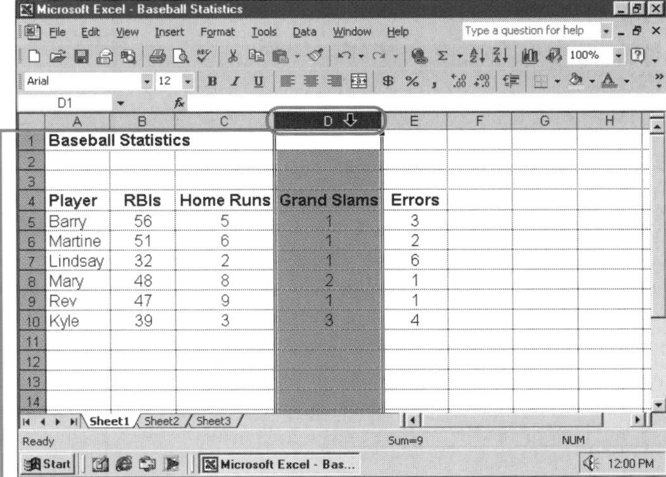

SELECT A ROW

1 Click the number of the row you want to select.

■ To select multiple rows, position the mouse ➡ over the number of the first row you want to select. Then drag the mouse ➡ until you highlight all the rows you want to select.

SELECT A COLUMN

1 Click the letter of the column you want to select.

■ To select multiple columns, position the mouse ⬇ over the letter of the first column you want to select. Then drag the mouse ⬇ until you highlight all the columns you want to select.

COMPLETE A SERIES

Excel can save you time by completing a text or number series for you.

You can complete a series across a row or down a column in a worksheet. Excel completes a text series based on the text you enter in one cell. Excel completes a number series based on the numbers you enter in two cells.

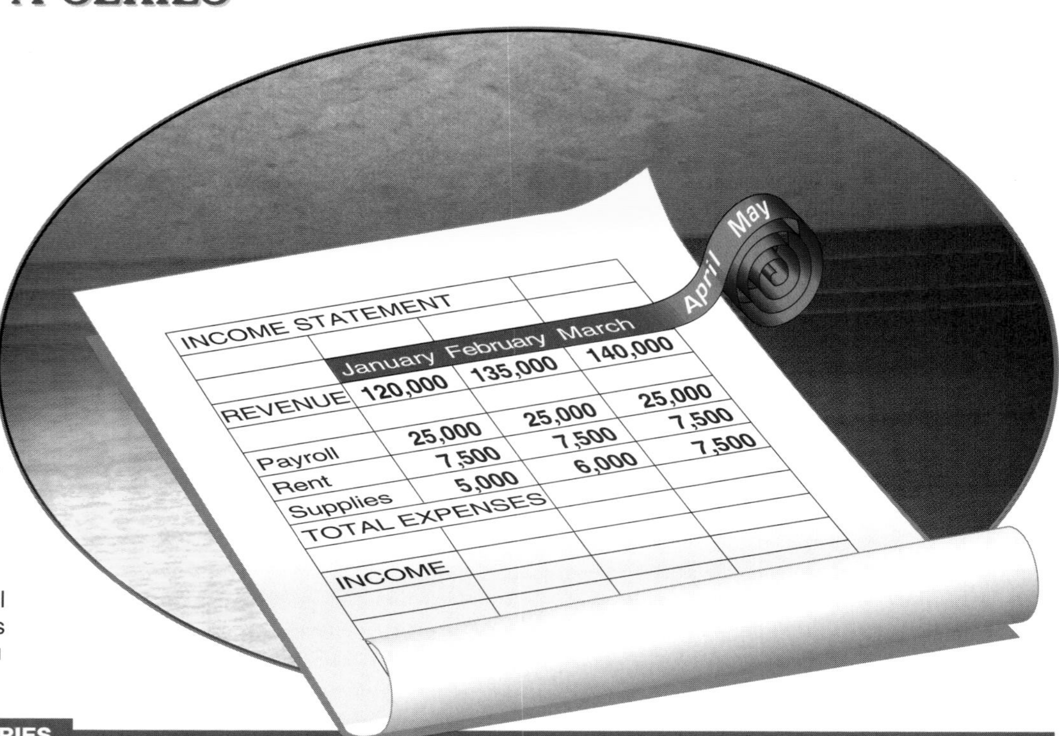

COMPLETE A TEXT SERIES

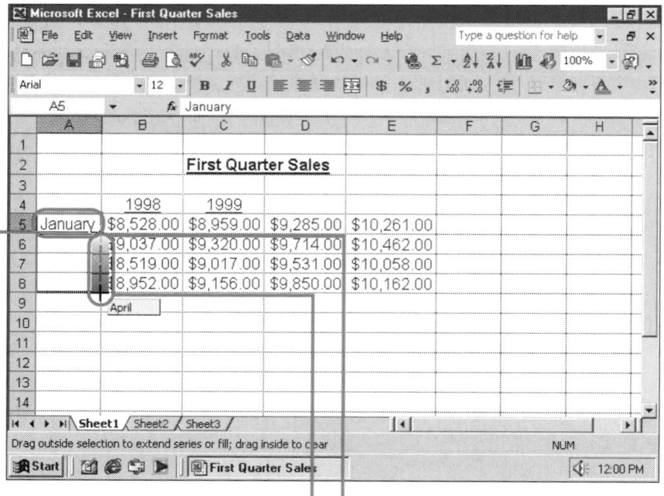

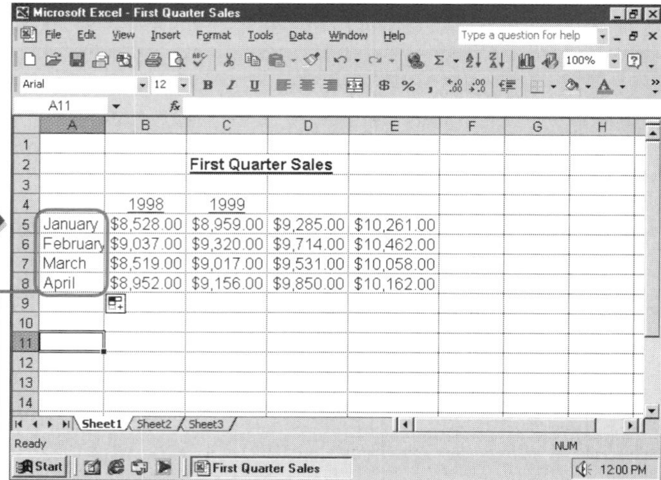

1 Enter the text you want to start the series.

2 Click the cell containing the text you entered.

3 Position the mouse ✥ over the bottom right corner of the cell (✥ changes to +).

4 Drag the mouse + over the cells you want to include in the series.

■ The cells display the text series.

Note: If Excel cannot determine the text series you want to complete, it will copy the text in the first cell to all the cells you select.

■ To deselect cells, click any cell.

Why does the Auto Fill Options button (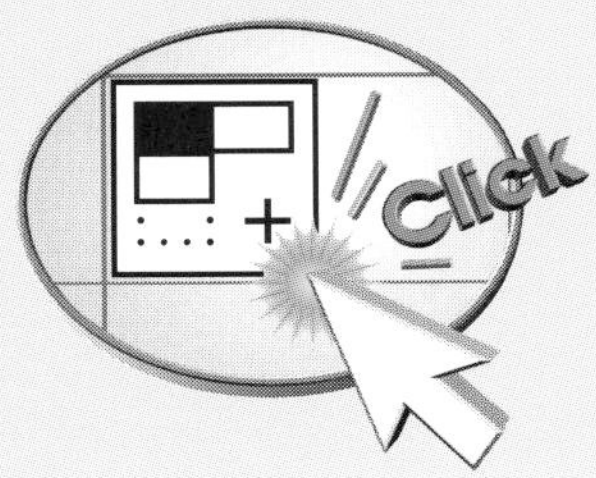) appear when I complete a series?

You can use the Auto Fill Options button to change the way Excel completes a series. Click the Auto Fill Options button to display a list of options and then select the option you want to use. The Auto Fill Options button is available only until you perform another task.

Can I complete a series that will repeat data in several cells?

Yes. Perform steps 1 to 4 below, except enter the same text or data into the first two cells in step 1. Excel will repeat the information in all the cells you select.

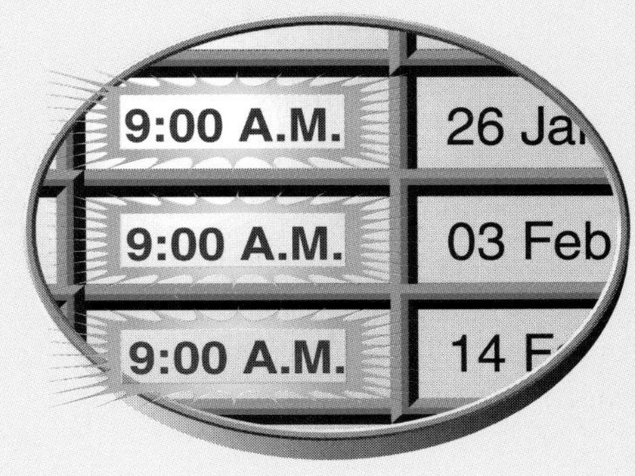

COMPLETE A NUMBER SERIES

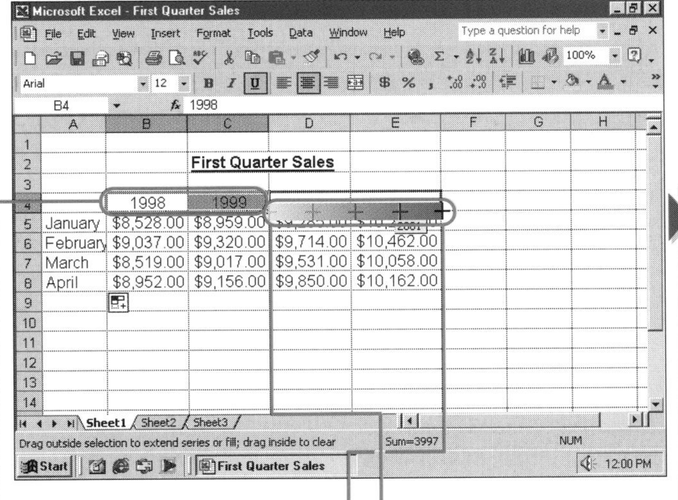

1 Enter the first two numbers you want to start the series.

2 Select the cells containing the numbers you entered. To select cells, see page 106.

3 Position the mouse over the bottom right corner of the selected cells (changes to +).

4 Drag the mouse + over the cells you want to include in the series.

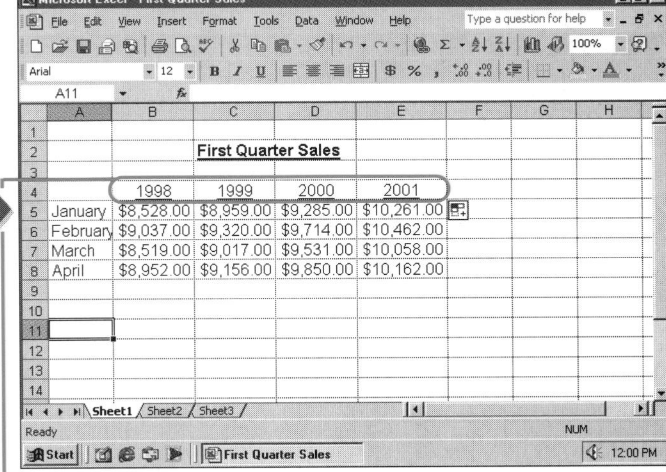

■ The cells display the number series.

■ To deselect cells, click any cell.

SWITCH BETWEEN WORKSHEETS

A workbook contains several worksheets. You can easily switch from one worksheet to another.

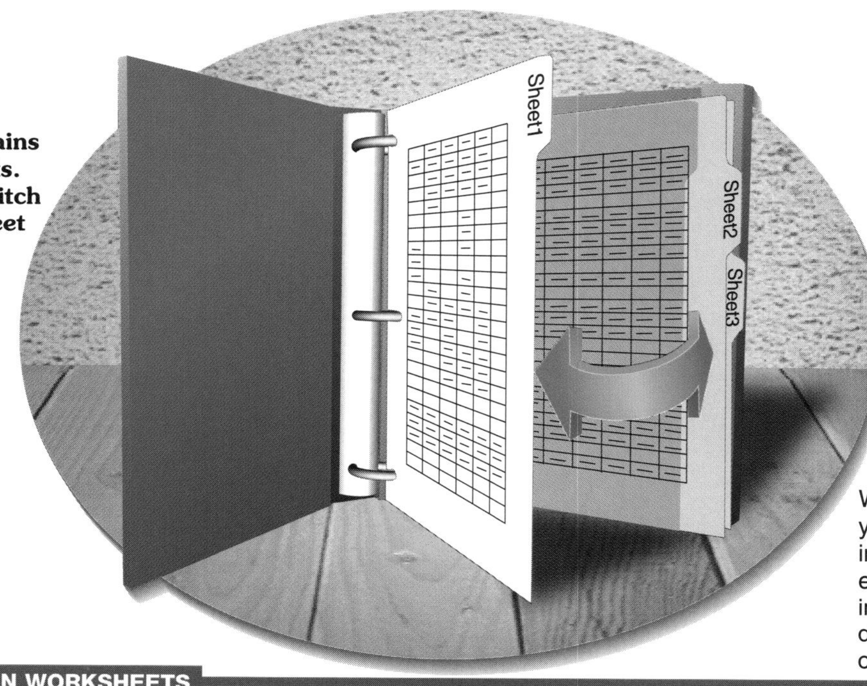

Worksheets can help you organize information in your workbook. For example, you can store information for each division of a company on a separate worksheet.

SWITCH BETWEEN WORKSHEETS

	A	B	C	D	E	F
1	My Monthly Budget					
2						
3	**Expenses**	**Costs**		**Monthly Income:**	$2,975.00	
4	Rent	$1,050.00		**Monthly Costs:**	$2,265.00	
5	Utilities	$45.00				
6	Cable	$40.00		**Total Savings:**	$710.00	
7	Car lease payment	$340.00				
8	Gas	$80.00				
9	Loan payment	$215.00				
10	Phone bill	$55.00				
11	IRA contribution	$150.00				
12	Groceries	$250.00				
13	Entertainment	$40.00				
14						

■ This area displays a tab for each worksheet in your workbook. The displayed worksheet has a white tab.

1 Click the tab for the worksheet you want to display.

■ The worksheet you selected appears. The contents of the other worksheets in your workbook are hidden behind the displayed worksheet.

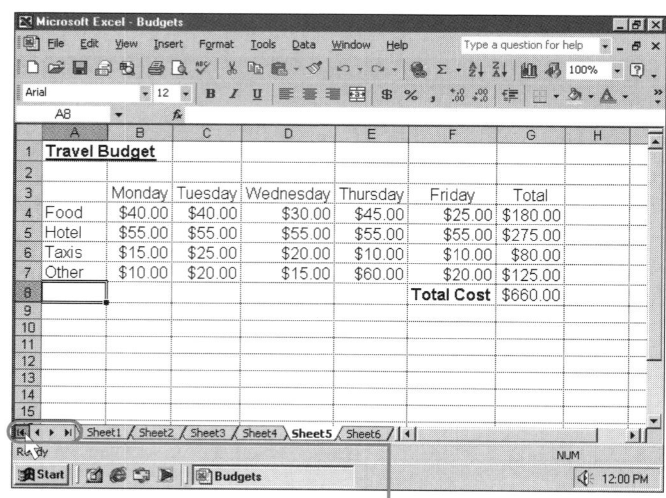

	A	B	C	D	E	F	G	H
1	Travel Budget							
2								
3		Monday	Tuesday	Wednesday	Thursday	Friday	Total	
4	Food	$40.00	$40.00	$30.00	$45.00	$25.00	$180.00	
5	Hotel	$55.00	$55.00	$55.00	$55.00	$55.00	$275.00	
6	Taxis	$15.00	$25.00	$20.00	$10.00	$10.00	$80.00	
7	Other	$10.00	$20.00	$15.00	$60.00	$20.00	$125.00	
8						**Total Cost**	$660.00	

BROWSE THROUGH WORKSHEET TABS

■ If you have many worksheets in your workbook, you may not be able to see all the worksheet tabs.

Note: To insert additional worksheets, see page 112.

1 Click one of the following buttons to browse through the worksheet tabs.

- Display first tab
- Display previous tab
- Display next tab
- Display last tab

RENAME A WORKSHEET

You can rename a worksheet in your workbook to better describe the contents of the worksheet.

RENAME A WORKSHEET

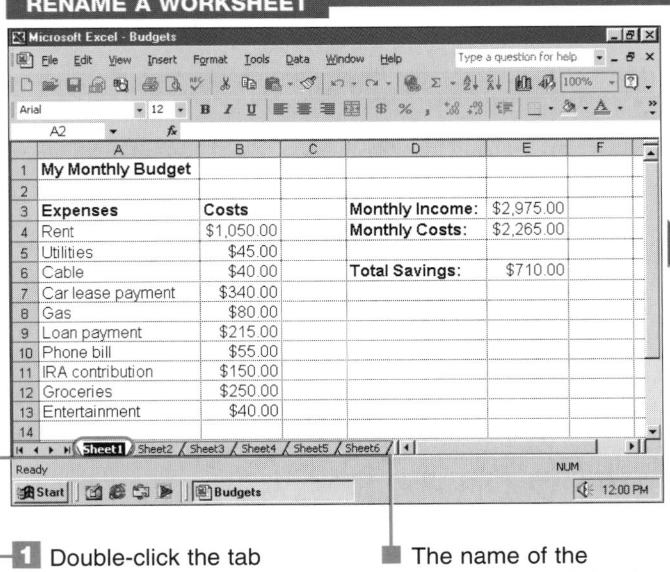

1 Double-click the tab for the worksheet you want to rename.

■ The name of the worksheet is highlighted.

2 Type a new name for the worksheet and then press the Enter key.

Note: A worksheet name can contain up to 31 characters, including spaces.

INSERT A WORKSHEET

You can insert a new worksheet to include additional information in your workbook.

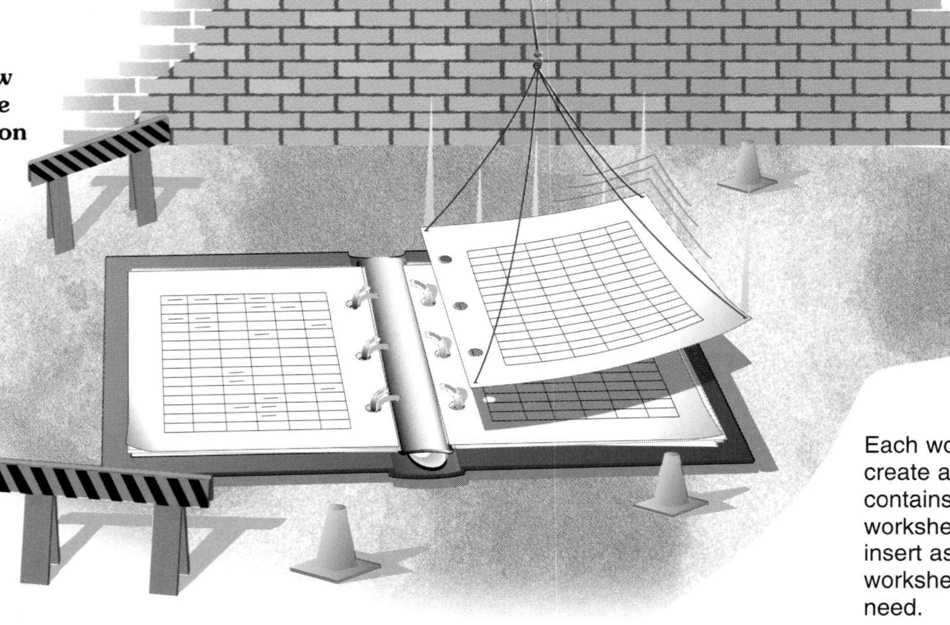

Each workbook you create automatically contains three worksheets. You can insert as many new worksheets as you need.

INSERT A WORKSHEET

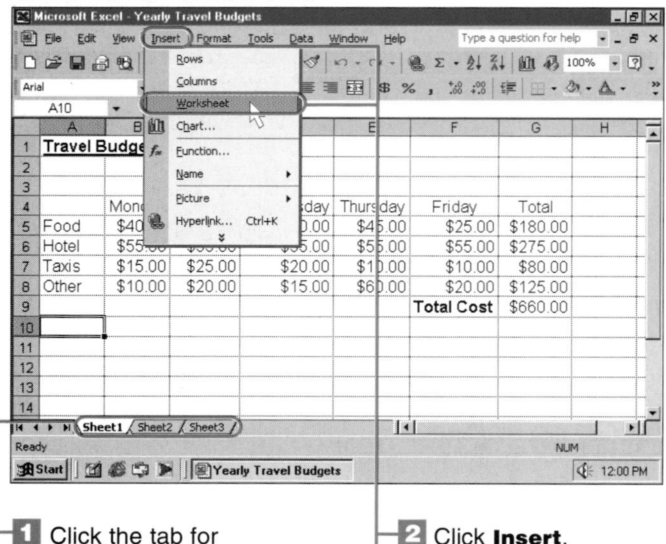

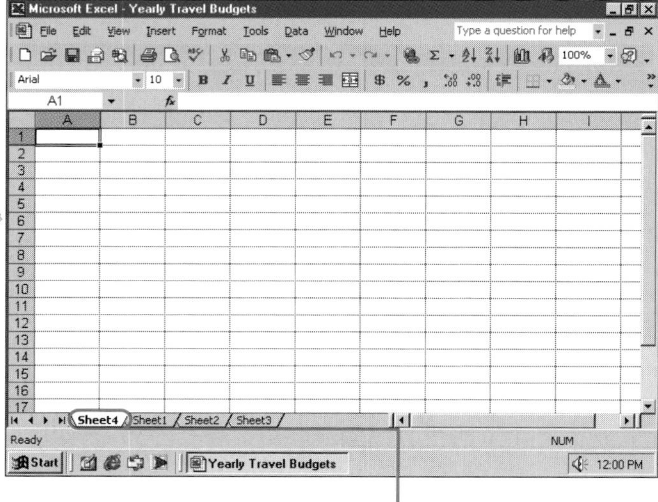

1 Click the tab for the worksheet you want to appear after the new worksheet.

2 Click **Insert**.

3 Click **Worksheet**.

■ The new worksheet appears.

■ Excel displays a tab for the new worksheet.

DELETE A WORKSHEET

You can permanently remove a worksheet you no longer need from your workbook.

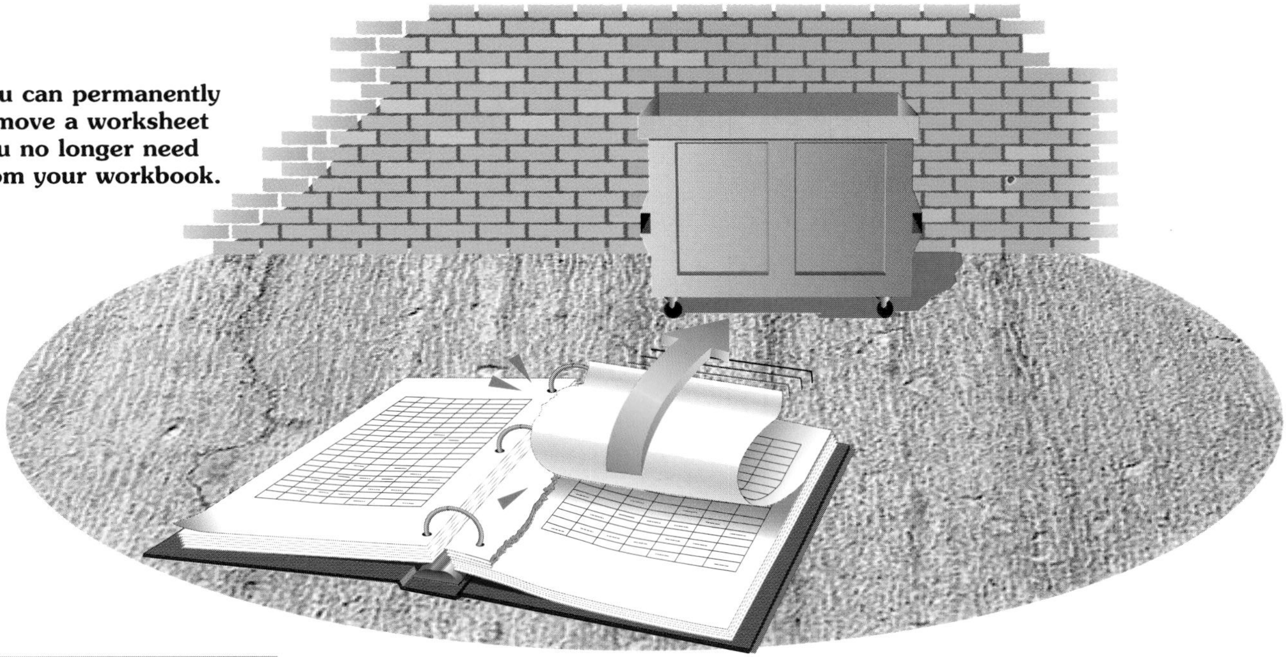

DELETE A WORKSHEET

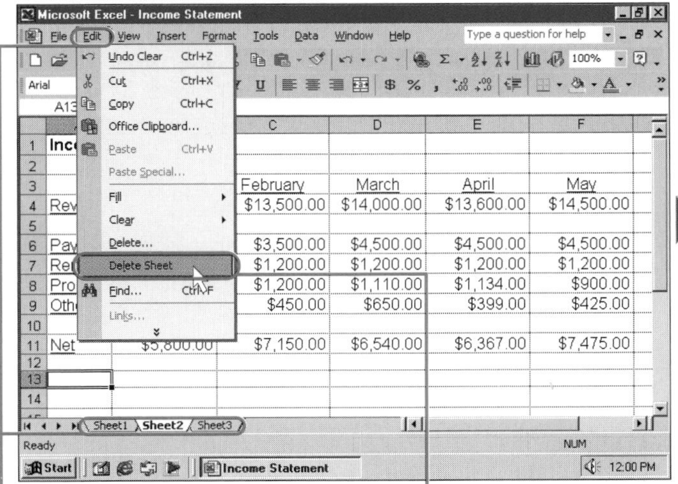

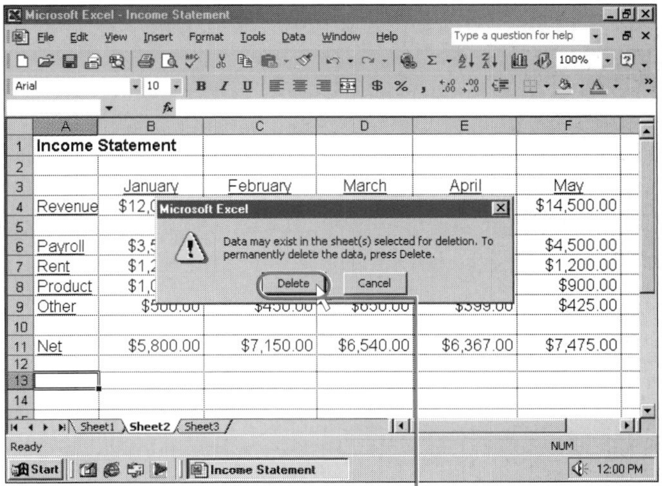

Microsoft Excel

Data may exist in the sheet(s) selected for deletion. To permanently delete the data, press Delete.

Delete Cancel

1 Click the tab for the worksheet you want to delete.

2 Click **Edit**.

3 Click **Delete Sheet**.

Note: If Delete Sheet does not appear on the menu, position the mouse over the bottom of the menu to display all the menu options.

■ A warning dialog box may appear, stating that Excel will permanently delete the data in the worksheet.

4 Click **Delete** to permanently delete the worksheet.

MOVE A WORKSHEET

You can move a worksheet to a new location in your workbook. This allows you to re-organize the data in your workbook.

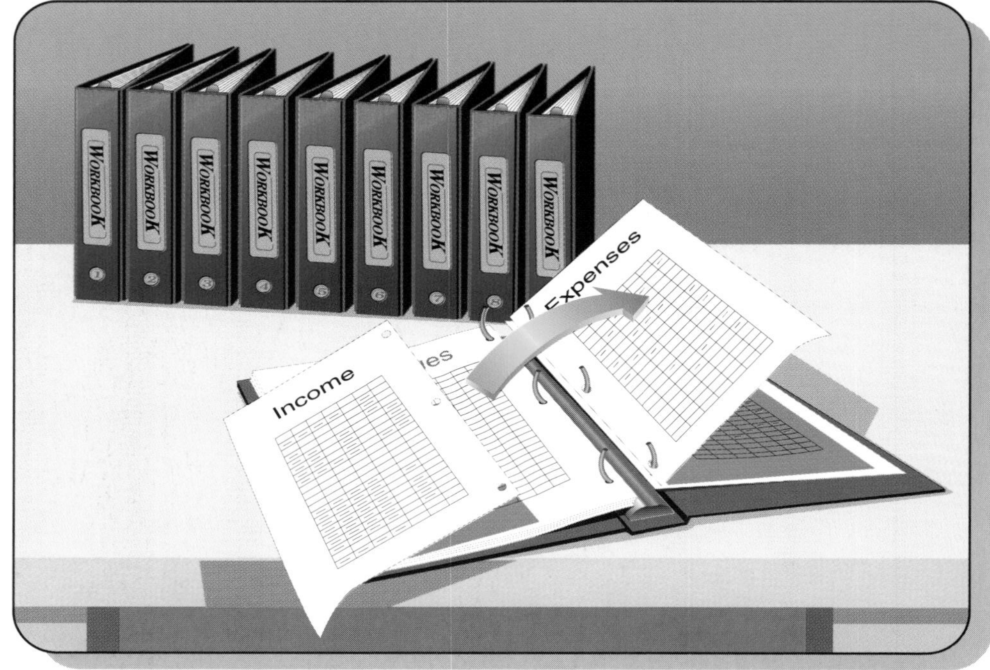

MOVE A WORKSHEET

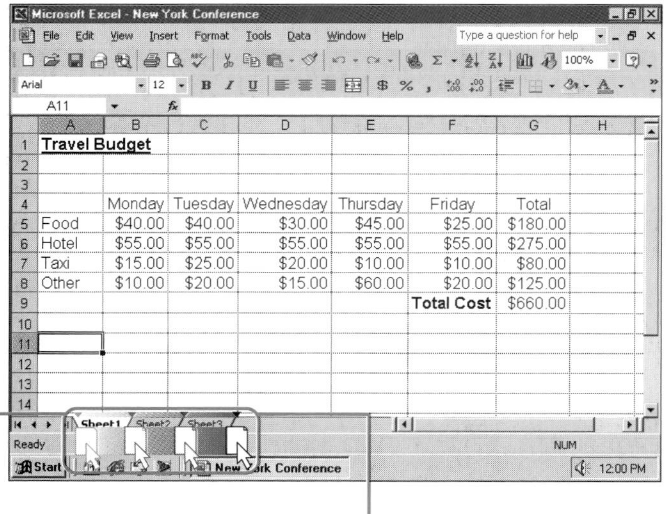

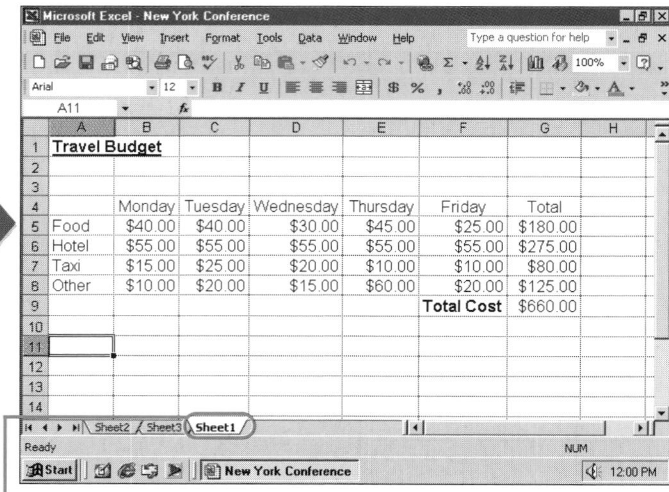

1 Position the mouse over the tab for the worksheet you want to move.

2 Drag the worksheet to a new location.

■ An arrow (▼) shows where the worksheet will appear.

■ The worksheet appears in the new location.

COLOR A WORKSHEET TAB

You can add color to the tab for a worksheet. Adding color to a worksheet tab is useful for marking a worksheet you want to stand out in your workbook.

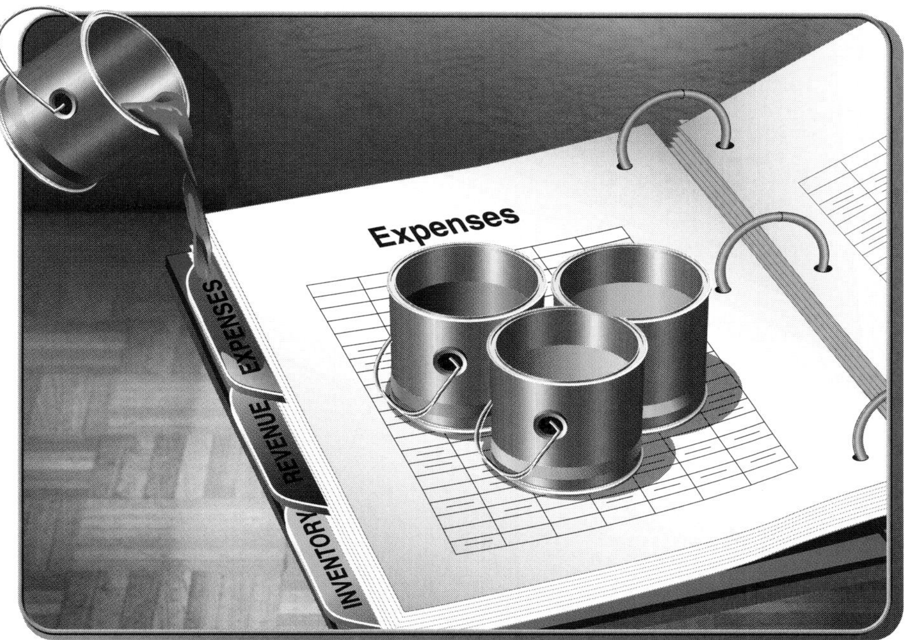

COLOR A WORKSHEET TAB

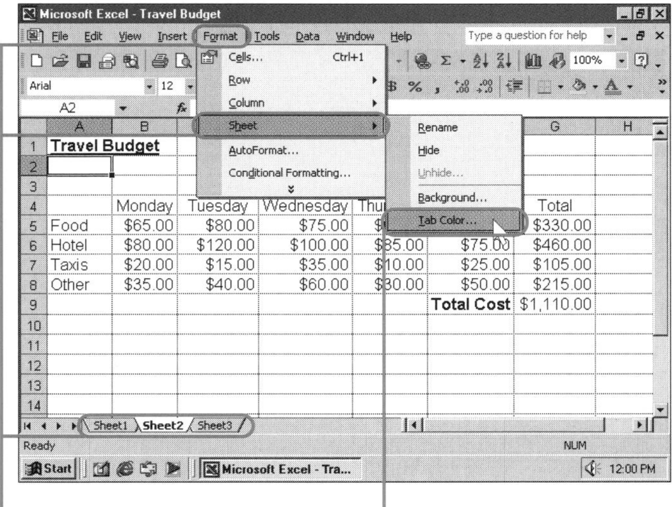

1 Click the worksheet tab you want to add color to.

2 Click **Format**.

3 Click **Sheet**.

4 Click **Tab Color**.

■ The Format Tab Color dialog box appears.

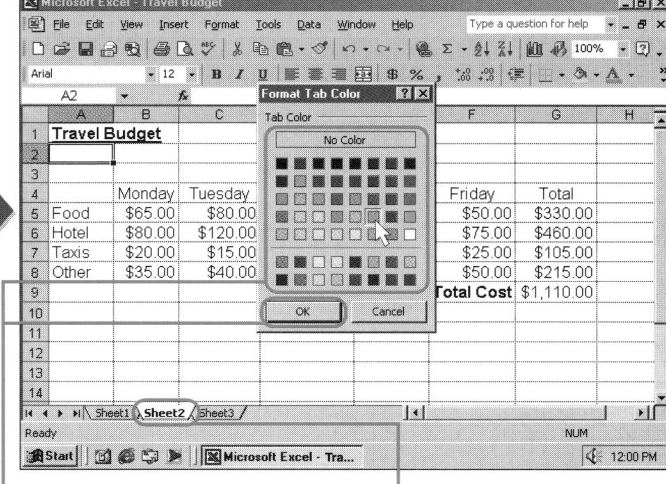

5 Click the color you want to use.

6 Click **OK**.

■ Excel adds the color you selected to the worksheet tab.

■ To remove color from a worksheet tab, repeat steps 1 to 6, selecting **No Color** in step 5.

SAVE A WORKBOOK

You can save your workbook to store the workbook for future use. Saving a workbook allows you to later review and make changes to the workbook.

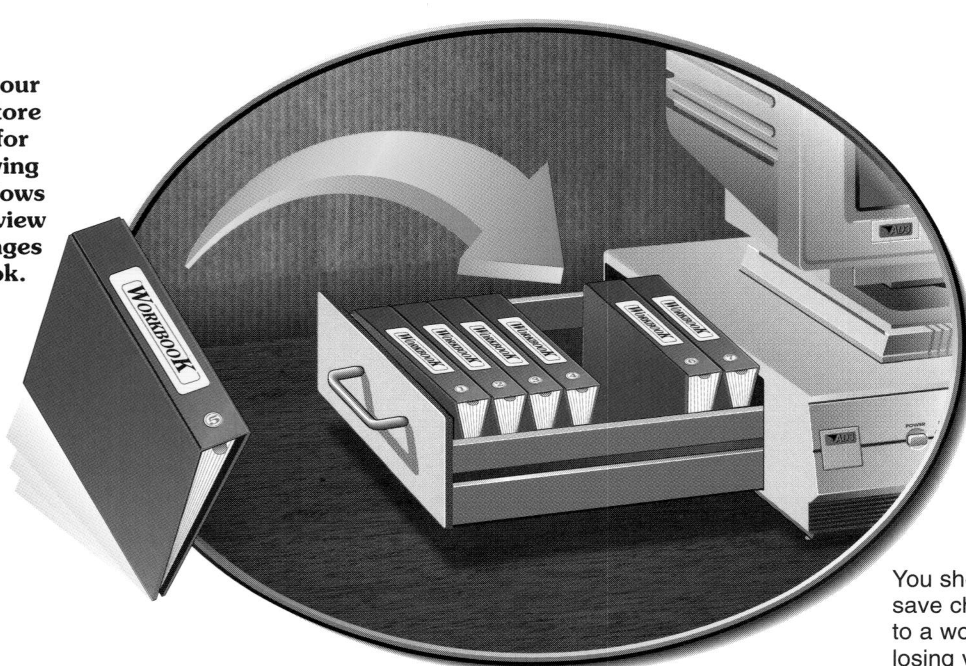

You should regularly save changes you make to a workbook to avoid losing your work.

SAVE A WORKBOOK

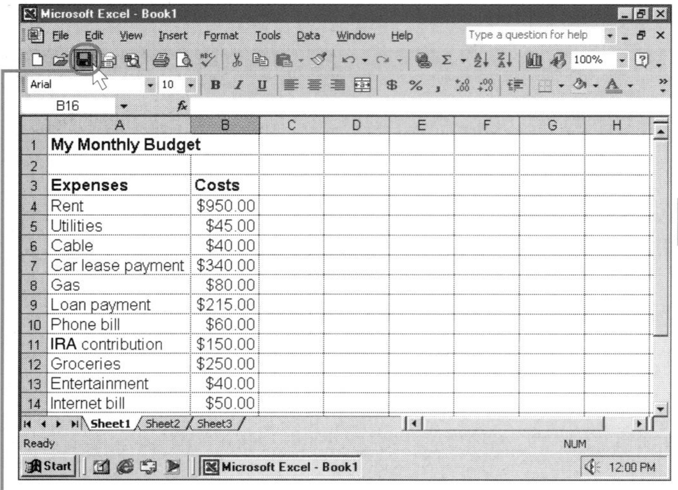

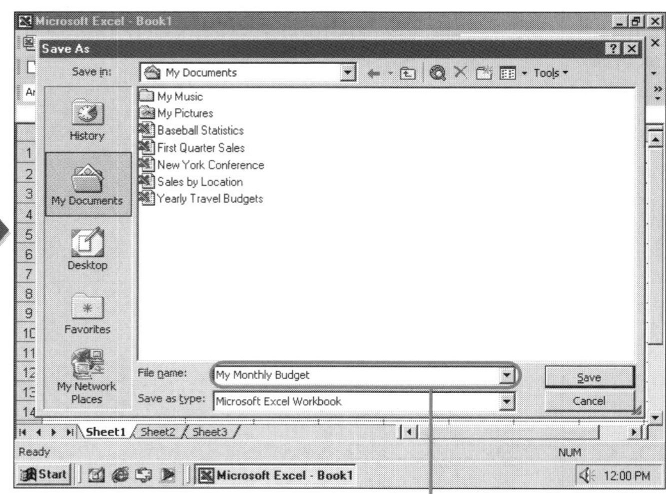

1 Click 💾 to save your workbook.

Note: If 💾 is not displayed, click » on the Standard toolbar to display all the buttons.

■ The Save As dialog box appears.

Note: If you previously saved your workbook, the Save As dialog box will not appear since you have already named the workbook.

2 Type a name for the workbook.

What are the commonly used locations that I can access?

History Provides access to folders and workbooks you recently worked with.	**My Documents** Provides a convenient place to store a workbook.	**Desktop** Allows you to store a workbook on the Windows desktop.	**Favorites** Provides a place to store a workbook you will frequently use.	**My Network Places** Allows you to store a workbook on your network.

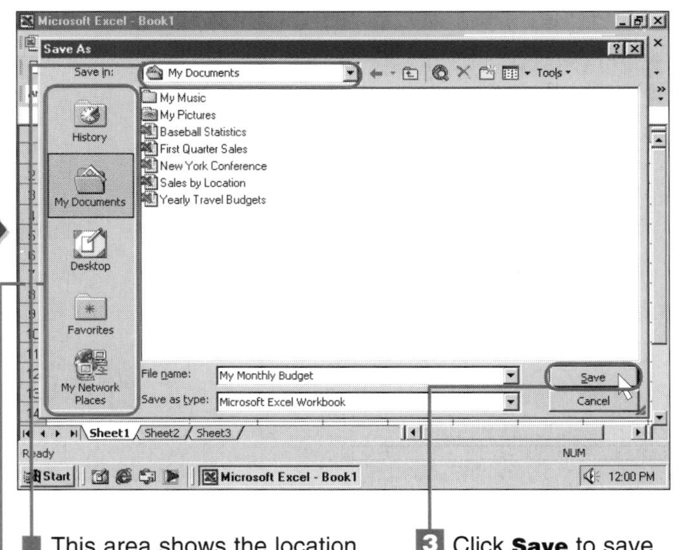

■ This area shows the location where Excel will store your workbook. You can click this area to change the location.

■ This area allows you to access commonly used locations. You can click a location to save your workbook in the location.

3 Click **Save** to save your workbook.

■ Excel saves your workbook.

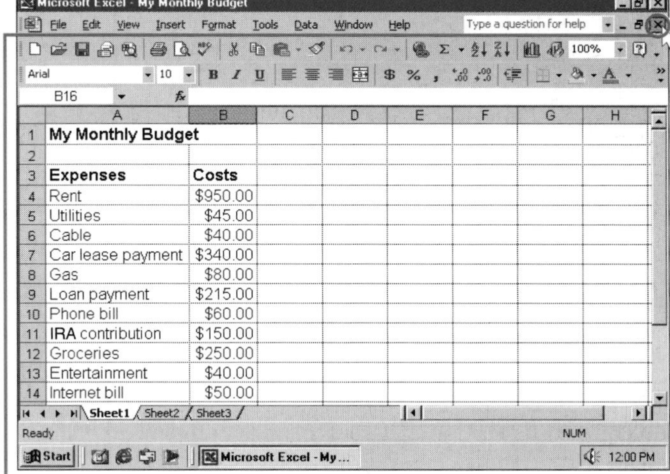

CLOSE A WORKBOOK

1 When you finish using a workbook, click ☒ to close the workbook.

■ The workbook disappears from your screen.

OPEN A WORKBOOK

You can open a saved workbook to view the workbook on your screen. This allows you to review and make changes to the workbook.

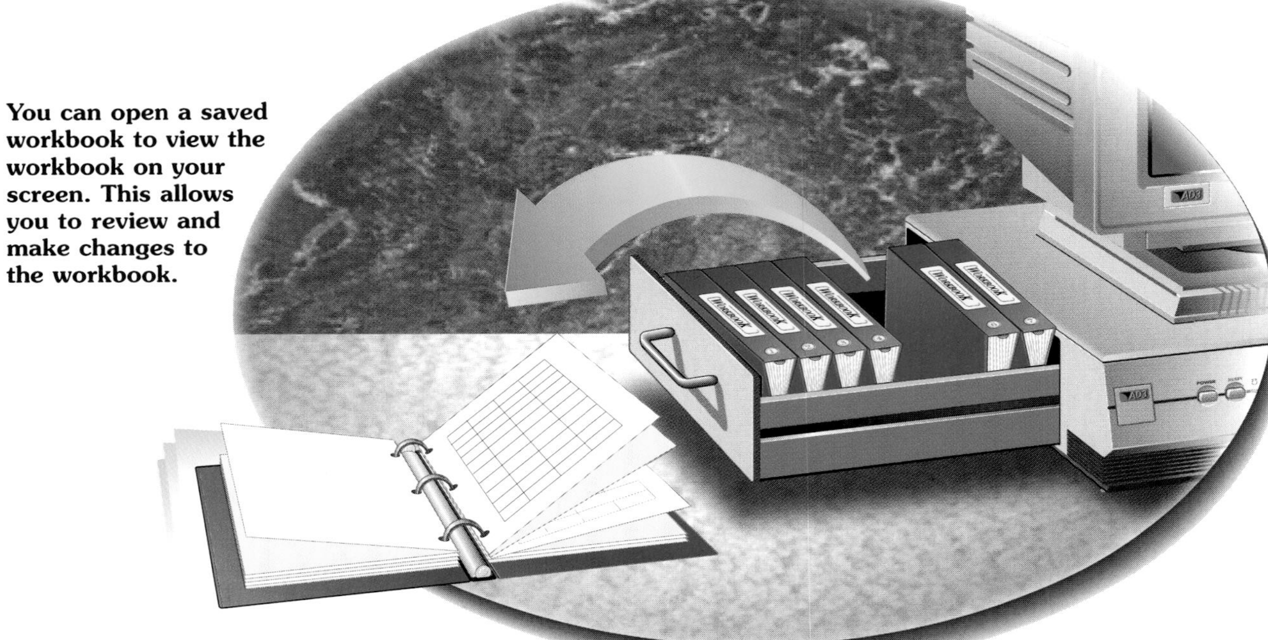

OPEN A WORKBOOK

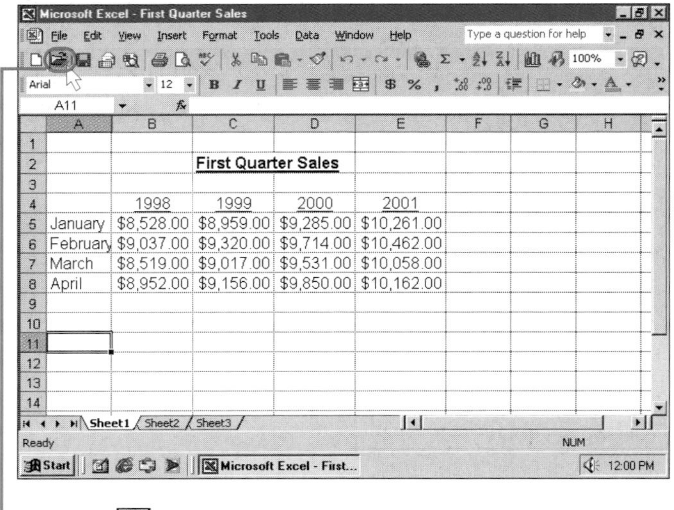

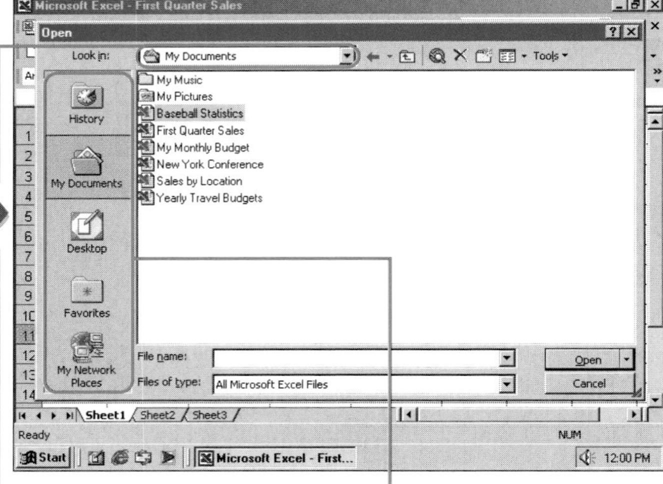

1 Click to open a workbook.

Note: If is not displayed, click on the Standard toolbar to display all the buttons.

■ The Open dialog box appears.

■ This area shows the location of the displayed workbooks. You can click this area to change the location.

■ This area allows you to access workbooks in commonly used locations. You can click a location to display the workbooks stored in the location.

Note: For information on the commonly used locations, see the top of page 117.

How can I quickly open a workbook I recently worked with?

Excel remembers the names of the last four workbooks you worked with. You can use one of the following methods to quickly open any of these workbooks.

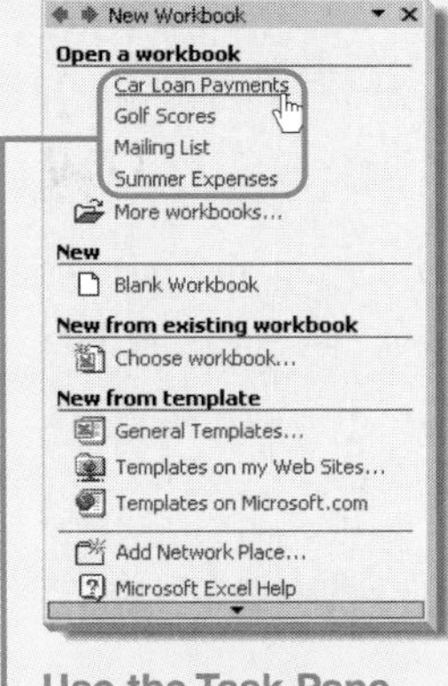

Use the Task Pane

The New Workbook task pane appears each time you start Excel. To display the New Workbook task pane, see page 12.

1 Click the name of the workbook you want to open.

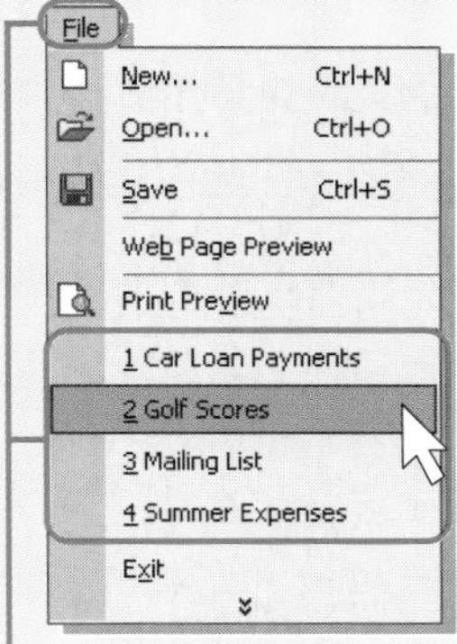

Use the File Menu

1 Click **File**.

2 Click the name of the workbook you want to open.

Note: If the names of the last four workbooks you worked with are not all displayed, position the mouse over the bottom of the menu to display all the workbook names.

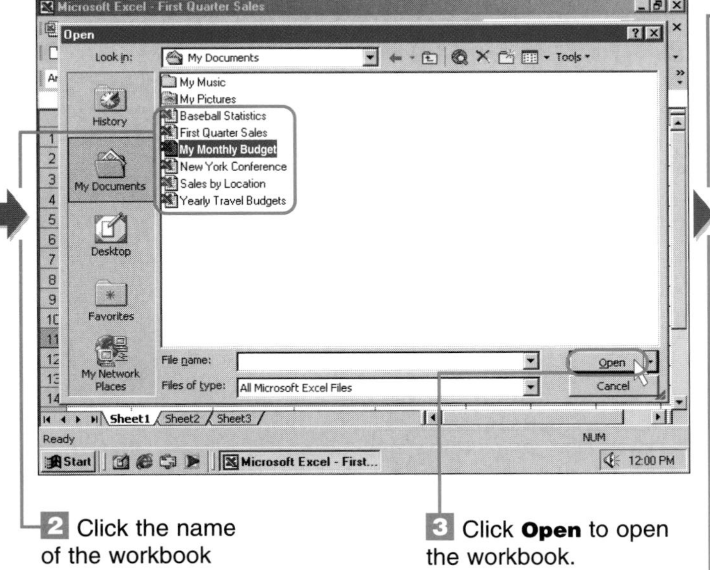

2 Click the name of the workbook you want to open.

3 Click **Open** to open the workbook.

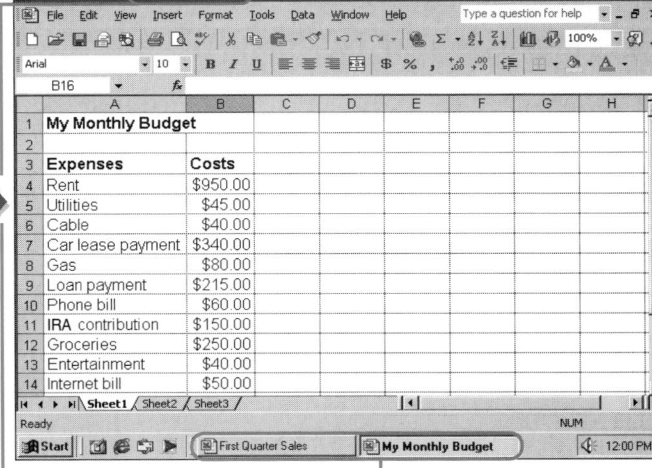

■ The workbook opens and appears on your screen. You can now review and make changes to the workbook.

■ This area displays the name of the open workbook.

■ If you already had a workbook open, the new workbook appears in a new Microsoft Excel window. You can click the buttons on the taskbar to switch between the open workbooks.

CREATE A NEW WORKBOOK

You can create a new workbook to store new information.

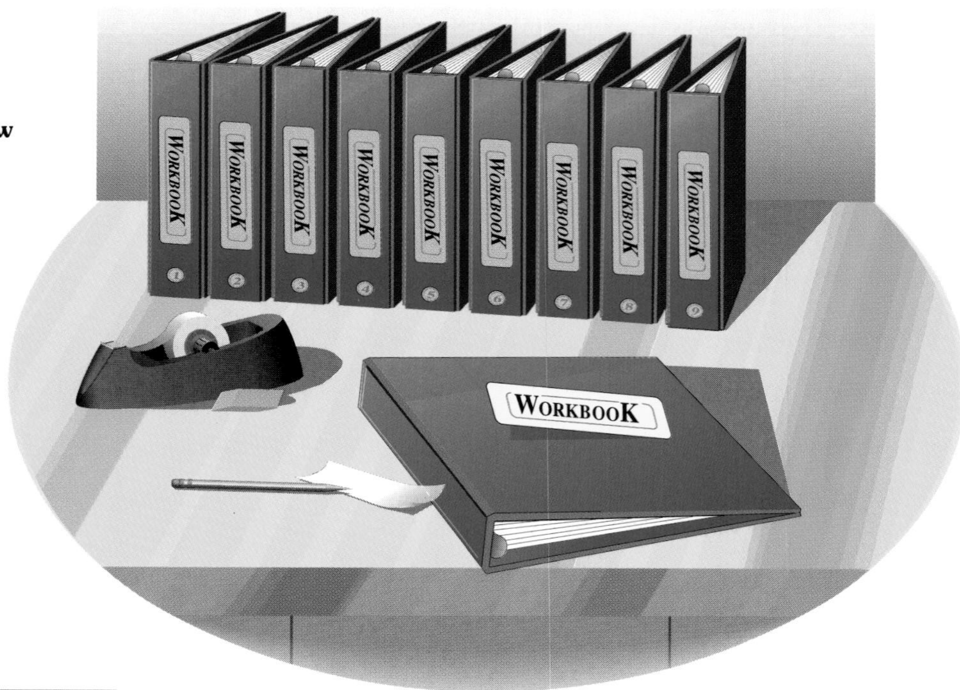

CREATE A NEW WORKBOOK

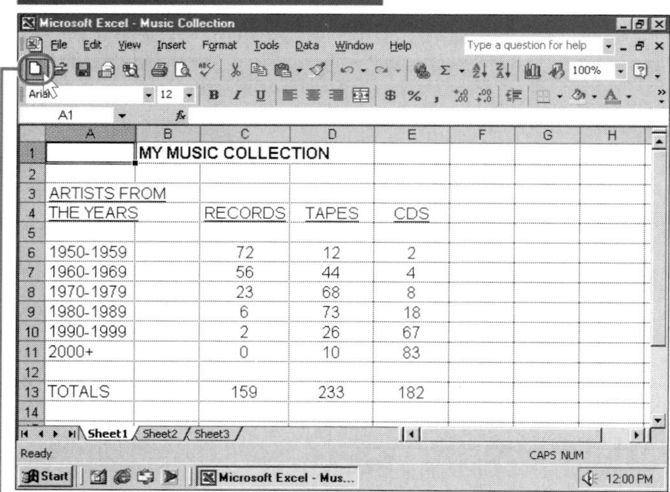

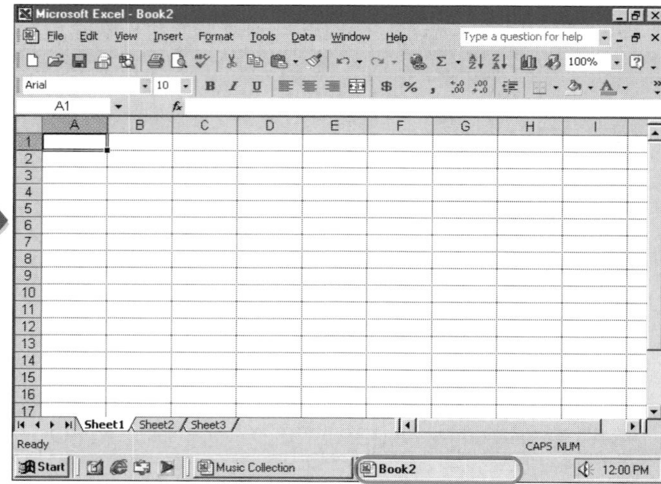

1 Click to create a new workbook.

Note: If is not displayed, click on the Standard toolbar to display all the buttons.

■ The new workbook appears in a new Microsoft Excel window.

■ A button for the new workbook appears on the taskbar.

SWITCH BETWEEN WORKBOOKS

You can have several workbooks open at once. Excel allows you to easily switch from one open workbook to another.

SWITCH BETWEEN WORKBOOKS

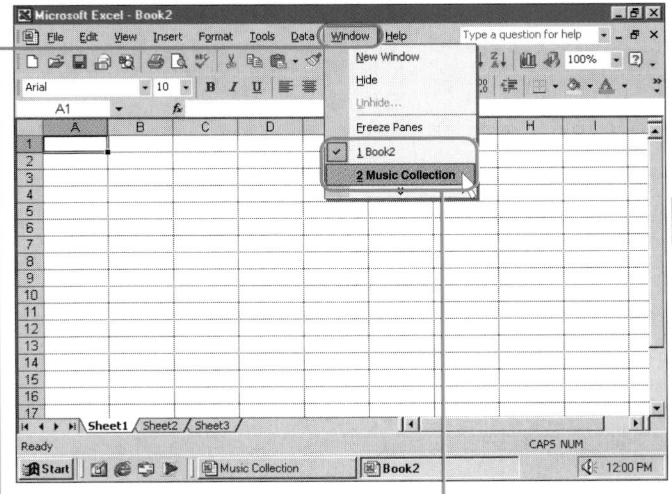

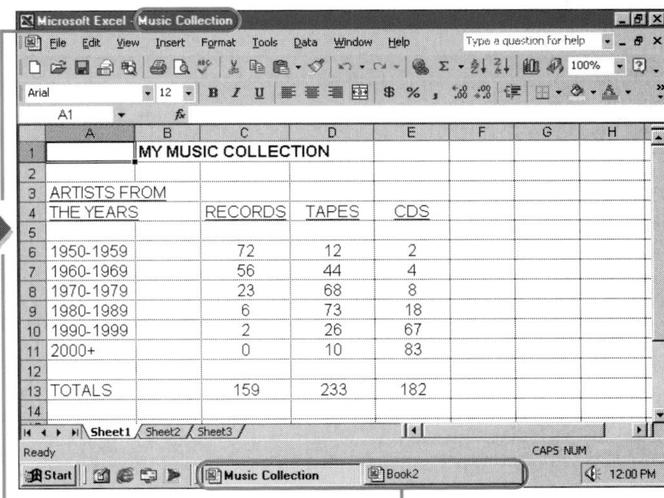

1 Click **Window** to display a list of all the workbooks you have open.

2 Click the name of the workbook you want to switch to.

■ The workbook you selected appears.

■ This area shows the name of the displayed workbook.

■ The taskbar displays a button for each open workbook. You can also click the buttons on the taskbar to switch between the open workbooks.

E-MAIL A WORKSHEET

You can e-mail the worksheet displayed on your screen to a friend, family member or colleague.

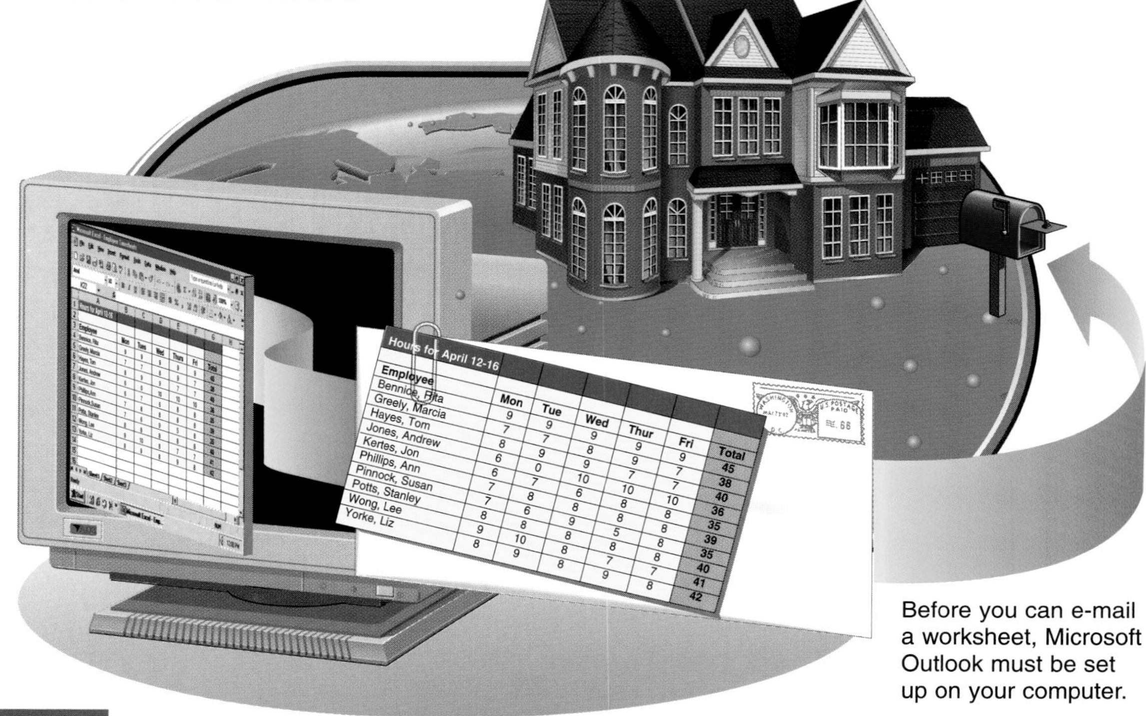

Before you can e-mail a worksheet, Microsoft Outlook must be set up on your computer.

E-MAIL A WORKSHEET

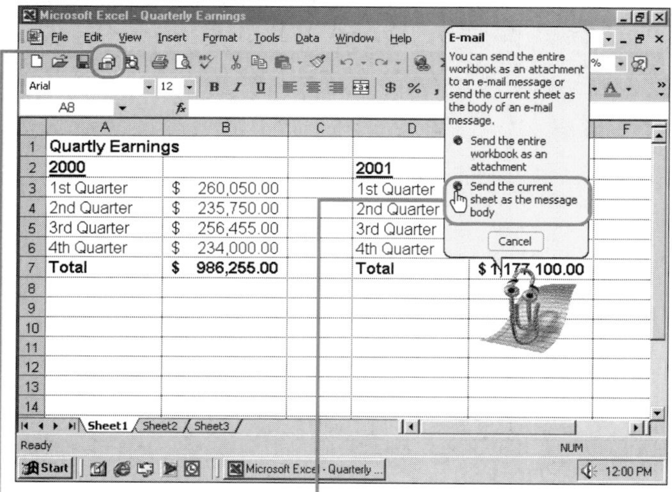

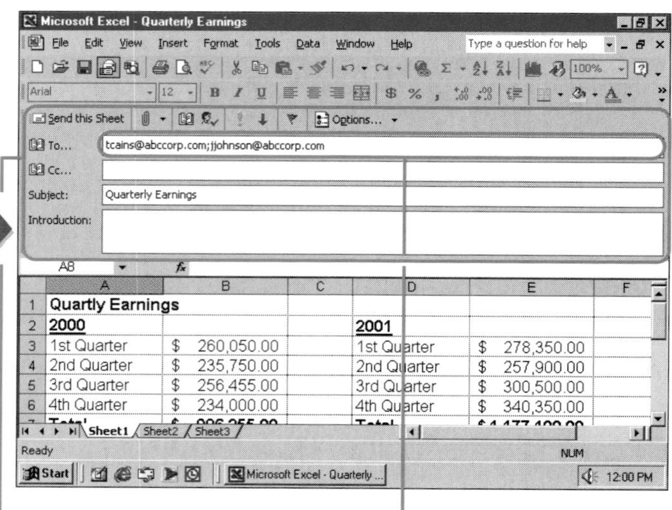

1 Click [icon] to e-mail the current worksheet.

Note: If [icon] is not displayed, click [icon] on the Standard toolbar to display all the buttons.

■ If the workbook contains data in more than one worksheet, a message appears, asking if you want to send the entire workbook or just the current worksheet.

2 Click this option to send the current worksheet.

■ An area appears for you to address the message.

3 Click this area and type the e-mail address of each person you want to receive the message. Separate each address with a semicolon (;).

Why would I include an introduction for a worksheet I am sending in an e-mail message?

Including an introduction allows you to provide the recipient of the message with additional information about the worksheet. For example, the recipient may require instructions or an explanation of the content of the worksheet.

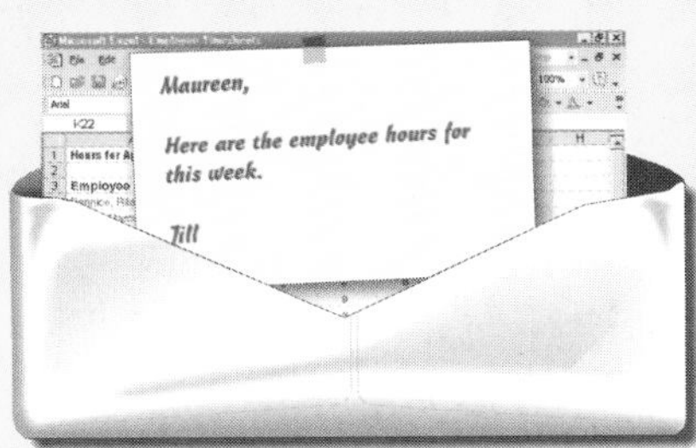

How do I e-mail an entire workbook?

To e-mail an entire workbook, perform steps 1 to 5 below, selecting **Send the entire workbook as an attachment** in step 2. Then click **Send** to send the message. When you e-mail an entire workbook, the workbook is sent as an attached file.

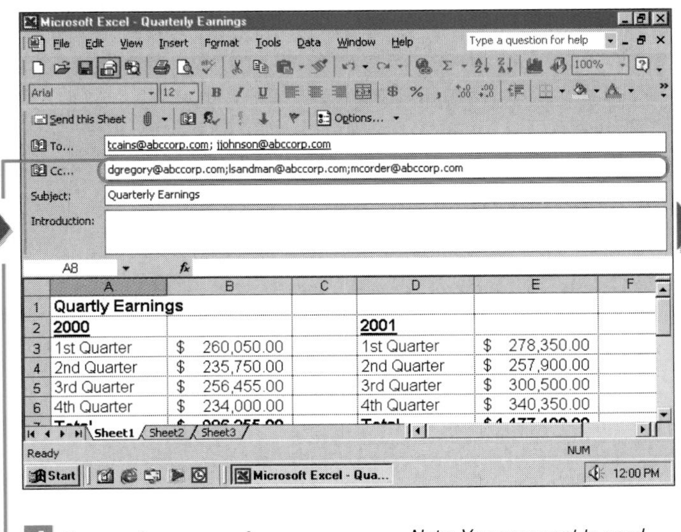

4 To send a copy of the message, click this area and type the e-mail address of each person you want to receive a copy. Separate each address with a semicolon (;).

Note: You may want to send a copy of the message to people who are not directly involved but would be interested in the message.

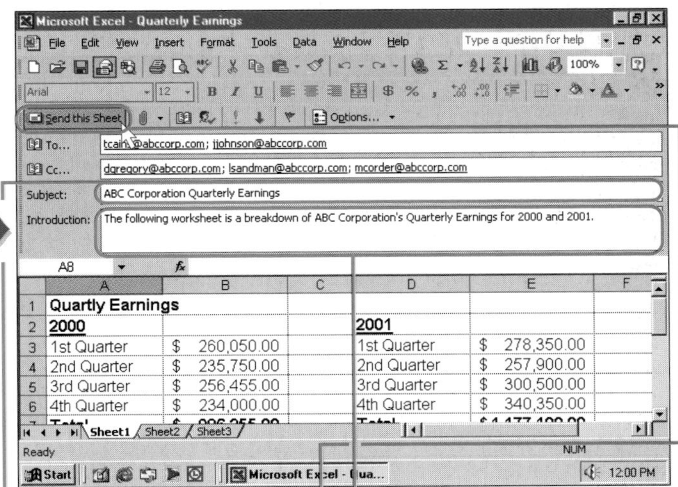

5 Click this area and type a subject for the message.

Note: If a subject already exists, you can drag the mouse I over the existing subject and then type a new subject.

6 To include an introduction for the worksheet you are sending in the message, click this area and type the introduction.

7 Click **Send this Sheet** to send the message.

EDIT OR DELETE DATA

You can edit data in your worksheet to correct a mistake or update data. You can also remove data you no longer need.

EDIT DATA

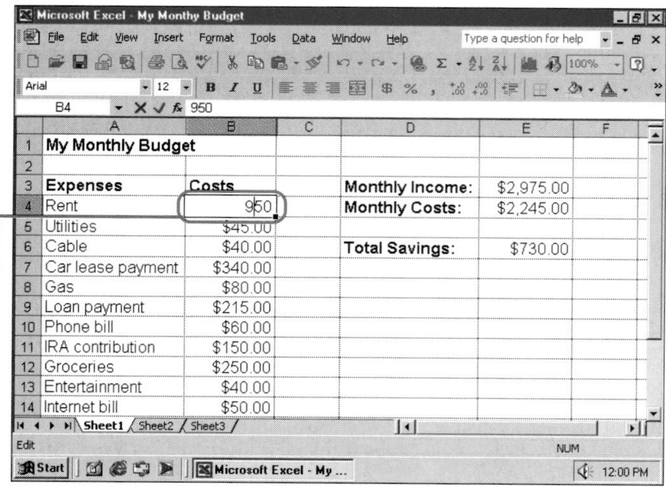

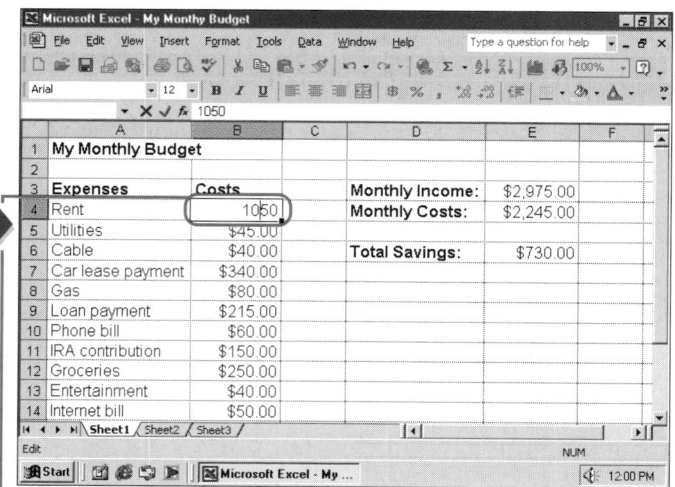

1 Double-click the cell containing the data you want to edit.

■ A flashing insertion point appears in the cell.

2 Press the ← or → key to move the insertion point to where you want to remove or add characters.

3 To remove the character to the left of the flashing insertion point, press the ←Backspace key.

4 To add data where the insertion point flashes on your screen, type the data.

5 When you finish making changes to the data, press the Enter key.

Can Excel automatically correct my typing mistakes?

Yes. Excel automatically corrects common spelling errors as you type. Here are a few examples.

adn → and
alot → a lot
comitee → committee
don;t → don't
nwe → new
occurence → occurrence
recieve → receive
seperate → separate
teh → the

When I delete the data in a cell, will Excel remove the formatting from the cell?

No. When you delete the data in a cell, Excel will not remove the formatting you applied to the cell, such as a new font or color. Any new data you enter into the cell will display the same formatting as the data you deleted.

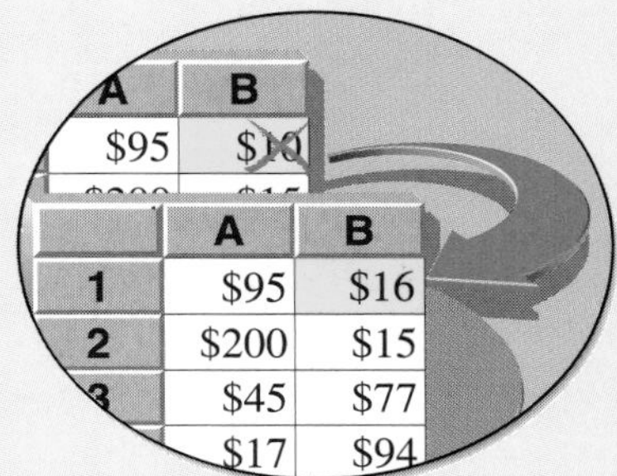

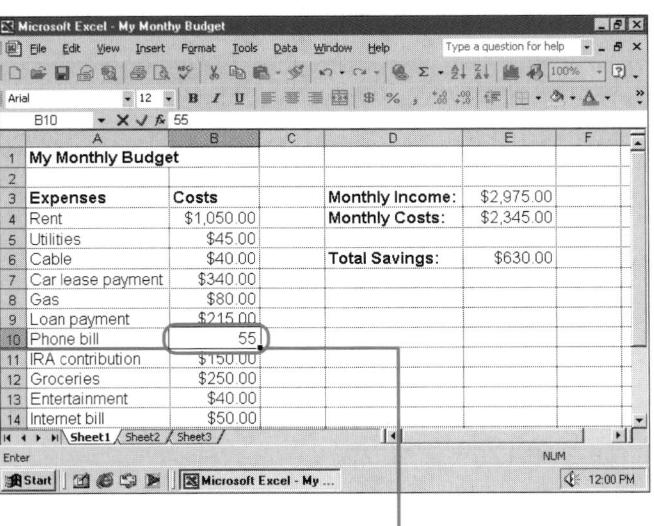

REPLACE ALL DATA IN A CELL

1 Click the cell containing the data you want to replace with new data.

2 Type the new data and then press the Enter key.

DELETE DATA

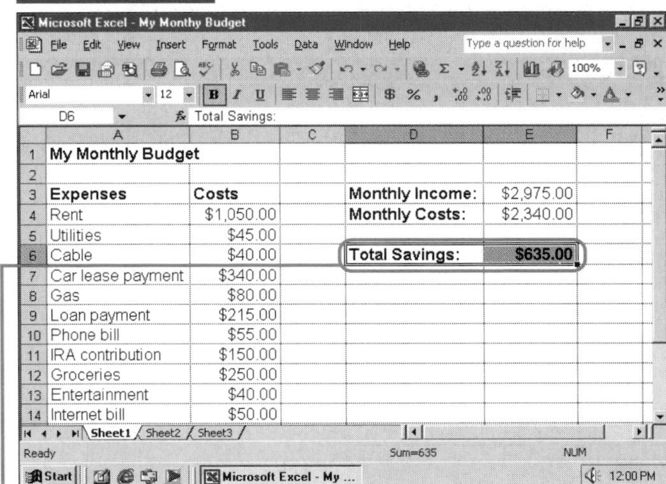

1 Select the cells containing the data you want to delete. To select cells, see page 106.

2 Press the Delete key.

■ The data in the cells you selected disappears.

■ To deselect cells, click any cell.

MOVE OR COPY DATA

You can move or copy data to a new location in your worksheet.

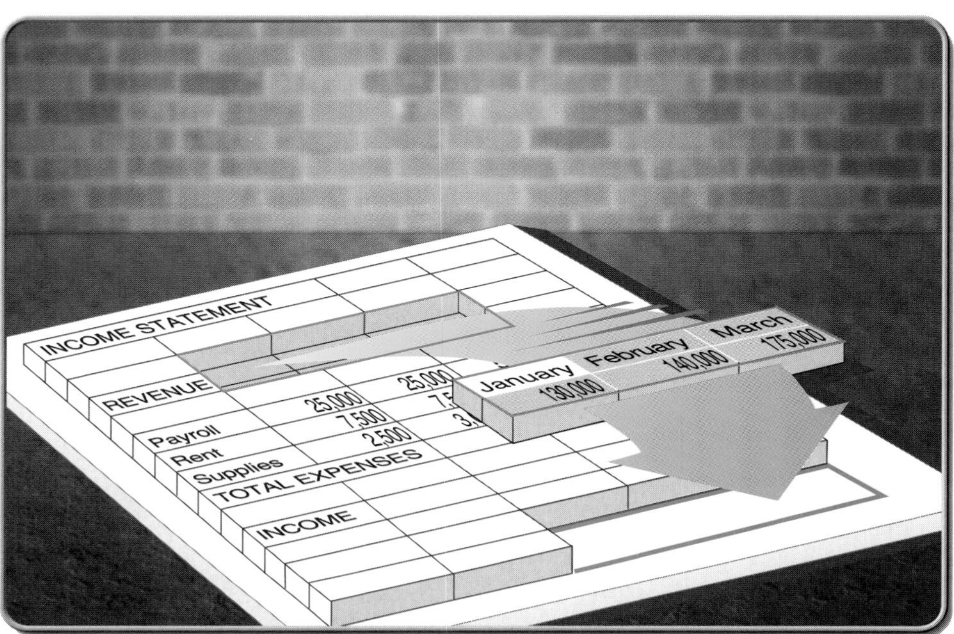

Moving data allows you to re-organize data in your worksheet. When you move data, the data disappears from its original location.

Copying data allows you to repeat data in your worksheet without having to retype the data. When you copy data, the data appears in both the original and new locations.

MOVE OR COPY DATA

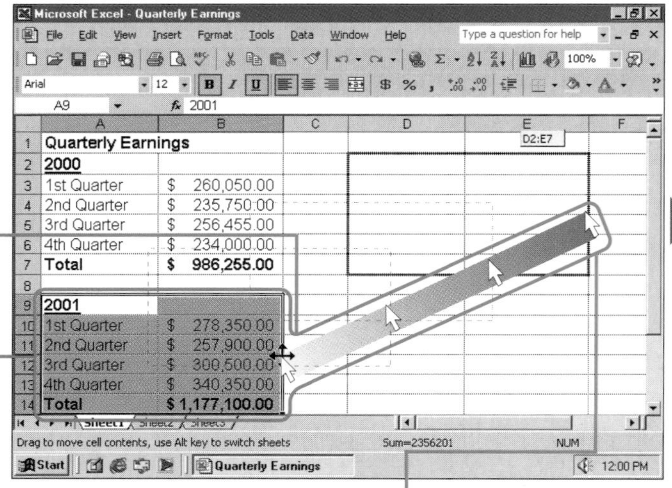

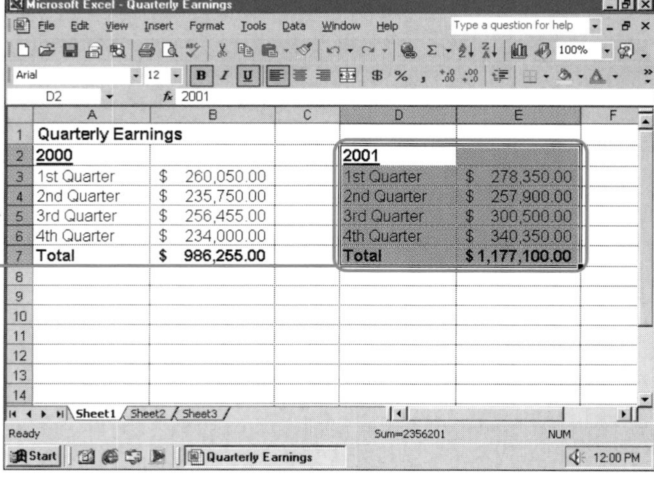

USING DRAG AND DROP

1 Select the cells containing the data you want to move. To select cells, see page 106.

2 Position the mouse over a border of the selected cells (changes to).

3 To move the data, drag the mouse to where you want to place the data.

Note: A gray box indicates where the data will appear.

■ The data moves to the new location.

■ To copy data, perform steps 1 to 3, except press and hold down the Ctrl key as you perform step 3.

How can I use the Clipboard task pane to move or copy data?

The Clipboard task pane displays the last 24 items you have selected to move or copy using the toolbar buttons. To display the Clipboard task pane, see page 12. To place a clipboard item into your worksheet, click the cell where you want to place the item and then click the item in the task pane.

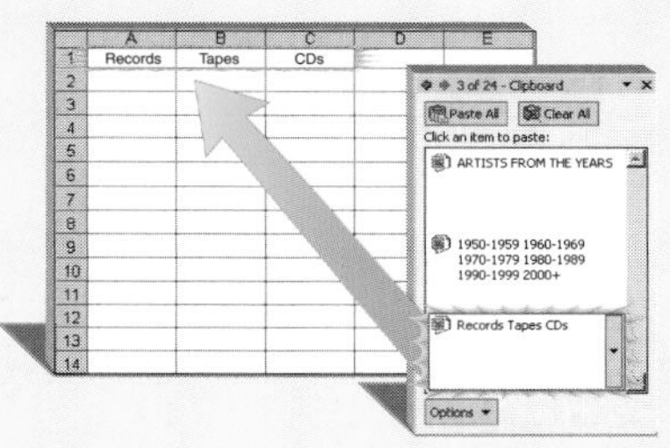

Why does the Paste Options button ([Paste Options icon]) appear when I copy data?

You can use the Paste Options button ([Paste Options icon]) to change the way Excel copies data when you use the Copy button ([Copy icon]). For example, you can specify that you want to copy only the formatting of the original cells to the new location. Click the Paste Options button to display a list of options and then select the option you want to use. The Paste Options button is available only until you perform another task.

- Keep Source Formatting
- Match Destination Formatting
- Values and Number Formatting
- Keep Source Column Widths
- Formatting Only
- Link Cells

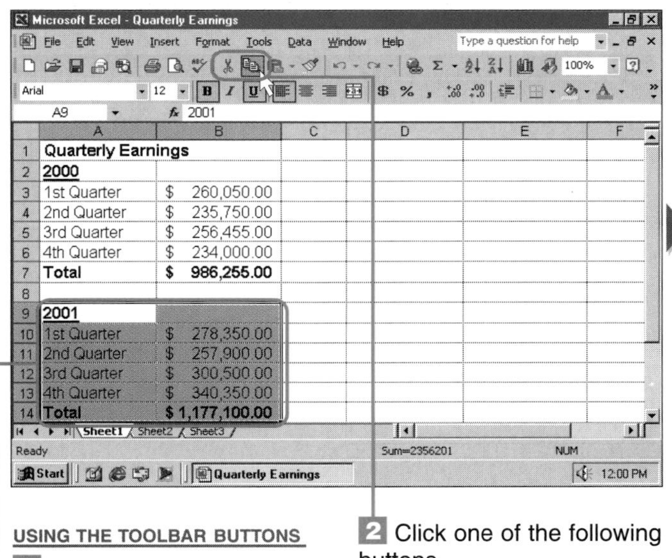

USING THE TOOLBAR BUTTONS

1 Select the cells containing the data you want to move or copy. To select cells, see page 106.

2 Click one of the following buttons.

[Cut icon] Move data

[Copy icon] Copy data

Note: If the button you want is not displayed, click [toolbar options icon] on the Standard toolbar to display all the buttons.

3 Click the cell where you want to place the data. This cell will become the top left cell of the new location.

4 Click [Paste icon] to place the data in the new location.

Note: If [Paste icon] is not displayed, click [toolbar options icon] on the Standard toolbar to display all the buttons.

■ The data appears in the new location.

INSERT A ROW OR COLUMN

You can add a row or column to your worksheet to insert additional data.

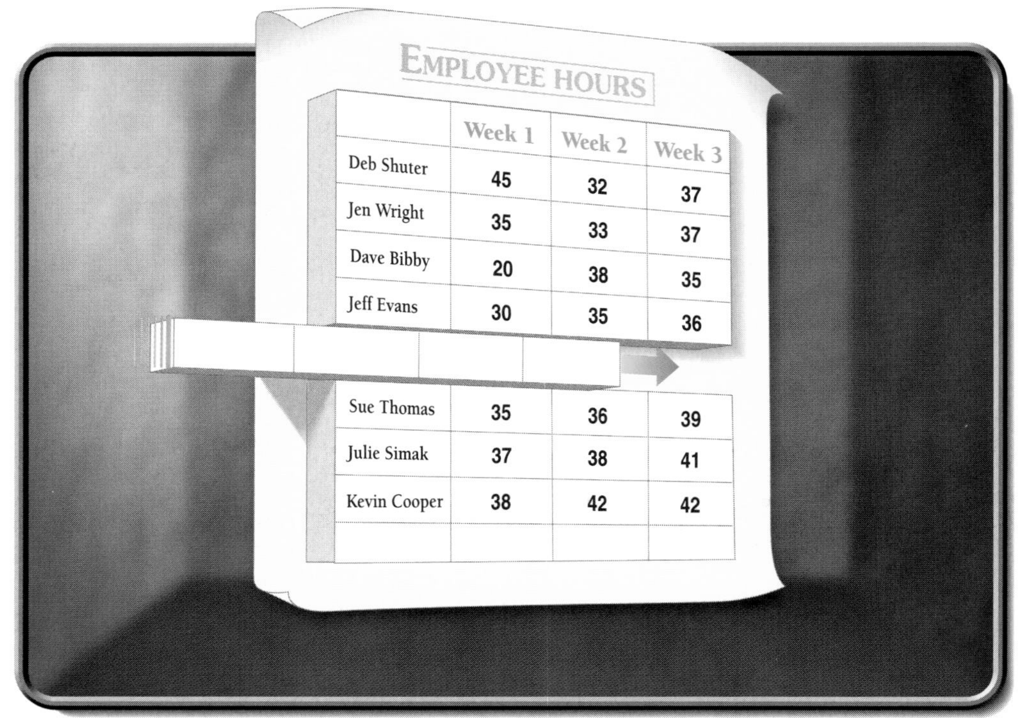

INSERT A ROW

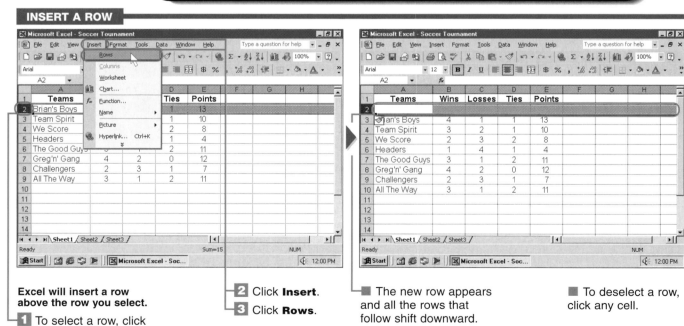

Excel will insert a row above the row you select.

1 To select a row, click the row number.

2 Click **Insert**.

3 Click **Rows**.

■ The new row appears and all the rows that follow shift downward.

■ To deselect a row, click any cell.

Do I need to adjust my formulas when I insert a row or column?

No. When you insert a row or column, Excel automatically updates any formulas affected by the insertion. For information on formulas, see pages 134 to 147.

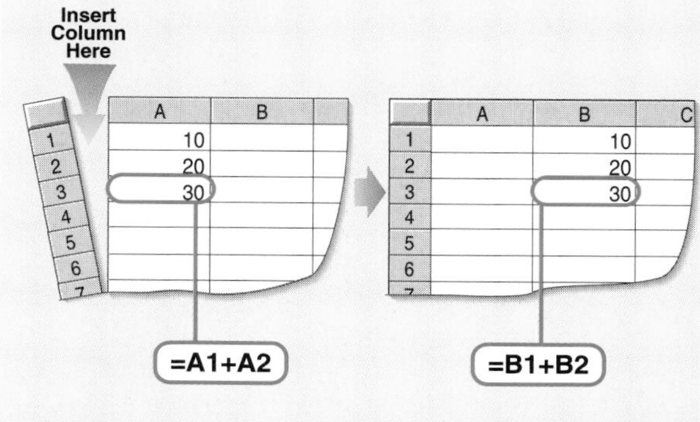

How do I insert several rows or columns at once?

You can use one of the methods shown below to insert several rows or columns at once, but you must first select the number of rows or columns you want to insert. For example, to insert two columns, select two columns and then perform steps 2 and 3 below. To select multiple rows or columns, see page 107.

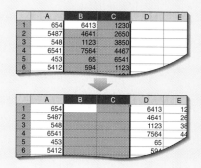

INSERT A COLUMN

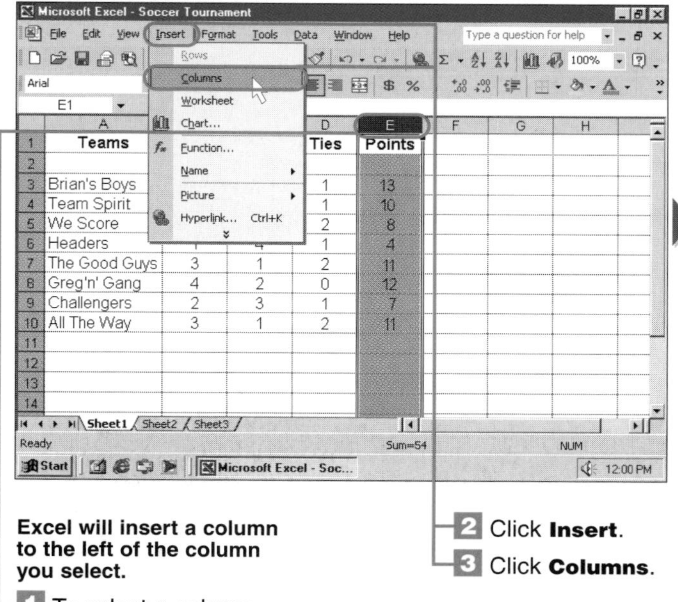

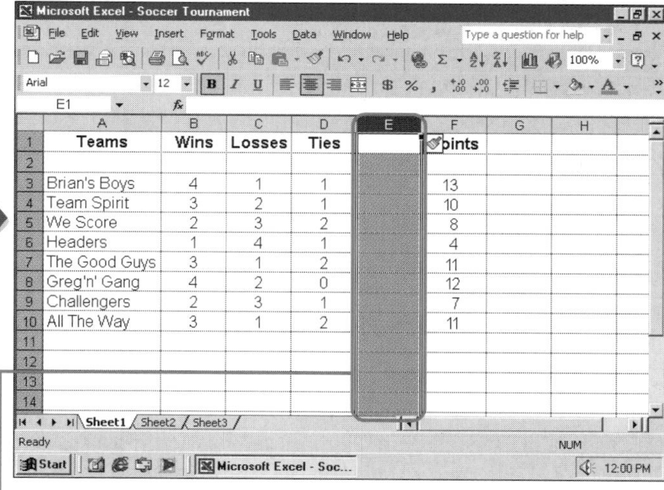

Excel will insert a column to the left of the column you select.

1 To select a column, click the column letter.

2 Click **Insert**.

3 Click **Columns**.

■ The new column appears and all the columns that follow shift to the right.

■ To deselect a column, click any cell.

DELETE A ROW OR COLUMN

You can delete a row or column to remove data you no longer want to display in your worksheet.

DELETE A ROW

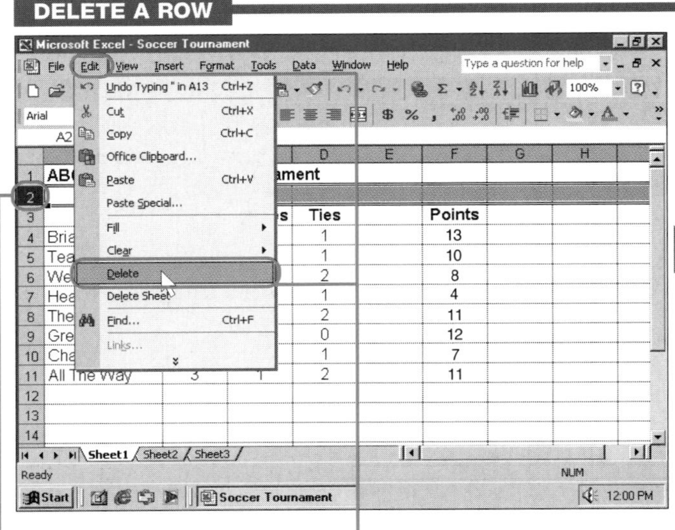

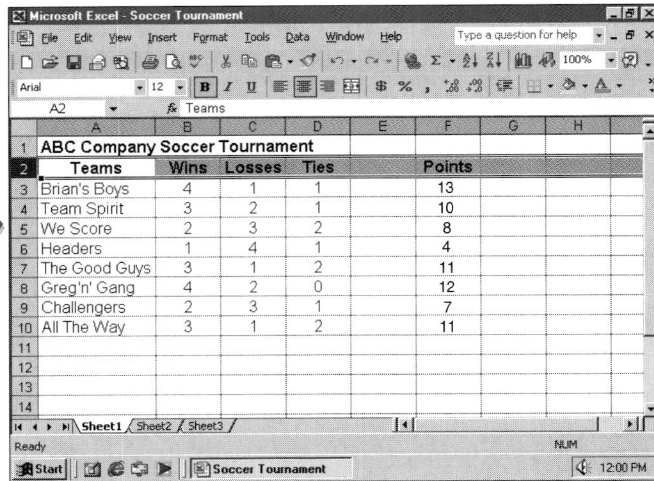

1 To select the row you want to delete, click the row number.

2 Click **Edit**.

3 Click **Delete** to delete the row.

■ The row disappears and all the rows that follow shift upward.

■ To deselect a row, click any cell.

Why did #REF! appear in a cell after I deleted a row or column?

If #REF! appears in a cell in your worksheet, you may have deleted data needed to calculate a formula. Before you delete a row or column, make sure the row or column does not contain data that is used in a formula. For information on formulas, see pages 134 to 147.

How do I delete several rows or columns at once?

You can use one of the methods shown below to delete several rows or columns at once, but you must first select the rows or columns you want to delete. For example, to delete three columns, select the columns and then perform steps 2 and 3 below. To select multiple rows or columns, see page 107.

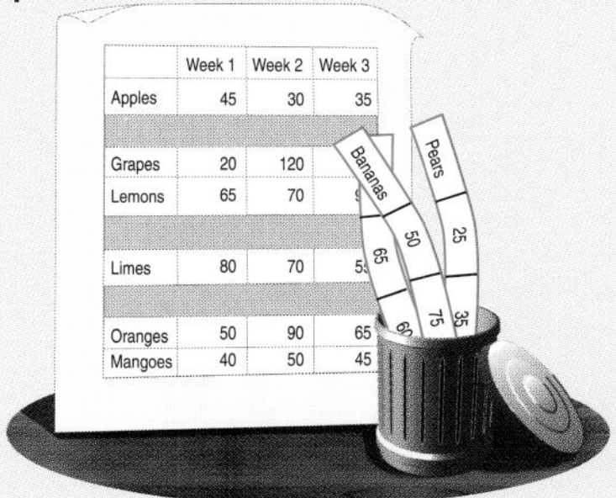

DELETE A COLUMN

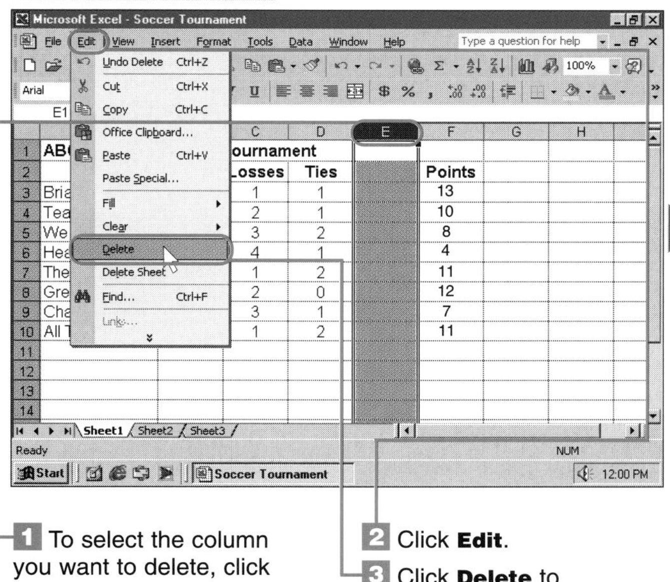

1 To select the column you want to delete, click the column letter.

2 Click **Edit**.

3 Click **Delete** to delete the column.

■ The column disappears and all the columns that follow shift to the left.

■ To deselect a column, click any cell.

ZOOM IN OR OUT

You can enlarge or reduce the display of data on your screen.

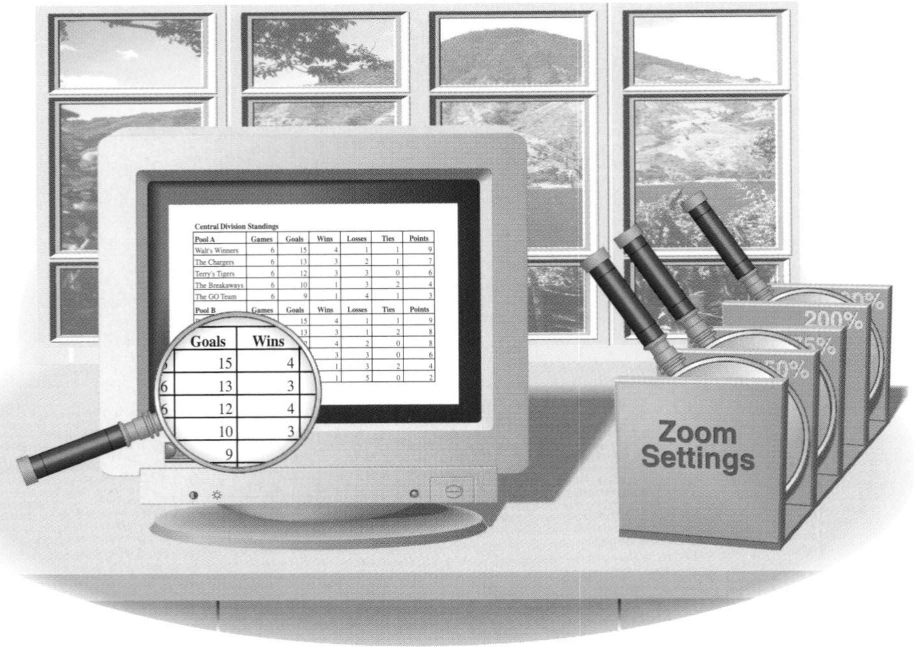

Changing the zoom setting will not affect the way data appears on a printed page.

ZOOM IN OR OUT

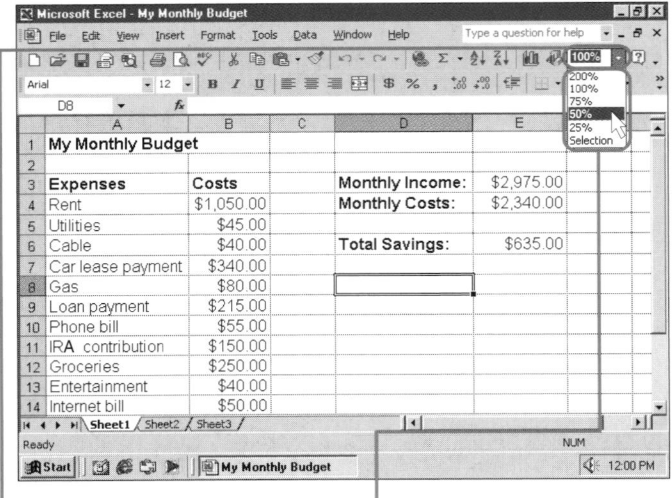

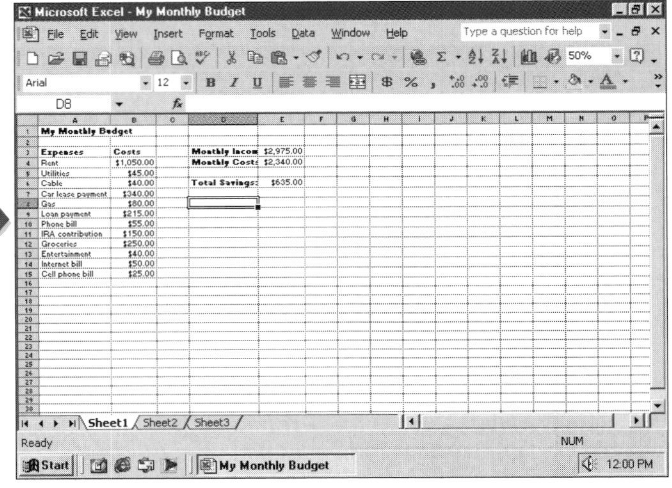

1 Click ▾ in this area to display a list of zoom settings.

Note: If the Zoom area is not displayed, click » on the Standard toolbar to display the area.

2 Click the zoom setting you want to use.

Note: If you select cells before performing step **1**, *the* ***Selection*** *setting enlarges the selected cells to fill the window. To select cells, see page 106.*

■ The worksheet appears in the new zoom setting. You can edit the worksheet as usual.

■ To return to the normal zoom setting, repeat steps **1** and **2**, selecting **100%** in step **2**.

UNDO CHANGES

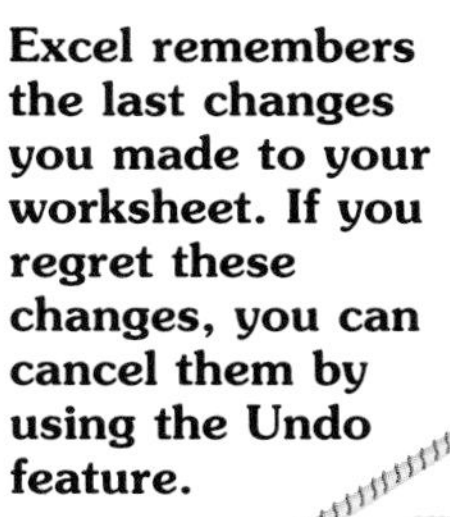
Excel remembers the last changes you made to your worksheet. If you regret these changes, you can cancel them by using the Undo feature.

The Undo feature can cancel your last editing and formatting changes.

UNDO CHANGES

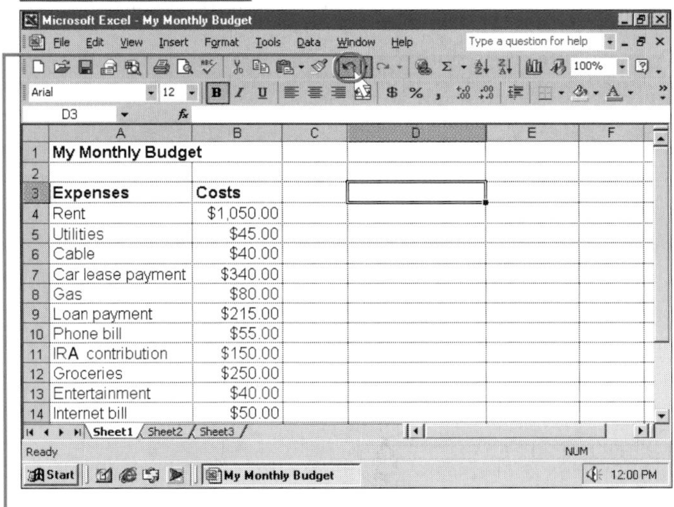

1 Click ↶ to undo the last change you made to your worksheet.

Note: If ↶ is not displayed, click » on the Standard toolbar to display all the buttons.

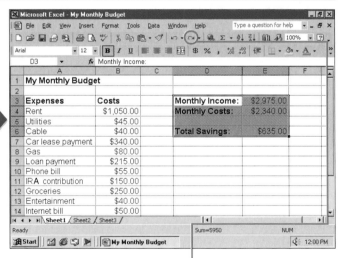

■ Excel cancels the last change you made to your worksheet.

■ You can repeat step **1** to cancel previous changes you made.

■ To reverse the results of using the Undo feature, click ↷.

Note: If ↷ is not displayed, click » on the Standard toolbar to display all the buttons.

INTRODUCTION TO FORMULAS AND FUNCTIONS

A formula allows you to calculate and analyze data in your worksheet.

A formula always begins with an equal sign (=).

OPERATORS

A formula can contain one or more operators. An operator specifies the type of calculation you want to perform.

Arithmetic Operators

You can use arithmetic operators to perform mathematical calculations.

	A	B
1	5	5
2		
3	10	

=A1+B1

Operator	Description
+	Addition (A1+B1)
-	Subtraction (A1-B1)
*	Multiplication (A1*B1)
/	Division (A1/B1)
%	Percent (A1%)
^	Exponentiation (A1^B1)

Comparison Operators

You can use comparison operators to compare two values. Comparison operators return a value of TRUE or FALSE.

	A	B
1	5	5
2		
3	TRUE	

=A1=B1

Operator	Description
=	Equal to (A1=B1)
>	Greater than (A1>B1)
<	Less than (A1<B1)
>=	Greater than or equal to (A1>=B1)
<=	Less than or equal to (A1<=B1)
<>	Not equal to (A1<>B1)

ORDER OF CALCULATIONS

1	Percent (%)
2	Exponentiation (^)
3	Multiplication (*) and Division (/)
4	Addition (+) and Subtraction (-)
5	Comparison operators

	A
1	2
2	4
3	6
4	8
5	
6	

=A1+A2+A3*A4
=2+4+6*8=54

=A1+(A2+A3)*A4
=2+(4+6)*8=82

=A1*(A3-A2)+A4
=2*(6-4)+8=12

=A2^A1+A3
$=4^2+6=22$

When a formula contains more than one operator, Excel performs the calculations in a specific order.

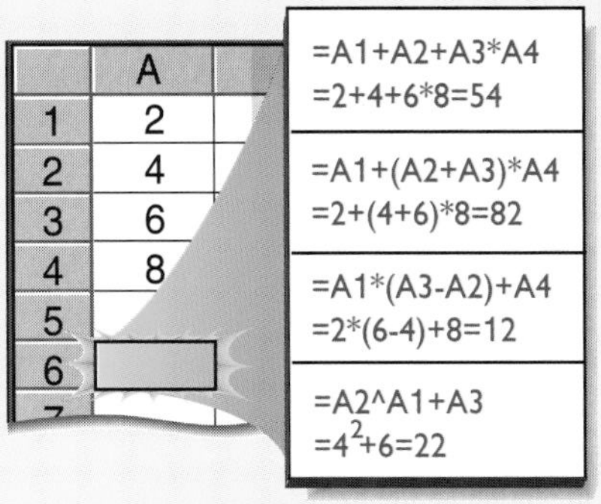

You can use parentheses ( ) to change the order in which Excel performs calculations. Excel will perform the calculations inside the parentheses first.

CELL REFERENCES

When entering formulas, use cell references instead of actual data whenever possible. For example, enter the formula =A1+A2 instead of =10+20.

When you use cell references and you change a number used in a formula, Excel will automatically redo the calculation for you.

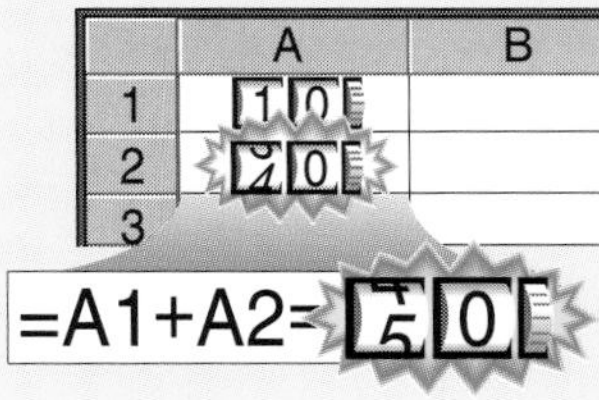

	A	B
1	10	
2	20	
3		

=A1+A2=50

FUNCTIONS

A function is a ready-to-use formula that you can use to perform a calculation on the data in your worksheet. Examples of commonly used functions include AVERAGE, COUNT, MAX and SUM.

- A function always begins with an equal sign (=).
- The data Excel will use to calculate a function is enclosed in parentheses ( ).

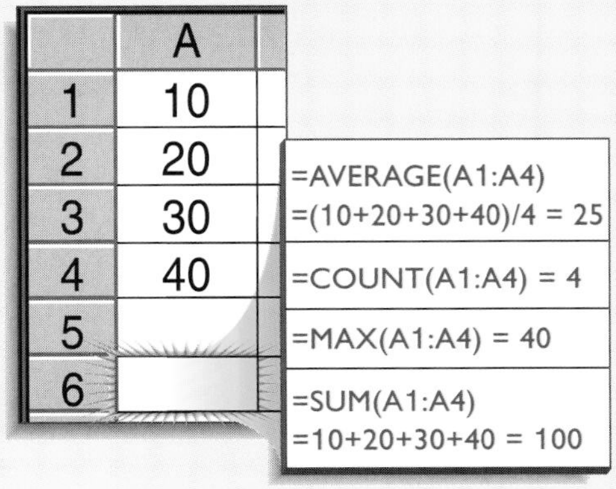

	A
1	10
2	20
3	30
4	40
5	
6	

=AVERAGE(A1:A4)
=(10+20+30+40)/4 = 25

=COUNT(A1:A4) = 4

=MAX(A1:A4) = 40

=SUM(A1:A4)
=10+20+30+40 = 100

Specify Individual Cells

When a comma (,) separates cell references in a function, Excel uses each cell to perform the calculation. For example, =SUM(A1,A2,A3) is the same as the formula =A1+A2+A3.

Specify a Group of Cells

When a colon (:) separates cell references in a function, Excel uses the specified cells and all cells between them to perform the calculation.

For example, =SUM(A1:A3) is the same as the formula =A1+A2+A3.

ENTER A FORMULA

You can enter a formula into any cell in your worksheet. A formula helps you calculate and analyze data in your worksheet.

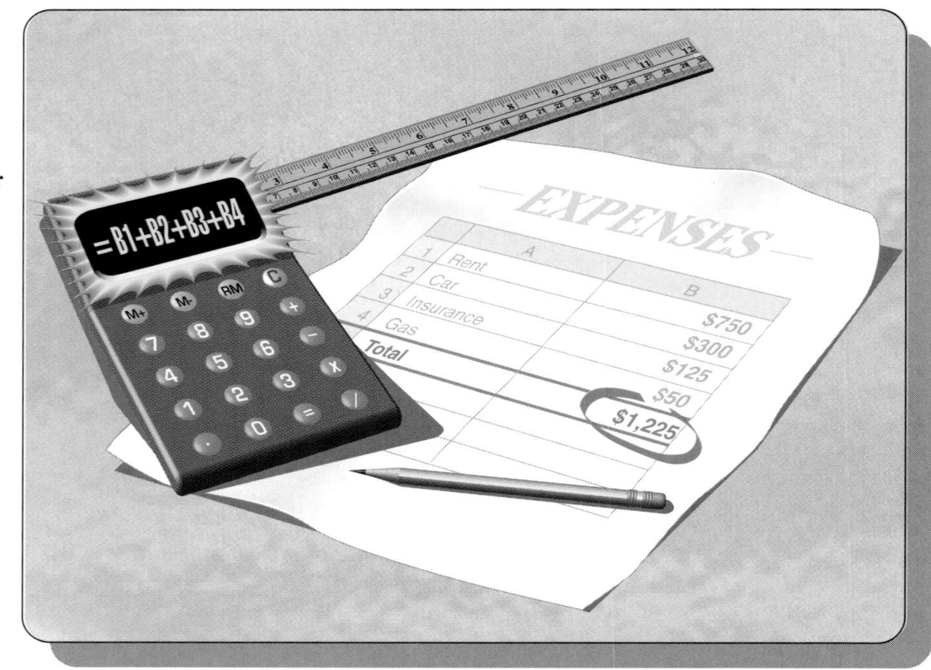

When entering formulas, you should use cell references instead of actual data whenever possible.

A formula always begins with an equal sign (=).

ENTER A FORMULA

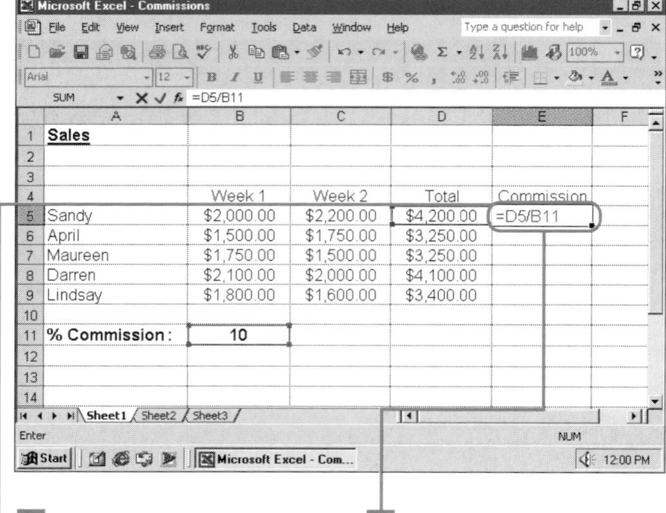

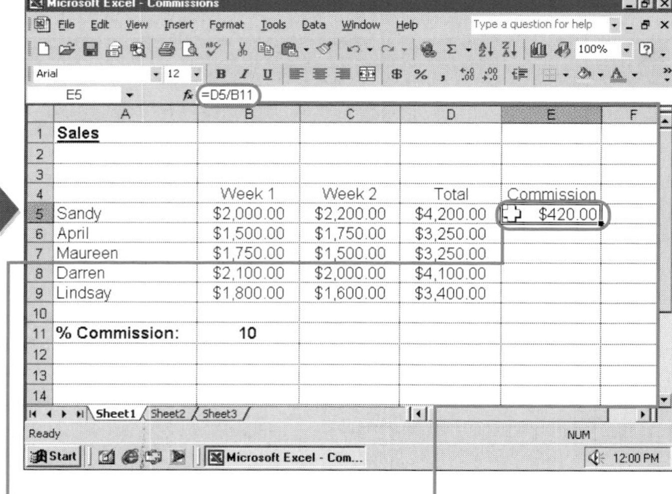

1 Click the cell where you want to enter a formula.

2 Type an equal sign (=) to begin the formula.

3 Type the formula and then press the Enter key.

■ The result of the calculation appears in the cell.

4 To view the formula you entered, click the cell containing the formula.

■ The formula bar displays the formula for the cell.

What happens if I change a number used in a formula?

When you use cell references and you change a number used in a formula, Excel will automatically redo the calculation for you.

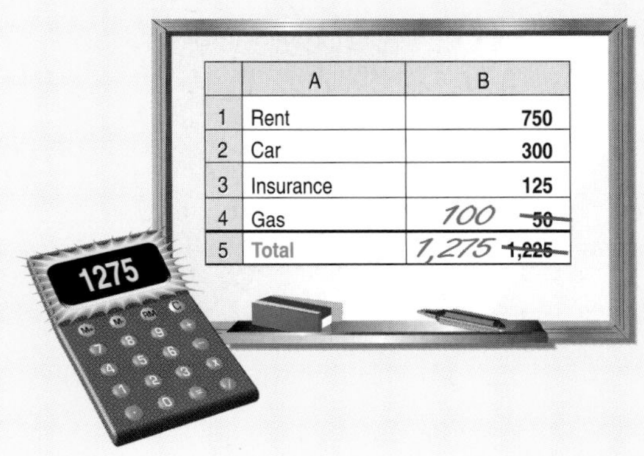

How can I quickly enter cell references into a formula?

To quickly enter cell references, perform steps 1 and 2 on page 136 and then click the first cell you want to use in the formula. Type the operator you want to use to perform the calculation and then click the next cell you want to use in the formula. When you finish entering cell references and operators, press the Enter key to perform the calculation.

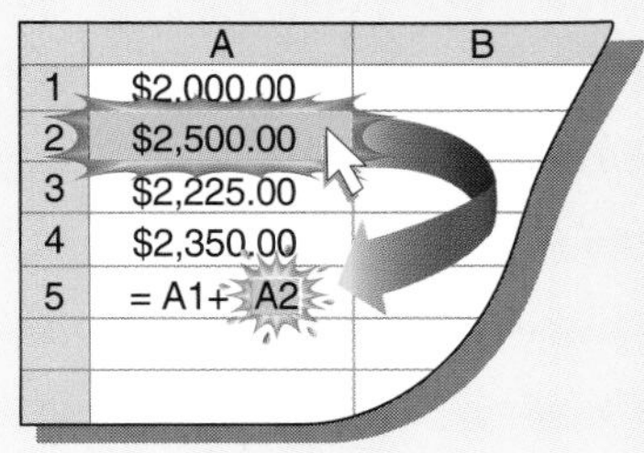

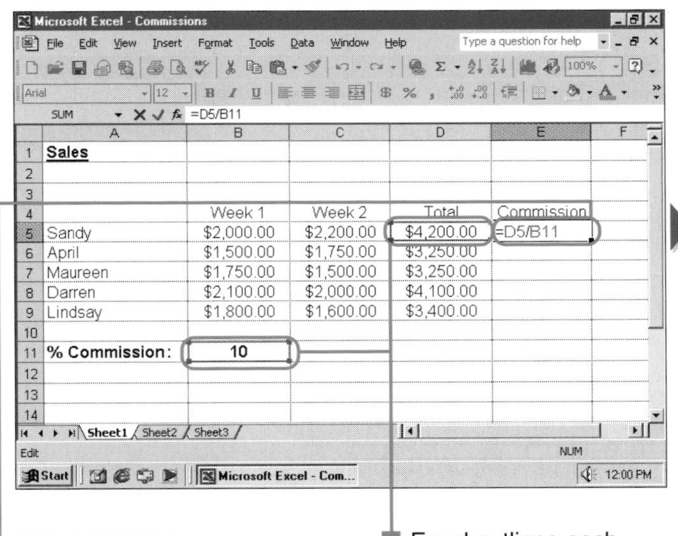

EDIT A FORMULA

1 Double-click the cell containing the formula you want to change.

■ The formula appears in the cell.

■ Excel outlines each cell used in the formula with a different color.

2 Press the ← or → key to move the flashing insertion point to where you want to remove or add characters.

3 To remove the character to the left of the insertion point, press the ←Backspace key.

4 To add data where the insertion point flashes on your screen, type the data.

5 When you finish making changes to the formula, press the Enter key.

Excel helps you enter functions into your worksheet. Functions allow you to perform calculations without typing long, complex formulas.

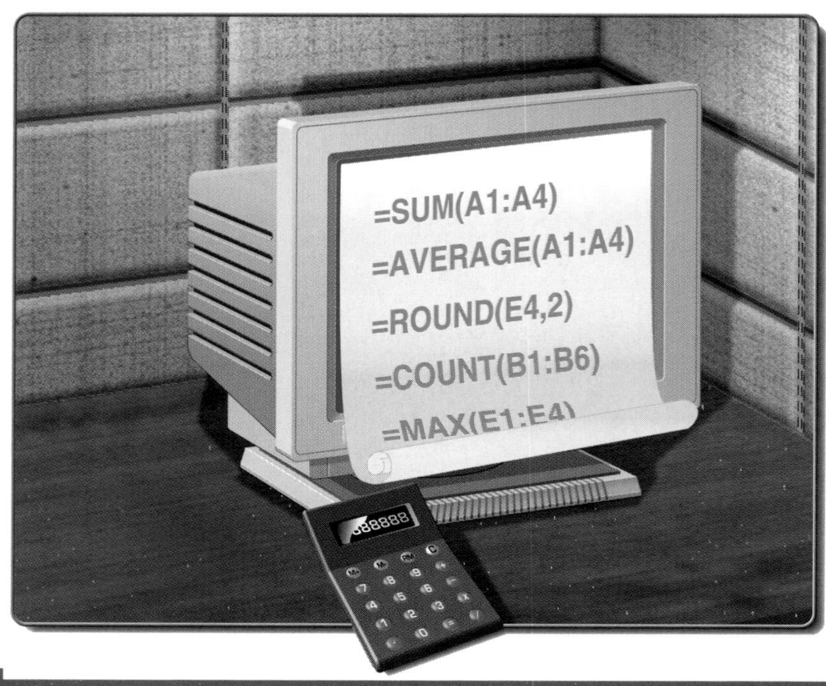

Excel offers over 200 functions to help you analyze data in your worksheet. There are financial functions, math and trigonometry functions, date and time functions, statistical functions and many more.

ENTER A FUNCTION

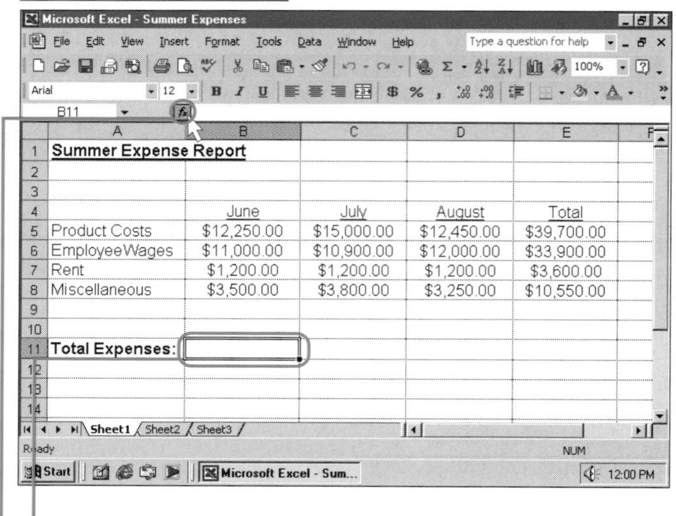

1 Click the cell where you want to enter a function.

2 Click [fx] to enter a function.

■ The Insert Function dialog box appears.

*Note: The Office Assistant may also appear. Click **No** to remove the Office Assistant from your screen.*

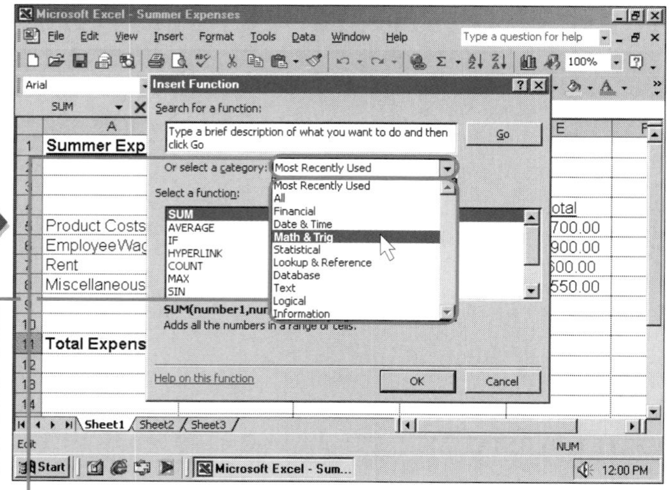

3 Click this area to display the categories of available functions.

4 Click the category containing the function you want to use.

*Note: If you do not know which category contains the function you want to use, select **All** to display a list of all the functions.*

Can Excel help me find the function I should use to perform a calculation?

If you do not know which function to use to perform a calculation, you can have Excel recommend a function.

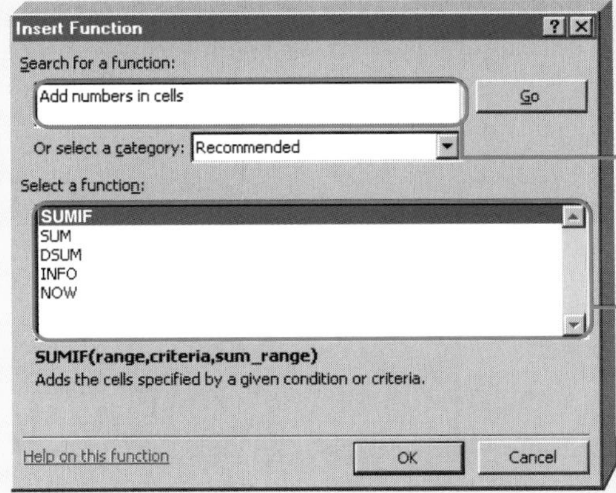

1 Perform steps 1 and 2 below to display the Insert Function dialog box.

2 Type a brief description of the calculation you want to perform and then press the Enter key.

■ This area displays a list of recommended functions you can use to perform the calculation. You can perform steps 5 to 11 below to use a function Excel recommends.

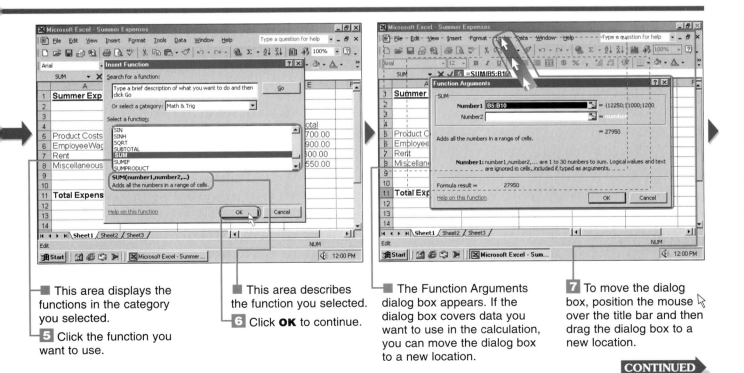

■ This area displays the functions in the category you selected.

5 Click the function you want to use.

■ This area describes the function you selected.

6 Click **OK** to continue.

■ The Function Arguments dialog box appears. If the dialog box covers data you want to use in the calculation, you can move the dialog box to a new location.

7 To move the dialog box, position the mouse over the title bar and then drag the dialog box to a new location.

CONTINUED

When entering a function, you must specify which numbers you want to use in the calculation.

ENTER A FUNCTION (CONTINUED)

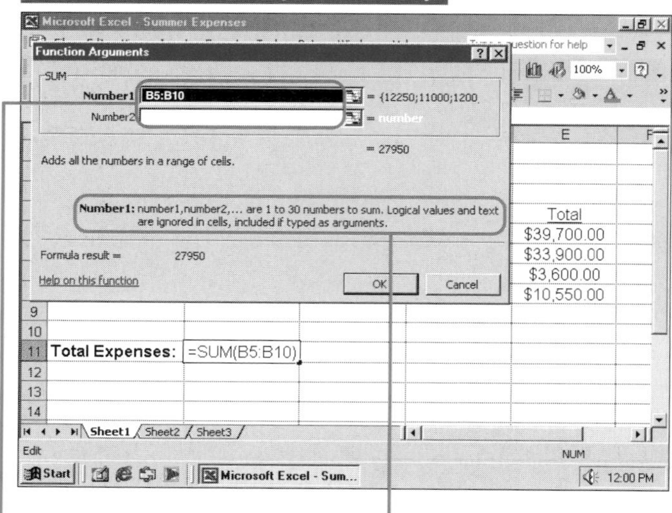

■ This area displays boxes where you enter the numbers you want to use in the calculation.

■ This area describes the numbers you need to enter.

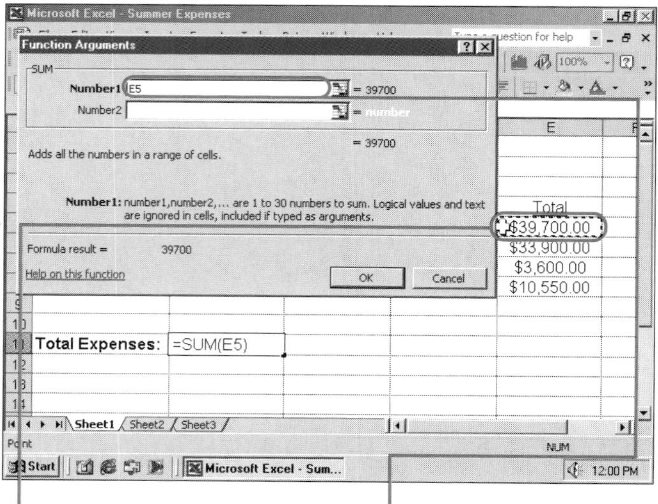

8 To enter the first number for the function, click the cell that contains the number.

Note: If the number you want to use does not appear in your worksheet, type the number.

■ The cell reference for the number appears in this area.

Can I enter a function myself?

If you know the name of the function you want to use, you can type the function and cell references directly into a cell in your worksheet. You must start the function with an equal sign (=), enclose the cell references in parentheses ( ) and separate the cell references with commas (,) or a colon (:).

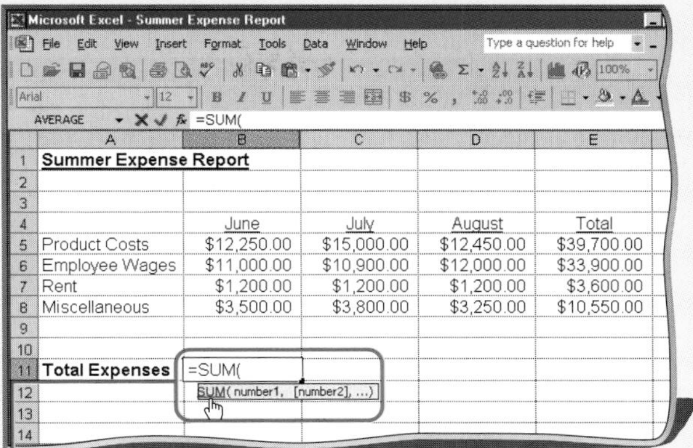

■ When you type a function directly into a cell, a yellow box appears, displaying the name of the function. You can click the name of the function to display help information about the function.

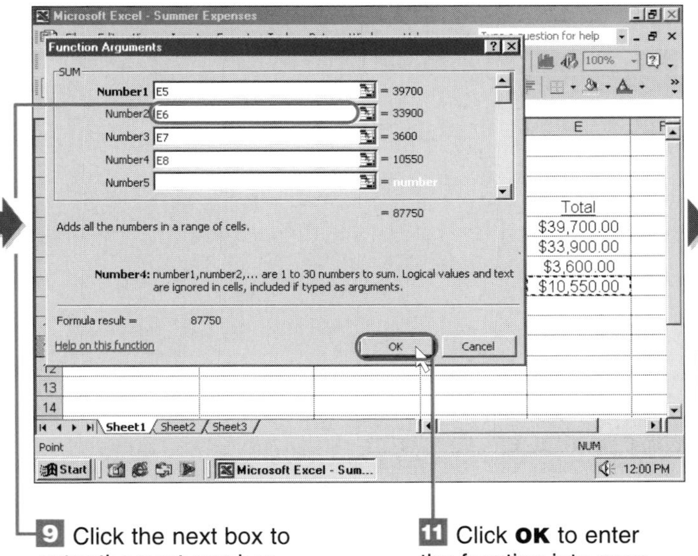

9 Click the next box to enter the next number.

10 Repeat steps **8** and **9** until you have entered all the numbers you want to use in the calculation.

11 Click **OK** to enter the function into your worksheet.

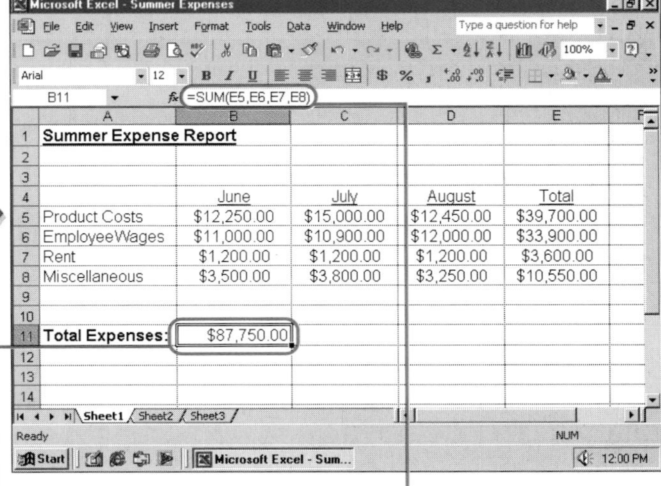

■ The result of the function appears in the cell.

■ The formula bar displays the function for the cell.

PERFORM COMMON CALCULATIONS

You can quickly perform common calculations on numbers in your worksheet. For example, you can calculate the sum of a list of numbers.

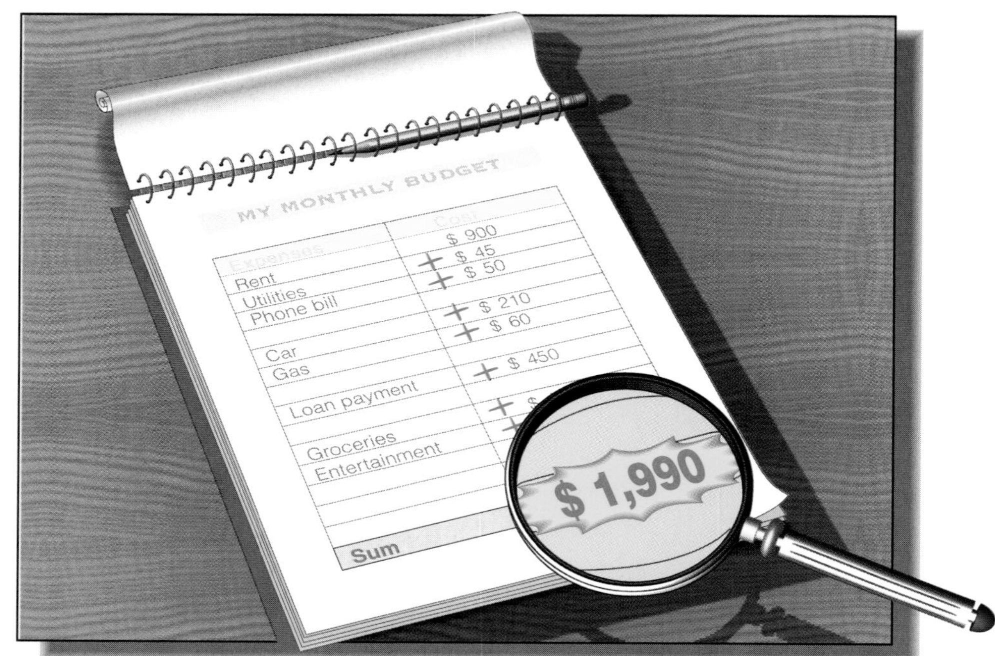

PERFORM COMMON CALCULATIONS

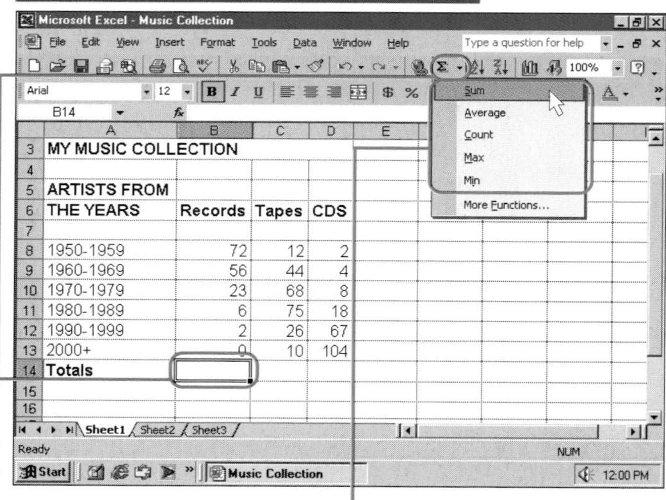

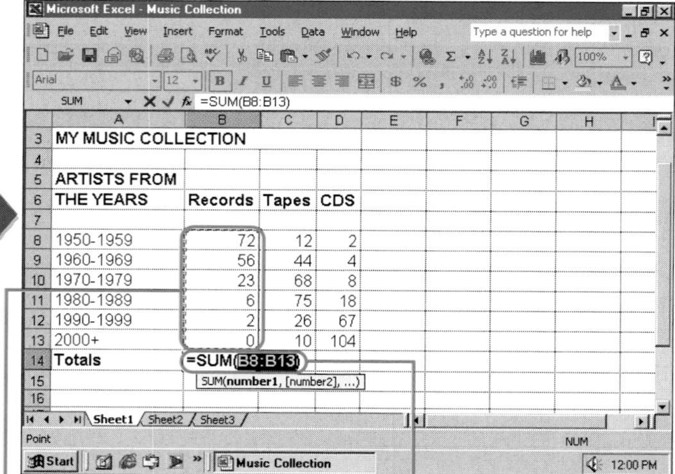

1 Click the cell below or to the right of the cells containing the numbers you want to include in the calculation.

2 Click ▾ in this area to display a list of common calculations.

Note: If Σ ▾ is not displayed, click » on the Standard toolbar to display all the buttons.

3 Click the calculation you want to perform.

Note: If you want to quickly add the numbers, you can click Σ instead of performing steps 2 and 3.

■ A moving outline appears around the cells that Excel will include in the calculation.

■ If Excel outlines the wrong cells, you can select the cells that contain the numbers you want to include in the calculation. To select cells, see page 106.

■ The cell you selected in step 1 displays the function Excel will use to perform the calculation.

What common calculations can I perform?

Sum	Adds a list of numbers.
Average	Calculates the average value of a list of numbers.
Count	Calculates the number of values in a list.
Max	Find the largest value in a list of numbers.
Min	Finds the smallest value in a list of numbers.

Can I perform calculations on several columns or rows of data at the same time?

Yes. Select the cells below or to the right of the cells that contain the numbers you want to include in the calculation. To select cells, see page 106. Then perform steps 2 and 3 on page 142.

	Product A	Product B	Month Totals
January	10	5	
February	20	6	
March	30	3	

	Product A	Product B	Month Totals
January	10	5	15
February	20	6	26
March	30	3	33

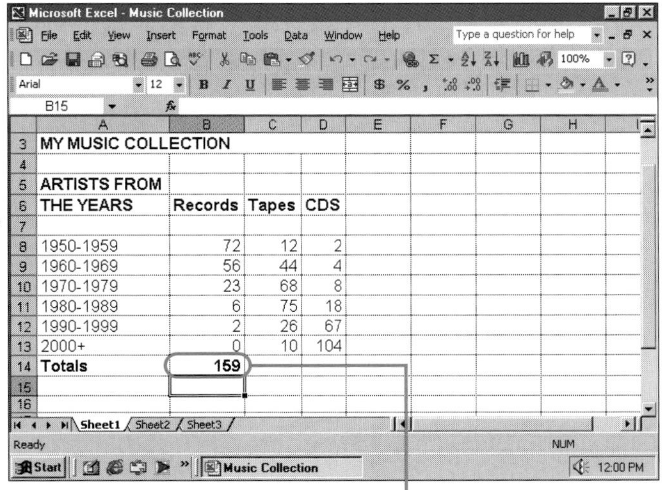

4 Press the Enter key to perform the calculation.

■ The result of the calculation appears.

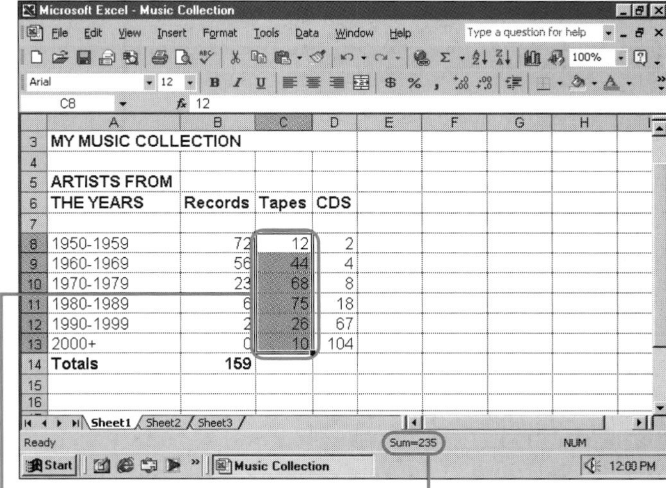

QUICKLY ADD NUMBERS

You can quickly display the sum of a list of numbers without entering a formula into your worksheet.

1 Select the cells containing the numbers you want to add. To select cells, see page 106.

■ This area displays the sum of the cells you selected.

COPY A FORMULA

If you want to use the same formula several times in your worksheet, you can save time by copying the formula.

A relative reference is a cell reference that changes when you copy a formula.

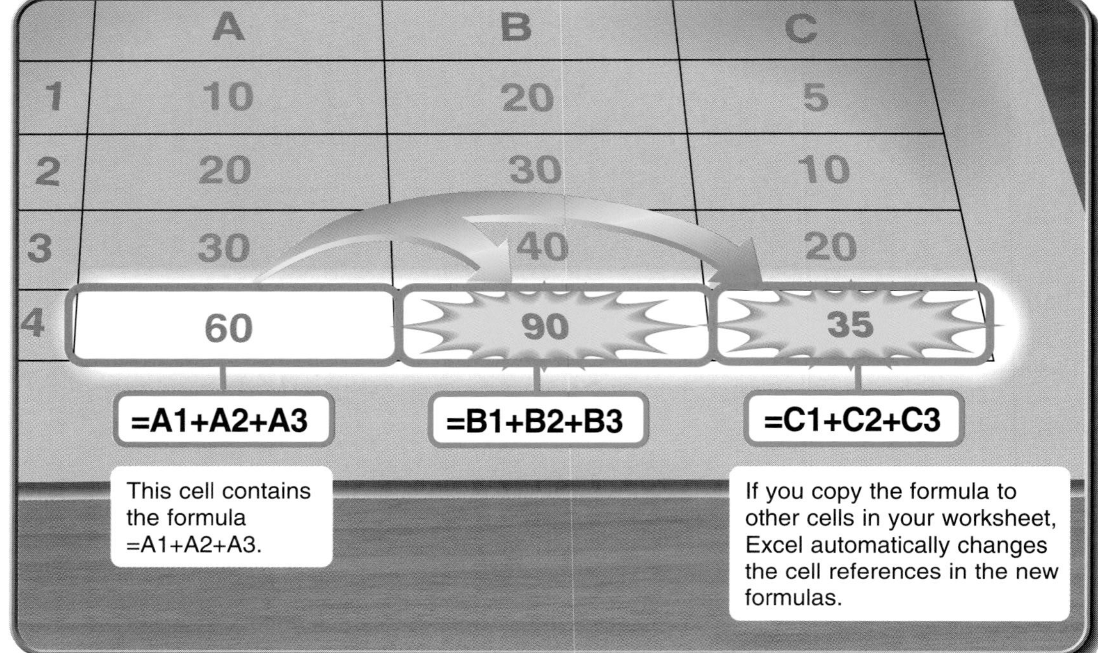

COPY A FORMULA

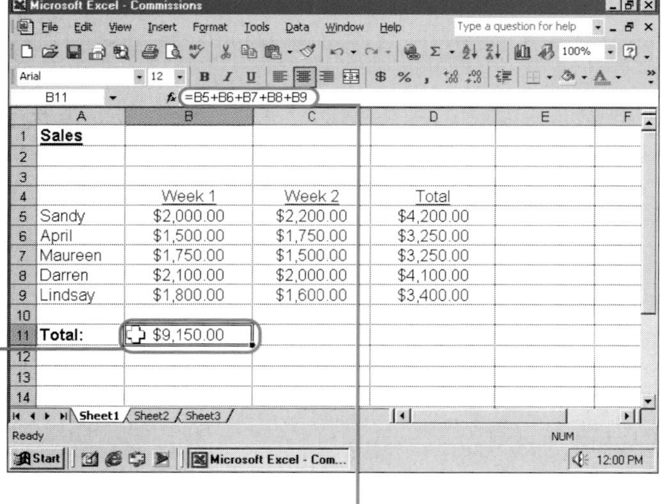

1 Enter the formula you want to copy to other cells. To enter a formula, see page 136.

2 Click the cell containing the formula you want to copy.

■ The formula bar displays the formula for the cell.

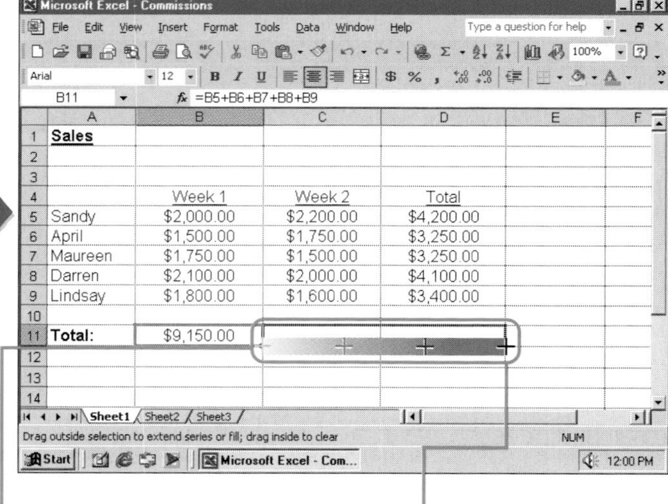

3 Position the mouse ✥ over the bottom right corner of the cell (✥ changes to +).

4 Drag the mouse + over the cells you want to receive a copy of the formula.

I do not want Excel to change a cell reference when I copy a formula. What can I do?

You can use an absolute reference in the formula. An absolute reference is a cell reference that does not change when you copy a formula. To make a cell reference absolute, type a dollar sign ($) before both the column letter and row number, such as A7.

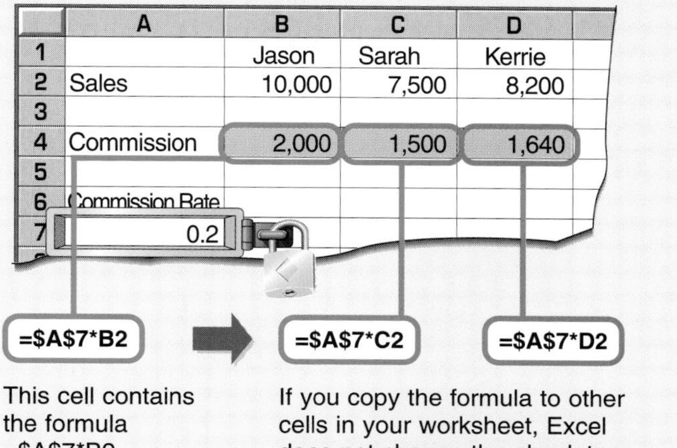

This cell contains the formula =A7*B2.

If you copy the formula to other cells in your worksheet, Excel does not change the absolute reference in the new formulas.

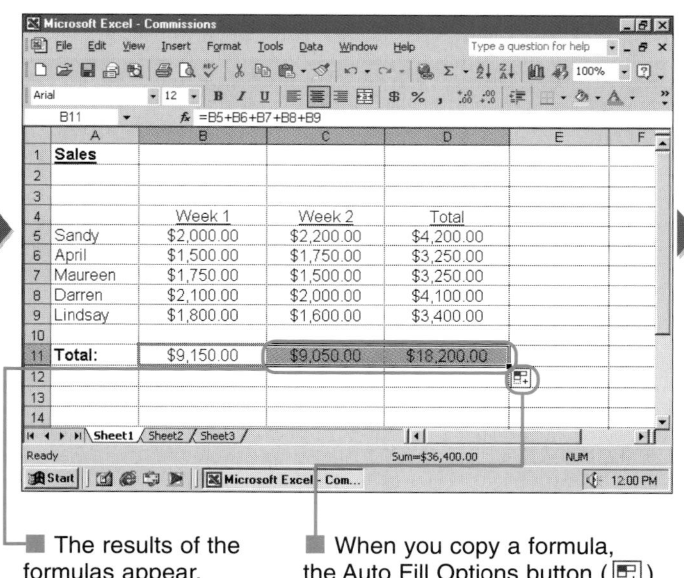

■ The results of the formulas appear.

■ When you copy a formula, the Auto Fill Options button ( ) appears. The Auto Fill Options button allows you to change the way Excel copies a formula. You can click the button to display a list of options and then select the option you want to use.

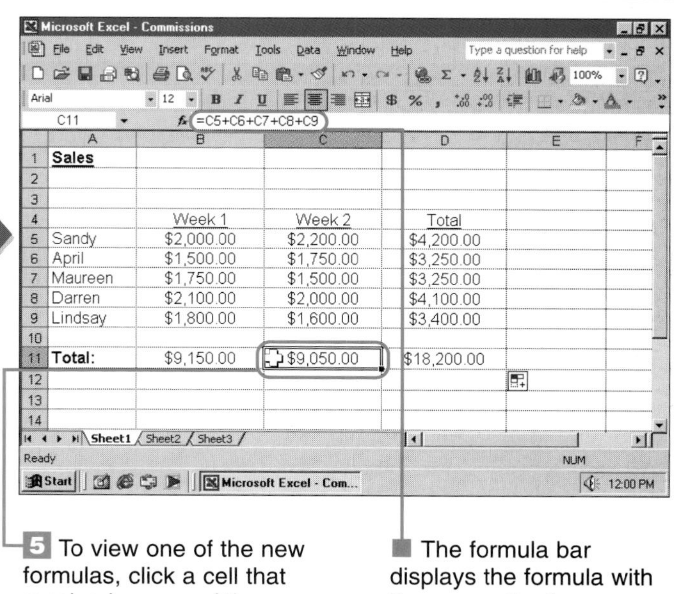

5 To view one of the new formulas, click a cell that received a copy of the formula.

■ The formula bar displays the formula with the new cell references.

CHECK ERRORS IN FORMULAS

Excel can help you determine the cause of an error in a formula.

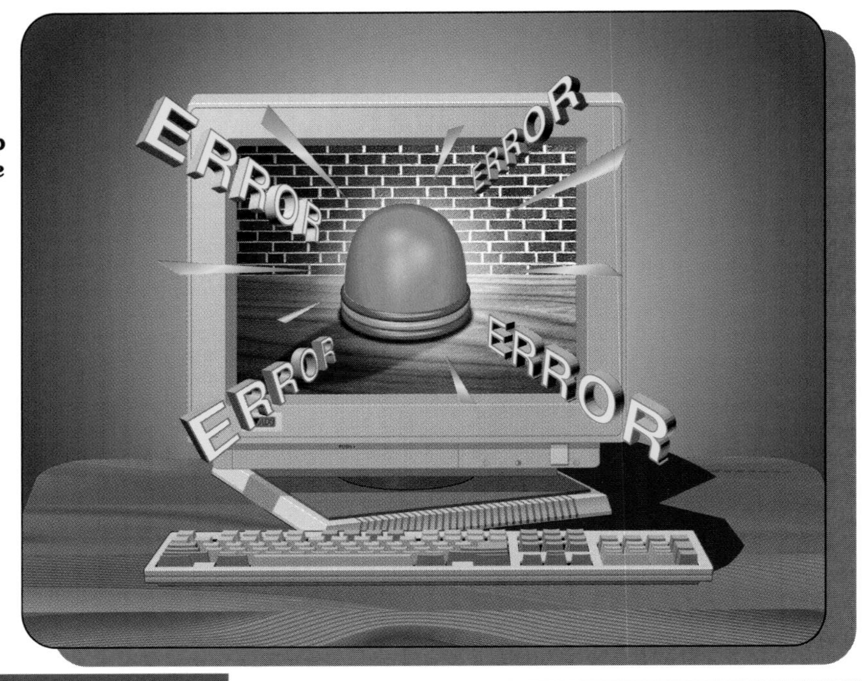

Excel checks your formulas for errors as you work and marks cells that display the #DIV/0!, #NAME?, #REF! or #VALUE! error message. For information on error messages, see page 147.

Errors in formulas are often the result of typing mistakes. Once you determine the cause of an error, you can edit the formula to correct the error. To edit a formula, see page 137.

CHECK ERRORS IN FORMULAS

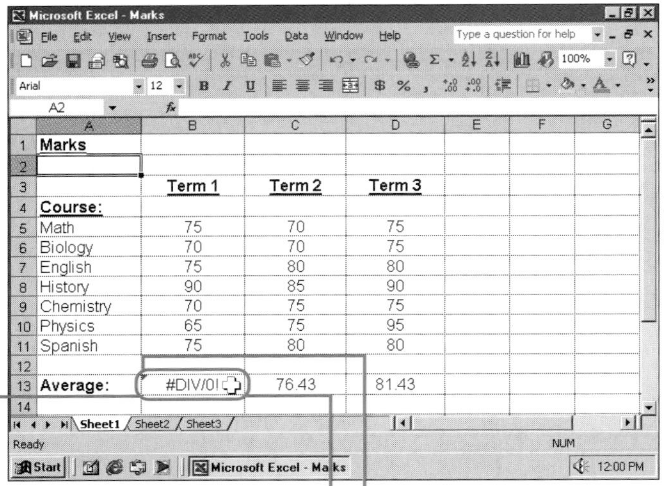

■ An error message appears in a cell when Excel cannot properly calculate the result of a formula.

■ A triangle appears in the top left corner of a cell displaying an error message when Excel can help you determine the cause of the error.

1 To determine the cause of an error, click a cell displaying a triangle.

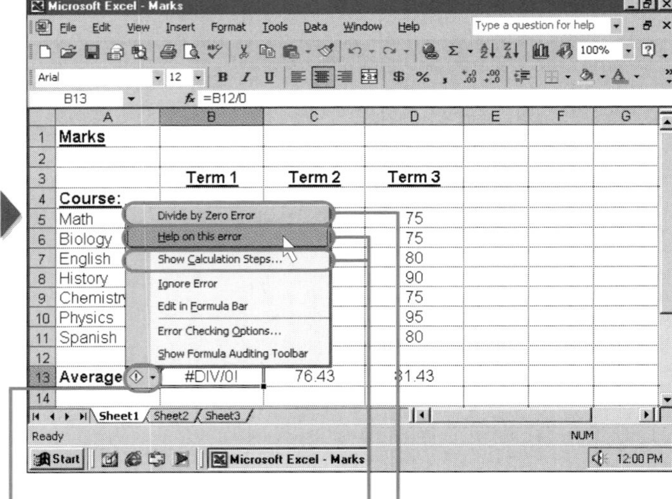

■ The Error Checking button ( ) appears.

2 Click the Error Checking button to display options you can use to determine the cause of the error.

■ This area displays the name of the error.

3 You can click **Help on this error** to view help information for the error.

■ You can click **Show Calculation Steps** to have Excel help you evaluate the cause of the error.

ERRORS IN FORMULAS

An error message appears when Excel cannot properly calculate or display the result of a formula.

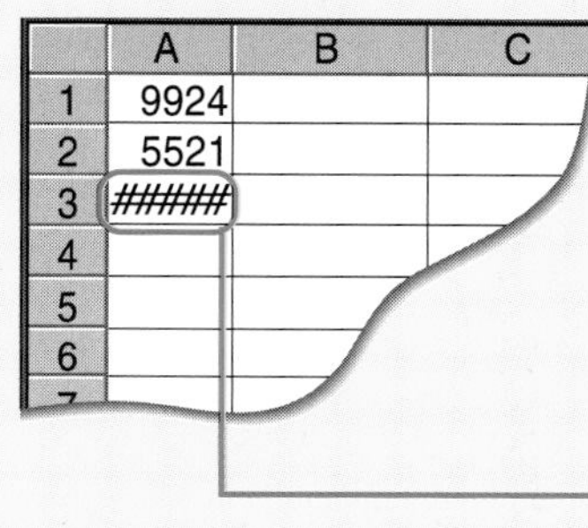

#####

The column is too narrow to display the result of the calculation. You can change the column width to display the result. To change the column width, see page 148.

■ This cell contains the formula: =A1*A2

#DIV/0!

The formula divides a number by zero (0). Excel considers a blank cell to have a value of zero.

■ This cell contains the formula: =A1/A2
=50/0

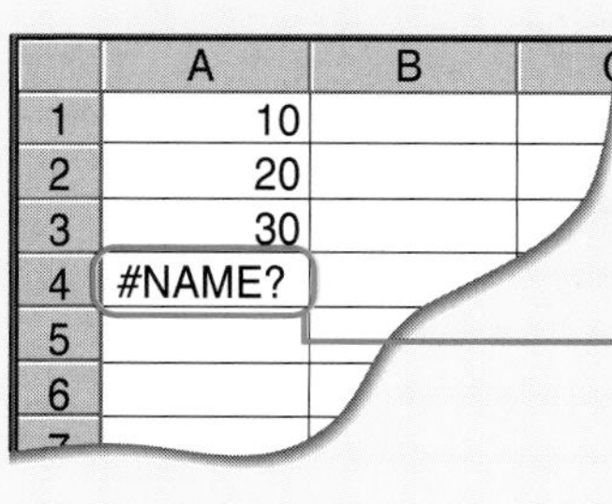

#NAME?

The formula contains a function name or cell reference Excel does not recognize.

■ This cell contains the formula: =AQ+A2+A3

In this example, the cell reference A1 was typed incorrectly.

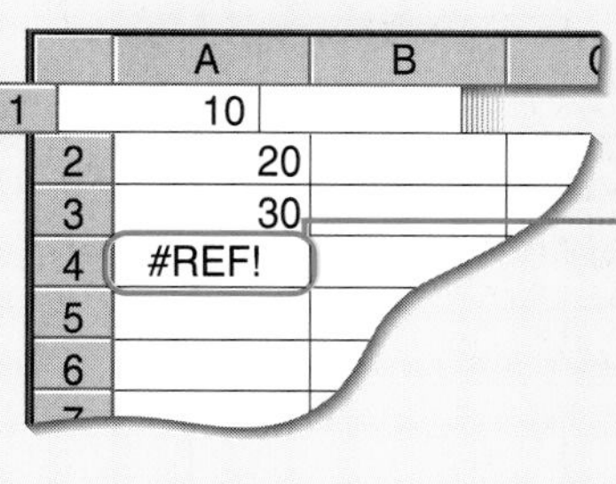

#REF!

The formula refers to a cell that is not valid.

■ This cell contains the formula: =A1+A2+A3

In this example, a row containing a cell used in the formula was deleted.

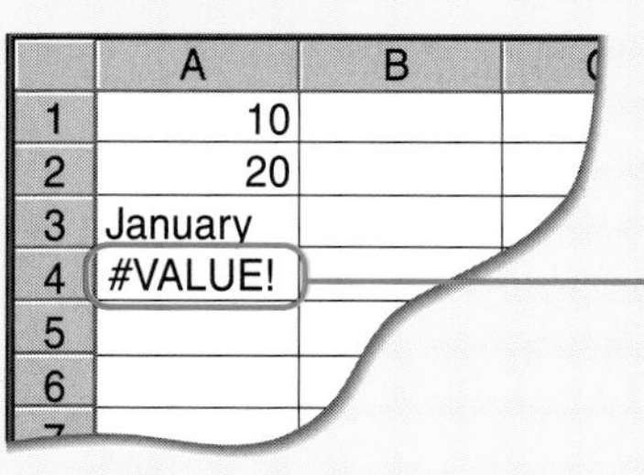

#VALUE!

The formula refers to a cell that Excel cannot use in a calculation.

■ This cell contains the formula: =A1+A2+A3

In this example, a cell used in the formula contains text.

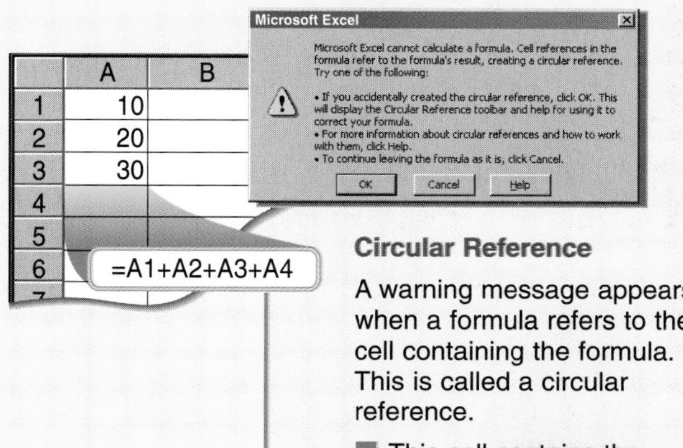

Circular Reference

A warning message appears when a formula refers to the cell containing the formula. This is called a circular reference.

■ This cell contains the formula: =A1+A2+A3+A4

CHANGE COLUMN WIDTH

You can change the width of columns to improve the appearance of your worksheet and display any hidden data.

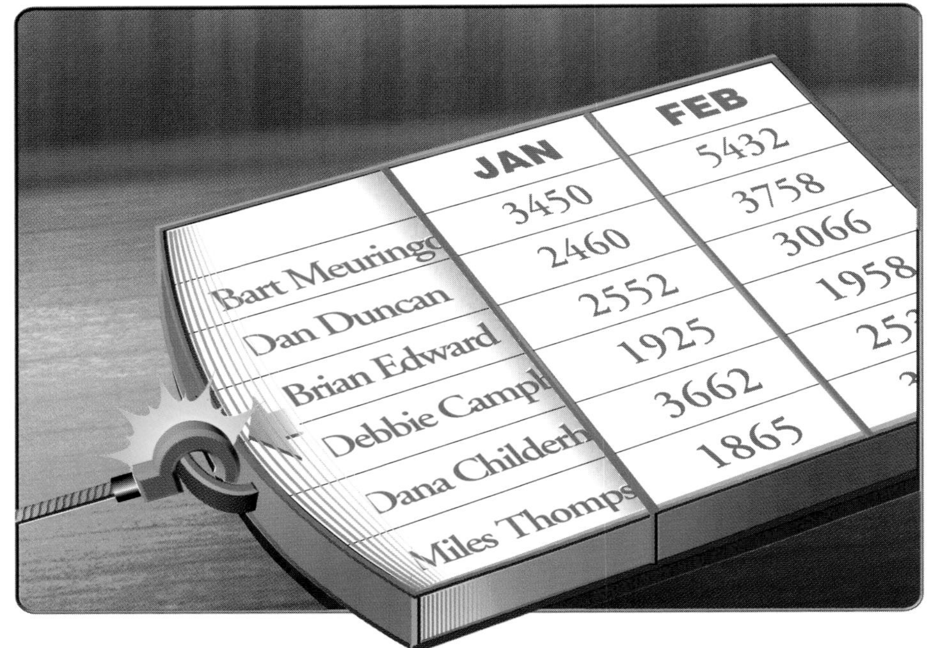

The text in a cell may be hidden if the text spills into a neighboring cell that contains data. You can increase the column width to display all the text in the cell.

CHANGE COLUMN WIDTH

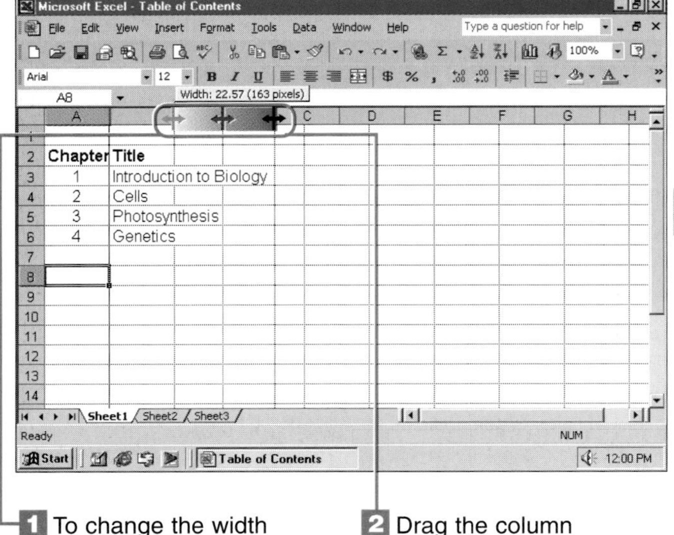

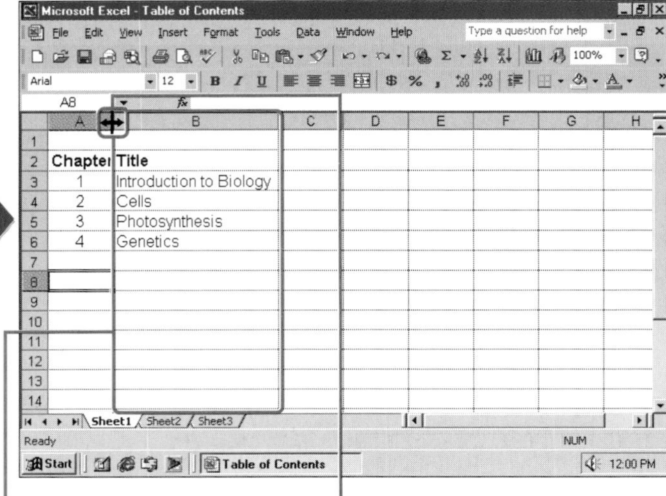

1 To change the width of a column, position the mouse ✥ over the right edge of the column heading (✥ changes to ↔).

2 Drag the column edge until the dotted line displays the column width you want.

■ The column displays the new width.

FIT LONGEST ITEM

1 To change a column width to fit the longest item in the column, double-click the right edge of the column heading.

CHANGE ROW HEIGHT

You can change the height of rows to add space between the rows of data in your worksheet.

CHANGE ROW HEIGHT

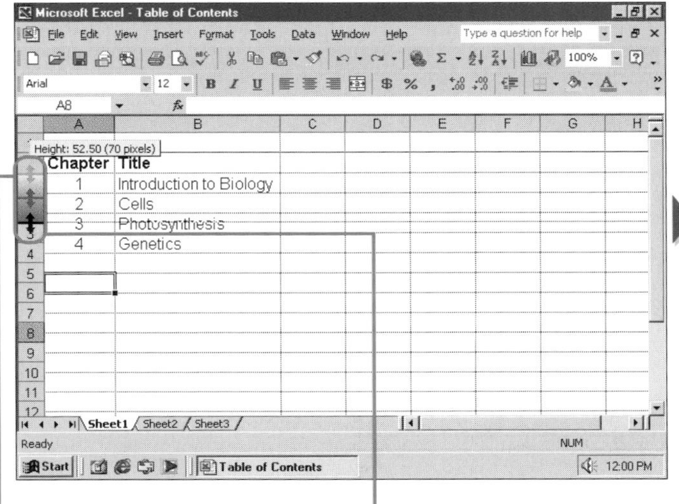

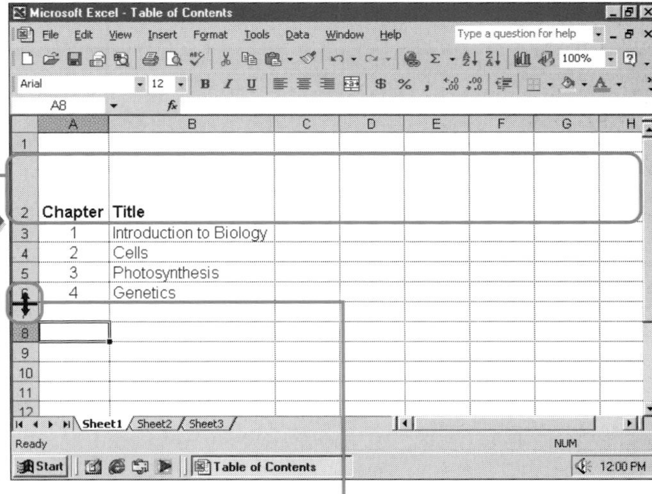

1 To change the height of a row, position the mouse ✥ over the bottom edge of the row heading (✥ changes to ✛).

2 Drag the row edge until the dotted line displays the row height you want.

■ The row displays the new height.

FIT TALLEST ITEM

1 To change a row height to fit the tallest item in the row, double-click the bottom edge of the row heading.

CHANGE FONT OF DATA

You can change the font of data to enhance the appearance of your worksheet.

CHANGE FONT OF DATA

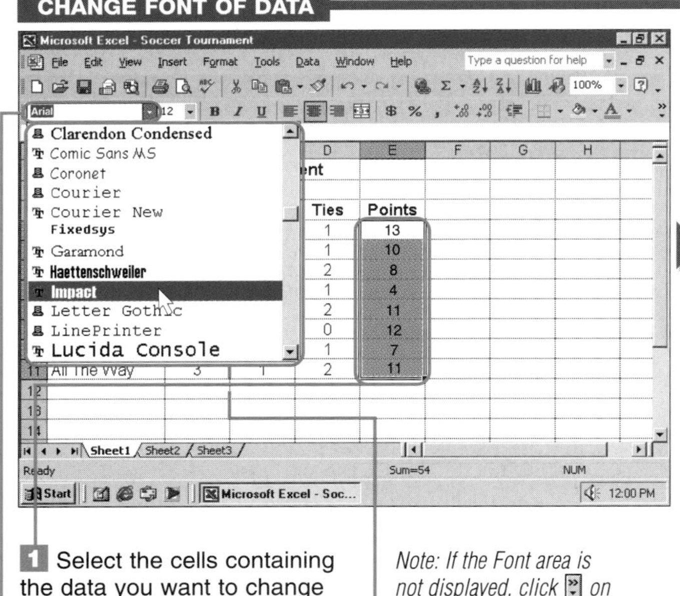

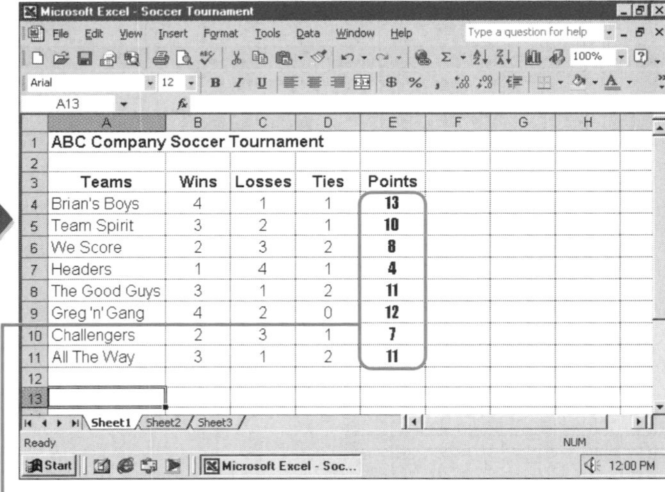

1 Select the cells containing the data you want to change to a different font. To select cells, see page 106.

2 Click ▾ in this area to display a list of the available fonts.

Note: If the Font area is not displayed, click » on the Formatting toolbar to display the area.

3 Click the font you want to use.

■ The data changes to the font you selected.

■ To deselect cells, click any cell.

CHANGE SIZE OF DATA

You can increase or decrease the size of data in your worksheet.

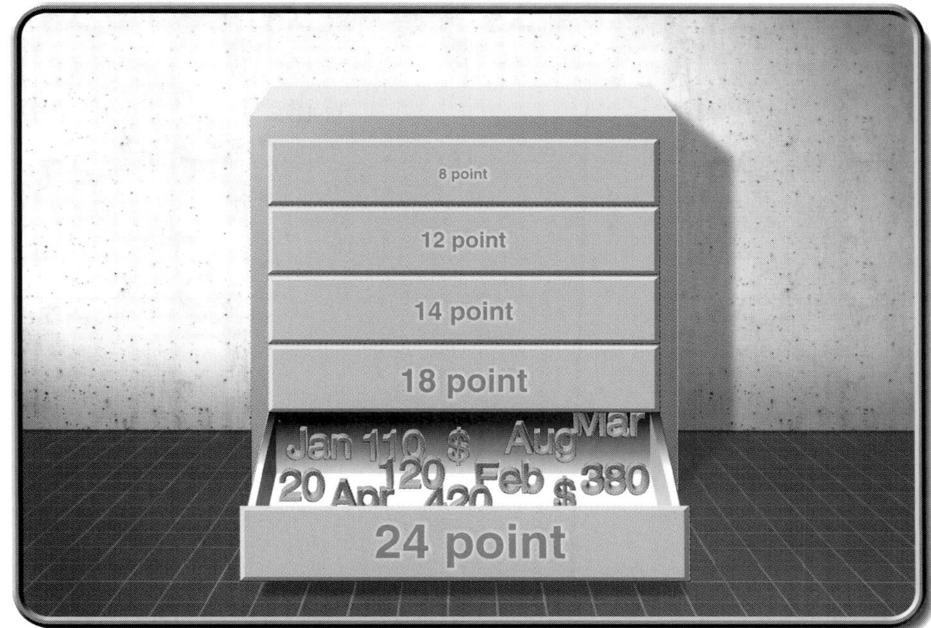

Larger data is easier to read, but smaller data allows you to fit more information on a page.

CHANGE SIZE OF DATA

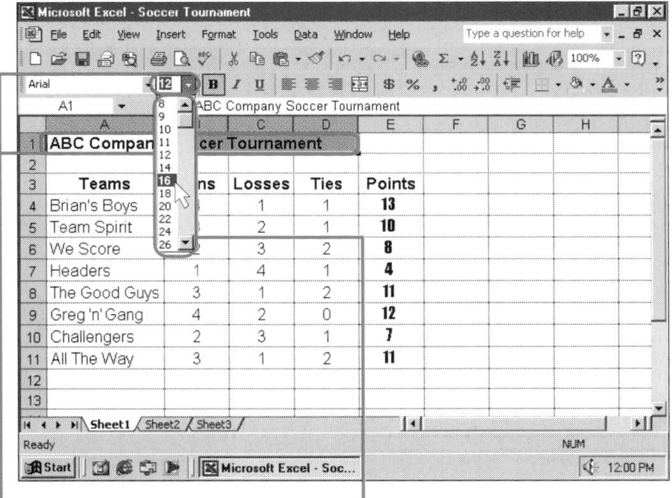

1 Select the cells containing the data you want to change to a new size. To select cells, see page 106.

2 Click ▾ in this area to display a list of the available sizes.

Note: If the Font Size area is not displayed, click » on the Formatting toolbar to display the area.

3 Click the size you want to use.

■ The data changes to the size you selected.

■ To deselect cells, click any cell.

CHANGE NUMBER FORMAT

You can change the appearance of numbers in your worksheet without retyping the numbers.

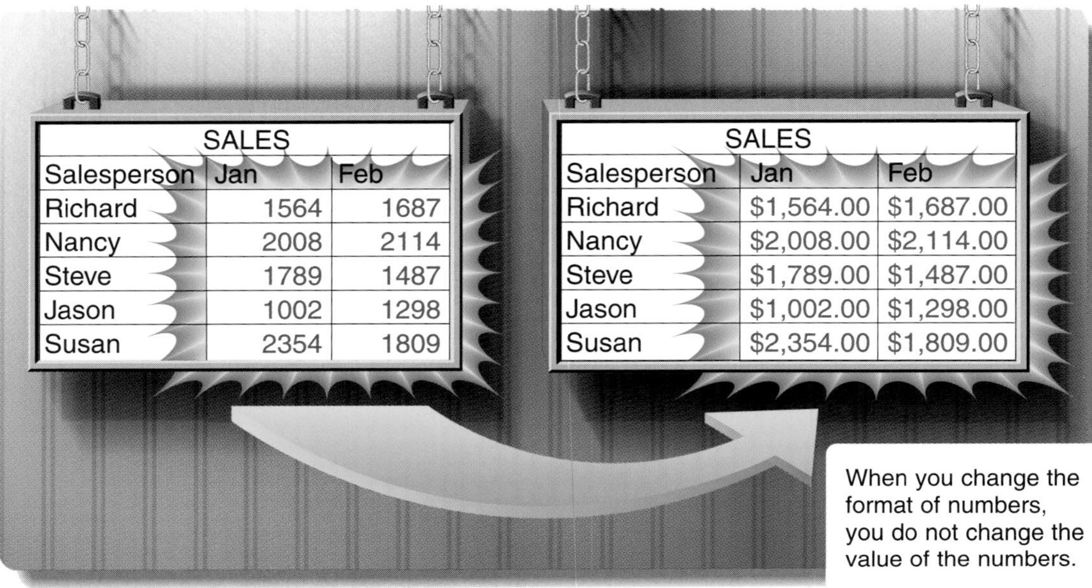

When you change the format of numbers, you do not change the value of the numbers.

CHANGE NUMBER FORMAT

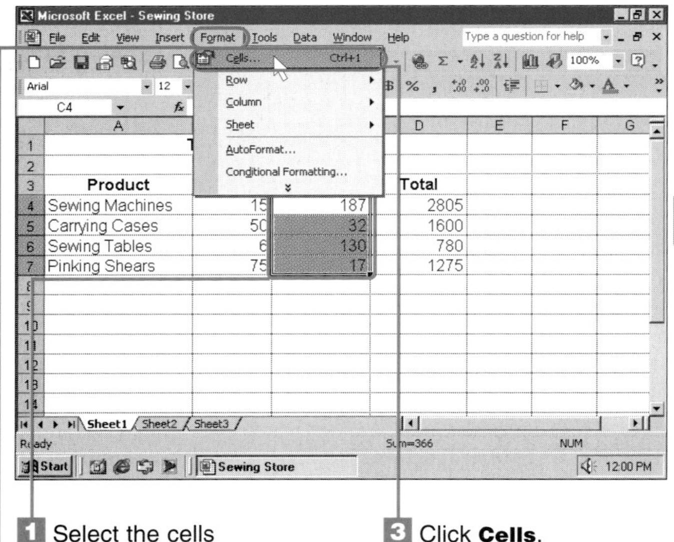

1 Select the cells containing the numbers you want to format. To select cells, see page 106.

2 Click **Format**.

3 Click **Cells**.

■ The Format Cells dialog box appears.

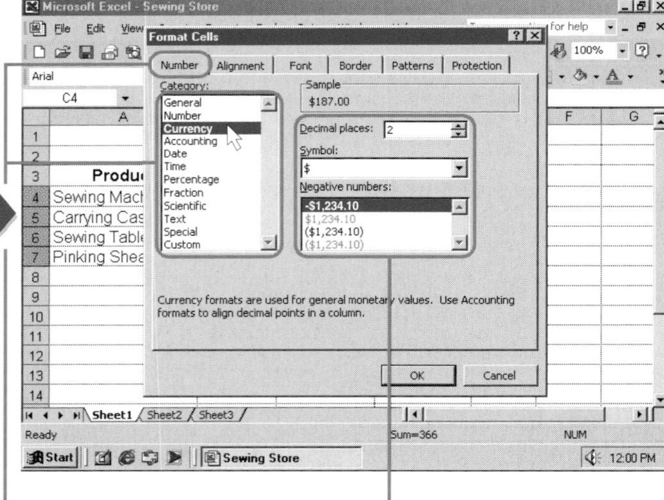

4 Click the **Number** tab.

5 Click the category that describes the numbers in the cells you selected.

■ This area displays the options for the category you selected. The available options depend on the category you selected.

What categories are available for formatting numbers?

Category:	Description:	Example:
General	Applies no specific number format.	100
Number	Used to format numbers for general display.	100.00
Currency	Used to format monetary values.	$100.00
Accounting	Aligns the currency symbols and decimal points in a column of monetary values.	$ 100.00 $ 1200.00
Date	Used to format dates.	23-Apr-01
Time	Used to format times.	12:00 PM
Percentage	Used to format percentages.	25.00%
Fraction	Used to format fractions.	1/4
Scientific	Used to format numbers in scientific notation.	1.00E+02
Text	Treats numbers as text.	135 Hillcrest Street
Special	Used to format special numbers, such as ZIP codes.	90210
Custom	Allows you to apply your own number format.	3-45-678

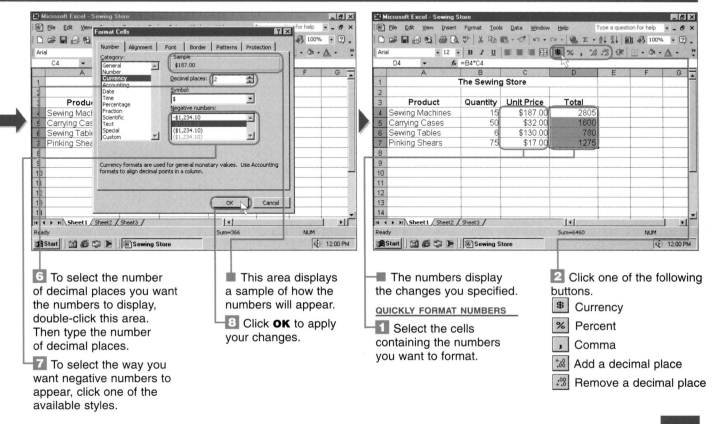

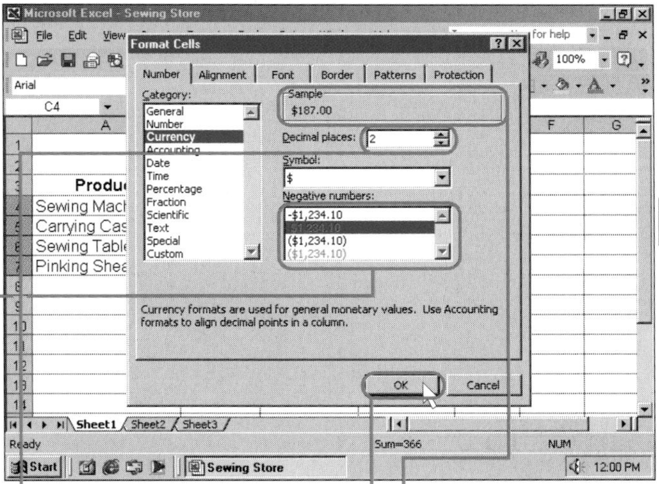

6 To select the number of decimal places you want the numbers to display, double-click this area. Then type the number of decimal places.

7 To select the way you want negative numbers to appear, click one of the available styles.

■ This area displays a sample of how the numbers will appear.

8 Click **OK** to apply your changes.

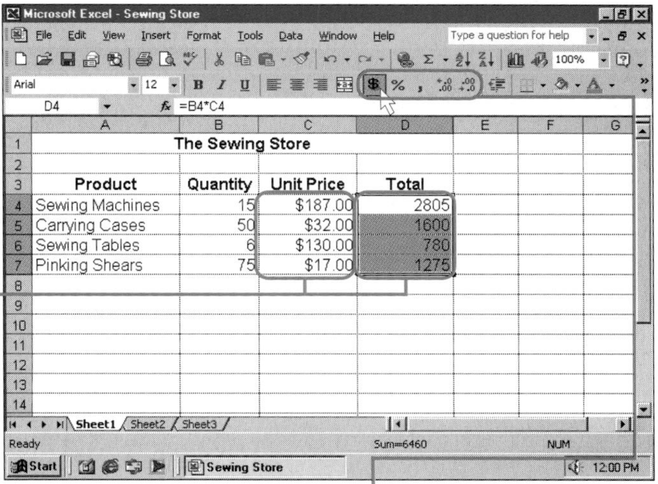

■ The numbers display the changes you specified.

QUICKLY FORMAT NUMBERS

1 Select the cells containing the numbers you want to format.

2 Click one of the following buttons.

- $ Currency
- % Percent
- , Comma
- +.0 .00 Add a decimal place
- .00 +.0 Remove a decimal place

CHANGE DATA COLOR

You can change the color of data in your worksheet to draw attention to headings or important information.

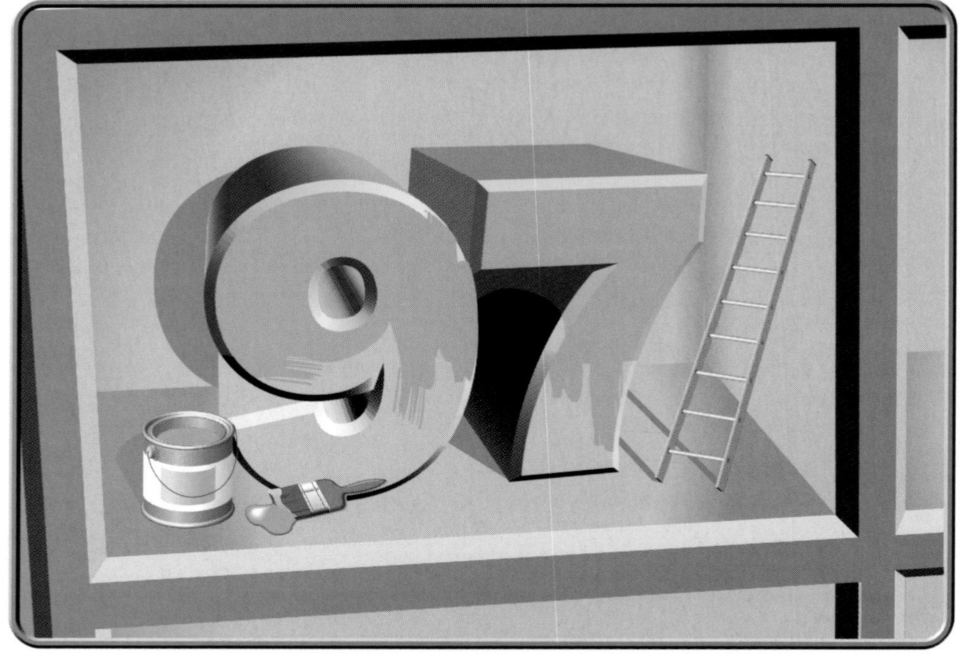

CHANGE DATA COLOR

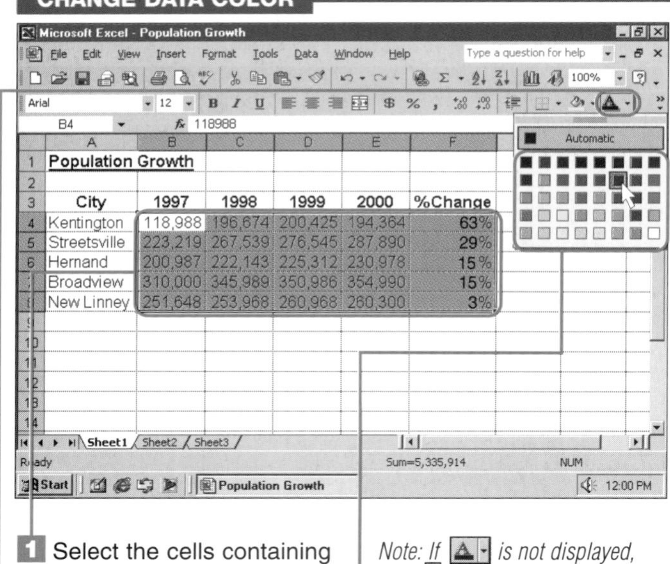

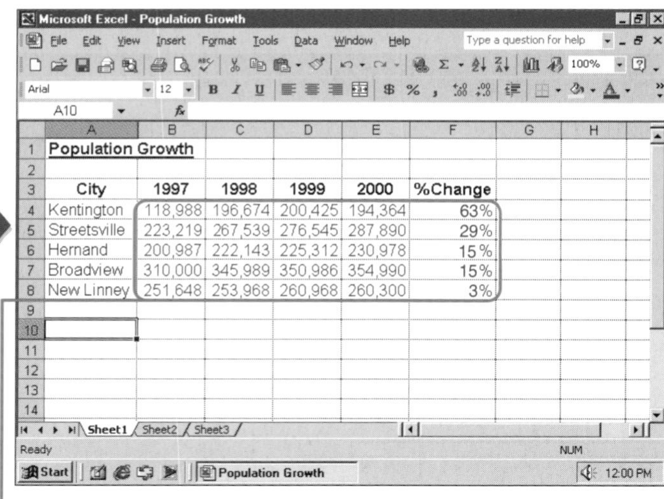

1 Select the cells containing the data you want to change to a different color. To select cells, see page 106.

2 Click ▾ in this area to display the available colors.

Note: If A ▾ *is not displayed, click* » *on the Formatting toolbar to display all the buttons.*

3 Click the color you want to use.

■ The data appears in the color you selected.

■ To deselect cells, click any cell.

■ To return data to its original color, repeat steps **1** to **3**, selecting **Automatic** in step **3**.

CHANGE CELL COLOR

You can add color to cells to make the cells stand out in your worksheet.

Adding color to cells is useful for marking data you want to review or verify later.

CHANGE CELL COLOR

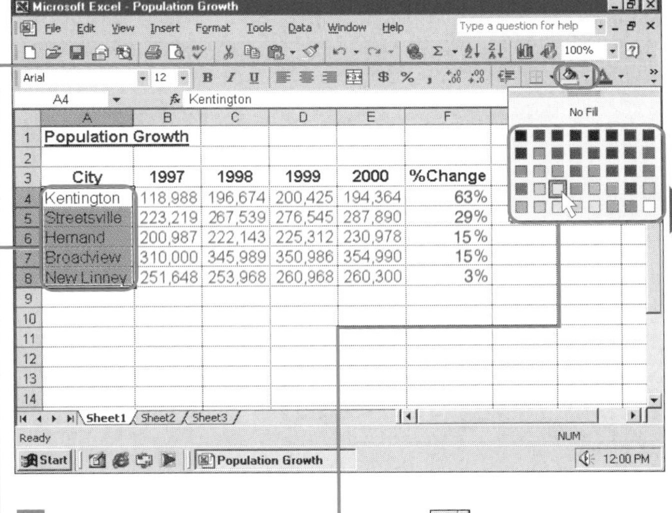

Microsoft Excel - Population Growth

	A	B	C	D	E	F
1	Population Growth					
2						
3	City	1997	1998	1999	2000	%Change
4	Kentington	118,988	196,674	200,425	194,364	63%
5	Streetsville	223,219	267,539	276,545	287,890	29%
6	Hernand	200,987	222,143	225,312	230,978	15%
7	Broadview	310,000	345,989	350,986	354,990	15%
8	New Linney	251,648	253,968	260,968	260,300	3%

1 Select the cells you want to change to a different color. To select cells, see page 106.

2 Click ▾ in this area to display the available colors.

Note: If the Fill Color button is not displayed, click » on the Formatting toolbar to display all the buttons.

3 Click the color you want to use.

■ The cells appear in the color you selected.

■ To deselect cells, click any cell.

■ To remove color from cells, repeat steps 1 to 3, selecting **No Fill** in step 3

CHANGE ALIGNMENT OF DATA

You can align data in different ways to enhance the appearance of your worksheet.

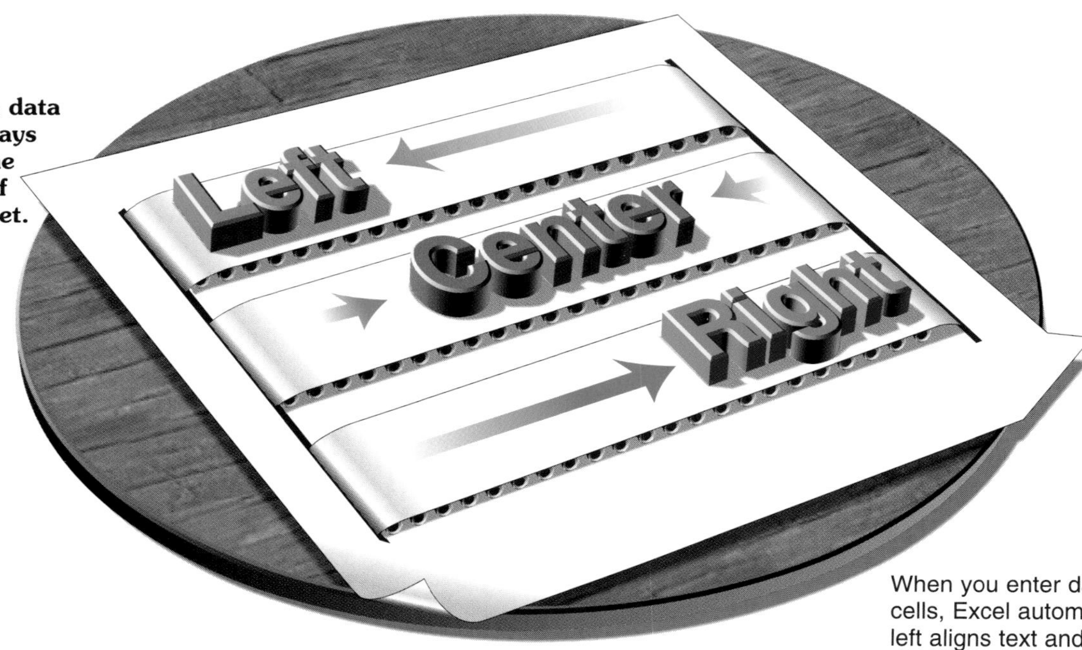

When you enter data into cells, Excel automatically left aligns text and right aligns numbers and dates.

CHANGE ALIGNMENT OF DATA

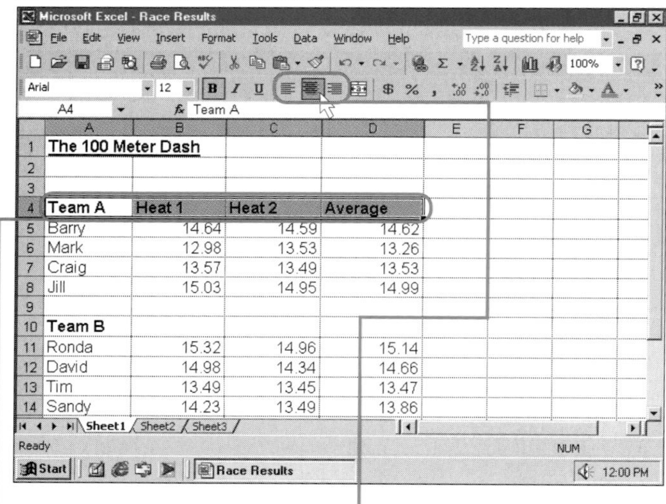

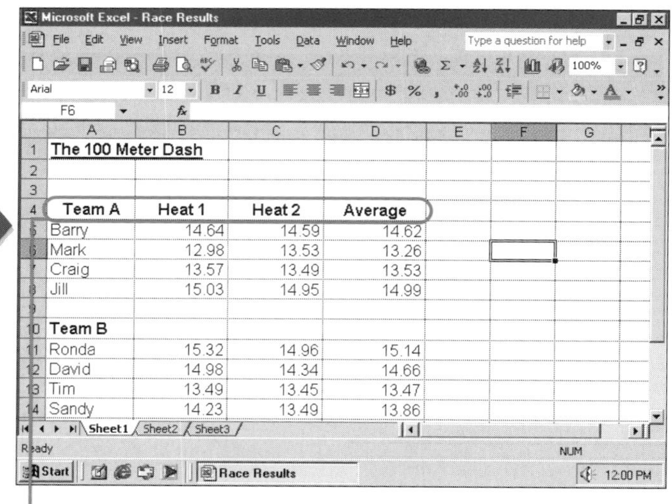

1 Select the cells containing the data you want to align differently. To select cells, see page 106.

2 Click one of the following buttons.

- Left align
- Center
- Right align

Note: If the button you want is not displayed, click » on the Formatting toolbar to display all the buttons.

■ The data appears in the new alignment.

■ To deselect cells, click any cell.

CENTER DATA ACROSS COLUMNS

You can center data across several columns in your worksheet. This is useful for centering titles over your data.

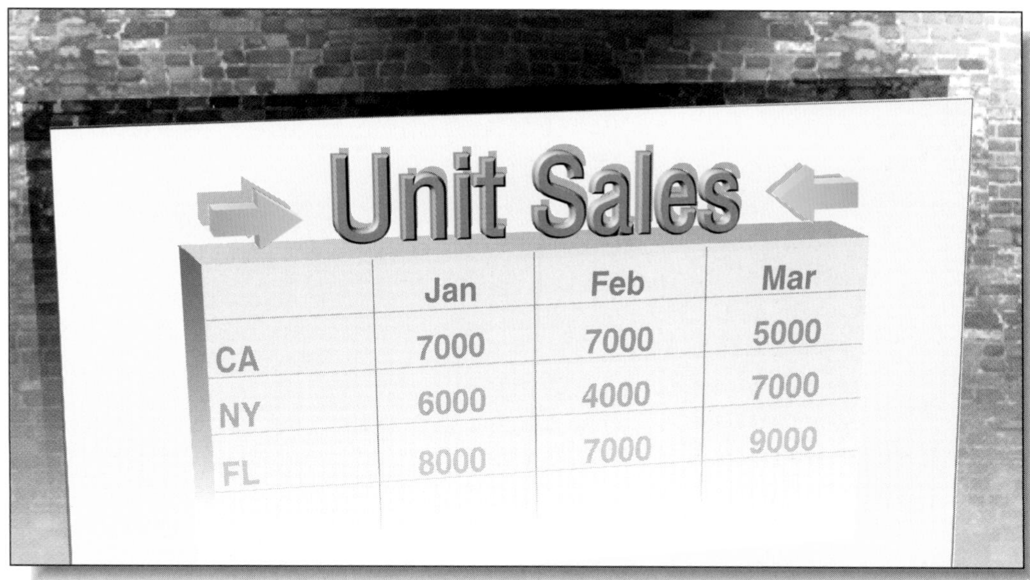

CENTER DATA ACROSS COLUMNS

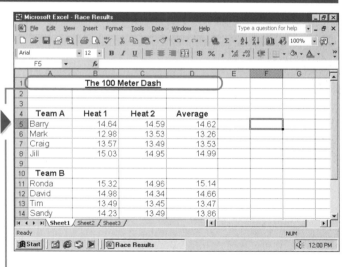

Microsoft Excel - Race Results

A1 | The 100 Meter Dash

	A	B	C	D
1	The 100 Meter Dash			
2				
3				
4	Team A	Heat 1	Heat 2	Average
5	Barry	14.64	14.59	14.62
6	Mark	12.98	13.53	13.26
7	Craig	13.57	13.49	13.53
8	Jill	15.03	14.95	14.99
9				
10	Team B			
11	Ronda	15.32	14.96	15.14
12	David	14.98	14.34	14.66
13	Tim	13.49	13.45	13.47
14	Sandy	14.23	13.49	13.86

Microsoft Excel - Race Results

F5

	A	B	C	D
1		The 100 Meter Dash		
2				
3				
4	Team A	Heat 1	Heat 2	Average
5	Barry	14.64	14.59	14.62
6	Mark	12.98	13.53	13.26
7	Craig	13.57	13.49	13.53
8	Jill	15.03	14.95	14.99
9				
10	Team B			
11	Ronda	15.32	14.96	15.14
12	David	14.98	14.34	14.66
13	Tim	13.49	13.45	13.47
14	Sandy	14.23	13.49	13.86

1 Select the cells you want to center the data across. To select cells, see page 106.

Note: The first cell you select should contain the data you want to center.

2 Click ⊞ to center the data across the columns.

Note: If ⊞ is not displayed, click » on the Formatting toolbar to display all the buttons.

■ Excel centers the data across the columns.

■ If you no longer want to center the data across the columns, click the cell that contains the data and then repeat step **2**.

BOLD, ITALICIZE OR UNDERLINE DATA

You can bold, italicize or underline data to emphasize data in your worksheet.

BOLD, ITALICIZE OR UNDERLINE DATA

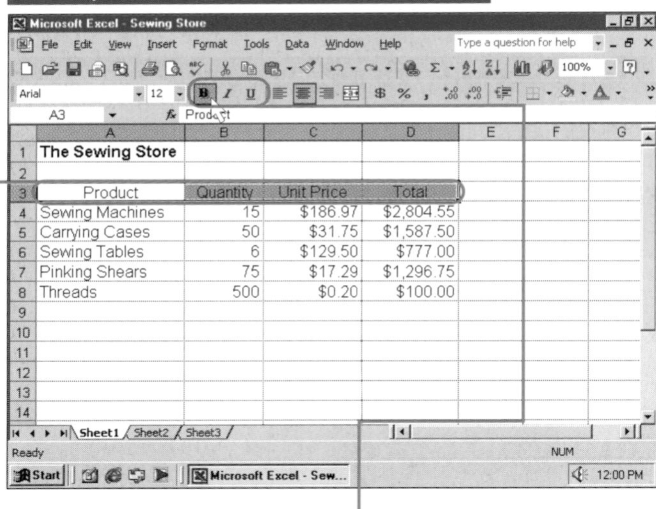

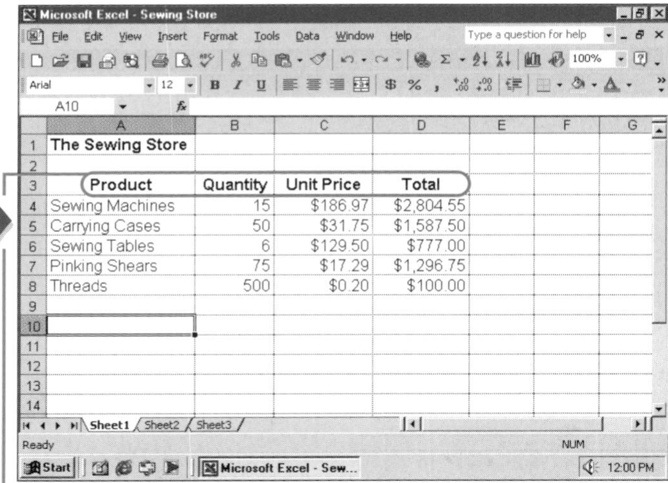

1 Select the cells containing the data you want to bold, italicize or underline. To select cells, see page 106.

2 Click one of the following buttons.

- **B** Bold
- *I* Italic
- U Underline

Note: If the button you want is not displayed, click » on the Formatting toolbar to display all the buttons.

■ The data appears in the style you selected.

■ To deselect cells, click any cell.

■ To remove a bold, italic or underline style, repeat steps **1** and **2**.

COPY FORMATTING

You can copy the formatting of a cell to make other cells in your worksheet look exactly the same.

You may want to copy the formatting of cells to make all the titles in your worksheet look the same. This will give the information in your worksheet a consistent appearance.

COPY FORMATTING

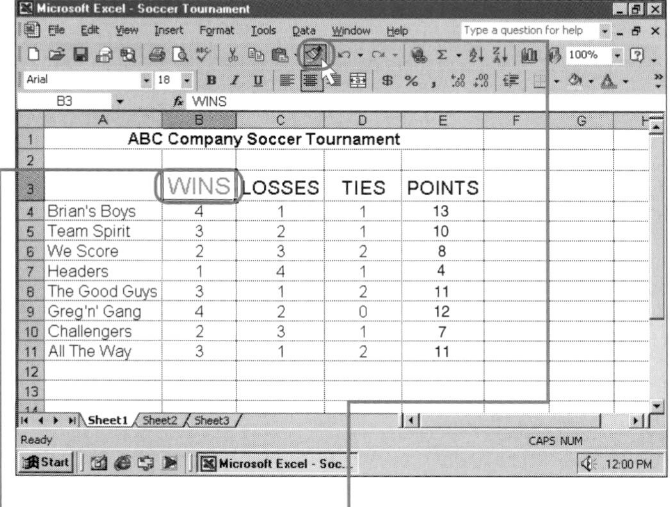

1 Click a cell that displays the formatting you want to copy to other cells.

2 Click to copy the formatting of the cell.

Note: If is not displayed, click on the Standard toolbar to display all the buttons.

■ The mouse changes to when over your worksheet.

3 Select the cells you want to display the same formatting. To select cells, see page 106.

■ The cells you selected display the formatting.

■ To deselect cells, click any cell.

APPLY AN AUTOFORMAT

Excel offers many ready-to-use designs that you can choose from to give your worksheet a professional appearance.

APPLY AN AUTOFORMAT

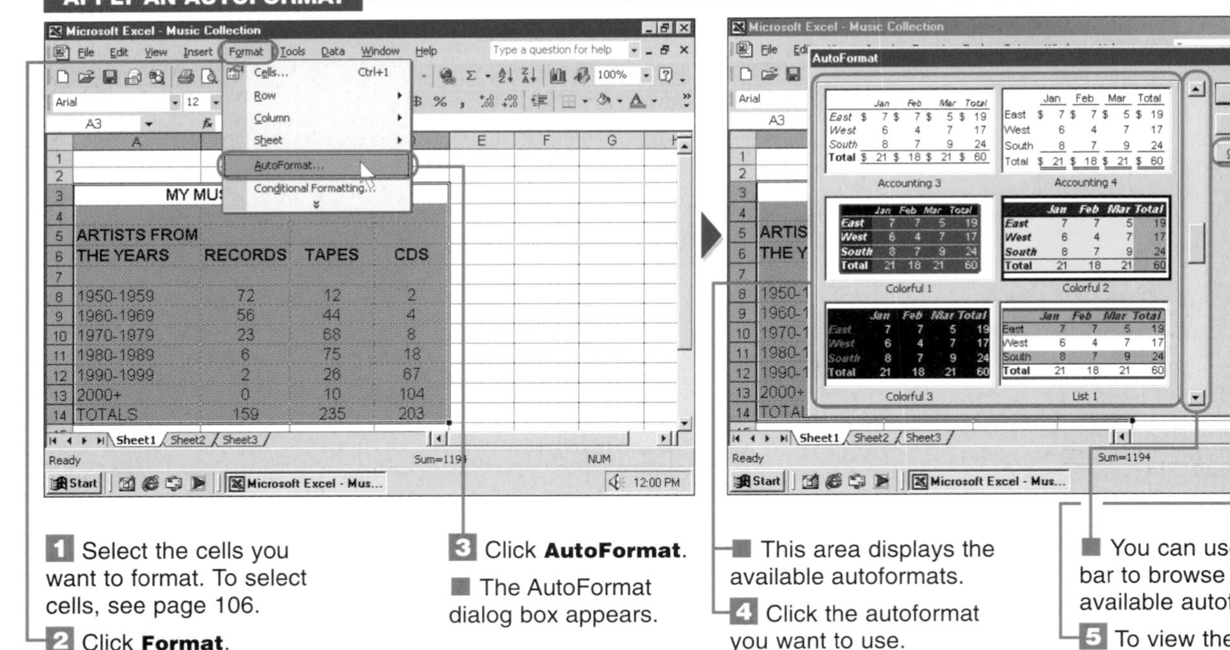

1 Select the cells you want to format. To select cells, see page 106.

2 Click **Format**.

3 Click **AutoFormat**.

■ The AutoFormat dialog box appears.

■ This area displays the available autoformats.

4 Click the autoformat you want to use.

■ You can use the scroll bar to browse through the available autoformats.

5 To view the formatting options for the autoformats, click **Options**.

What formatting will Excel apply to the cells in my worksheet?

Each autoformat includes a combination of formats, such as fonts, colors, borders, alignments and number styles. When you apply an autoformat, Excel may also adjust the column width and row height of the cells to best fit the information in the cells.

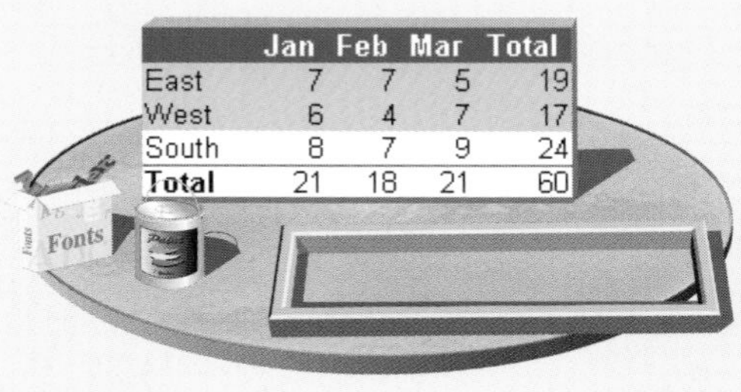

What happens if I add data to my worksheet after applying an autoformat?

If you enter data directly to the right or below the cells you applied an autoformat to, Excel may automatically format the new data.

If Excel does not automatically format the new data, you can select all the cells you want to display the autoformat and then perform steps **2** to **7** below.

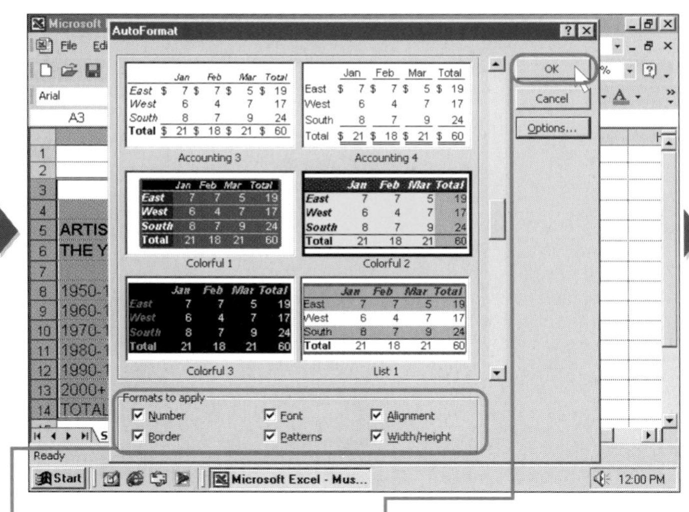

■ The formatting options appear in this area. A check mark (✔) beside an option indicates that Excel will apply the option to the cells.

6 You can click an option to turn the option on (✔) or off (☐).

7 Click **OK** to apply the autoformat to the cells you selected.

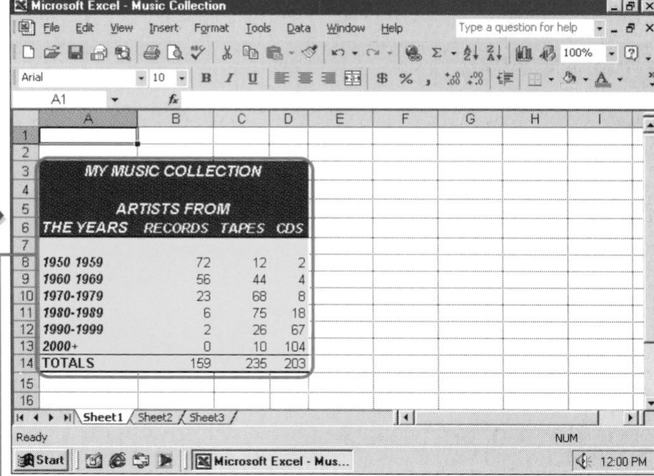

■ The cells display the autoformat you selected.

■ To deselect cells, click any cell.

■ To remove an autoformat, repeat steps **1** to **4**, selecting **None** in step **4**. Then perform step **7**.

PREVIEW A WORKSHEET BEFORE PRINTING

You can use the Print Preview feature to see how your worksheet will look when printed. This allows you to confirm that the worksheet will print the way you expect.

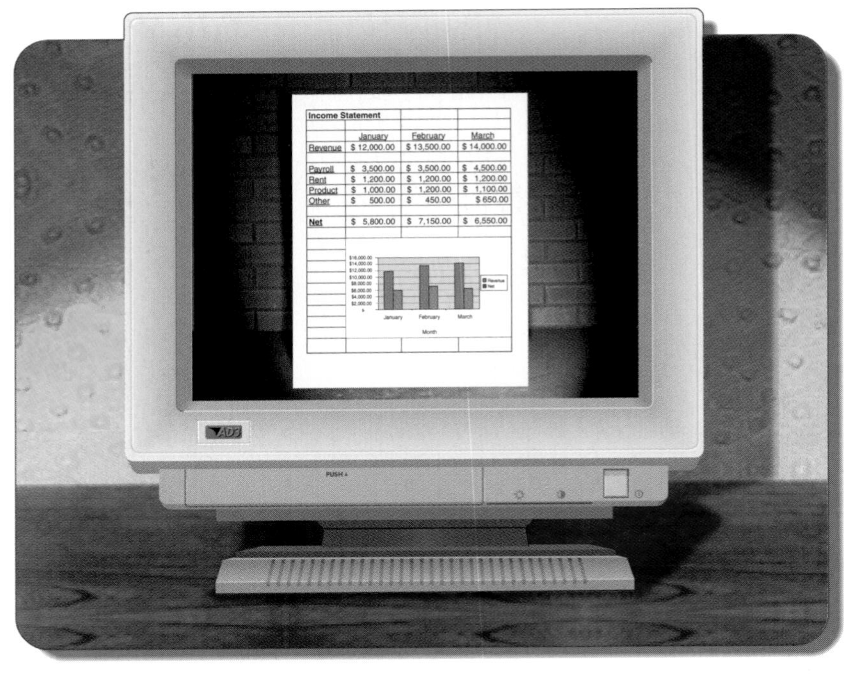

PREVIEW A WORKSHEET BEFORE PRINTING

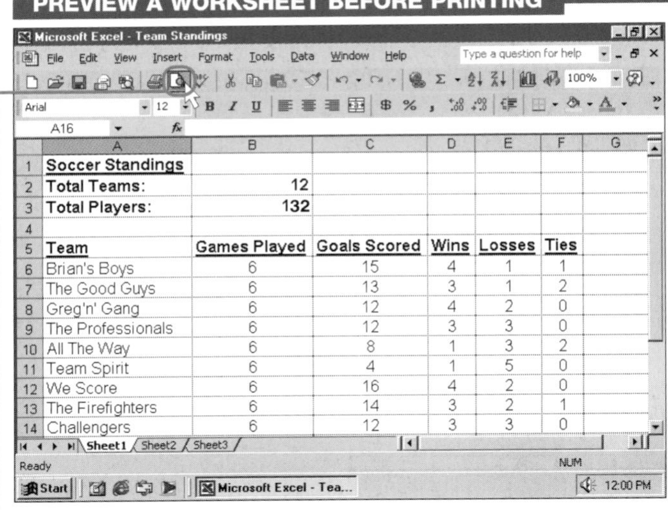

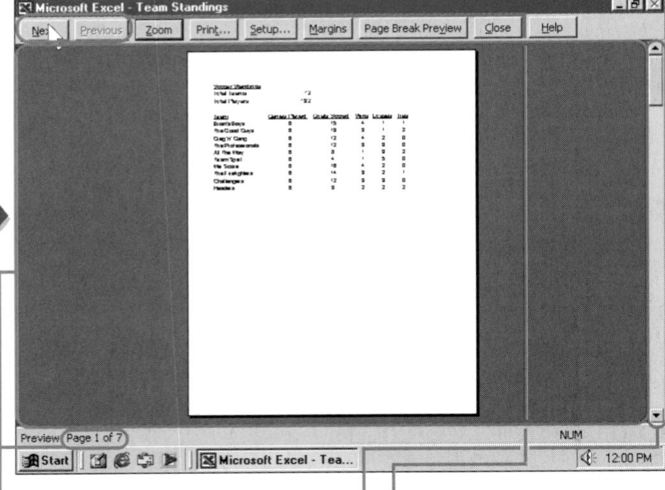

1 Click [print preview icon] to preview your worksheet before printing.

Note: If [print preview icon] is not displayed, click [toolbar options icon] on the Standard toolbar to display all the buttons.

■ The Print Preview window appears.

■ This area displays a page from your worksheet.

■ This area indicates which page is displayed and the total number of pages in your worksheet.

2 If your worksheet contains more than one page, you can click **Next** or **Previous** to view the next or previous page.

■ You can also use the scroll bar to view other pages.

Why does my worksheet appear in black and white in the Print Preview window?

If you are using a black-and-white printer, your worksheet appears in black and white in the Print Preview window. If you are using a color printer, your worksheet will appear in color.

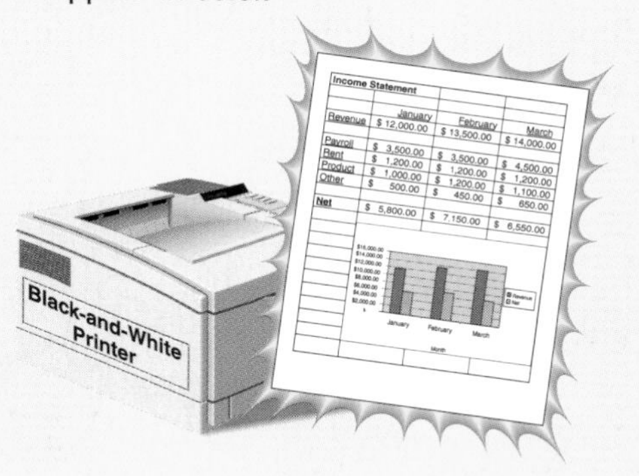

Why don't the gridlines appear on my worksheet in the Print Preview window?

By default, Excel will not print the gridlines that appear around each cell in your worksheet. To print gridlines and change other printing options, see page 168.

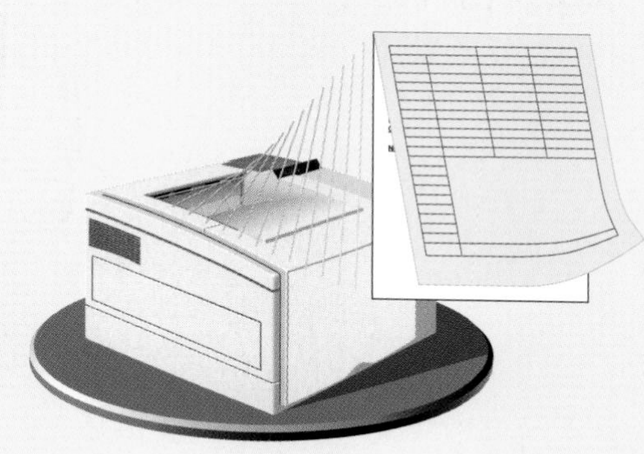

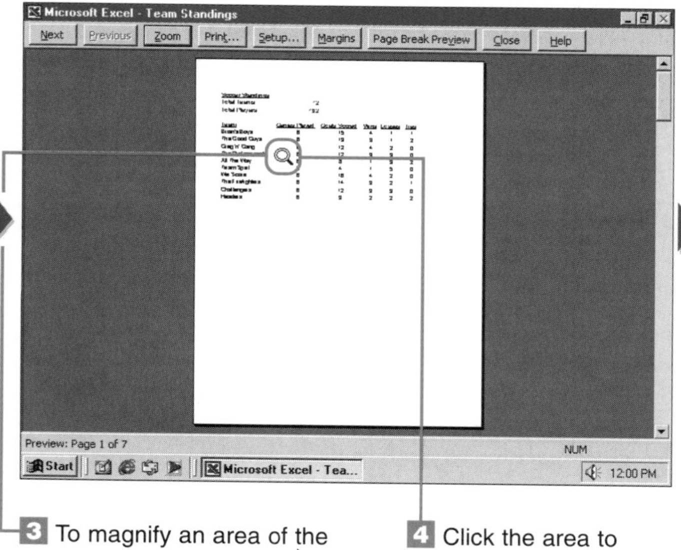

3 To magnify an area of the page, position the mouse ↖ over the area you want to magnify (↖ changes to 🔍).

4 Click the area to magnify the area.

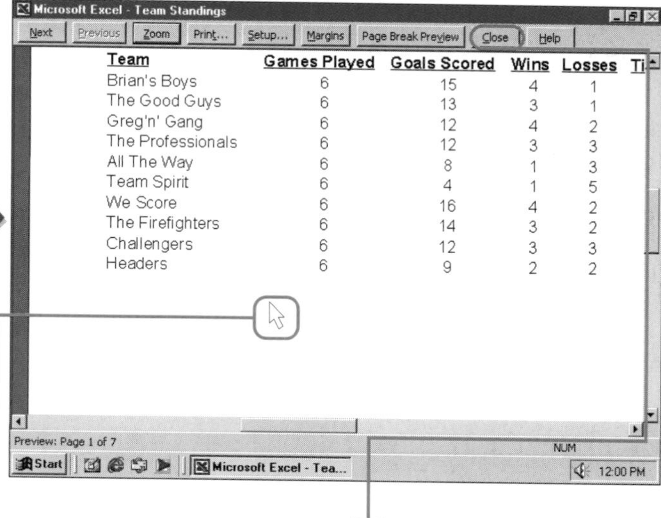

■ A magnified view of the area appears.

5 To once again display the entire page, click anywhere on the page.

6 When you finish previewing your worksheet, click **Close** to close the Print Preview window.

PRINT A WORKSHEET

You can produce a paper copy of the worksheet displayed on your screen.

Before printing your worksheet, make sure your printer is turned on and contains paper.

PRINT A WORKSHEET

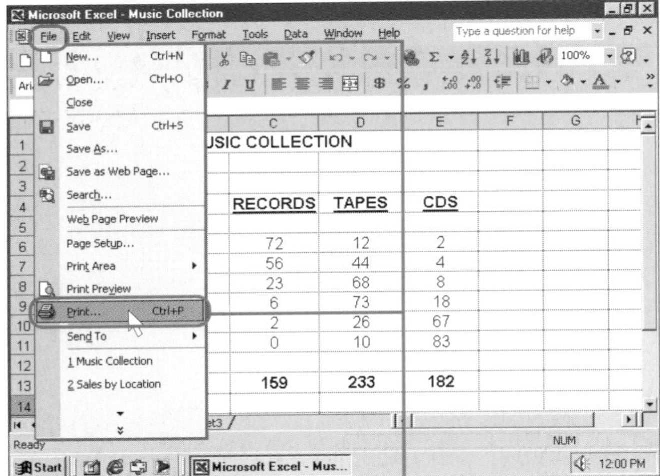

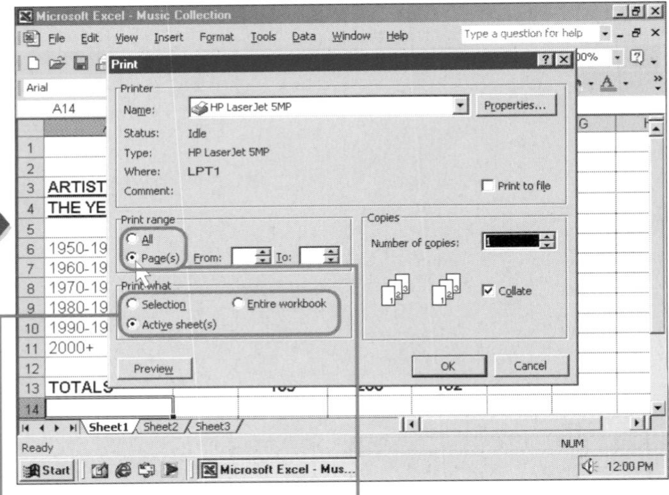

1 Click any cell in the worksheet you want to print.

■ To print only specific cells in your worksheet, select the cells you want to print. To select cells, see page 106.

2 Click **File**.

3 Click **Print**.

■ The Print dialog box appears.

4 Click the part of the workbook you want to print (○ changes to ⊙).

Note: For information on the parts of the workbook that you can print, see the top of page 165.

5 If the part of the workbook you selected to print contains more than one page, click an option to specify which pages you want to print (○ changes to ⊙).

All - Prints every page.

Page(s) - Prints the pages you specify.

What part of a workbook can I print?

Excel allows you to specify which part of a workbook you want to print. Each workbook is divided into several worksheets.

For information on using multiple worksheets in a workbook, see pages 110 to 115.

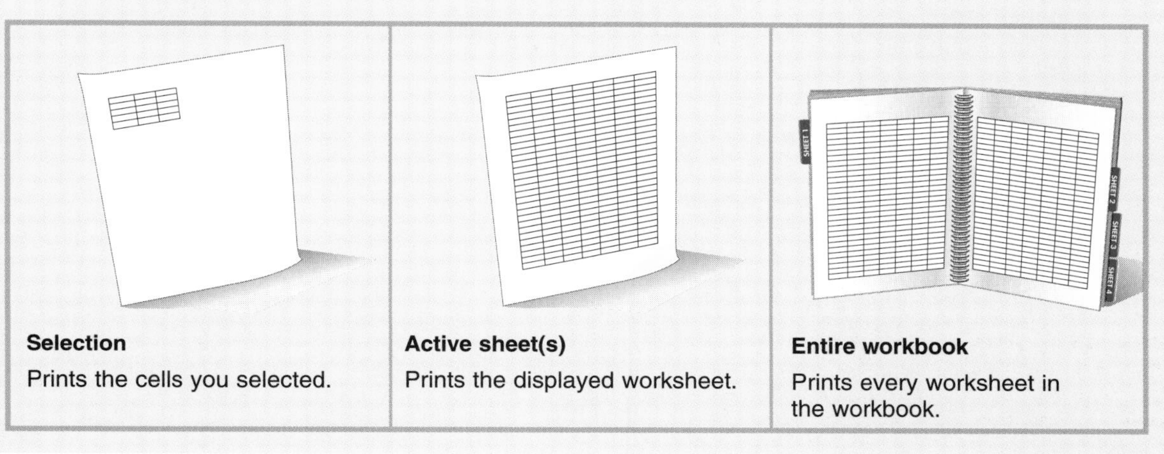

Selection

Prints the cells you selected.

Active sheet(s)

Prints the displayed worksheet.

Entire workbook

Prints every worksheet in the workbook.

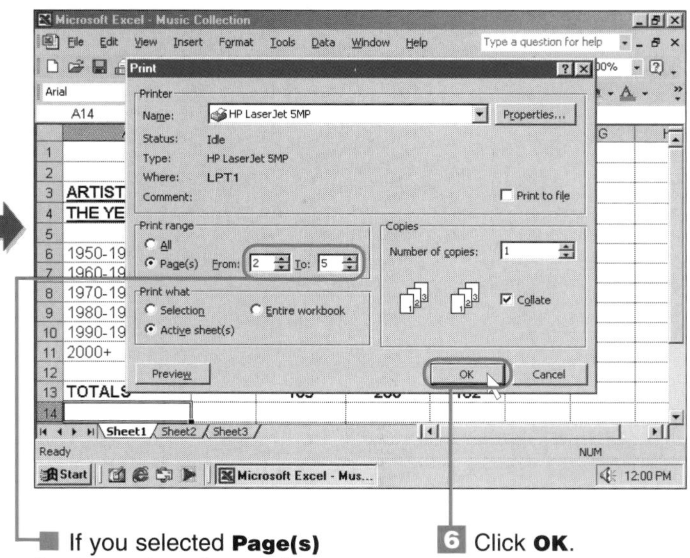

■ If you selected **Page(s)** in step 5, type the number of the first page you want to print. Press the Tab key and then type the number of the last page you want to print.

6 Click **OK**.

	A	B	C	D	E
1	MY MUSIC COLLECTION				
2					
3	ARTISTS FROM				
4	THE YEARS		RECORDS	TAPES	CDS
5					
6	1950-1959		72	12	2
7	1960-1969		56	44	4
8	1970-1979		23	68	8
9	1980-1989		6	73	18
10	1990-1999		2	26	67
11	2000+		0	10	83
12					
13	TOTALS		159	233	182

QUICKLY PRINT DISPLAYED WORKSHEET

1 Click 🖨 to quickly print the worksheet displayed on your screen.

Note: If 🖨 is not displayed, click » on the Standard toolbar to display all the buttons.

CHANGE PAGE ORIENTATION

You can change the page orientation to change the way your worksheet appears on a printed page.

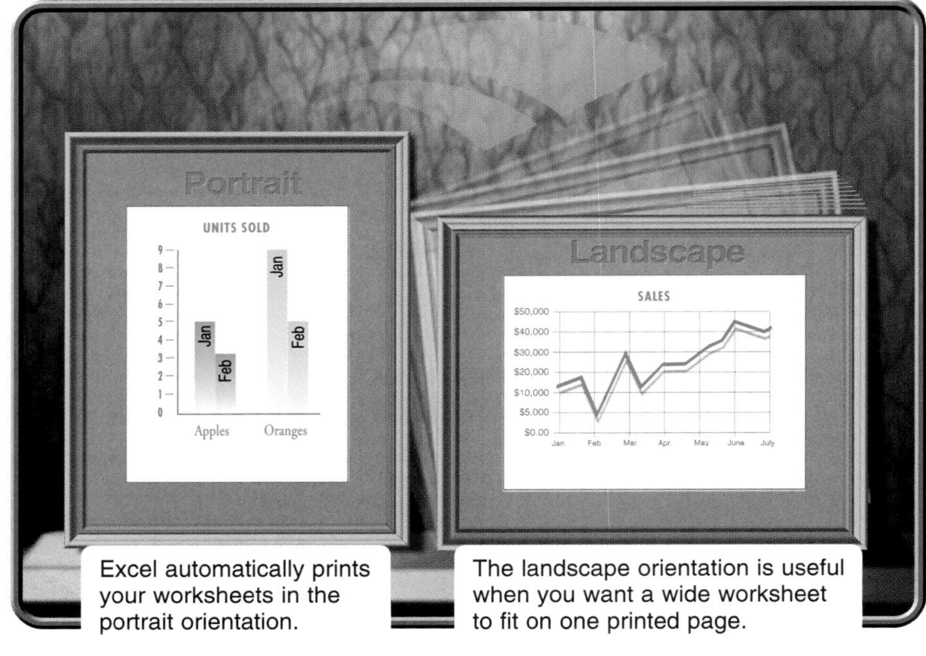

Excel automatically prints your worksheets in the portrait orientation.

The landscape orientation is useful when you want a wide worksheet to fit on one printed page.

Changing the page orientation will not affect the way your worksheet appears on your screen.

CHANGE PAGE ORIENTATION

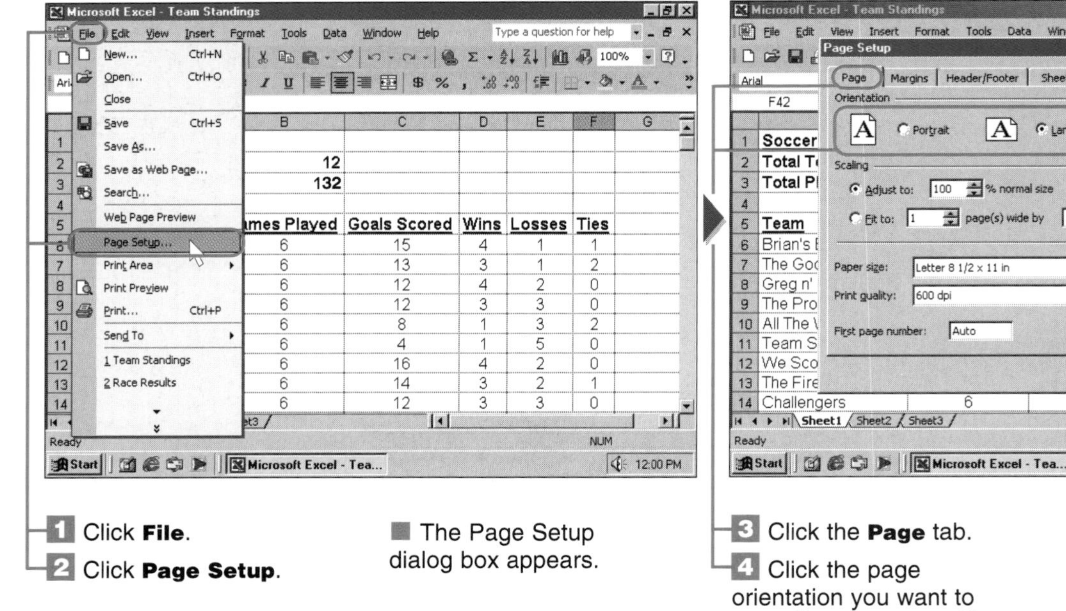

1 Click **File**.

2 Click **Page Setup**.

■ The Page Setup dialog box appears.

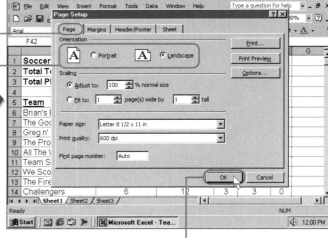

3 Click the **Page** tab.

4 Click the page orientation you want to use (○ changes to ⊙).

5 Click **OK** to confirm your change.

Note: You can use the Print Preview feature to see how your worksheet will appear on a printed page. For information on using the Print Preview feature, see page 162.

CHANGE MARGINS

You can change the margins in your worksheet. A margin is the amount of space between the data on a page and the edge of your paper.

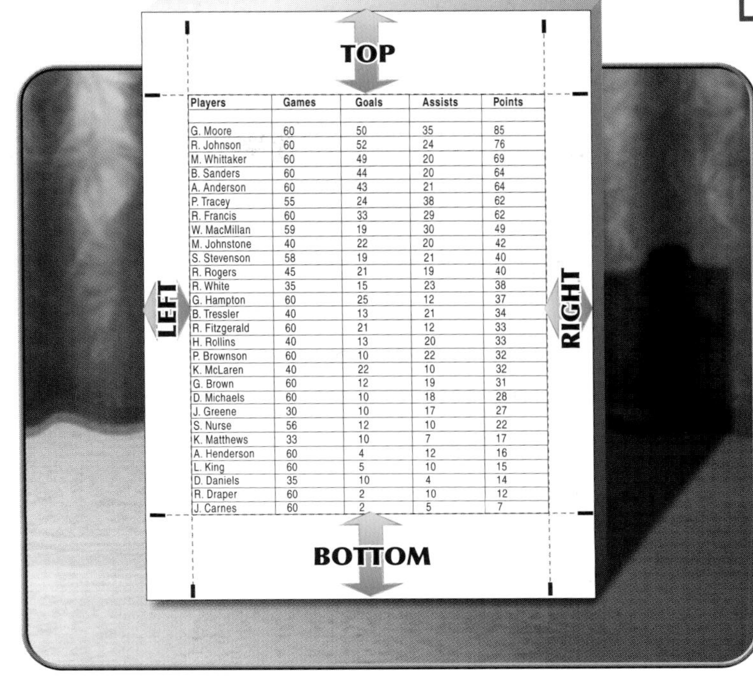

Players	Games	Goals	Assists	Points
G. Moore	60	50	35	85
R. Johnson	60	52	24	76
M. Whittaker	60	49	20	69
B. Sanders	60	44	20	64
A. Anderson	60	43	21	64
P. Tracey	55	24	38	62
R. Francis	60	33	29	62
W. MacMillan	59	19	30	49
M. Johnstone	40	22	20	42
S. Stevenson	58	19	21	40
R. Rogers	45	21	19	40
R. White	35	15	23	38
G. Hampton	60	25	12	37
B. Tressler	40	13	21	34
R. Fitzgerald	60	21	12	33
H. Rollins	40	13	20	33
P. Brownson	60	10	22	32
K. McLaren	40	22	10	32
G. Brown	60	12	19	31
D. Michaels	60	10	18	28
J. Greene	30	10	17	27
S. Nurse	56	12	10	22
K. Matthews	33	10	7	17
A. Henderson	60	4	12	16
L. King	60	5	10	15
D. Daniels	35	10	4	14
R. Draper	60	2	10	12
J. Carnes	60	2	5	7

Excel automatically sets the top and bottom margins to 1 inch and the left and right margins to 0.75 inches.

Changing the margins allows you to adjust the amount of information that can fit on a page. You may want to change the margins to accommodate letterhead or other specialty paper.

CHANGE MARGINS

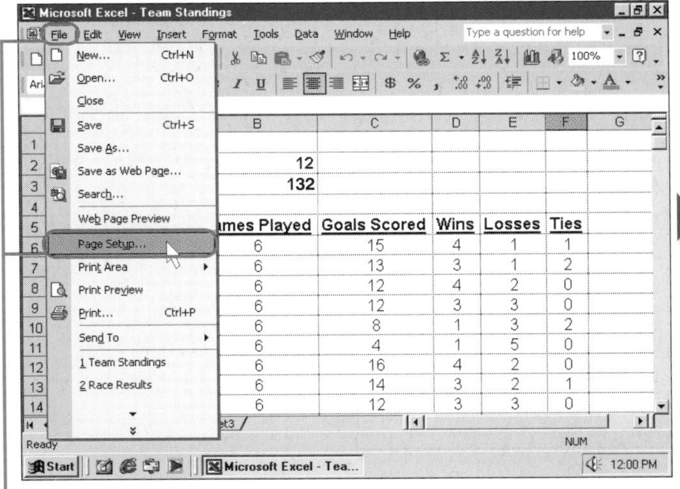

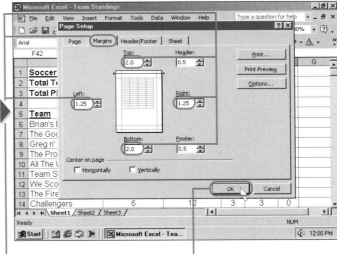

1 Click **File**.

2 Click **Page Setup**.

■ The Page Setup dialog box appears.

3 Click the **Margins** tab.

4 Double-click in the box for the margin you want to change. Then type a new margin in inches.

5 Repeat step 4 for each margin you want to change.

6 Click **OK** to confirm your changes.

Note: You can use the Print Preview feature to see how your worksheet will appear on a printed page. For information on using the Print Preview feature, see page 162.

CHANGE PRINT OPTIONS

You can use the print options that Excel offers to change the way your worksheet appears on a printed page.

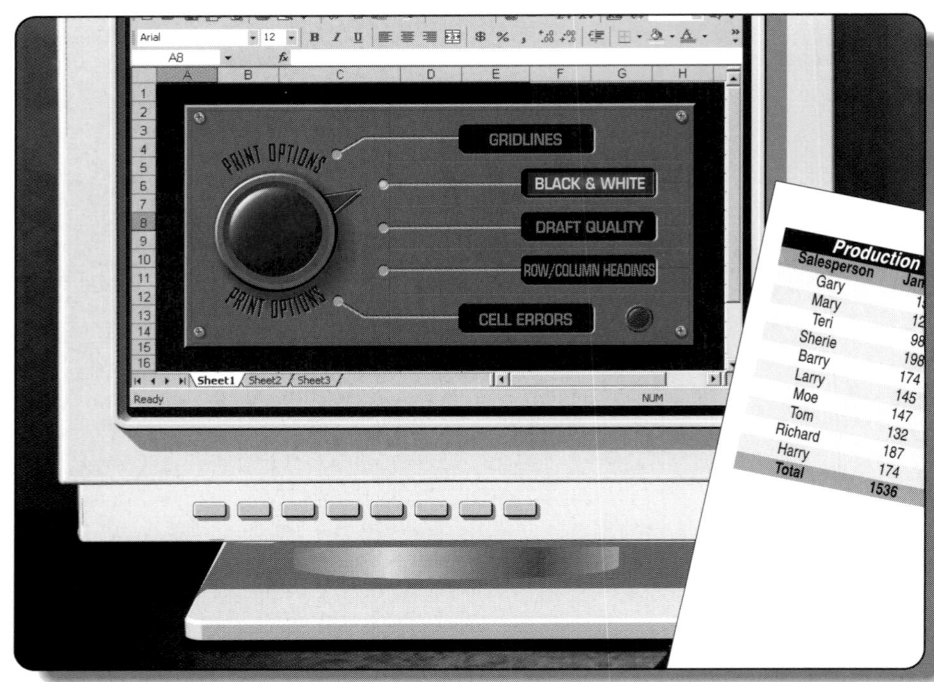

Changing the print options will not affect the way your worksheet appears on your screen.

CHANGE PRINT OPTIONS

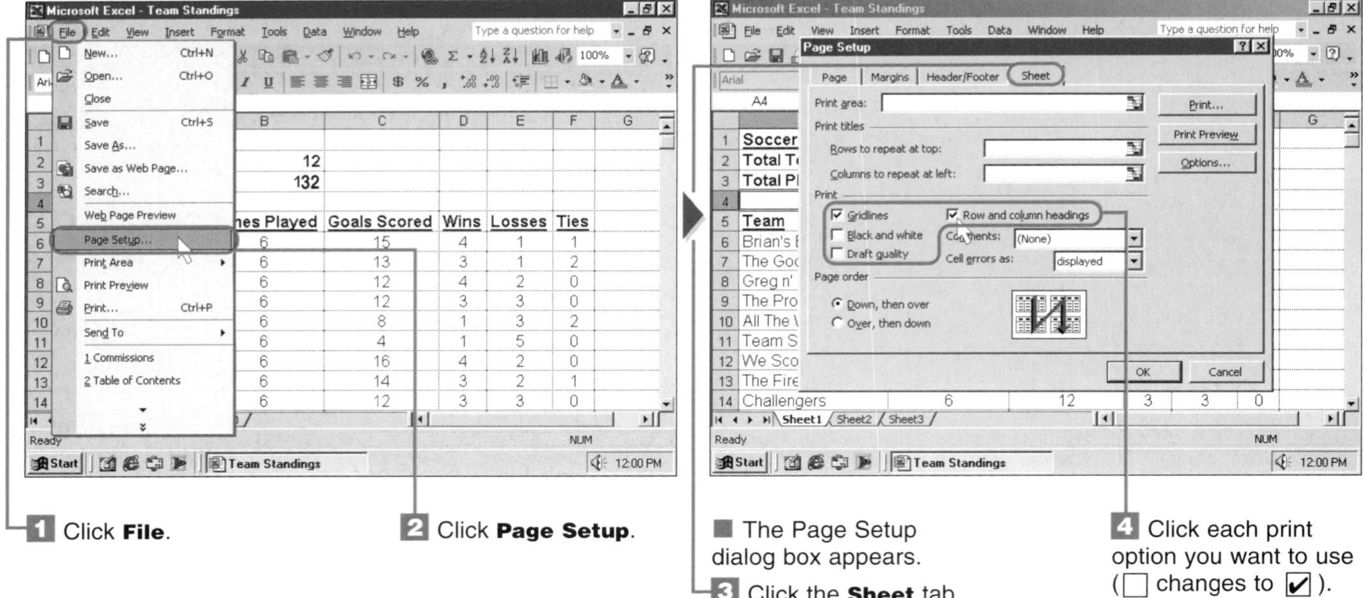

1 Click **File**.

2 Click **Page Setup**.

■ The Page Setup dialog box appears.

3 Click the **Sheet** tab.

4 Click each print option you want to use (☐ changes to ☑).

What print options does Excel offer?

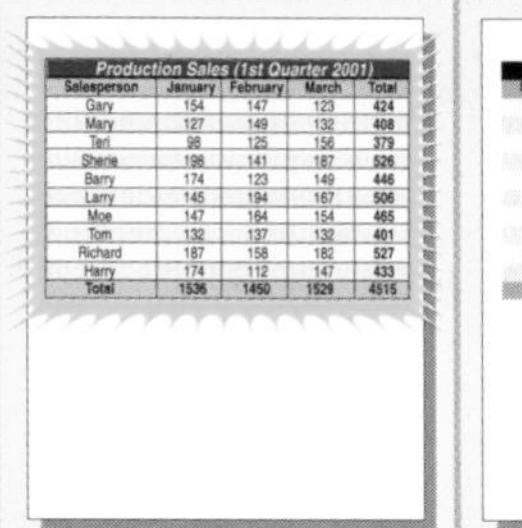

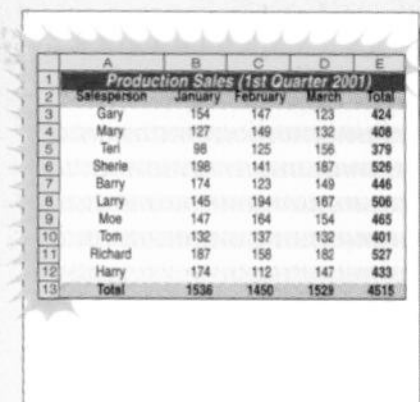

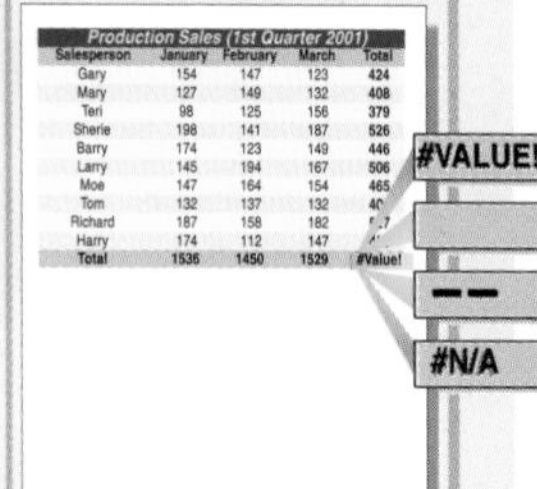

Gridlines

Prints lines around the cells in your worksheet.

Black and white

Prints a colored worksheet in black and white. This is useful when you want to print a colored worksheet on a black-and-white printer.

Draft quality

Reduces printing time by not printing gridlines and most graphics.

Row and column headings

Prints the row numbers and column letters.

Cell errors

Specifies the way cell errors appear on a printed page. For information on cell errors, see page 146.

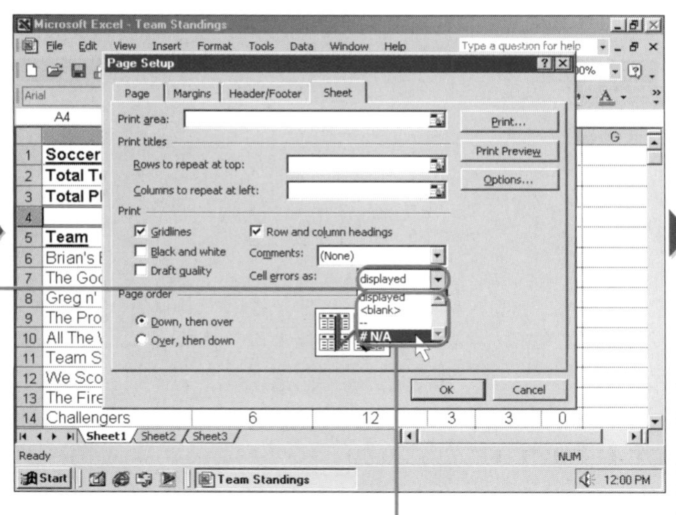

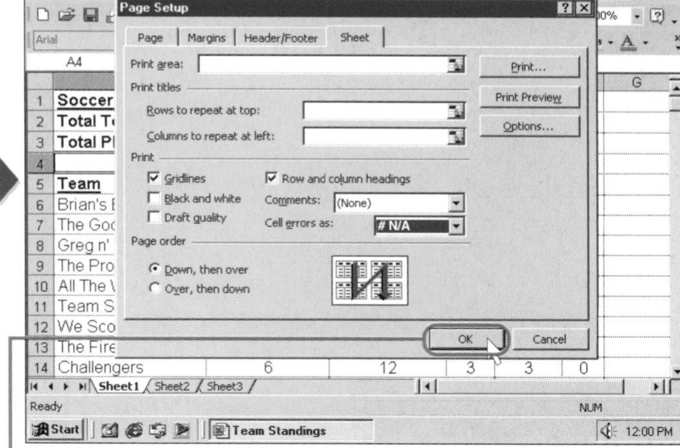

■ By default, Excel will print any cell errors that appear in your worksheet.

5 To specify how you want cell errors to appear when you print your worksheet, click this area.

6 Click the way you want cell errors to appear.

7 Click **OK** to confirm your changes.

Note: You can use the Print Preview feature to see how your worksheet will appear on a printed page. For information on using the Print Preview feature, see page 162.

CREATE A CHART

You can create a chart to graphically display your worksheet data. Charts allow you to easily compare data and view patterns and trends.

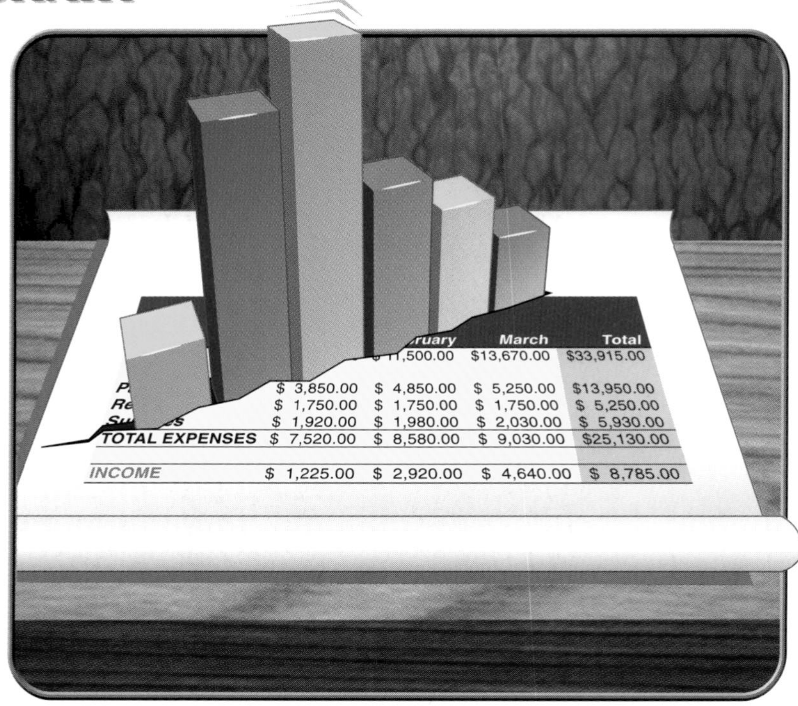

The Chart Wizard takes you step by step through the process of creating a chart.

CREATE A CHART

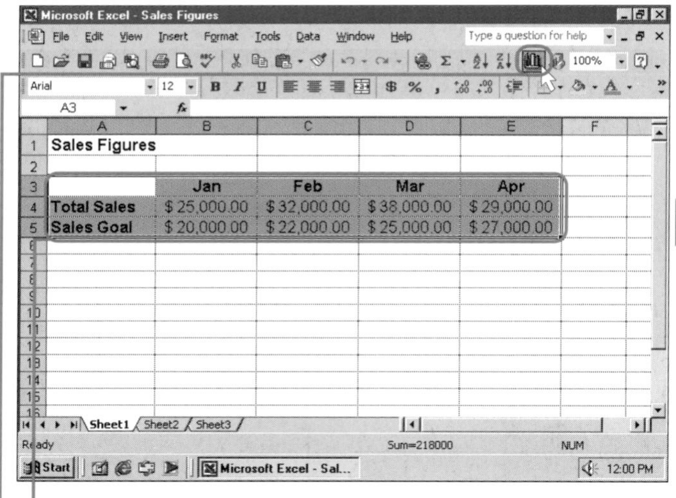

1 Select the cells containing the data you want to display in a chart, including the row and column labels. To select cells, see page 106.

2 Click to create a chart.

Note: If is not displayed, click on the Standard toolbar to display all the buttons.

■ The Chart Wizard appears.

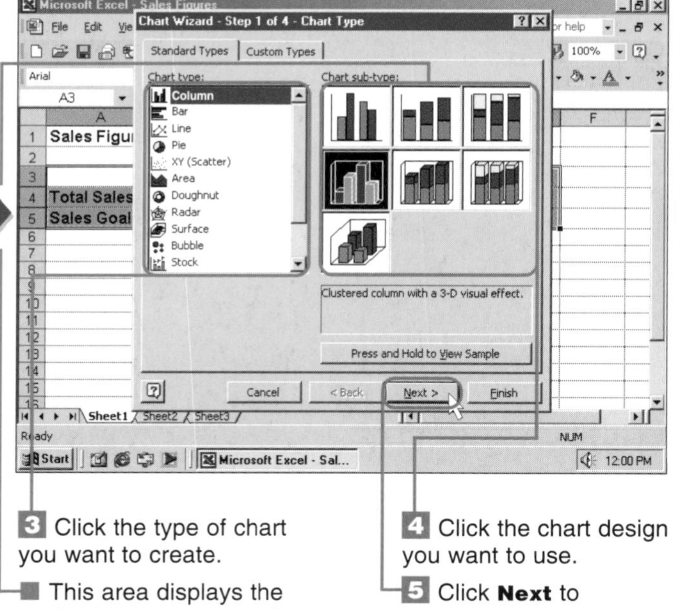

3 Click the type of chart you want to create.

■ This area displays the available chart designs for the type of chart you selected.

4 Click the chart design you want to use.

5 Click **Next** to continue.

What titles can I add to my chart?

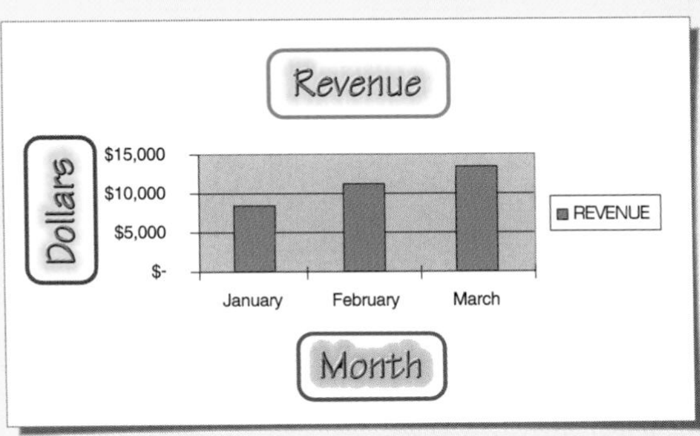

Chart title
Identifies the subject of your chart.

Value axis
Indicates the unit of measure used in your chart.

Category axis
Indicates the categories used in your chart.

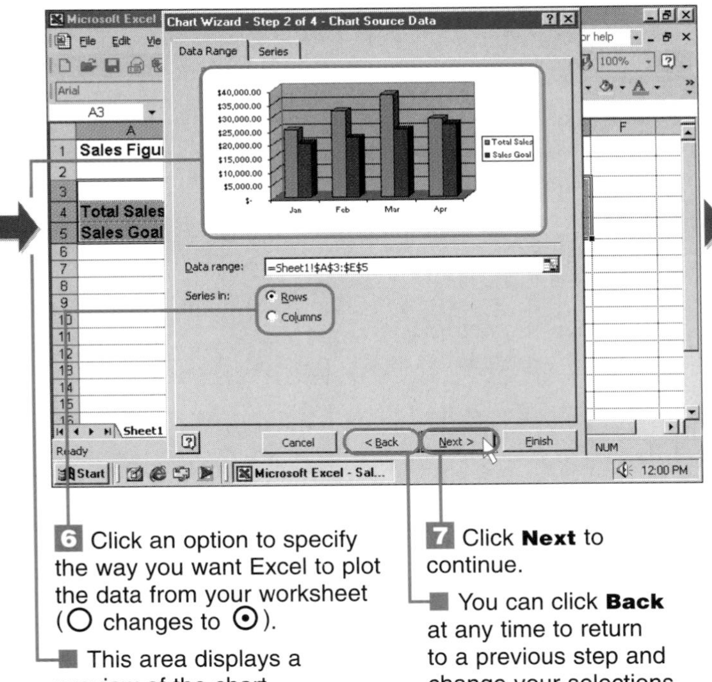

6 Click an option to specify the way you want Excel to plot the data from your worksheet (○ changes to ⊙).

■ This area displays a preview of the chart.

7 Click **Next** to continue.

■ You can click **Back** at any time to return to a previous step and change your selections.

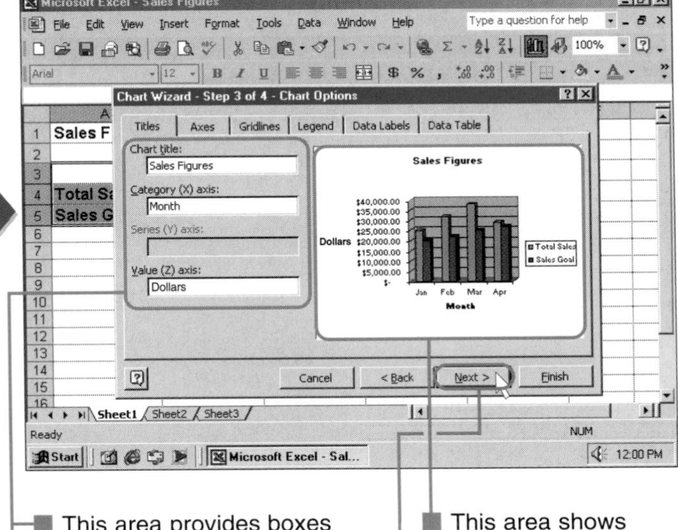

■ This area provides boxes you can use to add titles to the chart.

Note: Some boxes are not available for some chart types.

8 To add a title to the chart, click a box and type the title. Repeat this step for each title you want to add.

■ This area shows how the titles will appear in the chart.

9 Click **Next** to continue.

CONTINUED

CREATE A CHART

When creating a chart, you can choose to display the chart on the same worksheet as the data or on its own sheet, called a chart sheet.

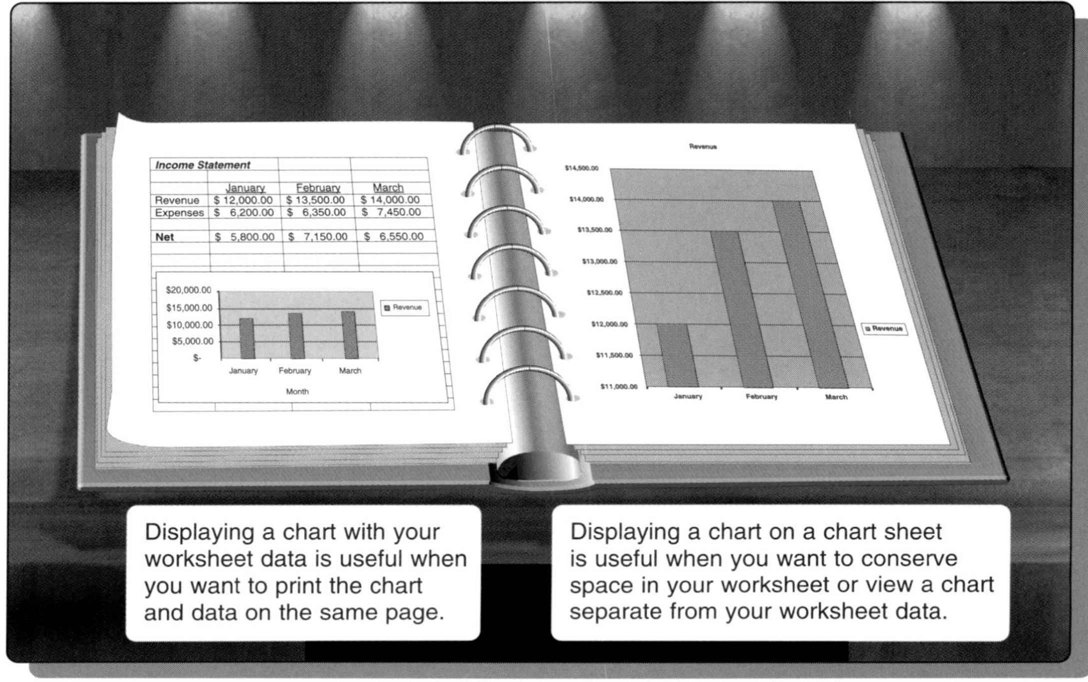

Displaying a chart with your worksheet data is useful when you want to print the chart and data on the same page.

Displaying a chart on a chart sheet is useful when you want to conserve space in your worksheet or view a chart separate from your worksheet data.

CREATE A CHART (CONTINUED)

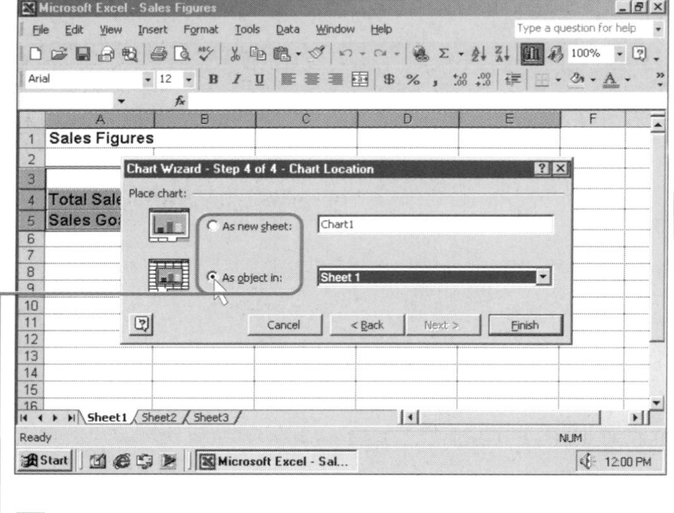

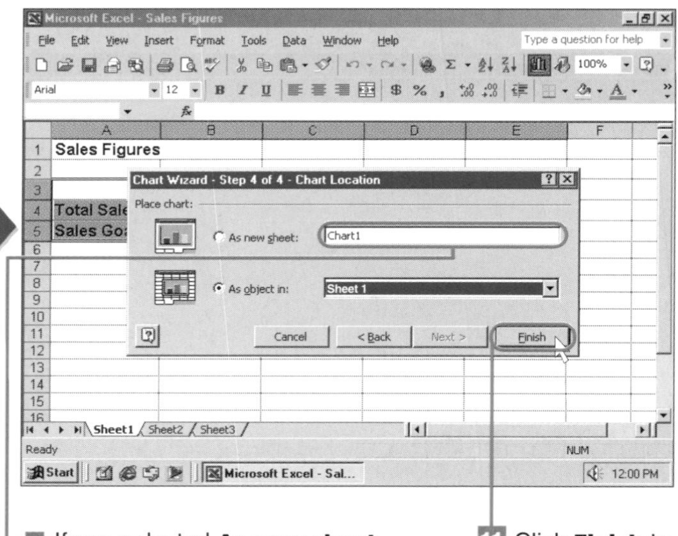

10 Click an option to specify where you want to display the chart (○ changes to ⊙).

As new sheet

Displays the chart on its own sheet, called a chart sheet.

As object in

Displays the chart on the same worksheet as the data.

■ If you selected **As new sheet** in step **10**, you can type a name for the chart sheet in this area.

11 Click **Finish** to create the chart.

What happens if I change the data I used to create a chart?

If you change the data you used to create a chart, Excel will automatically update the chart to display the changes.

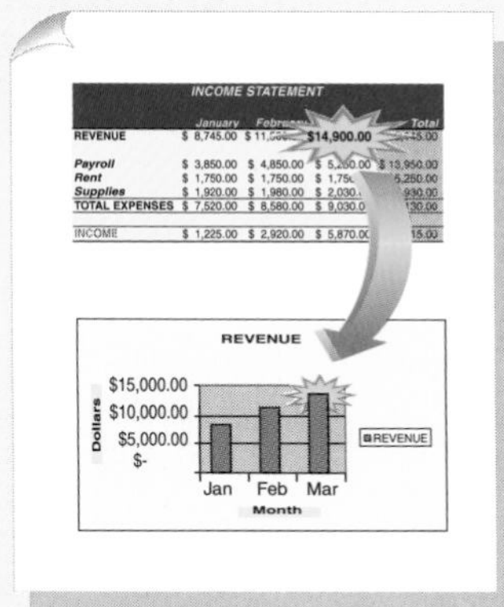

Can I change the chart titles?

Yes. After you create a chart, you can change the chart title and axis titles in the chart. Click the title you want to change. A box appears around the title. Drag the mouse I over the title until you select all the text. Type a new title and then click a blank area in the chart.

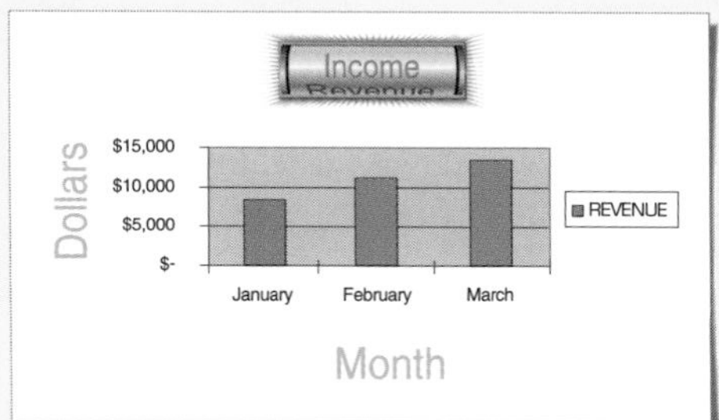

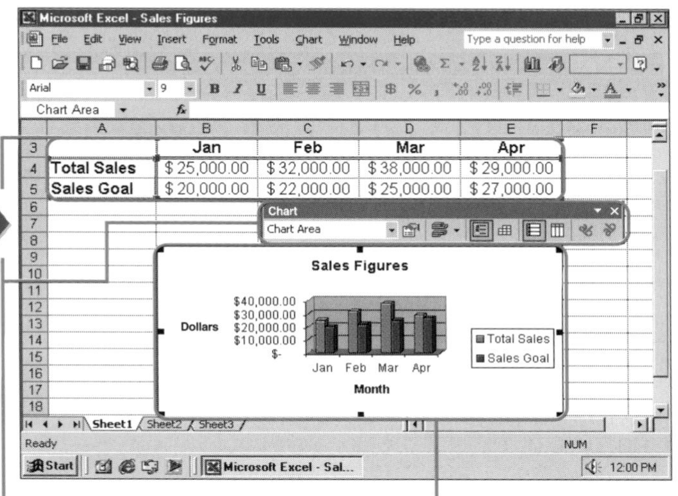

■ In this example, the chart appears on the same worksheet as the data.

■ The Chart toolbar also appears, displaying buttons that allow you to make changes to the chart.

■ Excel outlines the data you selected to create the chart.

■ The handles (■) around a chart let you change the size of the chart. To hide the handles, click outside the chart.

Note: To move or resize a chart, see page 174.

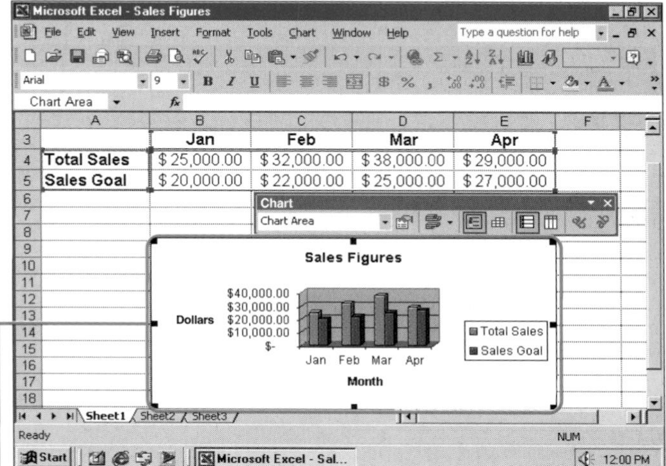

DELETE A CHART

1 Click a blank area in the chart you want to delete. Handles (■) appear around the chart.

2 Press the Delete key to delete the chart.

Note: To delete a chart displayed on a chart sheet, you must delete the sheet. To delete a worksheet, see page 113.

MOVE OR RESIZE A CHART

You can change the location and size of a chart displayed on your worksheet.

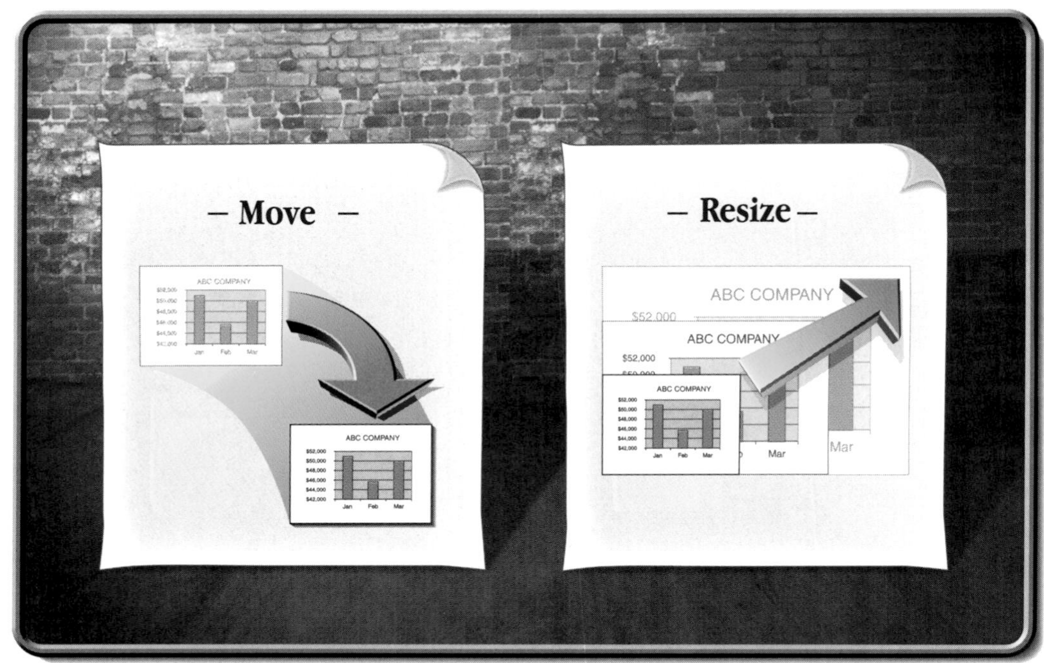

MOVE A CHART

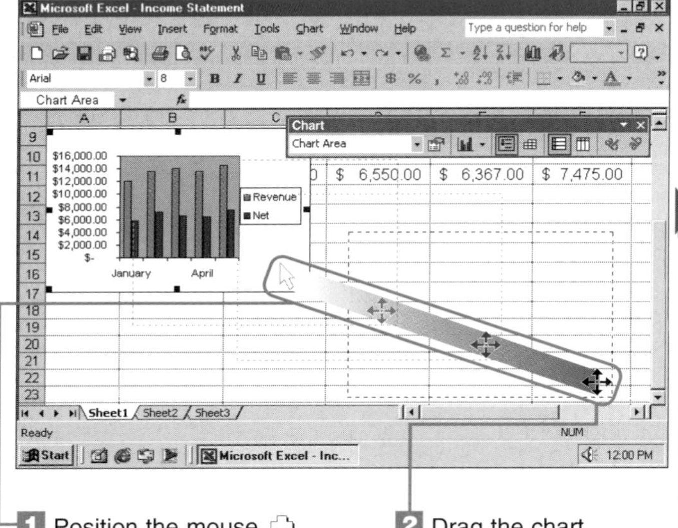

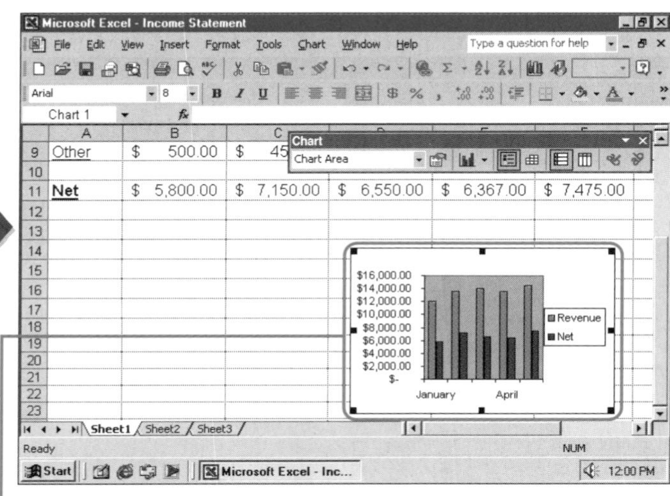

1 Position the mouse ✥ over a blank area in the chart you want to move (✥ changes to ↖).

2 Drag the chart to a new location in your worksheet.

■ A dashed line indicates where the chart will appear.

■ The chart appears in the new location.

What handle (■) should I use to resize a chart?

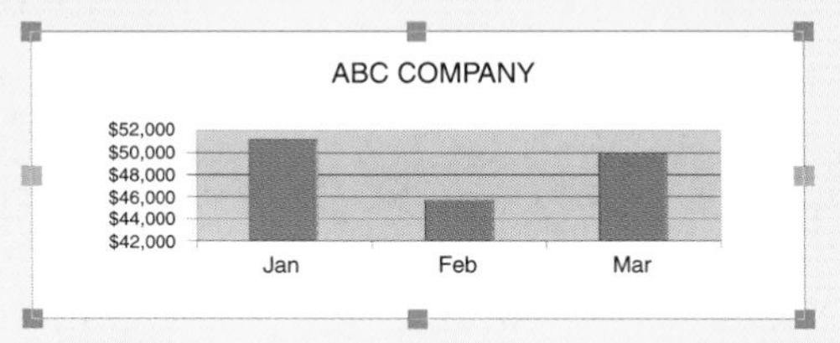

■ Changes the height of a chart

■ Changes the width of a chart

■ Changes the height and width of a chart at the same time

Can I move individual items in a chart?

Yes. To move the chart title, an axis title or the legend to a new location in a chart, position the mouse over the item. Then drag the item to a new location. You cannot move an item outside of the chart area.

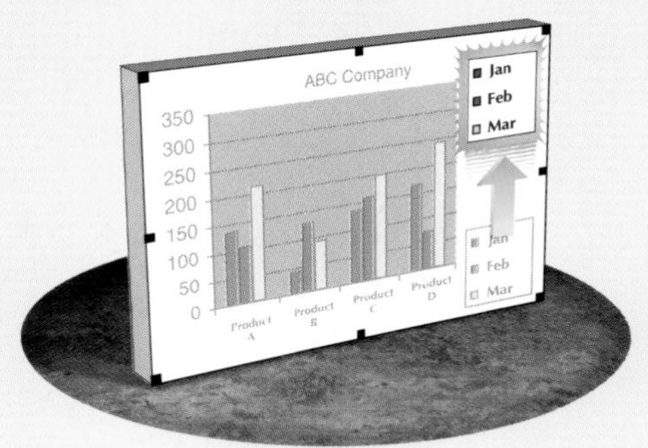

RESIZE A CHART

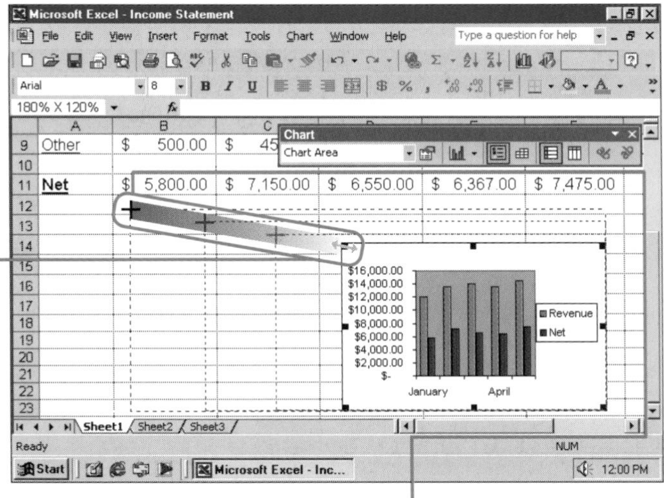

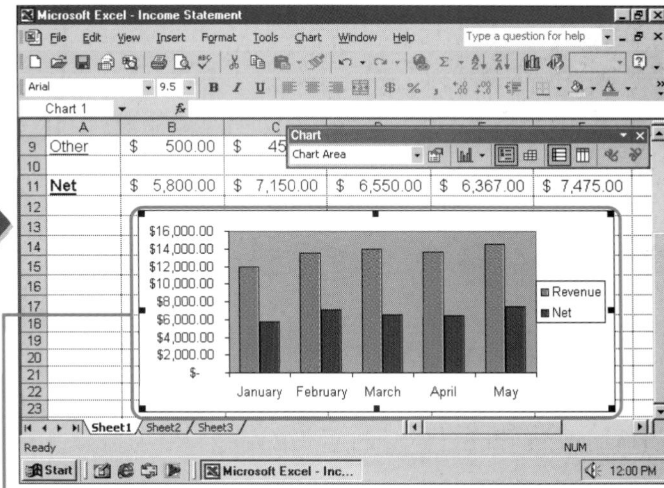

1 Click a blank area in the chart you want to resize. Handles (■) appear around the chart.

2 Position the mouse over one of the handles (changes to ↘, ↗, ↔ or ↕).

3 Drag the handle until the chart is the size you want.

■ A dashed line shows the new size.

■ The chart appears in the new size.

CHANGE THE CHART TYPE

After you create a chart, you can change the chart type to present your data more effectively.

The type of chart you should use depends on your data. For example, area, column and line charts are ideal for showing changes to values over time. Pie charts are ideal for showing percentages.

CHANGE THE CHART TYPE

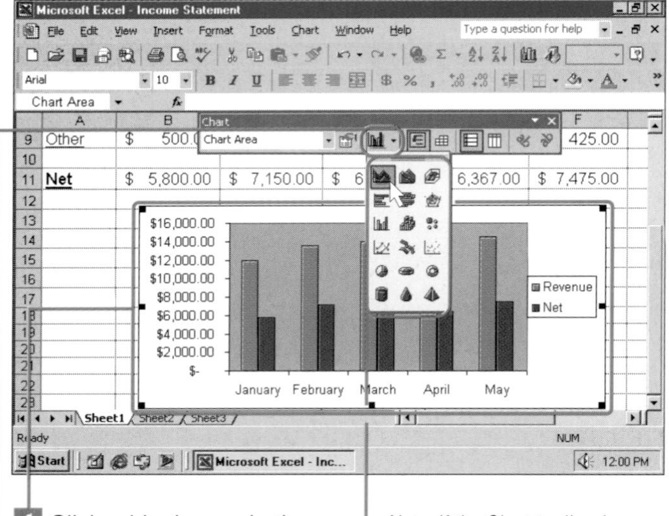

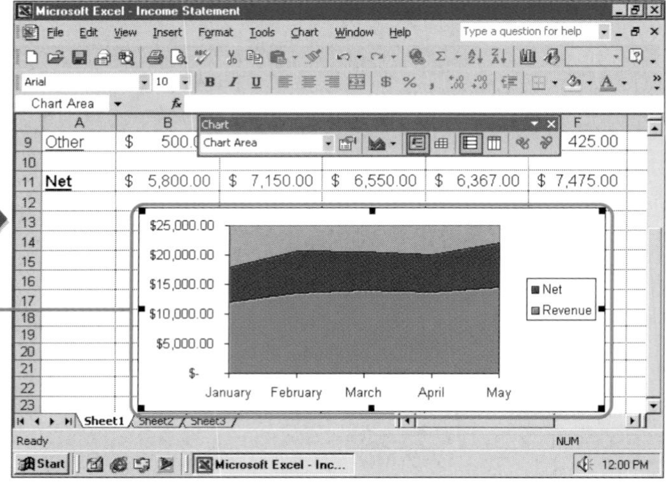

1 Click a blank area in the chart you want to change. Handle (■) appear around the chart.

2 Click ▾ in this area to display the available chart types.

Note: If the Chart toolbar is not displayed, see page 11 to display the toolbar.

3 Click the type of chart you want to use.

■ The chart displays the chart type you selected.

PRINT A CHART

You can print your chart with the worksheet data or on its own page.

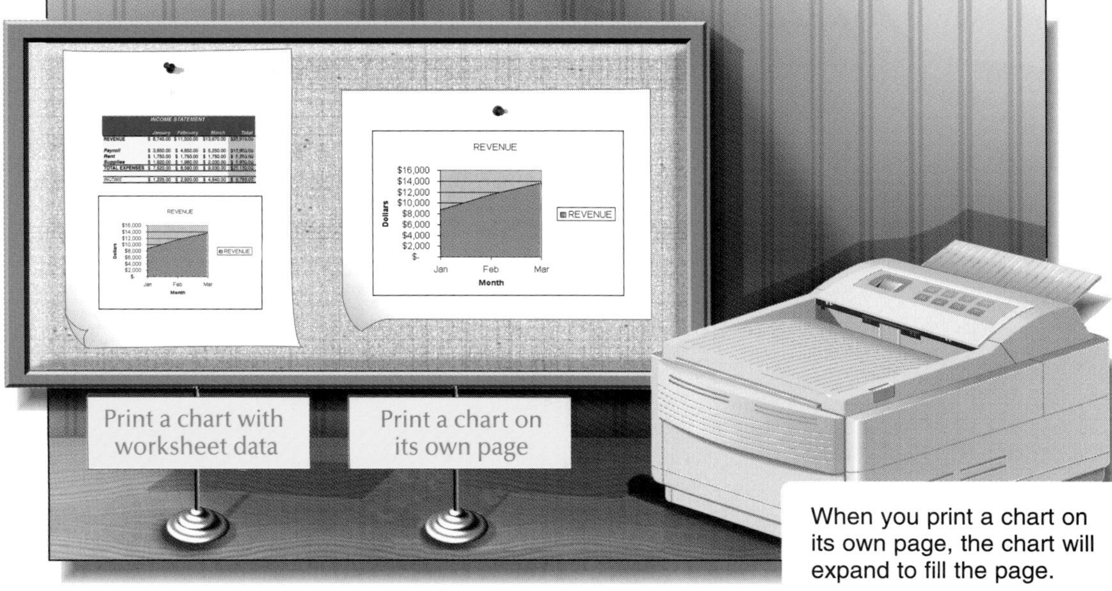

When you print a chart on its own page, the chart will expand to fill the page.

PRINT A CHART

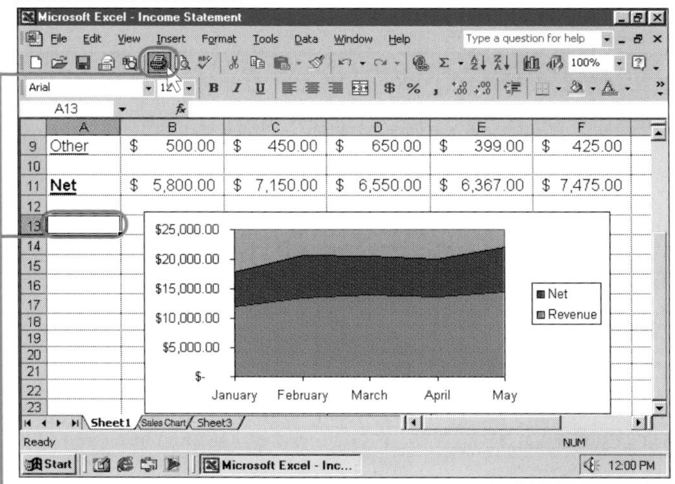

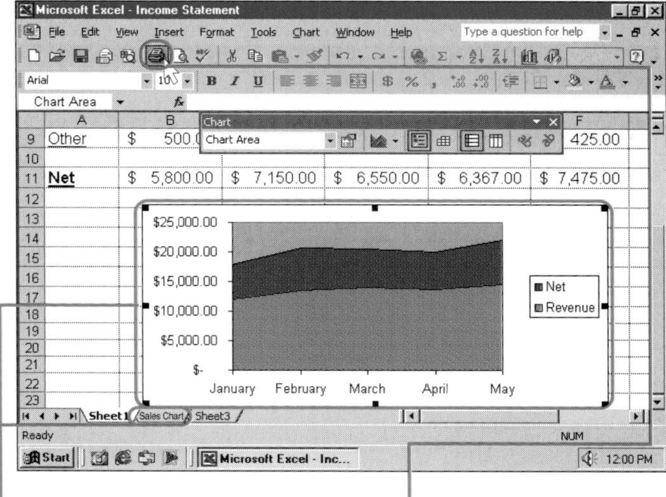

PRINT A CHART WITH WORKSHEET DATA

1 Click a cell outside the chart.

2 Click 🖨 to print the chart with your worksheet data.

Note: If 🖨 is not displayed, click » on the Standard toolbar to display all the buttons.

PRINT A CHART ON ITS OWN PAGE

1 To print a chart displayed on a worksheet, click a blank area in the chart.

■ To print a chart displayed on a chart sheet, click the tab for the chart sheet.

2 Click 🖨 to print the chart on its own page.

Note: If 🖨 is not displayed, click » on the Standard toolbar to display all the buttons.

Bill's Auto Body Shop
We perform body work on all makes and models of cars
Our fully trained mechanics will get your car up and running quickly and efficiently
Vrrroooomm

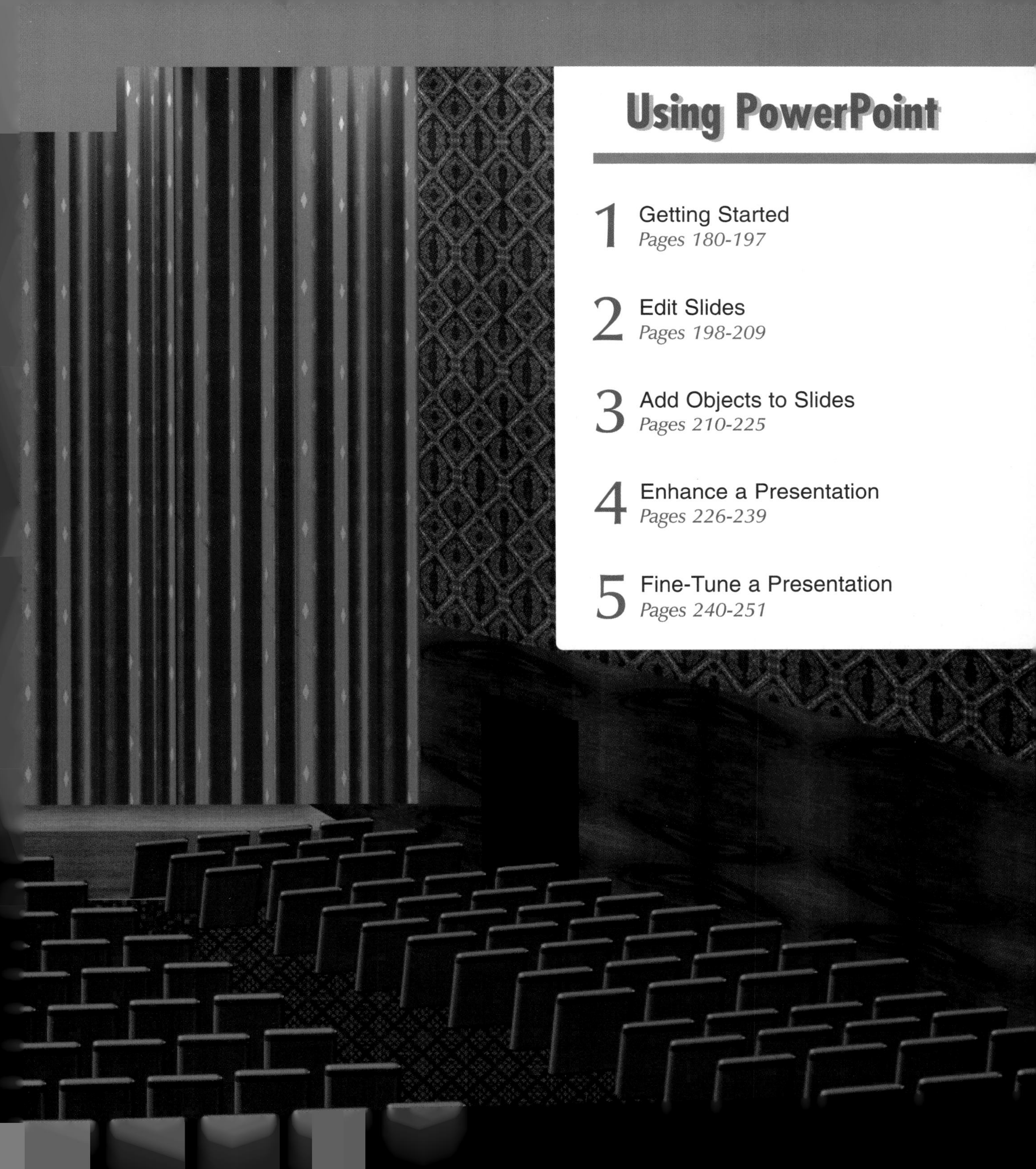

Using PowerPoint

PowerPoint helps you plan, organize, design and deliver professional presentations.

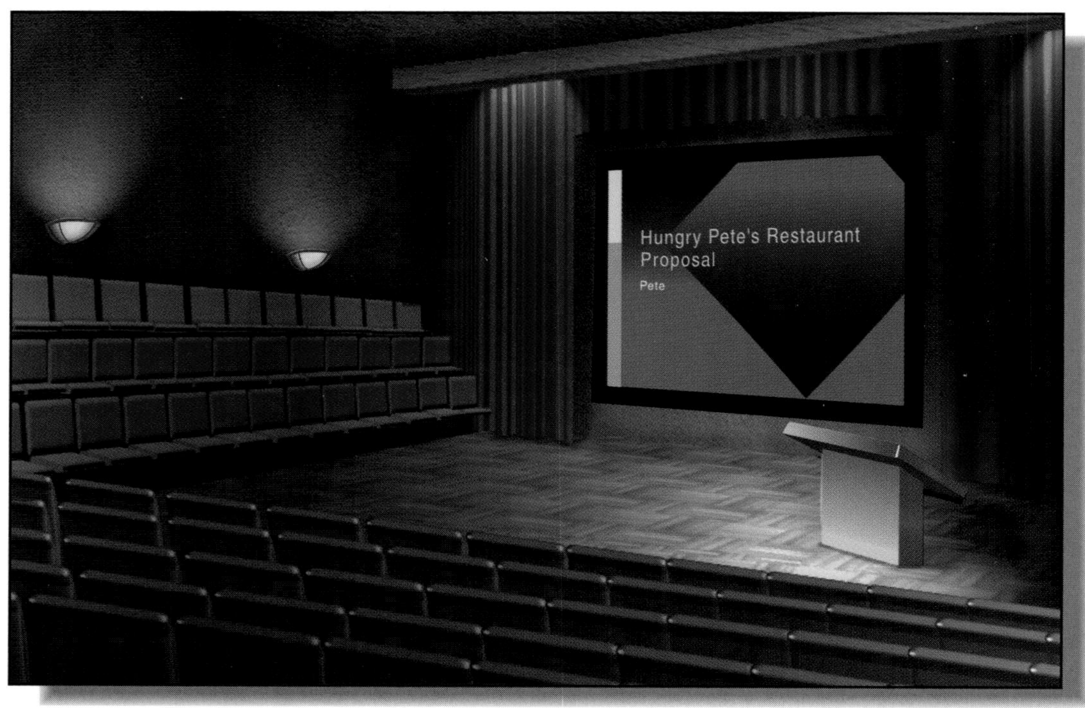

Create and Edit a Presentation

You can use PowerPoint's AutoContent Wizard to quickly create a presentation or design your own presentation one slide at a time. You can then add, delete and move text in the presentation and check the presentation for spelling errors.

Enhance a Presentation

You can emphasize the text on a slide using a bold, italic or underline style. You can also change the font, size and color of text. You can enhance your slides by adding objects such as clip art images, AutoShapes, charts and diagrams.

Fine-Tune a Presentation

If you plan to deliver a presentation on a computer screen, you can add special effects called transitions to help you move from one slide to the next. You can also re-organize the slides in your presentation and delete slides you no longer need.

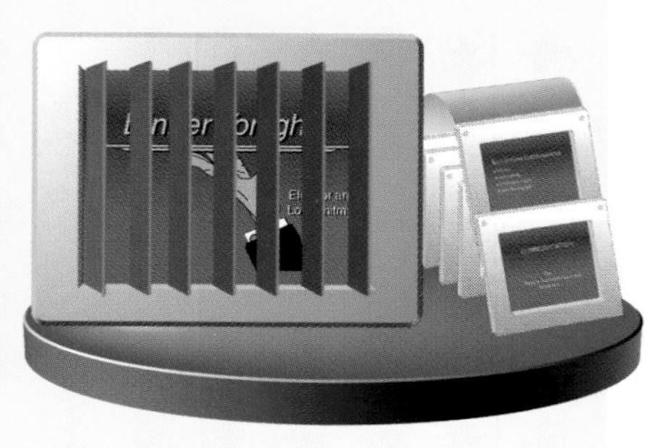

THE POWERPOINT WINDOW

The PowerPoint window displays several items to help you perform tasks efficiently.

Title Bar

Shows the name of the displayed presentation.

Menu Bar

Provides access to lists of commands available in PowerPoint and displays an area where you can type a question to get help information.

Standard Toolbar

Contains buttons you can use to select common commands, such as Save and Open.

Formatting Toolbar

Contains buttons you can use to select common formatting commands, such as Bold and Underline.

Outline and Slides Tabs

Provide two ways of viewing the slides in your presentation.

Slide Pane

Displays the current slide.

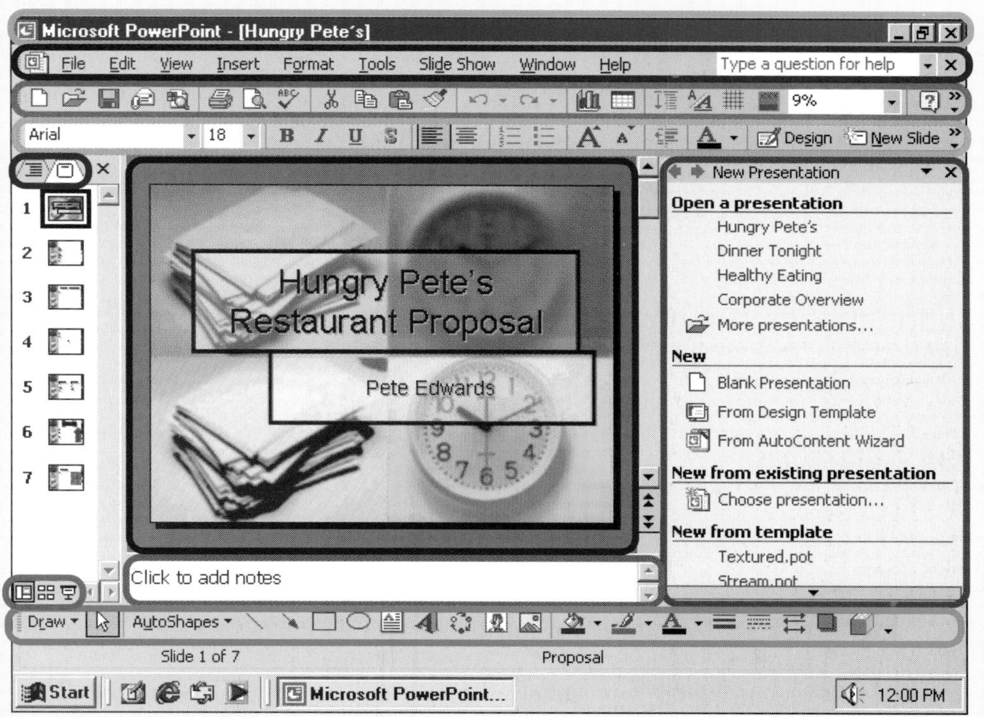

View Buttons

Allow you to quickly change the way your presentation is displayed on the screen.

Notes Pane

Displays the notes for the current slide.

Drawing Toolbar

Contains buttons to help you work with objects in your presentation.

Task Pane

Contains links you can select to perform common tasks, such as opening or creating a presentation.

CREATE A PRESENTATION USING THE AUTOCONTENT WIZARD

You can use the AutoContent Wizard to create a presentation. The wizard asks you a series of questions and then sets up a presentation based on your answers.

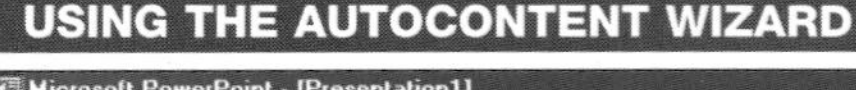

USING THE AUTOCONTENT WIZARD

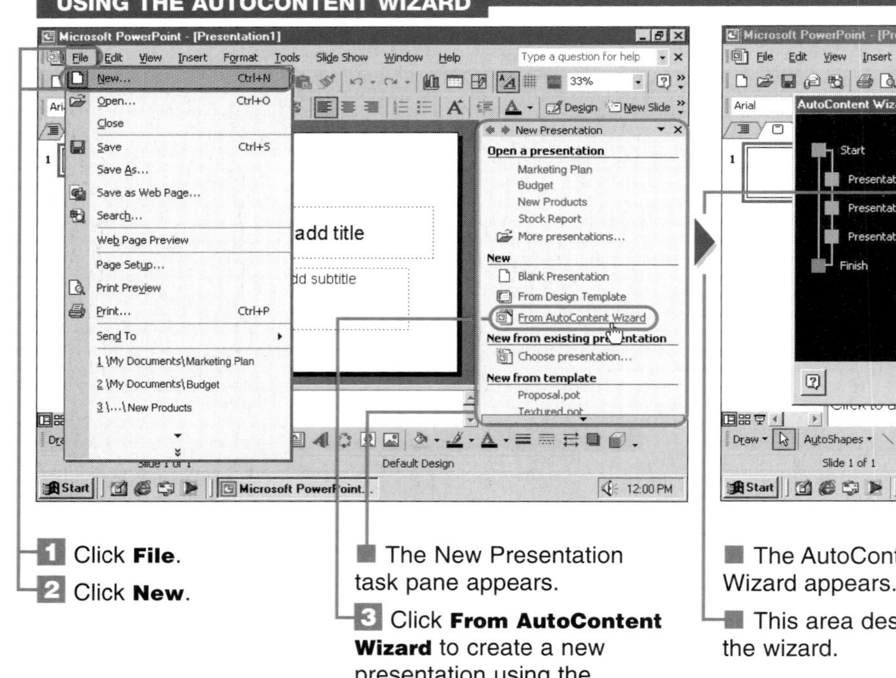

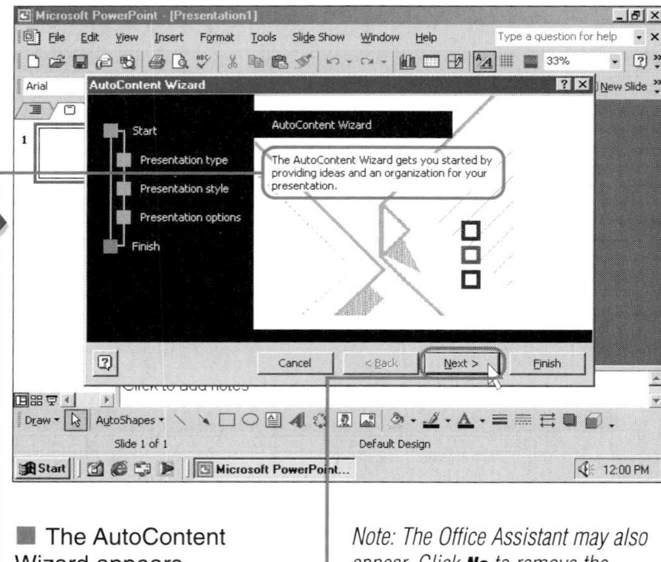

1 Click **File**.

2 Click **New**.

■ The New Presentation task pane appears.

3 Click **From AutoContent Wizard** to create a new presentation using the AutoContent Wizard.

■ The AutoContent Wizard appears.

■ This area describes the wizard.

*Note: The Office Assistant may also appear. Click **No** to remove the Office Assistant from your screen.*

4 Click **Next** to start creating your presentation.

Why did a dialog box appear after I selected a presentation in the AutoContent Wizard?

A dialog box appears if the presentation you selected is not installed on your computer. Insert the CD-ROM disc you used to install Office XP into your CD-ROM drive and then click **Yes** to install the presentation.

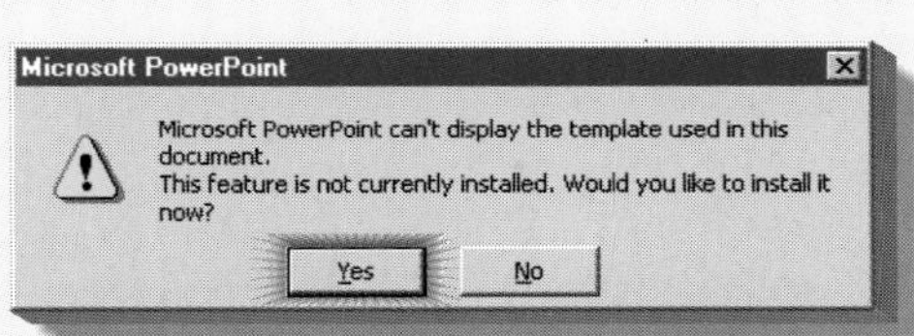

Is there another way to create a presentation?

If you want to design your own presentation without using the content PowerPoint suggests, you can create a blank presentation. Creating a blank presentation allows you to create and design each slide individually. To create a blank presentation, see page 186.

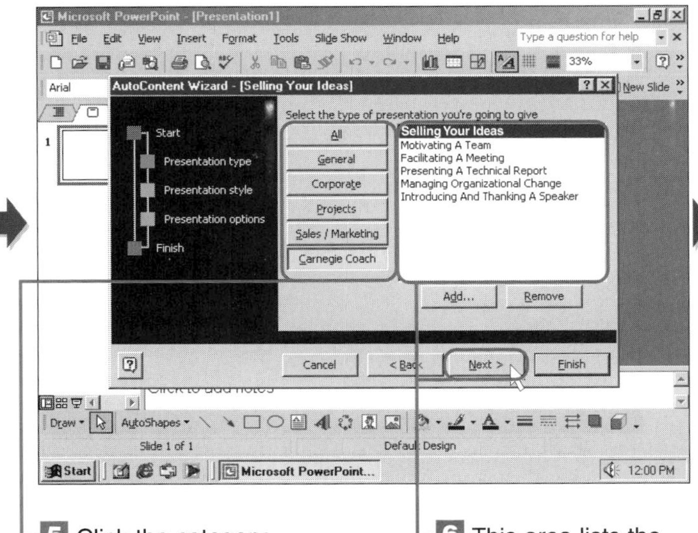

5 Click the category that best describes the type of presentation you want to create.

*Note: If you are not sure which category to select, click **All** to display all the available presentations.*

6 This area lists the presentations in the category you selected. Click the presentation that best suits your needs.

7 Click **Next** to continue.

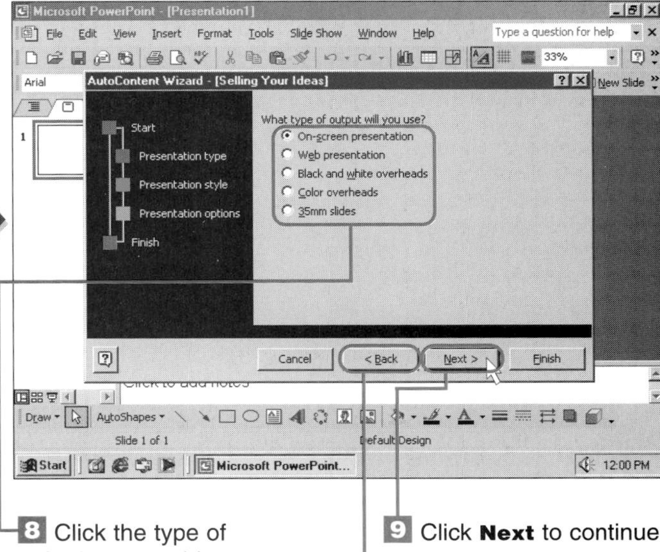

8 Click the type of output you want to use for your presentation (○ changes to ⊙).

9 Click **Next** to continue.

■ You can click **Back** at any time to return to a previous step and change your answers.

CONTINUED

CREATE A PRESENTATION USING THE AUTOCONTENT WIZARD

The AutoContent Wizard allows you to specify a title for the first slide in your presentation. You can also specify information you want to appear on each slide.

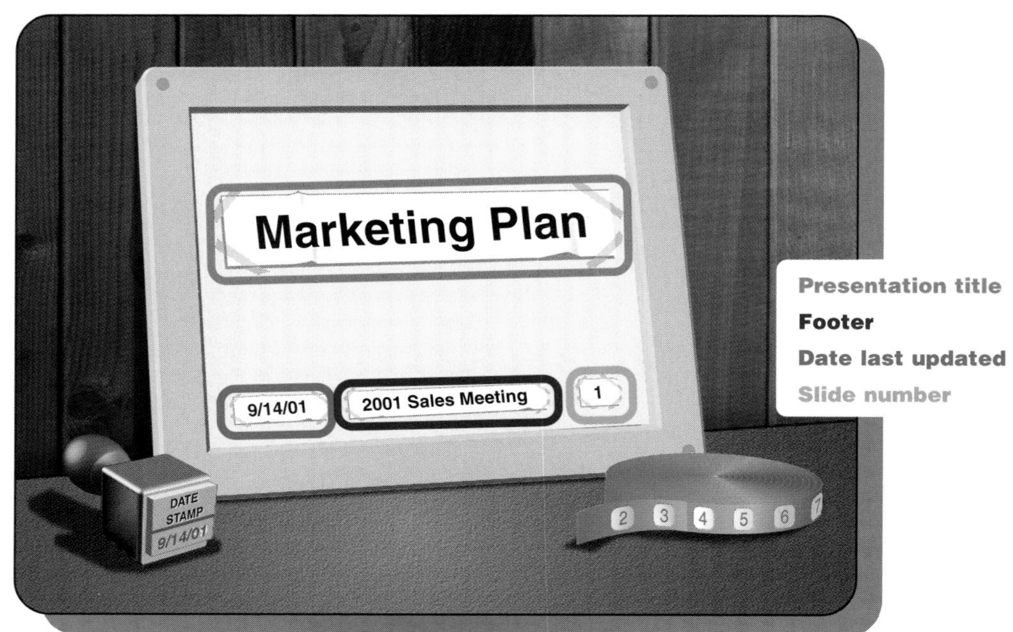

USING THE AUTOCONTENT WIZARD (CONTINUED)

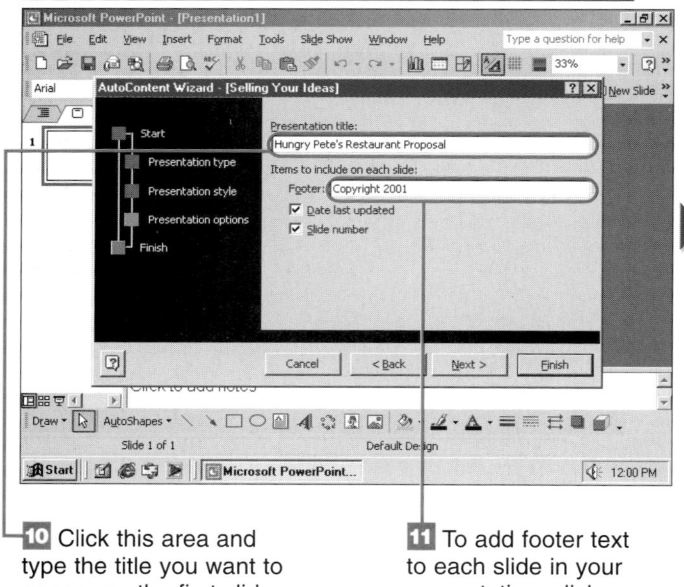

10 Click this area and type the title you want to appear on the first slide in your presentation.

11 To add footer text to each slide in your presentation, click this area and then type the text.

■ PowerPoint will add the current date and slide number to each slide in your presentation.

12 If you do not want to add the current date or slide number, click the option you do not want to add (☑ changes to ☐).

13 Click **Next** to continue.

How do I replace the sample text PowerPoint provides?

To replace the sample text, drag the mouse I over the text to select the text and then type the new text you want to use.

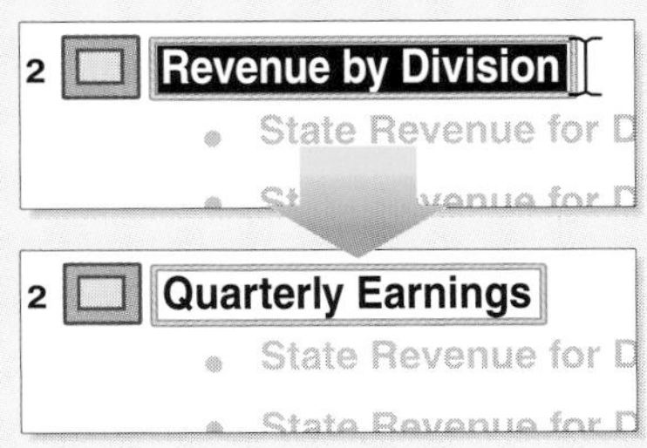

Can I change the design of the presentation I created using the AutoContent Wizard?

The design PowerPoint uses for the presentation depends on the presentation type you selected in the AutoContent Wizard. You can change the design of the presentation to give the presentation a new appearance. To change the design, see page 232.

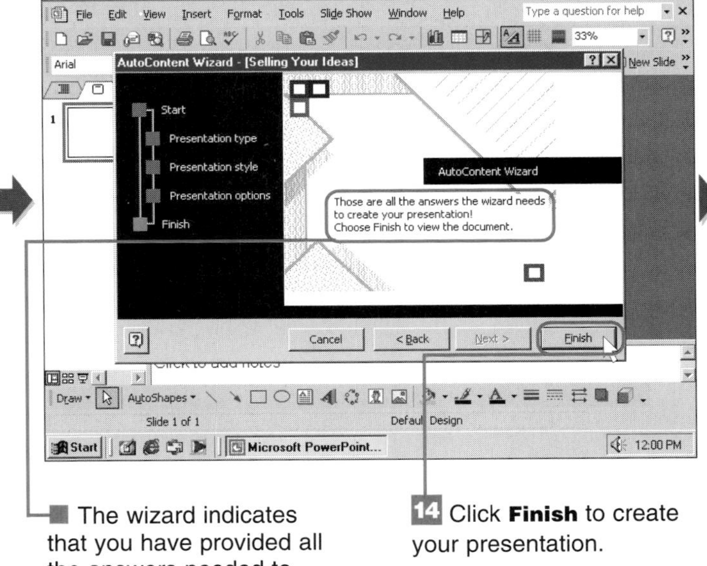

■ The wizard indicates that you have provided all the answers needed to create your presentation.

14 Click **Finish** to create your presentation.

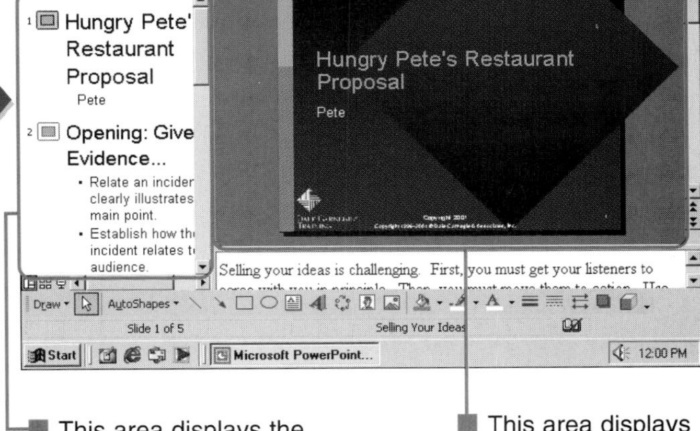

■ This area displays the sample text PowerPoint provides for each slide in your presentation. You can replace the sample text with your own text. For more information, see the top of this page.

■ This area displays the current slide.

CREATE A BLANK PRESENTATION

You can use PowerPoint to create a blank presentation. Blank presentations are useful when you want to create your own design and content for your slides.

CREATE A BLANK PRESENTATION

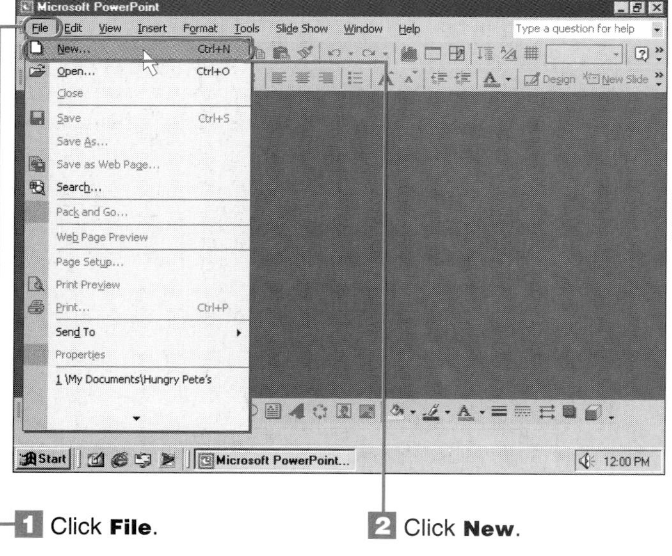

1 Click **File**.

2 Click **New**.

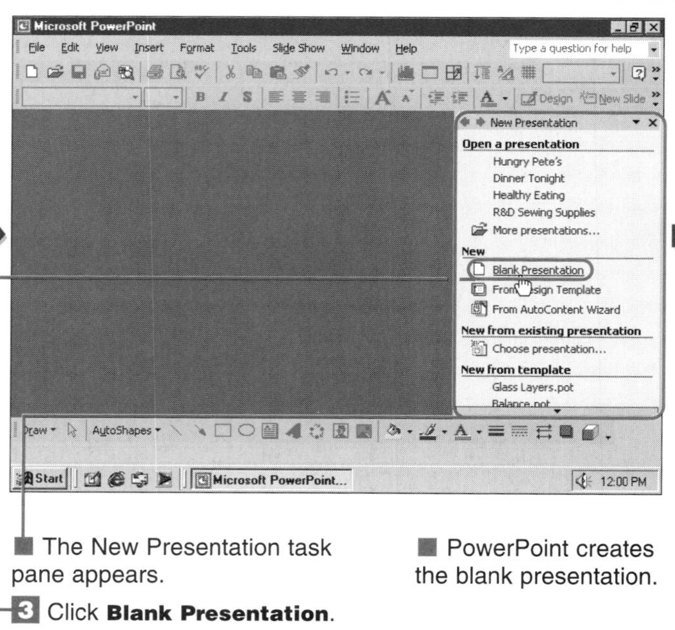

■ The New Presentation task pane appears.

3 Click **Blank Presentation**.

■ PowerPoint creates the blank presentation.

PowerPoint created only one slide in my presentation. What is wrong?

When you create a blank presentation, PowerPoint creates only the first slide. You can add additional slides to your presentation as you need them. To add a slide to your presentation, see page 208.

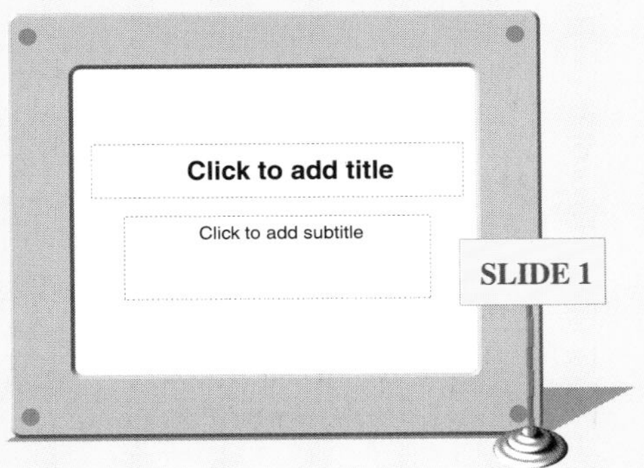

How can I quickly create a blank presentation?

While working in PowerPoint, you can click 🗋 to create a blank presentation at any time.

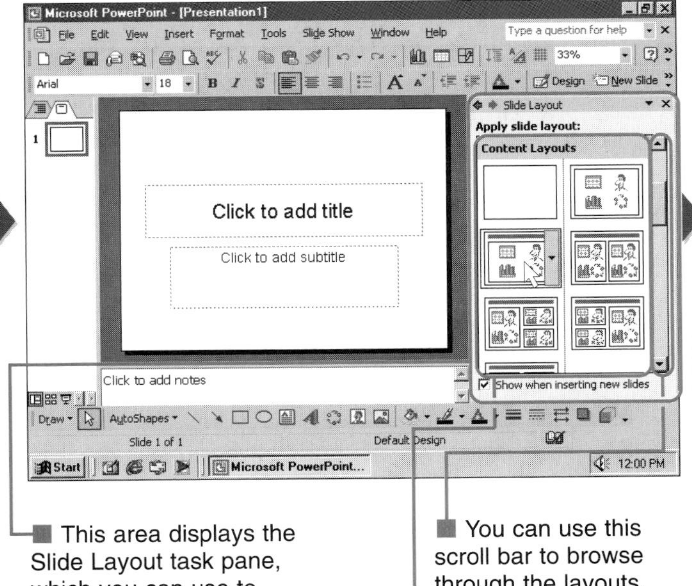

■ This area displays the Slide Layout task pane, which you can use to select a layout for the first slide in the presentation. For information on the slide layouts, see page 210.

■ You can use this scroll bar to browse through the layouts.

4 Click the layout you want to use.

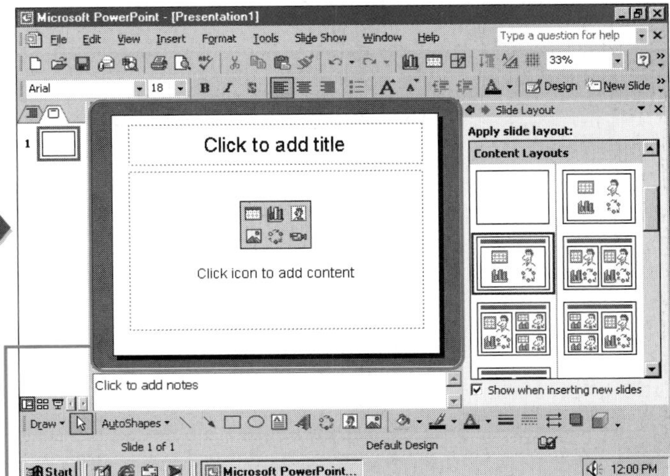

■ The slide displays the layout you selected.

■ You can now add text and objects to the slide. To add text, see page 200. To add objects, see pages 210 to 223.

CHANGE THE VIEW OF A PRESENTATION

PowerPoint offers several ways that you can view a presentation on your screen.

Each view displays the same presentation. If you make changes to your presentation in one view, the other views will also display the changes.

CHANGE THE VIEW OF A PRESENTATION

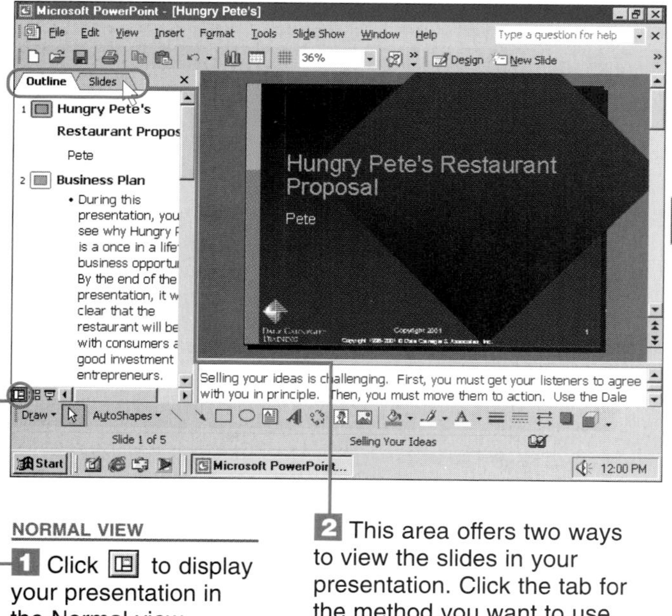

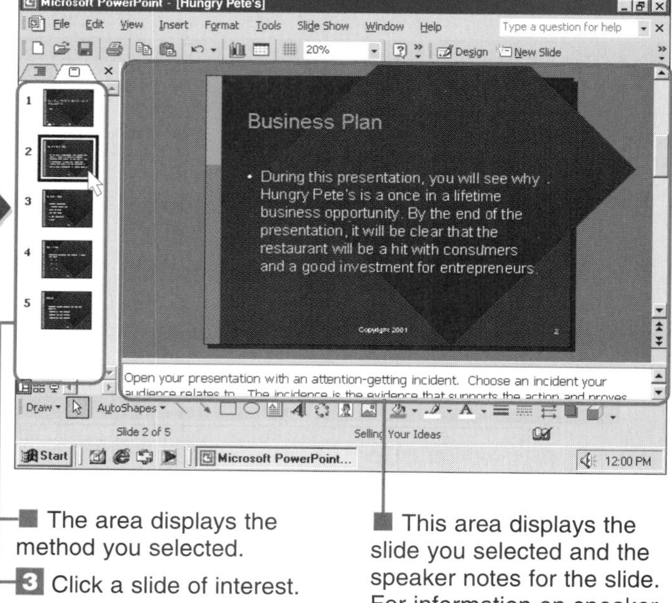

NORMAL VIEW

1 Click ▣ to display your presentation in the Normal view.

2 This area offers two ways to view the slides in your presentation. Click the tab for the method you want to use.

Outline - displays the text on each slide.

Slides - displays a miniature version of each slide.

■ The area displays the method you selected.

3 Click a slide of interest.

■ This area displays the slide you selected and the speaker notes for the slide. For information on speaker notes, see page 246.

When would I use each view?

Normal view

Useful for creating and editing your presentation. This view allows you to see different parts of your presentation, such as the current slide and your speaker notes, on a single screen.

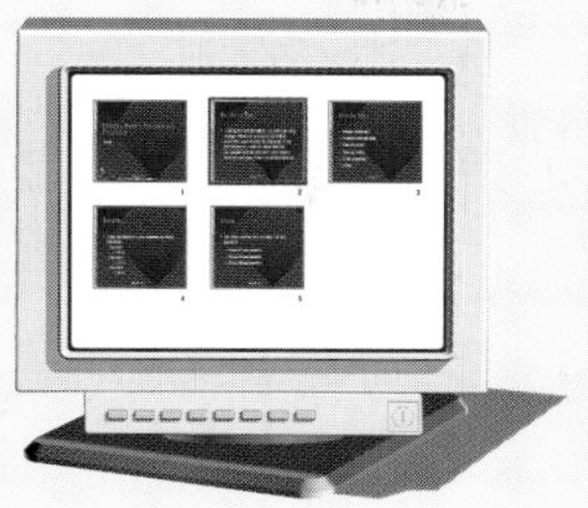

Slide Sorter view

Useful for reorganizing and deleting slides. This view allows you to see the overall organization of your presentation.

Slide Show view

Useful for previewing your presentation. This view allows you to see how your audience will view your presentation.

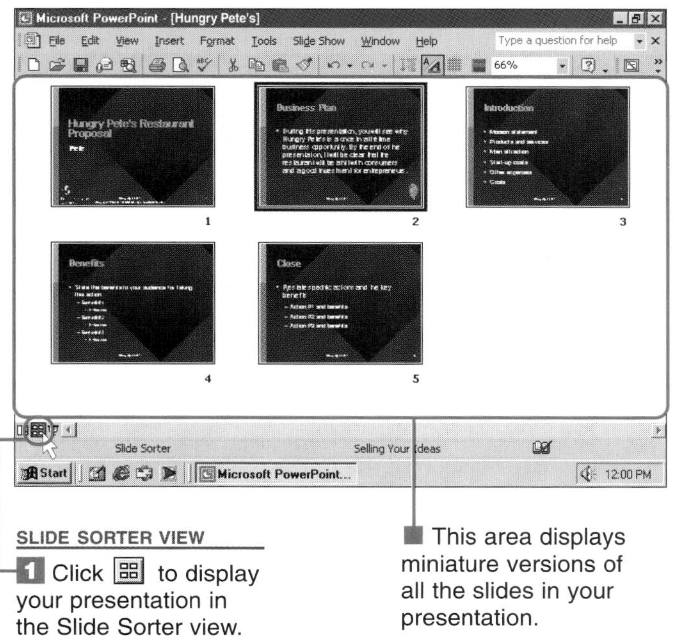

SLIDE SORTER VIEW

1 Click to display your presentation in the Slide Sorter view.

■ This area displays miniature versions of all the slides in your presentation.

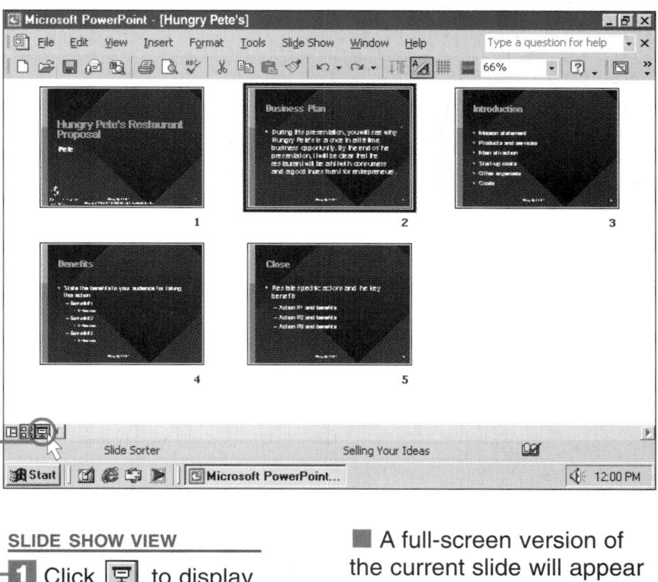

SLIDE SHOW VIEW

1 Click to display your presentation in the Slide Show view.

■ A full-screen version of the current slide will appear on your screen. You can move through the slides in your presentation to view your entire slide show. For information on viewing a slide show, see page 244.

BROWSE THROUGH A PRESENTATION

Your computer screen cannot display your entire presentation at once. You can browse through your presentation to view other areas of the presentation.

BROWSE THROUGH A PRESENTATION

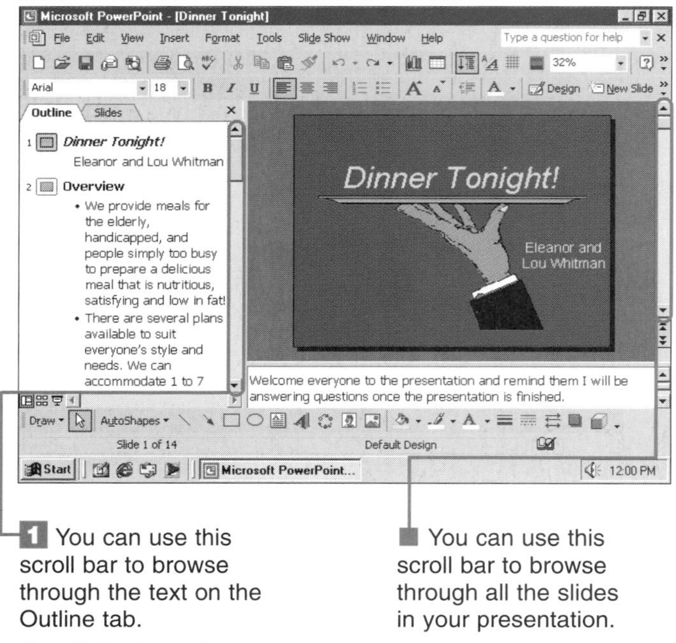

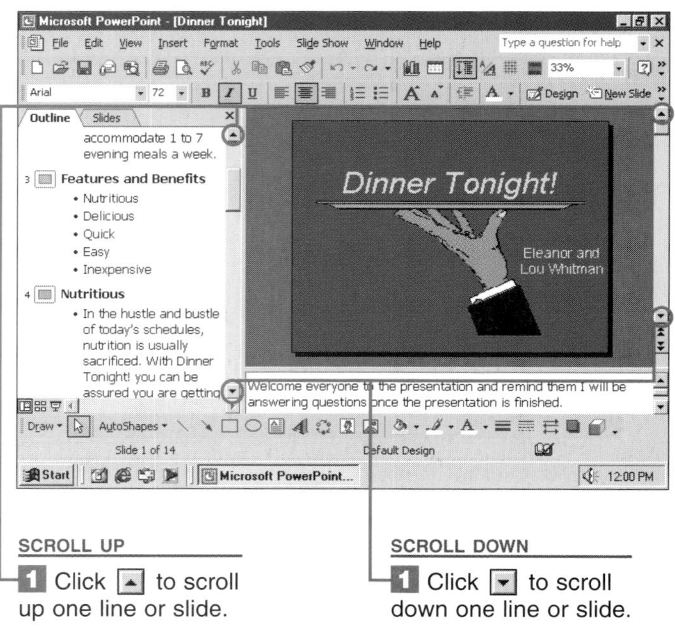

■1 You can use this scroll bar to browse through the text on the Outline tab.

Note: To display the Outline tab, see page 188.

■ You can use this scroll bar to browse through all the slides in your presentation.

SCROLL UP

■1 Click ▲ to scroll up one line or slide.

SCROLL DOWN

■1 Click ▼ to scroll down one line or slide.

How can I browse through the notes in my presentation?

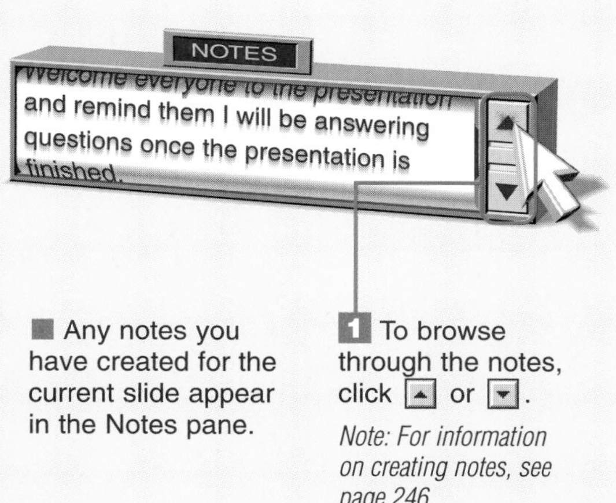

■ Any notes you have created for the current slide appear in the Notes pane.

1 To browse through the notes, click ▲ or ▼.

Note: For information on creating notes, see page 246.

How do I use a wheeled mouse to browse through my presentation?

A wheeled mouse has a wheel between the left and right mouse buttons. Moving this wheel lets you quickly browse through your presentation. The Microsoft IntelliMouse is a popular example of a wheeled mouse.

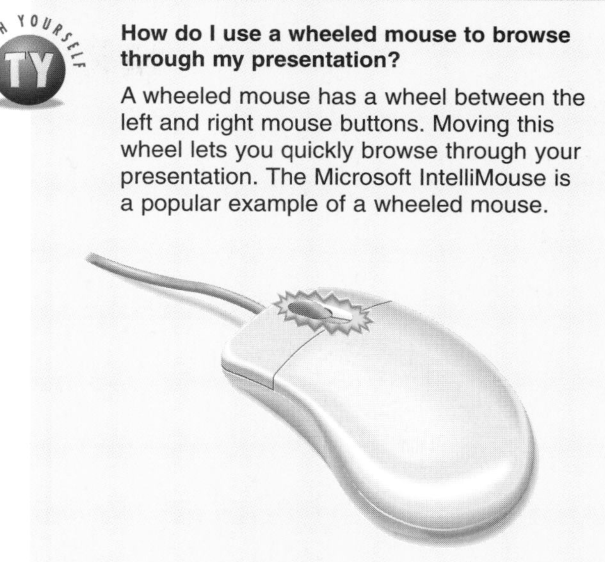

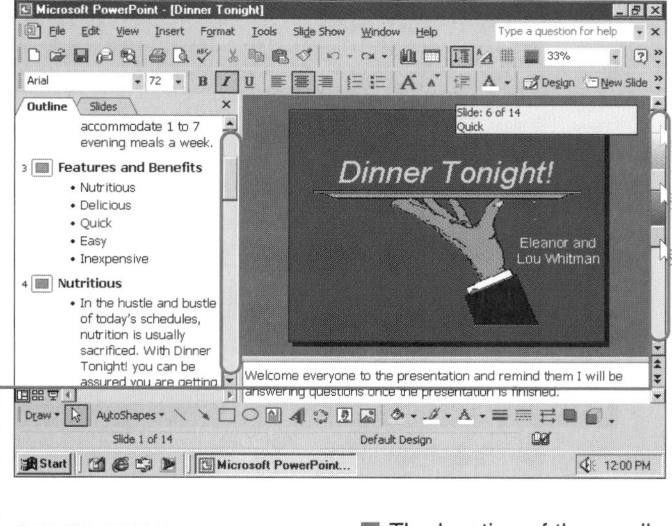

QUICKLY SCROLL

1 To quickly scroll through your presentation, drag the scroll box along the scroll bar.

■ The location of the scroll box indicates which part of your presentation you are viewing. To view the middle of your presentation, drag the scroll box halfway down the scroll bar.

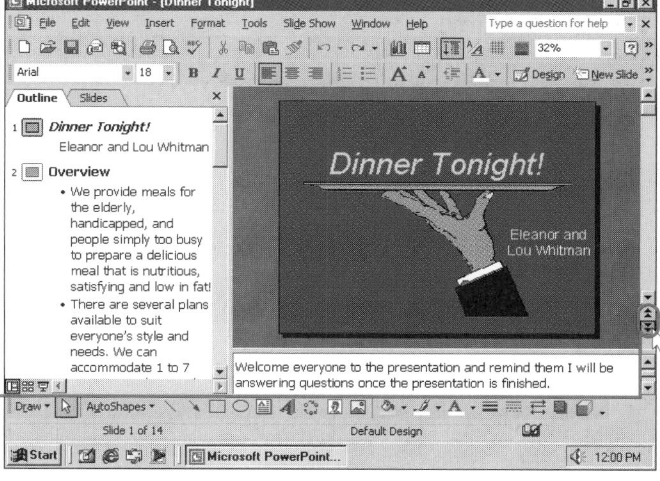

DISPLAY PREVIOUS OR NEXT SLIDE

1 Click one of the following buttons.

- ⏶ Display previous slide
- ⏷ Display next slide

SAVE A PRESENTATION

You can save your presentation to store the presentation for future use. This allows you to later review and make changes to the presentation.

You should regularly save changes you make to a presentation to avoid losing your work.

SAVE A PRESENTATION

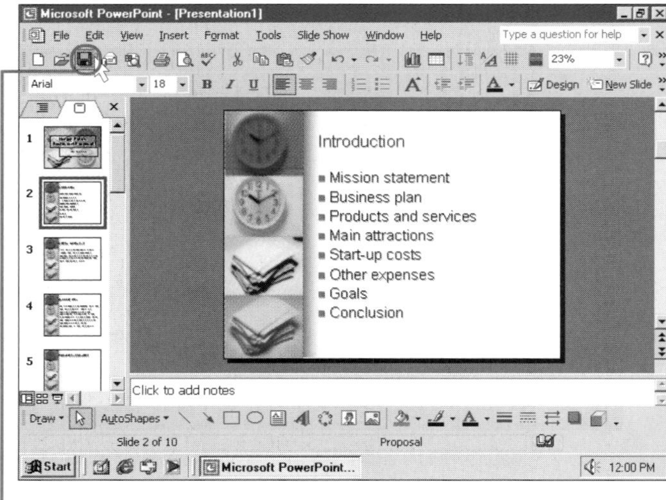

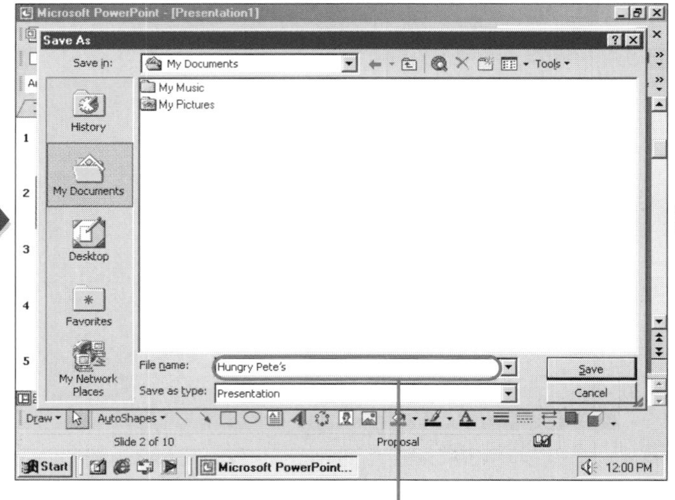

1 Click ▢ to save your presentation.

Note: If ▢ is not displayed, click » on the Standard toolbar to display all the buttons.

■ The Save As dialog box appears.

Note: If you previously saved your presentation, the Save As dialog box will not appear since you have already named the presentation.

2 Type a name for the presentation.

What are the commonly used locations that I can access?

History

Provides access to folders and presentations you recently worked with.

My Documents

Provides a convenient place to store a presentation.

Desktop

Allows you to store a presentation on the Windows desktop.

Favorites

Provides a place to store a presentation you will frequently use.

My Network Places

Allows you to store a presentation on your network.

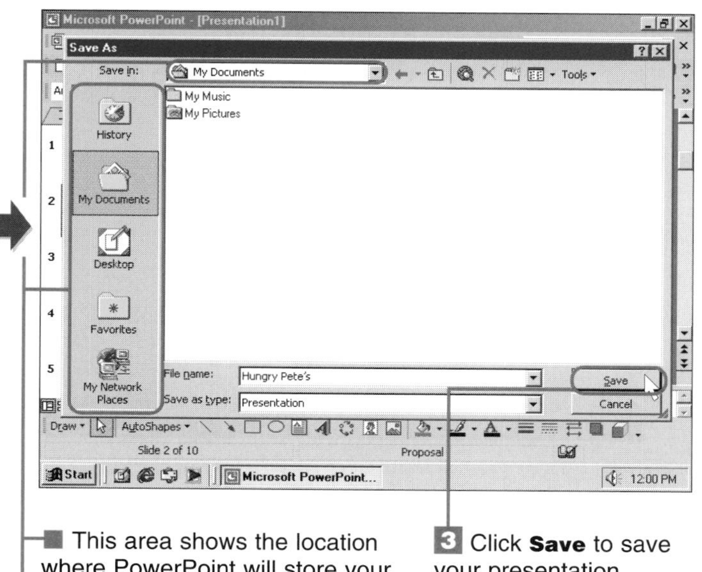

■ This area shows the location where PowerPoint will store your presentation. You can click this area to change the location.

■ This area allows you to access commonly used locations. You can click a location to save your presentation in the location.

3 Click **Save** to save your presentation.

■ PowerPoint saves your presentation.

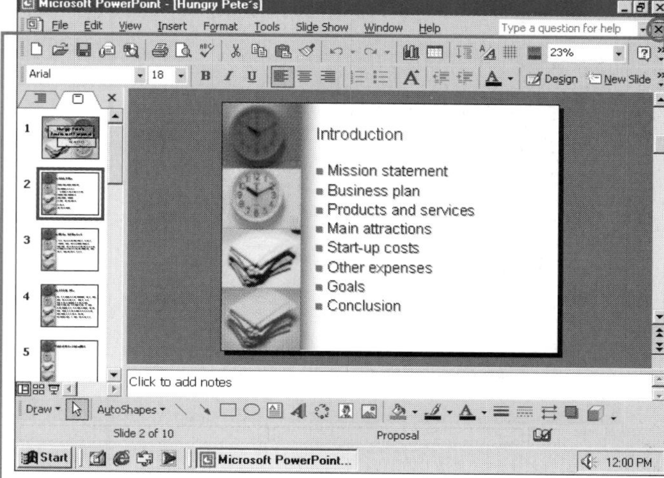

CLOSE A PRESENTATION

1 When you finish working with a presentation, click ☒ to close the presentation.

■ The presentation disappears from your screen.

OPEN A PRESENTATION

You can open a saved presentation to view the presentation on your screen. This allows you to review and make changes to the presentation.

OPEN A PRESENTATION

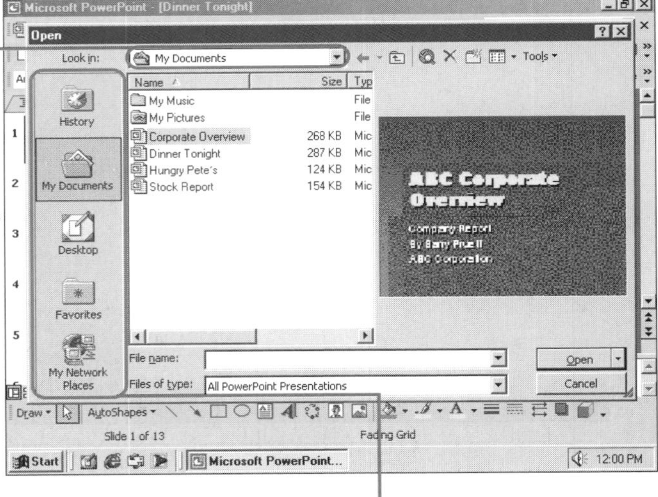

1 Click to open a presentation.

Note: If does not appear, click on the Standard toolbar to display all the buttons.

■ The Open dialog box appears.

■ This area shows the location of the displayed presentations. You can click this area to change the location.

■ This area allows you to access presentations in commonly used locations. You can click a location to display the presentations stored in the location.

Note: For information on the commonly used locations, *see the top of page 193.*

How can I quickly open a presentation I recently worked with?

PowerPoint remembers the names of the last four presentations you worked with. You can use one of the following methods to quickly open any of these presentations.

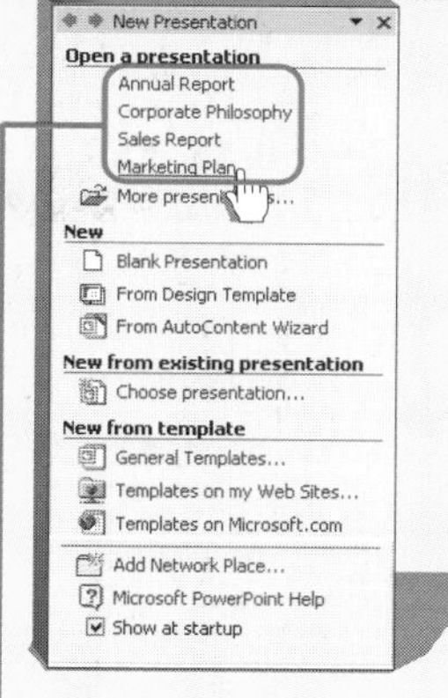

Use the Task Pane

The New Presentation task pane appears each time you start PowerPoint. To display the New Presentation task pane, see page 12.

1 Click the name of the presentation you want to open.

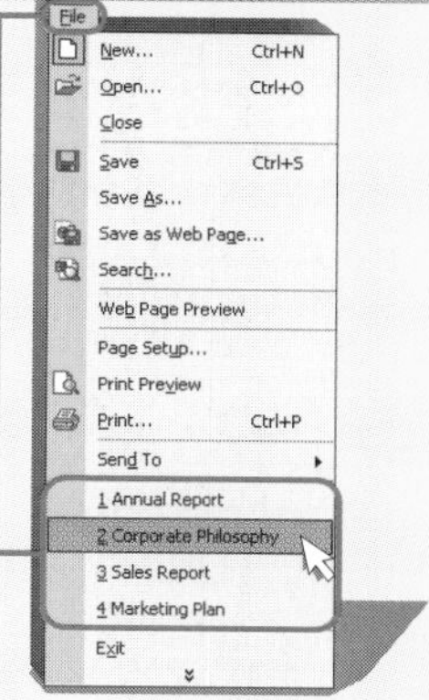

Use the File Menu

1 Click **File**.

2 Click the name of the presentation you want to open.

Note: If the names of the last four presentations you worked with are not all displayed, position the mouse over the bottom of the menu to display all the names.

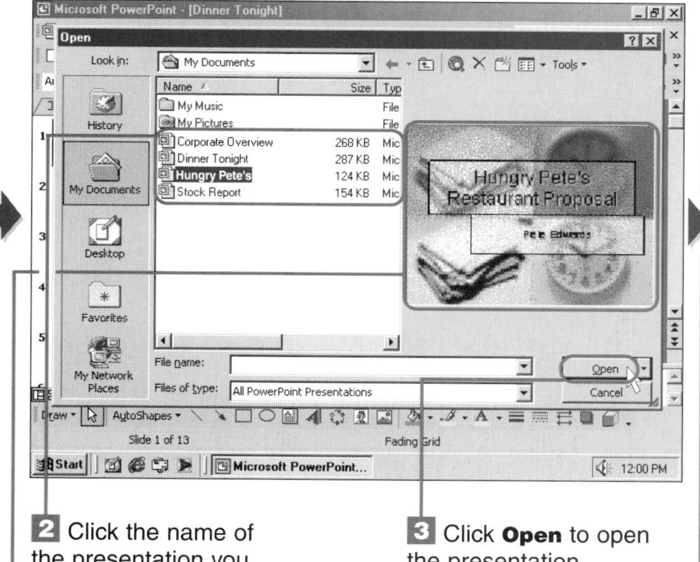

2 Click the name of the presentation you want to open.

■ This area displays the first slide in the presentation you selected.

3 Click **Open** to open the presentation.

■ The presentation opens and appears on your screen. You can now review and make changes to the presentation.

■ This area displays the name of the open presentation.

■ If you already had a presentation open, the new presentation appears in a new Microsoft PowerPoint window. You can click the buttons on the taskbar to switch between the open presentations.

E-MAIL A PRESENTATION

You can e-mail a presentation to a friend, family member or colleague.

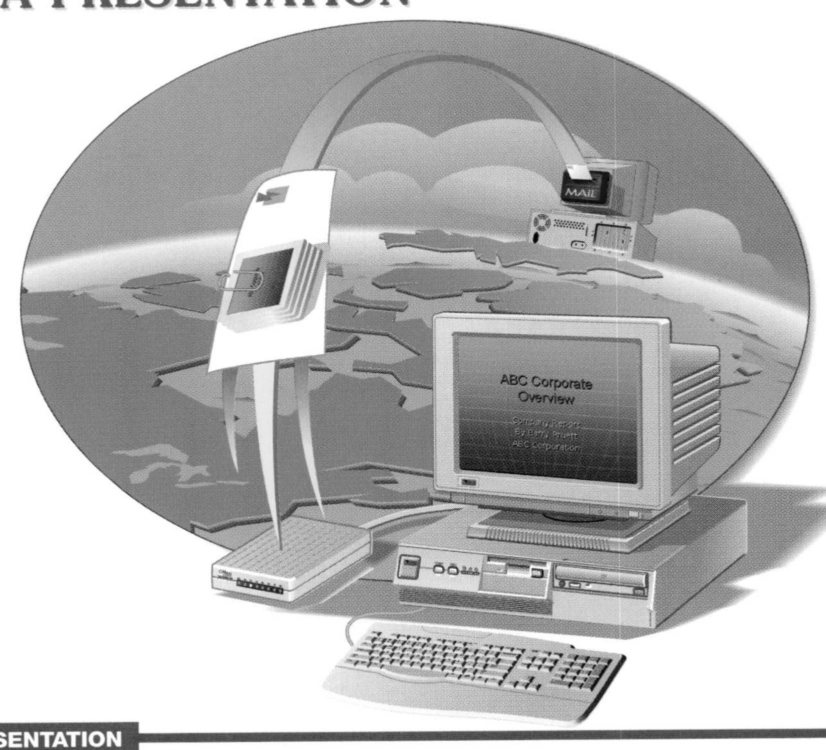

Before you can e-mail a presentation, Microsoft Outlook must be set up on your computer.

E-MAIL A PRESENTATION

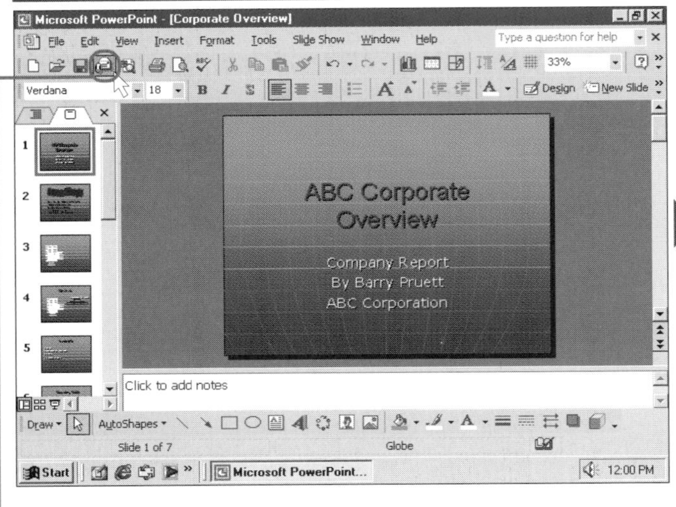

1 Click [icon] to e-mail the current presentation.

Note: If [icon] is not displayed, click [icon] on the Standard toolbar to display all the buttons.

■ The Choose Profile dialog box may appear. Click **OK** to close the dialog box.

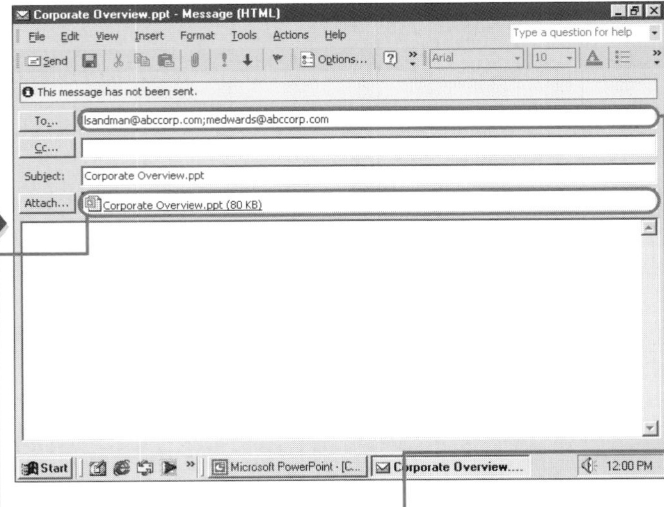

■ A window appears for the e-mail message.

■ This area displays the name and size of the presentation.

2 Click this area and type the e-mail address of each person you want to receive the message. Separate each address with a semicolon (;).

How can I address an e-mail message?

To

Sends the message to each person you specify.

Carbon Copy (Cc)

Sends a copy of the message to people who are not directly involved but would be interested in the message.

Why can't the person I sent my presentation to view the information?

When you e-mail a presentation, the presentation is sent as an attached file. The recipient must have PowerPoint 2000 or a later version of PowerPoint installed to open the file. For more information on attached files, see page 346.

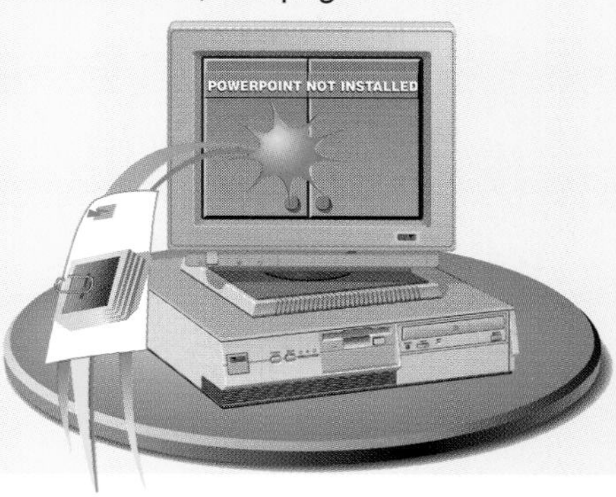

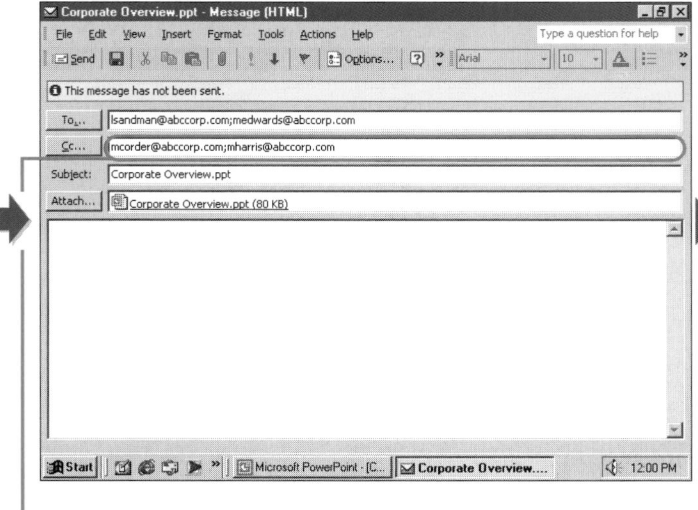

3 To send a copy of the message, click this area and type the e-mail address of each person you want to receive a copy. Separate each address with a semicolon (;).

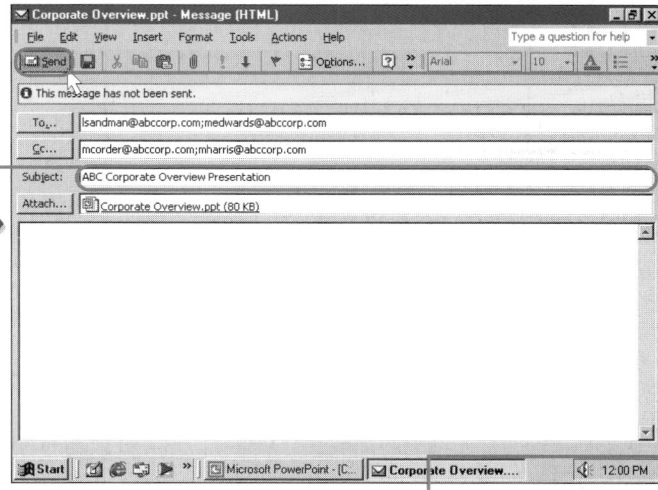

4 Click this area and type a subject for the message.

Note: If a subject already exists, you can drag the mouse I over the existing subject and then type a new subject.

5 Click **Send** to send the message.

SELECT TEXT

Before making changes to text in your presentation, you will often need to select the text you want to work with. Selected text appears highlighted on your screen.

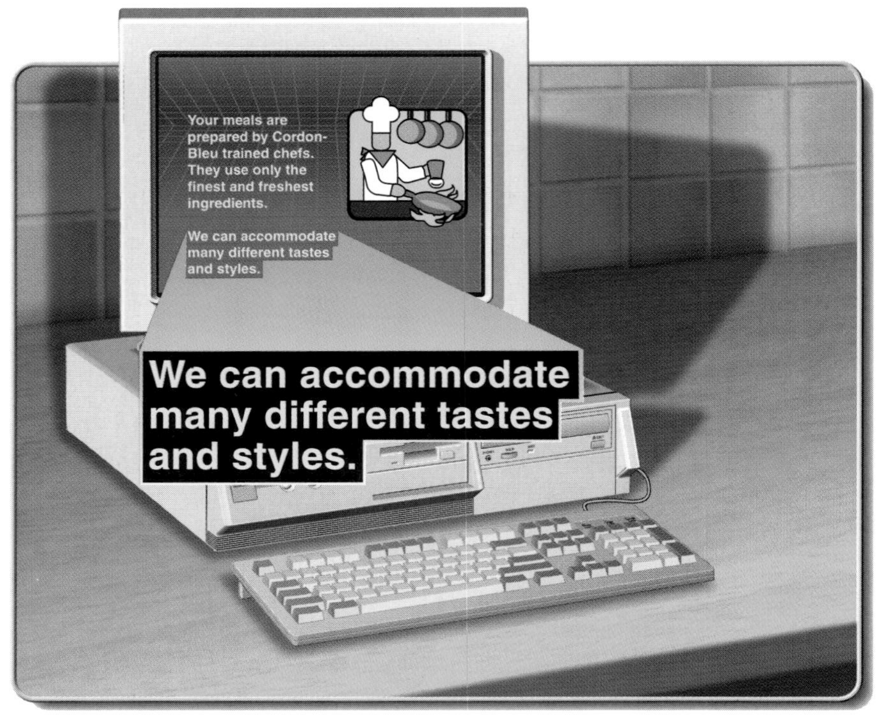

SELECT TEXT

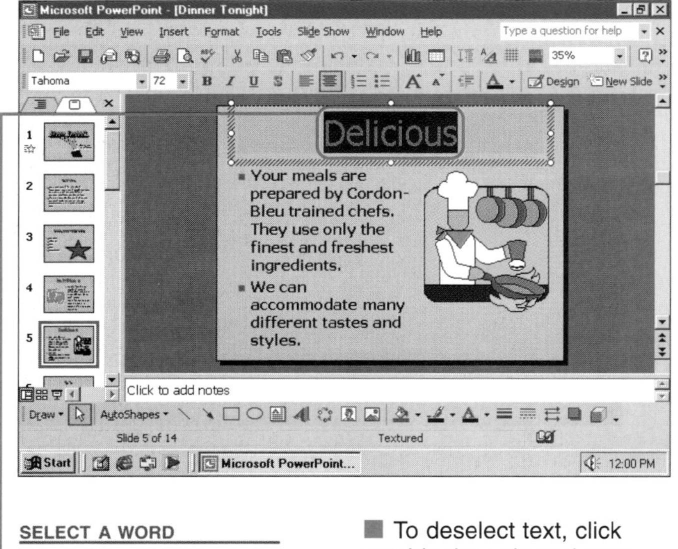

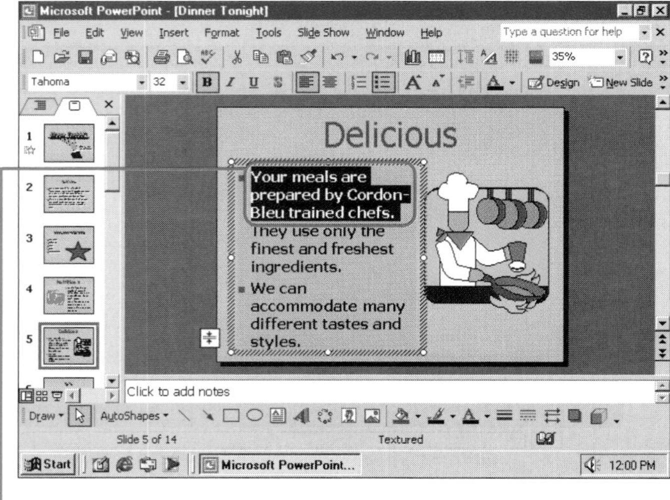

SELECT A WORD

1 Double-click the word you want to select.

■ To deselect text, click outside the selected area.

SELECT A SENTENCE

1 Click in the sentence you want to select.

2 Press and hold down the Ctrl key as you click in the sentence again.

Is there another way to select text in my presentation?

You can also perform the steps below to select text on the Outline tab in the Normal view. The Outline tab displays the text for all the slides in your presentation. For more information on the Outline tab, see page 188.

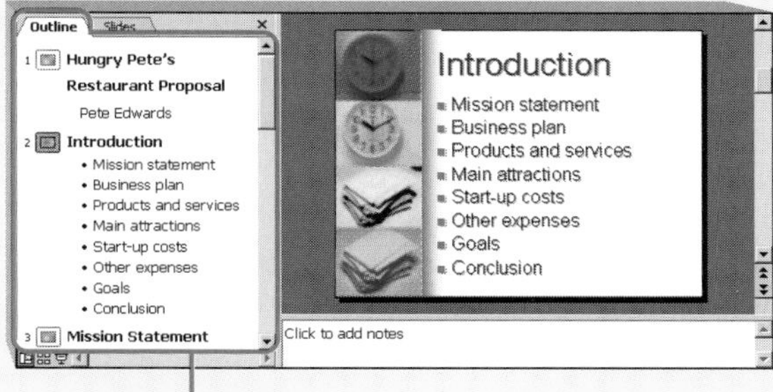

Outline tab

How can I quickly select all the text on a slide?

You can use the Outline tab to quickly select all the text on a slide.

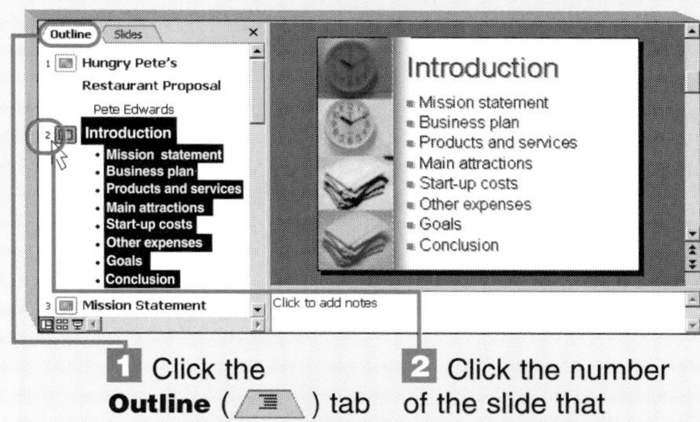

1 Click the **Outline** (≡) tab to display the text for all the slides in your presentation.

2 Click the number of the slide that contains the text you want to select.

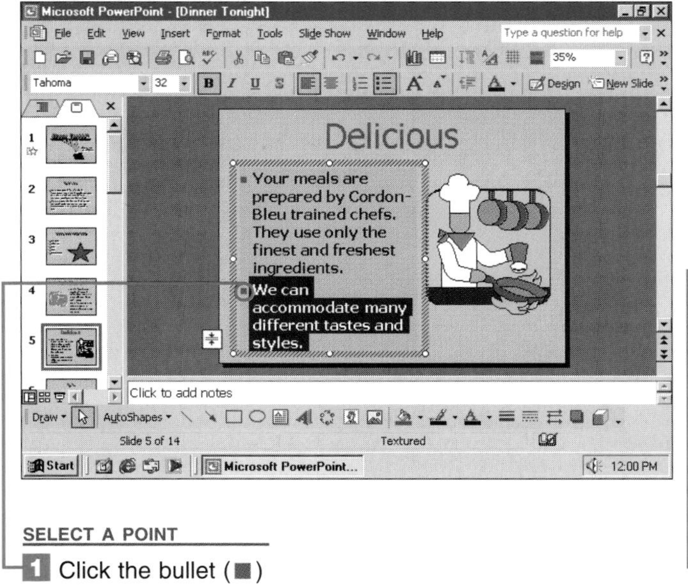

SELECT A POINT

1 Click the bullet (■) beside the point you want to select.

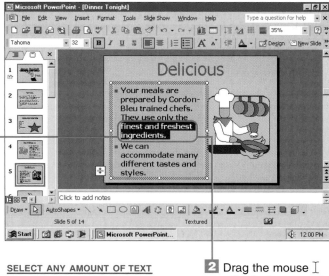

SELECT ANY AMOUNT OF TEXT

1 Position the mouse I over the first word you want to select.

2 Drag the mouse I over the text you want to select.

PowerPoint allows you to type text onto a slide in your presentation quickly and easily.

INSERT CHARACTERS

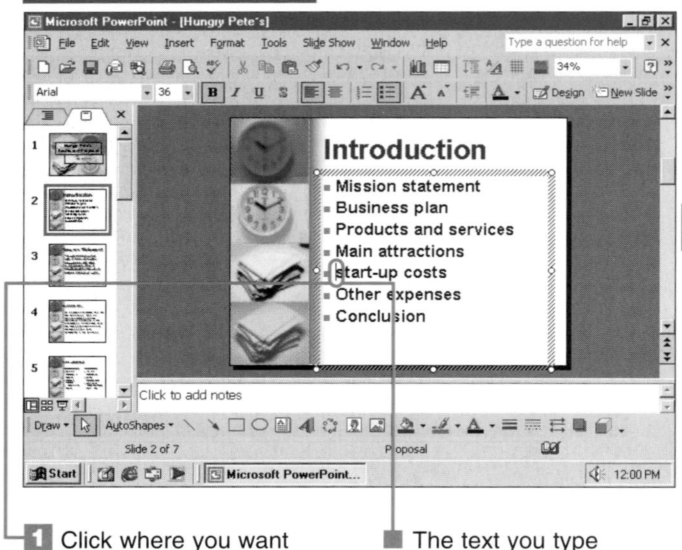

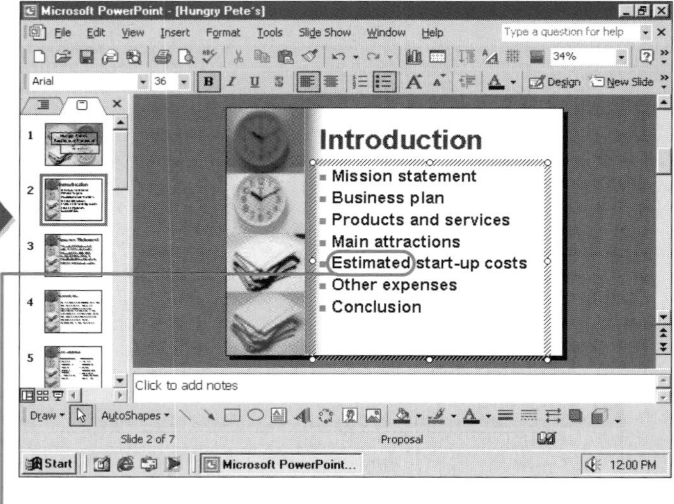

1 Click where you want to insert the new text.

■ The text you type will appear where the insertion point flashes on your screen.

Note: You can press the ←, ↓, ↑ or → key to move the insertion point.

2 Type the text you want to insert.

■ To insert a blank space, press the **Spacebar**.

Is there another way to insert text?

You can also insert text on the Outline tab in the Normal view. The Outline tab displays all the text for your presentation. Text you insert on the Outline tab will automatically appear on the slide in the Slide pane. For more information on the Outline tab, see page 188.

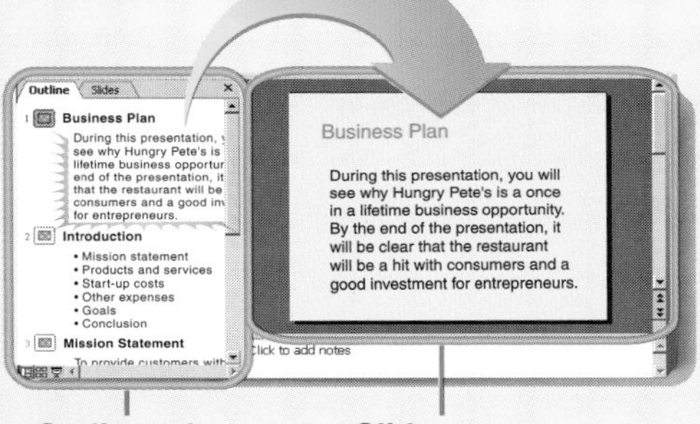

Outline tab

Slide pane

Why does the AutoFit Options button (⊞) appear when I insert text in a placeholder on a slide?

If you insert more text than a placeholder can hold, the AutoFit Options button (⊞) appears, allowing you to change how the text fits in the placeholder. For example, you can specify whether or not you want PowerPoint to resize the text to fit in the placeholder.

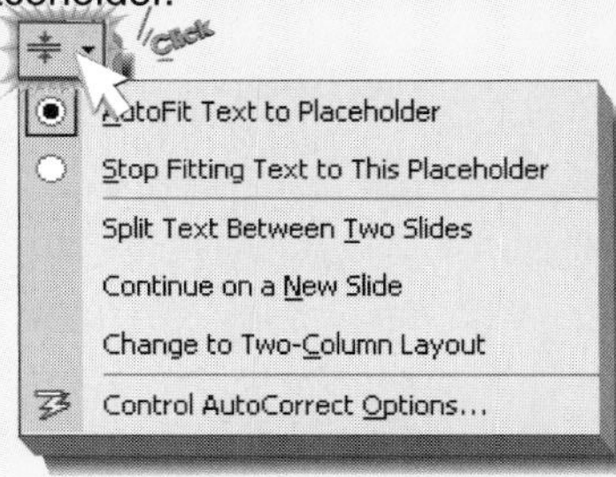

INSERT A NEW POINT

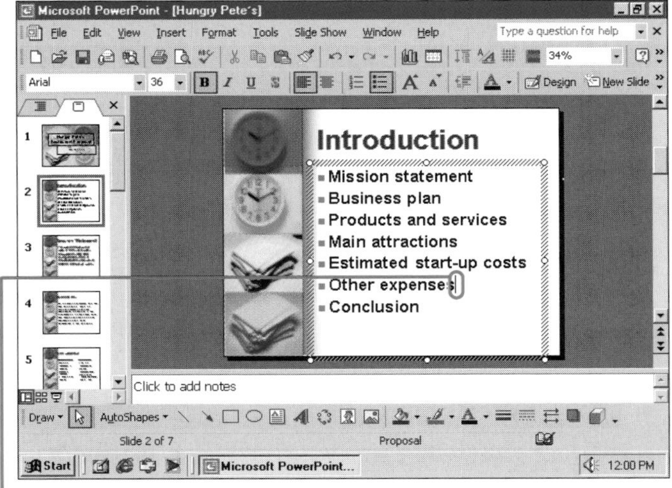

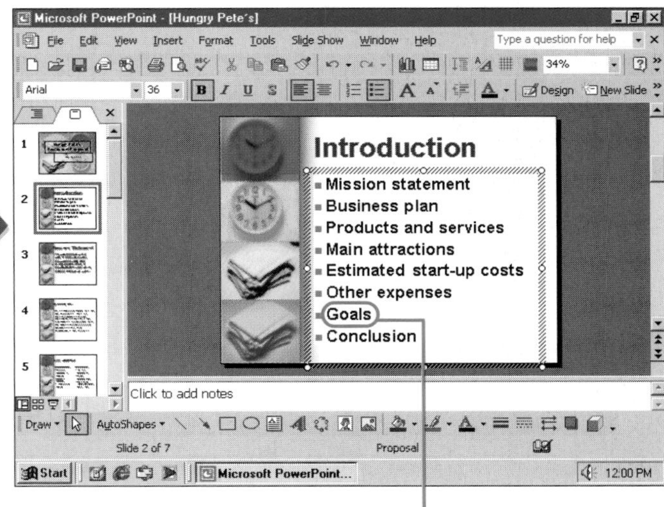

1 Click at the end of the point directly above where you want to insert a new point.

2 Press the Enter key to insert a blank line for the new point.

3 Type the text for the new point.

DELETE TEXT

You can delete text from a slide to remove information that you no longer need in your presentation.

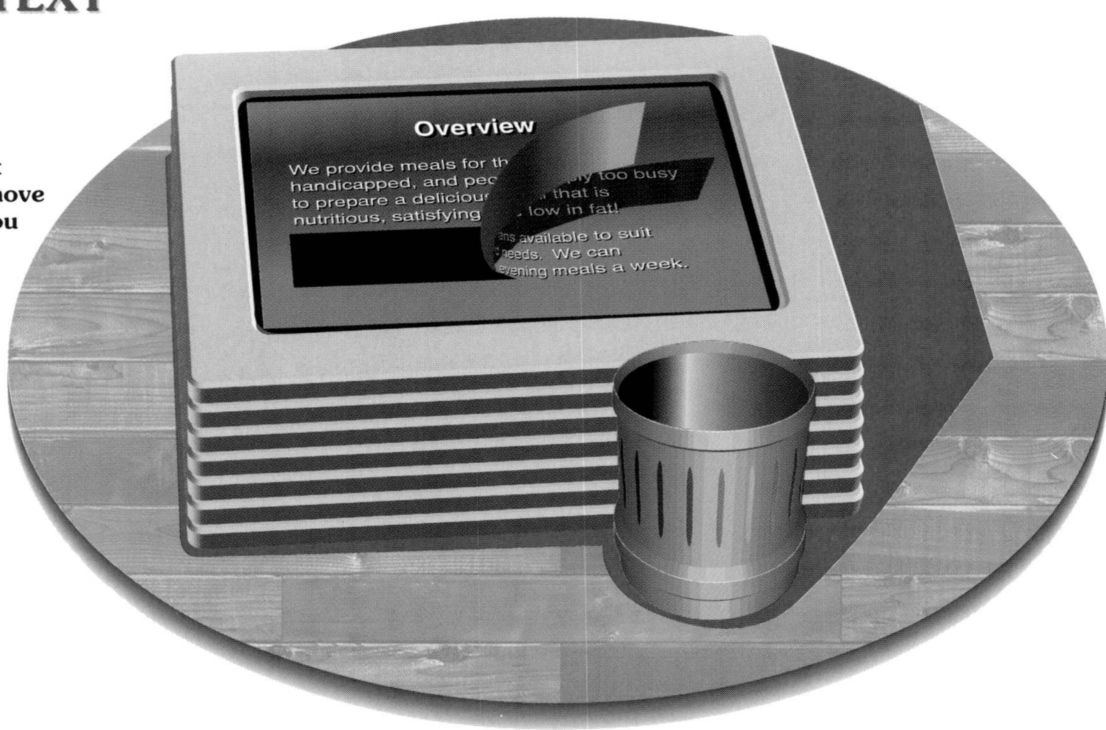

DELETE TEXT

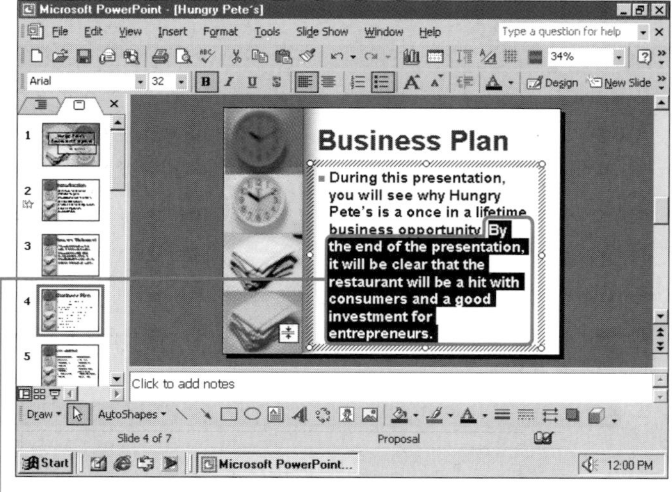

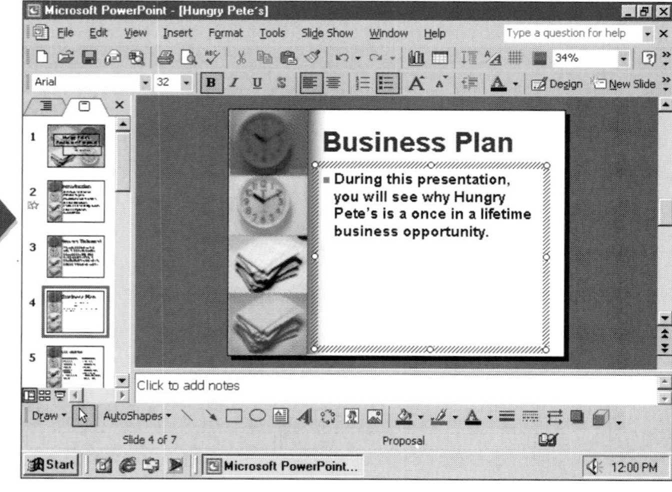

1 Select the text you want to delete. To select text, see page 198.

2 Press the Delete key to remove the text from your presentation.

■ The text disappears.

■ To delete a single character, click to the right of the character you want to delete and then press the ←Backspace key. PowerPoint will delete the character to the left of the flashing insertion point.

UNDO CHANGES

PowerPoint remembers the last changes you made to your presentation. If you regret these changes, you can cancel them by using the Undo feature.

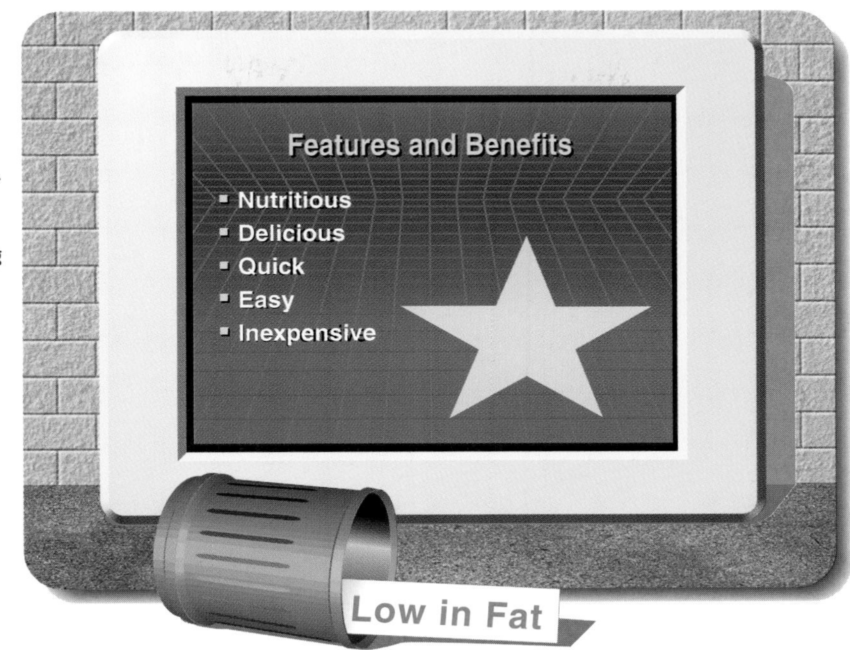

The Undo feature can cancel your last editing and formatting changes.

UNDO CHANGES

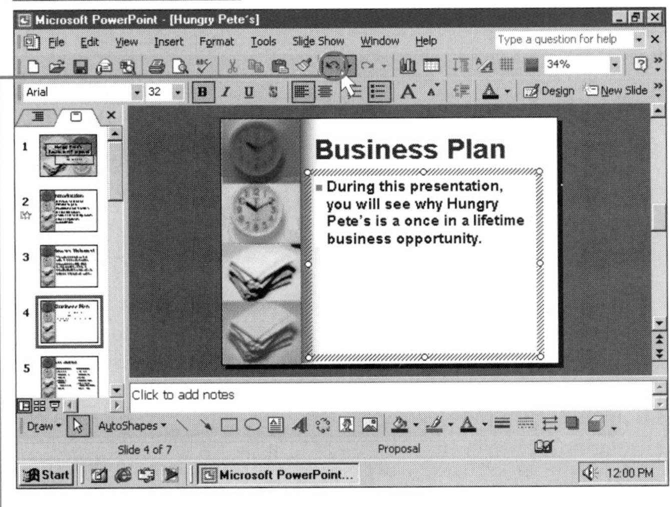

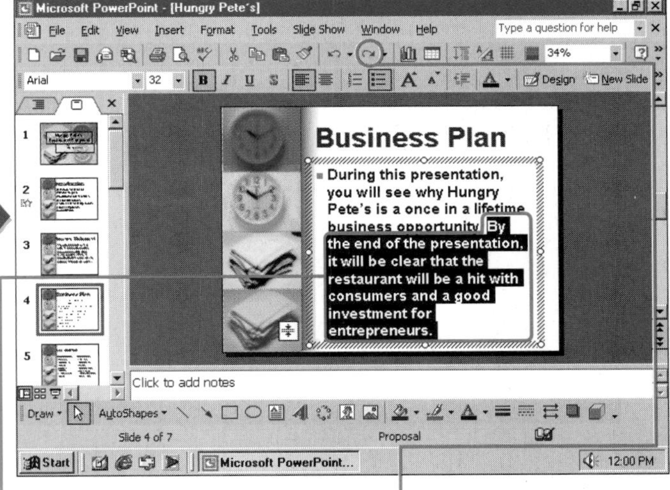

1 Click ↶ to undo the last change you made to your presentation.

Note: If ↶ is not displayed, click » on the Standard toolbar to display all the buttons.

■ PowerPoint cancels the last change you made to your presentation.

■ You can repeat step 1 to cancel previous changes you made.

■ To reverse the results of using the Undo feature, click ↷.

Note: If ↷ is not displayed, click » on the Standard toolbar to display all the buttons.

MOVE TEXT

You can move text to a new location in your presentation.

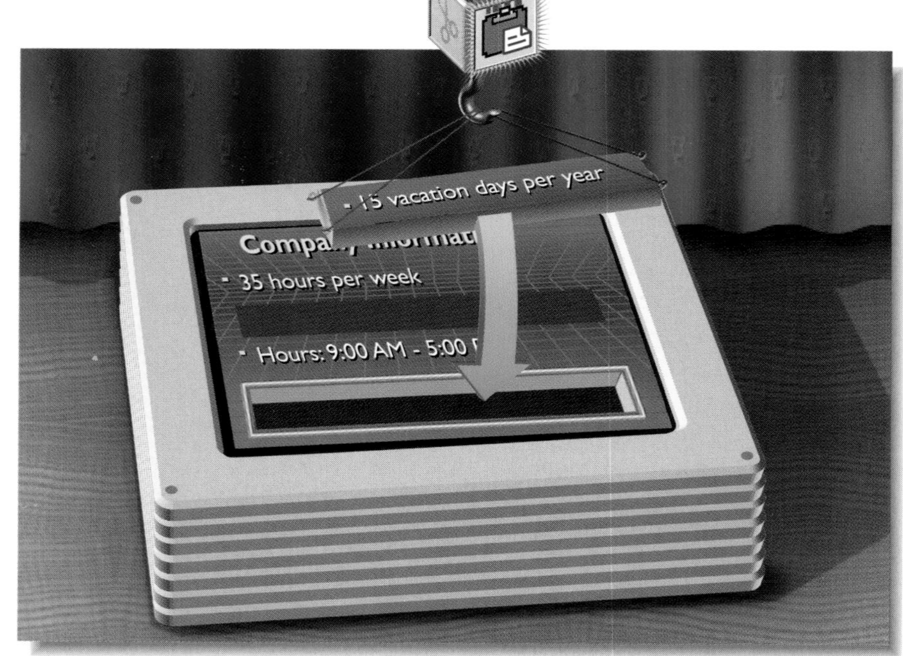

Moving text is useful when you want to re-organize the ideas on a slide.

MOVE TEXT

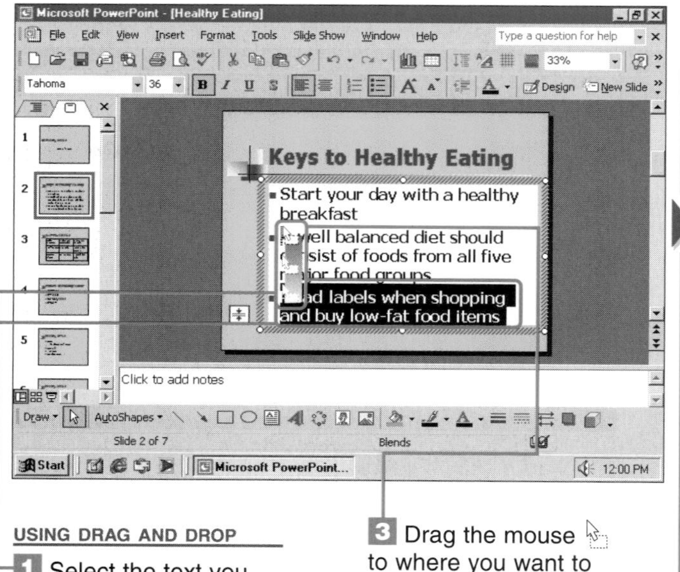

USING DRAG AND DROP

1 Select the text you want to move. To select text, see page 198.

2 Position the mouse I over the selected text (I changes to ↖).

3 Drag the mouse to where you want to place the text.

Note: The text will appear where you position the dotted insertion point on your screen.

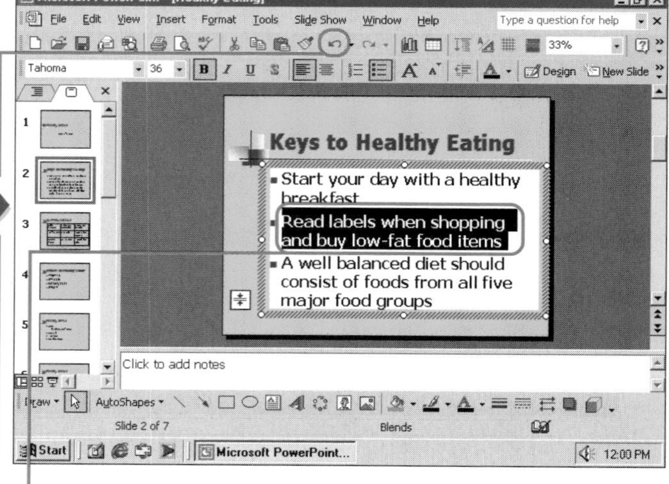

■ The text moves to the new location.

■ To immediately move the text back to its original location, click ↶.

Note: If ↶ is not displayed, click » on the Standard toolbar to display all the buttons.

How can I use the Clipboard task pane to move text?

The Clipboard task pane displays the last 24 items you have selected to move. To place a clipboard item in your presentation, click the location where you want the item to appear and then click the item in the task pane. For more information on using task panes, see page 12.

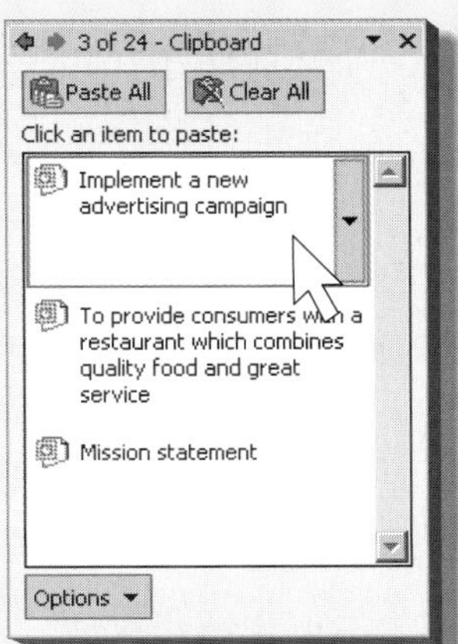

Why does the Paste Options button (📋) appear when I move text?

When you move text, the Paste Options button (📋) may appear, allowing you to change the format of the text. For example, you can choose to keep the original formatting of the text.

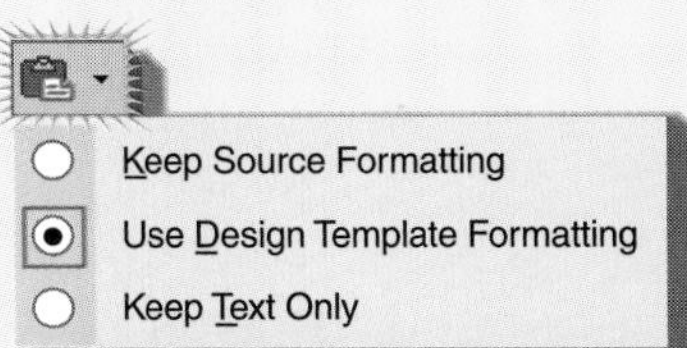

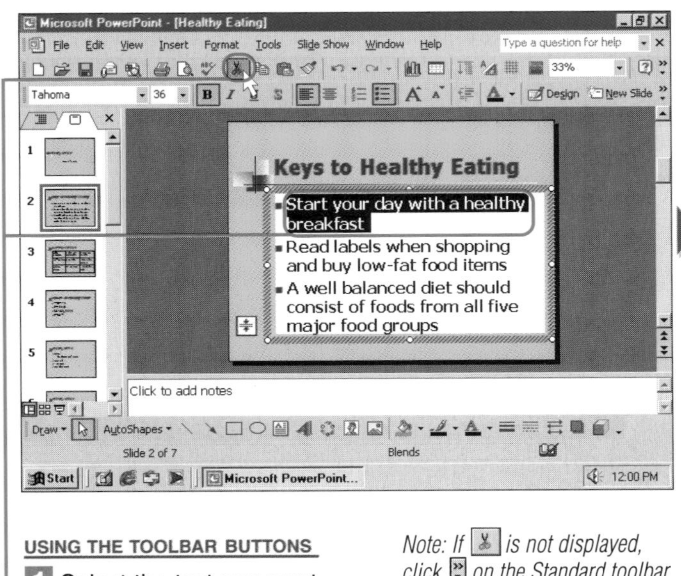

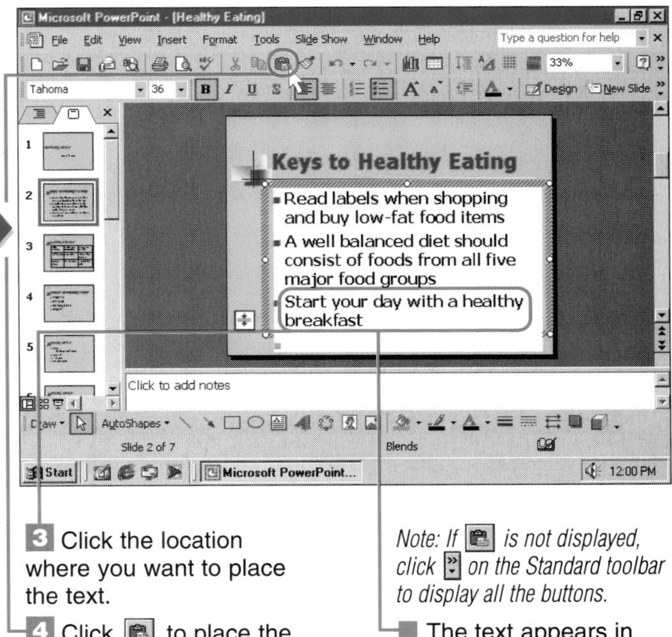

USING THE TOOLBAR BUTTONS

1 Select the text you want to move. To select text, see page 198.

2 Click ✂ to move the text.

Note: If ✂ is not displayed, click » on the Standard toolbar to display all the buttons.

■ The Clipboard task pane may appear. To use the Clipboard task pane, see the top of this page.

3 Click the location where you want to place the text.

4 Click 📋 to place the text in the new location.

Note: If 📋 is not displayed, click » on the Standard toolbar to display all the buttons.

■ The text appears in the new location.

CHECK SPELLING

You can find and correct all the spelling errors in your presentation.

PowerPoint automatically underlines misspelled words in red. The underlines will not appear when you print your presentation or view the slide show.

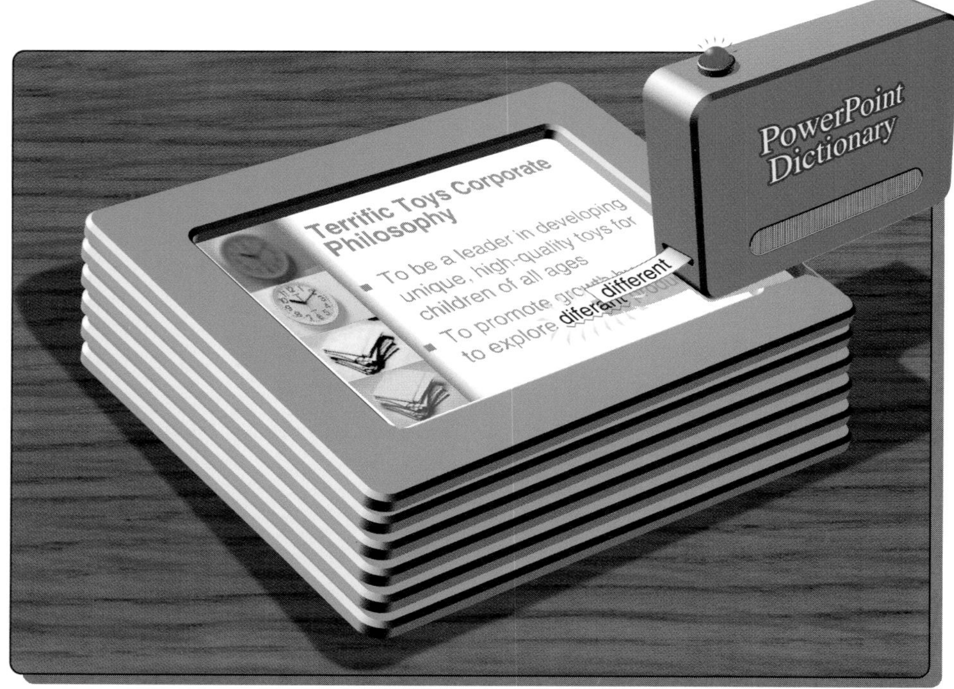

CHECK SPELLING

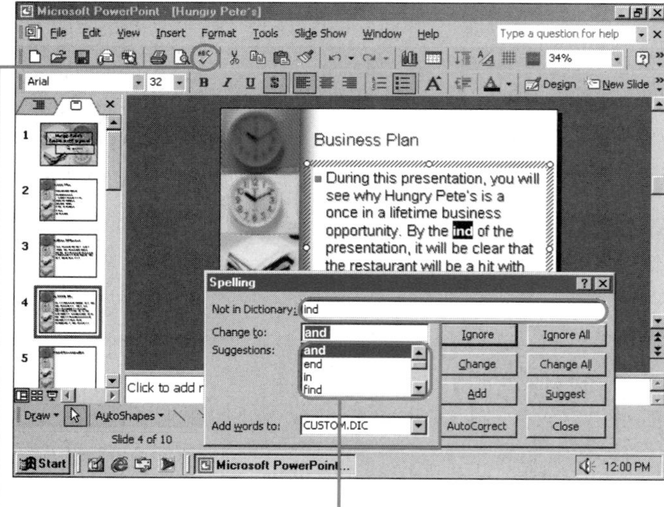

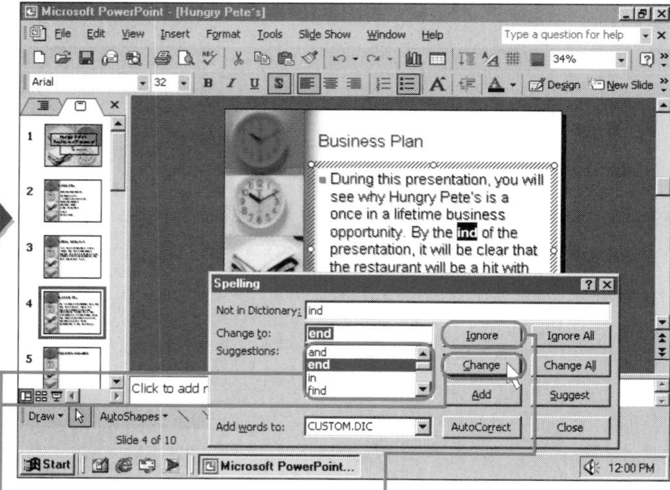

1 Click [icon] to start the spell check.

Note: If [icon] is not displayed, click [icon] on the Standard toolbar to display all the buttons.

■ The Spelling dialog box appears if PowerPoint finds a misspelled word in your presentation.

■ This area displays the first misspelled word.

■ This area displays suggestions for correcting the word.

2 Click the word you want to use to correct the misspelled word.

3 Click **Change** to replace the misspelled word with the word you selected.

■ To skip the word and continue checking your presentation, click **Ignore**.

*Note: To skip the word and all other occurrences of the word in your presentation, click **Ignore All**.*

Can PowerPoint automatically correct my typing mistakes?

PowerPoint automatically corrects common spelling errors as you type. Here are a few examples.

acheive → achieve
claer → clear
developement → development
foriegn → foreign
hte → the
occassion → occasion
recomend → recommend
statment → statement
wtih → with

How does PowerPoint find spelling errors in my presentation?

PowerPoint compares every word in your presentation to words in its dictionary. If a word in your presentation does not exist in the dictionary, the word is considered misspelled.

PowerPoint will not find a correctly spelled word used in the wrong context, such as "We have been in business for **sit** years." You should carefully review your presentation to find this type of error.

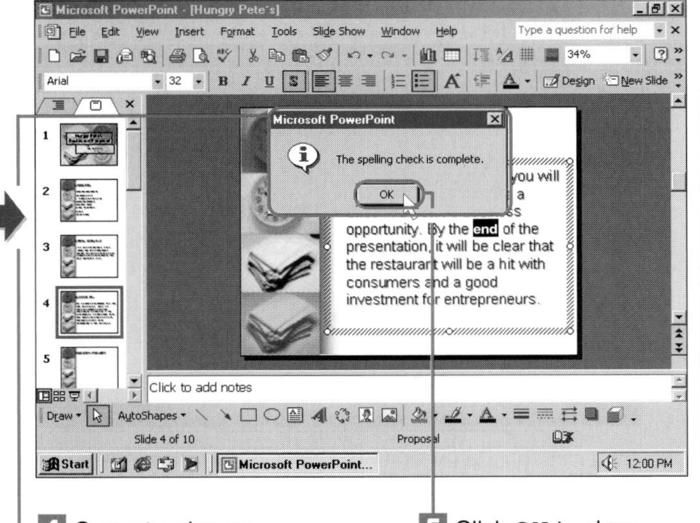

4 Correct or ignore misspelled words until this dialog box appears, telling you the spell check is complete.

5 Click **OK** to close the dialog box.

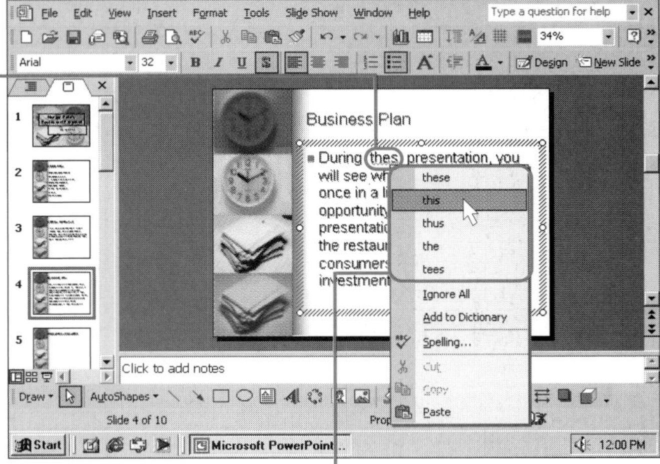

CORRECT ONE MISSPELLED WORD

1 Right-click the misspelled word you want to correct.

■ A menu appears with suggestions to correct the word.

2 To replace the misspelled word with one of the suggestions, click the suggestion.

Note: If you do not want to use any of the suggestions to correct the word, click outside the menu to close the menu.

ADD A NEW SLIDE

You can insert a new slide into your presentation to add a new topic you want to discuss.

ADD A NEW SLIDE

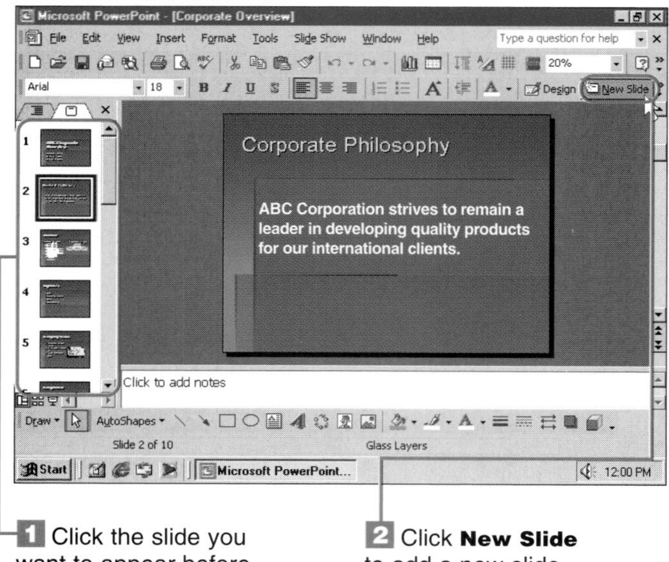

1 Click the slide you want to appear before the new slide.

2 Click **New Slide** to add a new slide.

Note: If the New Slide button is not displayed, click » on the Formatting toolbar to display all the buttons.

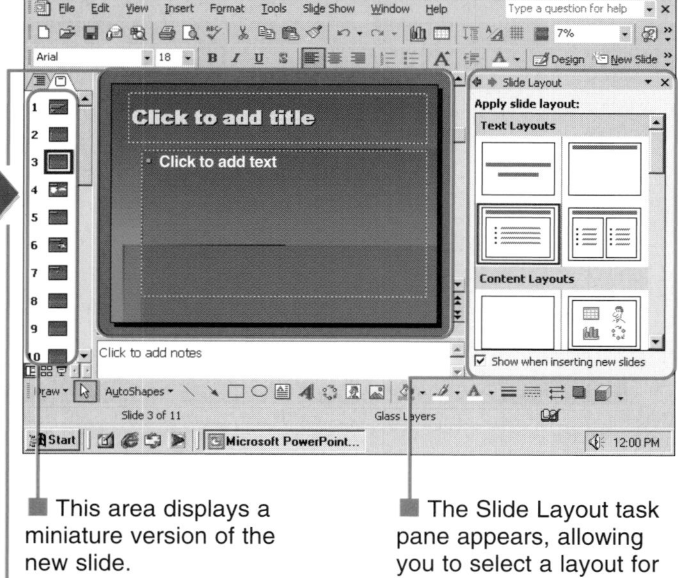

■ This area displays a miniature version of the new slide.

■ This area displays the new slide.

■ The Slide Layout task pane appears, allowing you to select a layout for the new slide.

How much text should I display on a slide?

You should be careful not to include too much text on a slide in your presentation. If you add too much text to a slide, the slide may be difficult to read and you will minimize the impact of important ideas. If a slide contains too much text, you should add a new slide to accommodate some of the text.

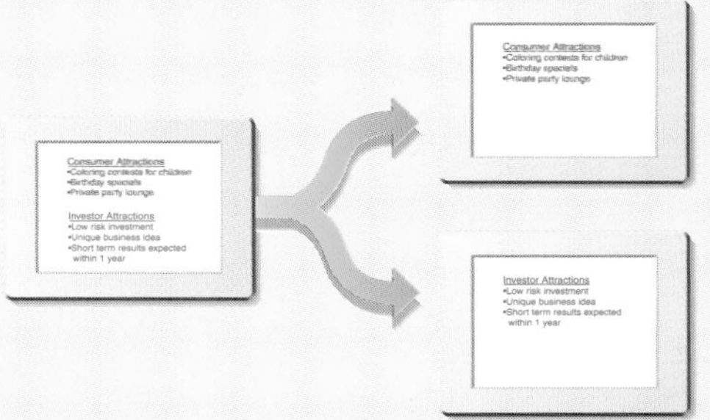

What types of layouts can I use for a new slide?

Each slide layout displays a different arrangement of placeholders, which determine the position of text and objects on a slide. The icons in the placeholders indicate the type of information you can add to the placeholder.

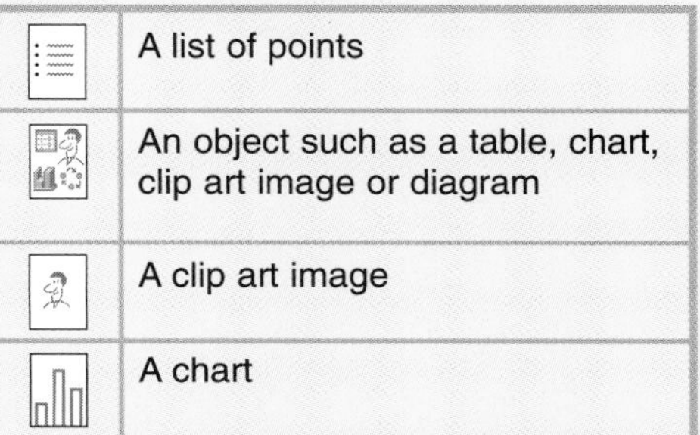

Icon	Description
	A list of points
	An object such as a table, chart, clip art image or diagram
	A clip art image
	A chart

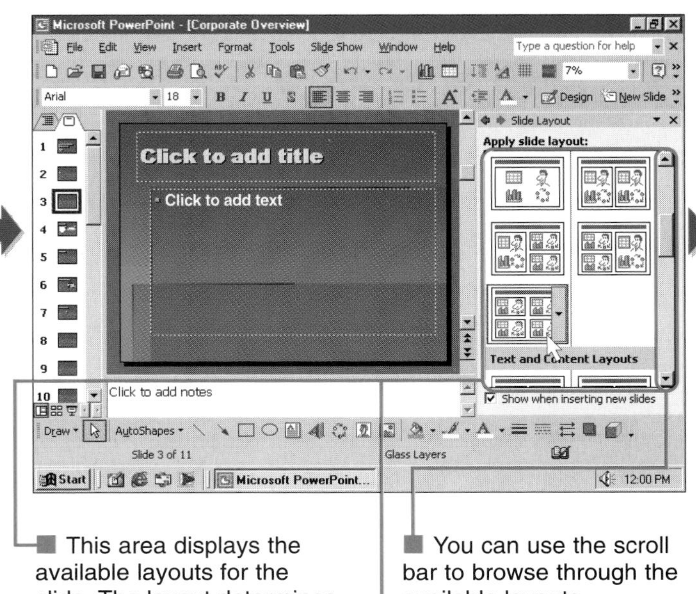

- This area displays the available layouts for the slide. The layout determines the position of text and objects on the slide.
- You can use the scroll bar to browse through the available layouts.

3 Click the layout you want to use for the new slide.

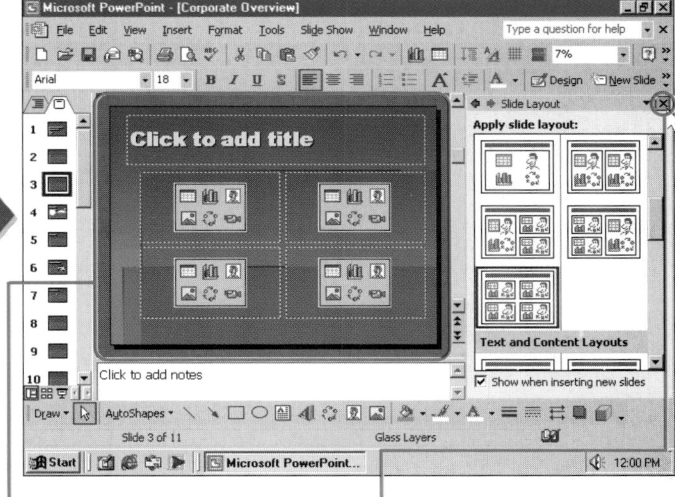

- The slide changes to the layout you selected.

*Note: To select a different layout, repeat step **3**.*

4 When the slide displays the layout you want to use, you can click ☒ to close the Slide Layout task pane.

CHANGE THE SLIDE LAYOUT

You can change the layout of a slide in your presentation to accommodate text and objects you want to add.

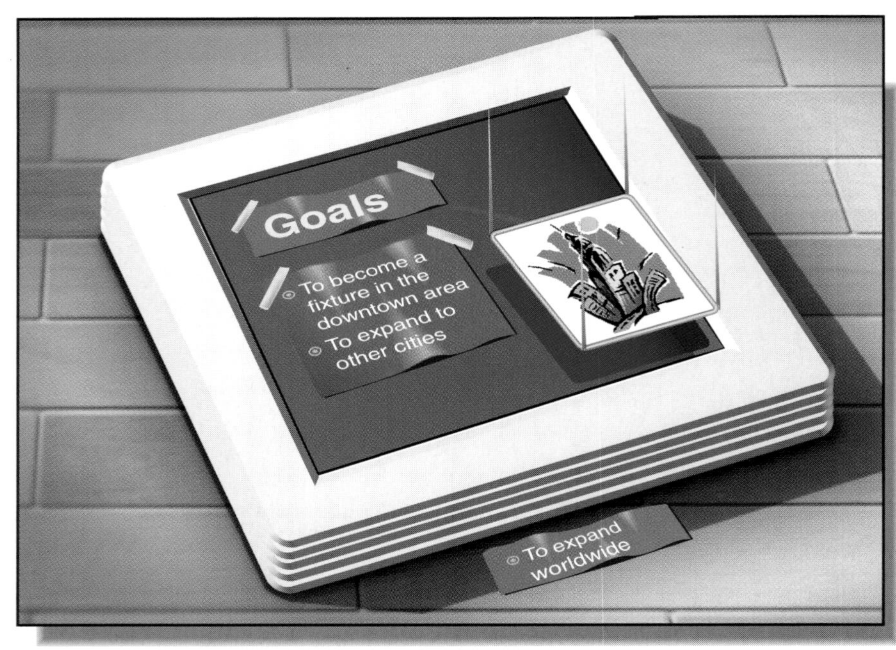

Each slide layout displays a different arrangement of placeholders. Placeholders allow you to easily add objects you want to appear on a slide, such as a clip art image or chart.

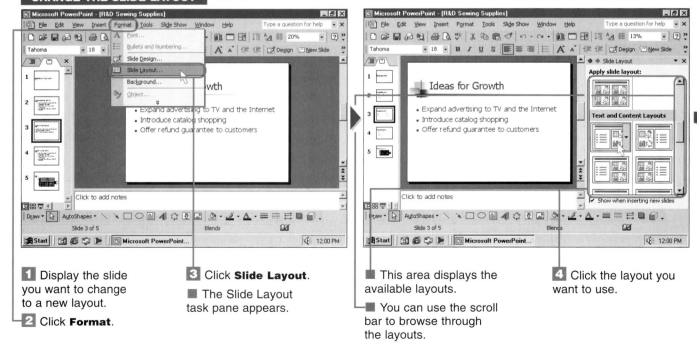

CHANGE THE SLIDE LAYOUT

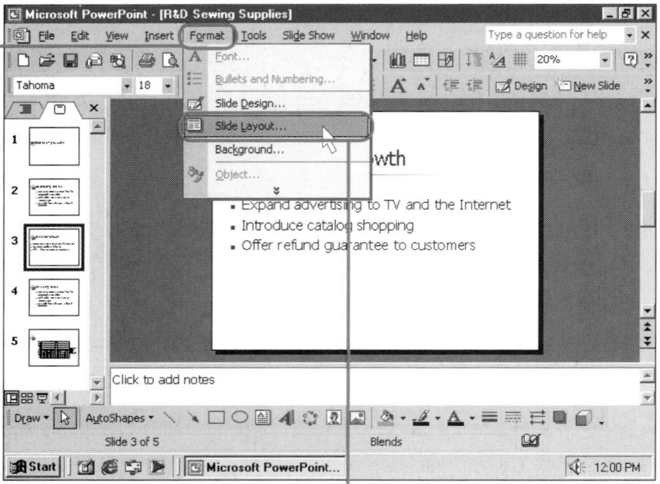

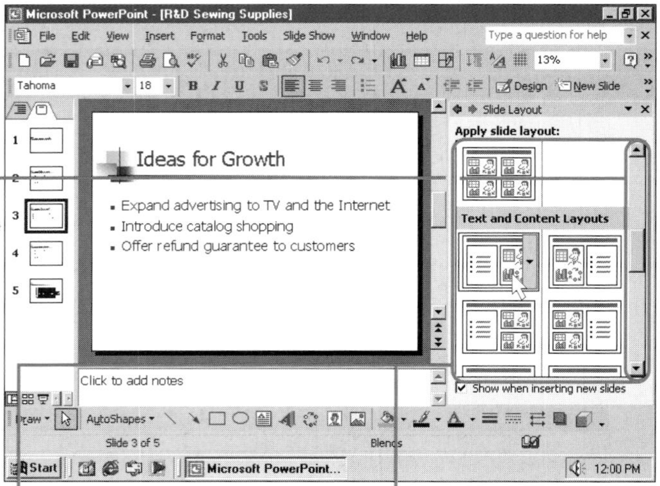

1 Display the slide you want to change to a new layout.

2 Click **Format**.

3 Click **Slide Layout**.

■ The Slide Layout task pane appears.

■ This area displays the available layouts.

■ You can use the scroll bar to browse through the layouts.

4 Click the layout you want to use.

What types of placeholders will a slide layout contain?

Each layout in the Slide Layout task pane contains icons that indicate the types of placeholders in the layout.

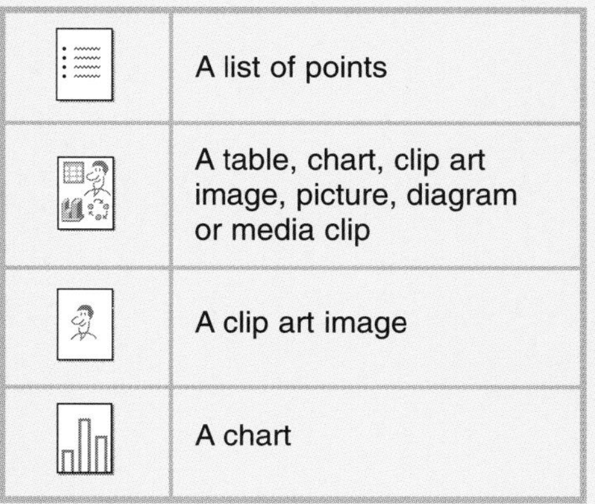

	A list of points
	A table, chart, clip art image, picture, diagram or media clip
	A clip art image
	A chart

What should I consider when changing the slide layout?

If you have already added text or an object to a slide, you should choose a slide layout that includes a placeholder for the type of information you added. This helps to ensure that the slide will not become cluttered with overlapping objects and placeholders.

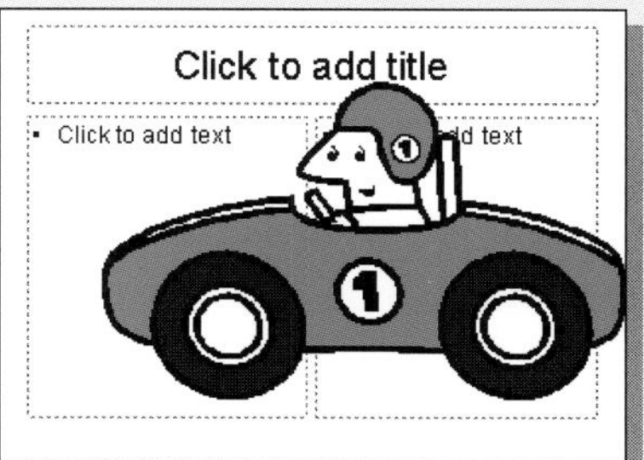

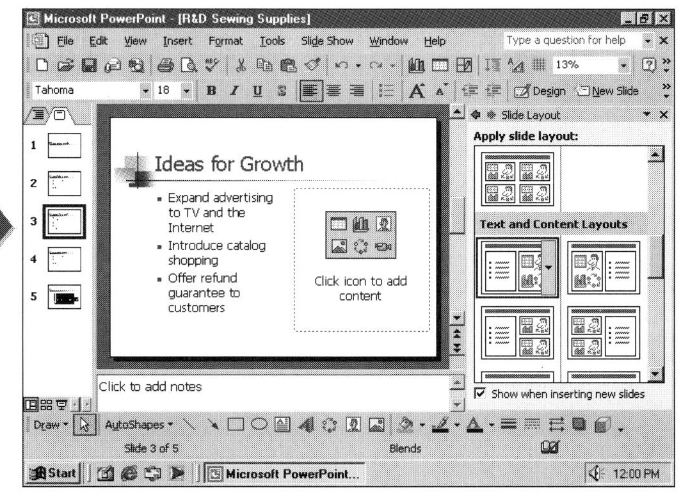

■ The slide changes to the layout you selected.

*Note: To select a different layout, repeat step **4**.*

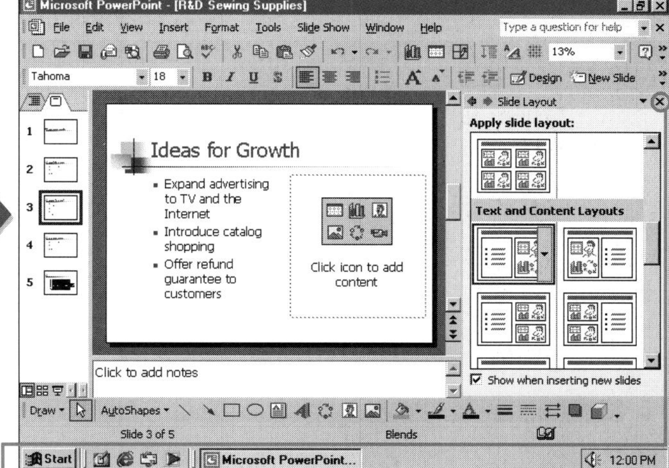

5 When you finish selecting a slide layout, you can click ☒ to close the Slide Layout task pane.

ADD AN AUTOSHAPE

PowerPoint provides many ready-made shapes, called AutoShapes, that you can add to your slides.

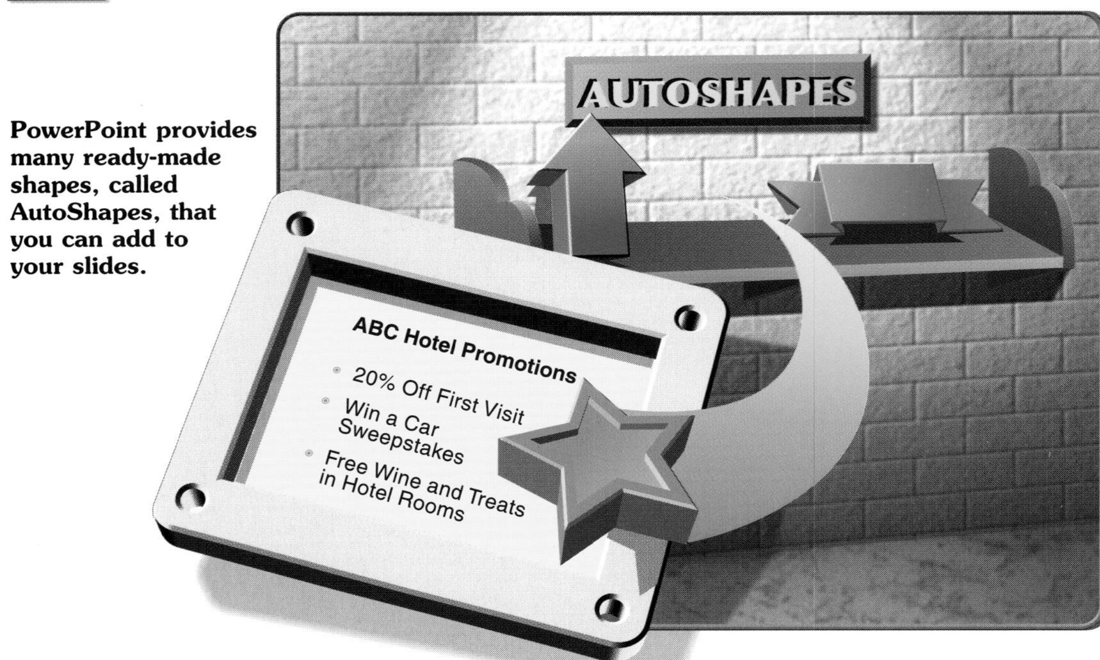

PowerPoint offers several types of AutoShapes, such as lines, arrows, stars and banners.

ADD AN AUTOSHAPE

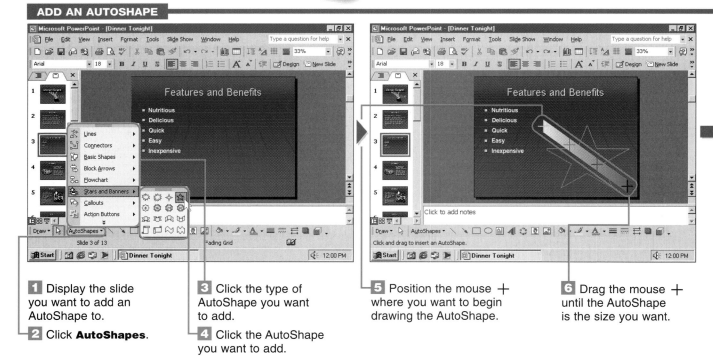

1 Display the slide you want to add an AutoShape to.

2 Click **AutoShapes**.

3 Click the type of AutoShape you want to add.

4 Click the AutoShape you want to add.

5 Position the mouse + where you want to begin drawing the AutoShape.

6 Drag the mouse + until the AutoShape is the size you want.

Can I add text to an AutoShape?

You can add text to most AutoShapes. This is particularly useful for AutoShapes such as banners and callouts. To add text to an AutoShape, click the AutoShape and then type the text you want the AutoShape to display. To change the size of the text, see page 227.

Why do green and yellow dots appear on some AutoShapes?

You can use the green and yellow dots to change the appearance of an AutoShape.

To rotate an AutoShape, position the mouse over the green dot (●) and then drag the mouse to a new position.

To change the design of an AutoShape, position the mouse over the yellow dot (◆) and then drag the mouse until the shape displays the design you want.

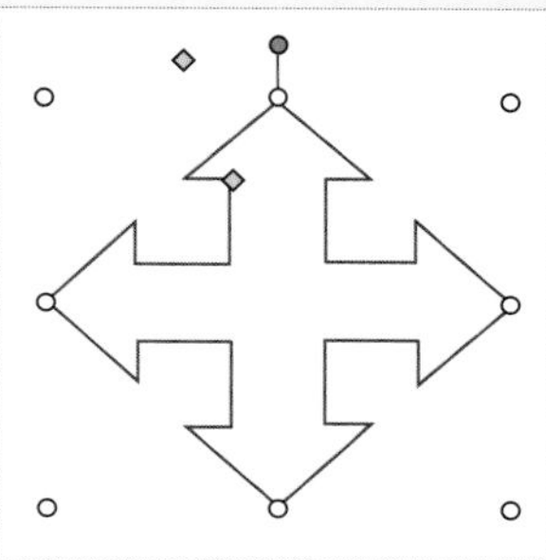

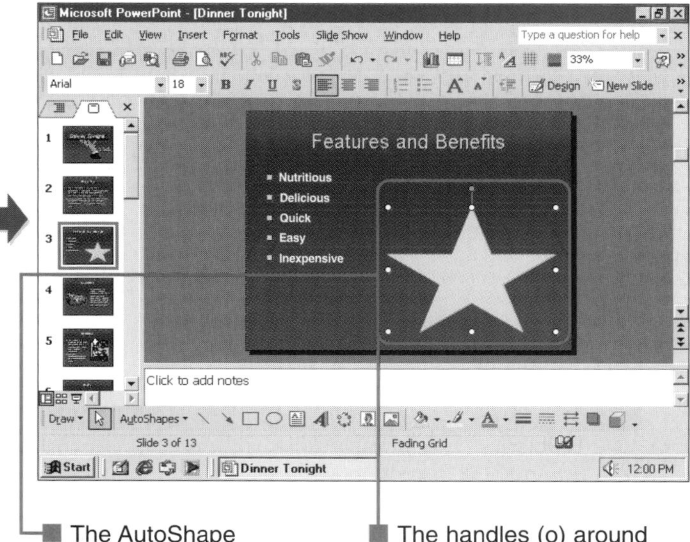

■ The AutoShape appears on the slide.

Note: To change the color of an AutoShape, see page 231.

■ The handles (o) around the AutoShape allow you to change the size of the AutoShape. To move or resize an AutoShape, see page 224.

■ To deselect an AutoShape, click outside the AutoShape.

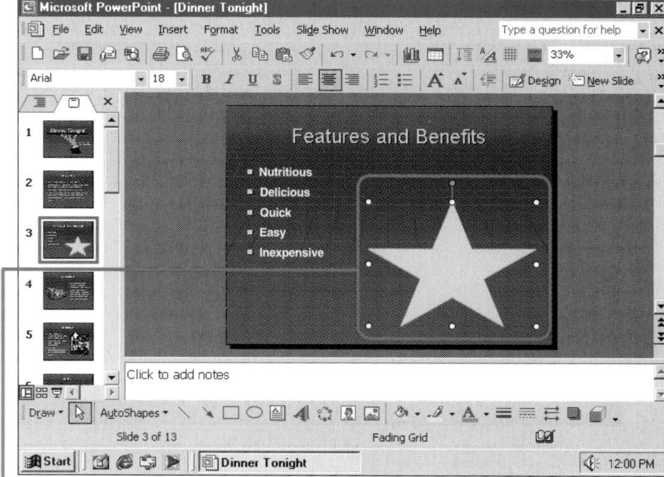

DELETE AN AUTOSHAPE

1 Click the AutoShape you want to delete.

2 Press the Delete key to remove the AutoShape from the slide.

ADD WORDART

You can add WordArt to a slide in your presentation to enhance a title or draw attention to important information.

ADD WORDART

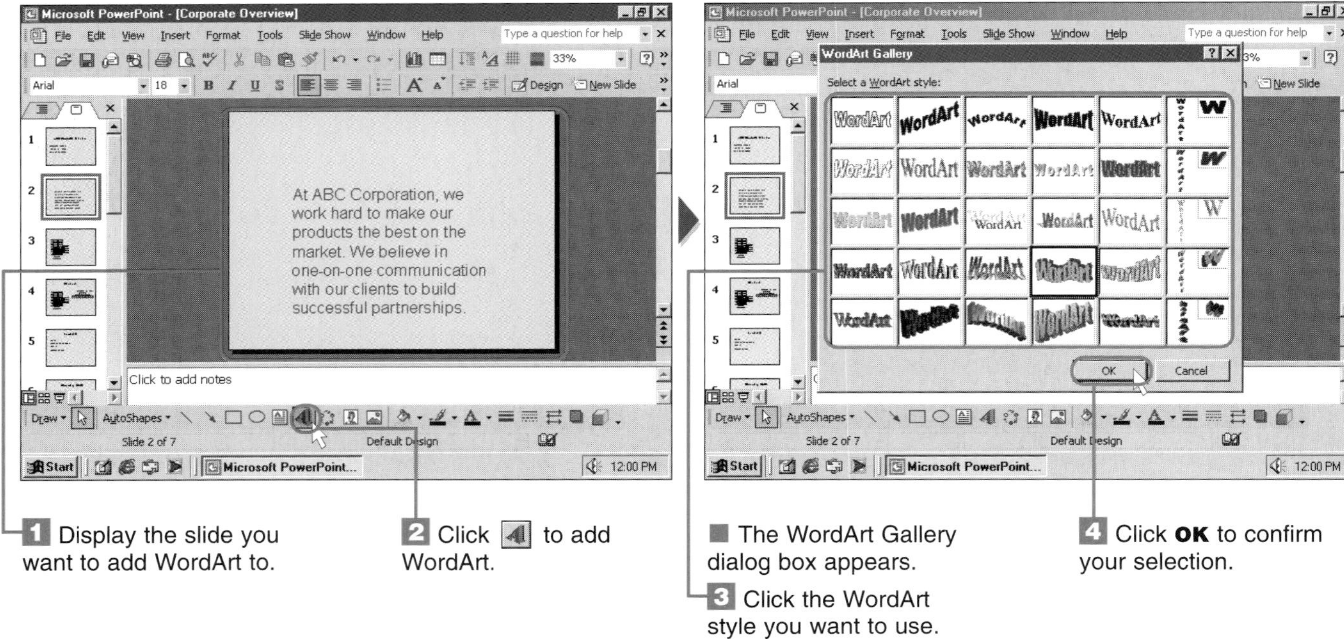

1 Display the slide you want to add WordArt to.

2 Click ![WordArt icon] to add WordArt.

■ The WordArt Gallery dialog box appears.

3 Click the WordArt style you want to use.

4 Click **OK** to confirm your selection.

How do I edit WordArt text?

To edit WordArt text, double-click the WordArt to display the Edit WordArt Text dialog box. Then perform steps 5 and 6 below to specify the new text you want the WordArt to display.

When I add WordArt to a slide, why does the WordArt toolbar appear?

The WordArt toolbar contains buttons that allow you to change the appearance of WordArt. For example, you can click Aa to display all the letters in the WordArt at the same height.

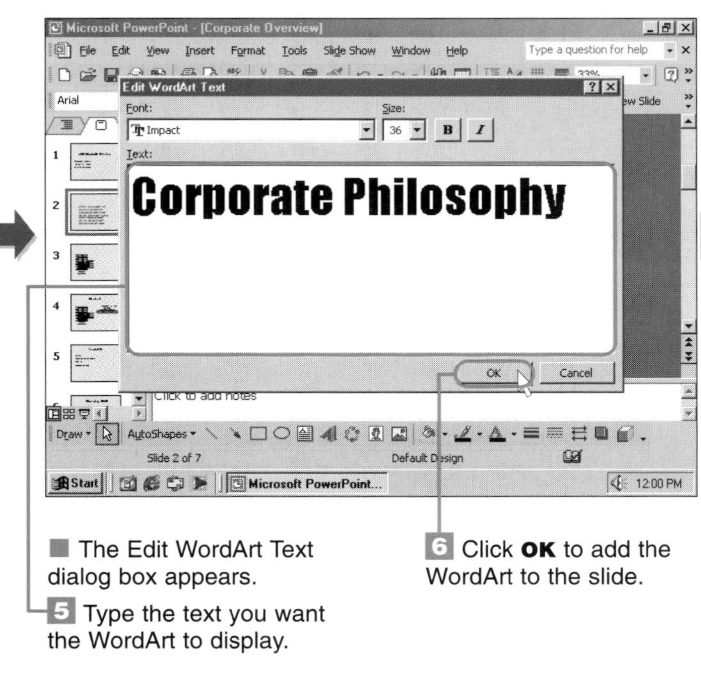

■ The Edit WordArt Text dialog box appears.

5 Type the text you want the WordArt to display.

6 Click **OK** to add the WordArt to the slide.

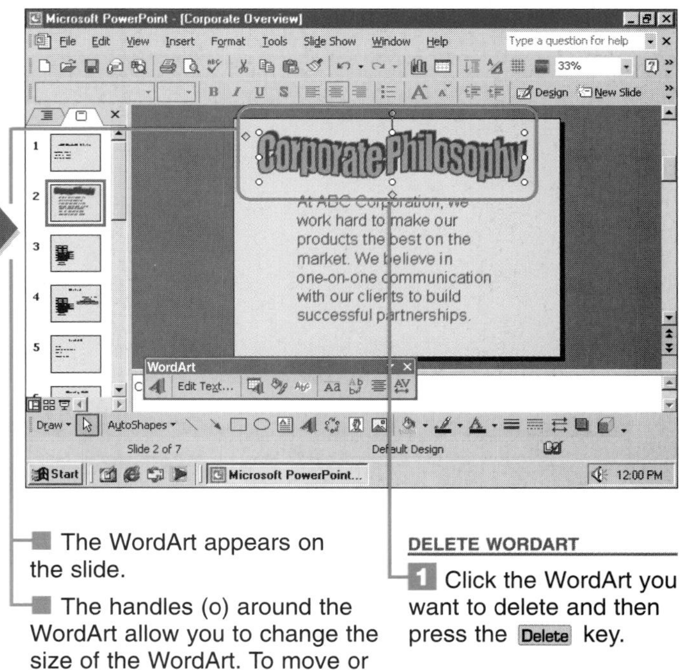

■ The WordArt appears on the slide.

■ The handles (o) around the WordArt allow you to change the size of the WordArt. To move or resize WordArt, see page 224.

■ To deselect WordArt, click outside the WordArt.

DELETE WORDART

1 Click the WordArt you want to delete and then press the Delete key.

ADD A PICTURE

You can add a picture stored on your computer to a slide in your presentation.

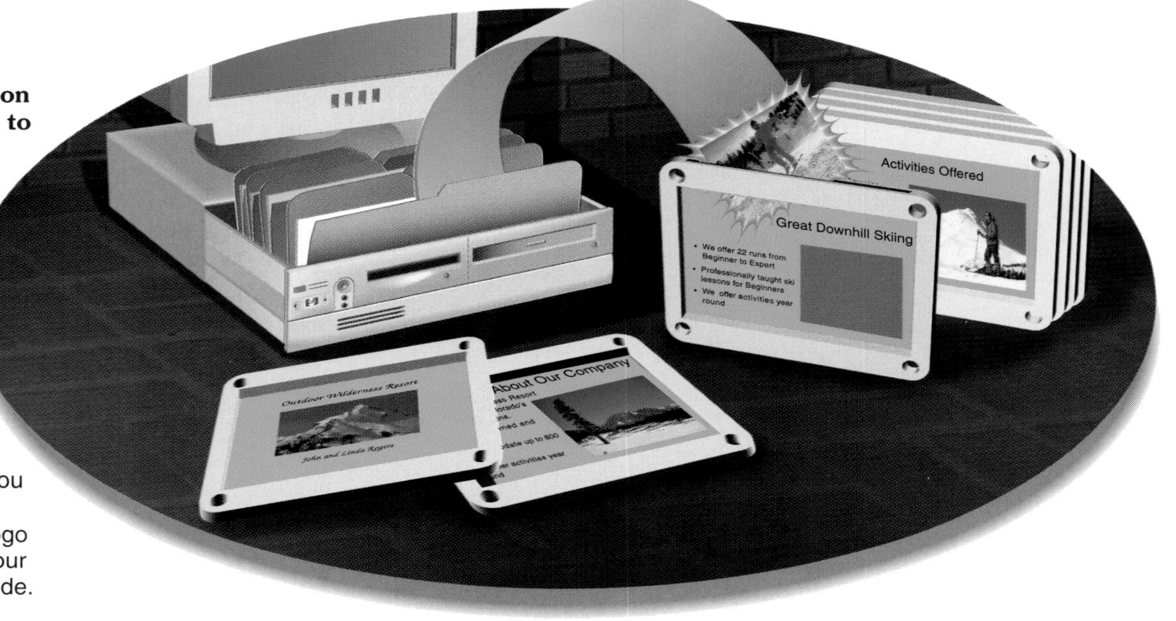

Adding a picture is useful when you want to display your company logo or a picture of your products on a slide.

ADD A PICTURE

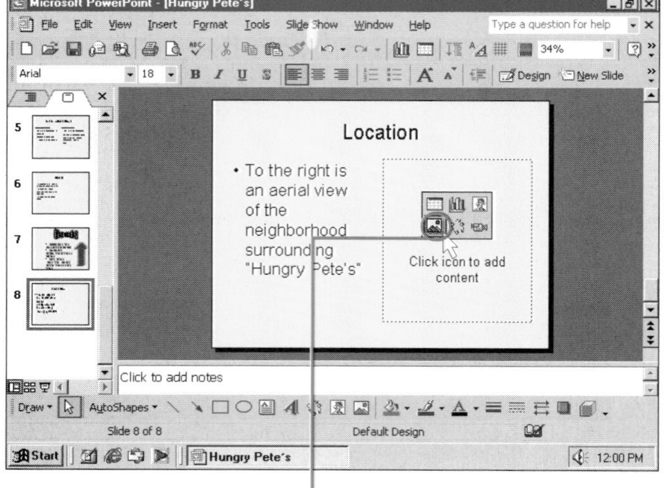

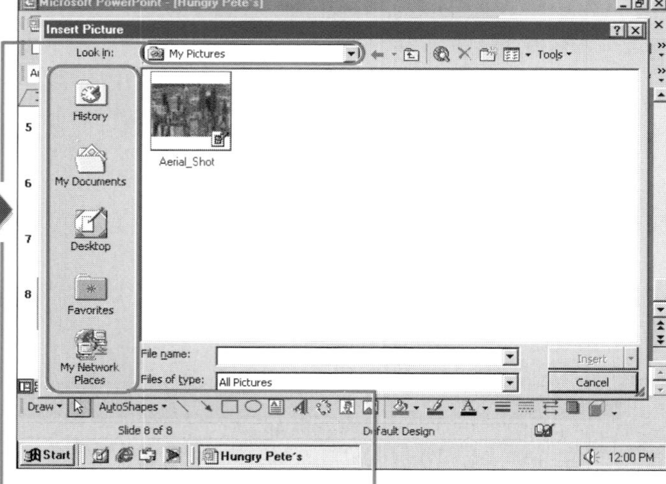

1 Display the slide you want to add a picture to.

2 Change the layout of the slide to one that includes a placeholder for a picture. To change the slide layout, see page 210.

3 Click the picture icon ( ) to add a picture to the slide.

■ The Insert Picture dialog box appears.

■ This area shows the location of the displayed pictures. You can click this area to change the location.

■ This area allows you to access pictures in commonly used locations. You can click a location to display the pictures stored in the location.

Note: For information on the commonly used locations, see the top of page 193.

Where can I obtain pictures?

There are many places that offer images you can use on your slides, such as Web sites and computer stores. You can also use a scanner to scan existing pictures into your computer or create your own pictures using an image editing program, such as Jasc Paint Shop Pro.

Why did the Picture toolbar appear when I added a picture to a slide?

The Picture toolbar contains buttons that allow you to change the appearance of a picture. For example, you can click or to increase or decrease the brightness of a picture. If the Picture toolbar does not appear, see page 11 to display the toolbar.

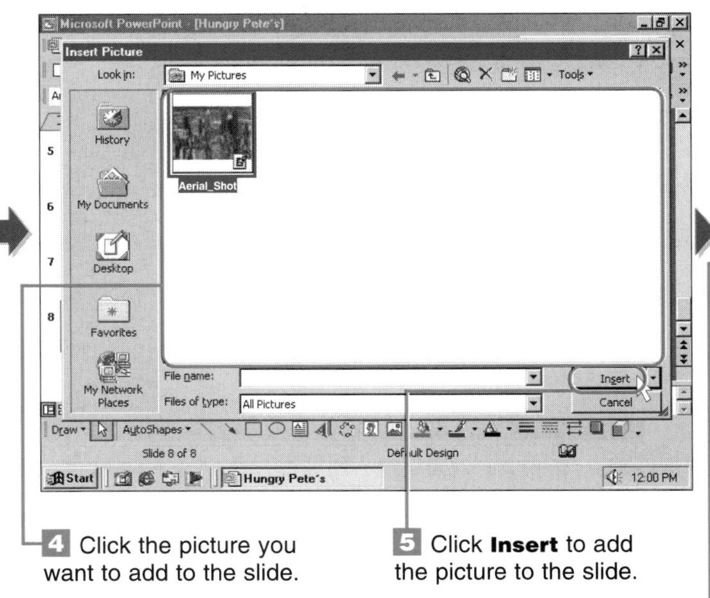

4 Click the picture you want to add to the slide.

5 Click **Insert** to add the picture to the slide.

■ The picture appears on the slide.

■ The handles (o) around the picture allow you to change the size of the picture. To move or resize a picture, see page 224.

■ To deselect the picture, click outside the picture.

DELETE A PICTURE

1 Click the picture you want to delete and then press the Delete key.

ADD A CLIP ART IMAGE

You can add a clip art image to a slide to make your presentation more interesting and entertaining.

ADD A CLIP ART IMAGE

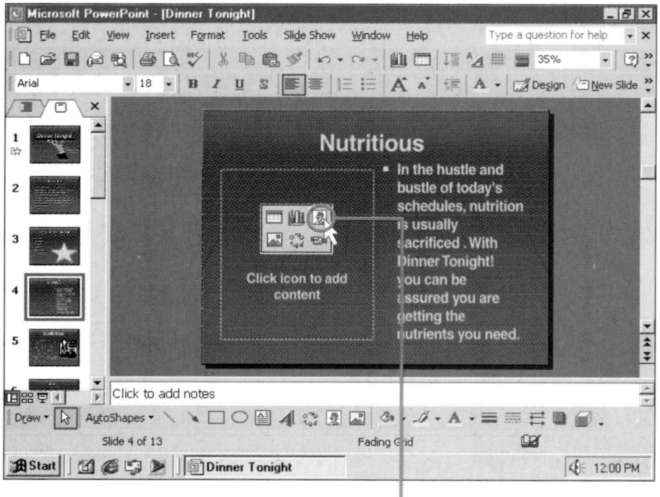

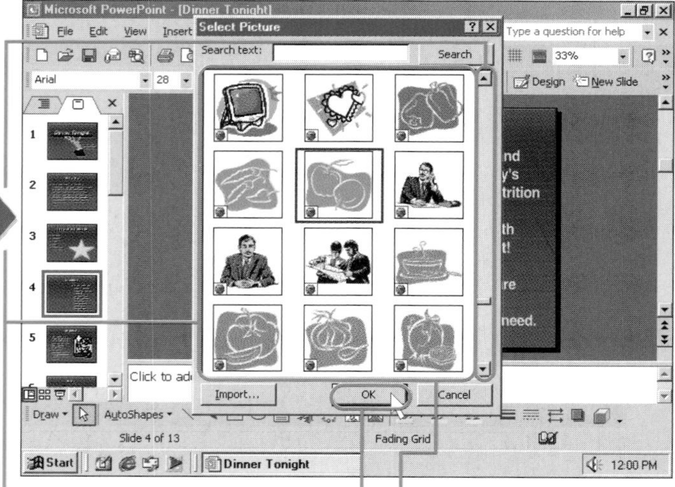

1 Display the slide you want to add a clip art image to.

2 Change the layout of the slide to one that includes a placeholder for a clip art image. To change the slide layout, see page 210.

3 Click the clip art icon ( ) to add a clip art image.

Note: Depending on the layout you chose in step 2, you may need to double-click the placeholder to add a clip art image.

■ The Select Picture dialog box appears.

■ This area displays the clip art images you can add to your slide.

■ You can use the scroll bar to browse through the clip art images.

4 Click the clip art image you want to add to your slide.

5 Click **OK** to add the clip art image to your slide.

Can I search for clip art images?

You can search for clip art images by specifying one or more words of interest in the Select Picture dialog box.

1 In the Select Picture dialog box, click this area and type a word that describes the clip art image you want to search for. Then press the Enter key.

■ The dialog box will display the clip art images that match the words you specify.

Where can I obtain more clip art images?

You can buy collections of clip art images at computer stores. Many Web sites, such as www.allfree-clipart.com and www.noeticart.com, also offer clip art images you can use on your slides.

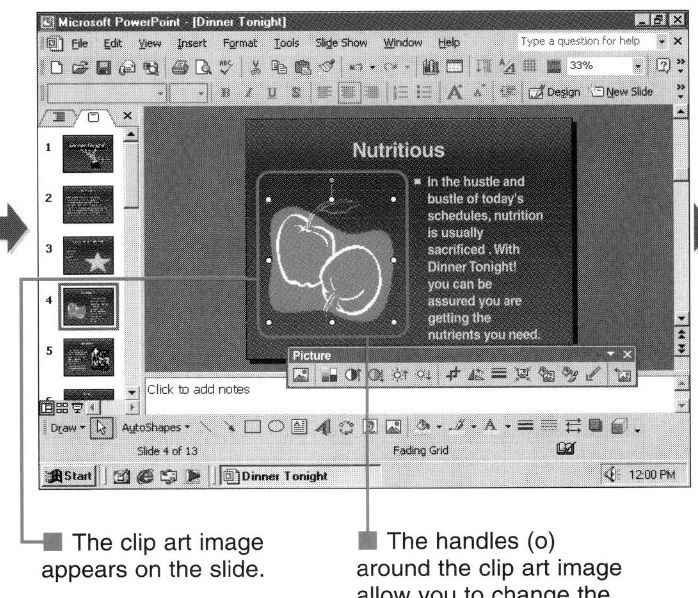

■ The clip art image appears on the slide.

■ The handles (o) around the clip art image allow you to change the size of the image. To move or resize a clip art image, see page 224.

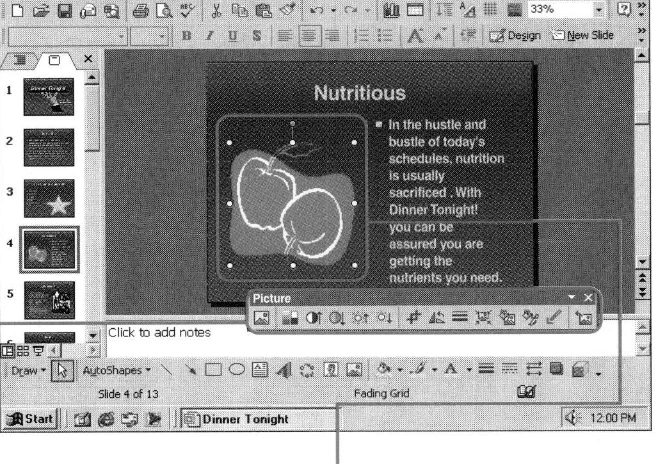

■ The Picture toolbar also appears, displaying buttons that allow you to change the clip art image.

■ To deselect a clip art image, click outside the image.

DELETE A CLIP ART IMAGE

1 Click the clip art image you want to delete and then press the Delete key.

ADD A CHART

You can add a chart to a slide to show trends and compare data.

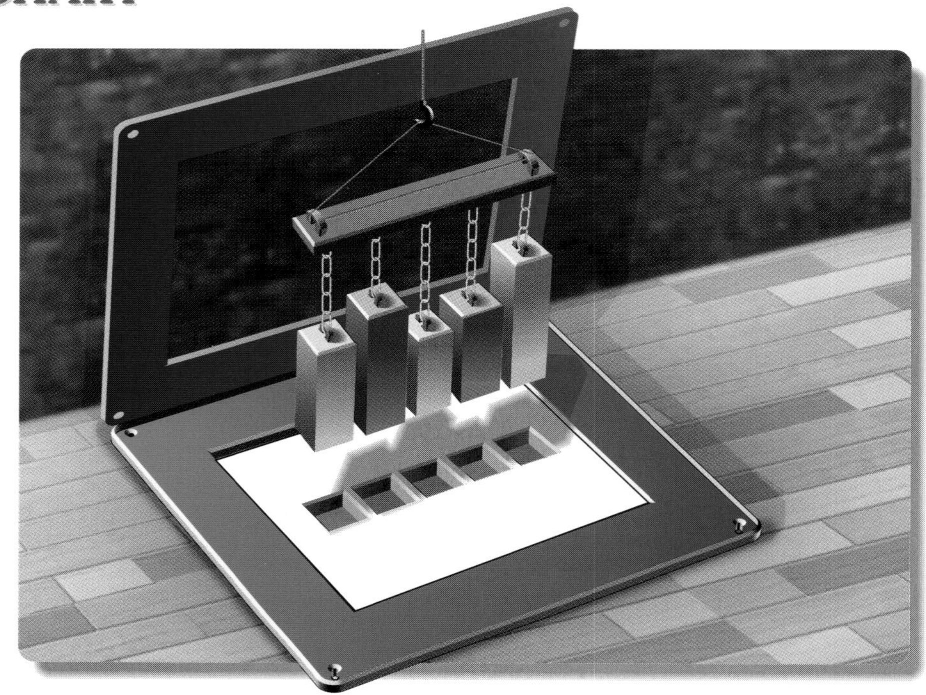

A chart is more appealing and often easier to understand than a list of numbers.

ADD A CHART

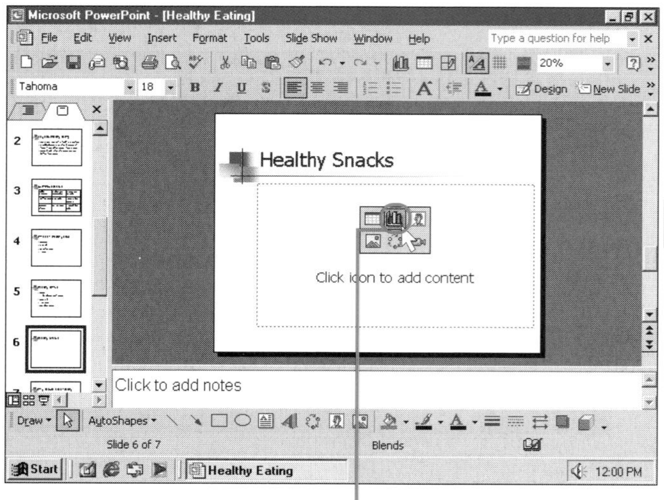

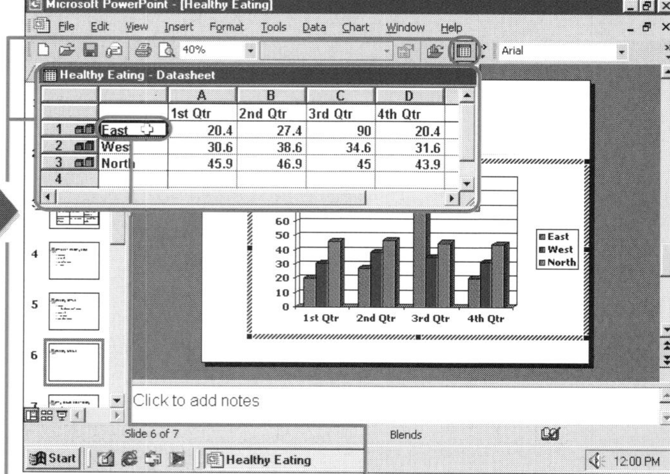

1 Display the slide you want to add a chart to.

2 Change the layout of the slide to one that includes a placeholder for a chart. To change the slide layout, see page 210.

3 Click the chart icon (chart icon) to add a chart.

Note: Depending on the layout you chose, you may need to double-click the placeholder to add a chart.

■ A datasheet appears, displaying sample data to show you where to enter information.

■ If the datasheet does not appear, click (datasheet icon) to display the datasheet.

Note: If (datasheet icon) is not displayed, click (more buttons icon) on the Standard toolbar to display all the buttons.

4 To replace the data in a cell, click the cell. A thick border appears around the cell.

How do I change the data displayed in a chart?

Double-click the chart to activate the chart and display the datasheet. You can then perform steps **4** to **7** below to change the data displayed in the chart.

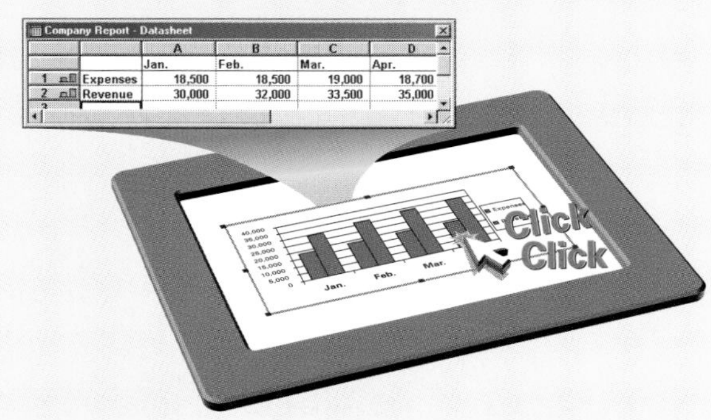

How can I add a chart without changing the slide layout?

You can click the Insert Chart button (📊) and then perform steps **4** to **7** below to add a chart to a slide without first changing the layout of the slide.

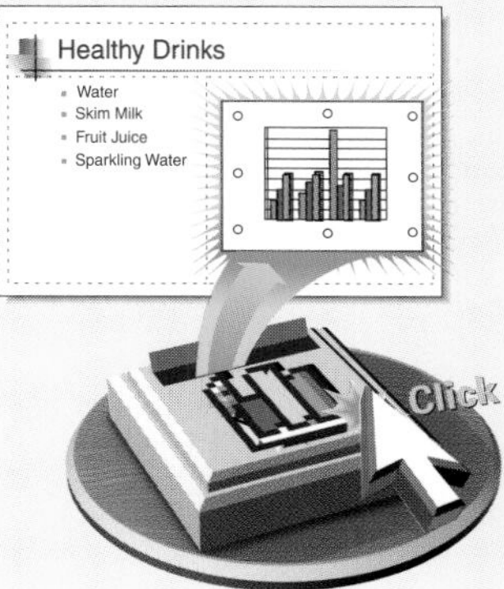

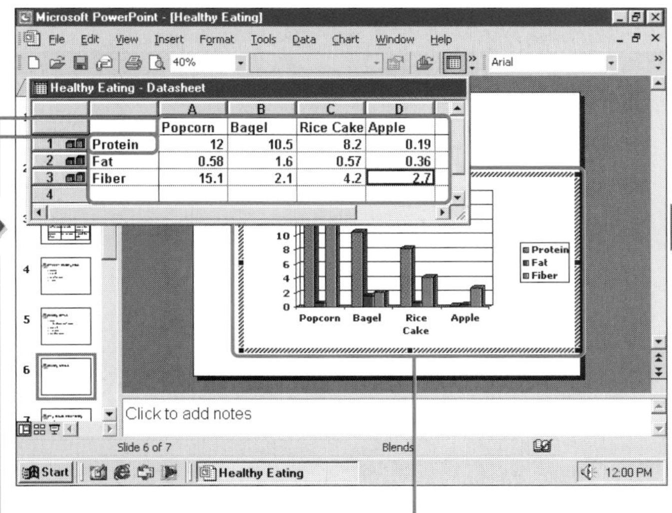

5 Type your data and then press the Enter key.

Note: To remove data from a cell and leave the cell empty, click the cell and then press the Delete *key.*

6 Repeat steps **4** and **5** until you finish entering all your data.

■ As you enter data, PowerPoint updates the chart on the slide.

7 When you finish entering data for the chart, click a blank area on your screen.

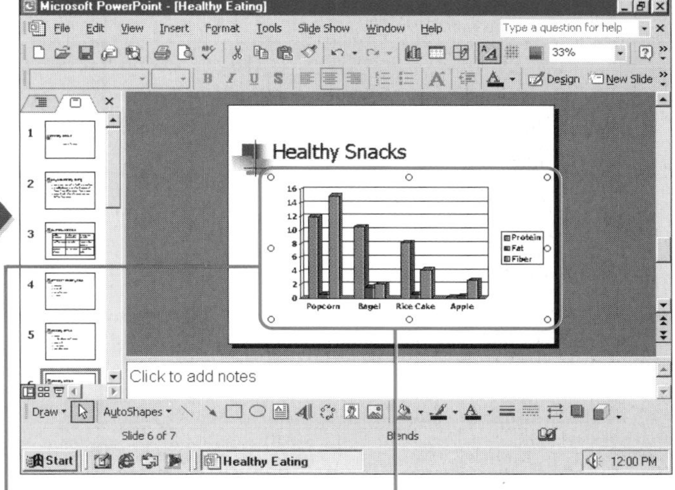

■ The datasheet disappears and you can clearly view the chart on the slide.

■ The handles (o) around the chart allow you to change the size of the chart. To move or resize a chart, see page 224.

DELETE A CHART

1 Click the chart you want to delete and then press the Delete key.

ADD A DIAGRAM

You can add a diagram to a slide in your presentation to illustrate data.

PowerPoint offers several types of diagrams you can choose from, such as Pyramid, Radial, Venn and Target.

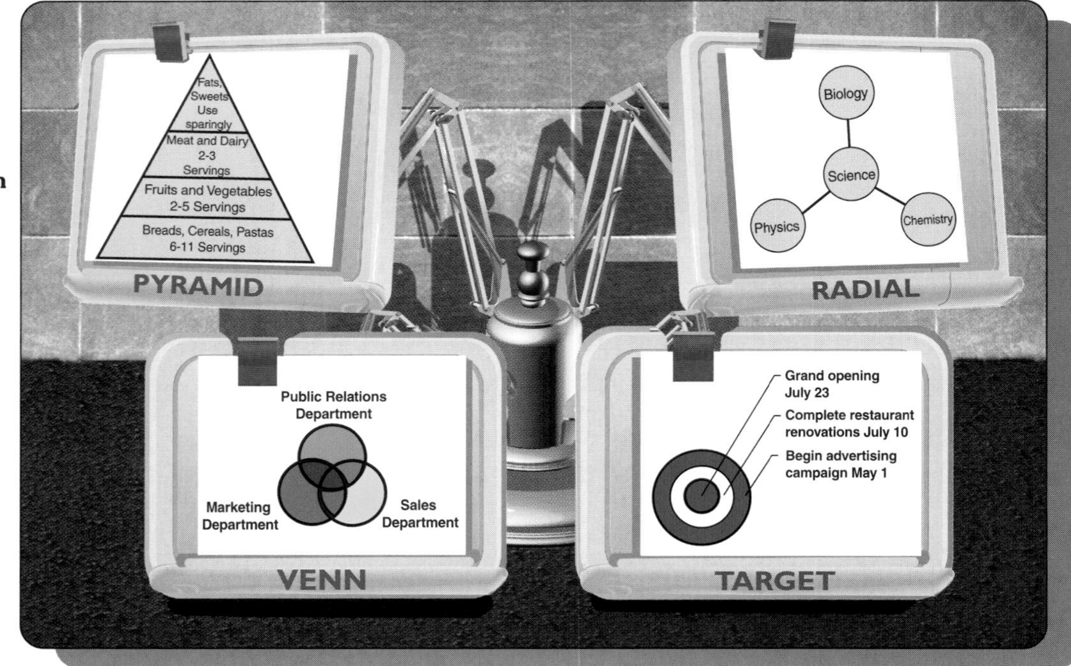

ADD A DIAGRAM

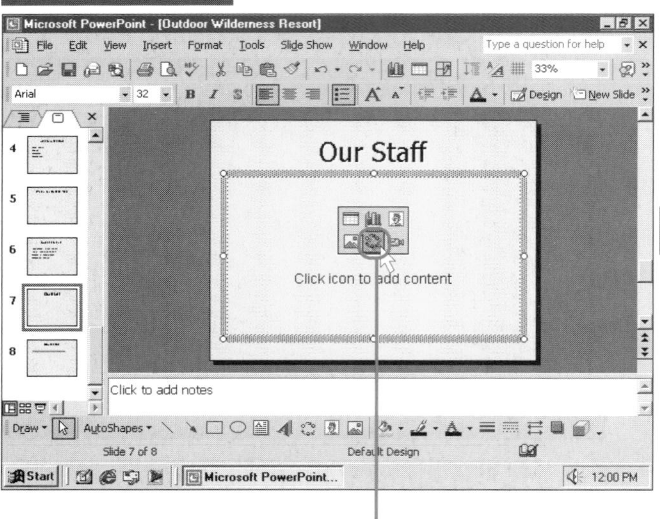

1 Display the slide you want to add a diagram to.

2 Change the layout of the slide to one that includes a placeholder for a diagram. To change the slide layout, see page 210.

3 Click the diagram icon ( ) to add a diagram to the slide.

Note: Depending on the layout you chose, you may need to double-click the placeholder to add a diagram.

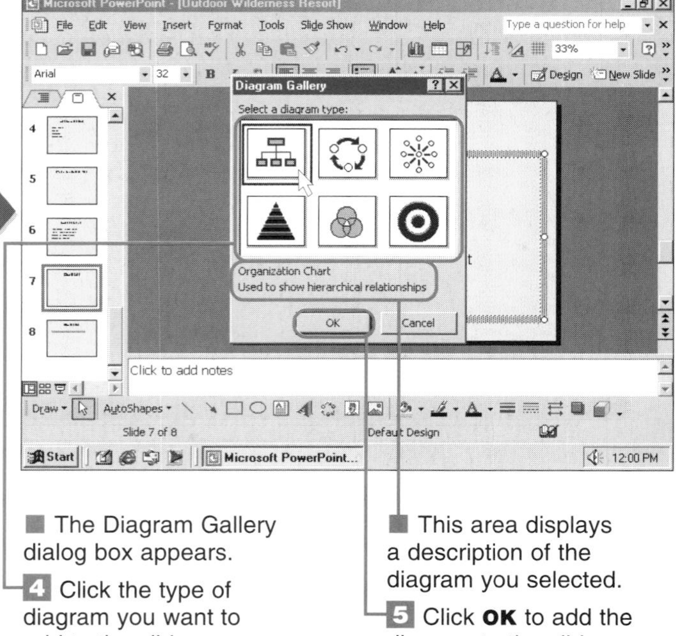

■ The Diagram Gallery dialog box appears.

4 Click the type of diagram you want to add to the slide.

■ This area displays a description of the diagram you selected.

5 Click **OK** to add the diagram to the slide.

When adding a shape to an organization chart, what options are available?

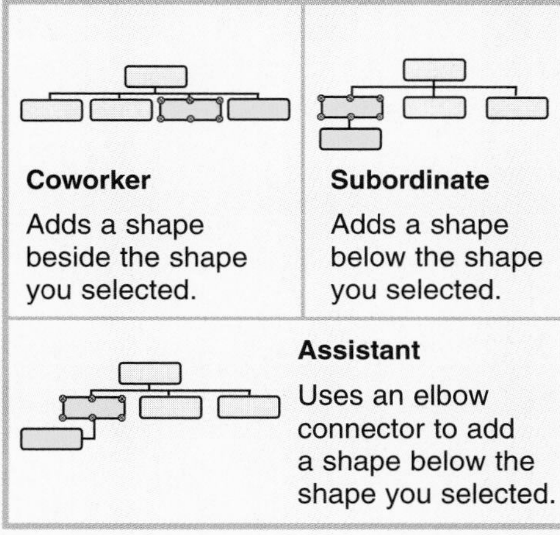

Coworker
Adds a shape beside the shape you selected.

Subordinate
Adds a shape below the shape you selected.

Assistant
Uses an elbow connector to add a shape below the shape you selected.

How do I delete a diagram?

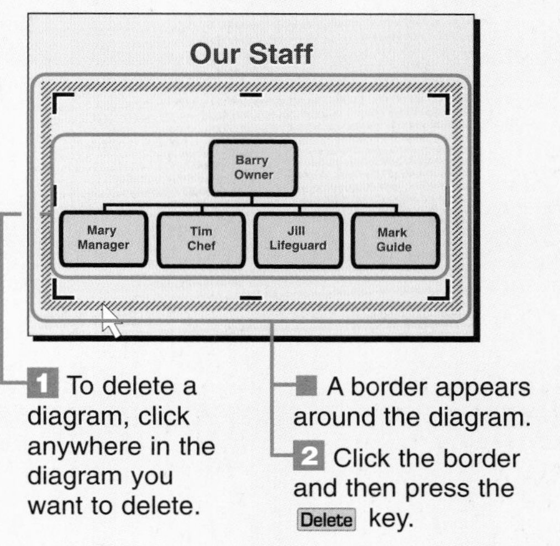

1 To delete a diagram, click anywhere in the diagram you want to delete.

■ A border appears around the diagram.

2 Click the border and then press the Delete key.

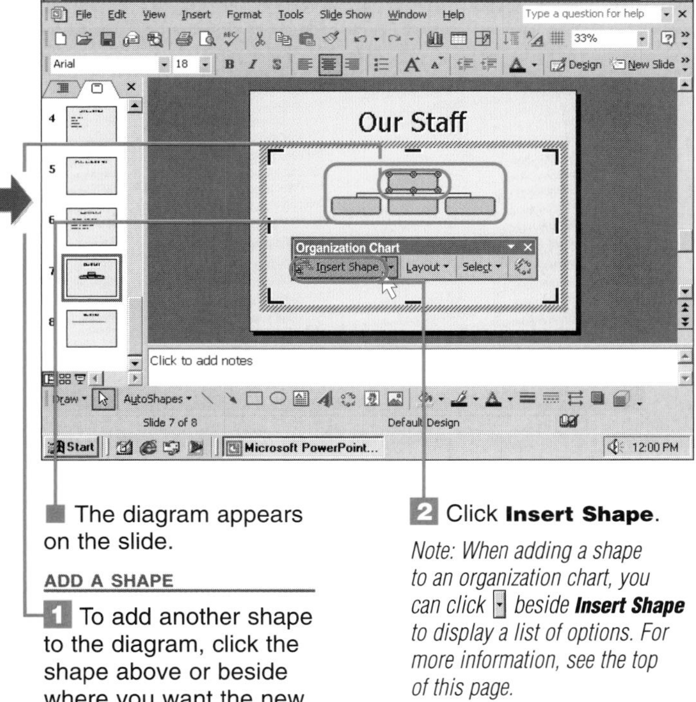

■ The diagram appears on the slide.

ADD A SHAPE

1 To add another shape to the diagram, click the shape above or beside where you want the new shape to appear.

2 Click **Insert Shape**.

*Note: When adding a shape to an organization chart, you can click ▾ beside **Insert Shape** to display a list of options. For more information, see the top of this page.*

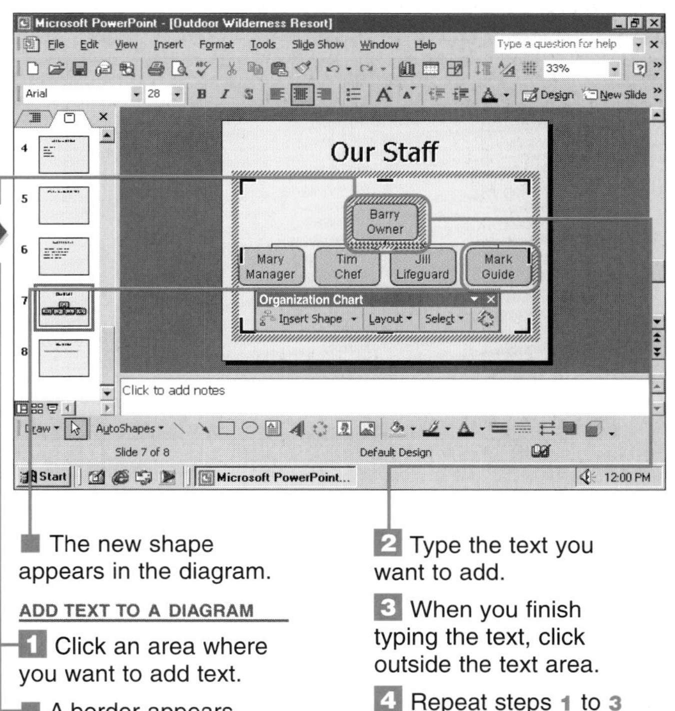

■ The new shape appears in the diagram.

ADD TEXT TO A DIAGRAM

1 Click an area where you want to add text.

■ A border appears around the area if you can add text to the area.

2 Type the text you want to add.

3 When you finish typing the text, click outside the text area.

4 Repeat steps 1 to 3 for each area of text you want to add.

MOVE OR RESIZE AN OBJECT

You can change the location and size of an object on a slide.

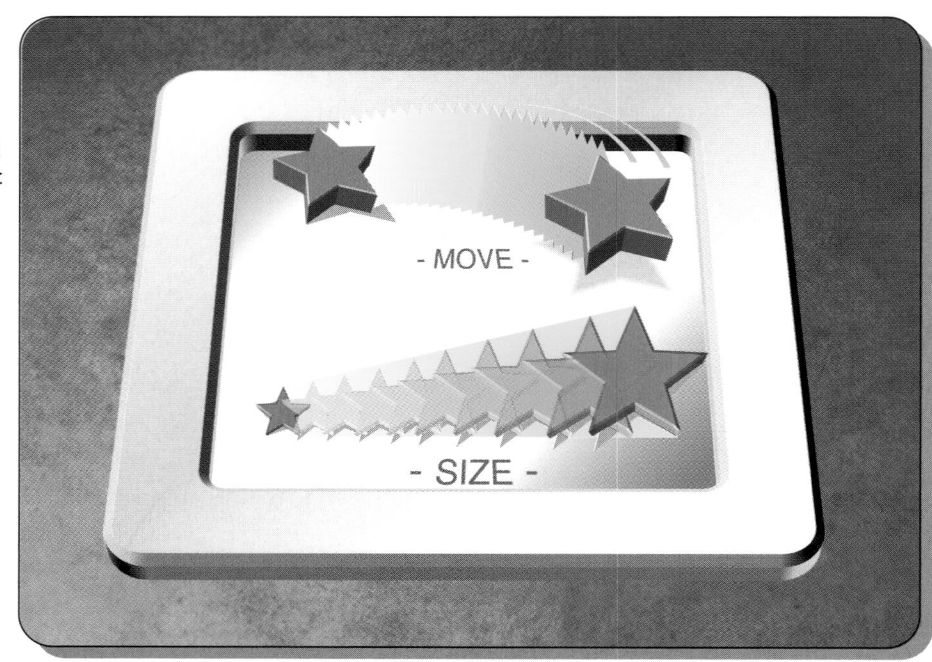

PowerPoint allows you to move and resize objects such as AutoShapes, WordArt, pictures, clip art images and charts.

MOVE AN OBJECT

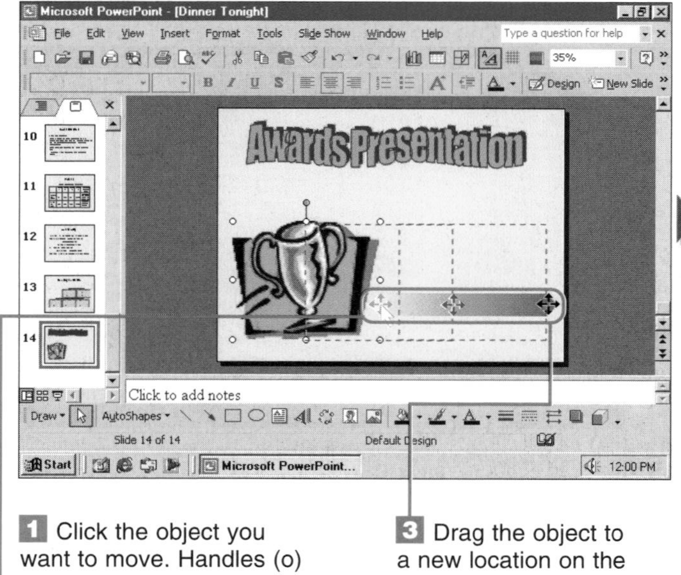

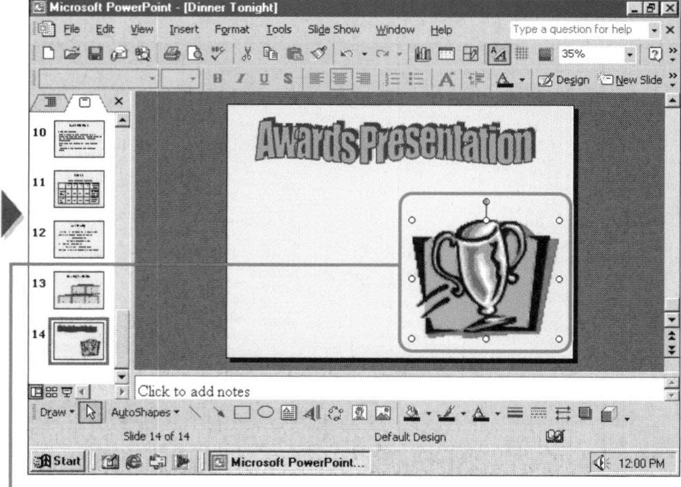

1 Click the object you want to move. Handles (o) appear around the object.

2 Position the mouse over an edge of the object (changes to).

3 Drag the object to a new location on the slide.

■ A dashed line indicates where the object will appear.

■ The object appears in the new location.

How can I change the way an object is moved or resized?

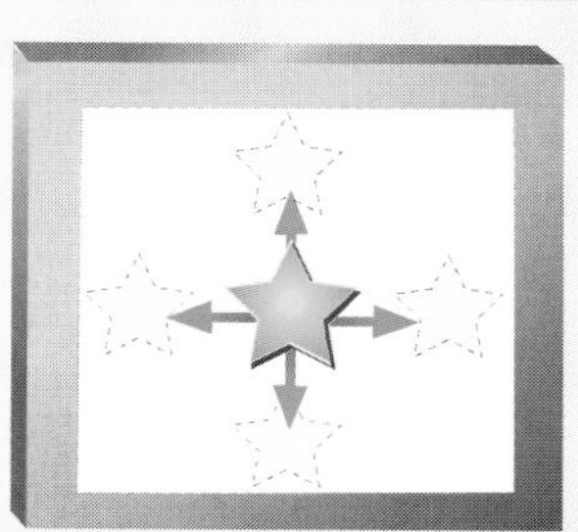

Move Only Horizontally or Vertically

To move an object only horizontally or vertically on a slide, press and hold down the Shift key as you move the object.

Maintain Object's Center When Resizing

To keep the center of an object in the same place while resizing the object, press and hold down the Ctrl key as you resize the object.

RESIZE AN OBJECT

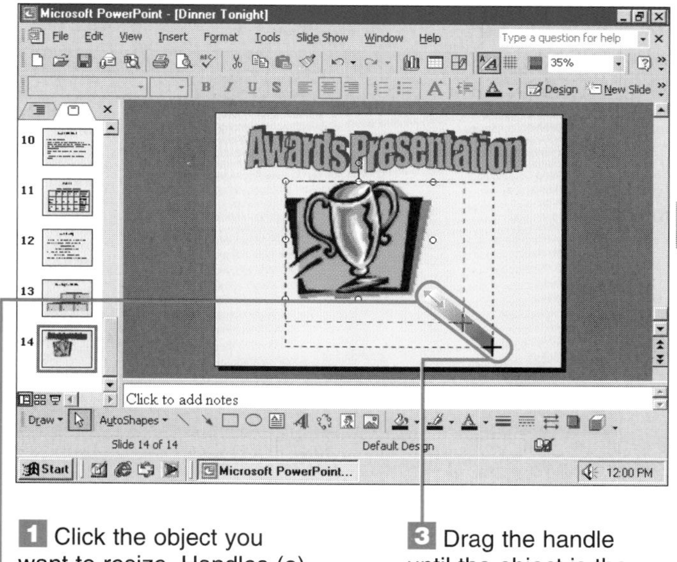

1 Click the object you want to resize. Handles (o) appear around the object.

2 Position the mouse over one of the handles (changes to ↖, ↗, ↔ or ↕).

3 Drag the handle until the object is the size you want.

■ A dashed line shows the new size.

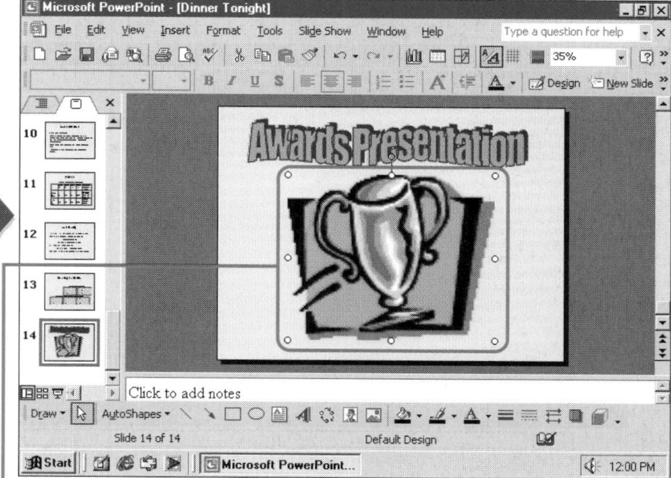

■ The object appears in the new size.

CHANGE FONT OF TEXT

You can change the font of text to enhance the appearance of a slide.

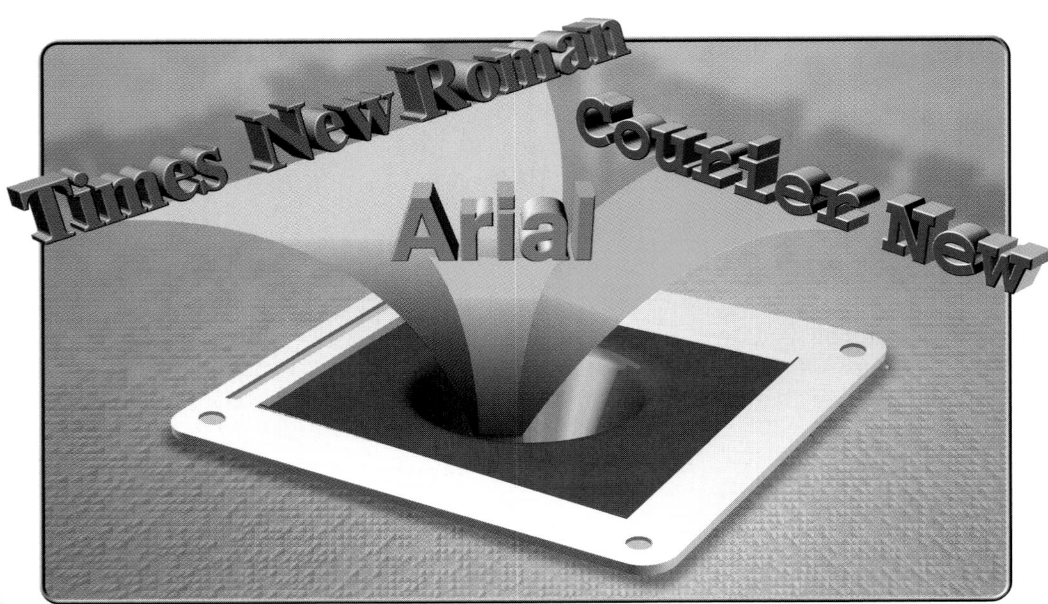

You should consider your audience when choosing a font. For example, choose an informal font, such as Comic Sans MS, for a presentation to your co-workers and a conservative font, such as Times New Roman, for a presentation to your clients.

CHANGE FONT OF TEXT

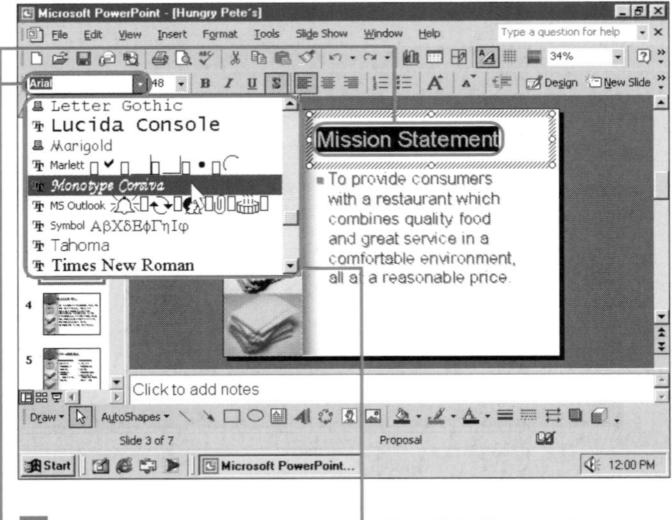

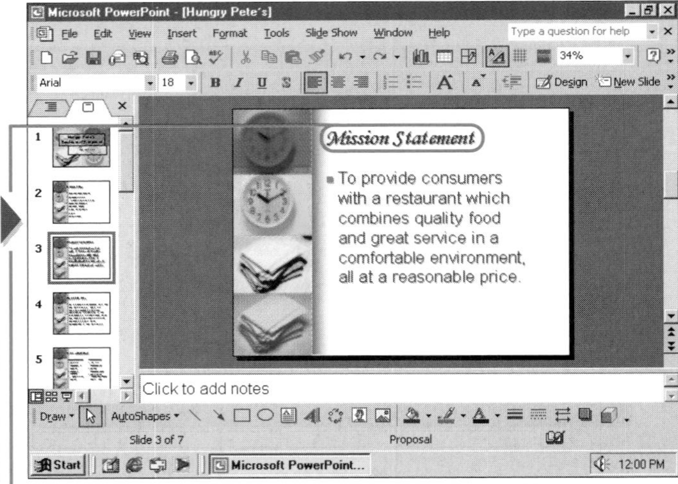

1 Select the text you want to change to a different font. To select text, see page 198.

2 Click in this area to display a list of the available fonts.

Note: If the Font area is not displayed, click on the Formatting toolbar to display the area.

3 Click the font you want to use.

Note: PowerPoint displays the fonts you have most recently used at the top of the list.

■ The text you selected changes to the new font.

■ To deselect text, click outside the selected area.

CHANGE SIZE OF TEXT

You can increase or decrease the size of text on a slide.

Larger text is easier to read, but smaller text allows you to fit more information on a slide.

CHANGE SIZE OF TEXT

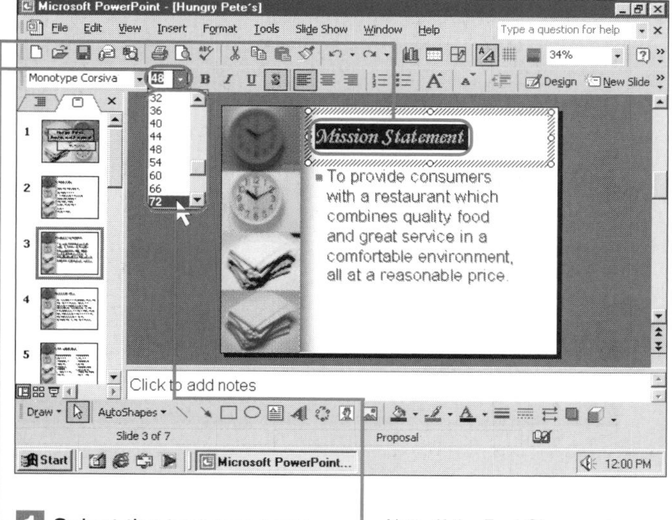

1 Select the text you want to change to a new size. To select text, see page 198.

2 Click ▾ in this area to display a list of the available sizes.

Note: If the Font Size area is not displayed, click » on the Formatting toolbar to display the area.

3 Click the size you want to use.

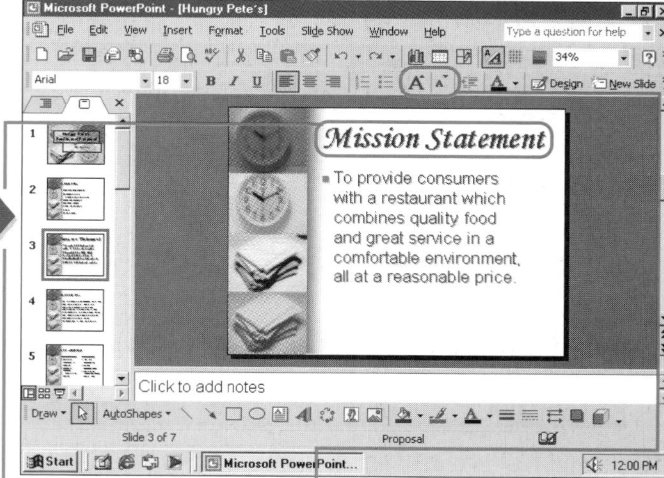

■ The text you selected changes to the new size.

■ To deselect text, click outside the selected area.

QUICKLY CHANGE SIZE OF TEXT

1 Select the text you want to change to a new size.

2 Click A or A to increase or decrease the size of the text.

Note: If the button you want is not displayed, click » on the Formatting toolbar to display all the buttons.

CHANGE STYLE OF TEXT

You can bold, italicize, underline or add a shadow to text to emphasize information on a slide.

CHANGE STYLE OF TEXT

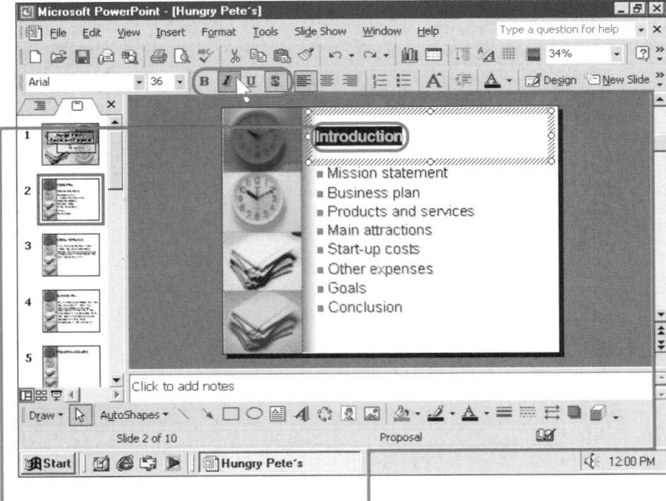

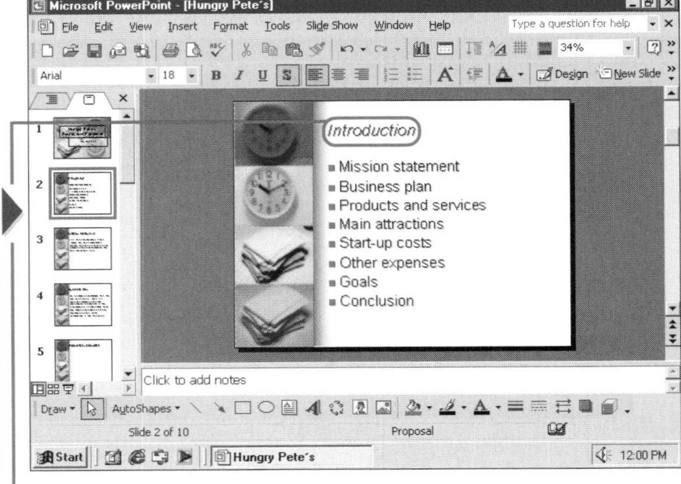

1 Select the text you want to bold, italicize, underline or add a shadow to. To select text, see page 198.

2 Click one of the following buttons.

- **B** Bold
- *I* Italic
- U Underline
- S Shadow

Note: If the button you want is not displayed, click » on the Formatting toolbar to display all the buttons.

■ The text you selected appears in the new style.

■ To deselect text, click outside the selected area.

■ To remove a bold, italic, underline or shadow style, repeat steps **1** and **2**.

CHANGE ALIGNMENT OF TEXT

You can change the alignment of text on a slide to enhance the appearance of the slide.

CHANGE ALIGNMENT OF TEXT

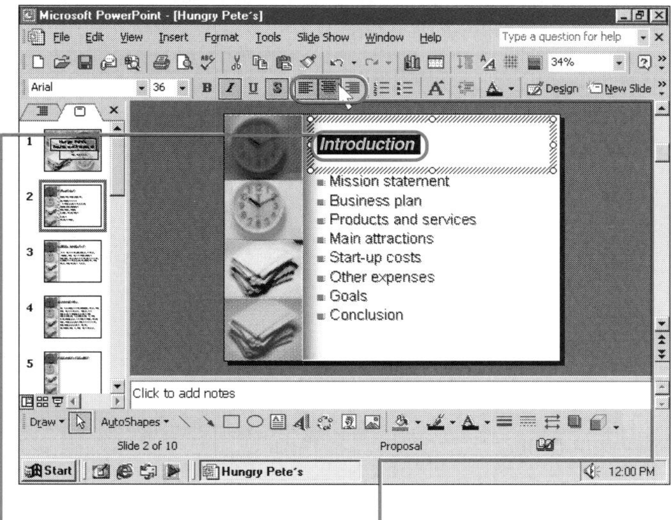

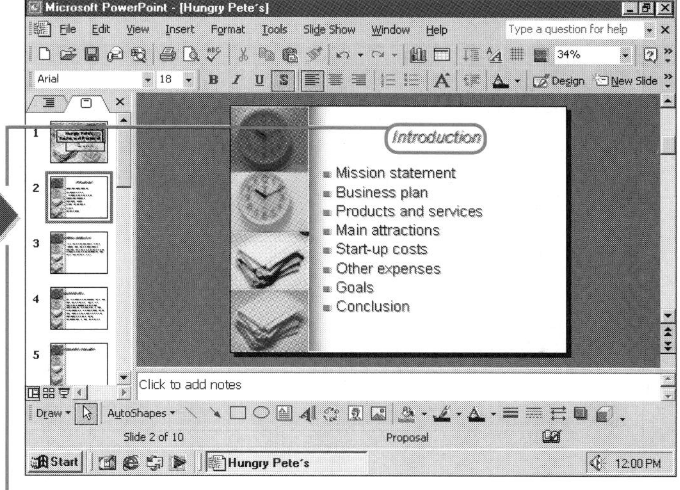

1 Select the text you want to align differently. To select text, see page 198.

2 Click one of the following buttons.

- Left align
- Center
- Right align

Note: If the button you want is not displayed, click on the Formatting toolbar to display all the buttons.

■ The text appears in the new alignment.

■ To deselect text, click outside the selected area.

CHANGE TEXT COLOR

You can change the color of text on a slide to enhance the appearance of the slide and draw attention to important information.

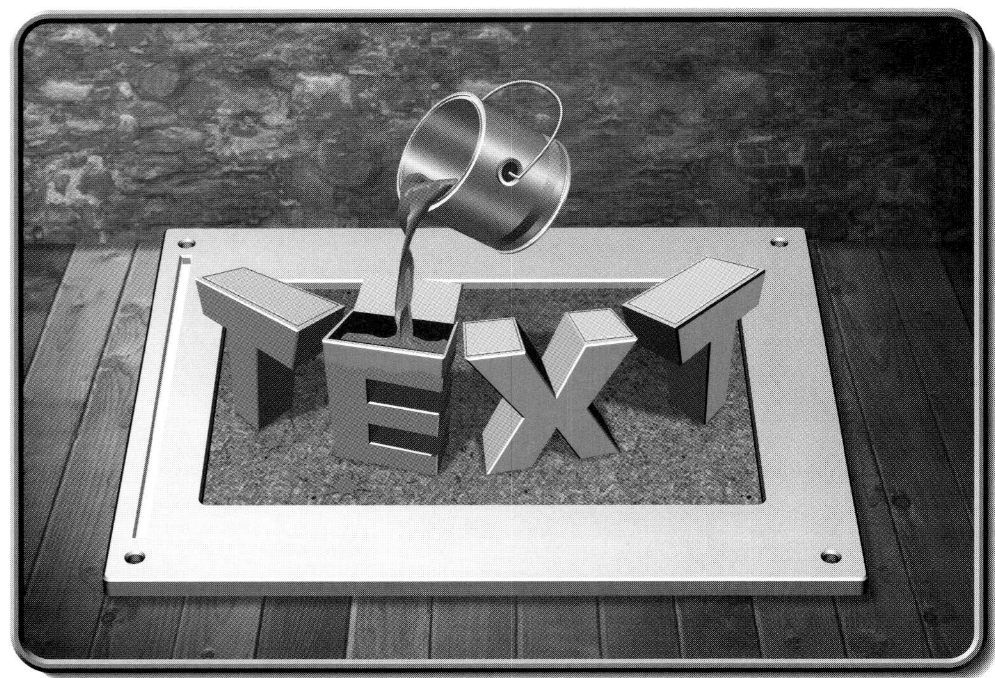

CHANGE TEXT COLOR

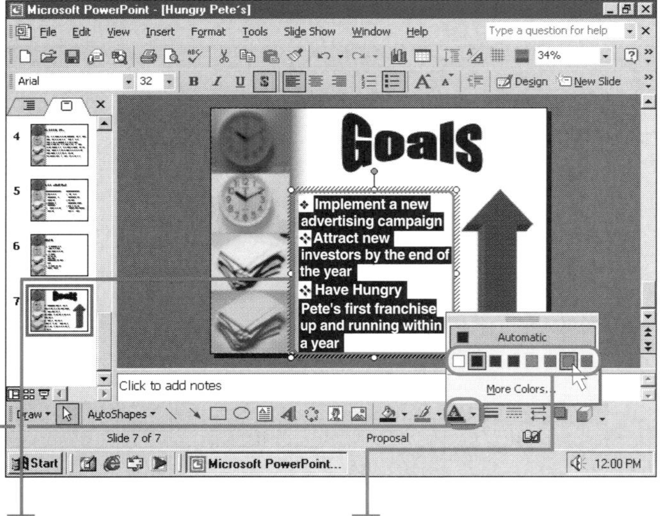

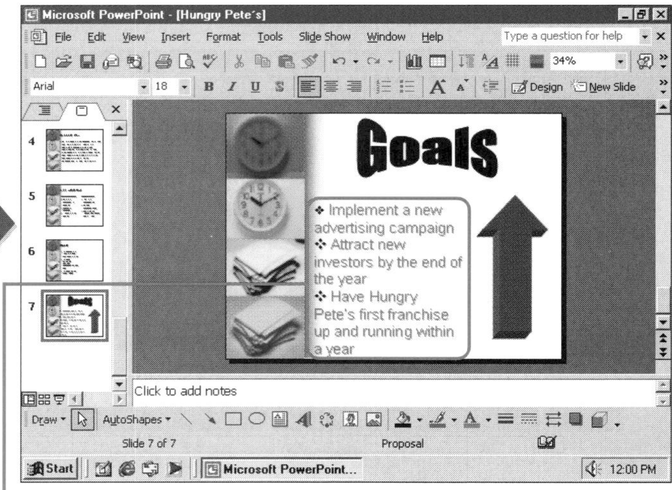

1 Select the text you want to change to a different color. To select text, see page 198.

2 Click ▾ in this area to display the available colors.

3 Click the color you want to use.

Note: The available colors depend on the color scheme of the slide. For information on color schemes, see page 234.

■ The text appears in the color you selected.

■ To deselect text, click outside the selected area.

■ To once again display the text in the default color, repeat steps 1 to 3, selecting **Automatic** in step 3.

CHANGE OBJECT COLOR

You can change the color of an object on a slide to better suit the design of the slide.

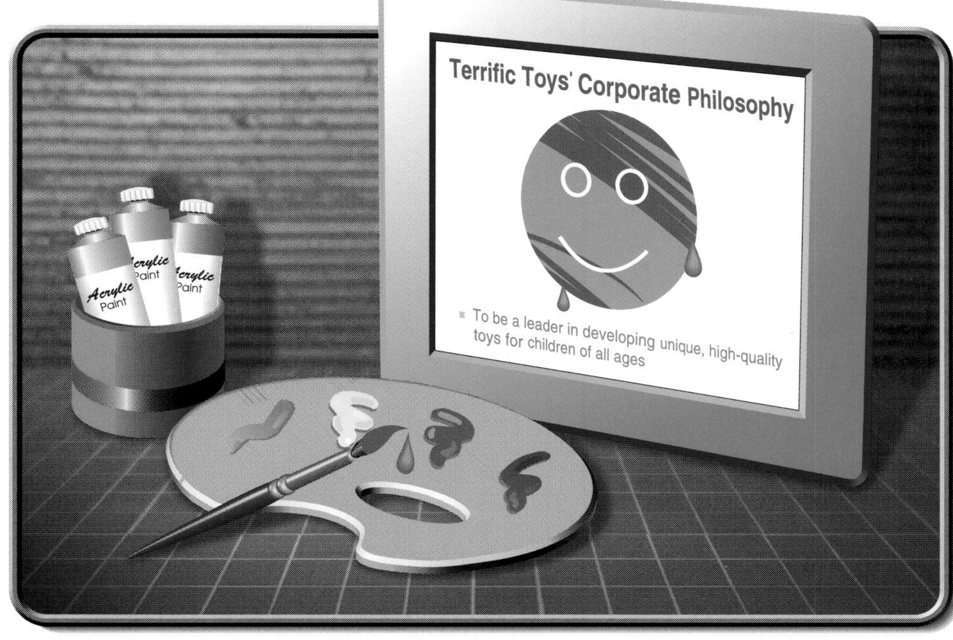

PowerPoint allows you to change the color of objects such as AutoShapes, WordArt, clip art images and charts.

CHANGE OBJECT COLOR

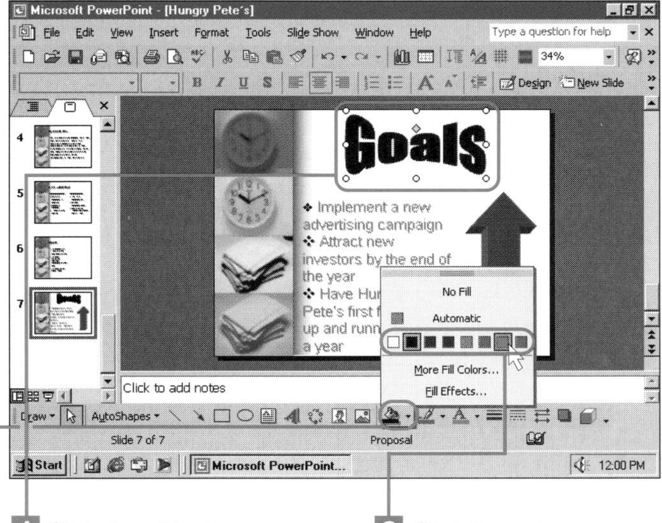

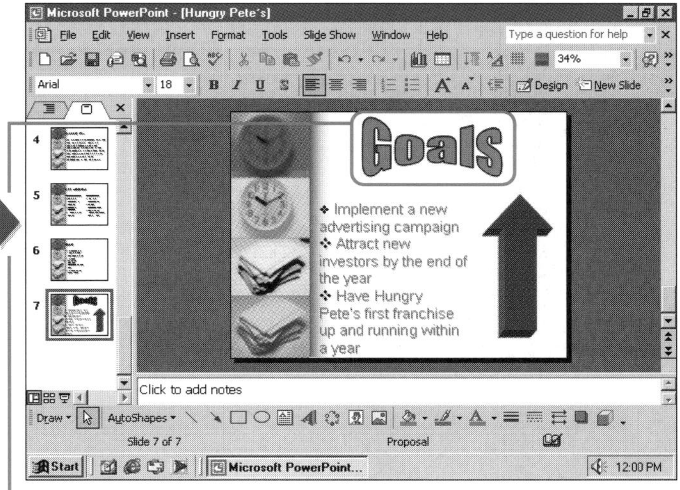

1 Click the object you want to change to a different color. Handles (o) appear around the object.

2 Click ▾ in this area to display the available colors.

3 Click the color you want to use.

Note: The available colors depend on the color scheme of the slide. For information on color schemes, see page 234.

■ The object appears in the color you selected.

■ To deselect the object, click outside the object.

■ To once again display the object in the default color, repeat steps 1 to 3, selecting **Automatic** in step 3.

CHANGE THE DESIGN TEMPLATE

PowerPoint offers many design templates that you can choose from to give the slides in your presentation a professional look.

You can change the design template for your entire presentation or for a single slide. Changing the design template for a single slide can make the slide stand out from the rest of your presentation.

CHANGE THE DESIGN TEMPLATE

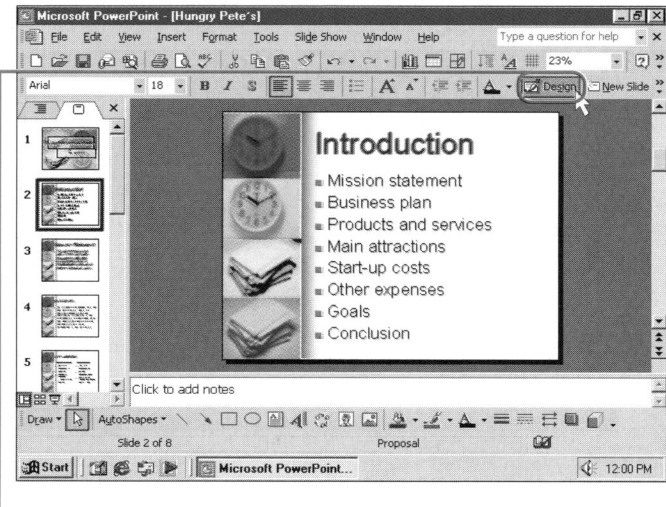

1 Click **Design** to display the Slide Design task pane.

Note: If the Design button is not displayed, click ⁝ on the Formatting toolbar to display all the buttons.

■ The Slide Design task pane appears.

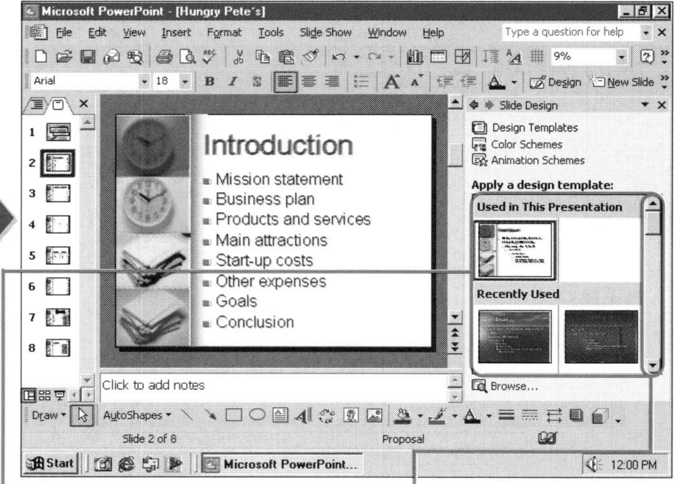

■ This area displays the available design templates.

Note: The design templates are organized into three sections— Used in This Presentation, Recently Used and Available For Use.

■ You can use the scroll bar to browse through the design templates.

When I changed the design template for my presentation, why did some parts of my slides not change?

The new design template may not affect parts of a slide you have previously formatted. For example, if you changed the color of text on a slide before changing the design template, the new design template will not affect the text you changed.

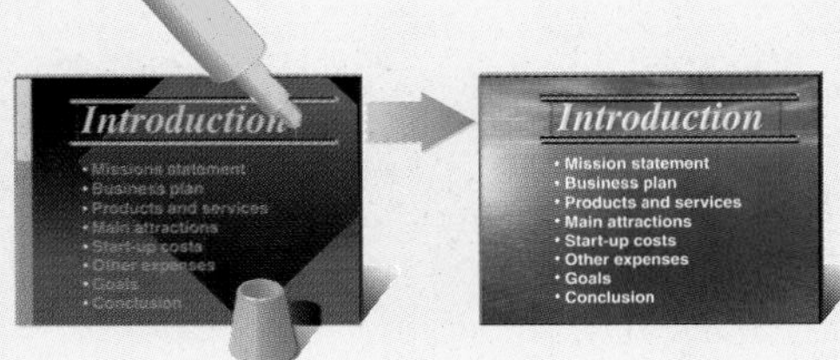

Can I apply a blank design template to my slides?

PowerPoint offers a blank template in the Available For Use section of the Slide Design task pane. Using a blank design template is useful if you find it difficult to work with the content of your presentation when colors are applied to the presentation. When you are finished working with your presentation, you can later change the design template to a more colorful template.

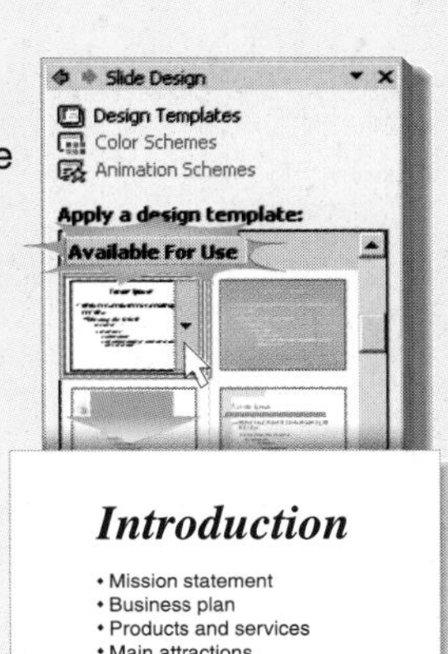

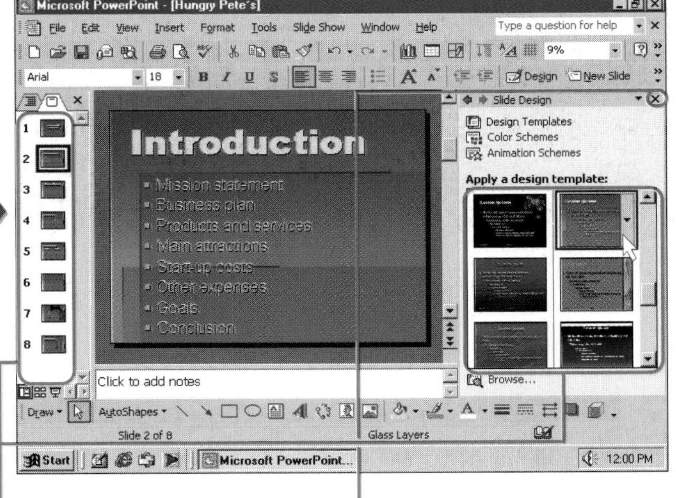

2 Click the design template you want to use.

■ All the slides in your presentation display the design template you selected.

Note: To select a different design template, repeat step 2.

3 When you finish selecting a design template, you can click ☒ to close the Slide Design task pane.

APPLY A DESIGN TEMPLATE TO ONE SLIDE

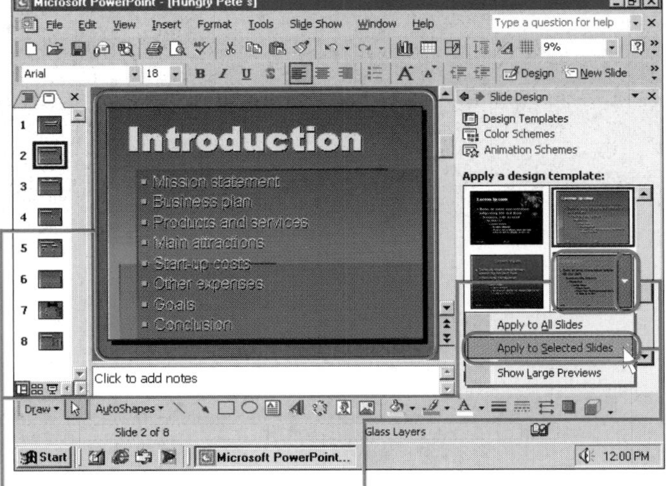

1 Display the slide you want to apply a design template to.

2 Position the mouse over the design template you want to use. An arrow (▾) appears.

3 Click the arrow (▾) to display a list of options.

4 Click **Apply to Selected Slides**.

CHANGE THE COLOR SCHEME

You can change the color scheme of all the slides in your presentation.

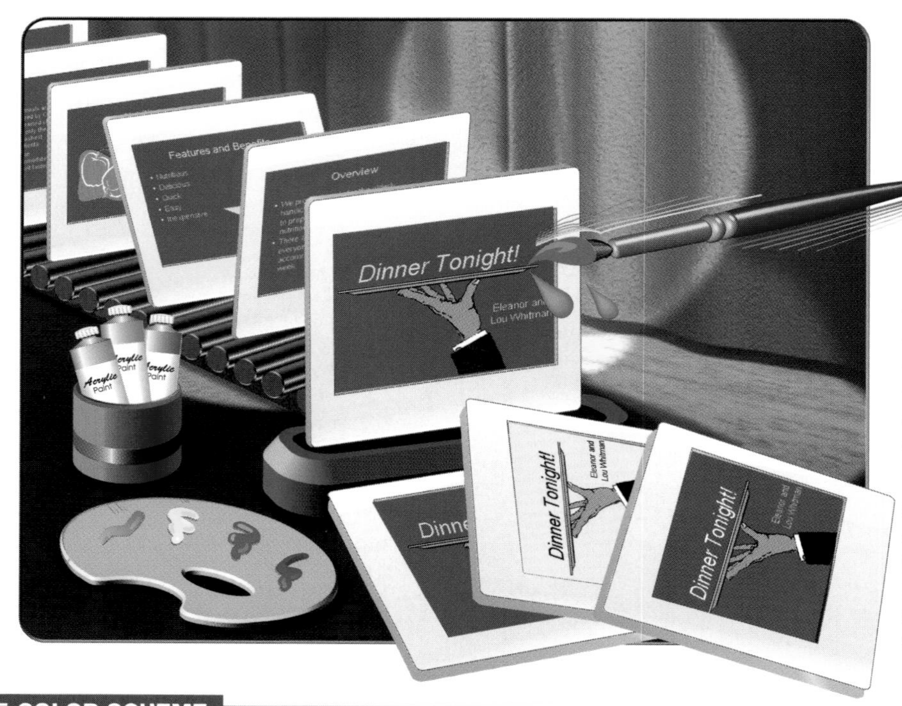

You can also change the color scheme of a single slide. Changing the color scheme for a single slide can make the slide stand out from the rest of your presentation.

Each color scheme contains a set of eight coordinated colors, including colors for the background, text, lines, shadows, titles and accents.

CHANGE THE COLOR SCHEME

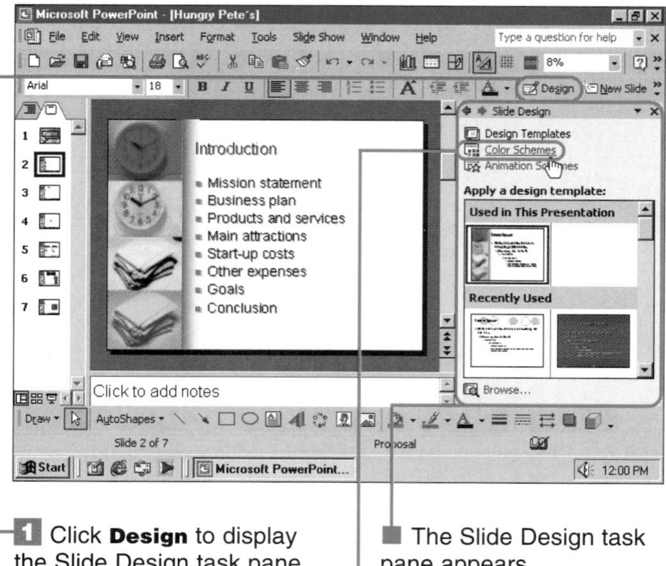

1 Click **Design** to display the Slide Design task pane.

Note: If the Design button is not displayed, click [»] on the Formatting toolbar to display all the buttons.

■ The Slide Design task pane appears.

2 Click **Color Schemes** to display the available color schemes.

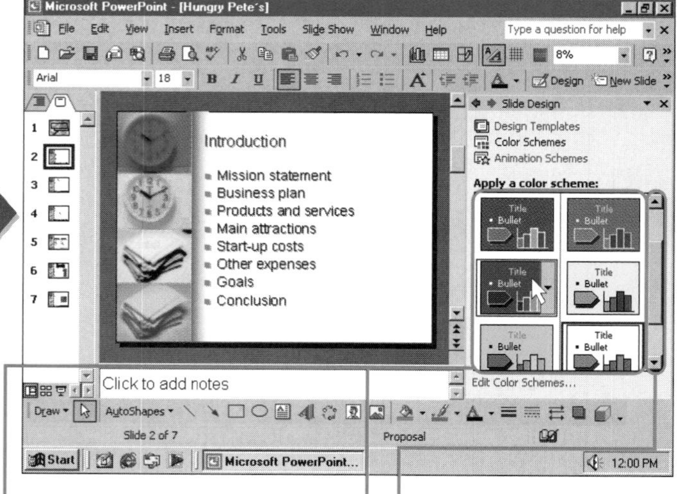

■ This area displays the available color schemes.

Note: The available color schemes depend on the current design template. For information on design templates, see page 232.

■ You can use the scroll bar to browse through the color schemes.

3 Click the color scheme you want to use.

What should I consider when changing the color scheme of slides?

When selecting a color scheme, you should consider how you will deliver the presentation. If you will be using overheads, you should choose a color scheme with a light background and dark text. If you will be using 35mm slides or delivering your presentation on a computer screen, you should choose a color scheme with a dark background and light text.

Some of the slides in my presentation did not change to the new color scheme. What is wrong?

You may have used more than one design template in your presentation. By default, PowerPoint only applies the new color scheme to slides with the same design template as the current slide. To apply the color scheme to all the slides in your presentation, perform steps 2 to 4 on page 235, selecting **Apply to All Slides** in step 4. For more information on design templates, see page 232.

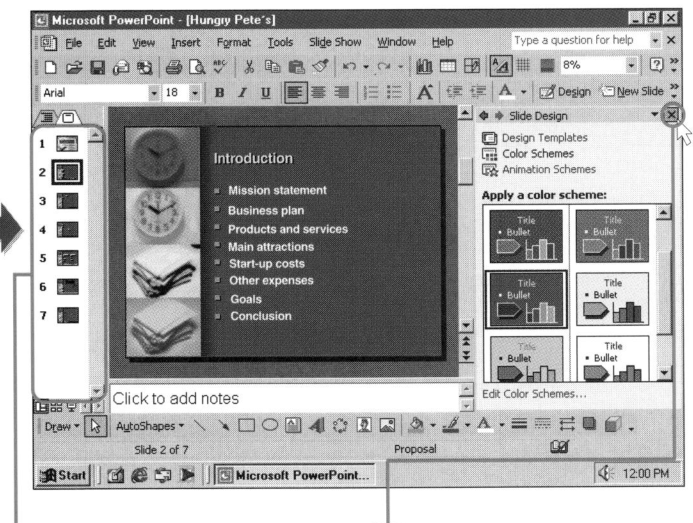

■ All the slides in your presentation display the color scheme you selected.

Note: To select a different color scheme, repeat step 3.

4 When you have finished selecting a color scheme, you can click ☒ to close the Slide Design task pane.

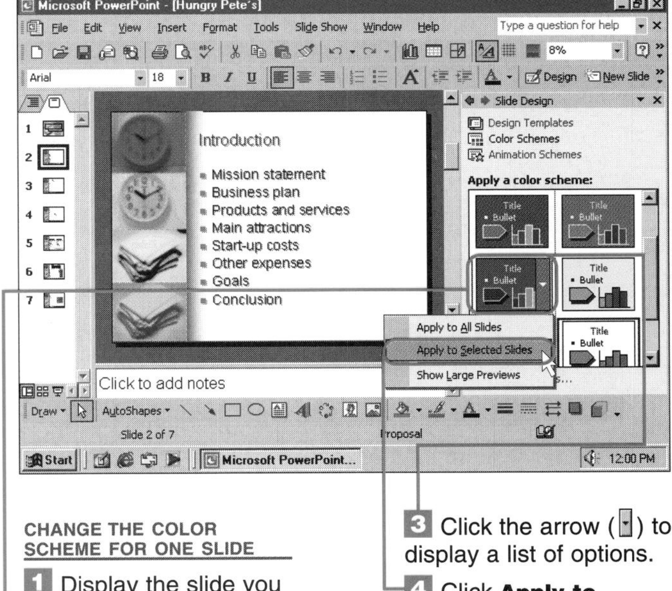

CHANGE THE COLOR SCHEME FOR ONE SLIDE

1 Display the slide you want to use a different color scheme.

2 Position the mouse over the color scheme you want to use. An arrow (▾) appears.

3 Click the arrow (▾) to display a list of options.

4 Click **Apply to Selected Slides**.

ANIMATE SLIDES

You can animate the objects on your slides. This can help keep your audience's attention throughout a presentation.

You can animate objects such as titles, lists of points, AutoShapes, WordArt and clip art images.

ANIMATE SLIDES

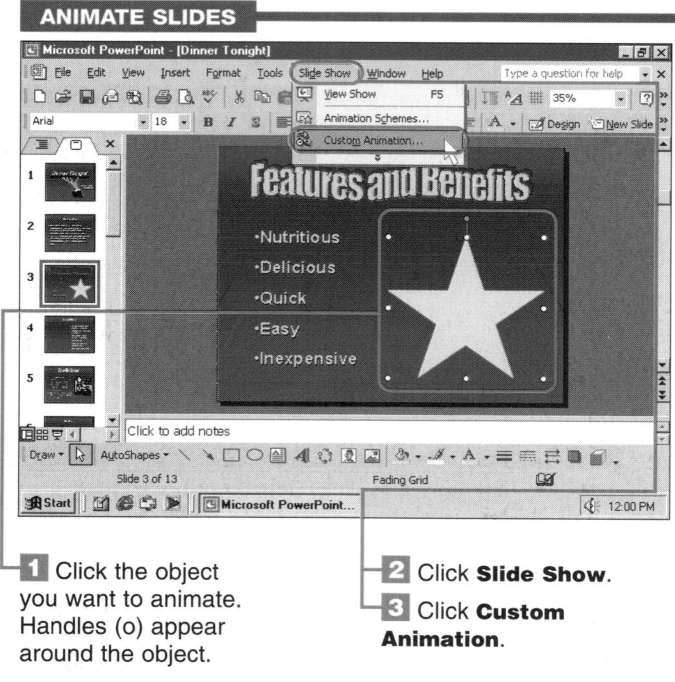

1 Click the object you want to animate. Handles (o) appear around the object.

2 Click **Slide Show**.

3 Click **Custom Animation**.

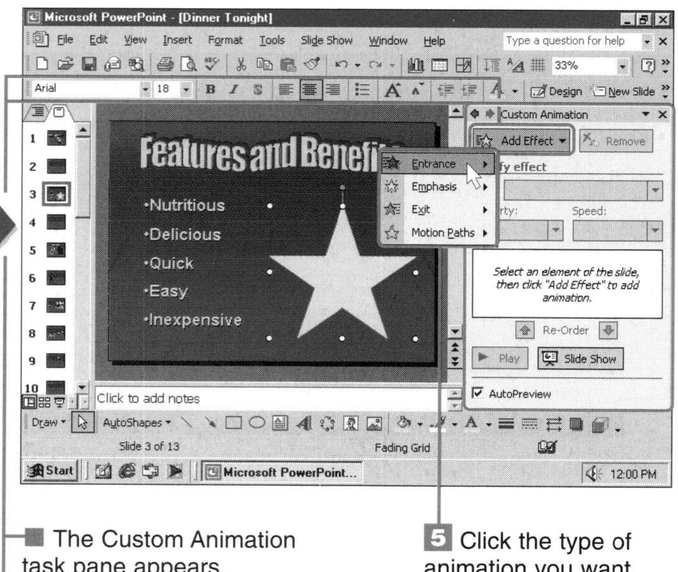

■ The Custom Animation task pane appears.

4 Click **Add Effect** to display the types of animations you can add.

5 Click the type of animation you want to add.

Note: For information about the types of animations, see the top of page 237.

What types of animations can I add to objects on my slides?

Entrance Animations that enter an object onto a slide.	**Emphasis** Animations that occur on a slide.	**Exit** Animations that exit an object from a slide.	**Motion Paths** Animations that move an object on a slide.

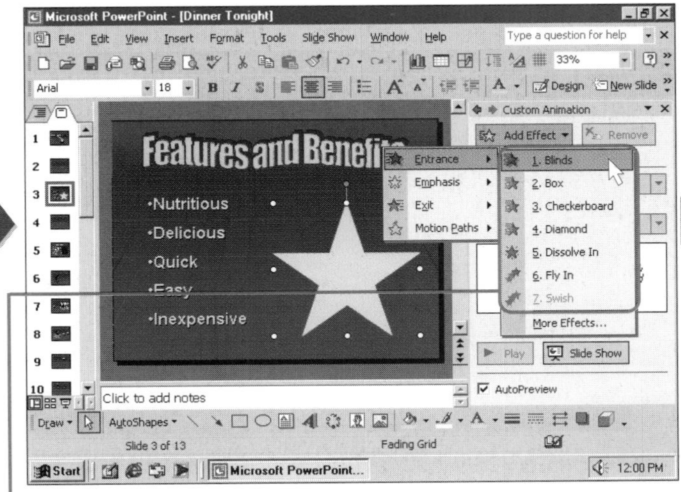

6 Click the animation you want to add. The available options depend on the type of animation you selected in step **5**.

*Note: To view more animations, click **More Effects**.*

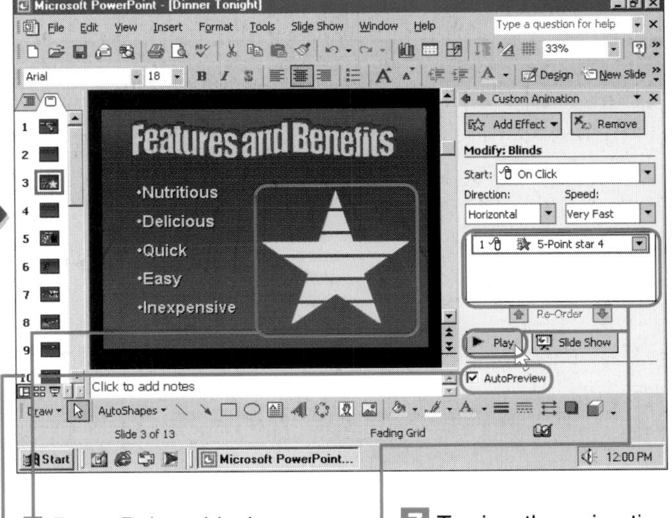

■ PowerPoint adds the animation to the selected object and displays a preview of the animation in this area.

■ If a preview for the animation does not automatically appear, click **AutoPreview** to turn the option on (☐ changes to ☑).

7 To view the animation again, click **Play**.

■ This area displays a description of the animation you added.

CONTINUED

ANIMATE SLIDES

You can specify properties for an animation you are adding to a slide. For example, you can specify a direction and speed for the animation.

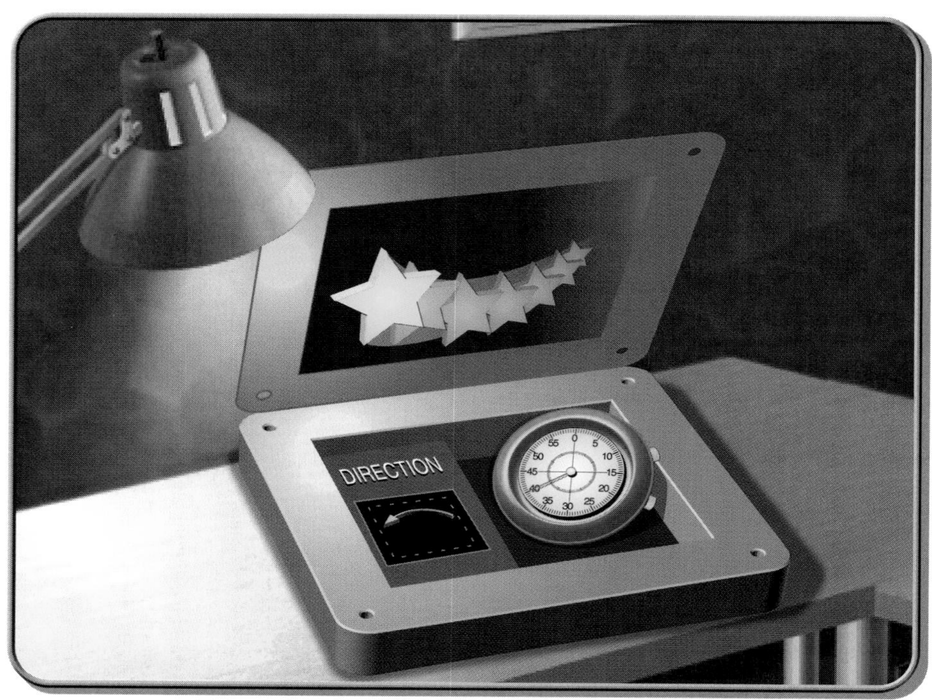

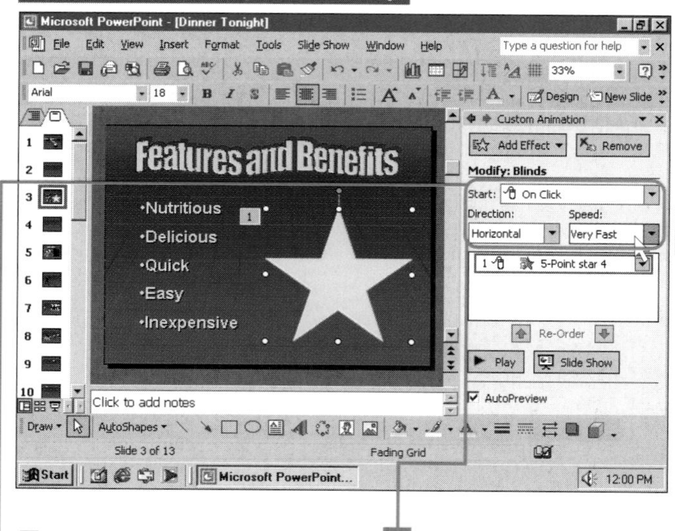

■ These areas allow you to change properties for the animation. The available properties depend on the animation you selected in step 6 on page 237.

8 To change a property for the animation, click an area to display a list of options.

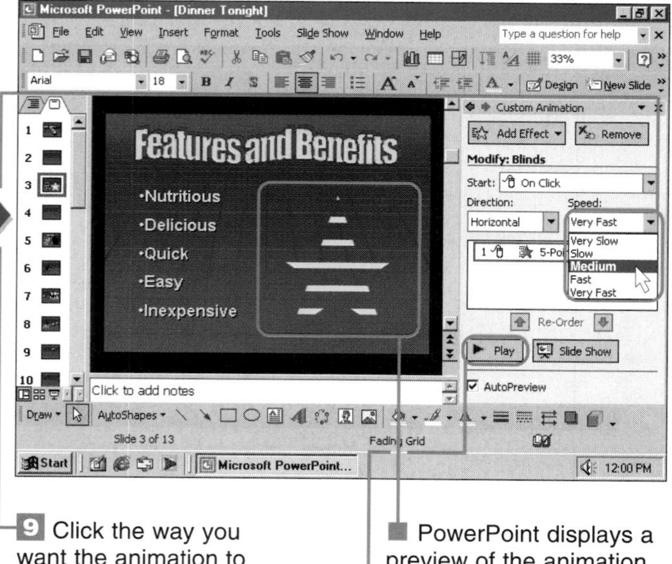

9 Click the way you want the animation to appear.

■ PowerPoint displays a preview of the animation with the option you selected.

■ To view the animation again, click **Play**.

How do I display animated objects in my slide show?

When viewing your slide show, you must click a slide to display each animated object on the slide. For example, if you animated a list of points, you will need to click the slide each time you want a point to appear.

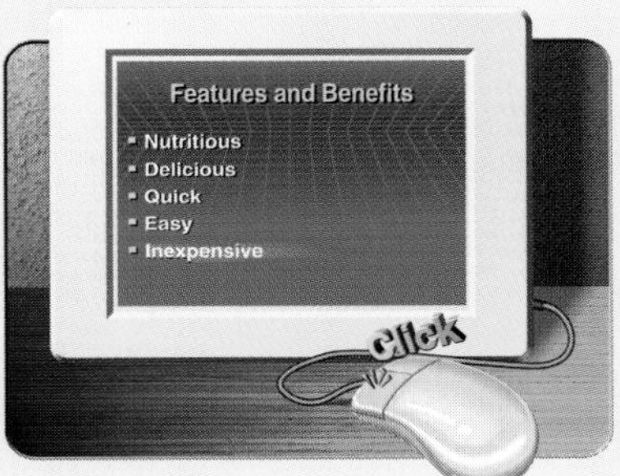

How can I change the order of the animations on a slide?

By default, animations appear in the order you added them to the slide.

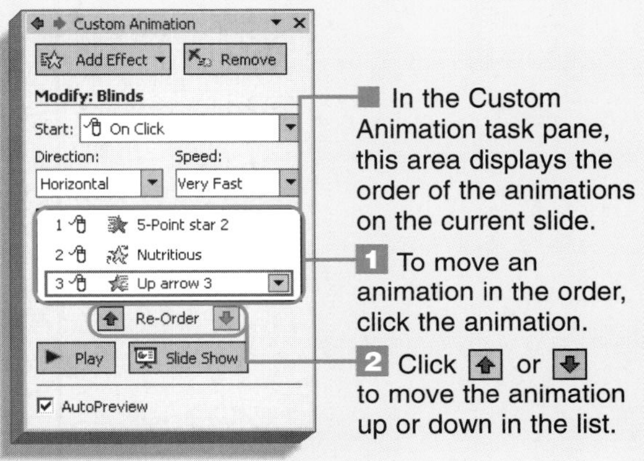

■ In the Custom Animation task pane, this area displays the order of the animations on the current slide.

1 To move an animation in the order, click the animation.

2 Click ⬆ or ⬇ to move the animation up or down in the list.

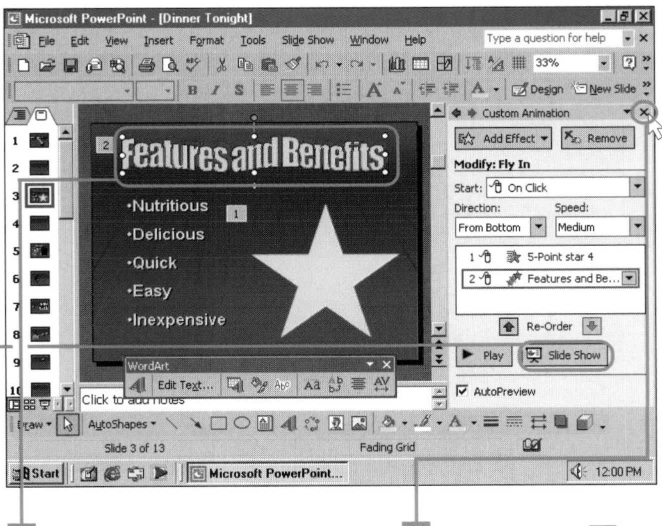

10 To animate another object, click the object and then repeat steps 4 to 9 starting on page 236.

■ When you finish animating objects on the slide, you can click **Slide Show** to view your presentation as a slide show. For information on viewing a slide show, see page 244.

11 You can click ☒ to close the Custom Animation task pane.

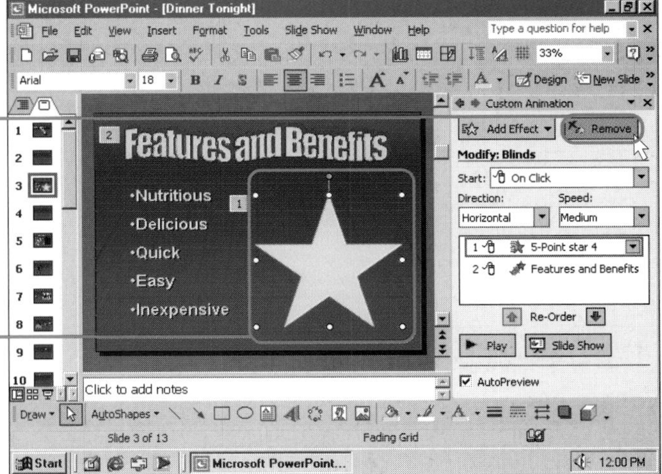

DELETE AN ANIMATION

1 Click the object you want to remove an animation from.

2 Click **Remove**.

Note: If the Custom Animation task pane is not displayed, perform steps 1 to 3 on page 236 to display the task pane.

■ PowerPoint removes the animation from the object.

REORDER SLIDES

You can change the order of the slides in your presentation. This is useful when you want to reorganize the ideas in your presentation.

REORDER SLIDES

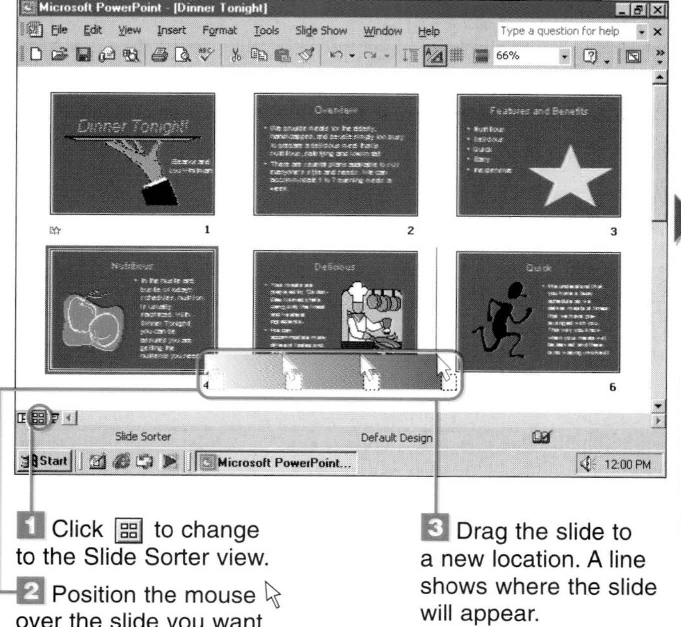

1 Click ⊞ to change to the Slide Sorter view.

2 Position the mouse ↖ over the slide you want to move.

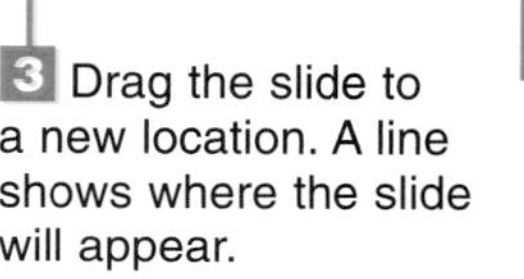

3 Drag the slide to a new location. A line shows where the slide will appear.

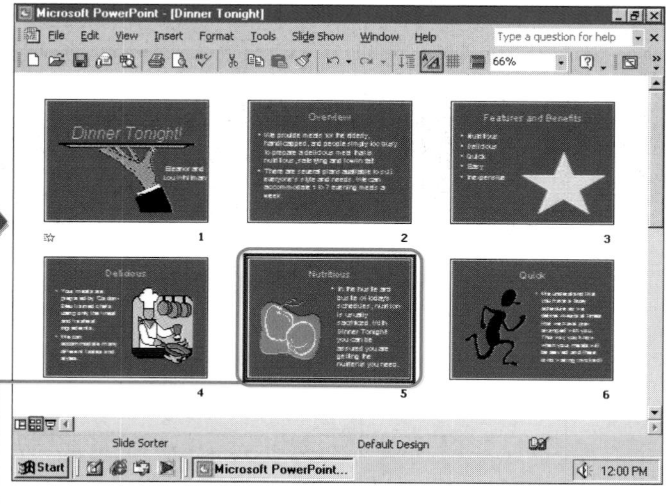

■ The slide appears in the new location.

DELETE A SLIDE

You can remove a slide you no longer need from your presentation. This is useful if a slide contains incorrect or outdated information.

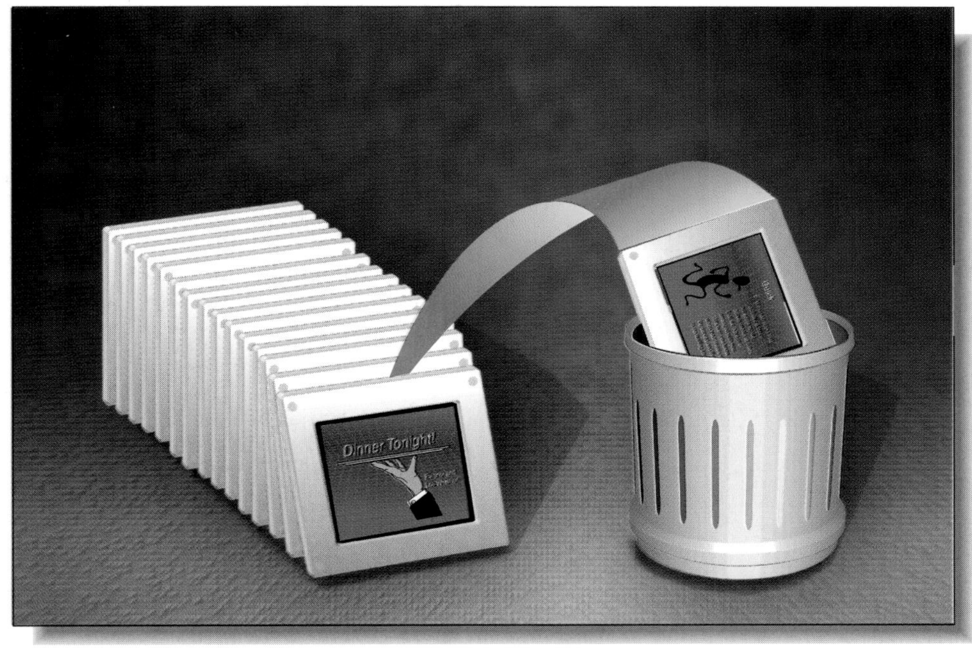

DELETE A SLIDE

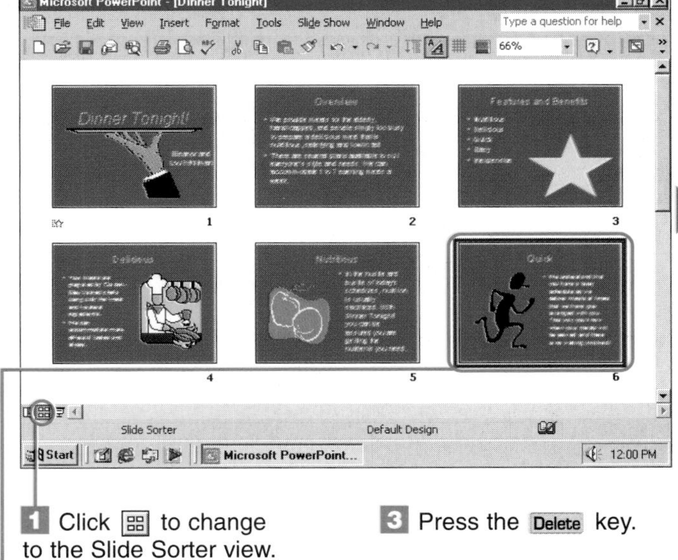

1 Click ▦ to change to the Slide Sorter view.

2 Click the slide you want to delete.

3 Press the Delete key.

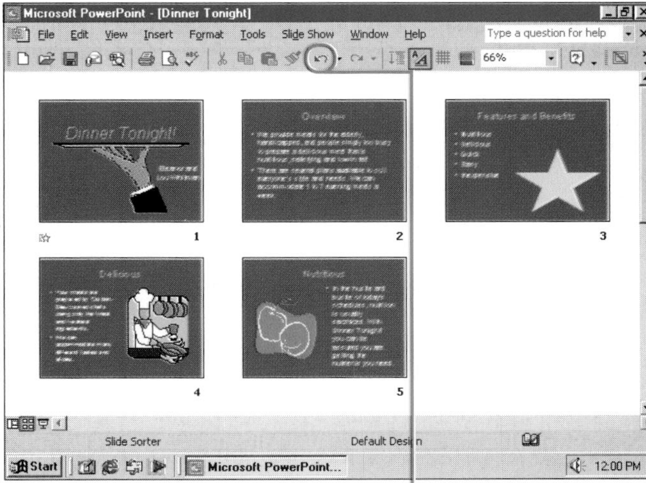

■ The slide disappears.

■ To immediately return the slide to the presentation, click ↶.

ADD SLIDE TRANSITIONS

You can add transitions to slides in your presentation. A transition is a visual effect that appears when you move from one slide to the next.

ADD SLIDE TRANSITIONS

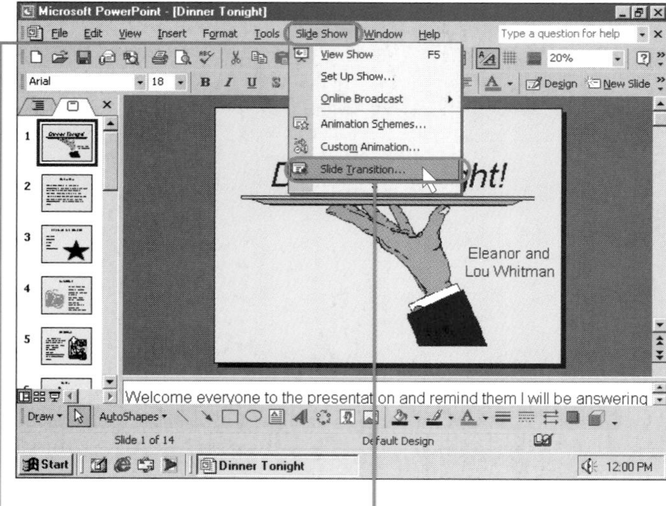

1 Display the slide you want to add a transition to.

2 Click **Slide Show**.

3 Click **Slide Transition**.

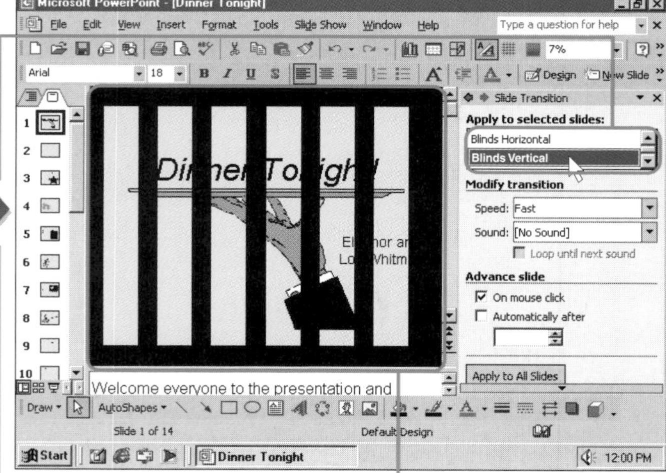

■ The Slide Transition task pane appears.

■ This area displays the available transitions. You can use the scroll bar to browse through the transitions.

4 Click the transition you want to use.

■ PowerPoint adds the transition to the displayed slide and displays a preview of the transition.

Note: To view the transition again, repeat step 4.

What should I consider when adding transitions to slides?

Although PowerPoint allows you to add a different transition to each slide in your presentation, using too many different transitions may distract the audience. The audience may focus on how each slide is introduced, rather than the information you are presenting.

How do I remove a transition from a slide?

Display the slide you want to remove a transition from and then perform steps 2 to 4 below, selecting **No Transition** in step 4.

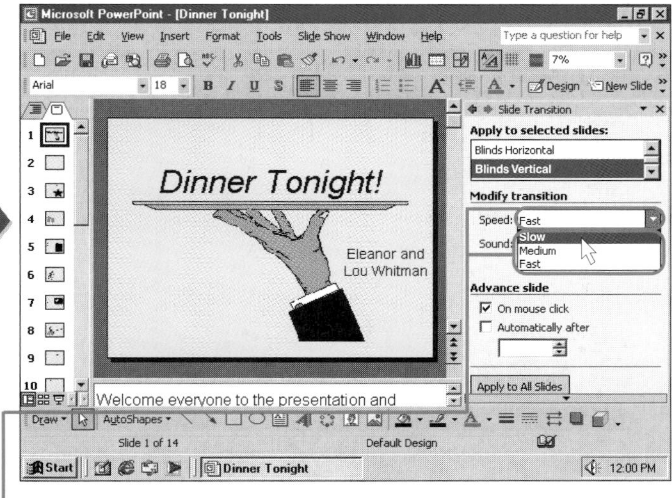

5 To change the speed of the transition, click this area to display a list of speed options.

6 Click the speed you want to use.

■ PowerPoint displays a preview of the transition with the speed you selected.

Note: To view the transition with the speed again, repeat steps 5 and 6.

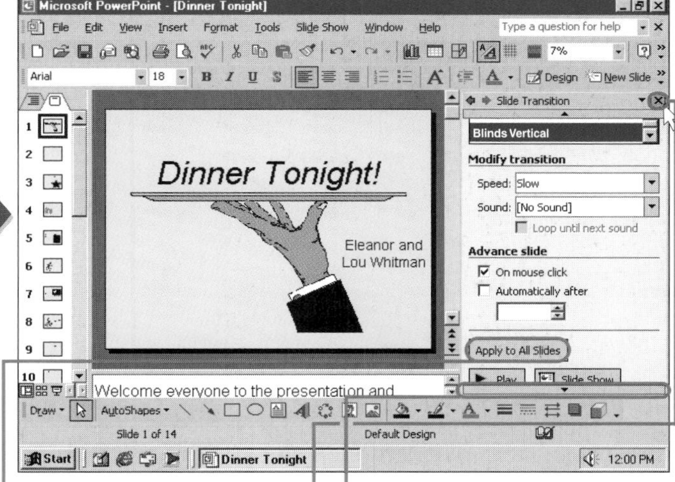

7 To add the transition to all the slides in your presentation, click **Apply to All Slides**.

■ If you cannot see the Apply to All Slides button, click ▼ to browse through the information in the task pane.

8 When you finish selecting a transition, you can click ☒ to close the Slide Transition task pane.

VIEW A SLIDE SHOW

You can view a slide show of your presentation on a computer screen. A slide show displays one slide at a time using the entire screen.

Before presenting a slide show to an audience, you can view the slide show to rehearse your presentation.

VIEW A SLIDE SHOW

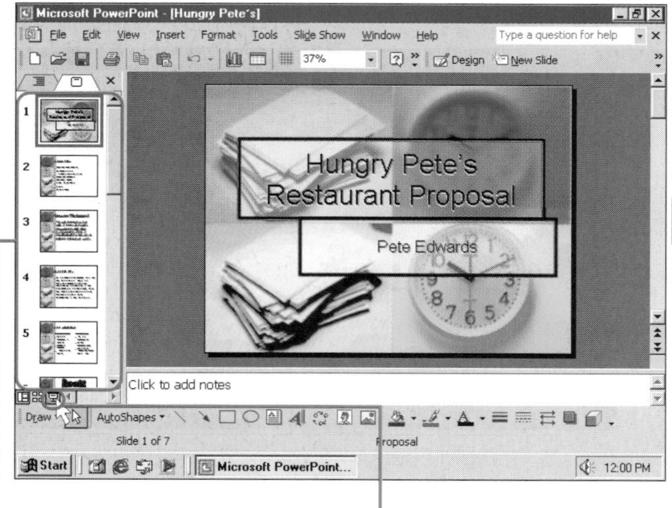

1 Click the first slide you want to view in the slide show.

2 Click the slide show button to start the slide show.

■ The slide you selected fills your screen.

Note: You can press the **Esc** *key to end the slide show at any time.*

3 To display the next slide, click anywhere on the current slide.

How can I use my keyboard to move through a slide show?

Task	Press this key
Display the next slide	Spacebar
Display the previous slide	Backspace
Display any slide	Type the number of the slide and then press Enter
End the slide show	Esc
Pause the slide show and turn the screen black	B (Press B again to return to the slide show)
Pause the slide show and turn the screen white	W (Press W again to return to the slide show)

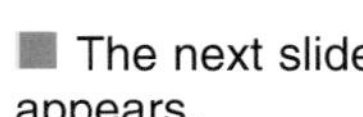

Introduction

- Mission statement
- Business plan
- Products and services
- Main attractions
- Start-up costs
- Other expenses
- Goals
- Conclusion

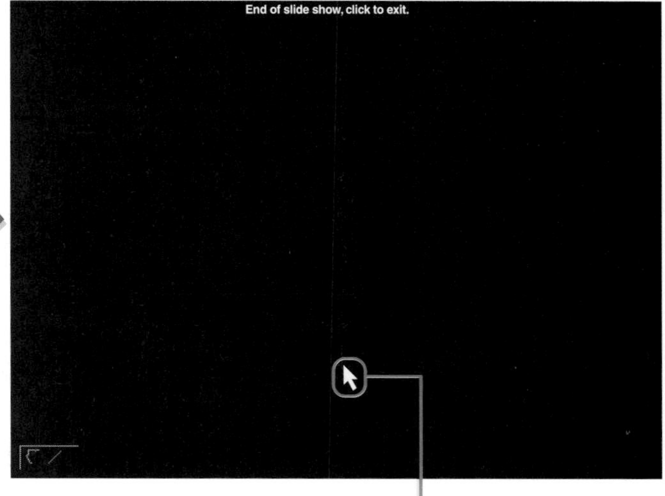
End of slide show, click to exit.

■ The next slide appears.

■ To return to the previous slide, press the Backspace key.

4 Repeat step **3** until this screen appears, indicating you have reached the end of the slide show.

5 Click the screen to exit the slide show.

CREATE NOTES

You can create notes that contain the ideas you want to discuss for each slide in your presentation. You can use your notes as a guide when delivering your presentation.

Notes can include statistics and information that you may need to answer questions from the audience.

CREATE NOTES

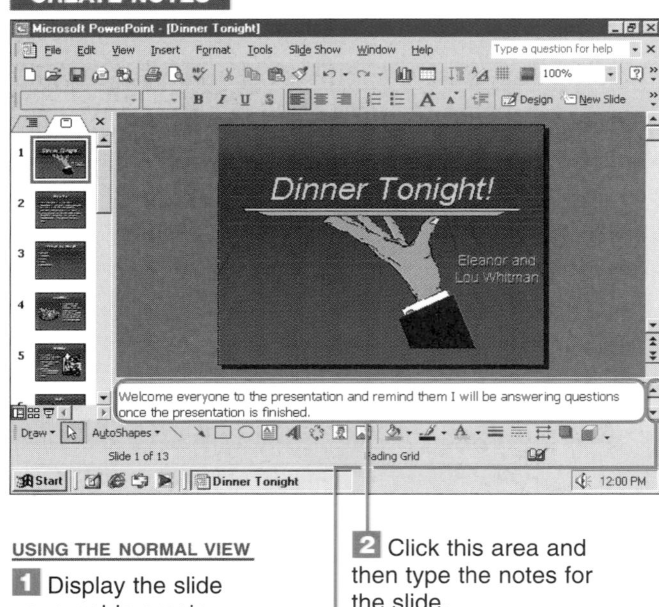

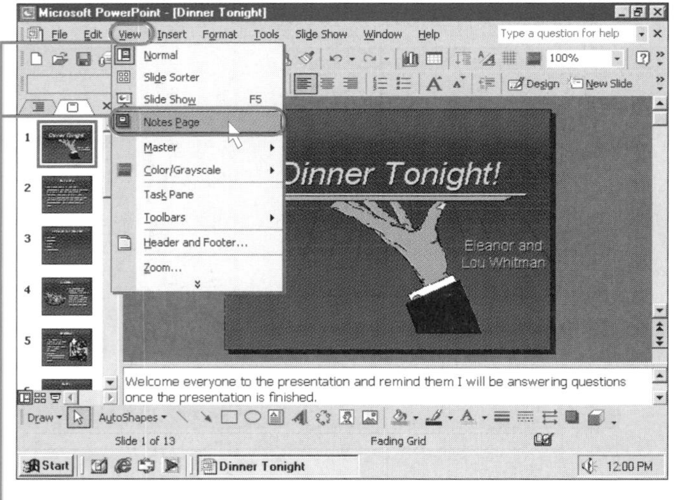

USING THE NORMAL VIEW

1 Display the slide you want to create notes for.

2 Click this area and then type the notes for the slide.

■ If you type more than one line of text, you can use the scroll bar to browse through the text.

USING NOTES PAGES

1 Click **View**.

2 Click **Notes Page** to display your notes pages.

Note: If Notes Page does not appear on the menu, position the mouse over the bottom of the menu to display all the menu options.

When using the Normal view to create notes, how do I increase the size of the notes area?

To increase the size of the notes area in the Normal view, position the mouse I over the top border of the area (I changes to ÷) and then drag the border to a new location.

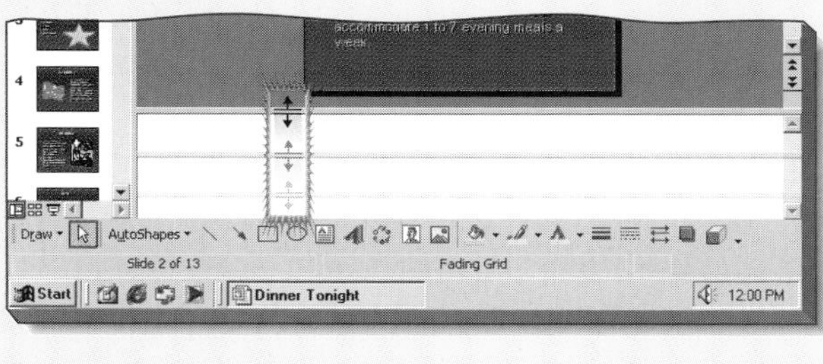

Can I print my notes pages?

You can print your notes pages so you will have a paper copy of the notes to refer to while delivering your presentation. Printing notes pages is also useful if you want to use the pages as handouts to help your audience follow your presentation. For information on printing notes pages, see page 250.

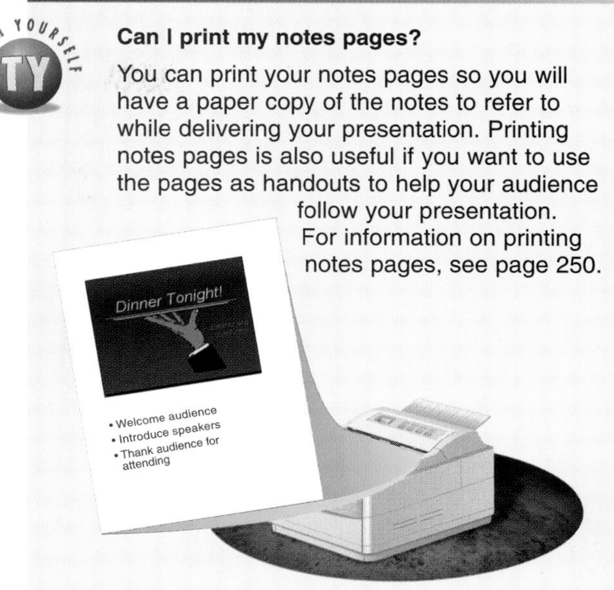

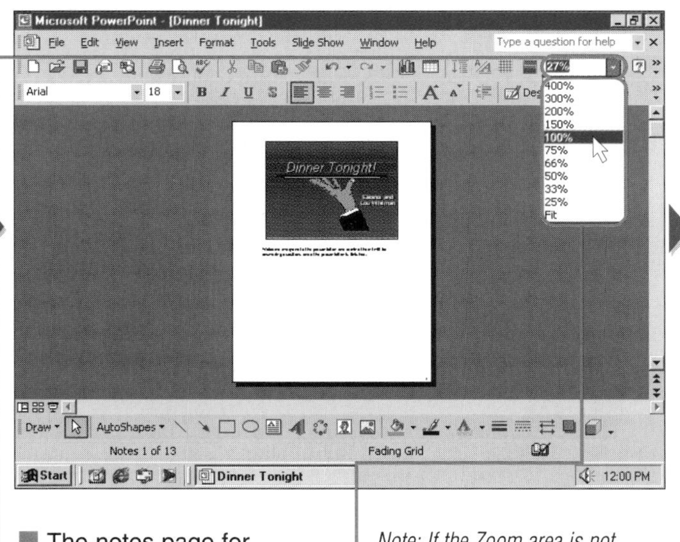

■ The notes page for the current slide appears.

Note: You can use the scroll bar to view the notes pages for other slides in the presentation.

3 To magnify the notes page so you can clearly view the notes, click ▾ in this area.

Note: If the Zoom area is not displayed, click » on the Standard toolbar to display the area.

4 Click the magnification you want to use.

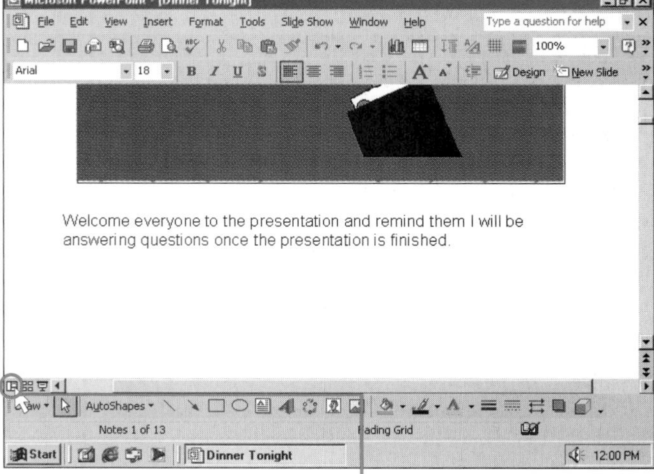

■ The notes page appears in the new magnification.

■ You can edit and format the text on the notes page as you would any text in your presentation.

*Note: To once again display the entire notes page, repeat steps 3 and 4, selecting **Fit** in step 4.*

5 When you finish reviewing your notes pages, click ⊞ to return to the Normal view.

PREVIEW A PRESENTATION BEFORE PRINTING

You can use the Print Preview feature to see how your presentation will look when printed. This allows you to confirm that the presentation will print the way you want.

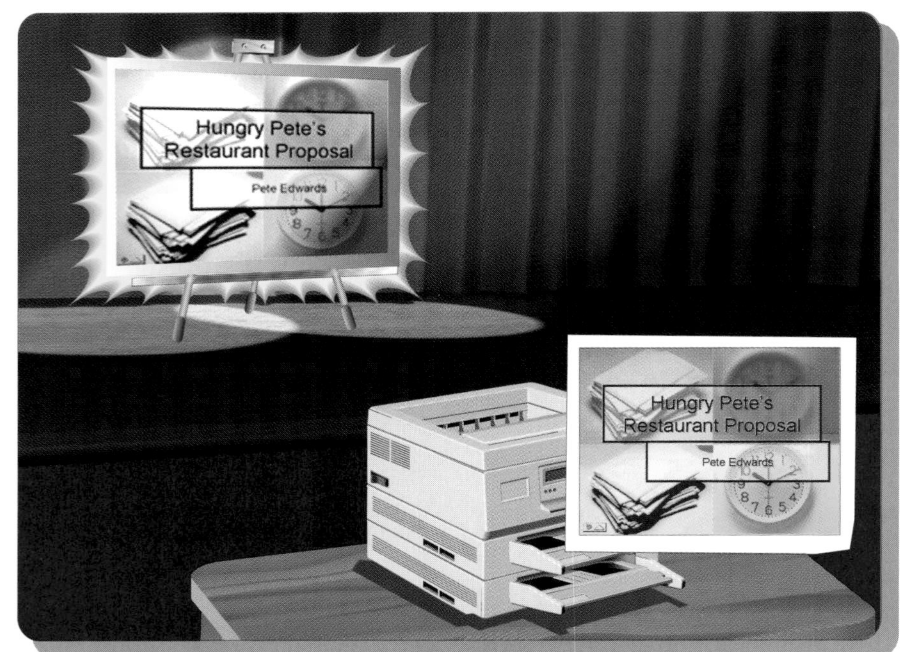

You can choose the part of your presentation that you want to preview, such as slides, handouts, notes pages or an outline.

PREVIEW A PRESENTATION BEFORE PRINTING

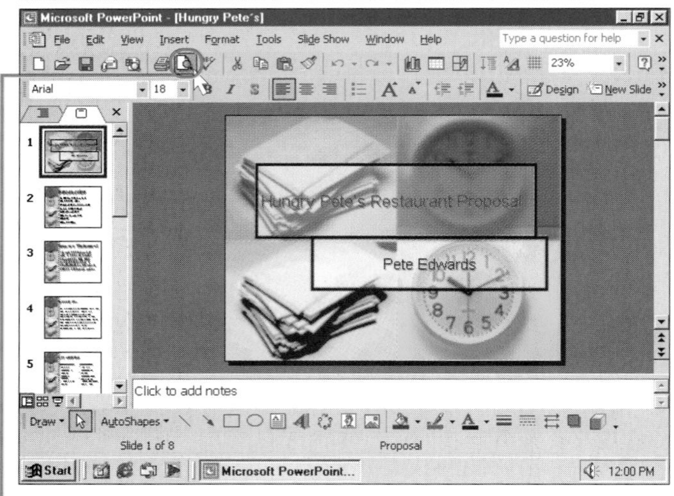

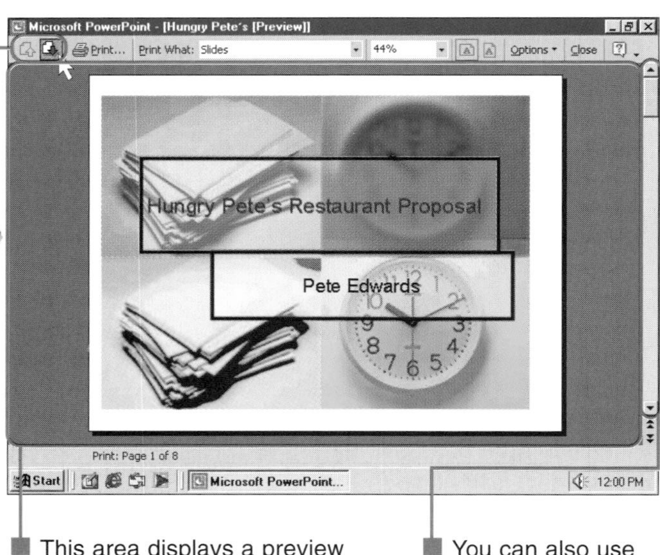

1 Click to preview your presentation before printing.

Note: If is not displayed, click on the Standard toolbar to display all the buttons.

■ The Print Preview window appears.

■ This area displays a preview of the slide that will appear on the first printed page.

2 To view the slides that will appear on the other printed pages, click one of the following buttons.

Display previous page

Display next page

■ You can also use the scroll bar to view the other pages.

How can I magnify an area of a page I am previewing?

Position the mouse over the area of the page you want to magnify (changes to) and then click the area to display a magnified view of the area. To once again display the entire page, you can click anywhere on the page.

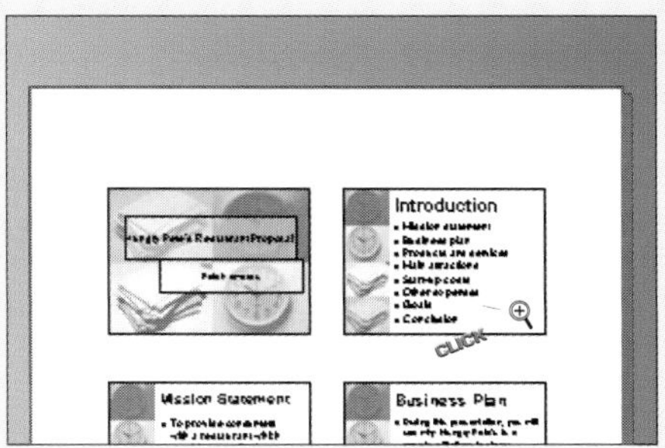

How can I quickly print my presentation while working in the Print Preview window?

You can click the Print button (Print...) to quickly print the presentation you are previewing.

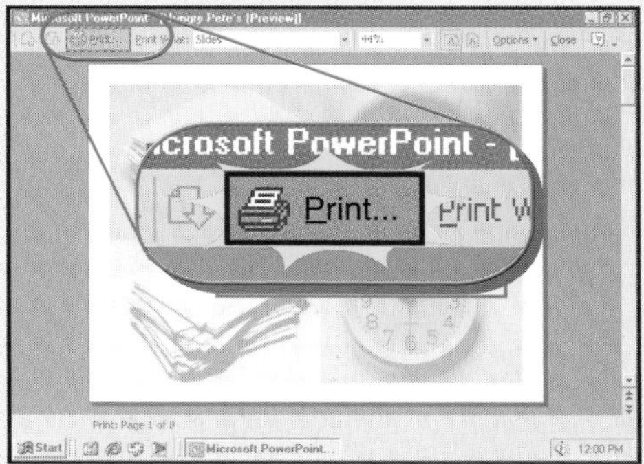

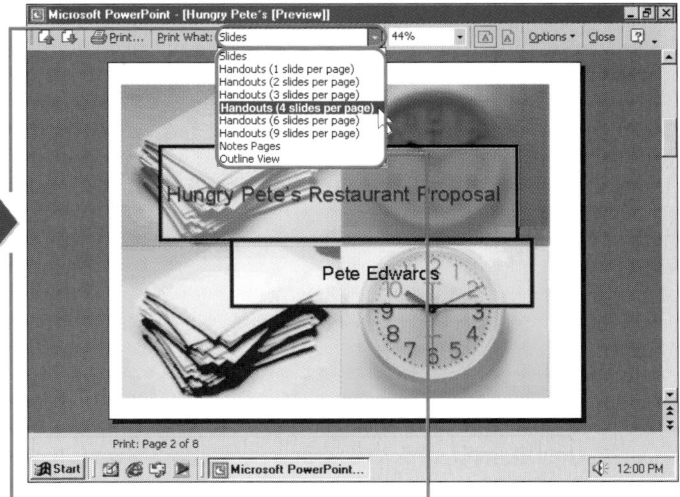

3 To preview a different part of your presentation before printing, click this area.

4 Click the part of the presentation you want to preview. For information on the parts of your presentation that you can print, see the top of page 251.

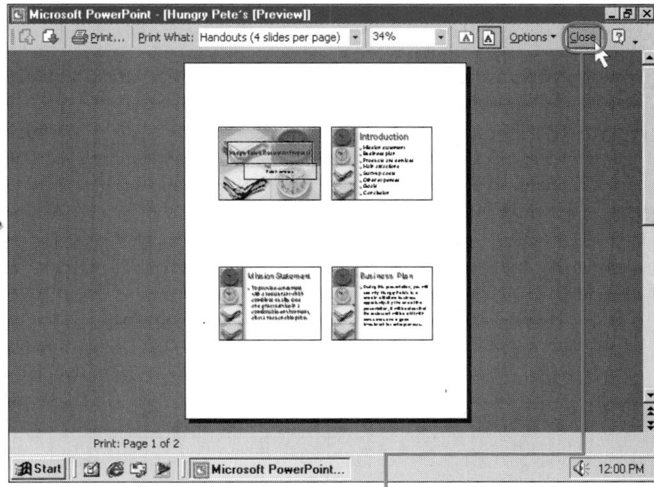

■ A preview of the part of the presentation you selected appears.

5 When you finish previewing your document, click **Close** to close the Print Preview window.

PRINT A PRESENTATION

You can produce a paper copy of a presentation for your own use or to hand out to your audience.

Before printing your presentation, make sure your printer is turned on and contains paper.

PRINT A PRESENTATION

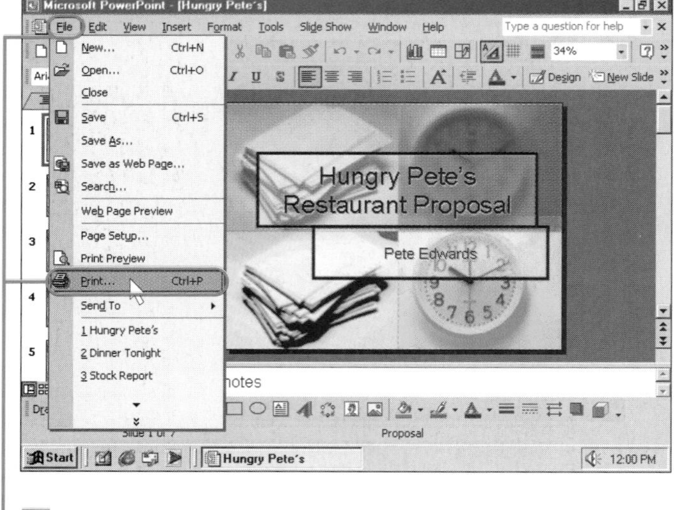

1 Click **File**.

2 Click **Print**.

■ The Print dialog box appears.

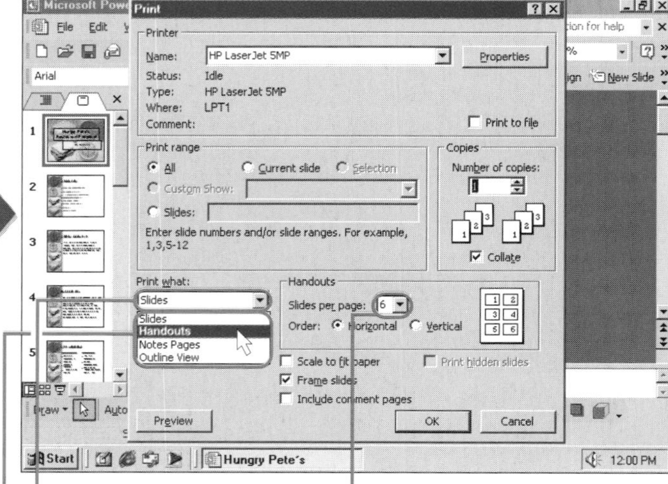

3 Click this area to select the part of the presentation you want to print.

4 Click the part of the presentation you want to print.

Note: For information on the available options, see the top of page 251.

■ If you selected **Handouts** in step 4, you can click this area to change the number of slides that will print on each page.

What parts of my presentation can I print?

Slides

Prints one slide on each page. This is useful when you are printing transparencies for an overhead projector.

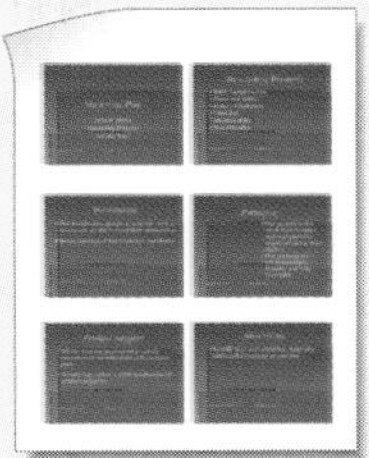

Handouts

Prints one or more slides on each page. You can give handouts to your audience to help them follow your presentation.

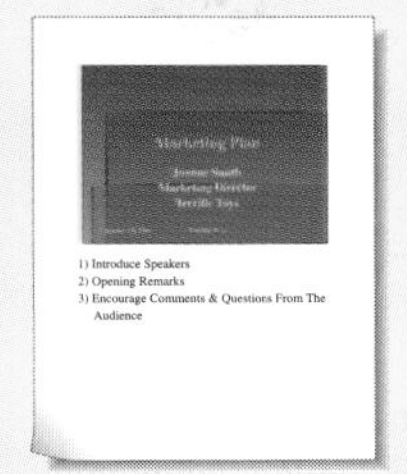

Notes Pages

Prints one slide and any notes you added to the slide on each page. You can use notes pages as a guide when delivering your presentation. To add notes to your slides, see page 246.

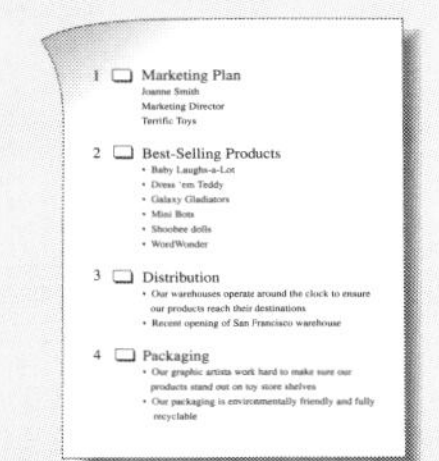

Outline View

Prints the text displayed in the Outline view of your presentation. For information on the Outline view, see page 188.

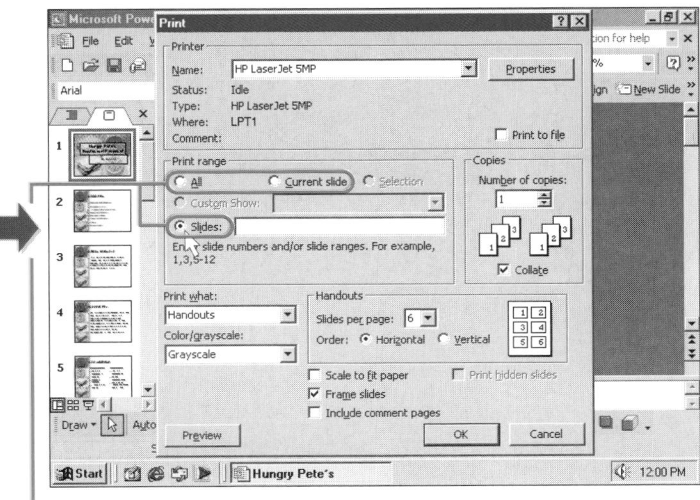

5 Click an option to specify which slides you want to print (○ changes to ⊙).

All - Print every slide in your presentation.

Current slide - Print the slide displayed on your screen.

Slides - Print the slides you specify.

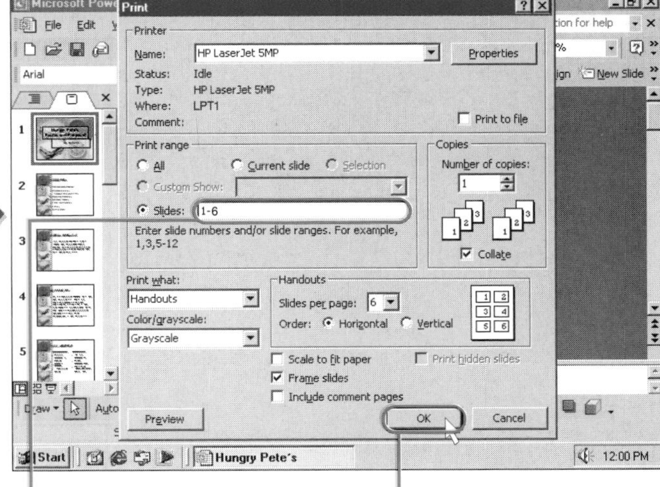

6 If you selected **Slides** in step 5, type the numbers of the slides you want to print in this area (example: 1,2,4 or 1-4).

7 Click **OK** to print your presentation.

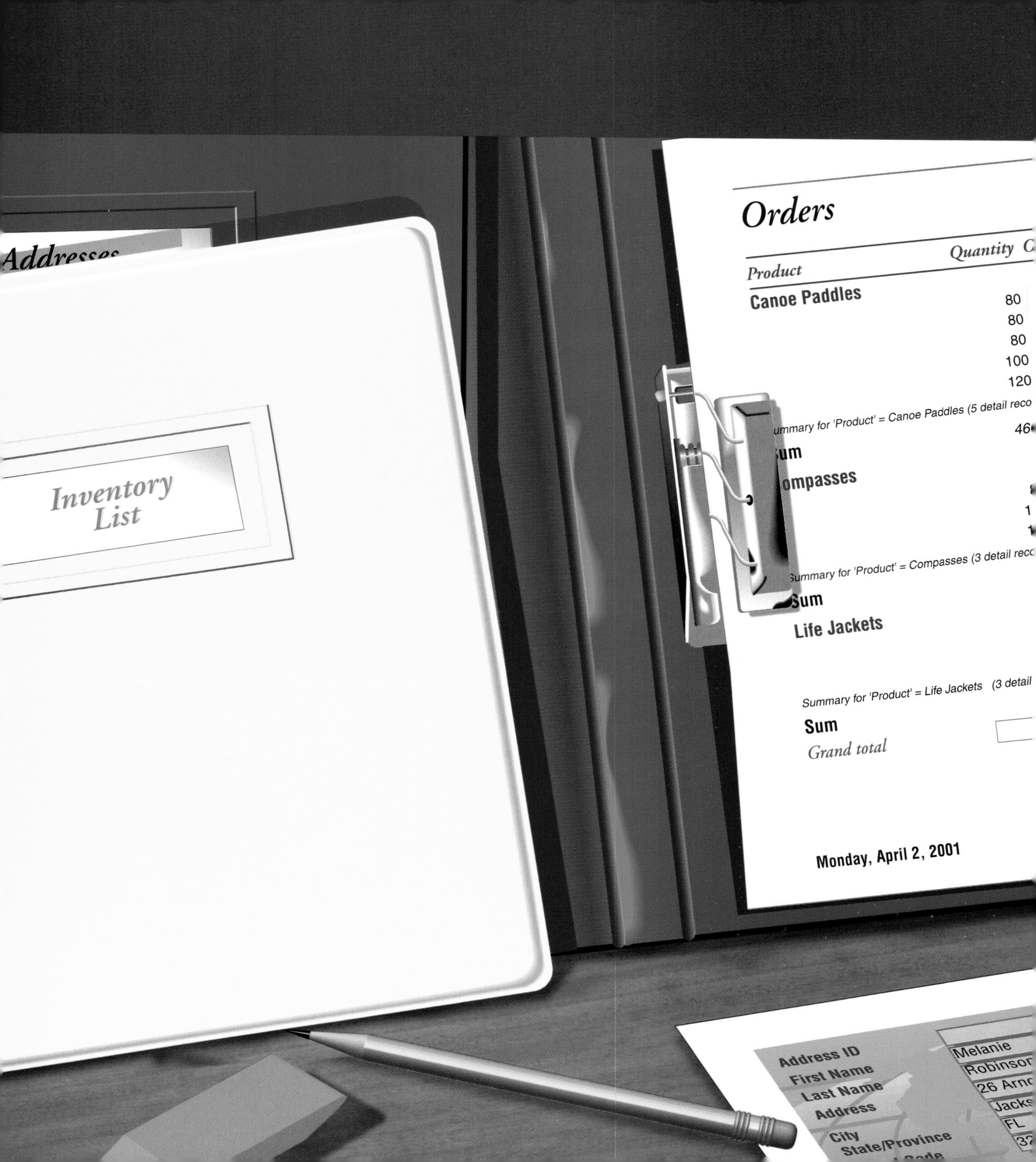

Inventory List
Orders
Quantity
Product
Canoe Paddles
80
80
80
100
120
Summary for 'Product' = Compasses
Sum
Life Jackets
Summary for 'Product' = Life Jackets
Sum
Grand total
Monday, April 2, 2001
Address ID
First Name
Last Name
Address
City
State/Province
Melanie
FL

Using Access

Access is a database program that allows you to store and manage large collections of information. Access provides you with all the tools you need to create an efficient and effective database.

A database contains a collection of information related to a particular topic. Databases are commonly used to store information such as contact, inventory or expense information. A database consists of objects such as tables, forms, queries and reports.

Tables

A table stores a collection of information about a specific topic, such as a mailing list. You can have one or more tables in a database. A table consists of fields and records.

Address ID	First Name	Last Name	Address	City	State/Province	Postal Code
1	Jim	Schmith	258 Linton Ave.	New York	NY	10010
2	Brenda	Petterson	50 Tree Lane	Boston	MA	02117
3	Todd	Talbot	68 Cracker Ave.	San Francisco	CA	94110
4	Chuck	Dean	47 Crosby Ave.	Las Vegas	NV	89116
5	Melanie	Robinson	26 Arnold Cres.	Jacksonville	FL	32256
6	Susan	Hughes	401 Idon Dr.	Nashville	TN	37243
7	Allen	Toppins	10 Heldon St.	Atlanta	GA	30375
8	Greg	Kilkenny	36 Buzzard St.	Boston	MA	02118
9	Jason	Marcuson	15 Bizzo Pl.	New York	NY	10020
10	Jim	Martin	890 Apple St.	San Diego	CA	92121

Field

A field is a specific category of information in a table, such as the first names of all your customers.

Record

A record is a collection of information about one person, place or thing in a table, such as the name and address of one customer.

Forms

Forms provide a quick way to view, enter and edit information in a database by presenting information in an easy-to-use format. Forms display boxes that clearly show you where to enter information.

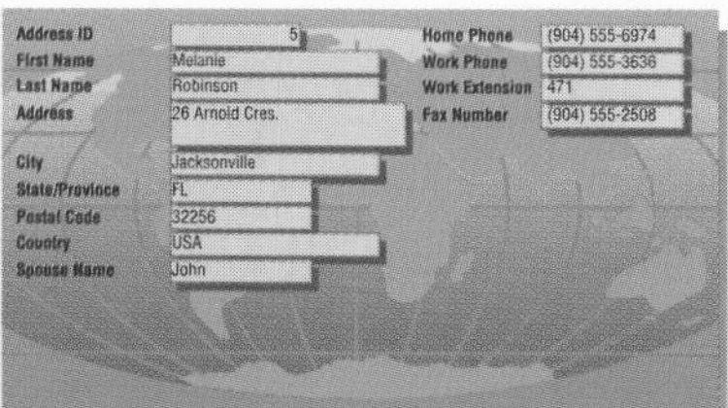

Queries

Queries allow you to ask Access to find information in a database that meets certain criteria or conditions. For example, you can create a query to find all customers who live in California.

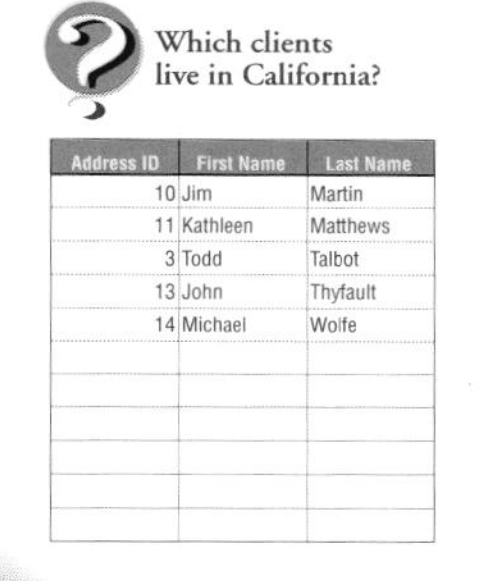

Address ID	First Name	Last Name
10	Jim	Martin
11	Kathleen	Matthews
3	Todd	Talbot
13	John	Thyfault
14	Michael	Wolfe

Reports

Reports are professional-looking documents that summarize information from a database. For example, you can create a report that displays the total sales for each product.

Orders

Product	Quantity	Order Number	Date
Canoe Paddles			
	80	7862	3/14/01
	80	938	3/2/01
	80	7921	3/11/01
	100	9126	3/12/01
	120	2386	3/12/01
Summary for 'Product' = Canoe Paddles (5 detail records)			
Sum	460		
Compasses			
	80	6892	3/12/01
	100	6124	3/18/01
	105	2935	2/20/01
Summary for 'Product' = Compasses (3 detail records)			
Sum	285		
Life Jackets			
	60	795	2/26/01
	65	1911	2/27/01
	110	6882	3/13/01
Summary for 'Product' = Life Jackets (3 detail records)			
Sum	235		
Grand total	980		

Friday, June 29, 2001 — *Page 1 of 1*

PLAN A DATABASE

You should take the time to plan your database. A well-planned database ensures that you will be able to perform tasks efficiently and accurately.

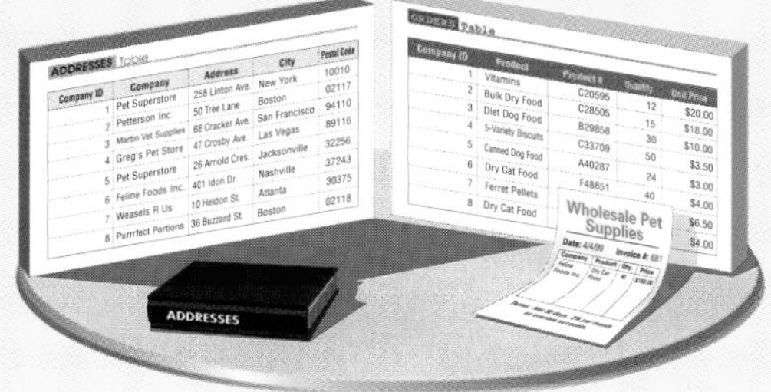

Determine the Tables You Need

Gather all the information you want to store in your database and then divide the information into separate tables. A table should contain information for only one subject.

The same information should not appear in more than one table in your database. You can work more efficiently and reduce errors if you only need to update information in one table.

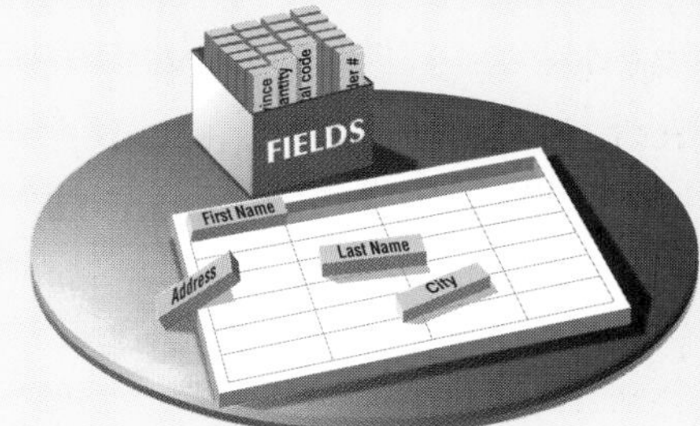

Determine the Fields You Need

Each field should relate directly to the subject of the table.

Make sure you break information down into its smallest parts. For example, break down names into two fields called First Name and Last Name.

CREATE A DATABASE USING A WIZARD

You can use the Database Wizard to quickly and easily create a database. The wizard saves you time by creating the tables, forms, queries and reports for your database.

You can use the Database Wizard to create many types of databases, such as databases for contact management, expenses, inventory control and order entry.

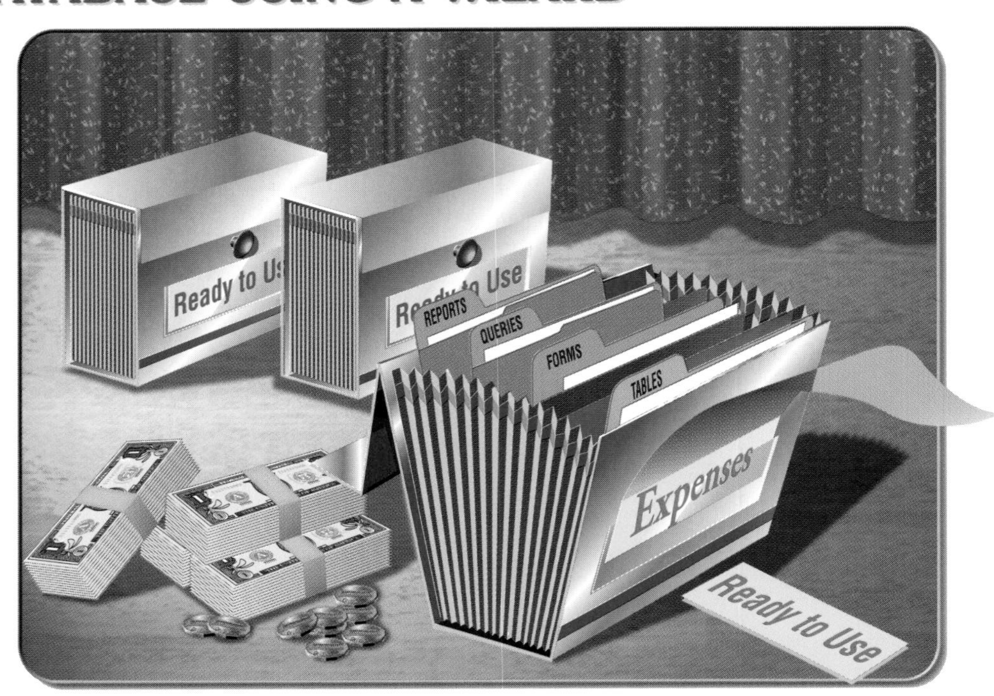

CREATE A DATABASE USING A WIZARD

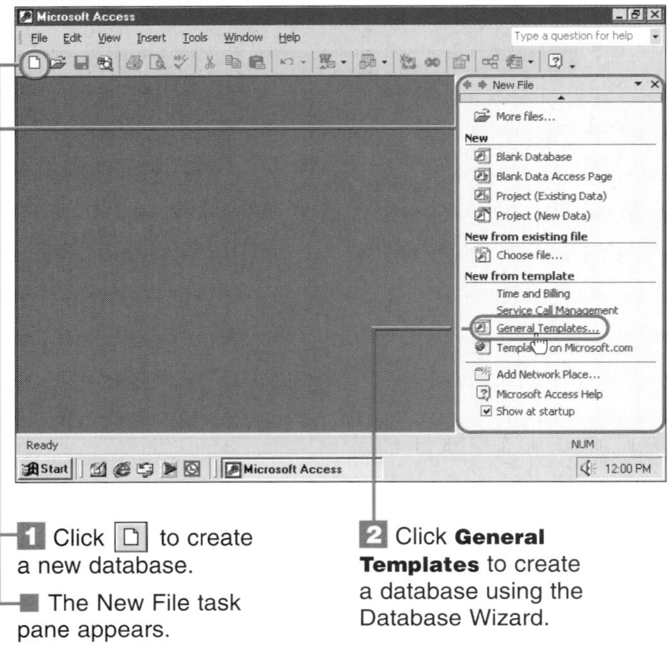

1 Click [ ] to create a new database.

■ The New File task pane appears.

2 Click **General Templates** to create a database using the Database Wizard.

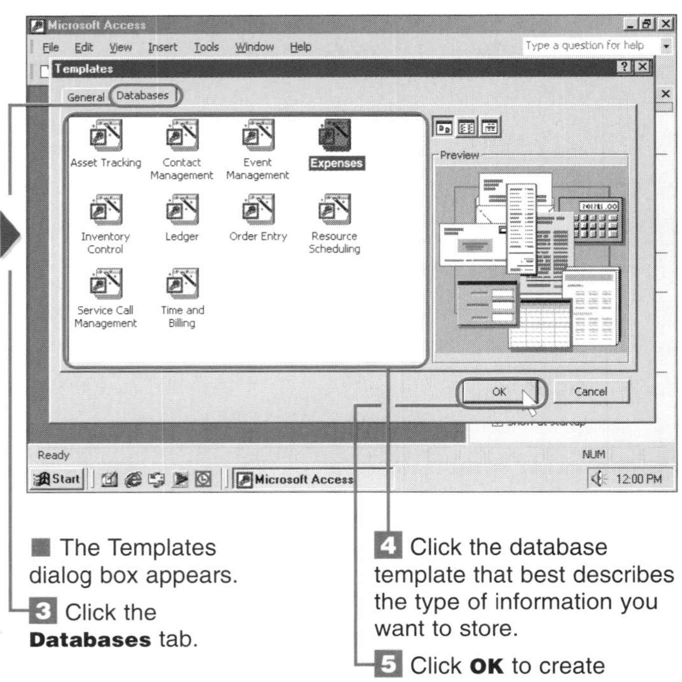

■ The Templates dialog box appears.

3 Click the **Databases** tab.

4 Click the database template that best describes the type of information you want to store.

5 Click **OK** to create the database.

■ The File New Database dialog box appears.

Can I have more than one database open at a time?

You can have only one database open at a time. If you are currently working with a database, Access will close the database when you create a new database.

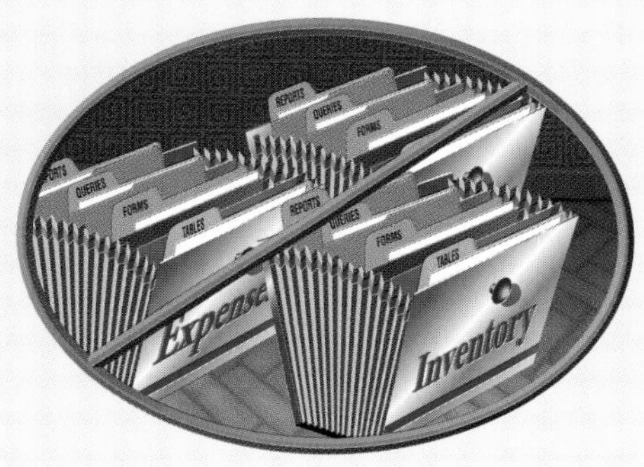

How can I quickly begin using a database template I recently worked with?

The New File task pane displays the names of the last two database templates you worked with. To display the New File task pane, perform step 1 on page 256.

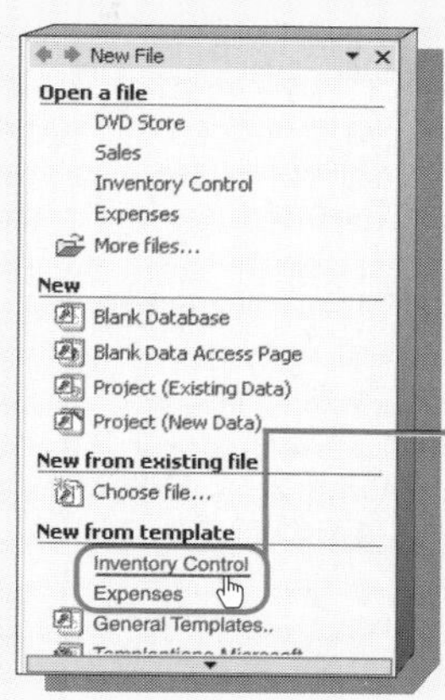

1 To quickly begin using a database template, click the name of the database template you want to use.

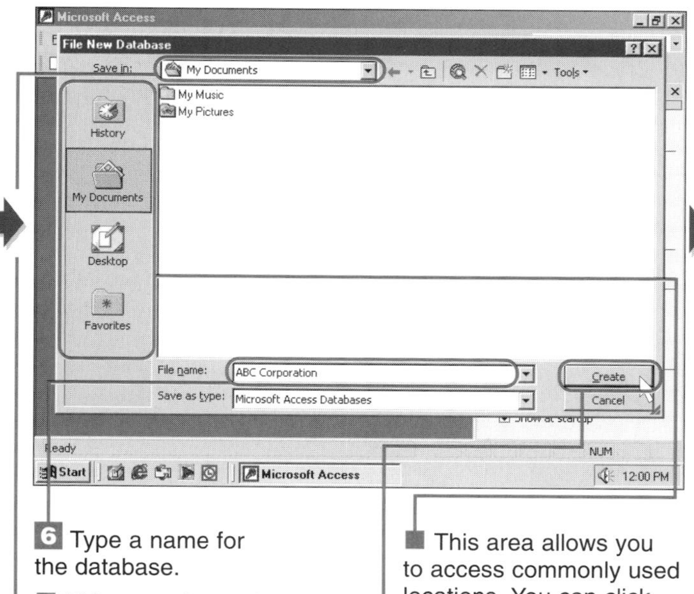

6 Type a name for the database.

■ This area shows the location where Access will store your database. You can click this area to change the location.

■ This area allows you to access commonly used locations. You can click a location to save your database in the location.

7 Click **Create** to create the database.

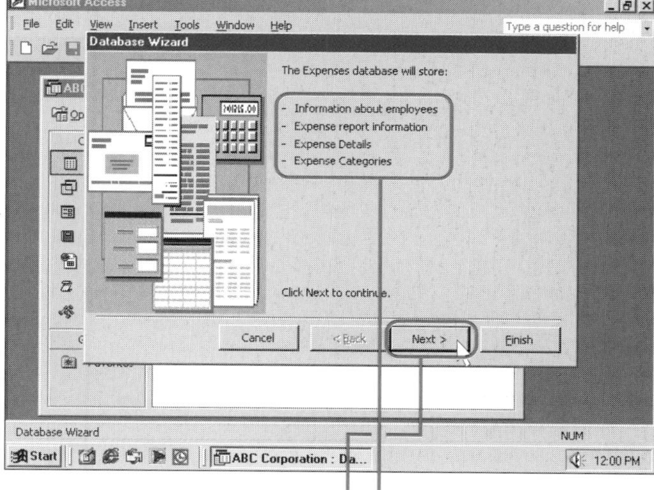

■ The Database Wizard appears.

■ This area describes the type of information the database will store.

8 Click **Next** to continue.

CONTINUED

The Database Wizard displays the fields that are included in each table in your database. You can choose to include other optional fields.

A field is a specific category of information in a table, such as the last names of all your customers.

CREATE A DATABASE USING A WIZARD (CONTINUED)

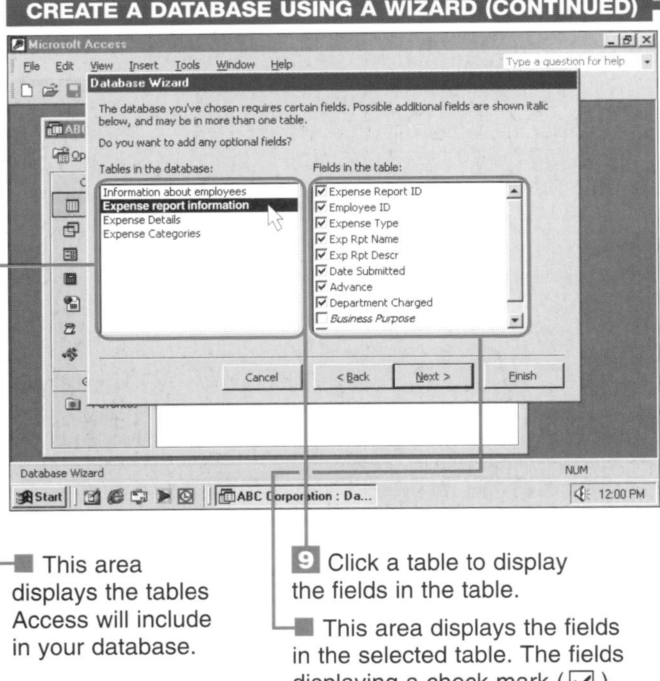

■ This area displays the tables Access will include in your database.

9 Click a table to display the fields in the table.

■ This area displays the fields in the selected table. The fields displaying a check mark (☑) are required fields and will be included in the table. The fields shown in *italics* are optional.

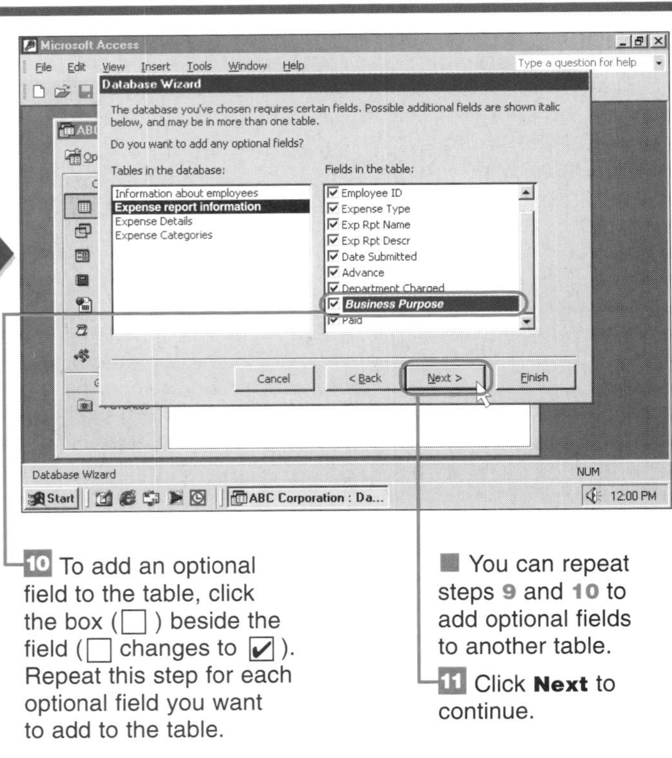

10 To add an optional field to the table, click the box (☐) beside the field (☐ changes to ☑). Repeat this step for each optional field you want to add to the table.

■ You can repeat steps **9** and **10** to add optional fields to another table.

11 Click **Next** to continue.

Do I have to answer all the questions in the Database Wizard?

No. You can click the **Finish** button at any time to create a database based on the answers you have provided so far. However, to ensure your database will appear the way you want, you should answer all the questions in the wizard.

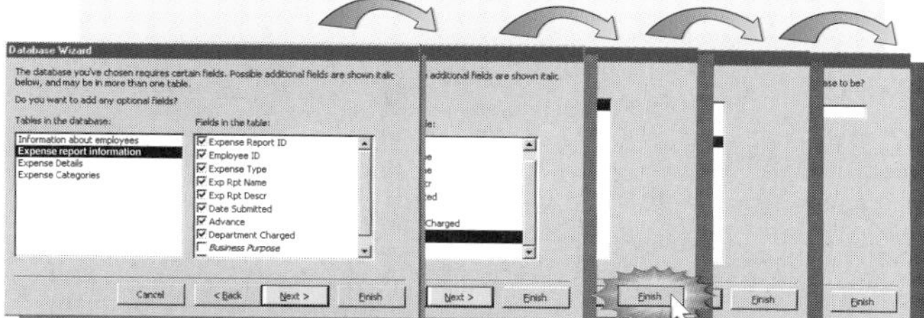

Can I remove a required field from a table in the Database Wizard?

No. You can only remove a required field after you finish creating the database. When you try to remove a required field from the Database Wizard, a dialog box appears, stating that the field is required and must be selected. To remove a field from a table in a database you have created, see page 275.

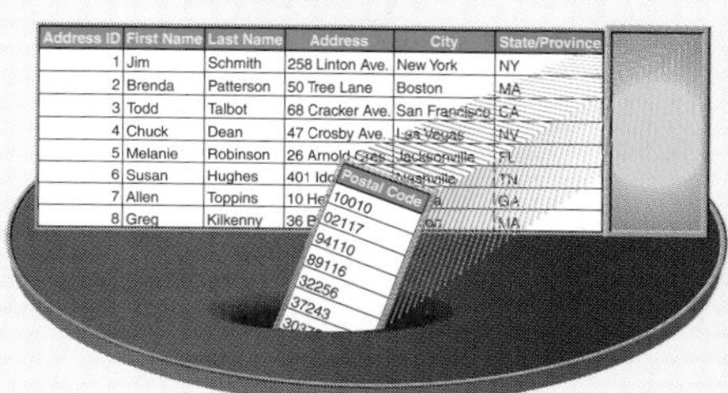

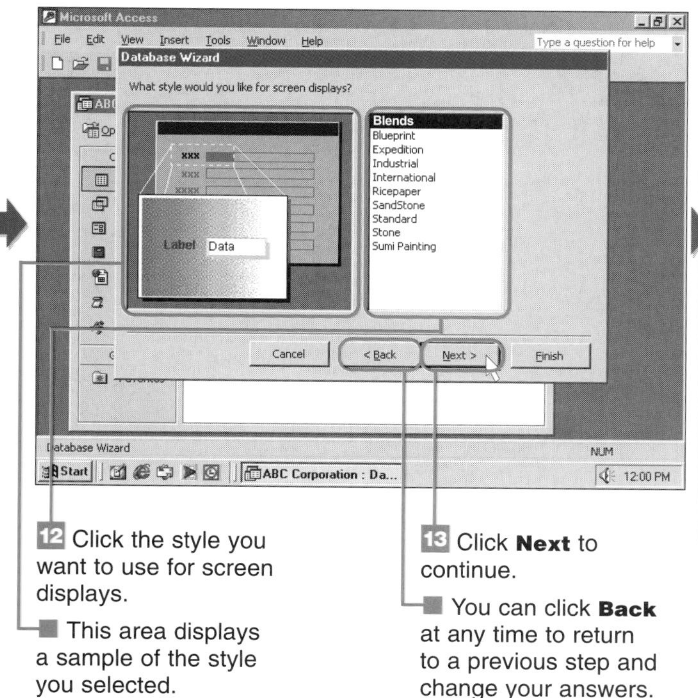

12 Click the style you want to use for screen displays.

- This area displays a sample of the style you selected.

13 Click **Next** to continue.

- You can click **Back** at any time to return to a previous step and change your answers.

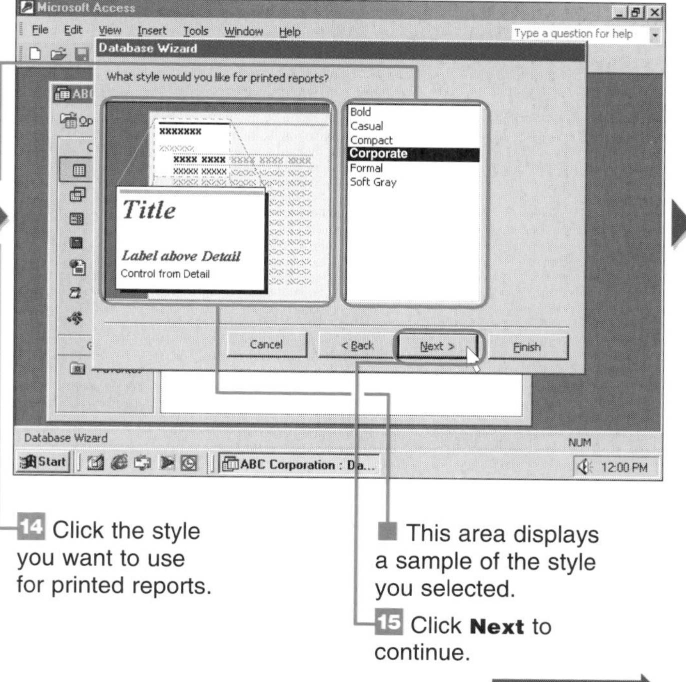

14 Click the style you want to use for printed reports.

- This area displays a sample of the style you selected.

15 Click **Next** to continue.

CONTINUED

CREATE A DATABASE USING A WIZARD

When you finish creating a database, Access displays a switchboard to help you perform common tasks in the database.

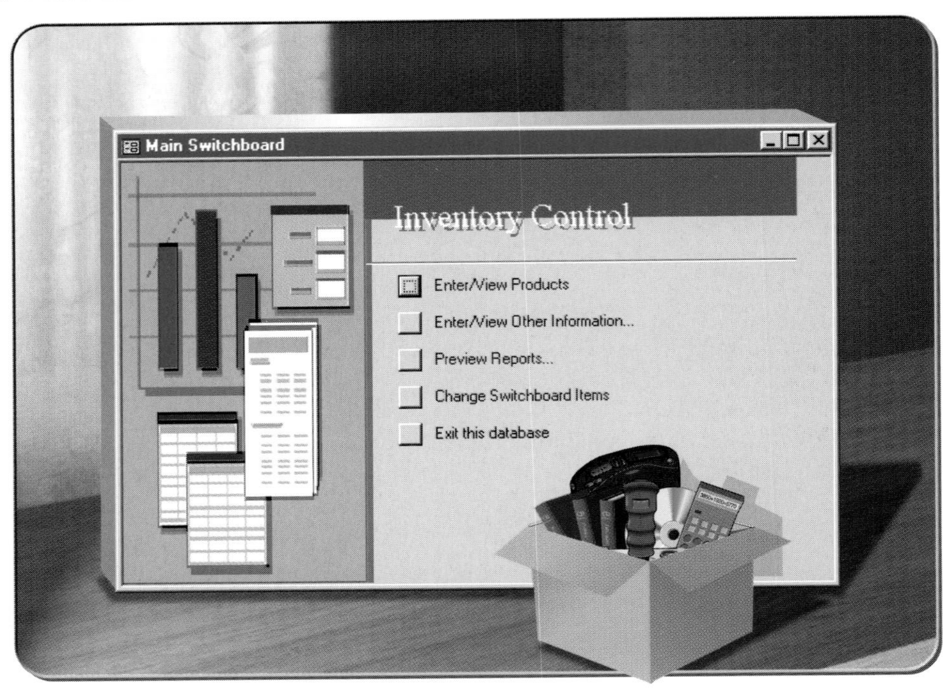

CREATE A DATABASE USING A WIZARD (CONTINUED)

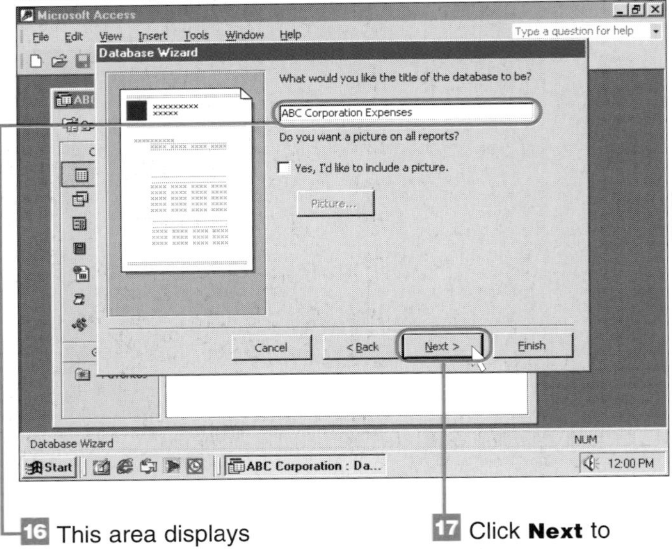

16 This area displays the title of the database. To use a different title, type the title.

17 Click **Next** to continue.

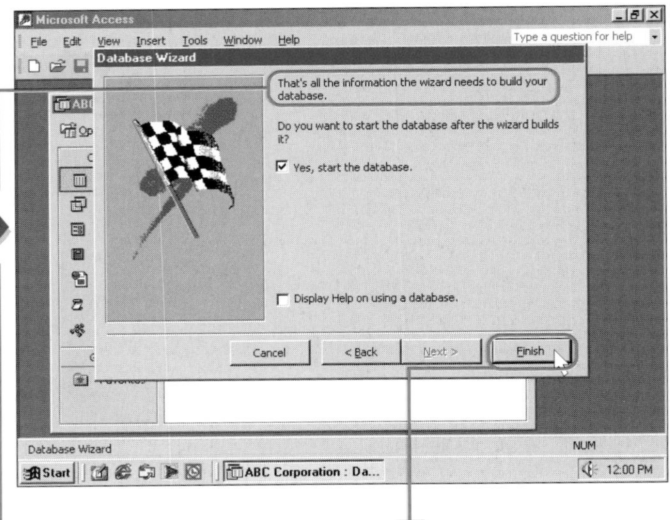

■ The Database Wizard indicates that you have provided all the information needed to create your database.

18 Click **Finish** to create your database.

Why does this dialog box appear when I finish using the Database Wizard?

Access may need you to enter information, such as your company name and address, to finish setting up the database.

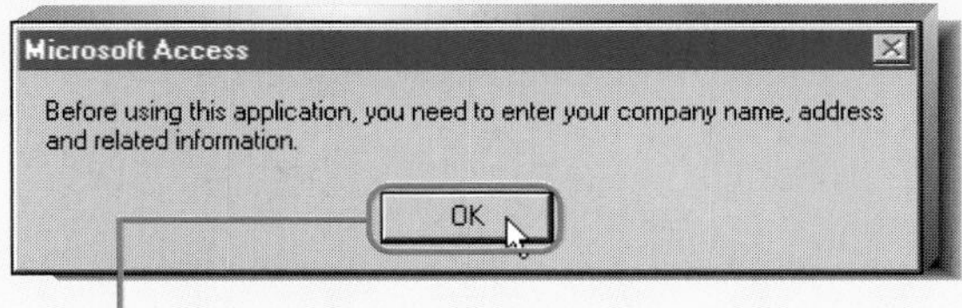

■ Click **OK** to display a form that provides areas for you to enter your information. To enter data into a form, see page 310.

Do I have to use the Main Switchboard window to work with my database?

Instead of the Main Switchboard window, you can use the Database window to work with your database. The Database window appears behind the Main Switchboard window. The Database window allows you to create and work with objects in your database. To quickly display the Database window, press the F11 key.

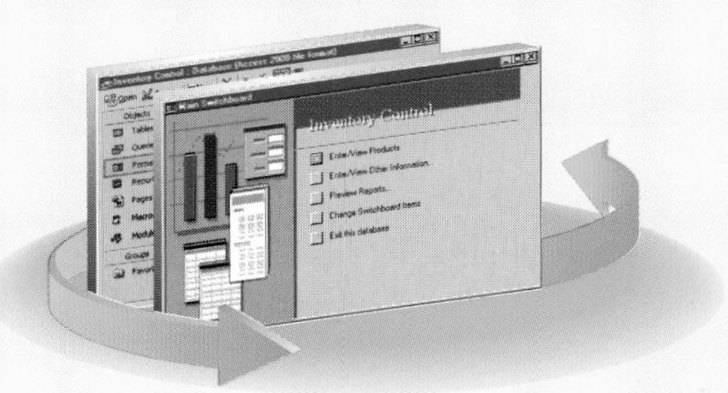

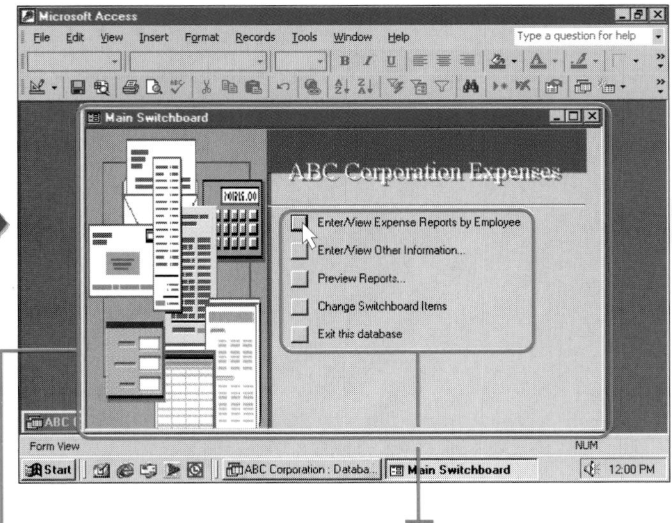

■ Access creates the objects for your database, including tables, forms, queries and reports.

■ The Main Switchboard window appears, which helps you perform common tasks.

19 To perform a task, click the task you want to perform.

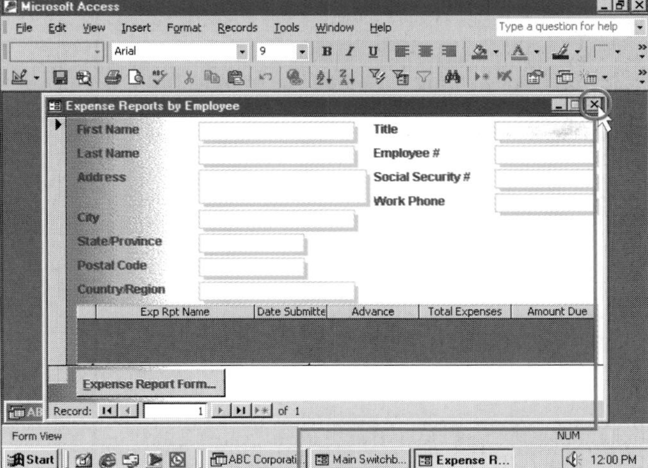

■ The database object that allows you to perform the task appears.

Note: If more tasks appear, repeat step 19 to display a database object.

20 When you finish using the object, click ☒ to close the object and return to the switchboard.

CREATE A BLANK DATABASE

If you want to design your own database, you can create a blank database. Creating a blank database gives you the most flexibility and control.

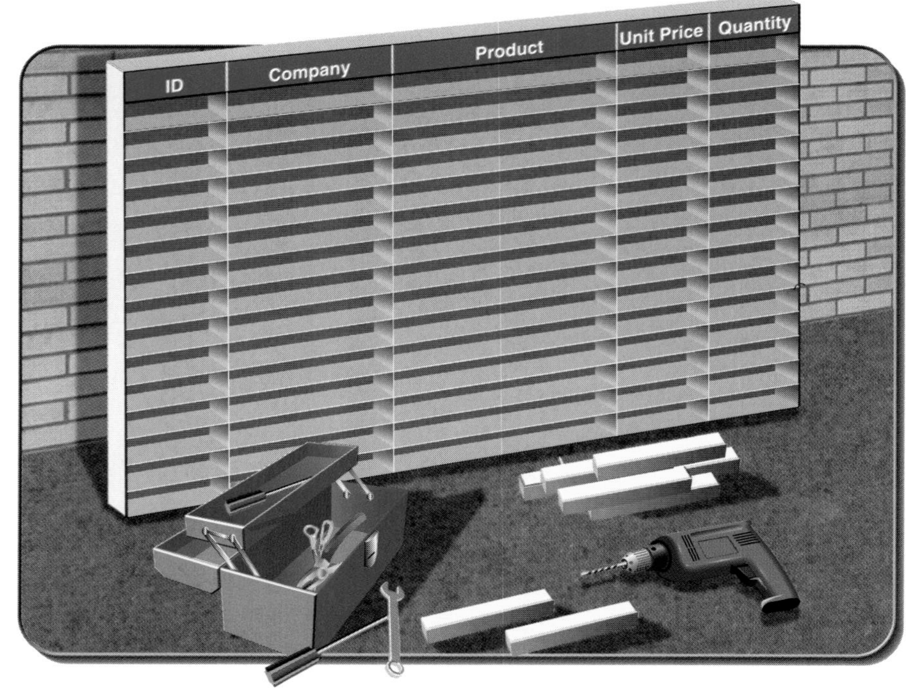

CREATE A BLANK DATABASE

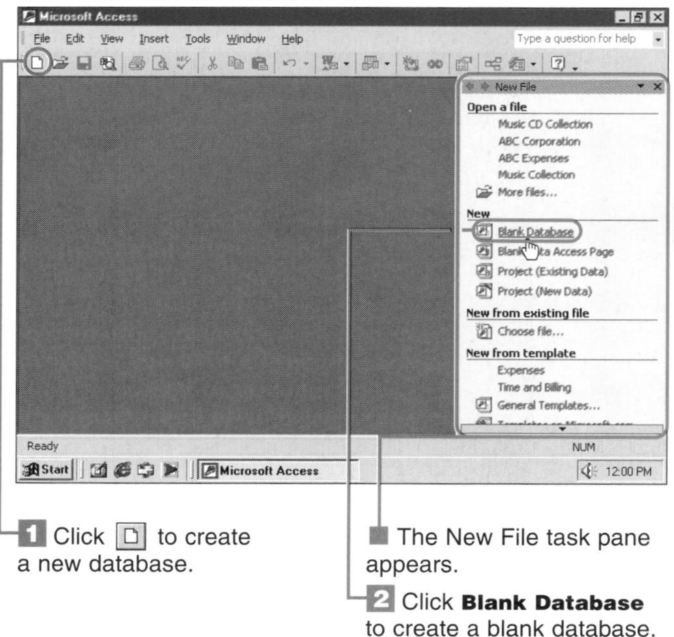

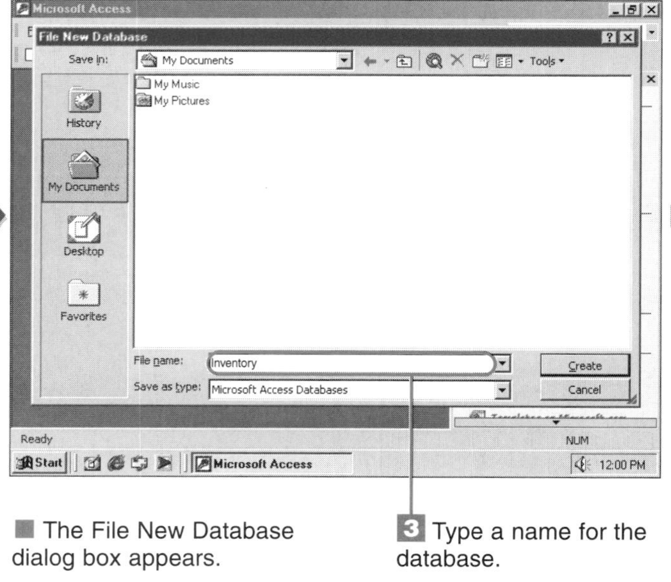

1 Click [New] to create a new database.

■ The New File task pane appears.

2 Click **Blank Database** to create a blank database.

■ The File New Database dialog box appears.

3 Type a name for the database.

What are the commonly used locations that I can access?

History

Provides access to folders and databases you recently worked with.

My Documents

Provides a convenient place to store a database.

Desktop

Allows you to store a database on the Windows desktop.

Favorites

Provides a place to store a database you will frequently use.

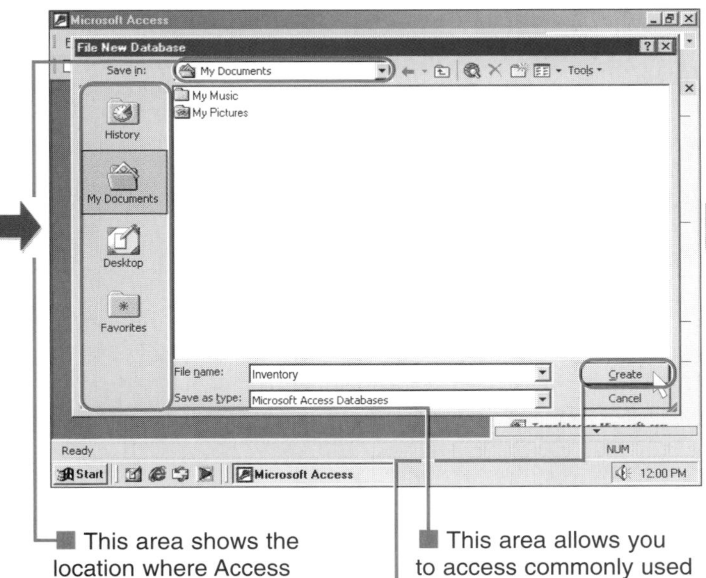

■ This area shows the location where Access will store your database. You can click this area to change the location.

■ This area allows you to access commonly used locations. You can click a location to save your database in the location.

4 Click **Create** to create the database.

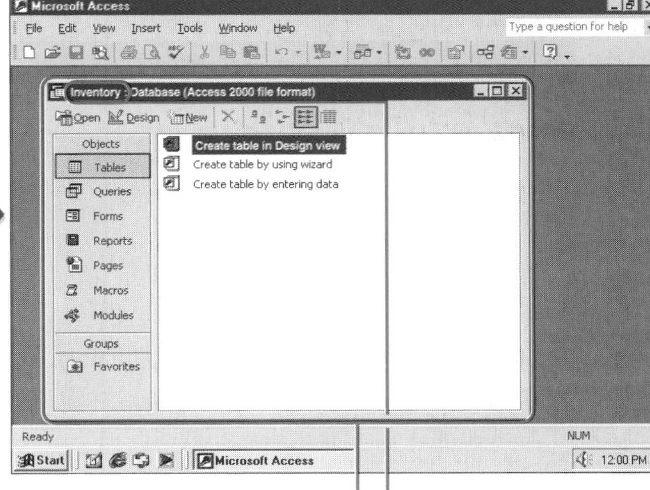

■ Access creates a blank database.

■ The Database window appears. This window allows you to create and work with objects in your database.

■ This area displays the name of the database.

■ You can now add objects, such as tables and reports, to your database. The objects you add will appear in the Database window.

OPEN A DATABASE OBJECT

You can use the Database window to open and work with objects in your database, including tables, queries, forms and reports.

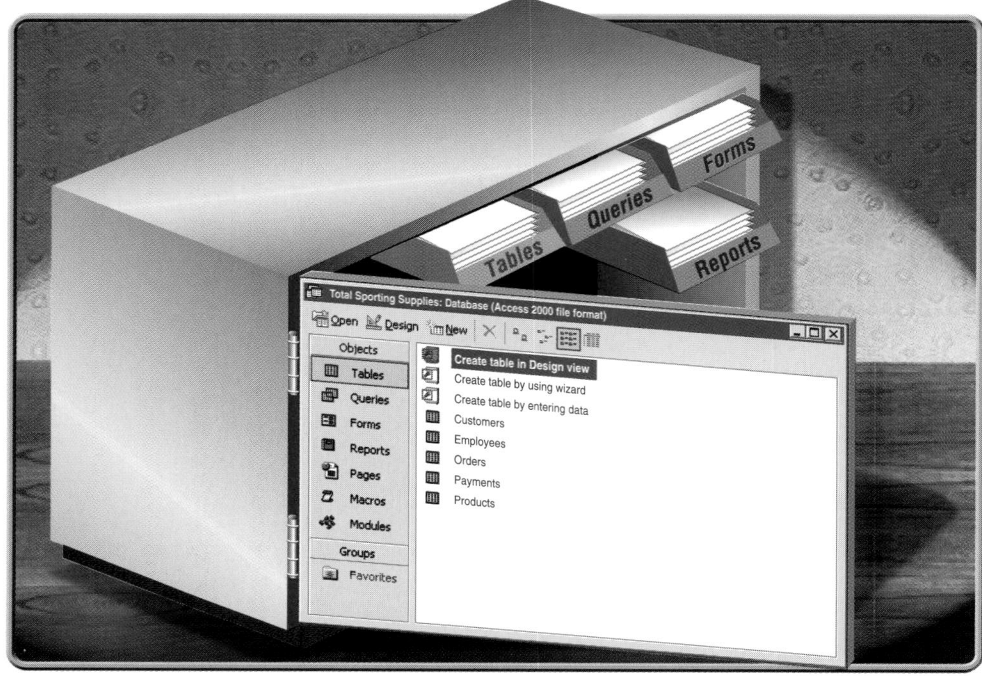

OPEN A DATABASE OBJECT

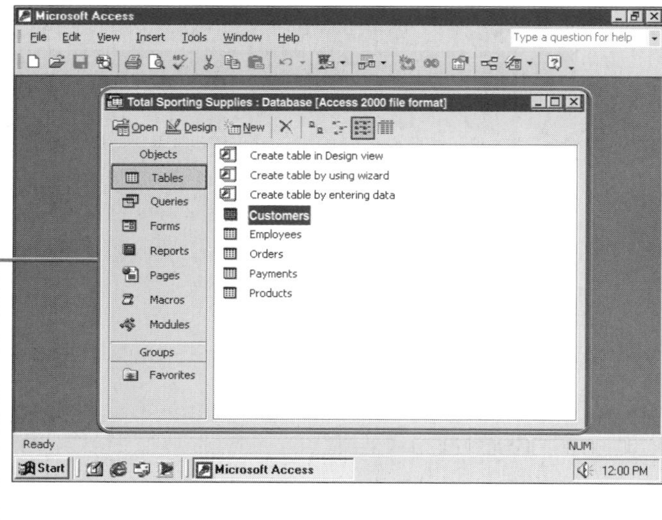

■ Each table, query, form and report in the database appears in the Database window.

■ If the Database window is hidden behind other windows, press the F11 key to display the window.

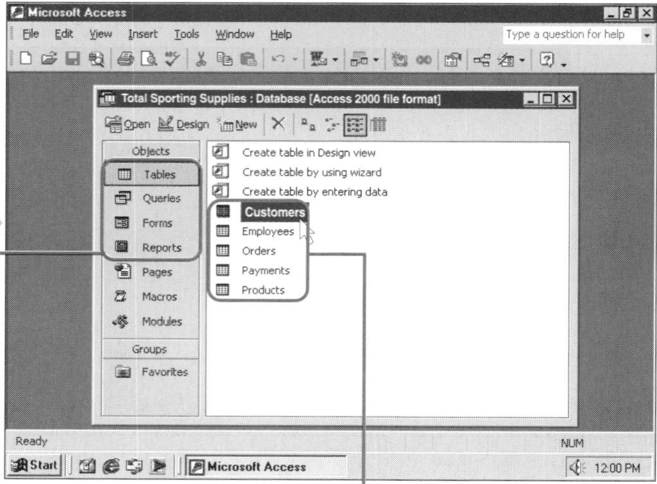

■ This area displays the types of objects in the database.

1 Click the type of object you want to work with.

■ This area displays all the objects for the type you selected.

2 Double-click an object to open the object.

What types of objects can I open in the Database window?

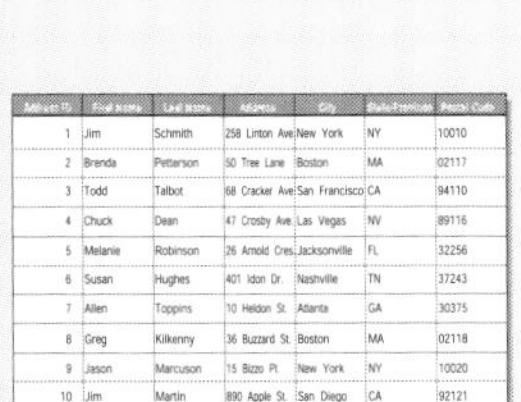

Tables

Contain information about a specific topic, such as a mailing list.

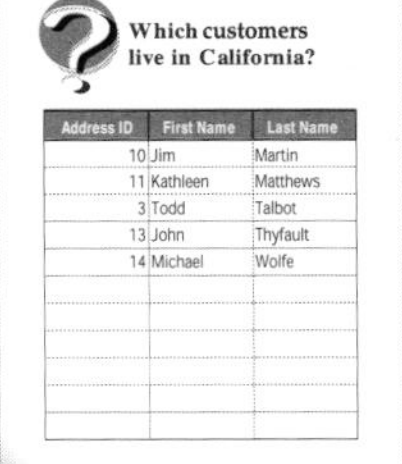

Queries

Allow you to find information of interest in your database.

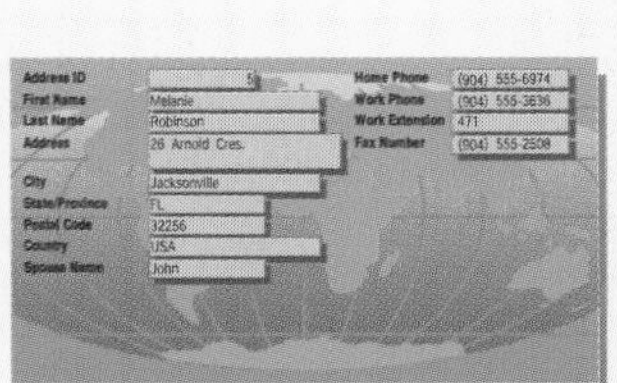

Forms

Provide a quick way to view, enter and change data in your database.

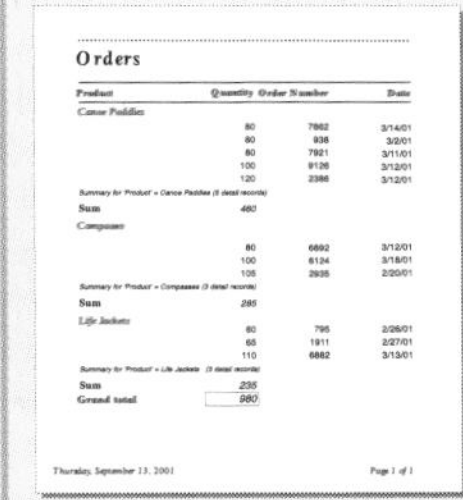

Reports

Summarize and display data from your database in professional-looking documents.

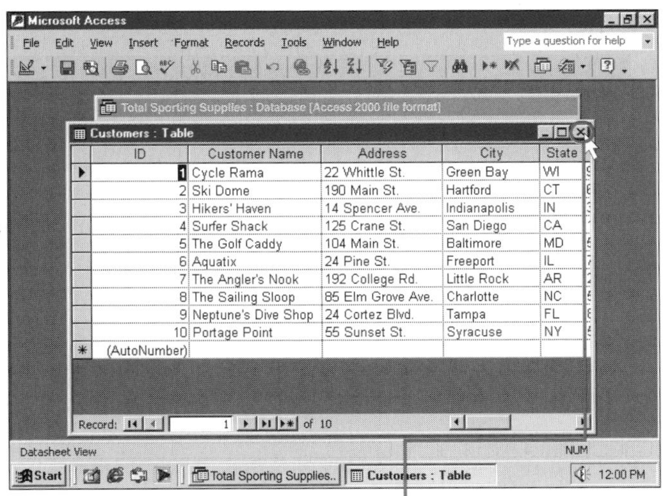

■ The object opens and appears on your screen.

3 When you finish working with the object, click ☒ to close the object and return to the Database window.

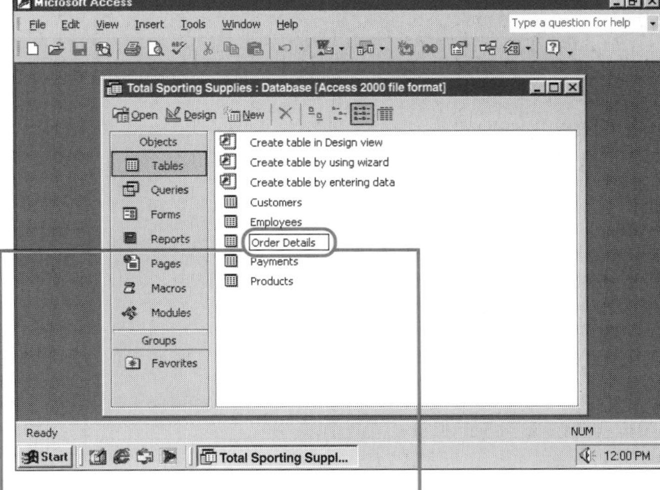

RENAME A DATABASE OBJECT

1 Click the name of the object you want to rename.

2 Press the F2 key.

A black border appears around the name of the object.

3 Type a new name for the object and then press the Enter key.

OPEN A DATABASE

You can open a database to view the database on your screen. This allows you to review and make changes to the database.

You can have only one database open at a time. Access will close a database displayed on your screen when you open another database.

OPEN A DATABASE

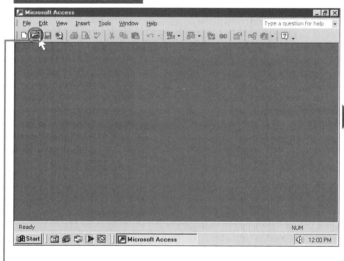

1 Click [Open] to open a database.

■ The Open dialog box appears.

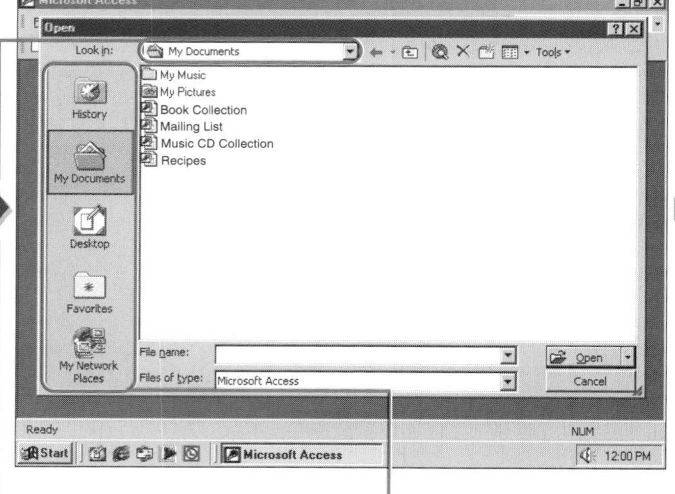

■ This area shows the location of the displayed databases. You can click this area to change the location.

■ This area allows you to access databases in commonly used locations. You can click a location to display the databases stored in the location.

Note: For information on the commonly used locations, see the top of page 263.

How can I quickly open a database I recently worked with?

Access remembers the names of the last four databases you worked with. You can use one of the following methods to quickly open any of these databases.

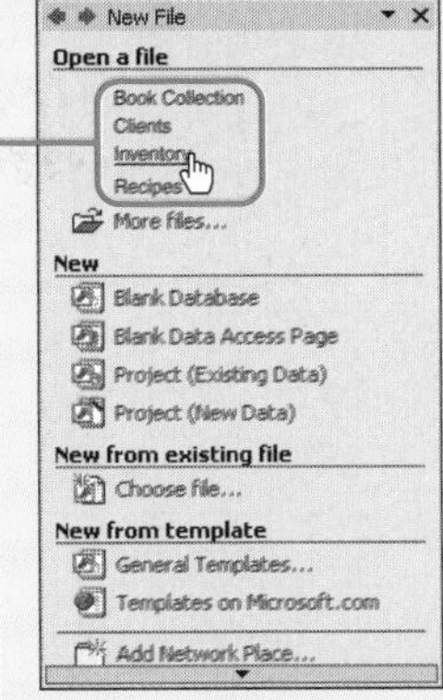

Use the Task Pane

The New File task pane appears each time you start Access. To display the New File task pane, see page 12.

1 Click the name of the database you want to open.

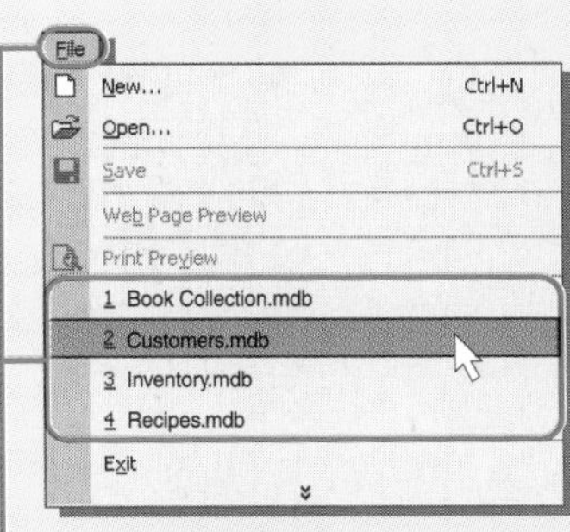

Use the File Menu

1 Click **File**.

2 Click the name of the database you want to open.

Note: If the names of the last four databases you worked with are not all displayed, position the mouse over the bottom of the menu to display all the names.

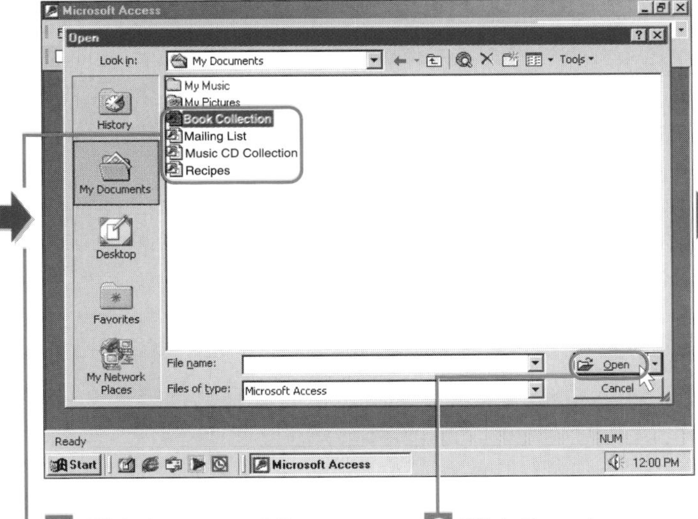

2 Click the name of the database you want to open.

3 Click **Open** to open the database.

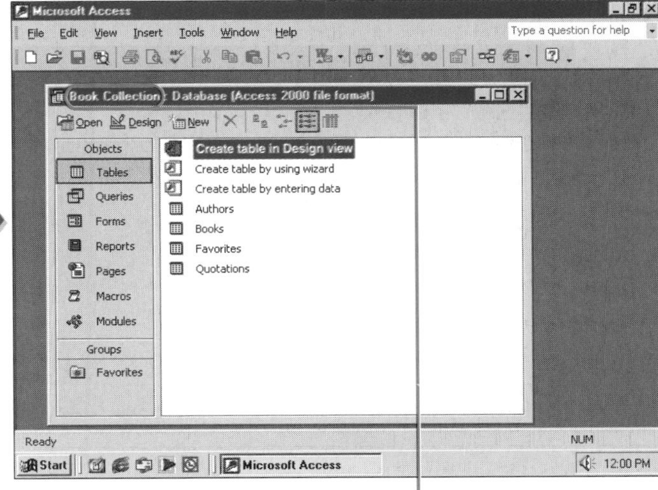

■ The database opens and appears on your screen.

■ The Database window allows you to create and work with objects, such as tables and forms, in your database.

■ This area displays the name of the open database.

CREATE A TABLE

A table stores a collection of information about a specific topic, such as a list of customer addresses. You can create a table to store new information in your database.

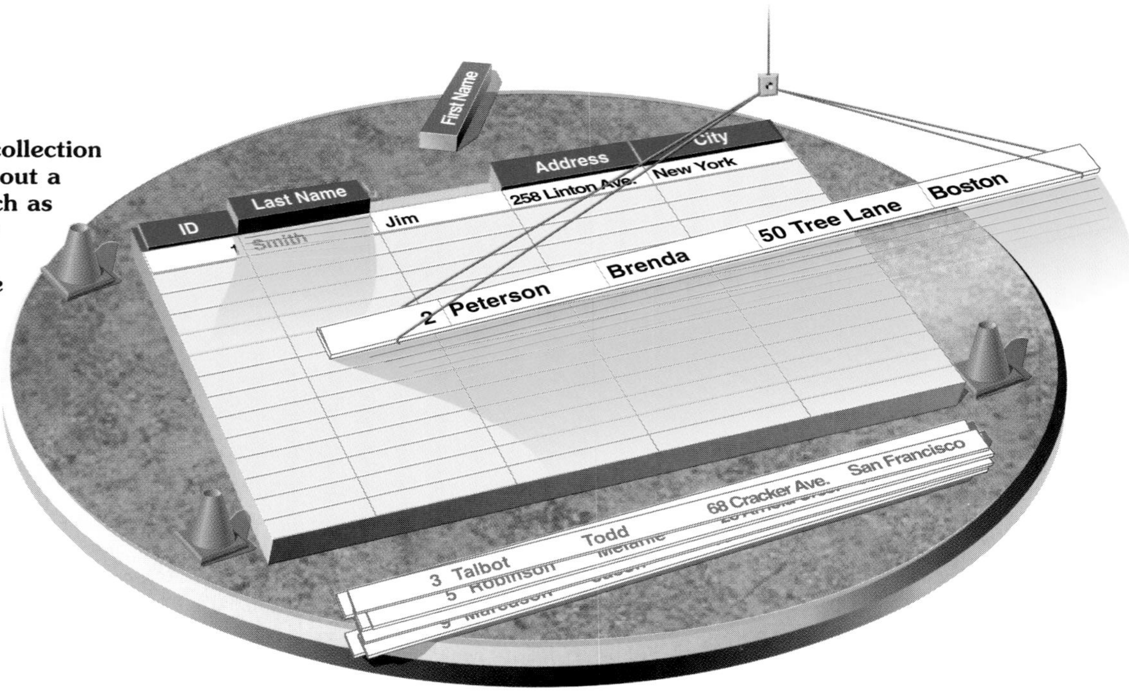

CREATE A TABLE

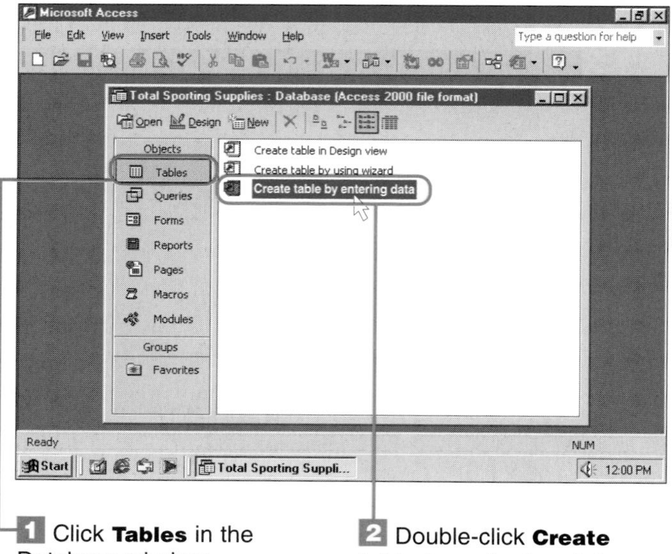

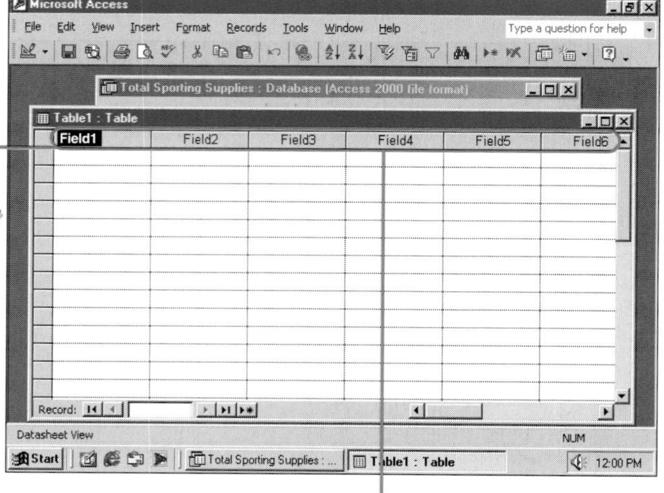

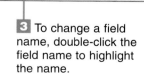

1 Click **Tables** in the Database window.

2 Double-click **Create table by entering data**.

■ A blank table appears.

■ This area displays the field names for each column in your table.

3 To change a field name, double-click the field name to highlight the name.

What are the parts of a table?

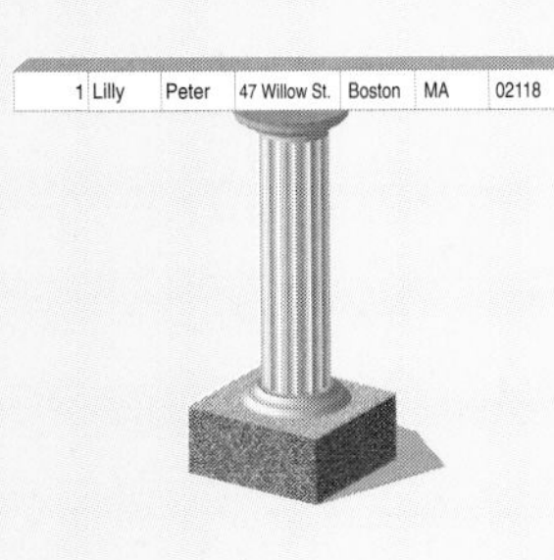

Record

A record is a collection of information about one person, place or thing.

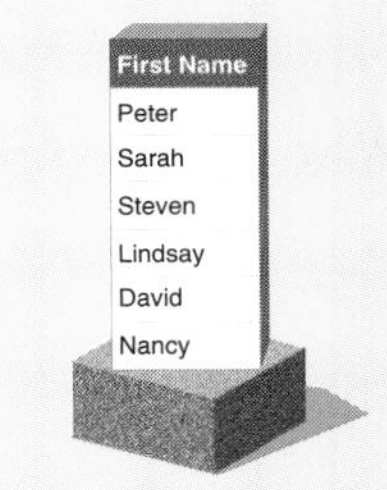

Field

A field is a specific category of information.

Field Name

A field name identifies the information in a field.

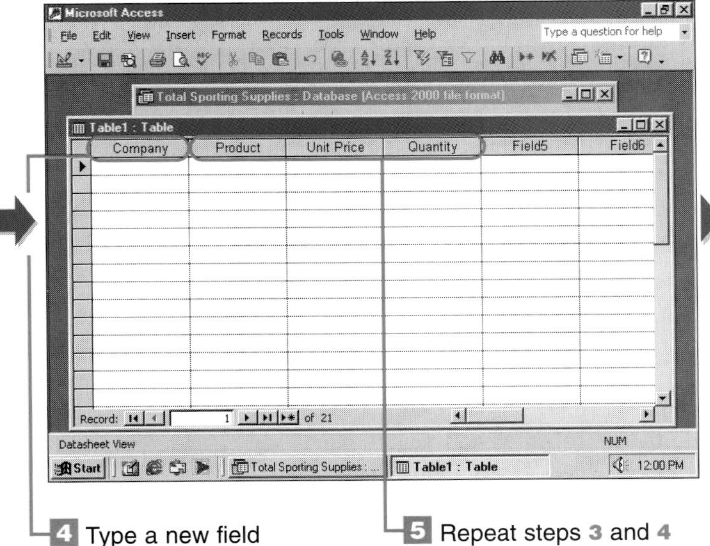

4 Type a new field name and then press the Enter key.

5 Repeat steps 3 and 4 for each field name you want to include in your table.

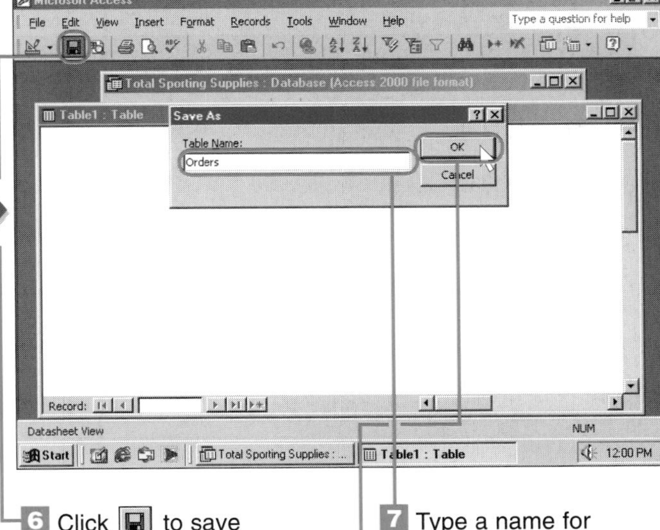

6 Click 🖫 to save your table.

■ The Save As dialog box appears.

7 Type a name for your table.

8 Click **OK** to save your table.

CONTINUED

CREATE A TABLE

You can have Access create a primary key for your table. A primary key is one or more fields that uniquely identifies each record in a table, such as a field containing ID numbers.

Each table in your database should have a primary key.

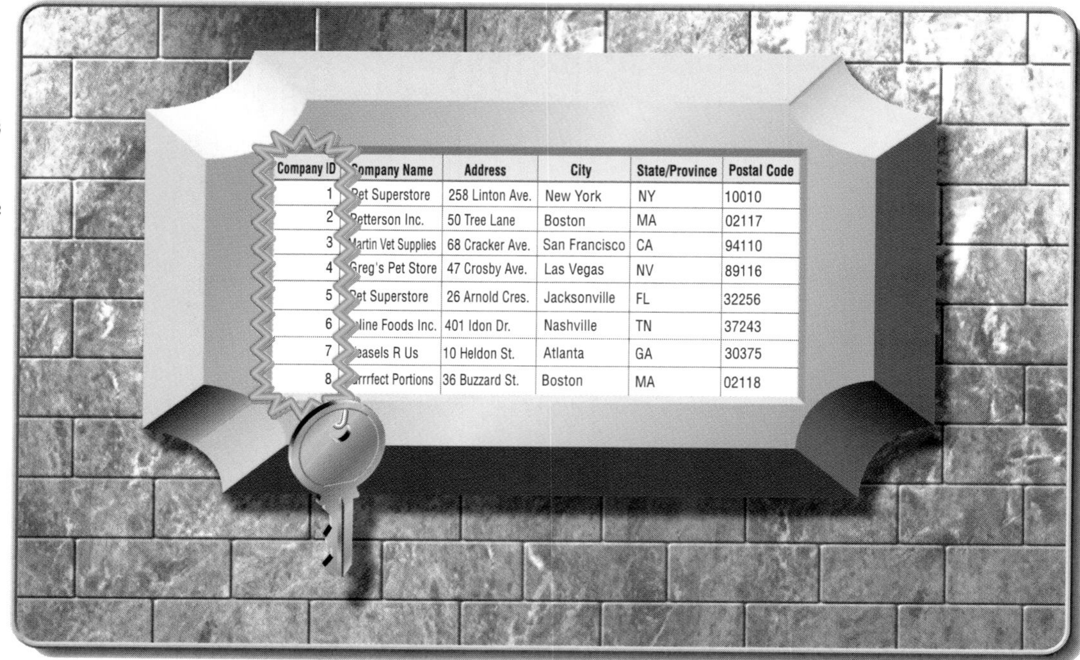

CREATE A TABLE (CONTINUED)

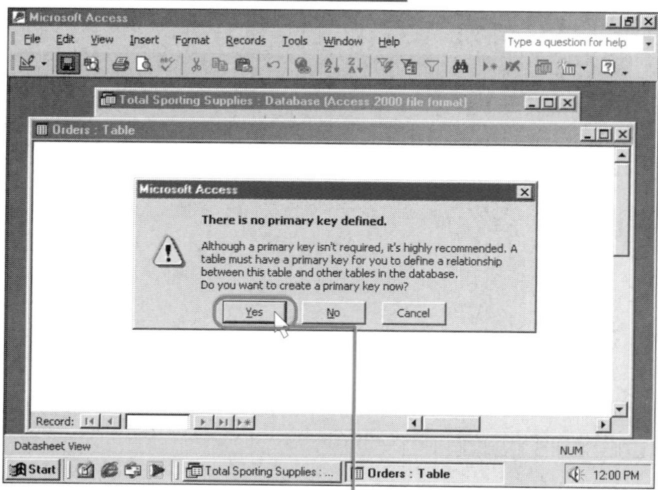

■ A dialog box appears, stating that your table does not have a primary key.

9 To have Access create a primary key for you, click **Yes**.

Note: You can later change the primary key. To change the primary key, see page 288.

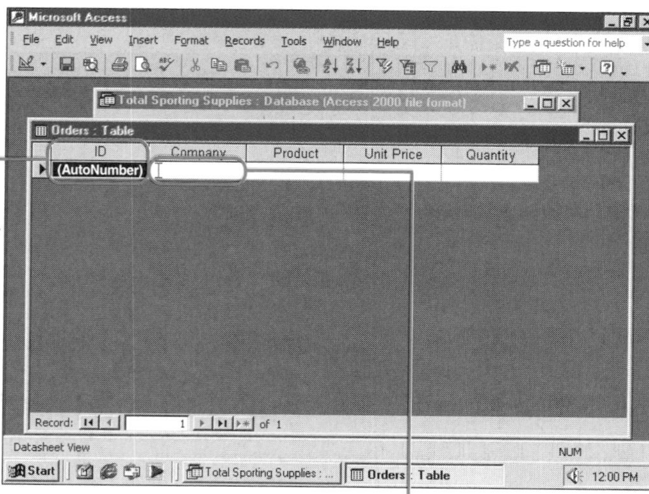

■ Access removes the rows and columns that do not contain data.

■ If you selected **Yes** in step **9**, Access adds an ID field to your table to serve as the primary key. The ID field will automatically number each record you add to your table.

10 To enter the data for a record, click the first empty cell in the row.

Why should each table in my database have a primary key?

Access uses the primary key in each table to create relationships between the tables. Relationships between tables allow you to bring together related information in your database. For information on relationships, see page 300.

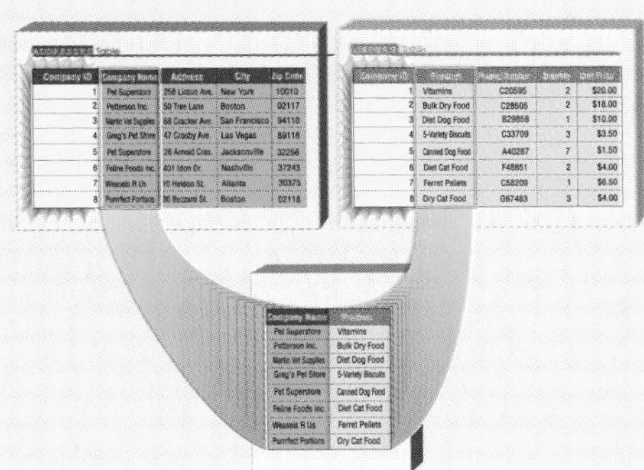

How do I delete a table from my database?

Before you delete a table, make sure the table is not used by any other objects in your database, such a query, form or report. When you delete a table, the table is permanently removed from your database.

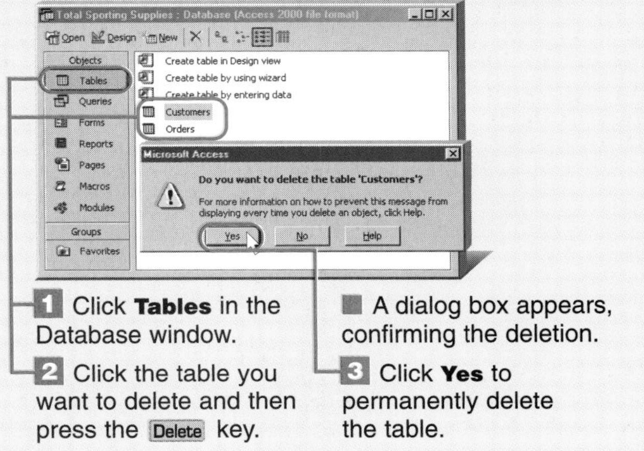

1 Click **Tables** in the Database window.

2 Click the table you want to delete and then press the Delete key.

■ A dialog box appears, confirming the deletion.

3 Click **Yes** to permanently delete the table.

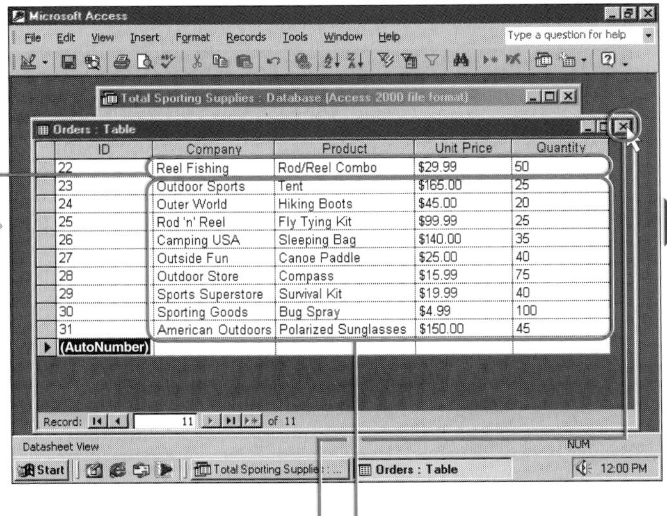

ID	Company	Product	Unit Price	Quantity
22	Reel Fishing	Rod/Reel Combo	$29.99	50
23	Outdoor Sports	Tent	$165.00	25
24	Outer World	Hiking Boots	$45.00	20
25	Rod 'n' Reel	Fly Tying Kit	$99.99	25
26	Camping USA	Sleeping Bag	$140.00	35
27	Outside Fun	Canoe Paddle	$25.00	40
28	Outdoor Store	Compass	$15.99	75
29	Sports Superstore	Survival Kit	$19.99	40
30	Sporting Goods	Bug Spray	$4.99	100
31	American Outdoors	Polarized Sunglasses	$150.00	45
(AutoNumber)				

11 Type the data that corresponds to the field and then press the Enter key to move to the next cell. Repeat this step until you finish entering all the data for the record.

12 Repeat steps 10 and 11 for each record you want to add to your table. Access automatically saves each record you enter.

13 When you finish entering records, click ☒ to close your table.

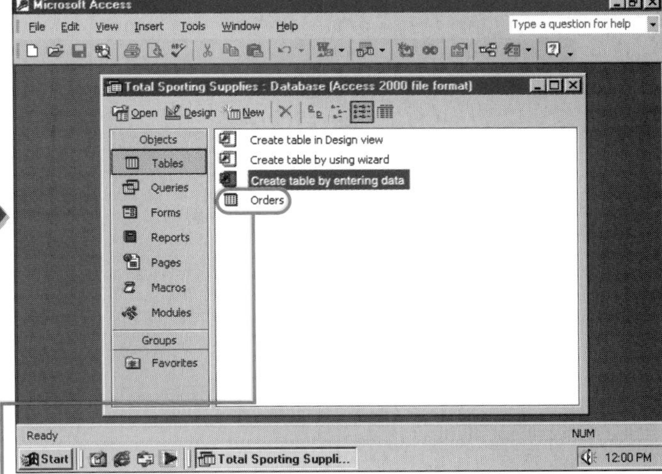

■ The name of your table appears in the Database window.

RENAME A FIELD

You can give a field a new name to more accurately describe the contents of the field.

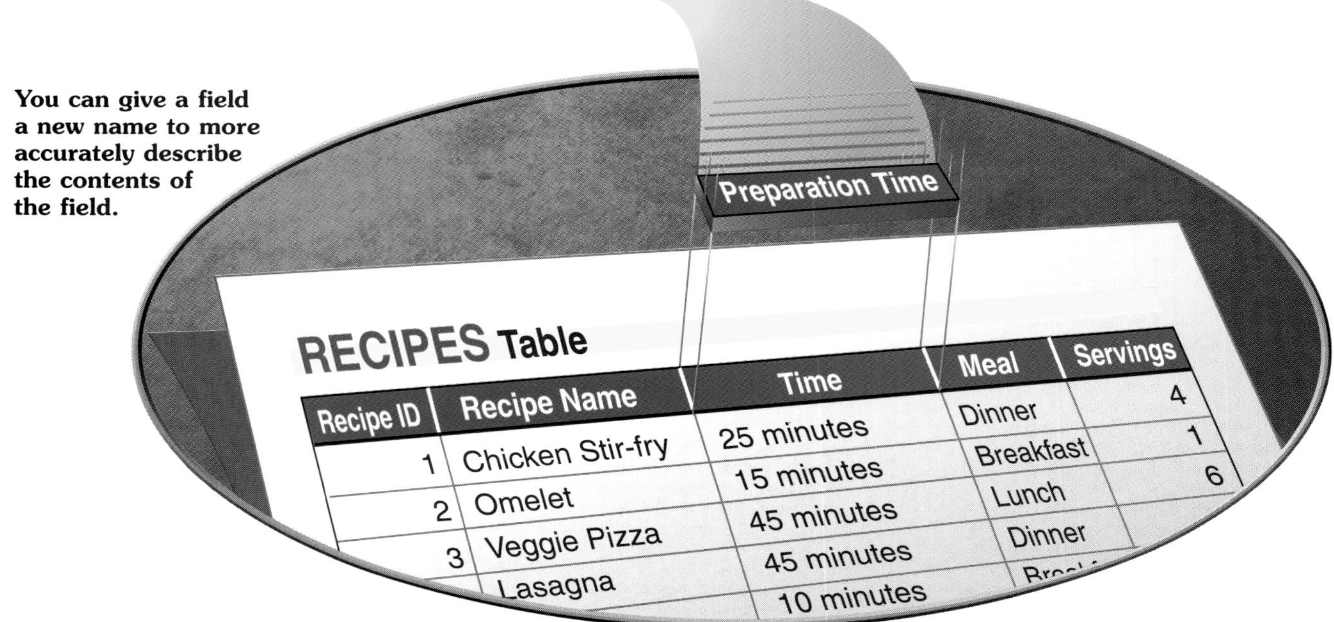

Preparation Time
RECIPES Table
Recipe ID
Recipe Name
Time
Meal
Servings
1
Chicken Stir-fry
25 minutes
Dinner
4
2
Omelet
15 minutes
Breakfast
1
3
Veggie Pizza
45 minutes
Lunch
6
Lasagna
45 minutes
Dinner
10 minutes

RENAME A FIELD

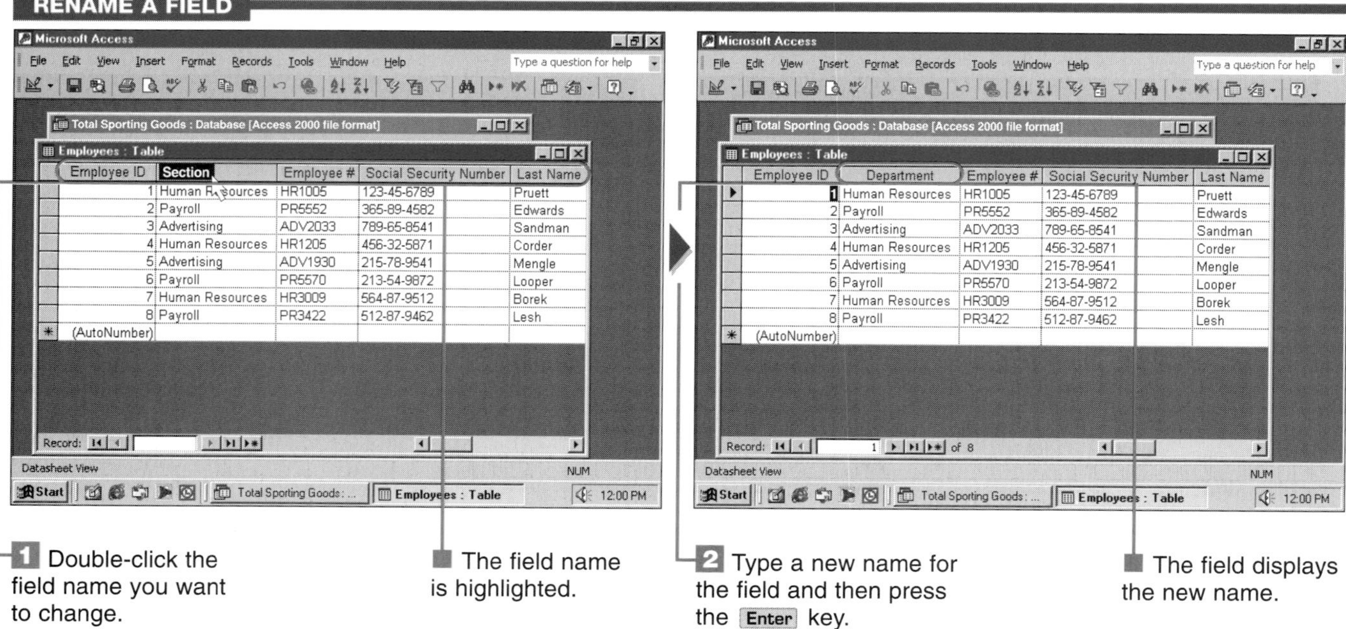

1 Double-click the field name you want to change.

■ The field name is highlighted.

2 Type a new name for the field and then press the **Enter** key.

■ The field displays the new name.

REARRANGE FIELDS

You can change the order of fields to better organize the information in your table.

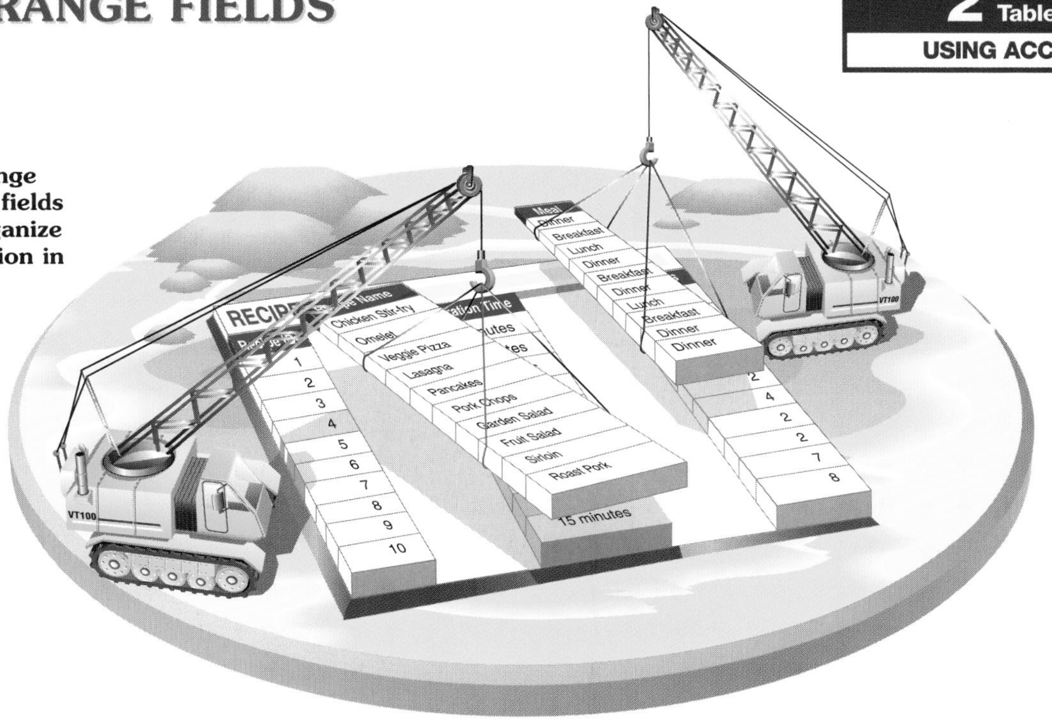

REARRANGE FIELDS

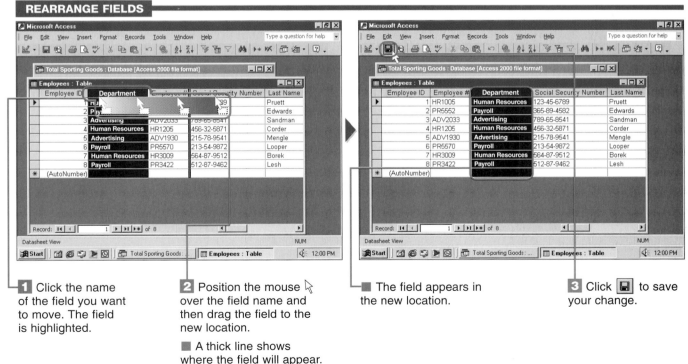

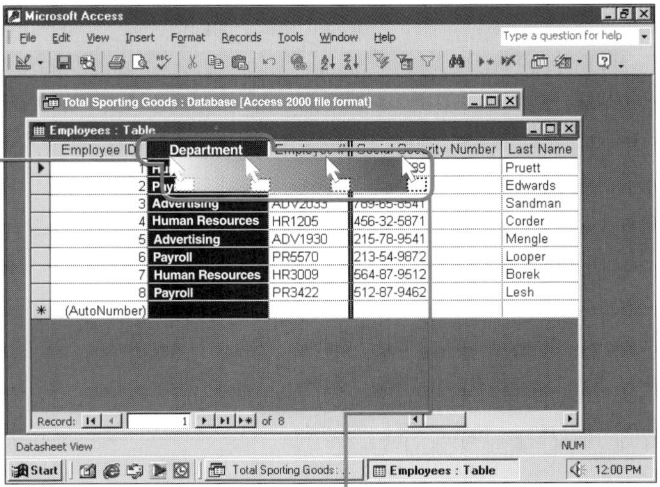

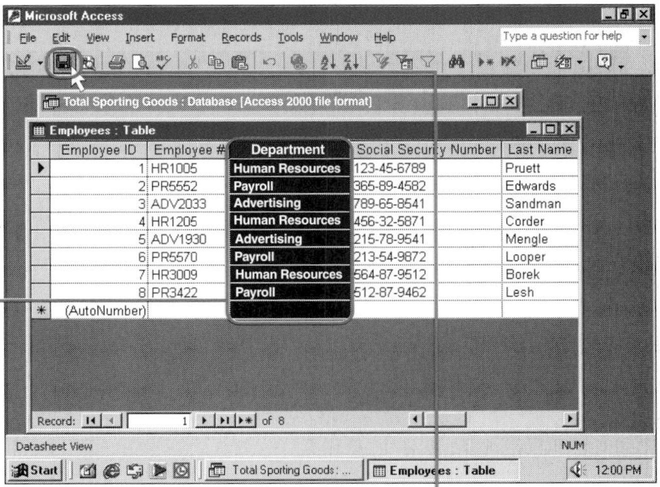

1 Click the name of the field you want to move. The field is highlighted.

2 Position the mouse over the field name and then drag the field to the new location.

■ A thick line shows where the field will appear.

■ The field appears in the new location.

3 Click (save icon) to save your change.

ADD A FIELD

You can add a field to a table when you want to include an additional category of information.

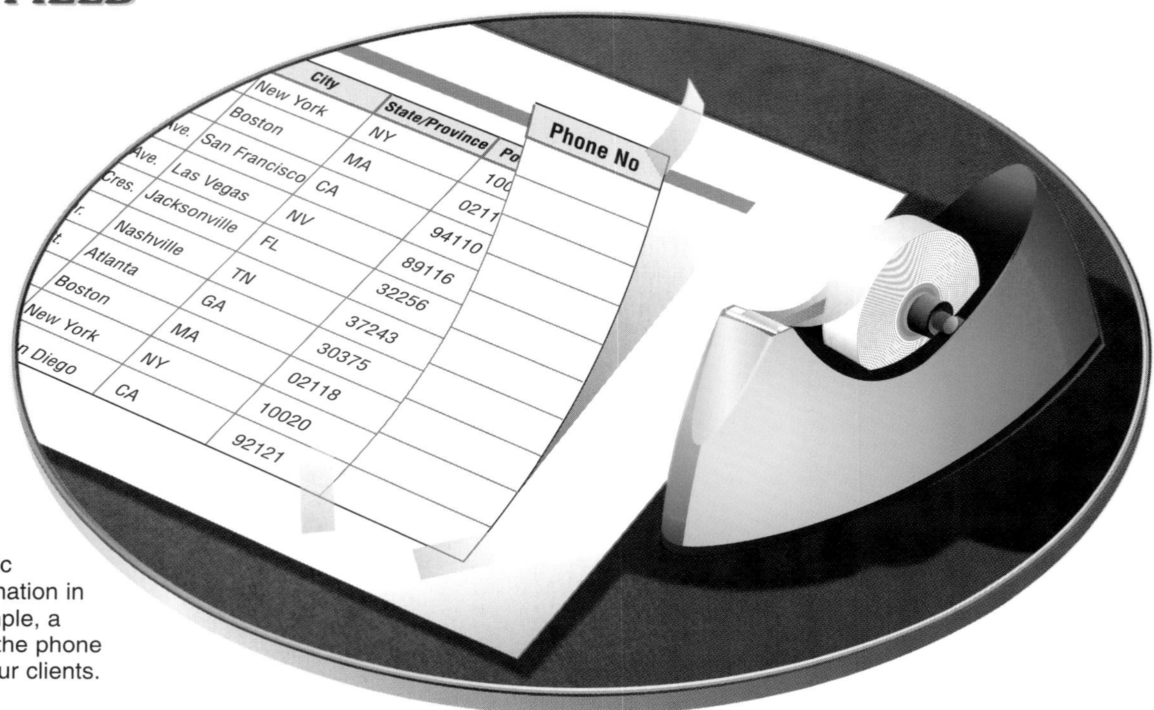

A field is a specific category of information in a table. For example, a field can contain the phone numbers of all your clients.

ADD A FIELD

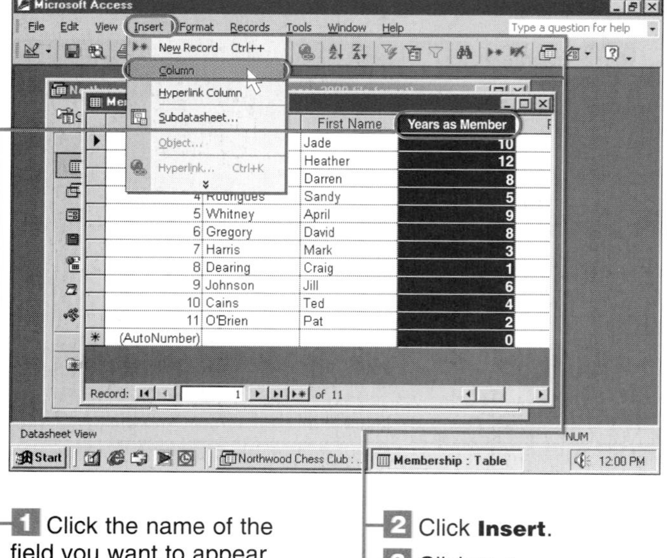

1 Click the name of the field you want to appear after the new field. The field is highlighted.

2 Click **Insert**.

3 Click **Column**.

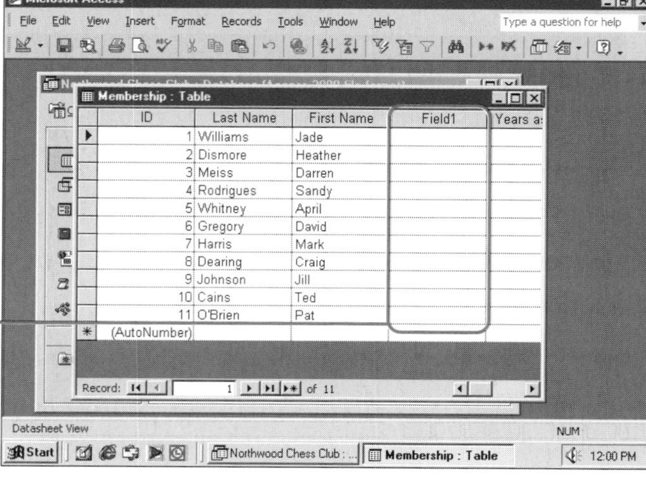

■ The new field appears in your table.

■ Access assigns a name to the new field. To give the field a descriptive name, see page 272.

DELETE A FIELD

If you no longer need a field, you can permanently delete the field from your table.

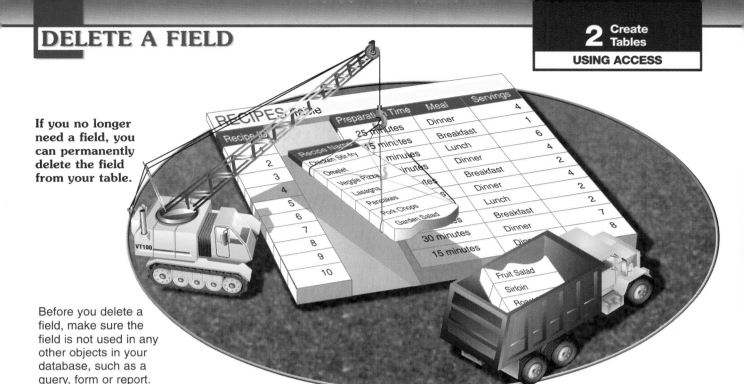

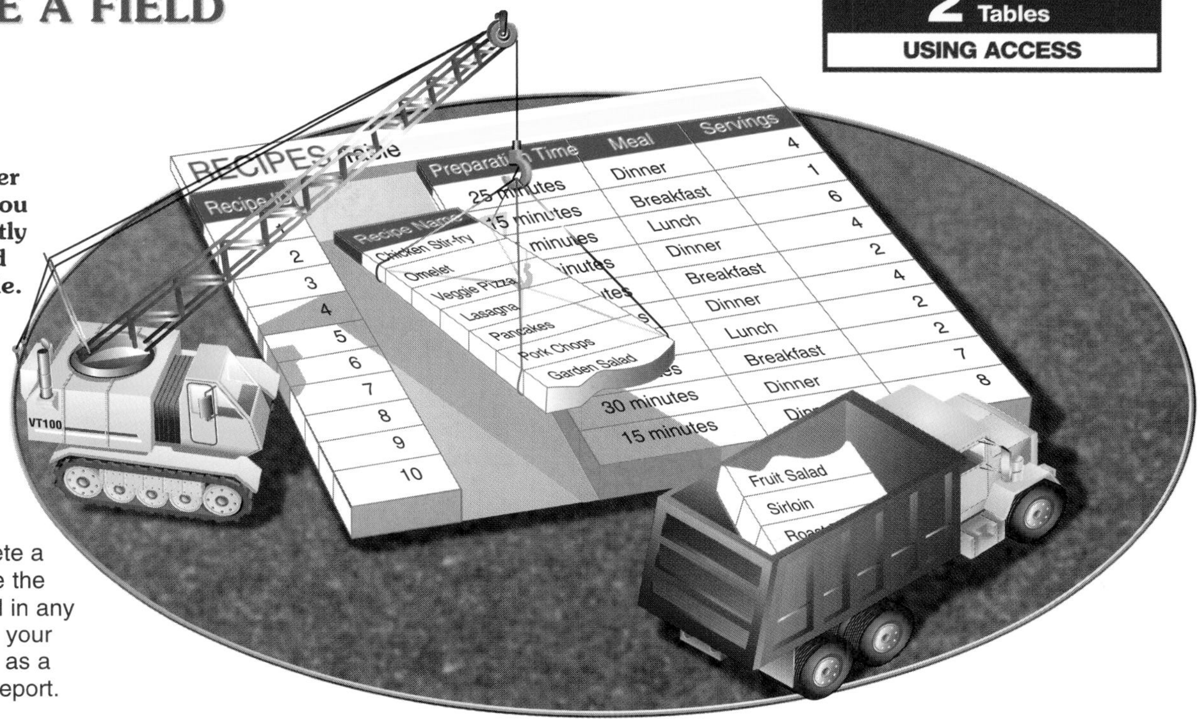

Before you delete a field, make sure the field is not used in any other objects in your database, such as a query, form or report.

DELETE A FIELD

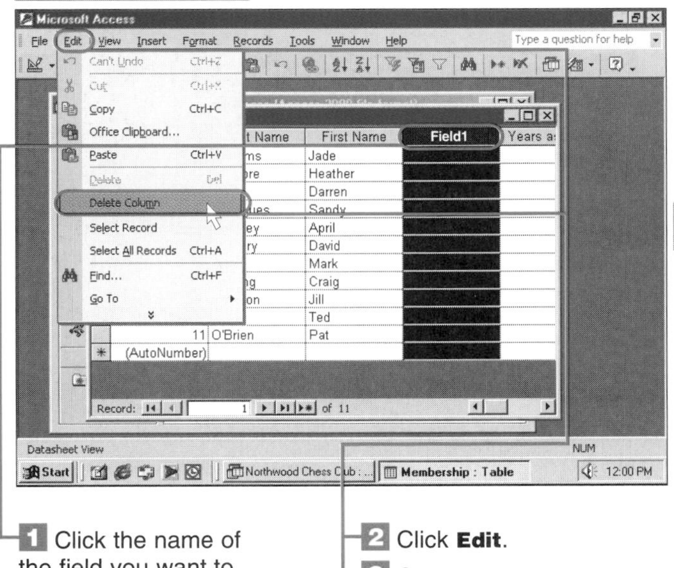

1 Click the name of the field you want to delete. The field is highlighted.

2 Click **Edit**.

3 Click **Delete Column**.

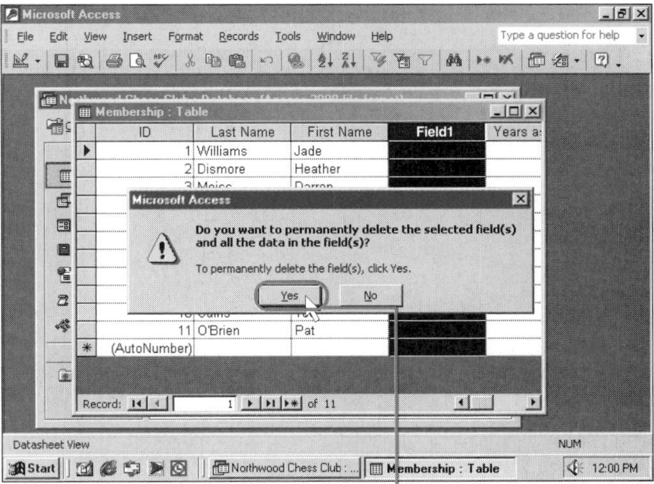

■ A dialog box appears, confirming the deletion.

4 Click **Yes** to permanently delete the field.

■ The field disappears from your table.

MOVE THROUGH DATA

You can move through the data in your table to review and edit information.

If your table contains a lot of data, your computer screen may not be able to display all the data at once. You can scroll through fields and records to display data that does not appear on your screen.

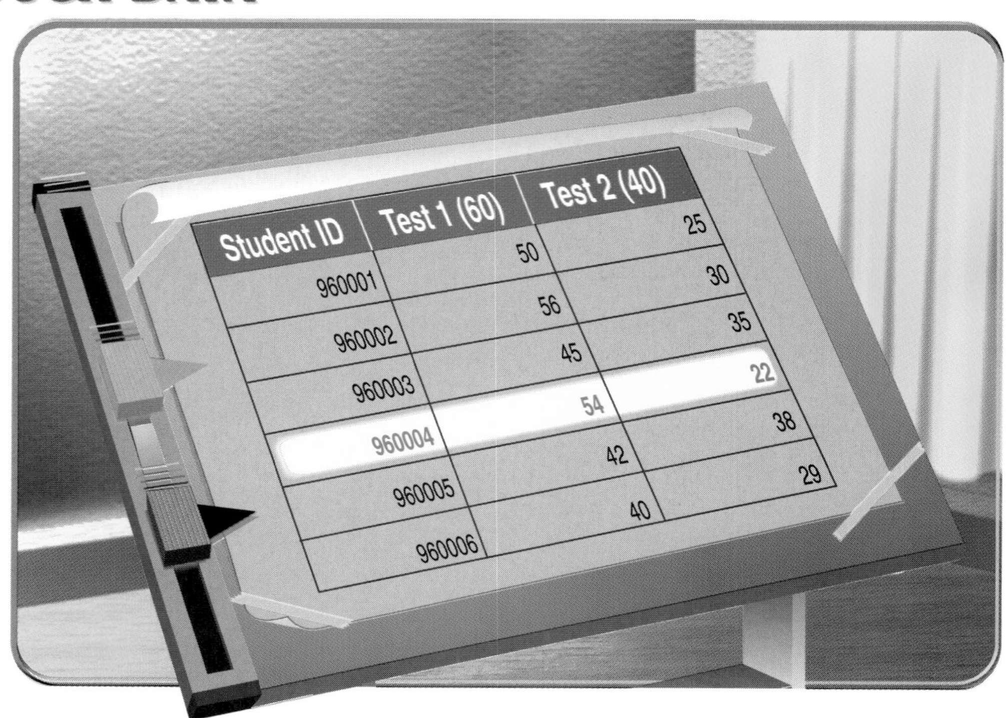

MOVE THROUGH DATA

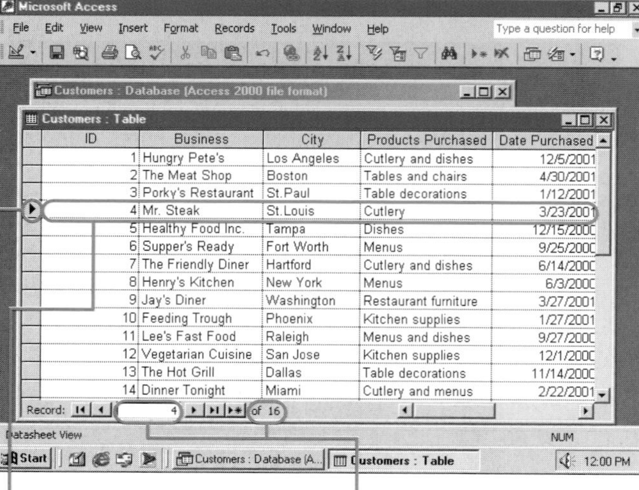

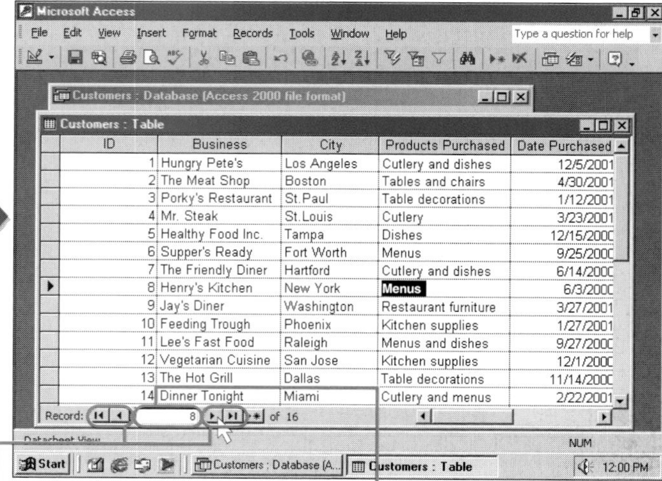

1 Click the record you want to make the current record.

■ An arrow (▸) appears beside the current record.

■ This area displays the number of the current record and the total number of records in the table.

2 To move through the records, click one of the following buttons.

- ⏮ First Record
- ◂ Previous Record
- ▸ Next Record
- ⏭ Last Record

■ To quickly move to a specific record, double-click this area and then type the number of the record you want to display. Then press the **Enter** key.

How do I use my keyboard to move through data in a table?

Press on Keyboard	Description
Page Up	Move up one screen of records
Page Down	Move down one screen of records
Tab	Move to the next field in the current record
↑	Move up one record in the same field
↓	Move down one record in the same field

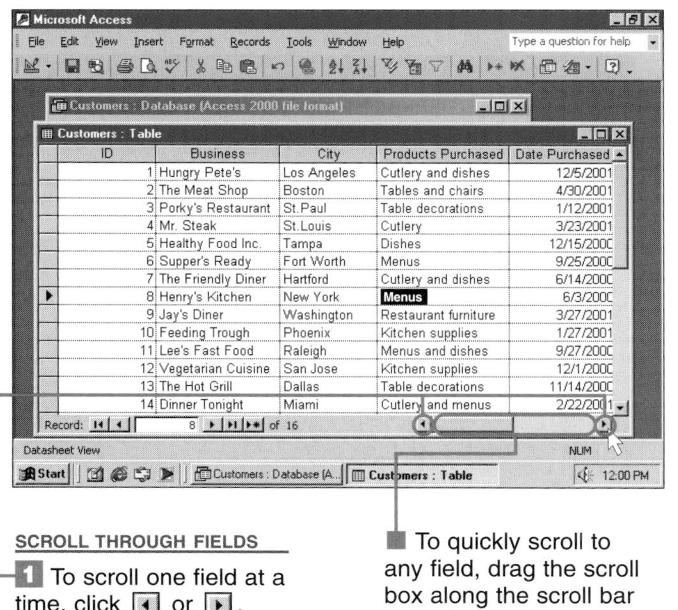

SCROLL THROUGH FIELDS

1 To scroll one field at a time, click ◄ or ►.

Note: You cannot scroll through fields if all the fields appear on your screen.

■ To quickly scroll to any field, drag the scroll box along the scroll bar until the field you want to view appears.

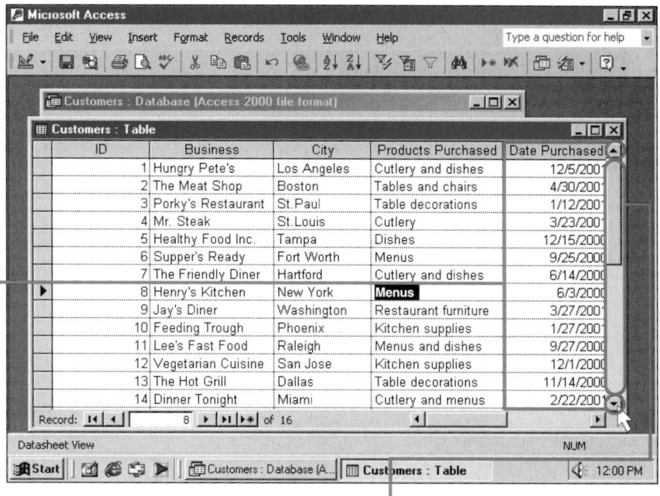

SCROLL THROUGH RECORDS

1 To scroll one record at a time, click ▲ or ▼.

Note: You cannot scroll through records if all the records appear on your screen.

■ To quickly scroll to any record, drag the scroll box along the scroll bar until a yellow box displays the number of the record you want to view.

SELECT DATA

Before performing many tasks in a table, you must select the data you want to work with. Selected data appears highlighted on your screen.

SELECT DATA

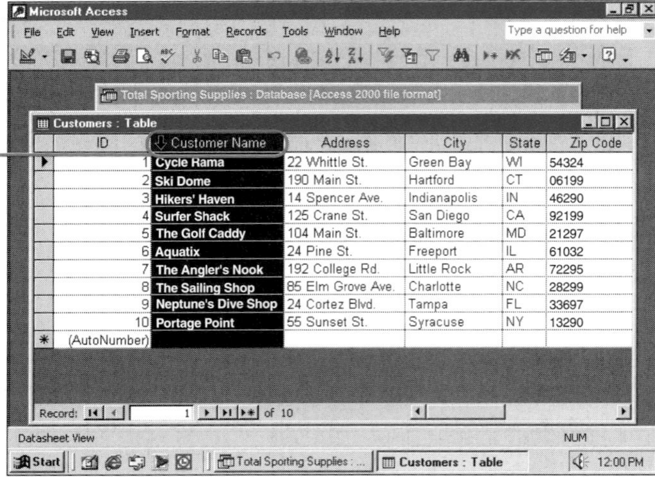

SELECT A FIELD

1 Position the mouse ⇖ over the name of the field you want to select (⇖ changes to ⬇) and then click to select the field.

■ To select multiple fields, position the mouse ⇖ over the name of the first field (⇖ changes to ⬇). Then drag the mouse ⬇ until you highlight all the fields you want to select.

SELECT A RECORD

1 Position the mouse ⇖ over the area to the left of the record you want to select (⇖ changes to ➡) and then click to select the record.

■ To select multiple records, position the mouse ⇖ over the area to the left of the first record (⇖ changes to ➡). Then drag the mouse ➡ until you highlight all the records you want to select.

How do I select all the records in a table?

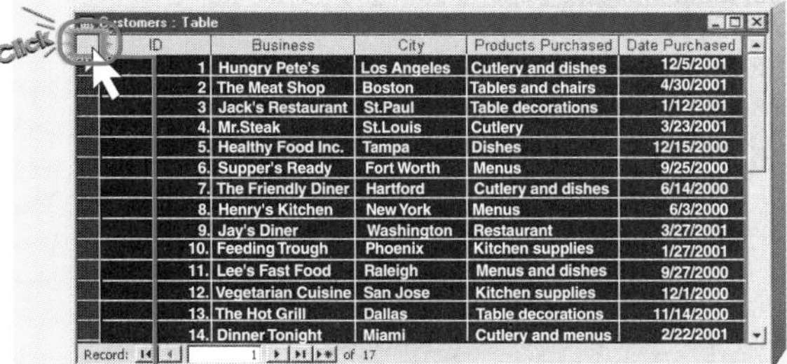

■ To select all the records in a table, click the blank area ( ) to the left of the field names.

How do I deselect data?

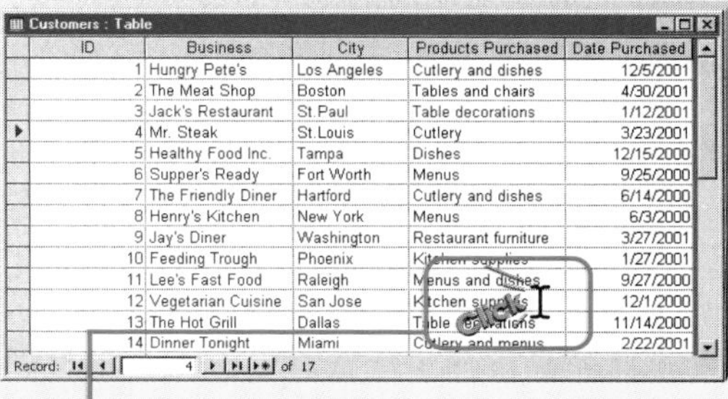

■ To deselect data, click anywhere in the table.

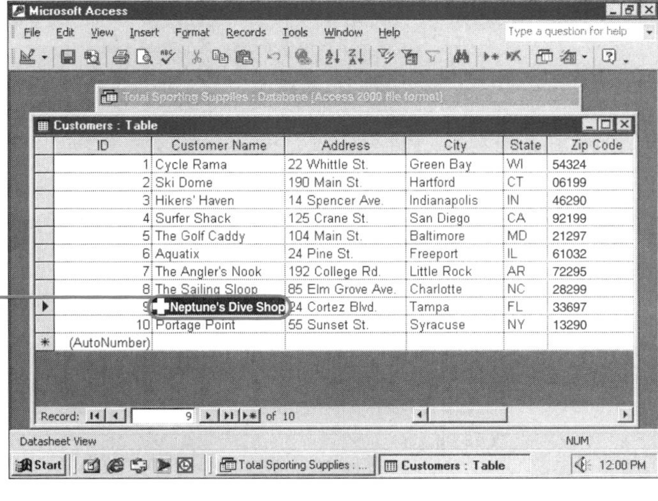

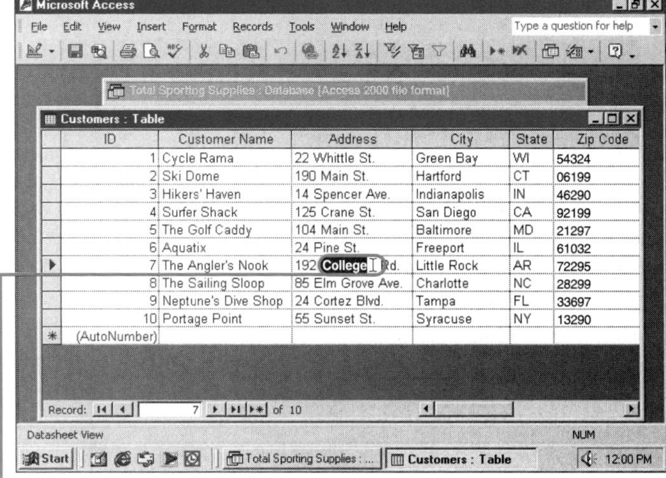

SELECT A CELL

1 Position the mouse I over the left edge of the cell you want to select (I changes to ✚) and then click to select the cell.

■ To select multiple cells, position the mouse I over the left edge of the first cell (I changes to ✚). Then drag the mouse ✚ until you highlight all the cells you want to select.

SELECT DATA IN A CELL

1 Position the mouse I over the left edge of the data and then drag the mouse I until you highlight all the data you want to select.

■ To quickly select a word, double-click the word.

EDIT DATA

You can edit the data in a table to correct a mistake or update the data.

Access automatically saves changes you make to data in a table.

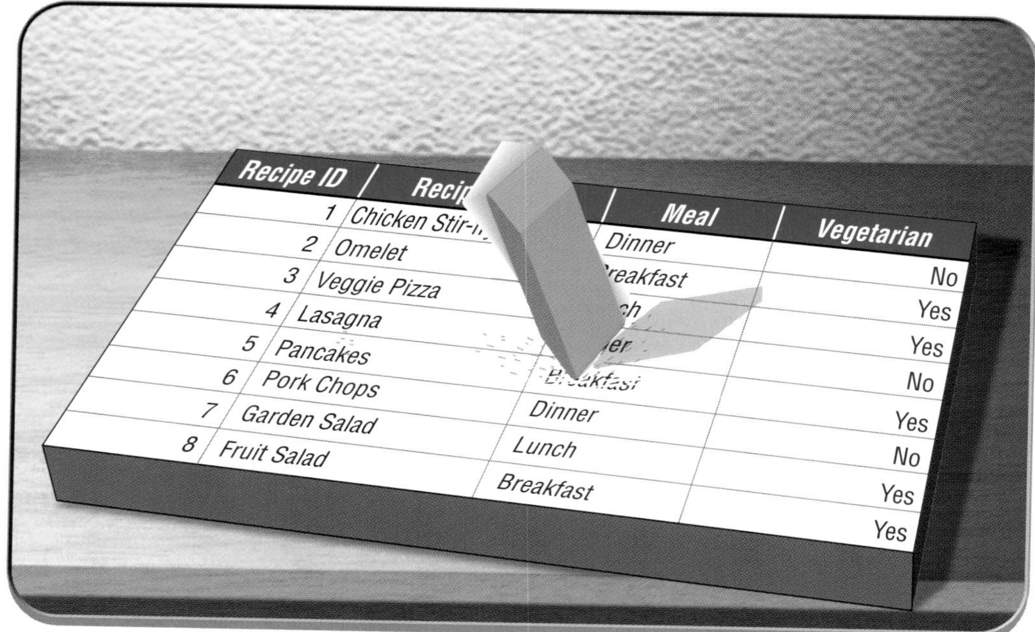

EDIT DATA

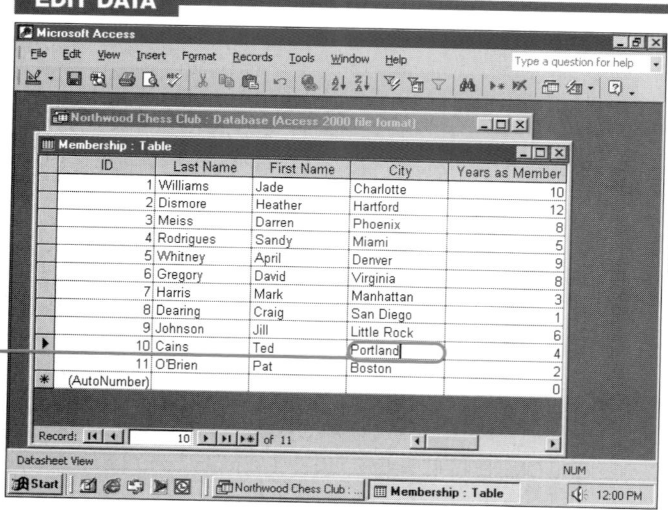

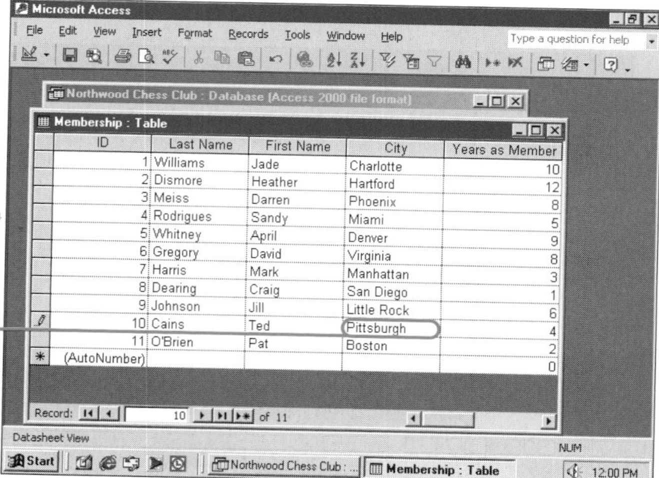

1 Click the location in the cell where you want to edit data.

■ A flashing insertion point appears in the cell.

Note: You can press the ← *or* → *key to move the insertion point to where you want to edit data.*

2 To remove the character to the left of the flashing insertion point, press the **Backspace** key.

3 To add data where the insertion point flashes on your screen, type the data.

4 When you finish making changes to the data, press the **Enter** key.

What are the symbols that appear to the left of the records?

▶	This is the current record.
✎	You are editing this record.
✱	You can enter data for a new record here.

Why can't I edit the data in a cell?

You may be trying to edit data in a field that has the AutoNumber data type. A field that has the AutoNumber data type automatically numbers records for you. You cannot edit the data in an AutoNumber field. For more information on data types, see page 291.

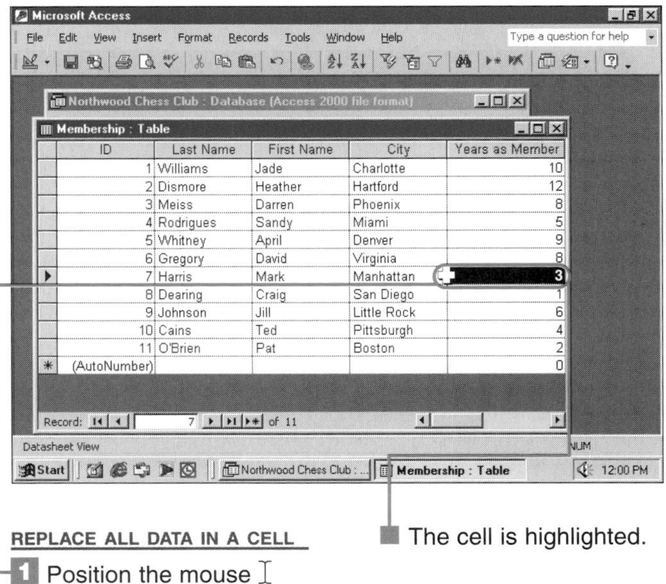

REPLACE ALL DATA IN A CELL

1 Position the mouse I over the left edge of the cell containing the data you want to replace with new data (I changes to ✚) and then click to select the cell.

■ The cell is highlighted.

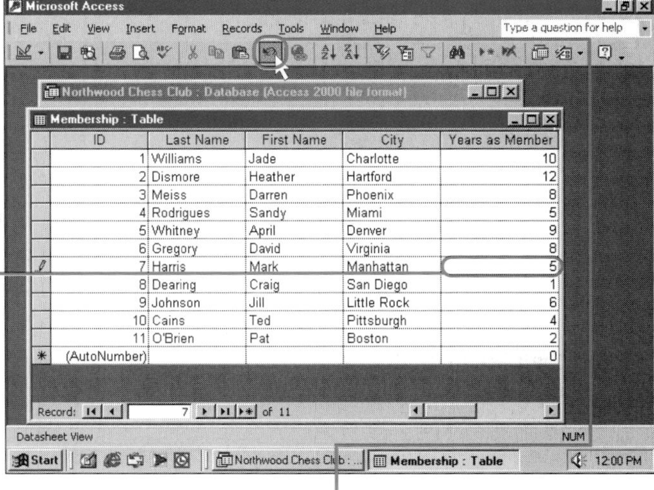

2 Type the new data and then press the Enter key.

UNDO CHANGES

1 Click ↶ to immediately undo your most recent change.

ADD A RECORD

You can add a new record to insert additional information into your table. For example, you may want to add information about a new customer.

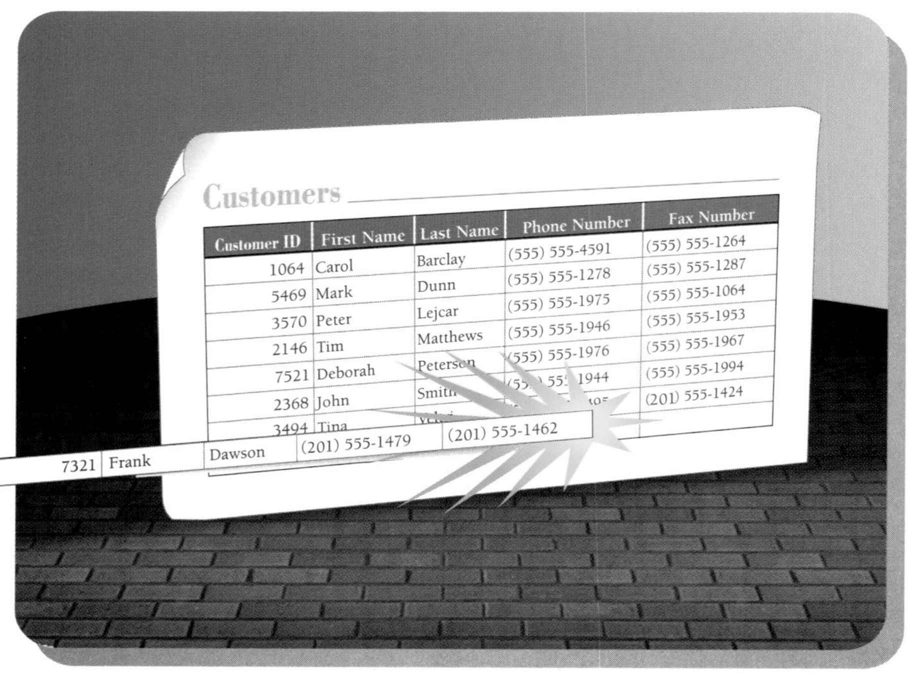

Customers
Customer ID | First Name | Last Name | Phone Number | Fax Number
1064 | Carol | Barclay | (555) 555-4591 | (555) 555-1264
5469 | Mark | Dunn | (555) 555-1278 | (555) 555-1287
3570 | Peter | Lejcar | (555) 555-1975 | (555) 555-1064
2146 | Tim | Matthews | (555) 555-1946 | (555) 555-1953
7521 | Deborah | Peterson | (555) 555-1976 | (555) 555-1967
2368 | John | Smith | (555) 555-1994
3494 | Tina | (201) 555-1424
7321 | Frank | Dawson | (201) 555-1479 | (201) 555-1462

You must add a new record to the end of your table. After adding a record, you can sort the records to change the order of the records. To sort records, see page 312.

ADD A RECORD

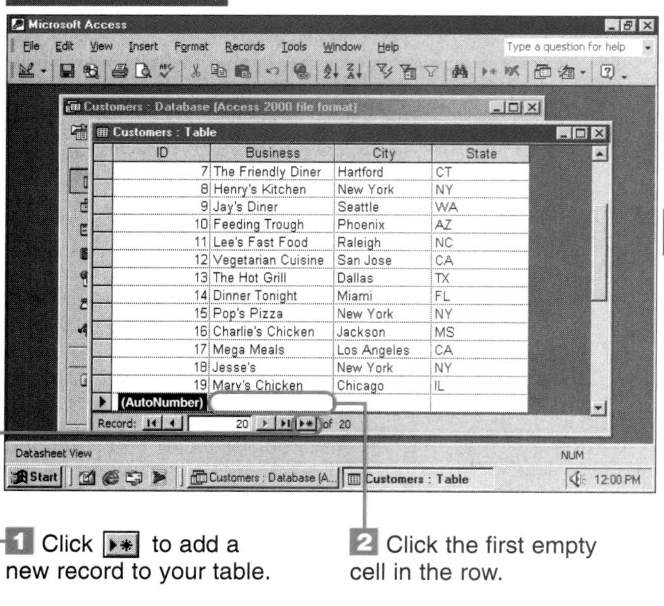

1 Click ▶* to add a new record to your table.

2 Click the first empty cell in the row.

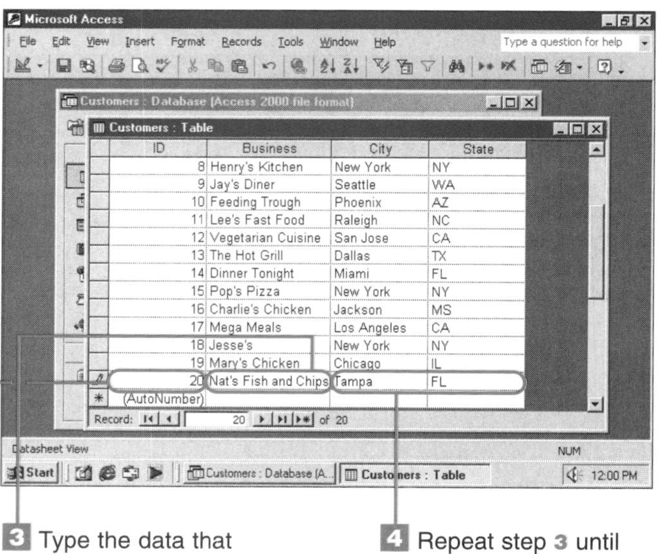

3 Type the data that corresponds to the field and then press the Enter key to move to the next cell.

■ In this example, the AutoNumber field automatically adds a number for the new record.

4 Repeat step **3** until you finish entering all the data for the record.

■ Access automatically saves each new record you add to the table.

DELETE A RECORD

You can delete a record from a table to permanently remove information you no longer need. For example, you may want to remove information about a customer who no longer orders your products.

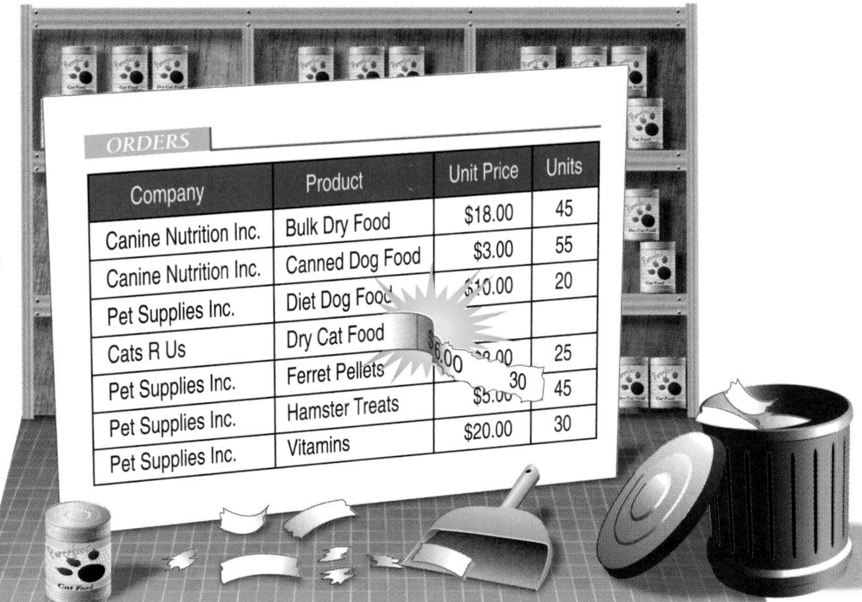

Deleting records saves storage space on your computer and keeps your database from becoming cluttered with unnecessary information.

DELETE A RECORD

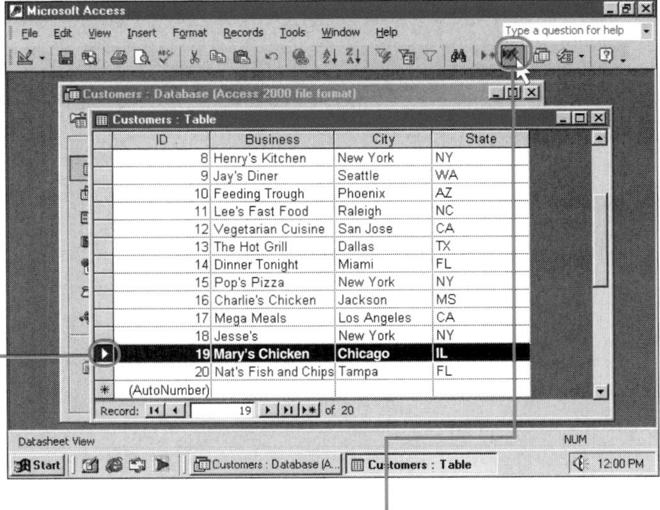

1 Position the mouse over the area to the left of the record you want to delete (changes to ➡) and then click to select the record.

2 Click to delete the record.

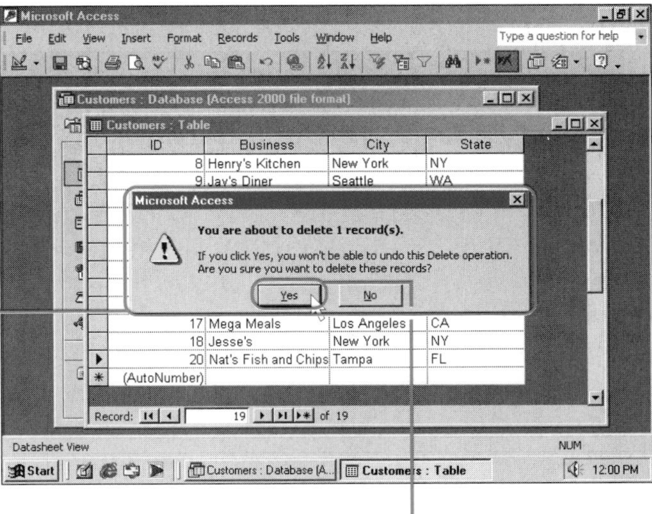

■ The record disappears from the table.

■ A warning dialog box appears, confirming the deletion.

3 Click **Yes** to permanently delete the record.

CHANGE COLUMN WIDTH

You can change the width of a column in your table. Increasing the width of a column lets you view data that is too long to display in the column.

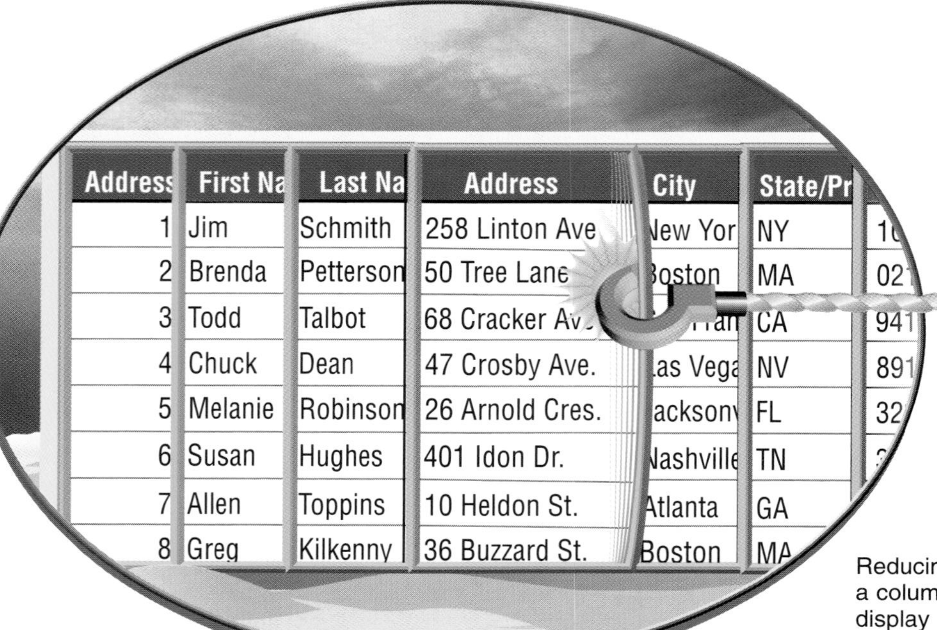

Reducing the width of a column allows you to display more fields on your screen at once.

CHANGE COLUMN WIDTH

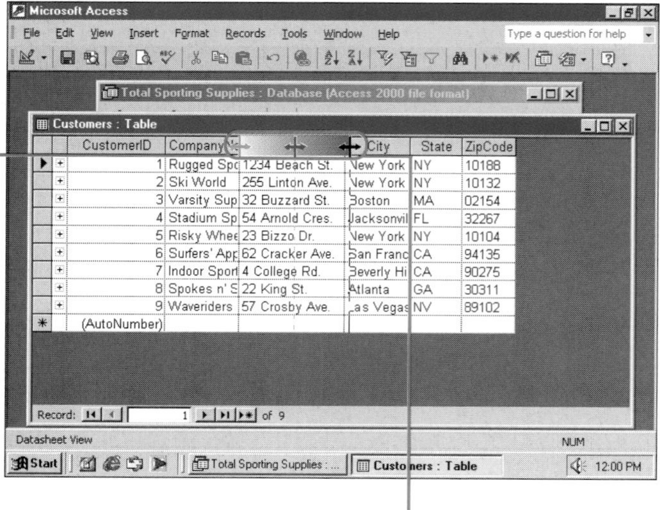

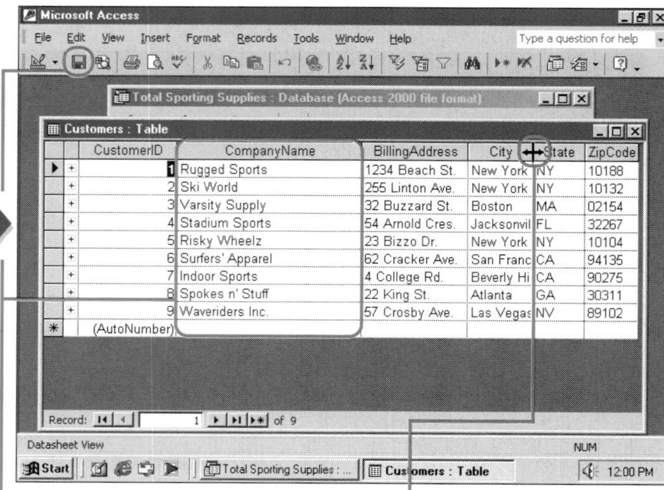

1 To change the width of a column, position the mouse over the right edge of the column heading (changes to ✛).

2 Drag the column edge until the line displays the column width you want.

■ The column displays the new width.

3 Click 💾 to save your change.

FIT LONGEST ITEM

1 To change a column width to fit the longest item in the column, double-click the right edge of the column heading.

DISPLAY A SUBDATASHEET

When viewing the records in a table, you can display a subdatasheet to view and edit related data from another table.

For example, in a table containing customer information, you can display a subdatasheet to view the orders for a customer.

You can only display a subdatasheet when the table you are working with has a relationship with another table in your database. For information on relationships, see page 300.

Customers : Table

	ID	Company Name	Billing Address	City
+	1	Sports Inc.	123 Bell Lane	Seattle
−	2	Racquets & Stuff	456 Tree Blvd.	Chicago
+	4	Born to Be Wild	991 Sunset Dr.	Tampa

Orders

OrderID	Item	Price	Quantity
45680	Skates	$2,458.70	10
74238	Helmets	$622.90	15
36749	Gloves	$714.03	15

DISPLAY A SUBDATASHEET

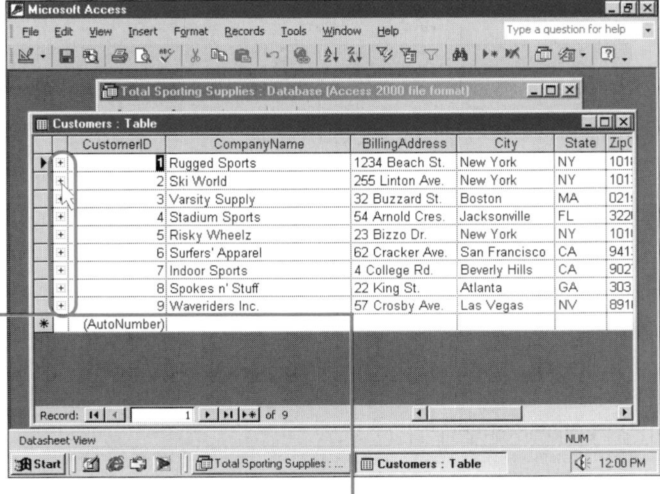

■ When records in a table relate to data in another table, a plus sign (+) appears beside each record.

1 Click the plus sign (+) beside a record to display the related data from the other table (+ changes to −).

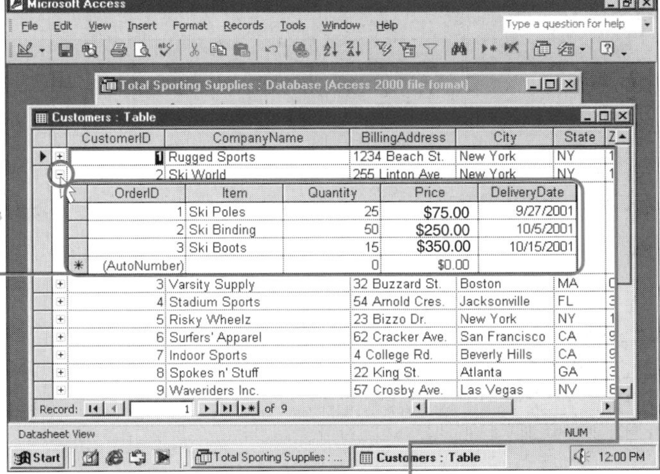

■ The related data from the other table appears. You can review and edit the data. To edit data, see page 280.

2 To once again hide the related data, click the minus sign (−) beside the record.

CHANGE THE VIEW OF A TABLE

Access offers several ways that you can view a table. Each view allows you to perform different tasks.

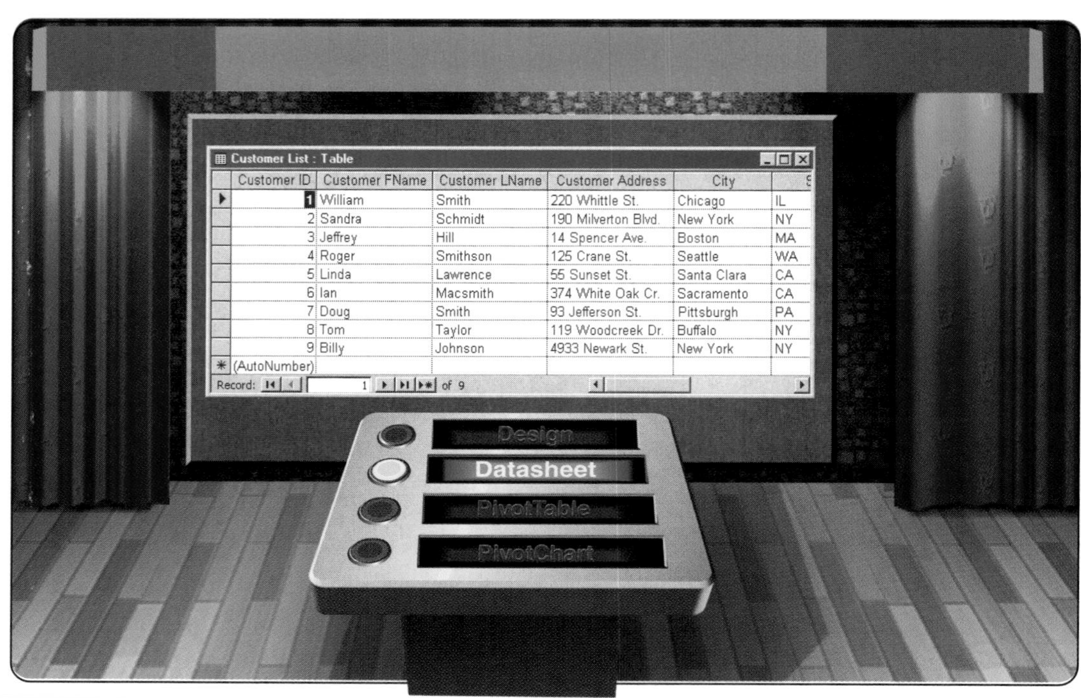

CHANGE THE VIEW OF A TABLE

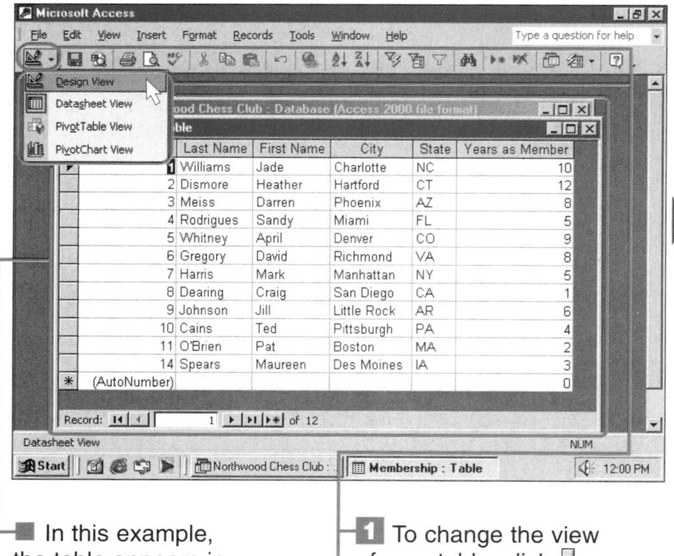

■ In this example, the table appears in the Datasheet view.

1 To change the view of your table, click ▾ in this area.

2 Click the view you want to use.

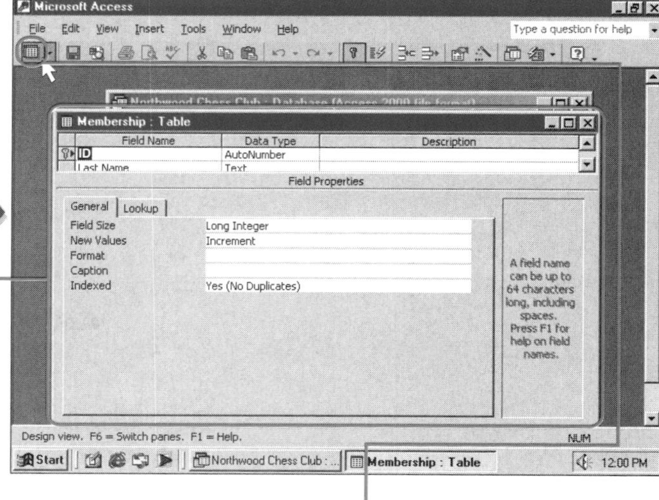

■ Your table appears in the view you selected.

■ In this example, the View button (Design) changes to (Datasheet). You can click the View button to quickly switch between the Datasheet (Datasheet) and Design (Design) views.

THE TABLE VIEWS

Design View

The Design view displays the structure of a table. You can change the settings in this view to specify the kind of information you can enter into a table.

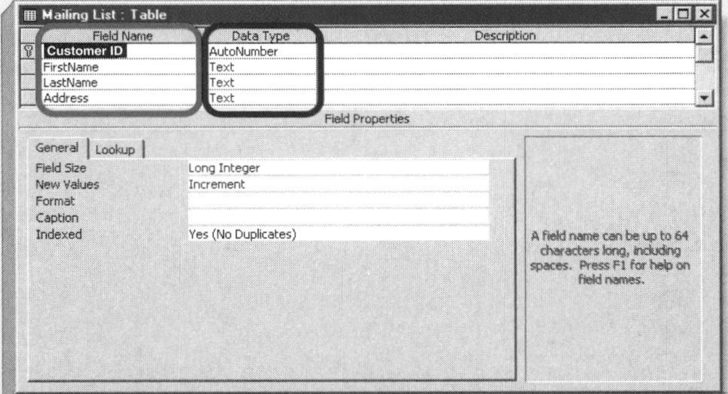

The **Field Name** area displays the name of each field in a table.

The **Data Type** area displays the data type for each field.

Datasheet View

The Datasheet view displays all the records in a table. You can enter, edit and review records in this view.

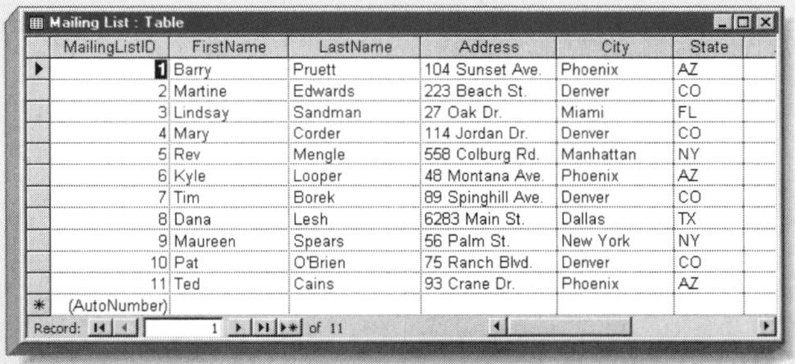

PivotTable View

The PivotTable view allows you to analyze and summarize the data in a table. The first time you display a table in this view, you must specify the fields you want to display. For information on using the PivotTable view, see page 292.

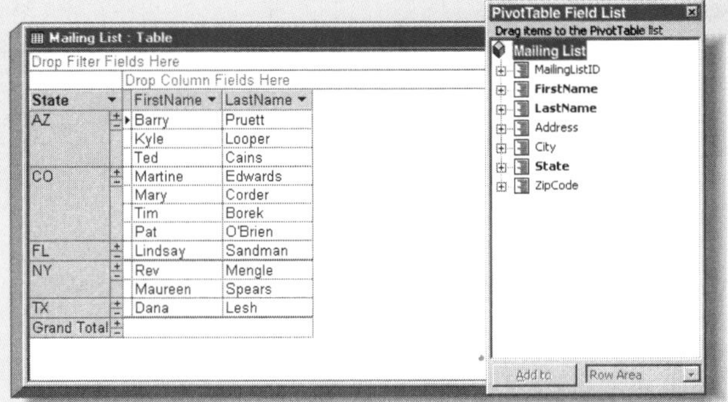

PivotChart View

The PivotChart view allows you to display a graphical summary of the data in a table. The first time you display a table in this view, you must specify the fields you want to display. For information on using the PivotChart view, see page 296.

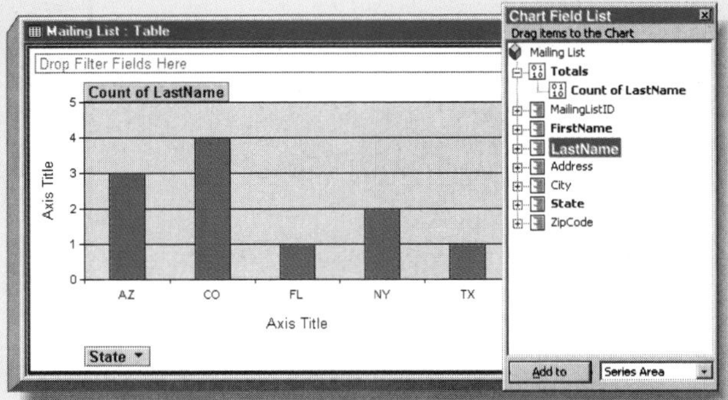

SET THE PRIMARY KEY

A primary key is one or more fields that uniquely identifies each record in a table. Each table in your database should have a primary key.

Access will not allow you to enter the same value into a primary key more than once.

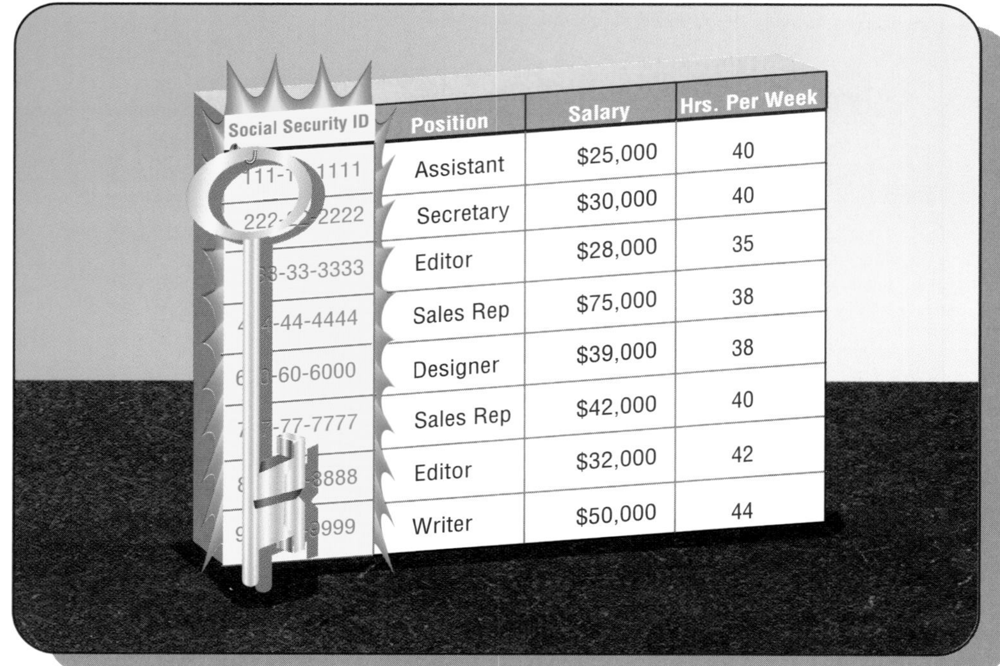

SET THE PRIMARY KEY

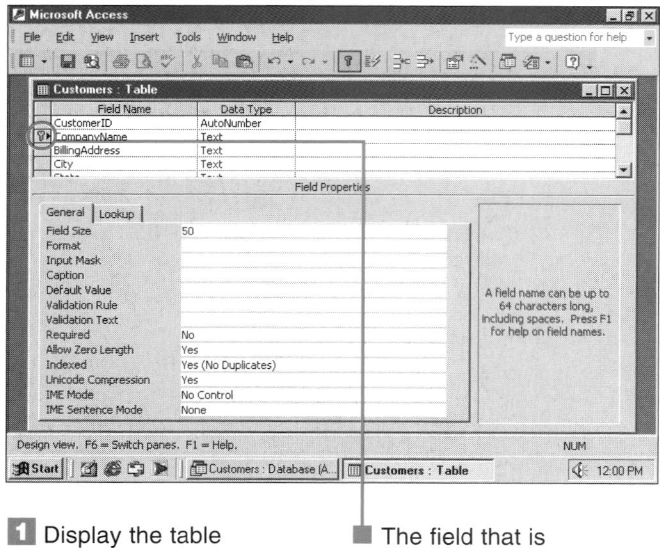

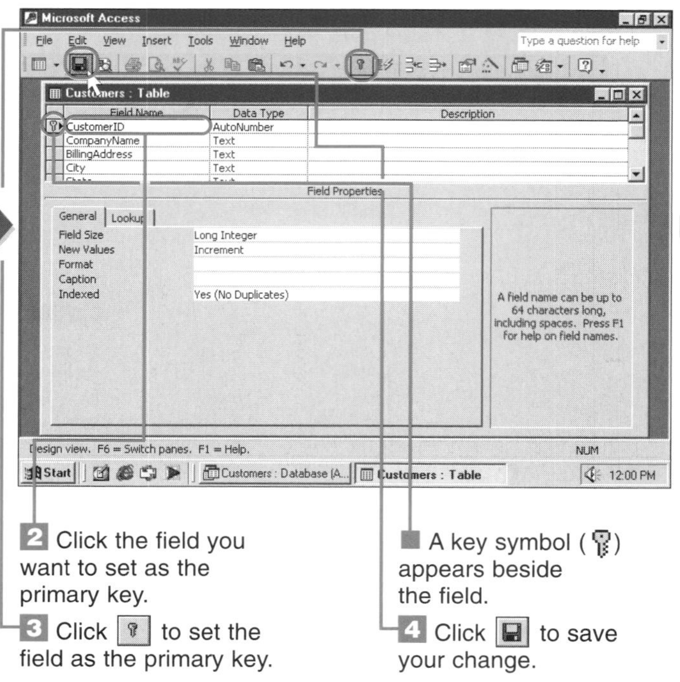

1 Display the table in the Design view.
To change the view of a table, see page 286.

■ The field that is currently set as the primary key displays a key symbol (🔑).

Note: Access may have set a primary key for you when you created the table.

2 Click the field you want to set as the primary key.

3 Click 🔑 to set the field as the primary key.

■ A key symbol (🔑) appears beside the field.

4 Click 💾 to save your change.

Why should each table in my database have a primary key?

Access uses the primary key in each table to create relationships between the tables. Relationships between tables allow you to bring together related information in your database. You should not change the primary key in a table that has a relationship with another table in your database. For information on relationships, see page 300.

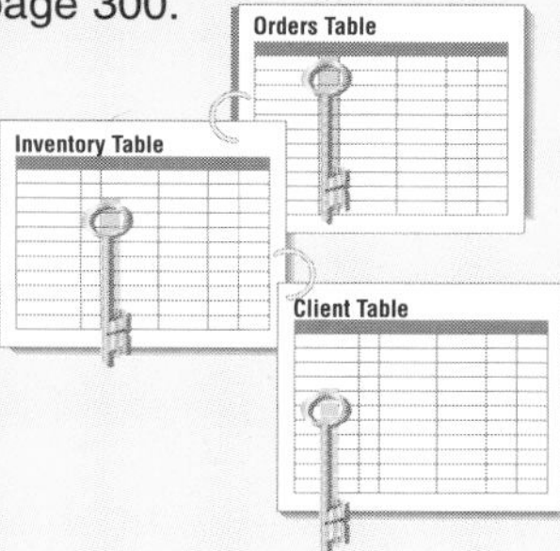

What types of primary keys can I create?

ID
1
2
3
4

AutoNumber

A field that automatically assigns a unique number to each record you add. When you create a table, Access can create an AutoNumber primary key for you.

Invoice No
6218
7410
8611
9431

Single-Field

A field that contains a unique value for each record.

Company Name	Company ID
Sports Superstore	4526
Reel Fishing	4527
American Outdoors	4528
Camping USA	4529

Multiple-Field

Two or more fields that together make up a unique value for each record.

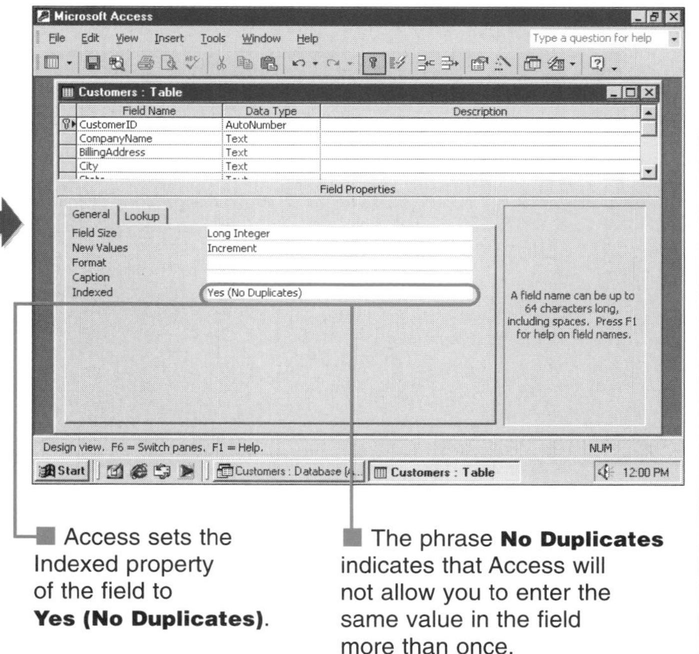

■ Access sets the Indexed property of the field to **Yes (No Duplicates)**.

■ The phrase **No Duplicates** indicates that Access will not allow you to enter the same value in the field more than once.

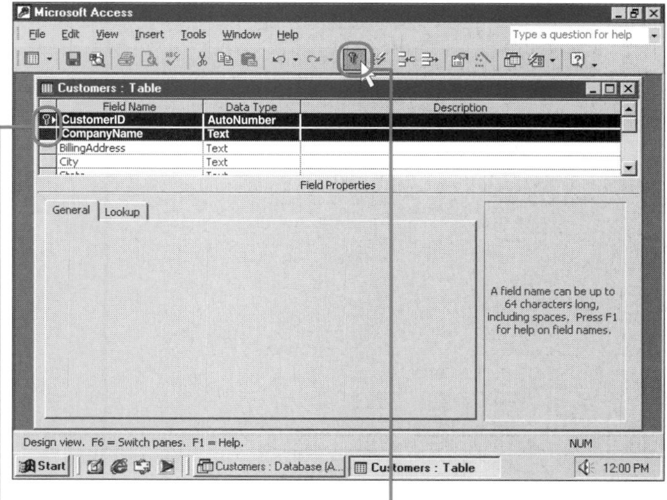

You can set more than one field as the primary key.

1 Press and hold down the Ctrl key.

2 While holding down the Ctrl key, click the area to the left of each field you want to set as the primary key.

3 Click the key button to set the fields as the primary key.

■ A key symbol appears beside each field.

CHANGE A FIELD'S DATA TYPE

You can change the type of data you can enter into a field.

Access will accept only entries that match the data type you specify for a field. This helps prevent errors when entering data. For example, you cannot enter text into a field with the Number data type.

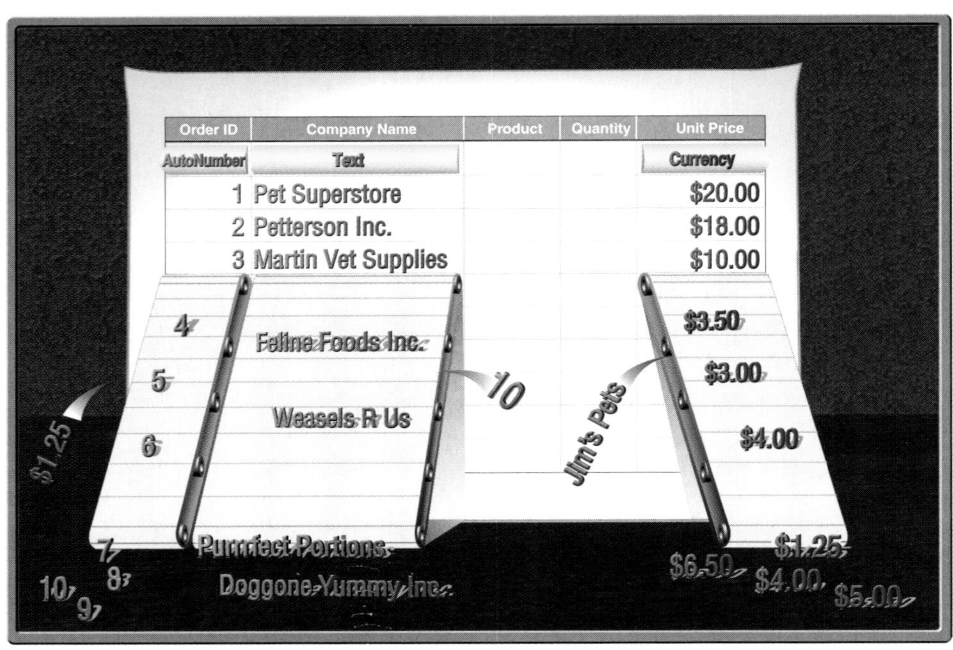

CHANGE A FIELD'S DATA TYPE

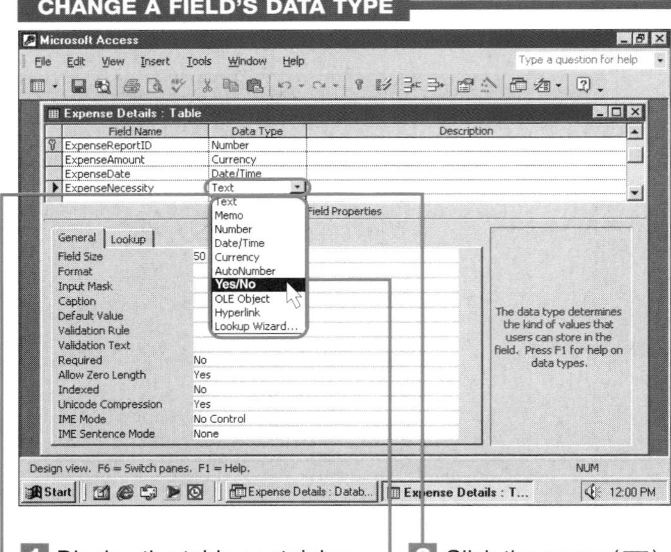

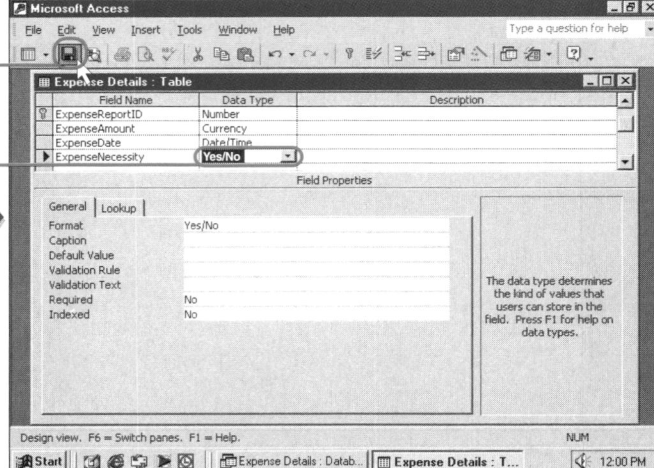

1 Display the table containing the field you want to change in the Design view. To change the view of a table, see page 286.

2 Click the Data Type area for the field you want to change. An arrow (▾) appears.

3 Click the arrow (▾) to display a list of data types.

4 Click the data type you want to use.

■ The field changes to the new data type.

5 Click 💾 to save your change.

*Note: If you change the data type for a field that contains data, Access will display an error message if it encounters errors while converting the data. Click **Yes** to continue or click **No** to cancel the change.*

DATA TYPES

Text

Accepts entries up to 255 characters long that include any combination of text and numbers, such as an address. Make sure you use this data type for numbers you do not want to use in calculations, such as phone numbers or zip codes.

AutoNumber

Automatically numbers each record for you.

Memo

Accepts entries up to 65,536 characters long that include any combination of text and numbers, such as notes, comments or lengthy descriptions.

Yes/No

Accepts only one of two values—Yes/No, True/False or On/Off.

Number

Accepts numbers you can use in calculations.

OLE Object

Accepts OLE objects. An OLE object is an object created in another program, such as a document created in Word or a spreadsheet created in Excel. OLE objects can also include sounds and pictures.

Date/Time

Accepts only dates and times.

Hyperlink

Accepts hyperlinks you can select to jump to another document or a Web page.

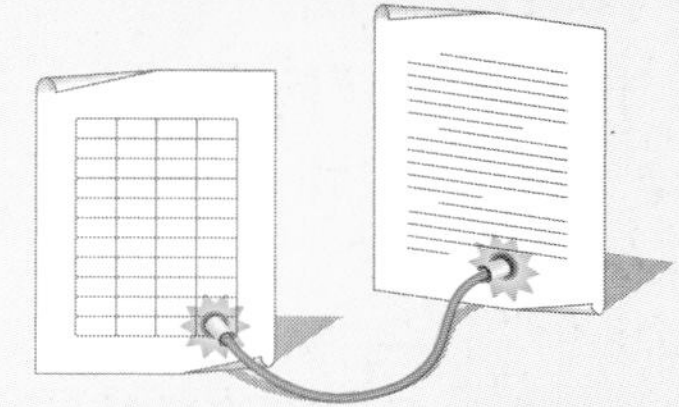

Currency

Accepts only monetary values.

USING THE PIVOTTABLE VIEW

You can use the PivotTable view to analyze and summarize the data in a table.

The first time you display a table in the PivotTable view, no fields are displayed. You must add the fields you want to display to the PivotTable view.

You can also use the method shown below to display a query or form in the PivotTable view.

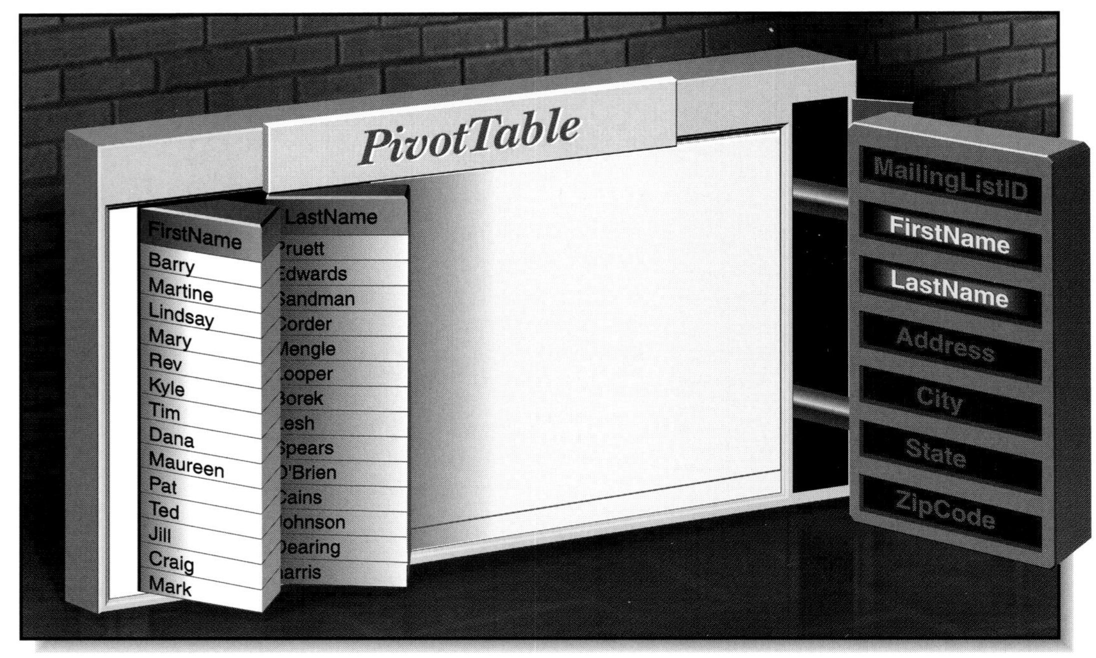

USING THE PIVOTTABLE VIEW

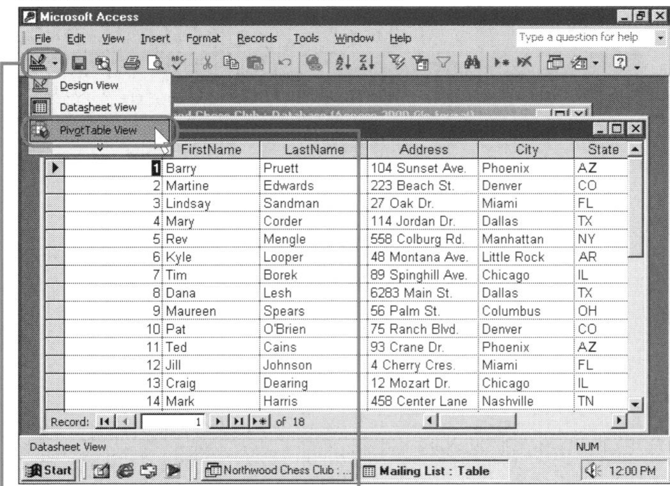

1 To change the view of a table, click ▾ in this area.

2 Click **PivotTable View**.

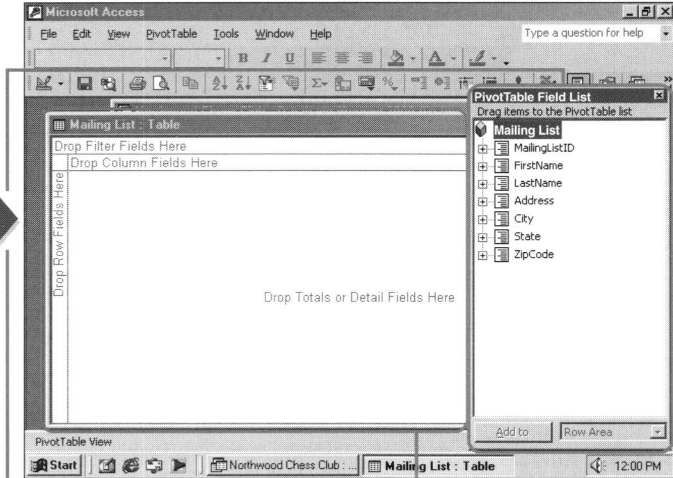

■ The PivotTable Field List dialog box appears, displaying the name of each field in your table.

*Note: If the PivotTable Field List dialog box does not appear, click **View** and then click **Field List**.*

■ This window displays areas you can use to summarize the data in your table.

Note: For information on the areas you can use to summarize data, see the top of page 293.

What areas can I use to summarize my data?

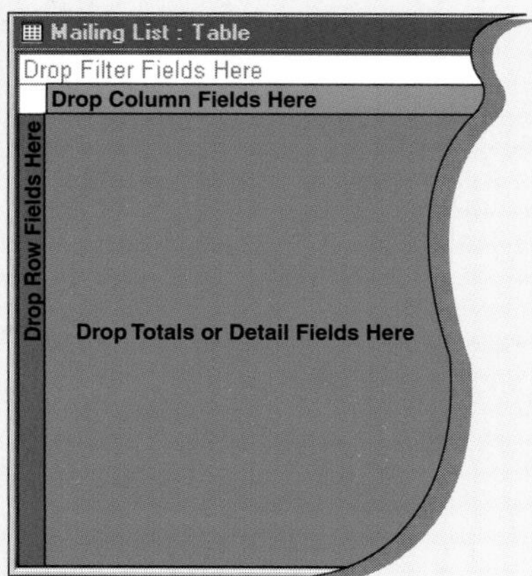

Detail area

You use the Detail area to specify the data you want to summarize.

Row area

You use the Row area to specify a field you want to use to summarize the data in the Detail area.

Column area

You use the Column area to specify a field you want to use to summarize the data in the Detail area.

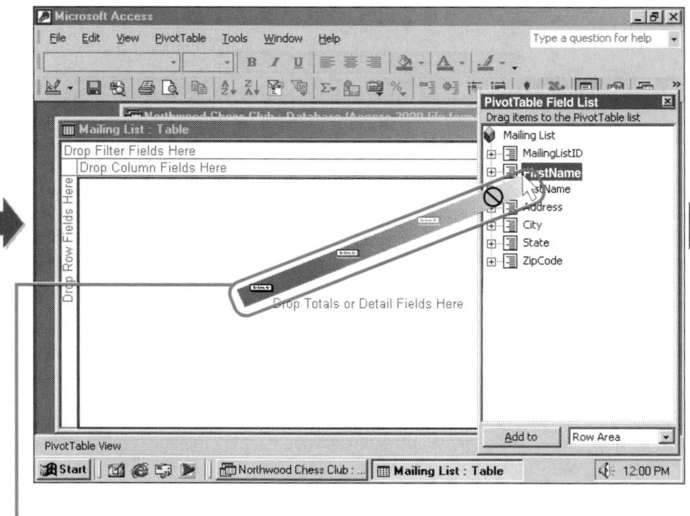

3 To add a field to the PivotTable view that contains data you want to summarize, position the mouse over the name of the field in the PivotTable Field List dialog box. Then drag the field name to the Detail area.

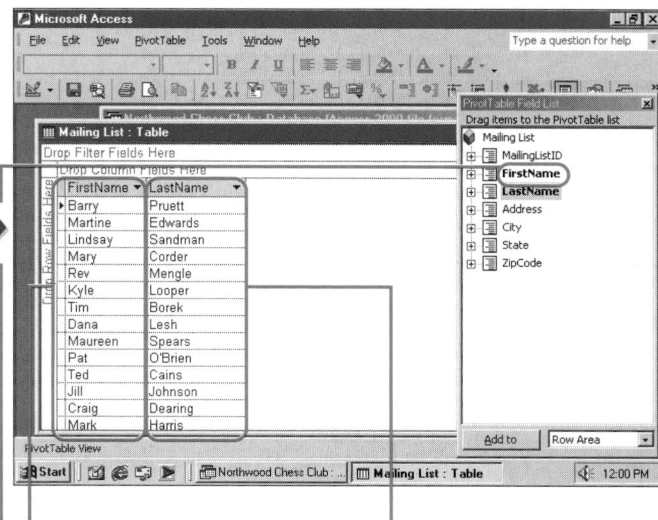

■ The field appears in the Detail area.

■ The name of the field in the PivotTable Field List dialog box appears in bold.

4 Repeat step 3 for each field you want to add to the Detail area.

CONTINUED

USING THE PIVOTTABLE VIEW

You can select the fields you want to use to summarize data in the PivotTable view.

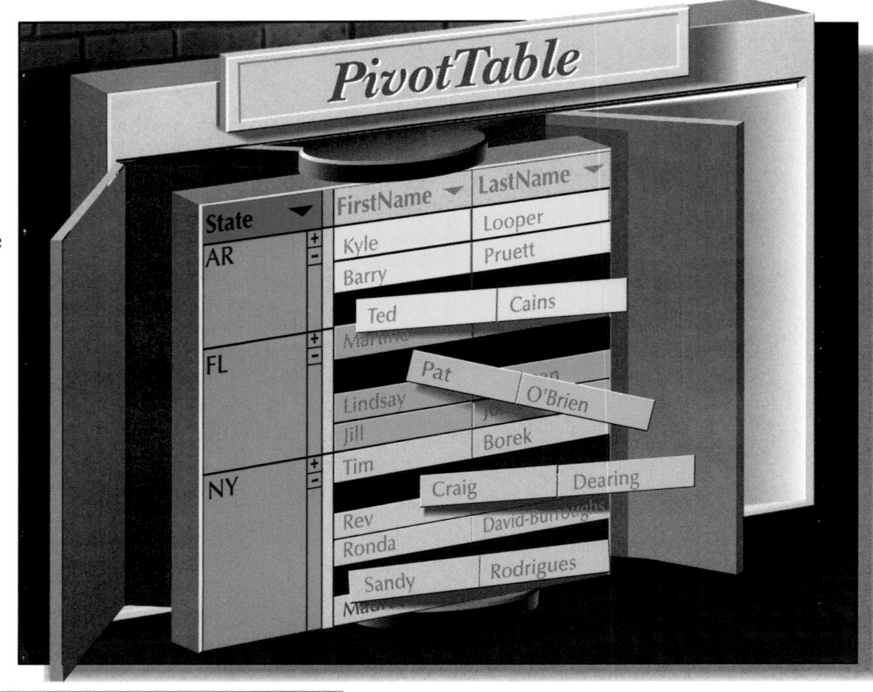

Summarizing data in the PivotTable view does not affect the table that contains the data.

You cannot edit data in the PivotTable view.

USING THE PIVOTTABLE VIEW (CONTINUED)

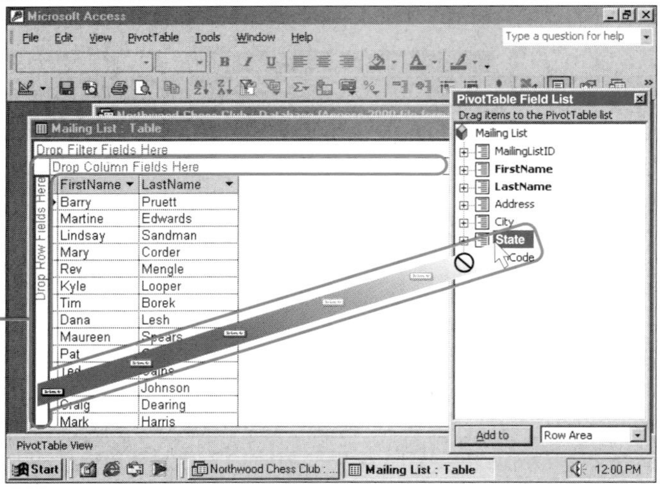

5 To add a field you want to use to summarize the data in the Detail area, position the mouse over the name of the field in the PivotTable Field List dialog box. Then drag the field name to the Row or Column area.

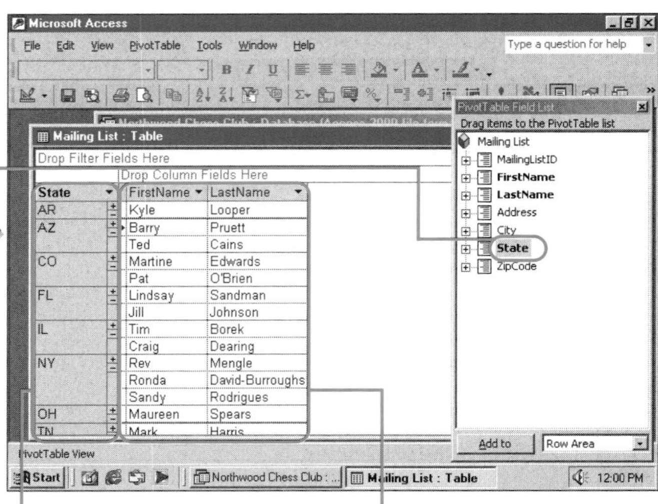

■ The name of the field and data from the field appear in the Row or Column area.

■ The name of the field in the PivotTable Field List dialog box appears in bold.

■ The PivotTable view displays a summary of your data. The data is summarized by the field you selected in step 5.

■ In this example, names are grouped by the State field.

Can I remove a field from the PivotTable view?

You can remove a field from the Detail, Row or Column area in the PivotTable view. Removing a field from the PivotTable view does not delete the field from the table.

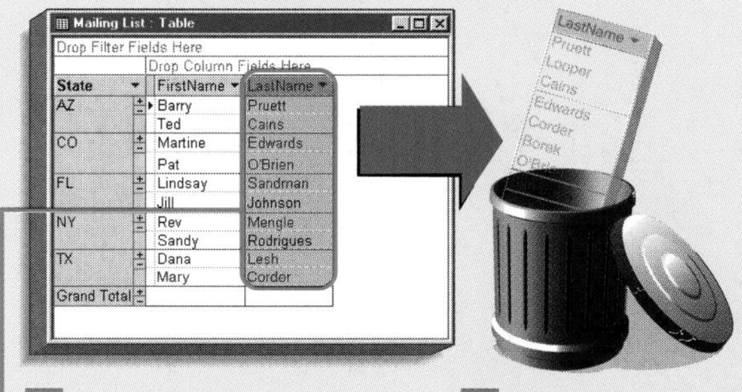

1 Click the name of the field you want to remove from the PivotTable view.

■ The field appears highlighted.

2 Press the Delete key.

■ The field disappears from the PivotTable view.

Can I summarize data by more than one field?

Yes. You can add more than one field to the Row or Column areas to summarize data. For example, you can group data by the State and City fields. To summarize data by more than one field, repeat step 5 on page 294 until the PivotTable view displays the fields you want.

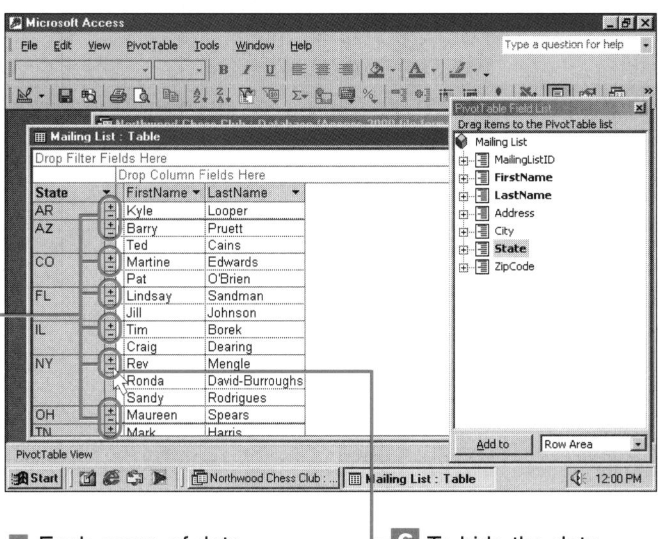

■ Each group of data displays a plus sign (+) and a minus sign (−).

6 To hide the data in a group, click the minus sign (−).

■ You can click the plus sign (+) to once again display the data.

SAVE THE PIVOTTABLE VIEW LAYOUT

1 Click the save button to save the layout of the PivotTable view.

■ The next time you display the table in the PivotTable view, the fields in the table will appear in the layout you saved.

Note: When you display a form in the PivotTable view, the layout you create is automatically saved.

USING THE PIVOTCHART VIEW

You can use the PivotChart view to display a graphical summary of the data in a table. The PivotChart view allows you to easily compare data in a table.

The first time you display a table in the PivotChart view, no fields are displayed. You must add the fields you want to display to the PivotChart view.

You can also use the method shown below to display a query or form in the PivotChart view.

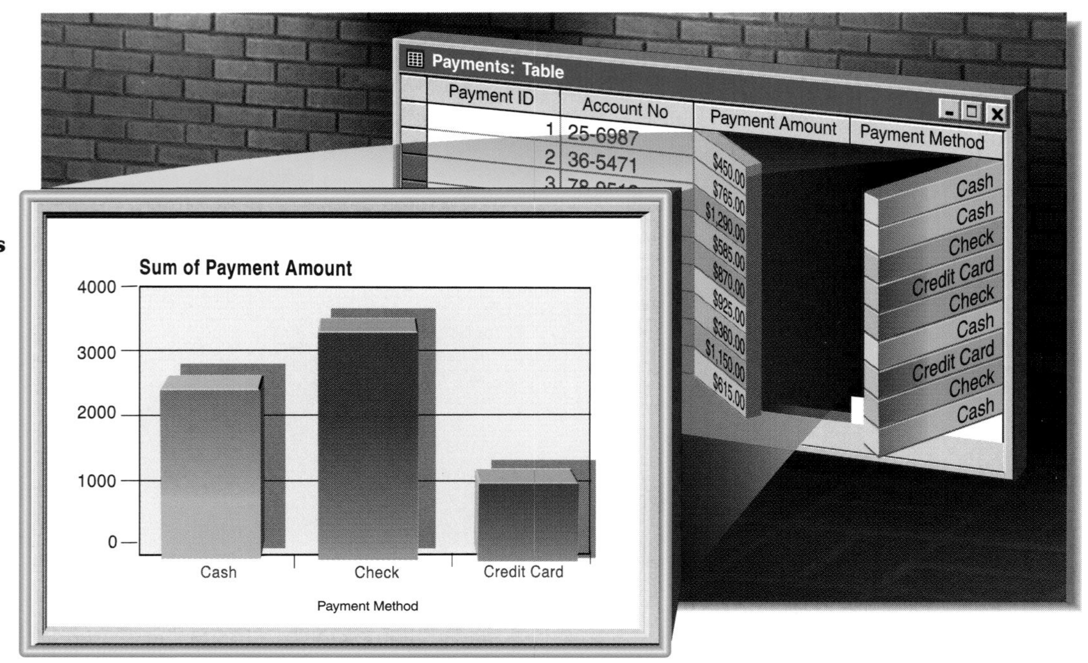

USING THE PIVOTCHART VIEW

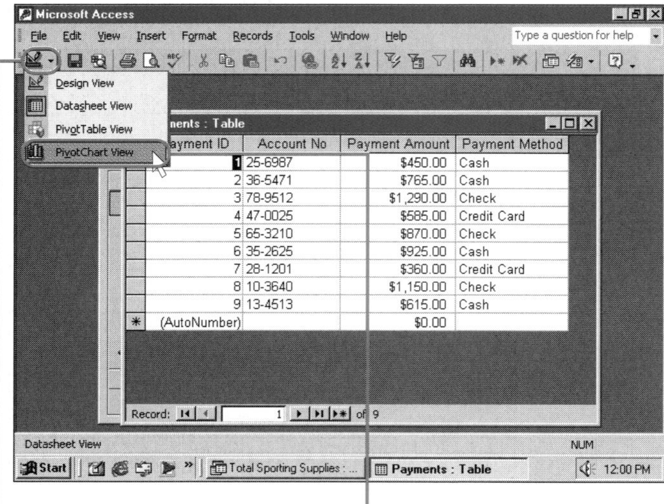

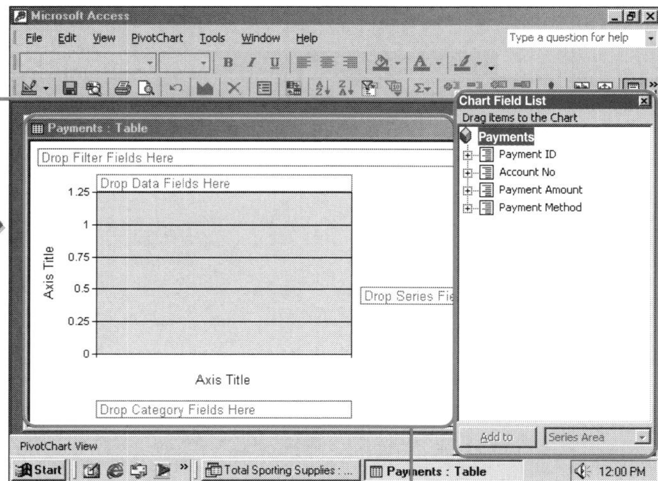

1 To change the view of a table, click ▾ in this area.

2 Click **PivotChart View**.

■ The Chart Field List dialog box appears, displaying the name of each field in your table.

*Note: If the Chart Field List dialog box does not appear, click **View** and then click **Field List**.*

■ This window displays areas you can use to create a chart that summarizes data from your table.

Note: For information on the areas you can use to create a chart, see the top of page 297.

What areas can I use to create a chart?

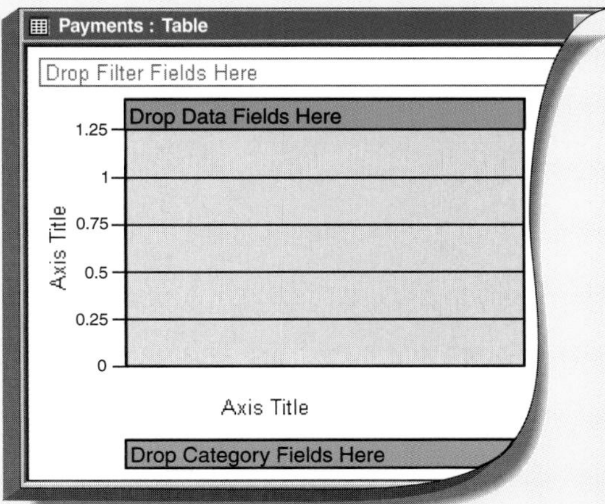

Category area

You use the Category area to specify the field that contains the categories you want the chart to display.

Data area

You use the Data area to specify the data you want to summarize in the chart. When you add a field to the Data area, Access performs a calculation on the data to compare or measure the data.

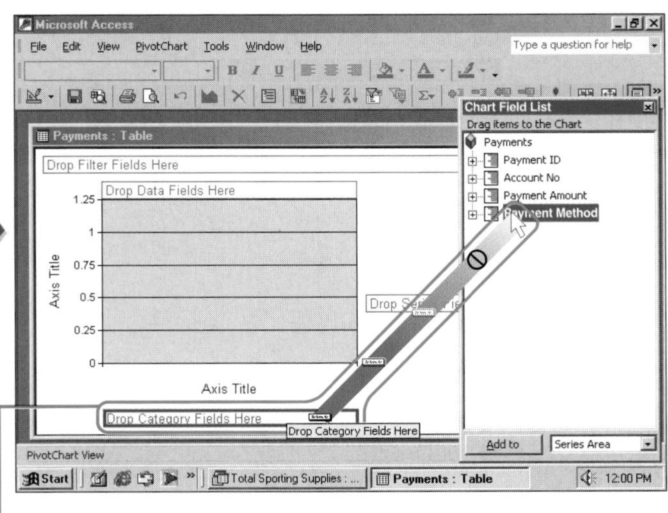

3 To add a field that contains categories for the chart, position the mouse over the name of the field in the Chart Field List dialog box. Then drag the field name to the Category area.

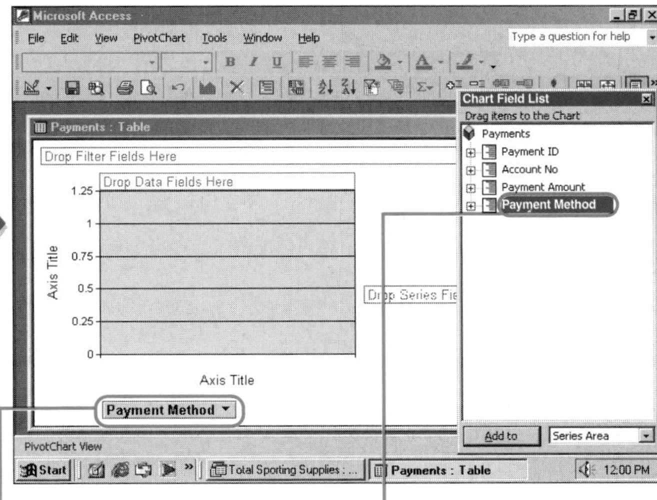

■ The name of the field appears in the Category area.

■ The name of the field in the Chart Field List dialog box appears in bold.

CONTINUED

USING THE PIVOTCHART VIEW

You can select the field containing the data you want to summarize in the PivotChart view.

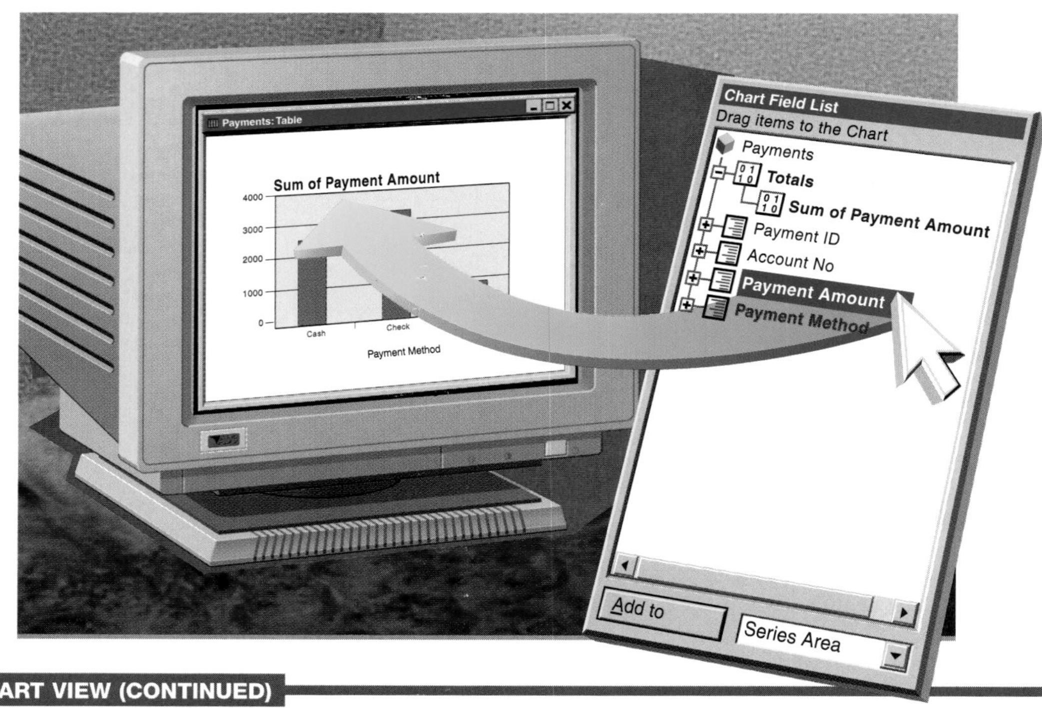

Summarizing data in the PivotChart view does not affect the table that contains the data.

You cannot edit data in the PivotChart view.

USING THE PIVOTCHART VIEW (CONTINUED)

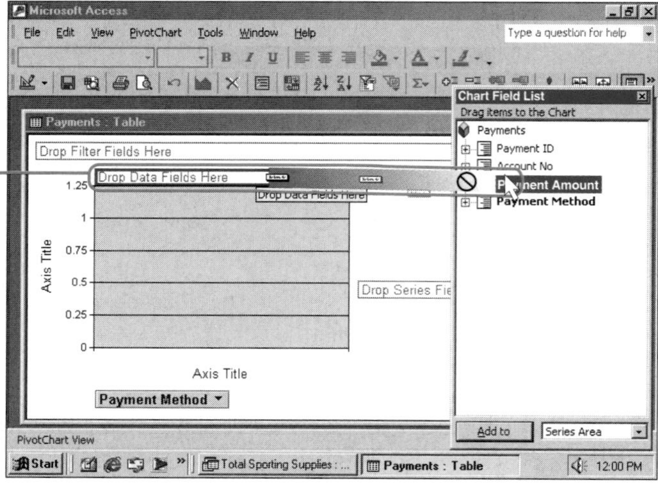

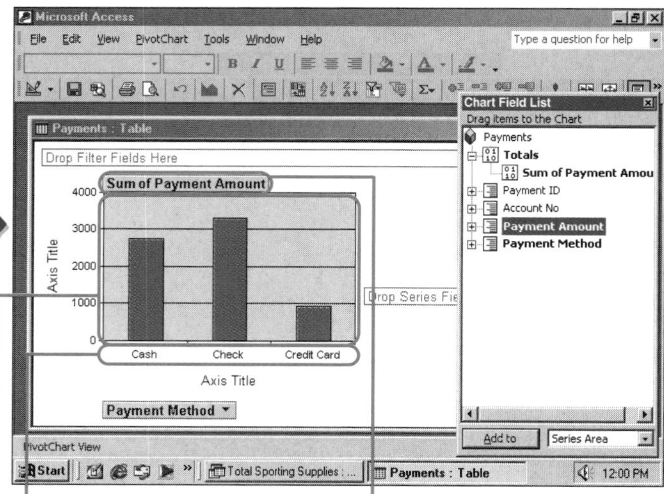

4 To add a field that contains data you want to summarize in the chart, position the mouse over the name of the field in the Chart Field List dialog box. Then drag the field name to the Data area.

■ The categories for the chart appear in this area.

■ The summarized data from the field you selected in step **4** appears in this area.

■ Access performs a calculation to summarize the data in the chart.

■ The type of calculation Access performed and the name of the field you selected in step **4** appear in the Data area.

Can I remove a field from the PivotChart view?

You can remove a field from the Category or Data area in the PivotChart view. Removing a field from the PivotChart view does not delete the field from the table.

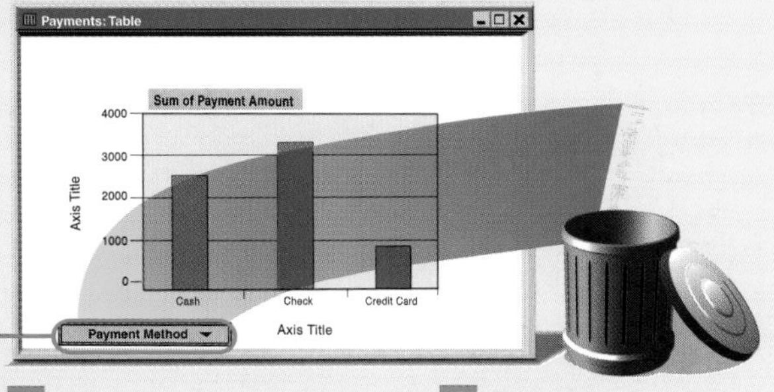

1 Click the name of the field you want to remove from the PivotChart view.

■ The field name appears highlighted.

2 Press the Delete key.

■ The field disappears from the PivotChart view.

How can I move the Chart Field List dialog box so it is not covering my chart?

To move the Chart Field List dialog box, position the mouse over the title bar and then drag the dialog box to a new location.

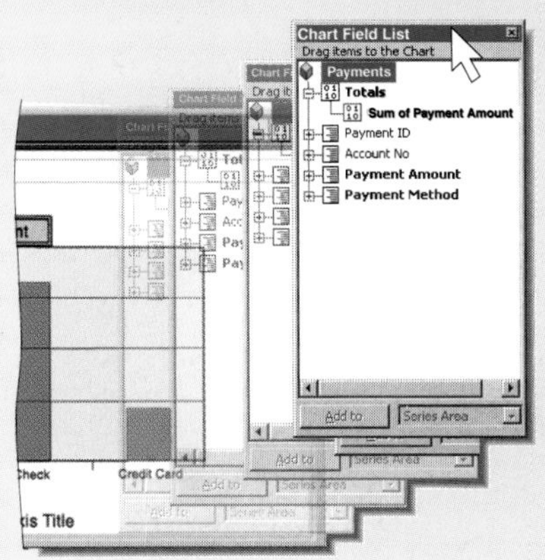

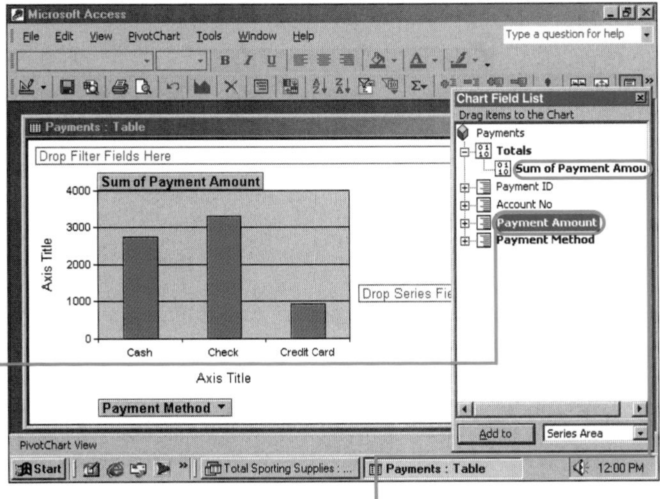

■ The name of the field you selected in step 4 appears in bold in the Chart Field List dialog box.

■ The type of calculation Access performed is also displayed in the Chart Field List dialog box.

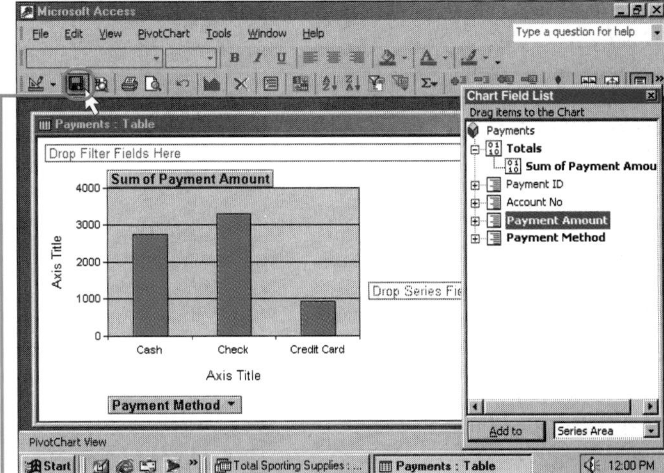

SAVE THE PIVOTCHART VIEW LAYOUT

1 Click to save the layout of the PivotChart view.

■ The next time you display the table in the PivotChart view, the fields in the table will appear in the layout you saved.

Note: When you display a form in the PivotChart view, the layout you create is automatically saved.

You can create relationships between tables. Relationships allow you to bring together related information in your database.

Relationships between tables are essential for creating a form, query or report that uses information from more than one table in your database.

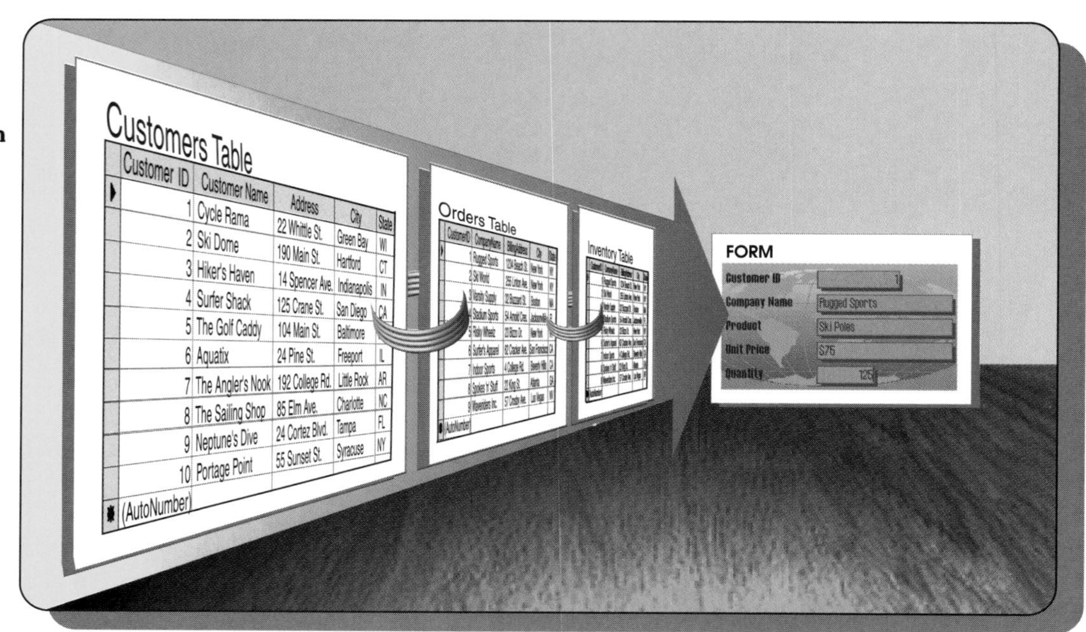

CREATE RELATIONSHIPS BETWEEN TABLES

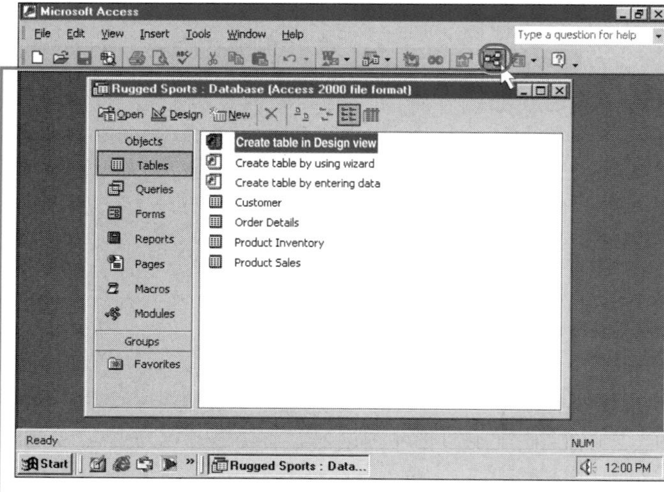

1 Click [icon] to display the Relationships window.

Note: If [icon] is not available, make sure the Database window is displayed and you do not have any other windows open on your screen. You can press the F11 key to display the Database window.

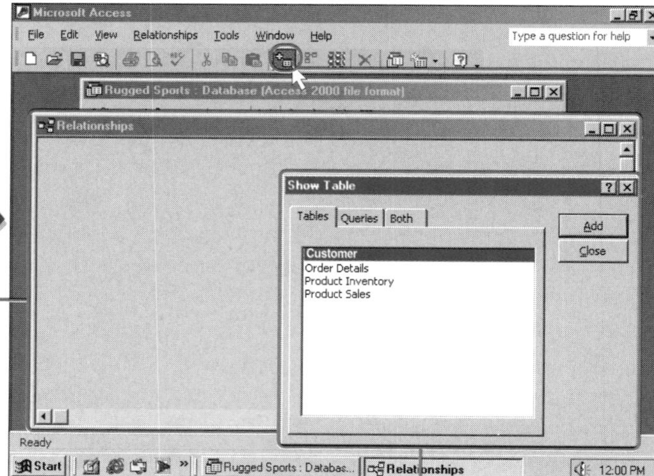

■ The Relationships window appears. If any relationships exist between the tables in your database, a box for each table appears in the window.

■ The Show Table dialog box may also appear, listing all the tables in your database.

2 If the Show Table dialog box does not appear, click [icon] to display the dialog box.

Why do relationships already exist between tables in my database?

If you used the Database Wizard to create your database, the wizard automatically created relationships between tables for you. For information on the Database Wizard, see page 256.

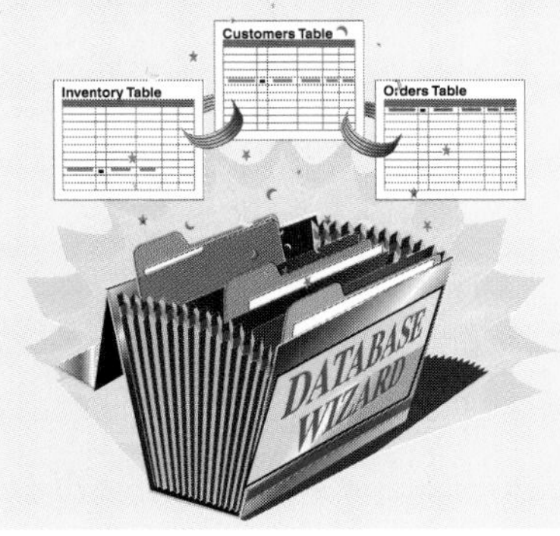

I accidentally added a table to the Relationships window. How do I remove the table from the window?

If you accidentally added a table to the Relationships window while performing the steps below, you can easily remove the table. Click the box for the table you want to remove and then press the Delete key. Removing a table from the Relationships window does not delete the table from the database.

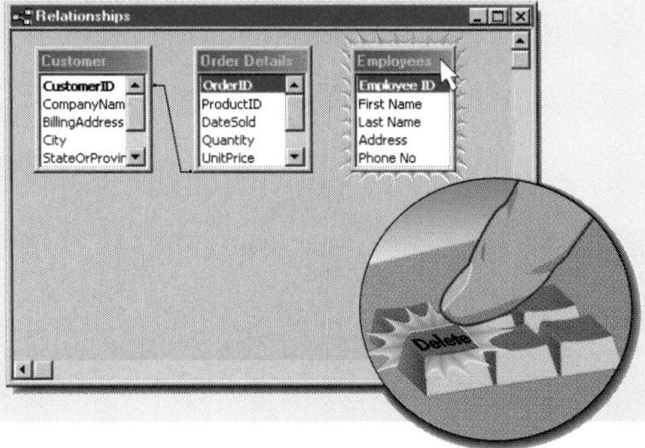

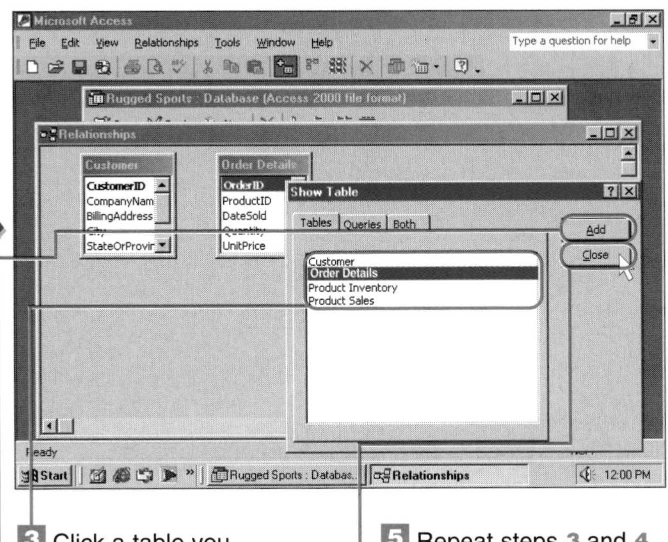

3 Click a table you want to add to the Relationships window.

4 Click **Add** to add the table to the window.

5 Repeat steps 3 and 4 for each table you want to add.

6 When you finish adding tables to the Relationships window, click **Close** to remove the Show Table dialog box.

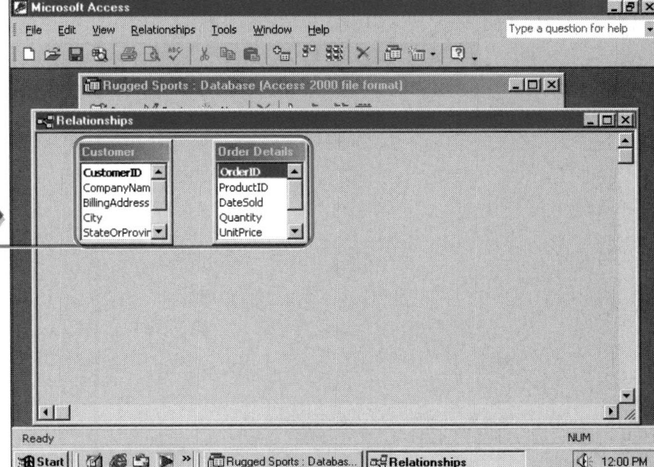

■ The Relationships window displays a box for each table. Each box displays the fields for one table.

■ The primary key for each table appears in **bold**. The primary key uniquely identifies each record in a table.

CONTINUED

CREATE RELATIONSHIPS BETWEEN TABLES

You create a relationship between tables by identifying the matching fields in the tables.

You will usually relate the primary key in one table to a matching field in the other table. The fields must use the same data type and contain the same kind of information. For information on data types, see page 290. In most cases, the fields will have the same name.

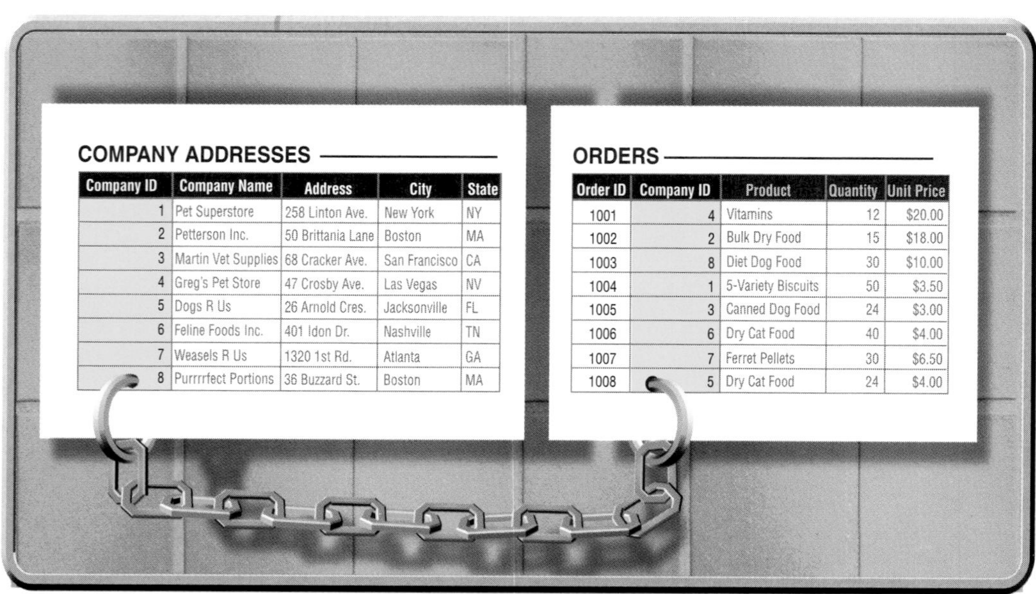

COMPANY ADDRESSES

Company ID	Company Name	Address	City	State
1	Pet Superstore	258 Linton Ave.	New York	NY
2	Petterson Inc.	50 Brittania Lane	Boston	MA
3	Martin Vet Supplies	68 Cracker Ave.	San Francisco	CA
4	Greg's Pet Store	47 Crosby Ave.	Las Vegas	NV
5	Dogs R Us	26 Arnold Cres.	Jacksonville	FL
6	Feline Foods Inc.	401 Idon Dr.	Nashville	TN
7	Weasels R Us	1320 1st Rd.	Atlanta	GA
8	Purrrrfect Portions	36 Buzzard St.	Boston	MA

ORDERS

Order ID	Company ID	Product	Quantity	Unit Price
1001	4	Vitamins	12	$20.00
1002	2	Bulk Dry Food	15	$18.00
1003	8	Diet Dog Food	30	$10.00
1004	1	5-Variety Biscuits	50	$3.50
1005	3	Canned Dog Food	24	$3.00
1006	6	Dry Cat Food	40	$4.00
1007	7	Ferret Pellets	30	$6.50
1008	5	Dry Cat Food	24	$4.00

CREATE RELATIONSHIPS BETWEEN TABLES (CONTINUED)

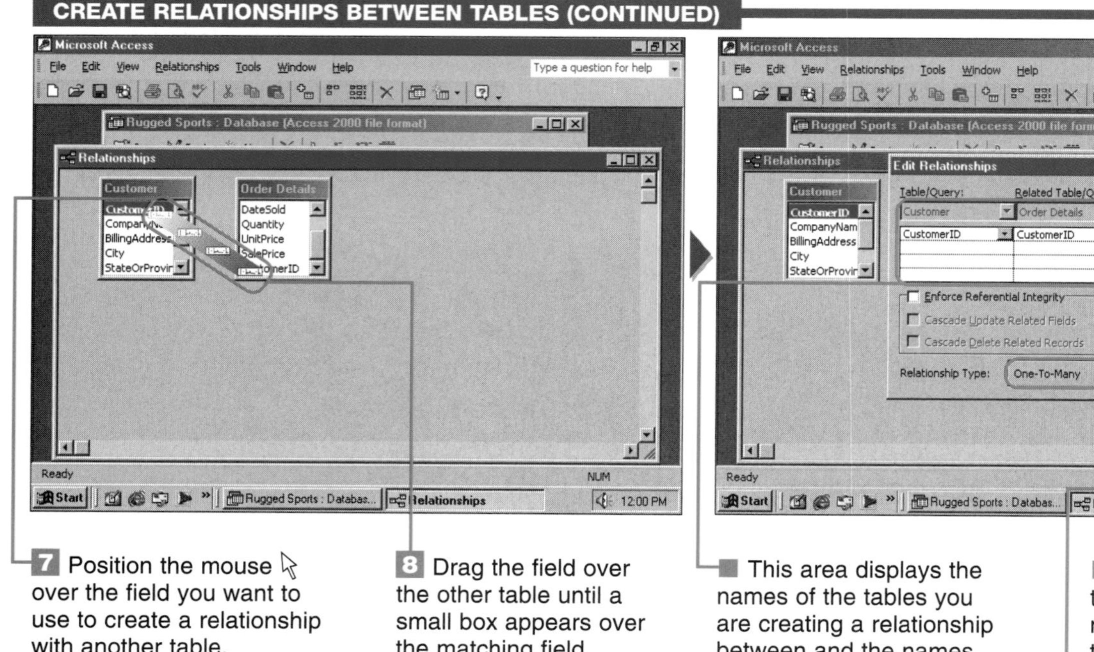

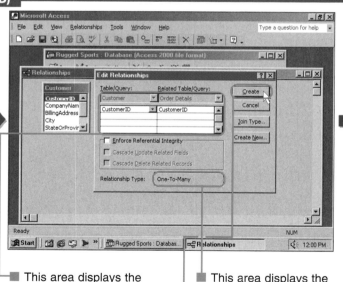

7 Position the mouse over the field you want to use to create a relationship with another table.

8 Drag the field over the other table until a small box appears over the matching field.

■ The Edit Relationships dialog box appears.

■ This area displays the names of the tables you are creating a relationship between and the names of the matching fields.

■ This area displays the type of relationship. For more information, see the top of page 303.

9 Click **Create** to create the relationship.

What types of relationships can I create between tables?

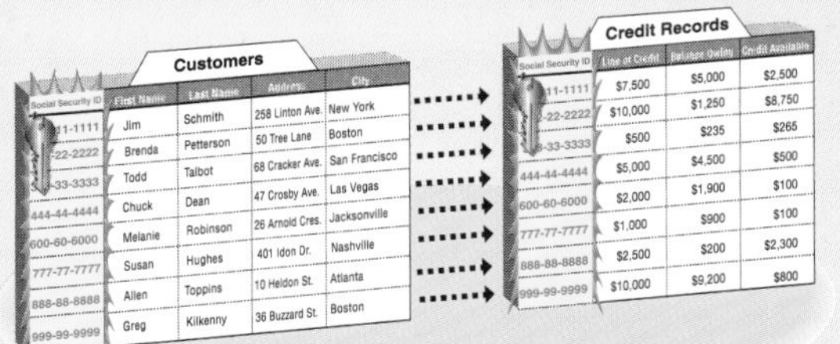

One-to-One

Each record in a table relates to one record in another table. For example, each customer has only one credit record. You create a one-to-one relationship by relating the primary key in one table to the primary key in another table.

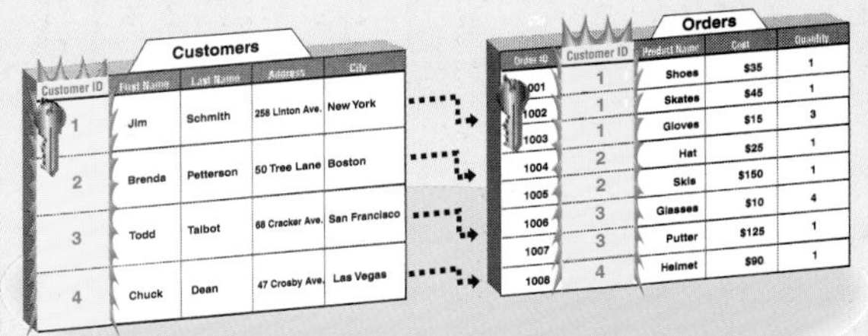

One-to-Many

Each record in a table relates to one or more records in another table. This is the most common type of relationship. For example, each customer can have more than one order. You create a one-to-many relationship by relating the primary key in one table to a matching field in another table.

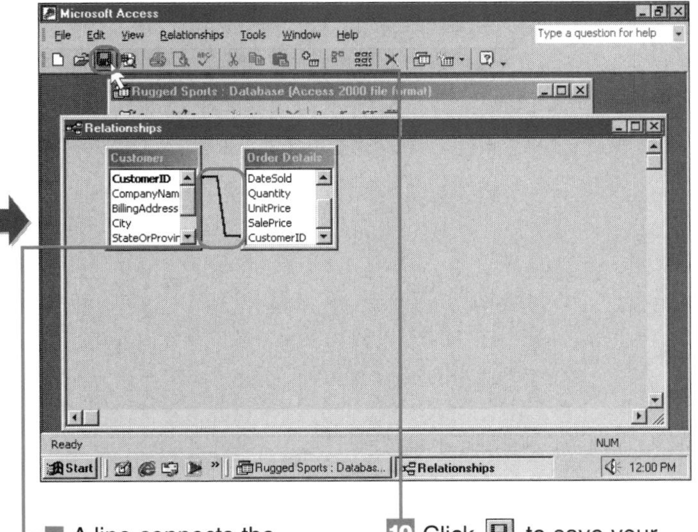

- A line connects the fields in the two tables to show the relationship.

10 Click the Save button to save your changes.

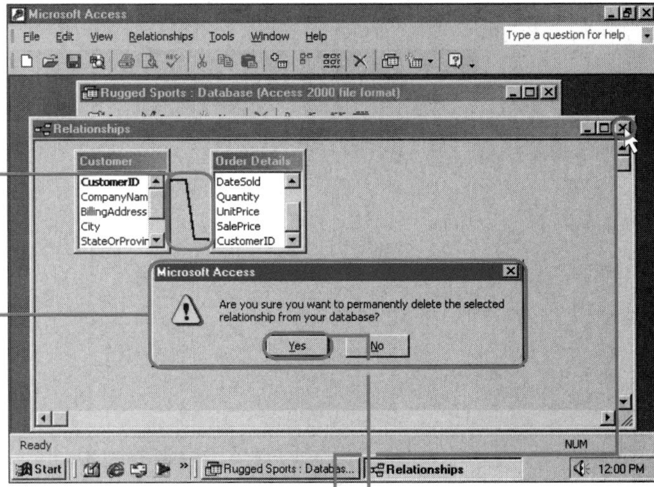

DELETE A RELATIONSHIP

1 Click the line for the relationship you want to delete.

2 Press the Delete key.

- A warning dialog box appears, confirming the deletion.

3 Click **Yes** to permanently delete the relationship.

- When you finish working in the Relationships window, click the Close button to close the window.

CREATE A FORM

You can use the Form Wizard to create a form that suits your needs. The wizard asks you a series of questions and then sets up a form based on your answers.

A form presents data from a table in an attractive, easy-to-use format. You can use a form to view, change, add or delete data in a table. Many people find forms easier to work with than tables.

CREATE A FORM

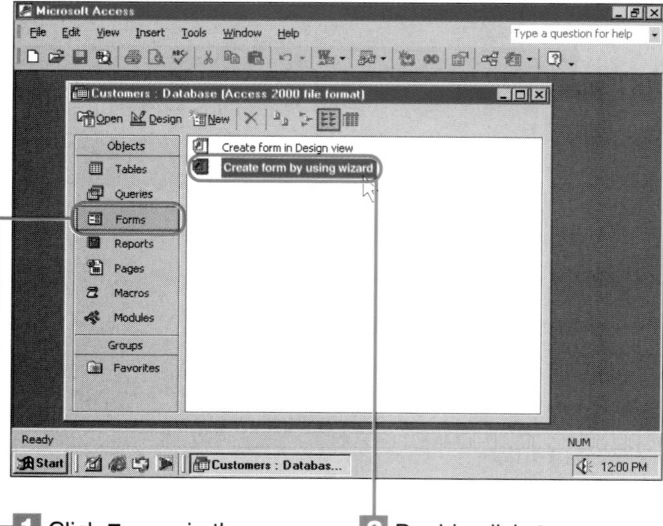

1 Click **Forms** in the Database window.

2 Double-click **Create form by using wizard**.

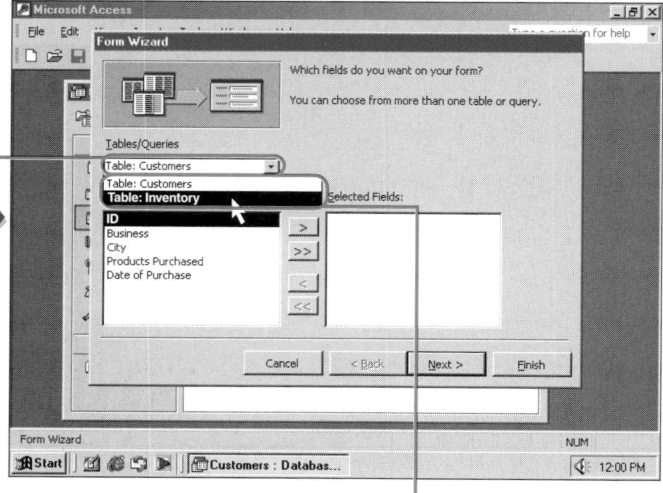

■ The Form Wizard appears.

3 Click ▾ in this area to display a list of tables in your database.

4 Click the table that contains the fields you want to include in your form.

In what order will the fields I select appear in my form?

The order you select the fields in the Form Wizard determines the order the fields will appear in the form. Make sure you select the fields in the order you want them to appear in your form.

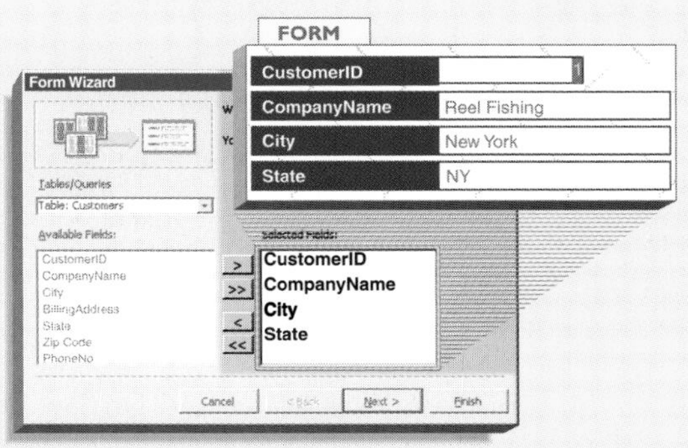

Can I create a form that includes fields from more than one table?

Yes. Perform steps 1 to 5 below to select the fields you want to include from one table. Then repeat steps 3 to 5 until you have selected all the fields you want to include in the form. When creating a form that uses fields from more than one table, the tables must be related. For information on relationships, see page 300.

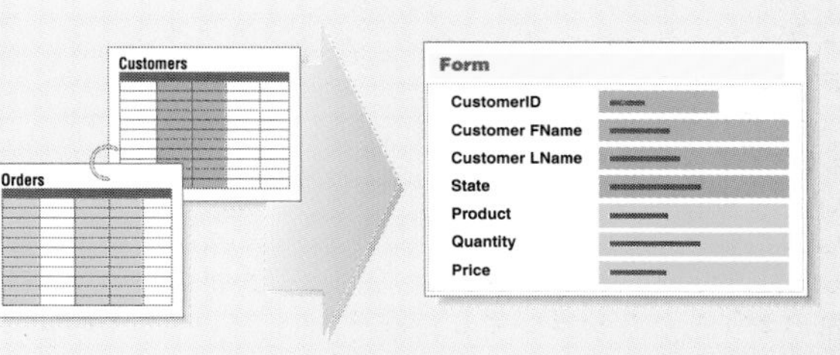

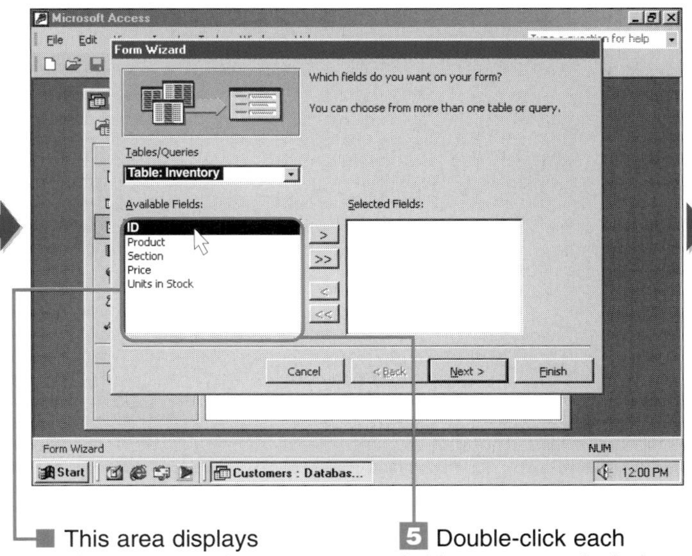

■ This area displays the fields in the table you selected.

5 Double-click each field you want to include in your form.

Note: To add all the fields at once, click >> .

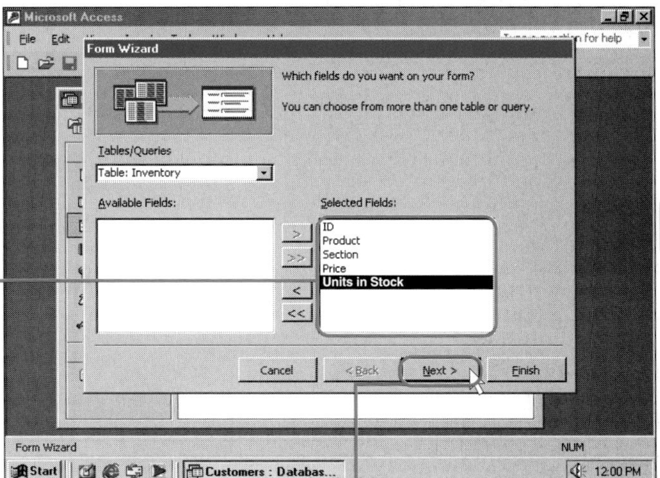

■ Each field you select appears in this area.

6 To remove a field you accidentally selected, double-click the field in this area.

Note: To remove all the fields at once, click << .

7 Click **Next** to continue.

CONTINUED

CREATE A FORM

When creating a form, you can choose from several different layouts. The layout of a form determines the arrangement of information on the form.

The Columnar and Justified layouts display one record at a time. The Tabular and Datasheet layouts display multiple records at a time.

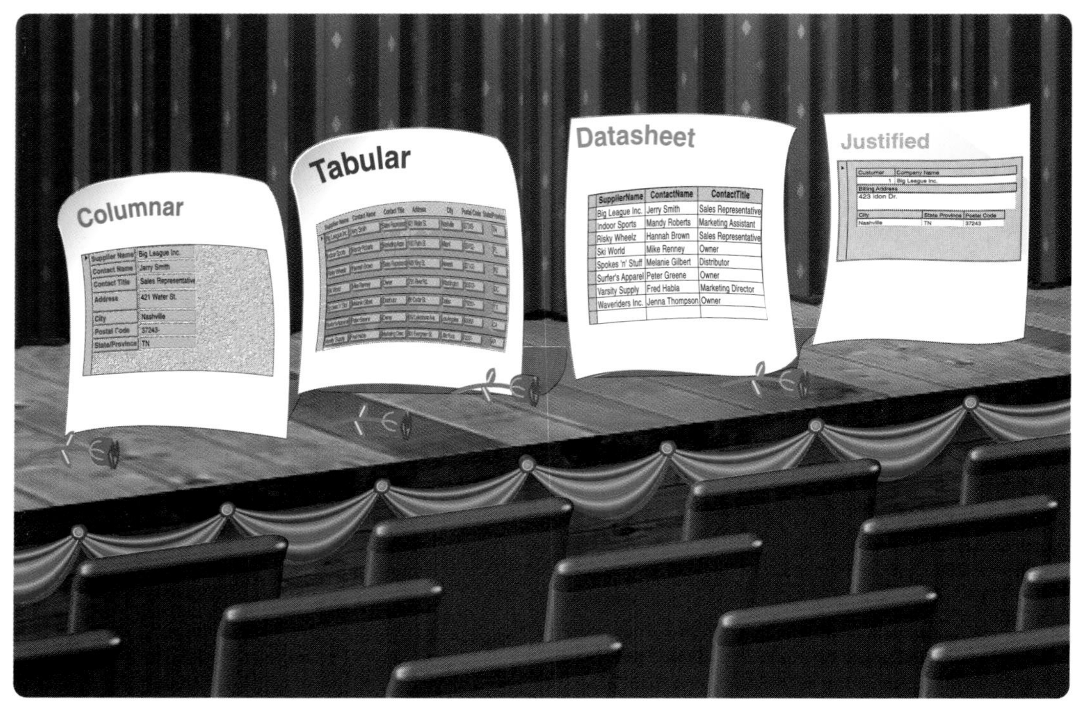

CREATE A FORM (CONTINUED)

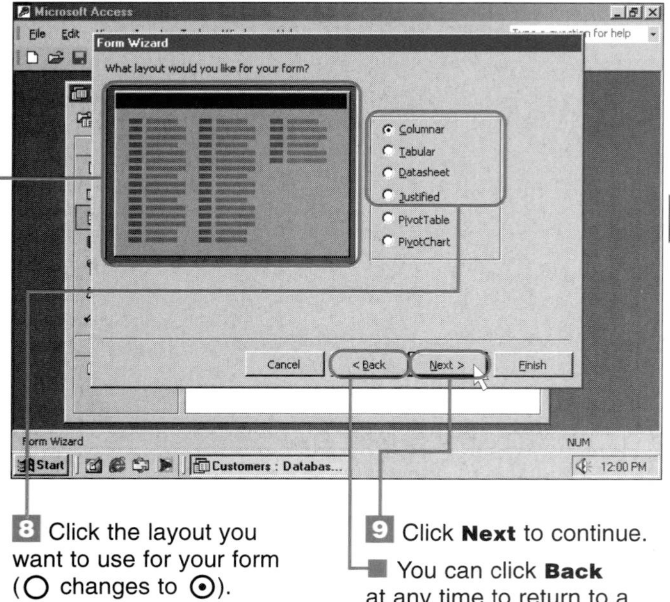

8 Click the layout you want to use for your form (○ changes to ⊙).

■ This area displays a sample of the layout you selected.

9 Click **Next** to continue.

■ You can click **Back** at any time to return to a previous step and change your answers.

10 Click the style you want to use for your form.

■ This area displays a sample of the style you selected.

11 Click **Next** to continue.

What are the PivotTable and PivotChart layouts used for?

The PivotTable and PivotChart layouts are special views that you can use to analyze the data in your form. The PivotTable view allows you to re-organize and summarize the data in your form. For information on using the PivotTable view, see page 292. The PivotChart view allows you to display a graphical summary of the data in your form. For information on using the PivotChart view, see page 296.

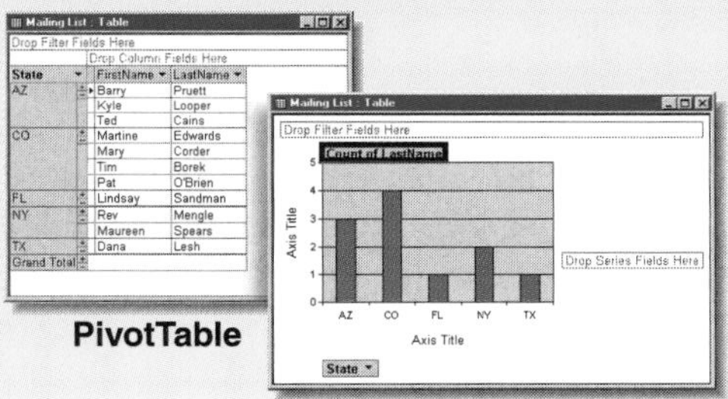

PivotTable

PivotChart

How do I delete a form from my database?

Each form you create appears in the Database window. If you no longer need a form, you can permanently delete the form from your database.

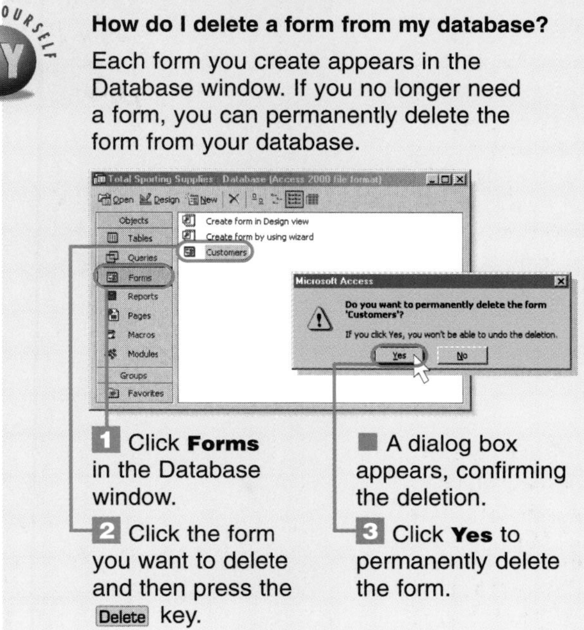

1 Click **Forms** in the Database window.

2 Click the form you want to delete and then press the Delete key.

■ A dialog box appears, confirming the deletion.

3 Click **Yes** to permanently delete the form.

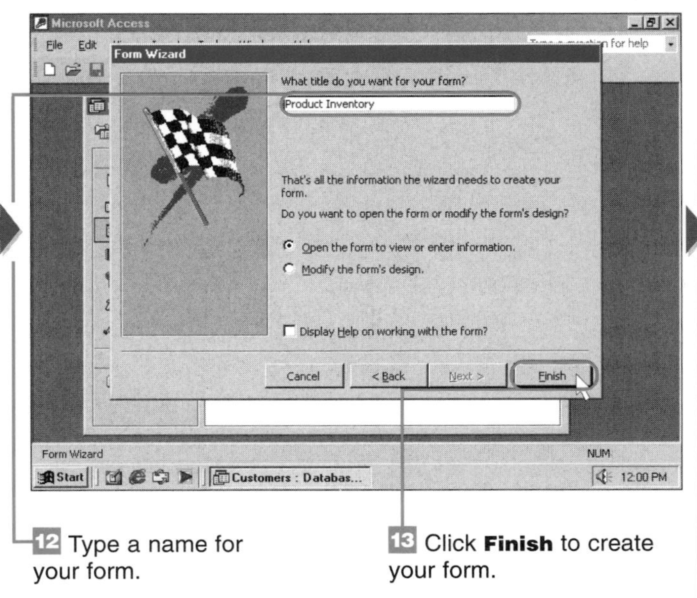

12 Type a name for your form.

13 Click **Finish** to create your form.

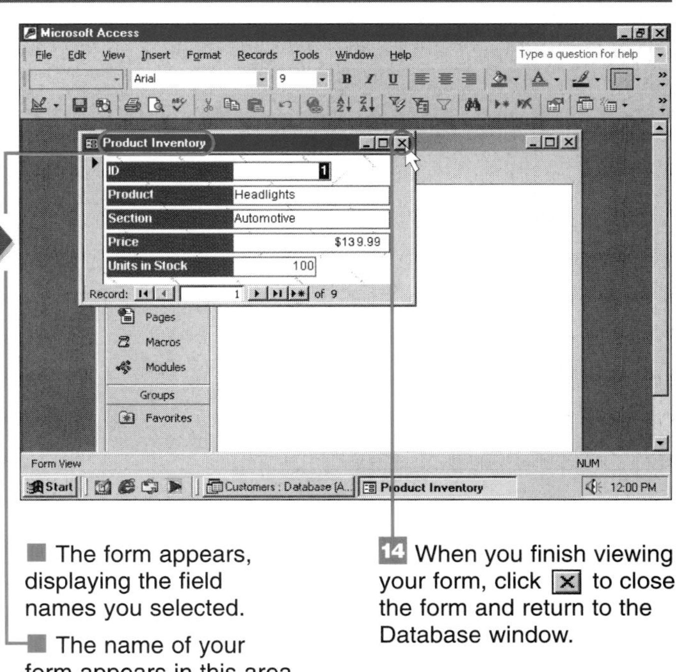

■ The form appears, displaying the field names you selected.

■ The name of your form appears in this area.

14 When you finish viewing your form, click ☒ to close the form and return to the Database window.

MOVE THROUGH RECORDS

You can move through the records in a form to review or edit information.

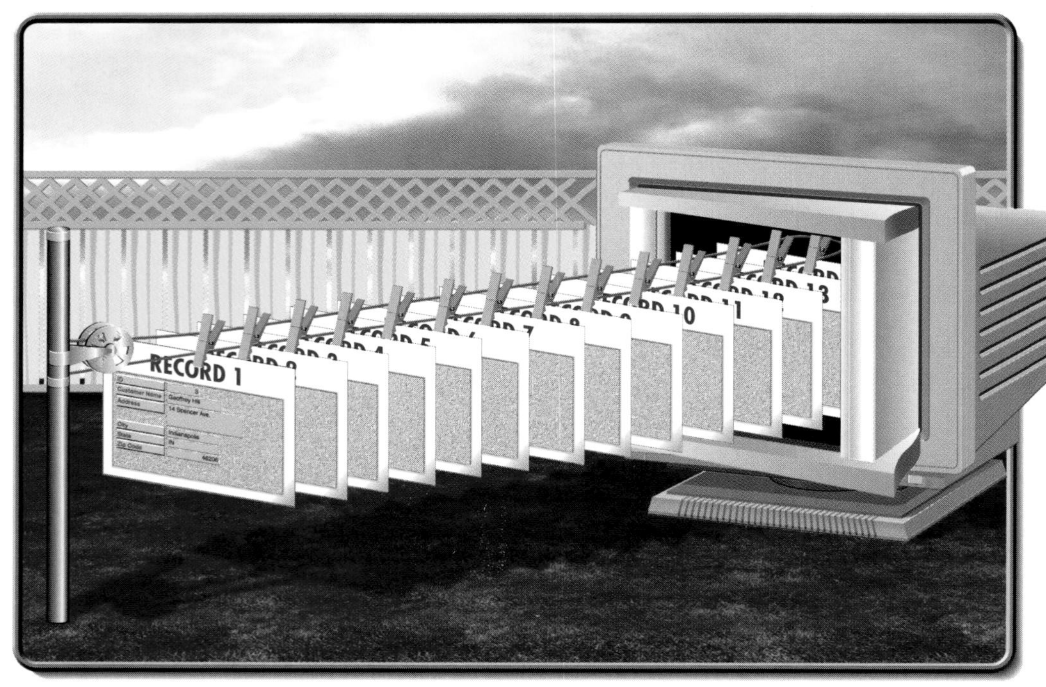

MOVE THROUGH RECORDS

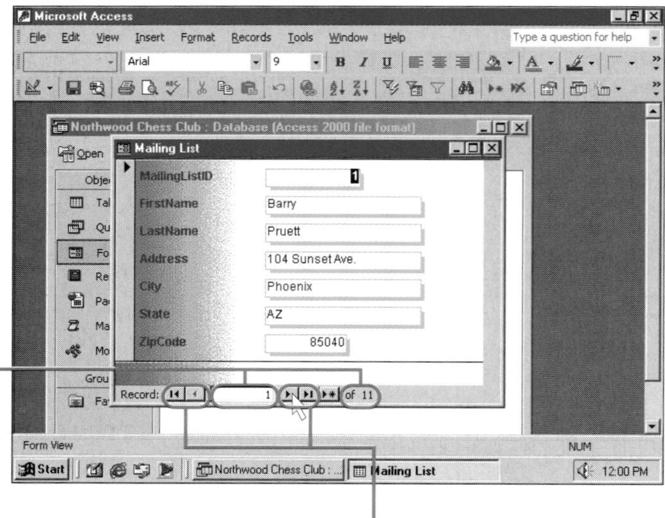

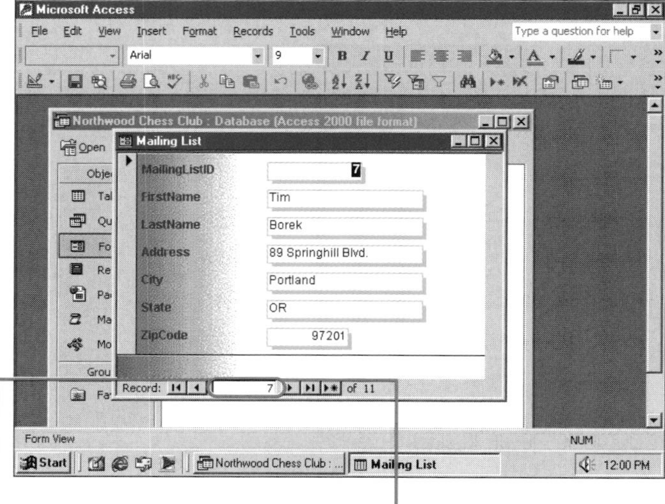

■ This area displays the number of the current record and the total number of records.

1 To move to another record, click one of the following buttons.

- ⏮ First record
- ◀ Previous record
- ▶ Next record
- ⏭ Last record

MOVE TO A SPECIFIC RECORD

1 Drag the mouse I over the number of the current record.

2 Type the number of the record you want to move to and then press the Enter key.

EDIT DATA

You can edit data displayed in a form to correct a mistake or update the data.

When you change data in a form, Access will also change the data in the table you used to create the form.

Access automatically saves changes you make to data in a form.

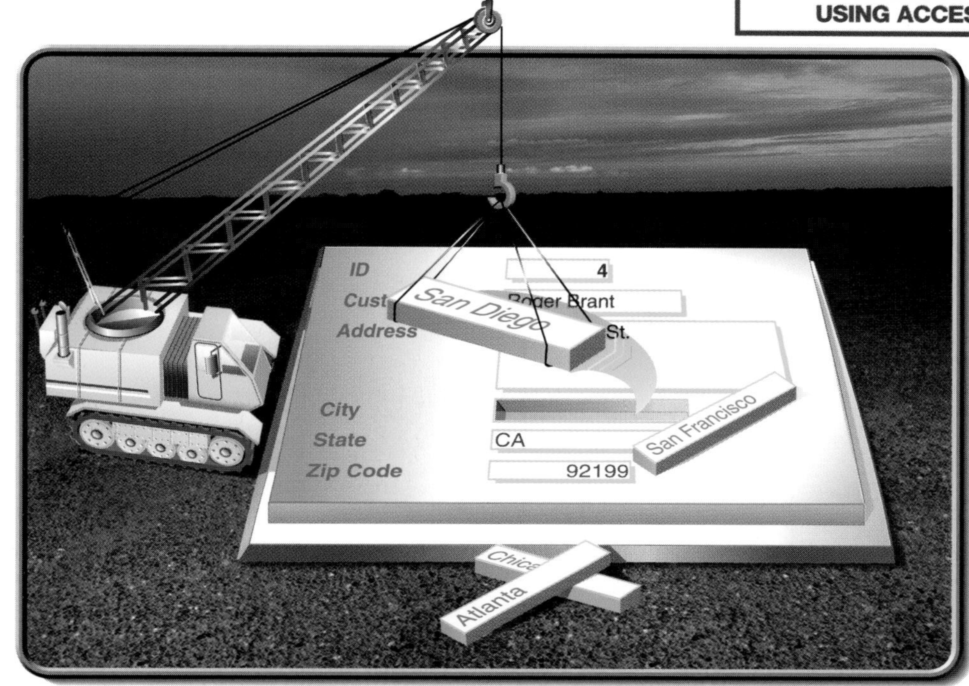

EDIT DATA

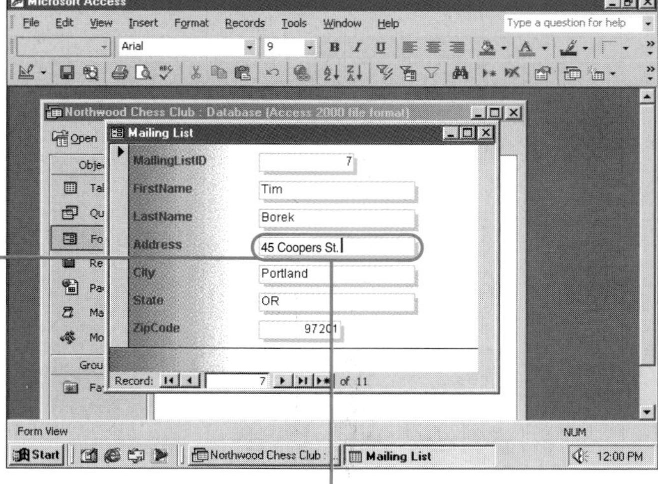

1 Click the location in the field where you want to edit data.

■ A flashing insertion point appears in the field.

Note: You can press the ← or → key to move the insertion point.

2 To remove the character to the left of the flashing insertion point, press the ←Backspace key.

3 To add data where the insertion point flashes on your screen, type the data.

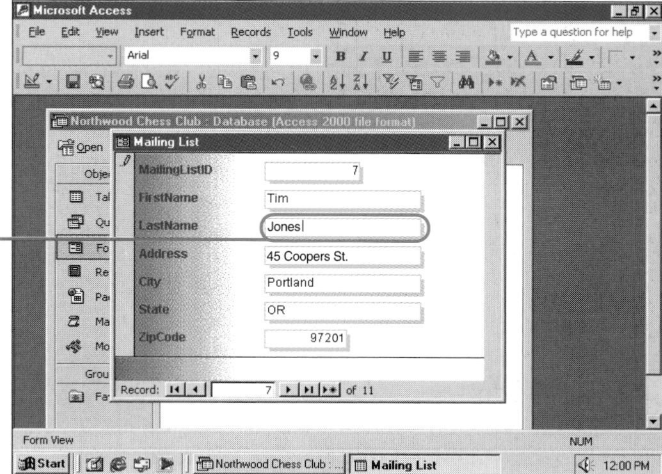

REPLACE ALL DATA IN A CELL

1 Drag the mouse I over the data until you highlight all the data in the field.

2 Type the new data.

■ The data you type replaces the data in the field.

ADD A RECORD

You can use a form to add a record to your database. For example, you may want to add a record to include information about a new client.

When you use a form to add a record, Access adds the record to the table you used to create the form.

ADD A RECORD

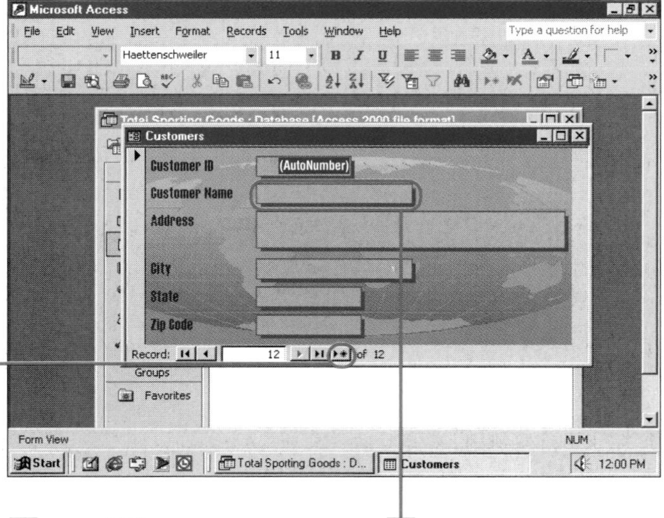

1 Click ▶* to add a record.

■ A blank form appears.

2 Click the first empty field in the form.

3 Type the data that corresponds to the field and then press the Tab key to move to the next field.

■ In this example, the AutoNumber field automatically adds a number for the new record.

4 Repeat step 3 until you finish entering all the data for the record.

■ Access automatically saves each new record you add using the form.

DELETE A RECORD

You can delete a record displayed in a form to permanently remove information you no longer need. For example, you may want to remove information about a product you no longer manufacture.

Deleting records saves storage space on your computer and keeps your database from becoming cluttered with unnecessary information.

When you delete a record displayed in a form, Access deletes the record from the table you used to create the form.

DELETE A RECORD

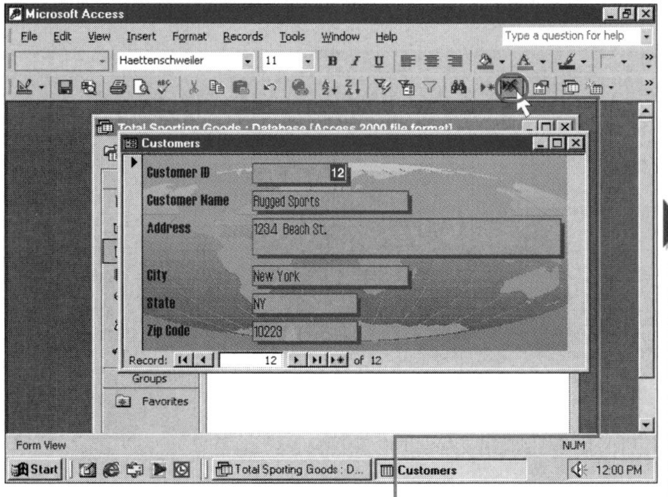

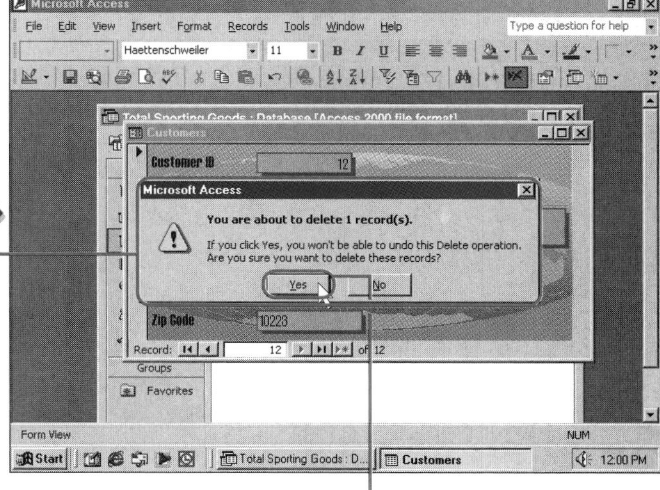

1 Display the record you want to delete.

2 Click [delete record icon] to delete the record.

■ The record disappears from the form.

■ A warning dialog box appears, confirming the deletion.

3 Click **Yes** to permanently delete the record.

SORT RECORDS

You can change the order of records in a table, in a form or in the results of a query. This can help you find, organize and analyze data.

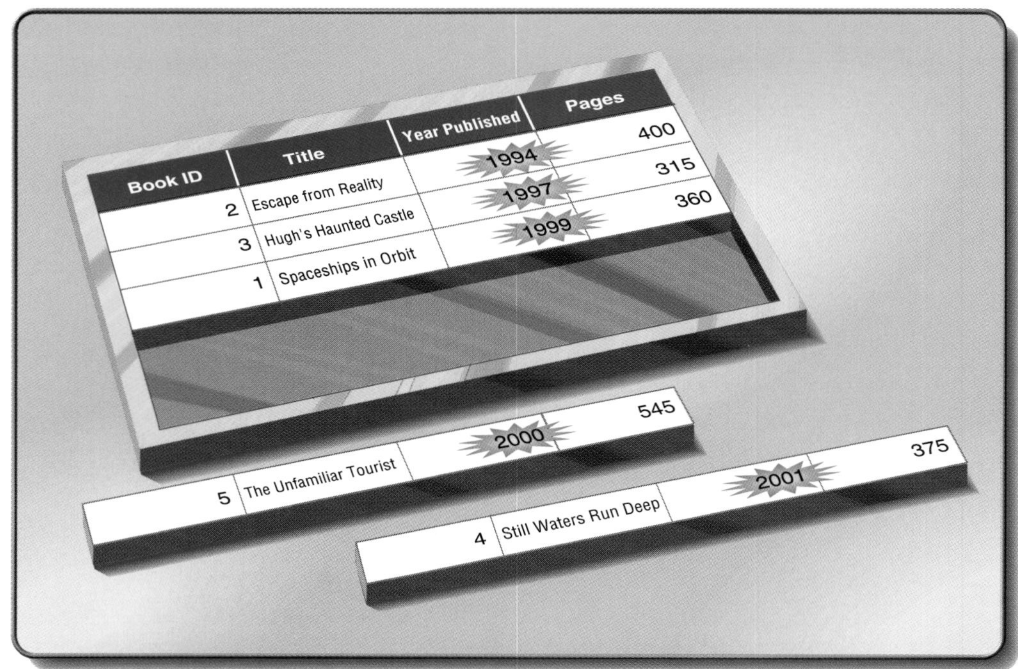

SORT RECORDS

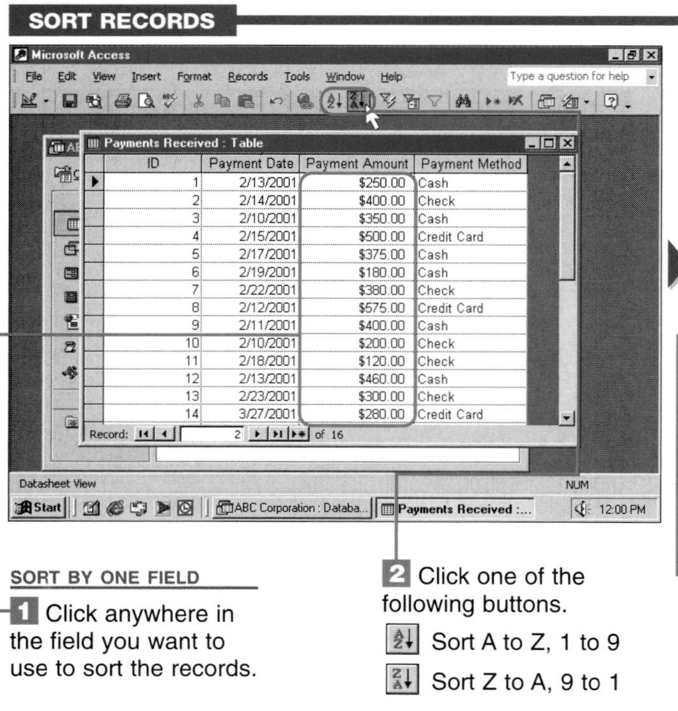

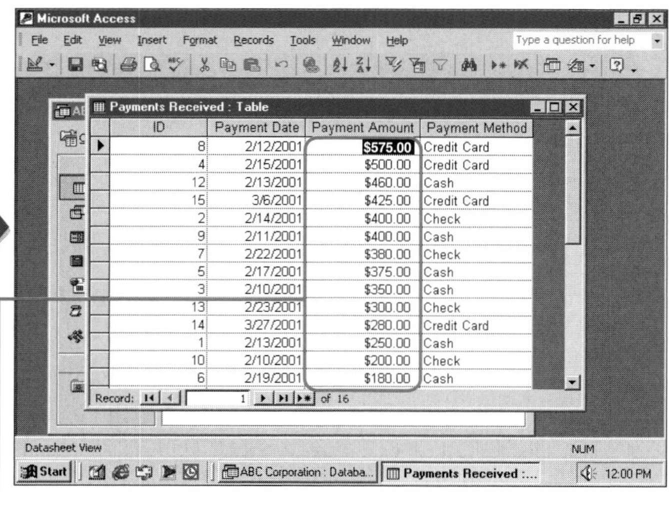

SORT BY ONE FIELD

1 Click anywhere in the field you want to use to sort the records.

2 Click one of the following buttons.

- Sort A to Z, 1 to 9
- Sort Z to A, 9 to 1

■ The records appear in the new order. In this example, the records are sorted by payment amount.

How do I remove a sort from my records?

After sorting records, you can return your records to the original sort order at any time.

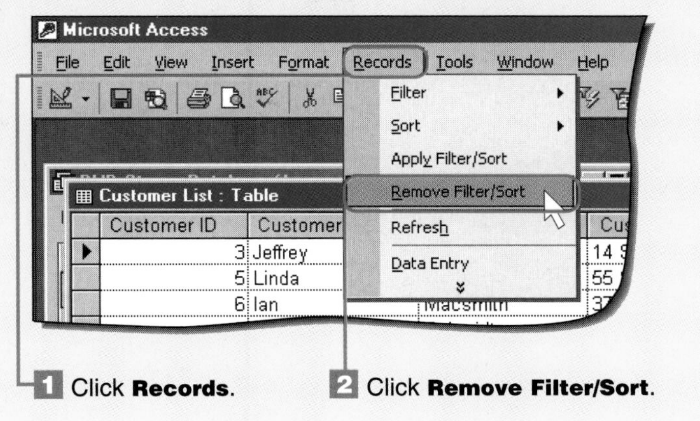

1 Click **Records**.

2 Click **Remove Filter/Sort**.

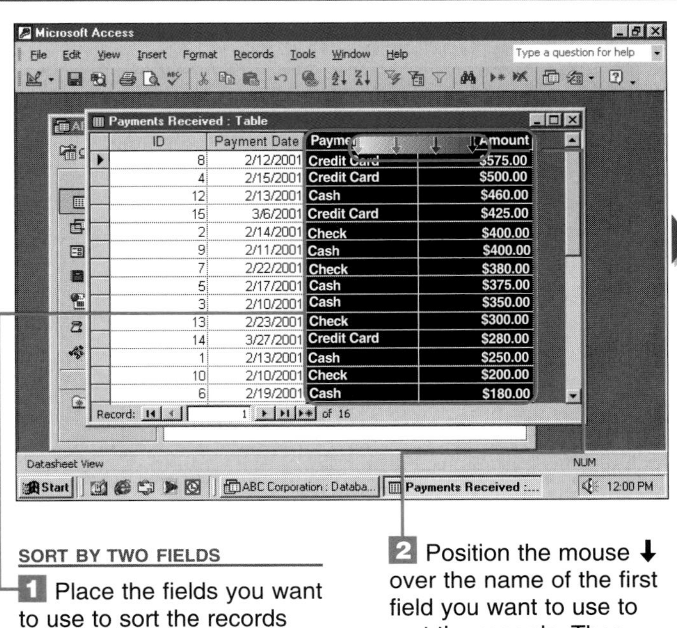

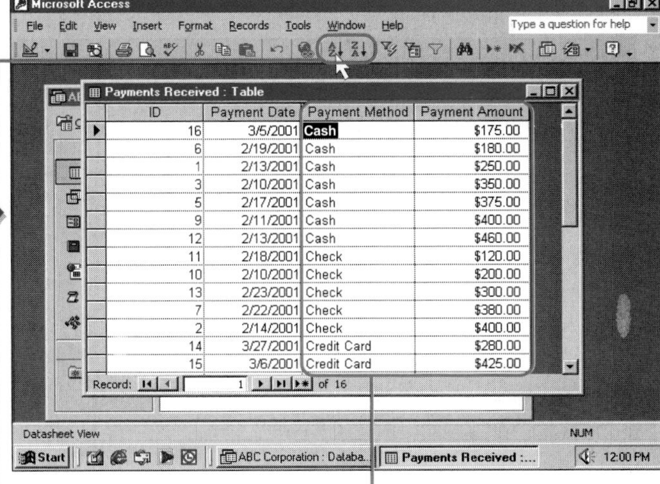

SORT BY TWO FIELDS

1 Place the fields you want to use to sort the records side by side and in the order you want to perform the sort. To re-arrange fields, see page 273.

2 Position the mouse ↓ over the name of the first field you want to use to sort the records. Then drag the mouse ↓ until you highlight the second field.

3 Click one of the following buttons.

Sort A to Z, 1 to 9

Sort Z to A, 9 to 1

■ The records appear in the new order. In this example, the records are sorted by payment method. All records with the same payment method are also sorted by payment amount.

FIND DATA

You can search for data in a table, in a form or in the results of a query.

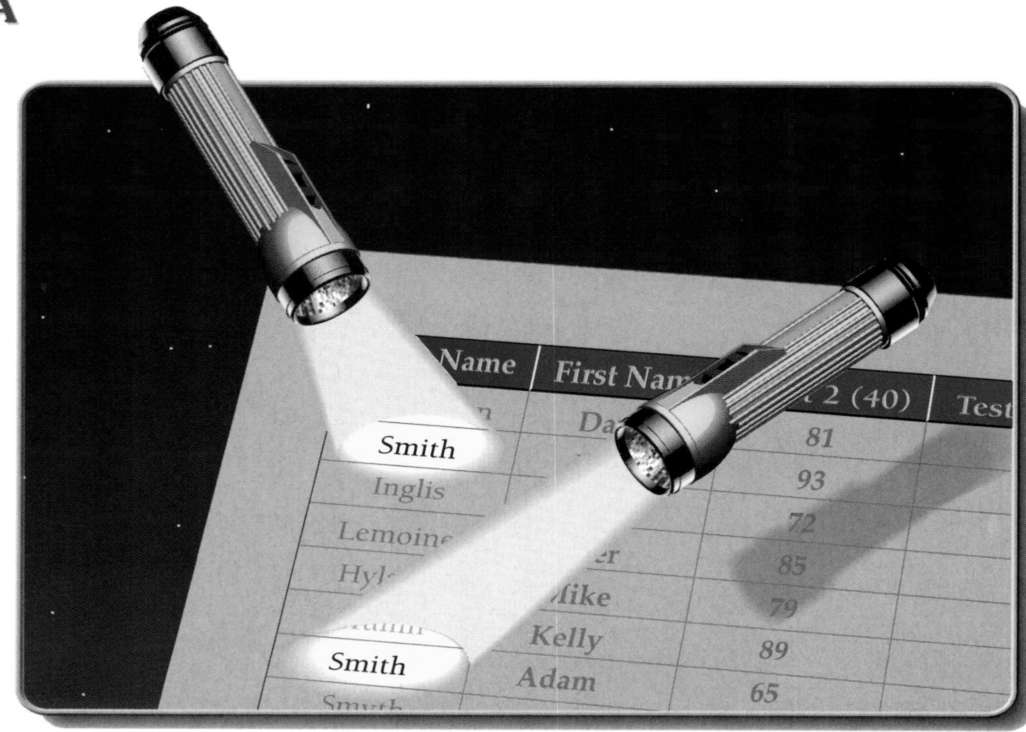

FIND DATA

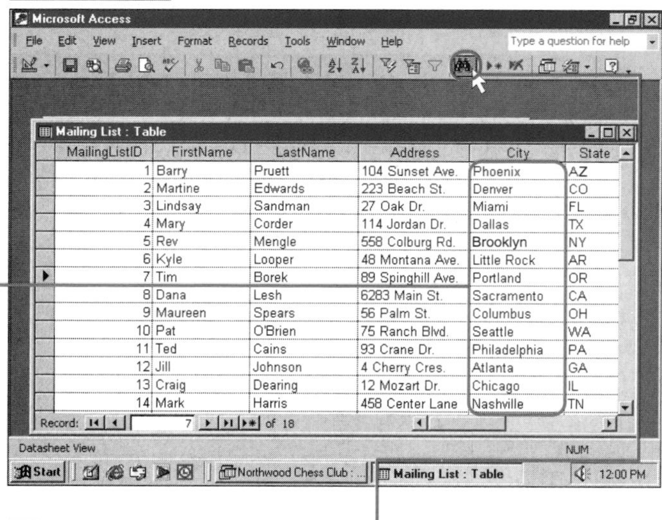

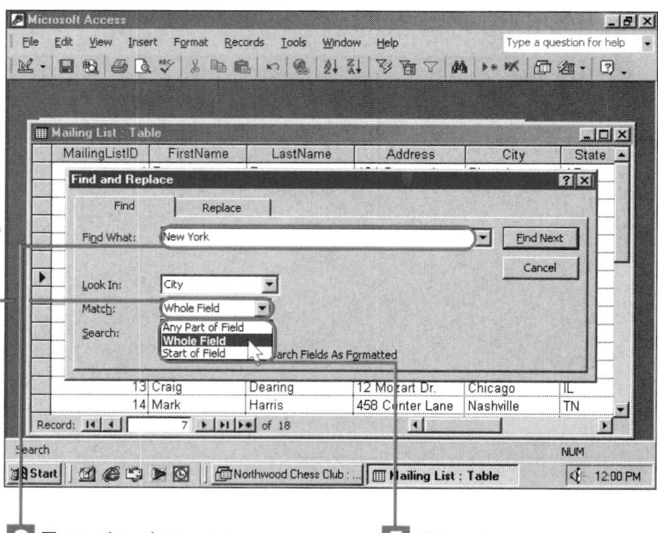

1 Click anywhere in the field that contains the data you want to find.

2 Click 🔍 to find the data.

■ The Find and Replace dialog box appears.

3 Type the data you want to find.

4 To specify how you want to search for the data, click this area.

5 Click the way you want to search for the data.

Note: For information on the ways you can search for data, see the top of page 315.

How can Access search for data in a field?

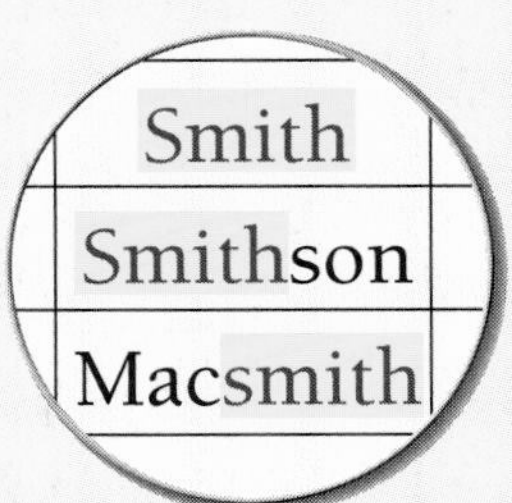

Any Part of Field

Finds data anywhere in the field. For example, a search for **smith** finds **Smith**, **Smithson** and **Macsmith**.

Whole Field

Finds data that is exactly the same as the data you specify. For example, a search for **smith** finds **Smith**, but not **Smithson** or **Macsmith**.

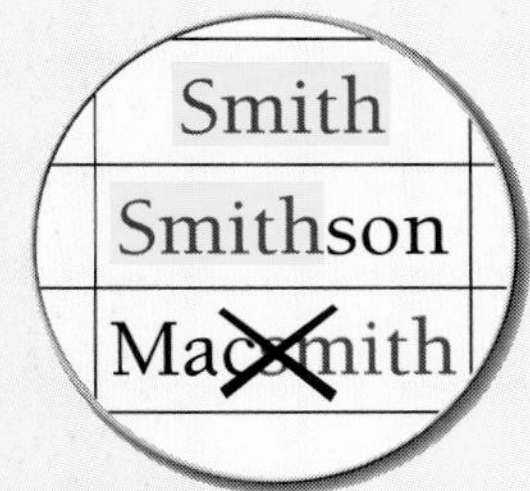

Start of Field

Finds data only at the beginning of the field. For example, a search for **smith** finds **Smith** and **Smithson**, but not **Macsmith**.

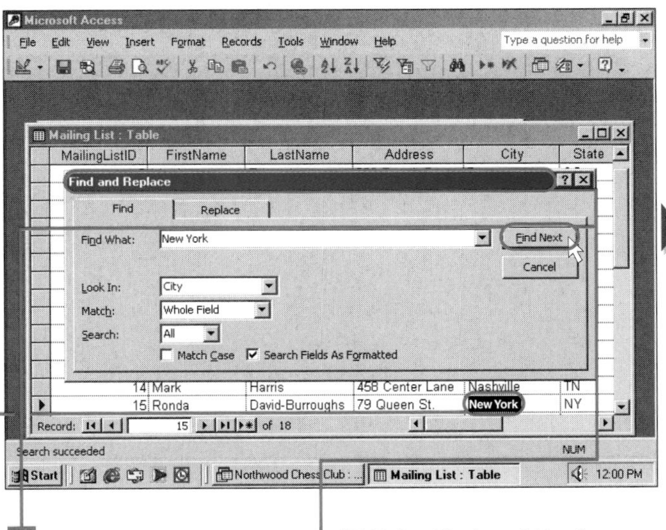

6 Click **Find Next** to start the search.

■ Access highlights the first instance of matching data in the field.

■ If the Find and Replace dialog box covers the highlighted data, position the mouse over the title bar and then drag the dialog box to a new location.

7 Click **Find Next** to find the next instance of matching data in the field.

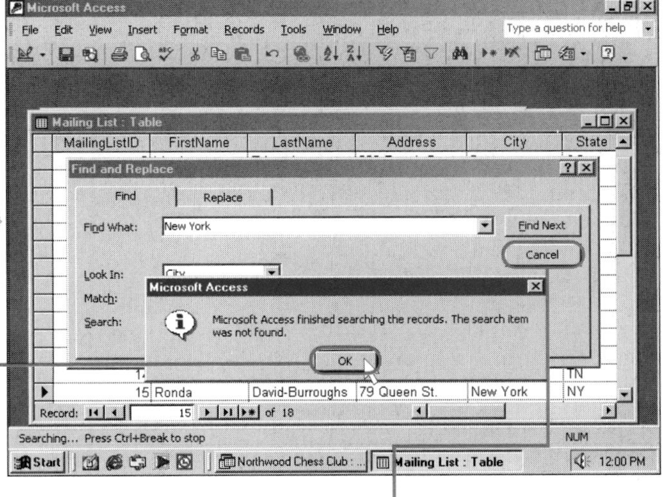

8 Repeat step 7 until a dialog box appears, telling you the search is complete.

9 Click **OK** to close the dialog box.

10 Click **Cancel** to close the Find and Replace dialog box.

FILTER DATA BY SELECTION

You can filter data in a table, in a form or in the results of a query to display only records containing data of interest. Filtering data can help you review and analyze information in your database.

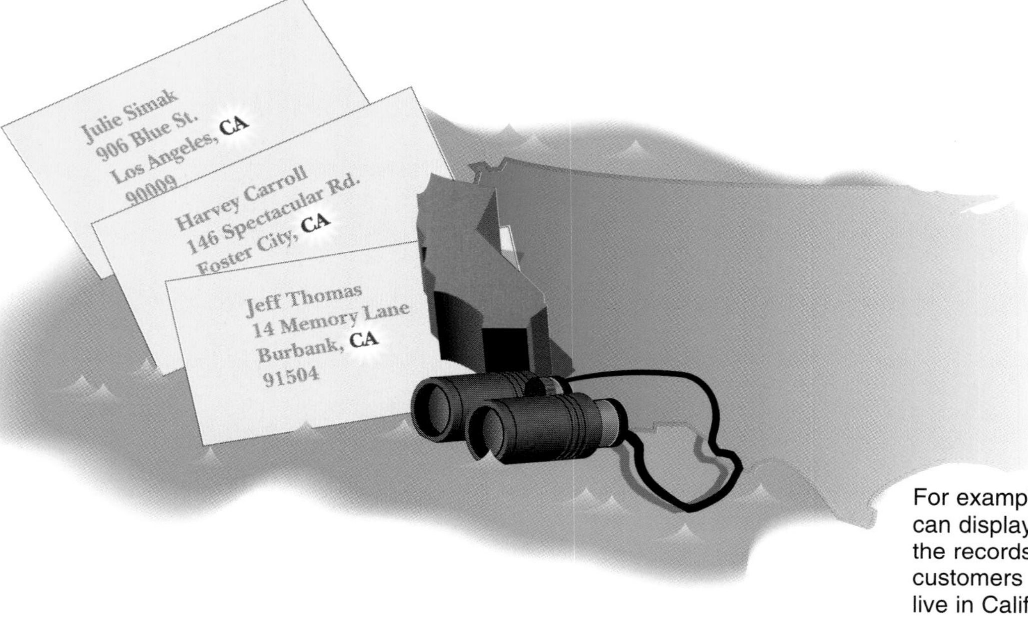

For example, you can display only the records for customers who live in California.

FILTER DATA BY SELECTION

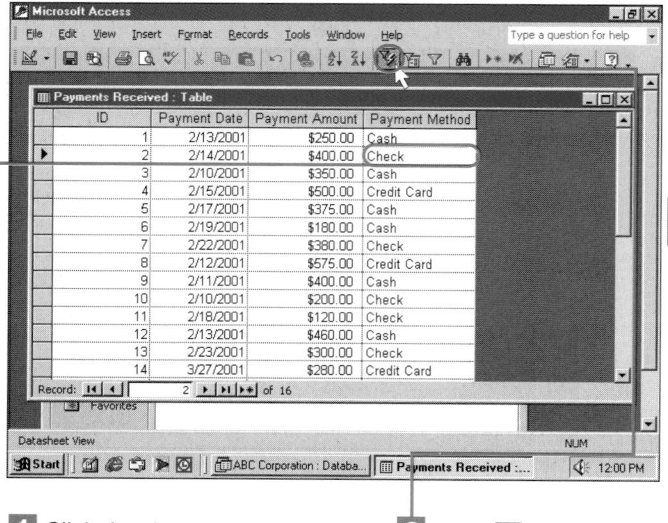

ID	Payment Date	Payment Amount	Payment Method
1	2/13/2001	$250.00	Cash
2	2/14/2001	$400.00	Check
3	2/10/2001	$350.00	Cash
4	2/15/2001	$500.00	Credit Card
5	2/17/2001	$375.00	Cash
6	2/19/2001	$180.00	Cash
7	2/22/2001	$380.00	Check
8	2/12/2001	$575.00	Credit Card
9	2/11/2001	$400.00	Cash
10	2/10/2001	$200.00	Check
11	2/18/2001	$120.00	Check
12	2/13/2001	$460.00	Cash
13	2/23/2001	$300.00	Check
14	3/27/2001	$280.00	Credit Card

1 Click the data you want to use to filter the records. Access will display only records that contain exactly the same data.

2 Click to filter the records.

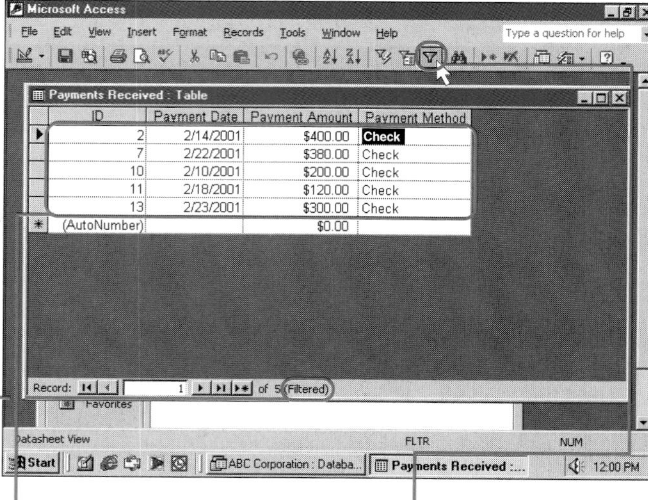

ID	Payment Date	Payment Amount	Payment Method
2	2/14/2001	$400.00	Check
7	2/22/2001	$380.00	Check
10	2/10/2001	$200.00	Check
11	2/18/2001	$120.00	Check
13	2/23/2001	$300.00	Check
(AutoNumber)		$0.00	

■ Access displays only the records containing the data. All other records are hidden.

■ The word **Filtered** appears in this area to indicate that you are viewing filtered records.

3 When you finish reviewing the filtered records, click to once again display all the records.

FILTER DATA USING CRITERIA

You can use criteria to filter data in a table, in a form or in the results of a query. Criteria are conditions that identify which records you want to display.

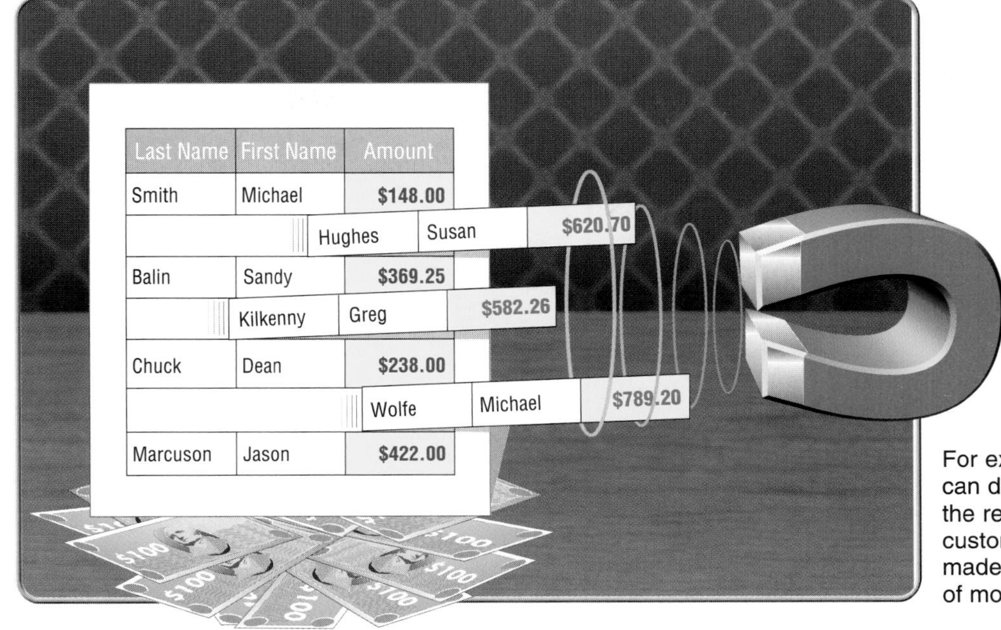

For example, you can display only the records for customers who made purchases of more than $500.

FILTER DATA USING CRITERIA

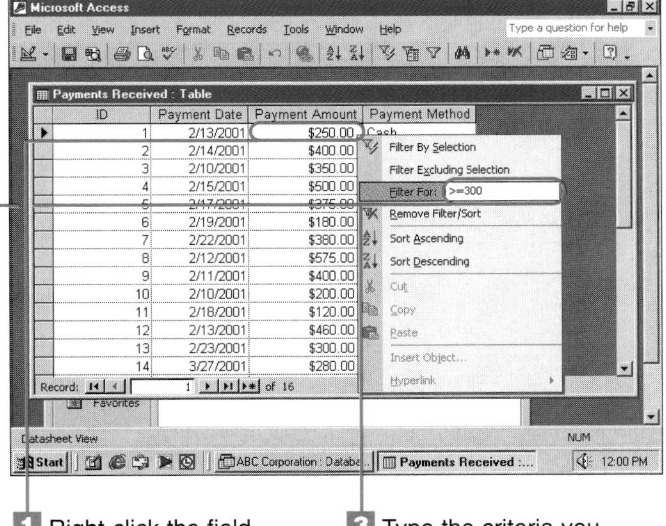

1 Right-click the field you want to use to filter the records. A menu appears.

2 Click this area.

3 Type the criteria you want to use to filter the records. Then press the Enter key.

Note: For examples of criteria you can use, see page 327.

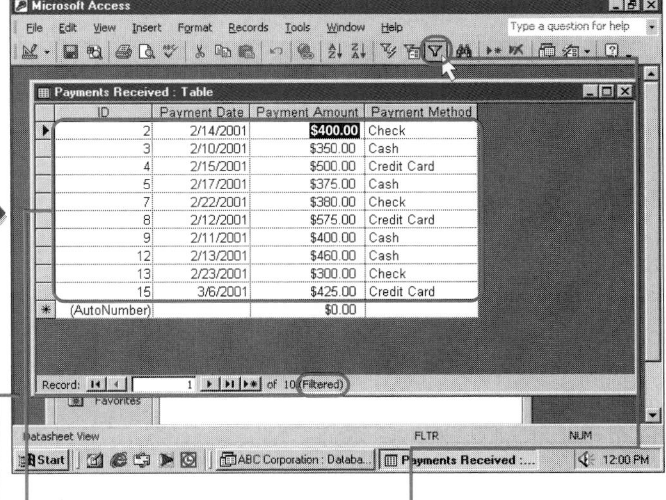

■ Access displays only the records that meet the criteria you specified. All other records are hidden.

■ The word **Filtered** appears in this area to indicate that you are viewing filtered records.

4 When you finish reviewing the filtered records, click [filter icon] to once again display all the records.

CREATE A QUERY

You can create a query to find information of interest in your database.

When you create a query, you ask Access to find information that meets certain criteria or conditions.

Which wines were made before 1965?

CREATE A QUERY

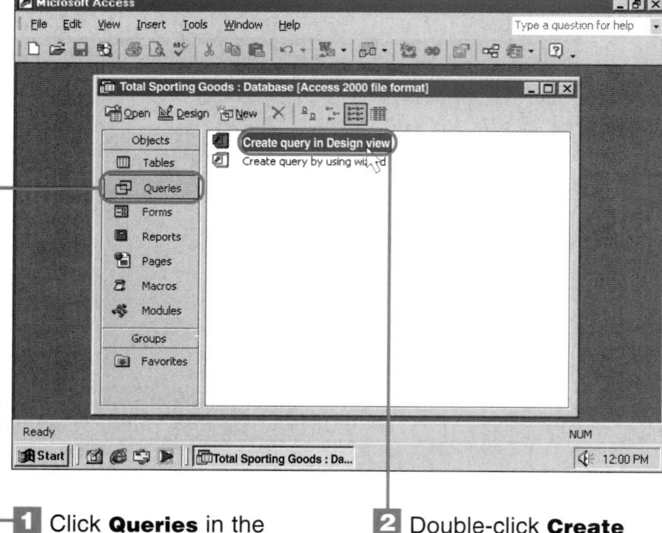

1 Click **Queries** in the Database window.

2 Double-click **Create query in Design view**.

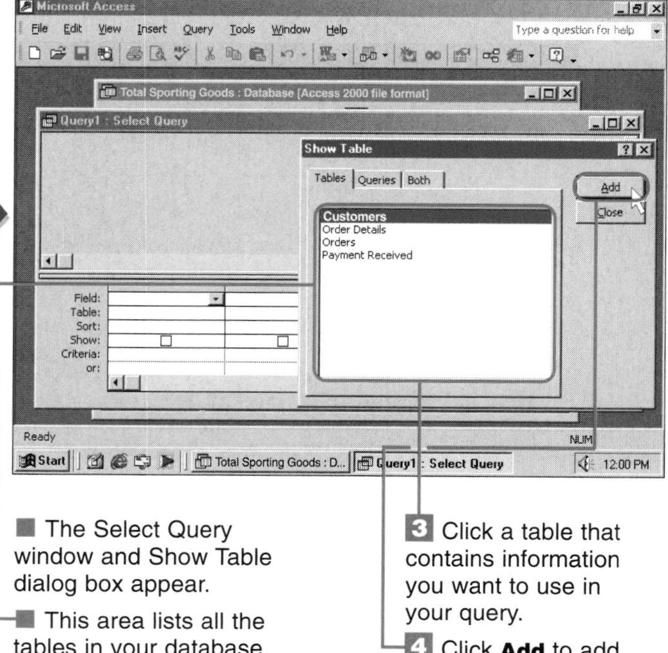

■ The Select Query window and Show Table dialog box appear.

■ This area lists all the tables in your database.

3 Click a table that contains information you want to use in your query.

4 Click **Add** to add the table to your query.

Why is there a line joining the tables in the Select Query window?

If the tables you select to use in a query are related, Access displays a line joining the related fields in the tables. When creating a query that uses more than one table, the tables should be related. For information on relationships, see page 300.

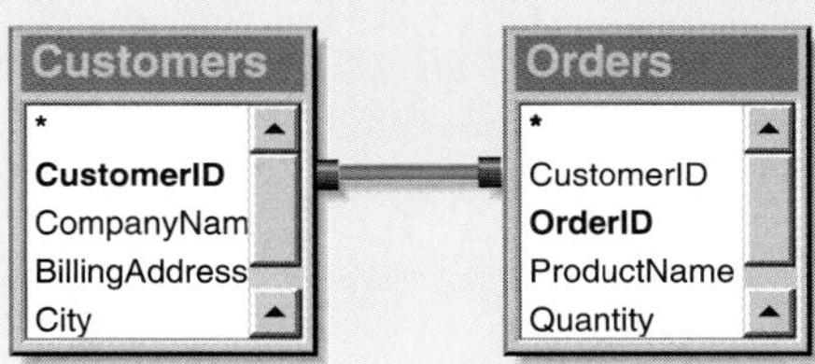

How do I add another table to my query?

You can click [icon] to redisplay the Show Table dialog box and add another table to your query. To add another table to your query, perform steps 3 and 4 on page 318.

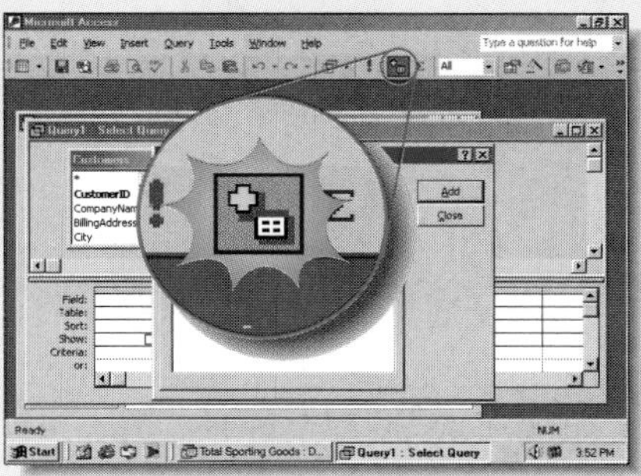

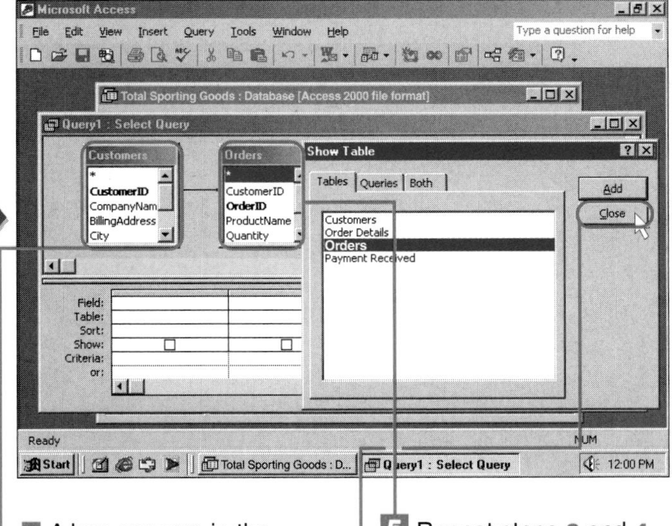

■ A box appears in the Select Query window, displaying the fields for the table you selected.

5 Repeat steps 3 and 4 for each table you want to use in your query.

6 Click **Close** to hide the Show Table dialog box.

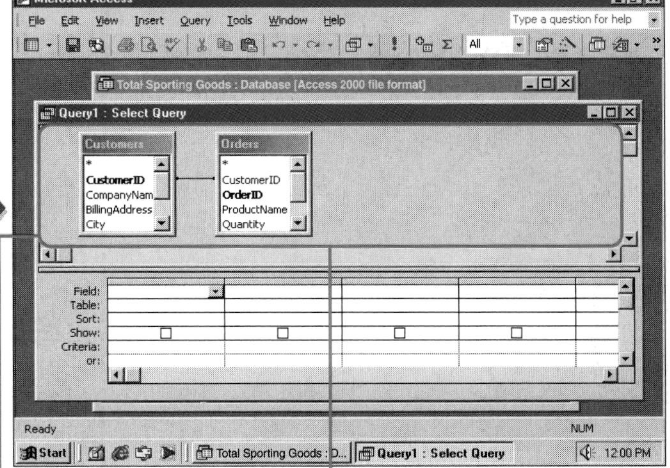

■ Each box in this area displays the fields for one table.

■ If you accidentally added a table to the query, click the table and then press the Delete key. This removes the table from the query, but not from the database.

CONTINUED

CREATE A QUERY

You can select the fields you want to include in your query.

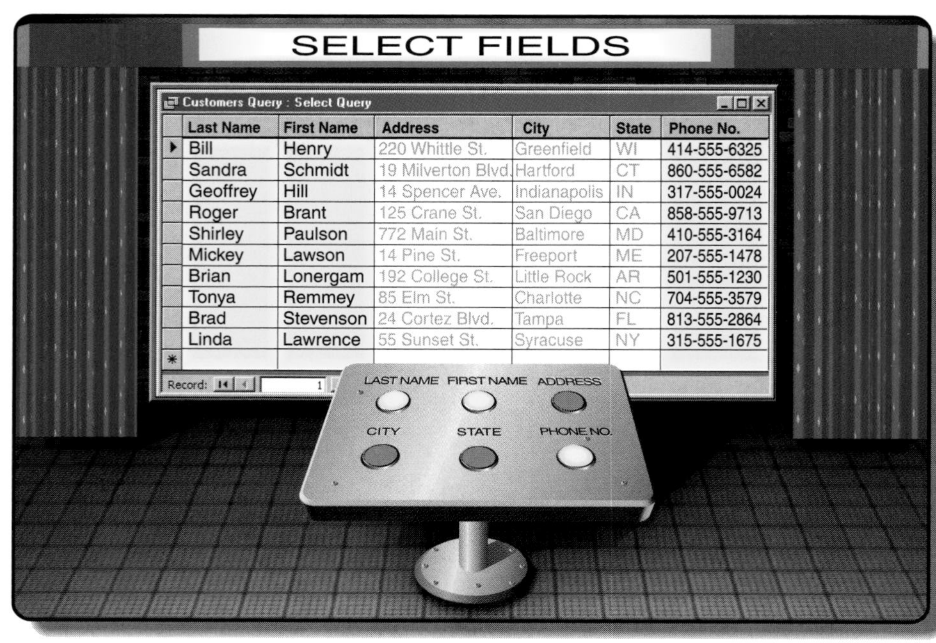

For example, you may want to include only the name and phone number of each customer.

CREATE A QUERY (CONTINUED)

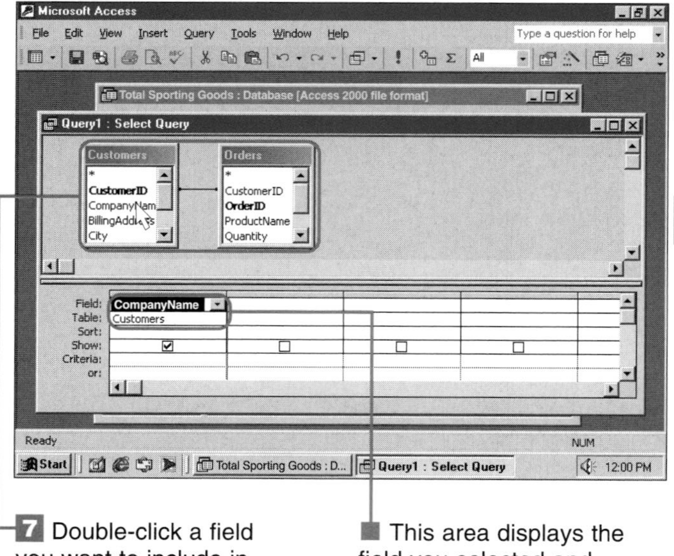

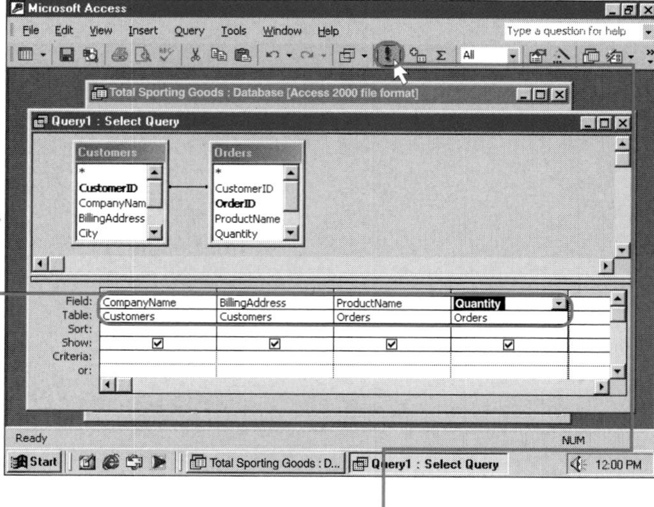

7 Double-click a field you want to include in your query.

■ This area displays the field you selected and the table that contains the field.

8 Repeat step **7** for each field you want to include in your query.

RUN THE QUERY

1 Click [!] to run the query.

Does a query store data?

No. When you save a query, Access saves only the design of the query. Each time you run a query, Access gathers the most current data from your database to determine the results of the query. You can open a saved query to run the query. To open a database object, see page 264.

How do I delete a query from my database?

Each query you save appears in the Database window. If you no longer need a query, you can permanently delete the query from your database.

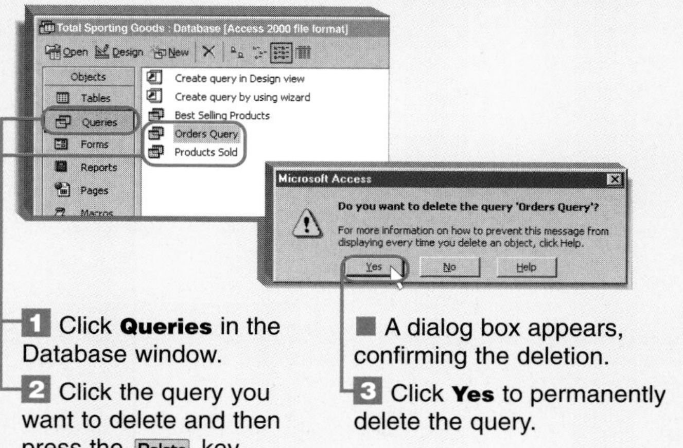

1 Click **Queries** in the Database window.

2 Click the query you want to delete and then press the Delete key.

■ A dialog box appears, confirming the deletion.

3 Click **Yes** to permanently delete the query.

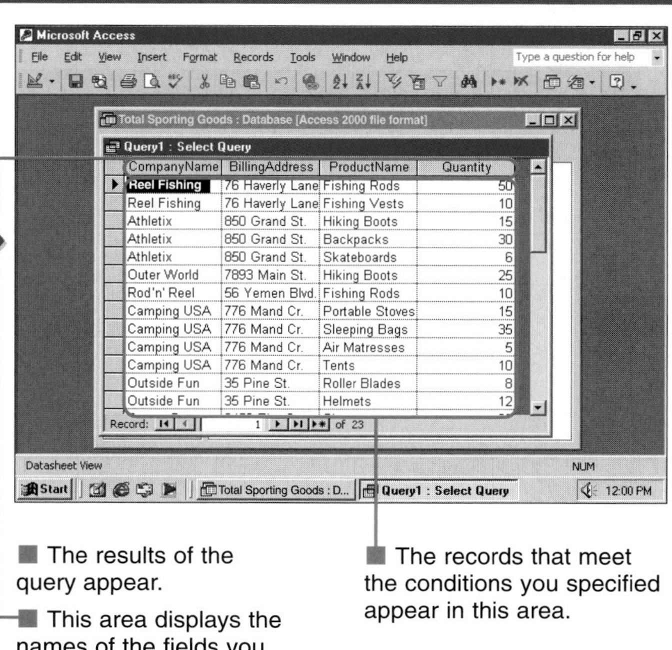

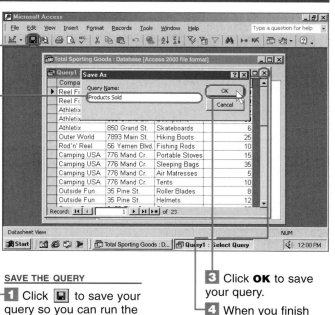

■ The results of the query appear.

■ This area displays the names of the fields you included in the query.

■ The records that meet the conditions you specified appear in this area.

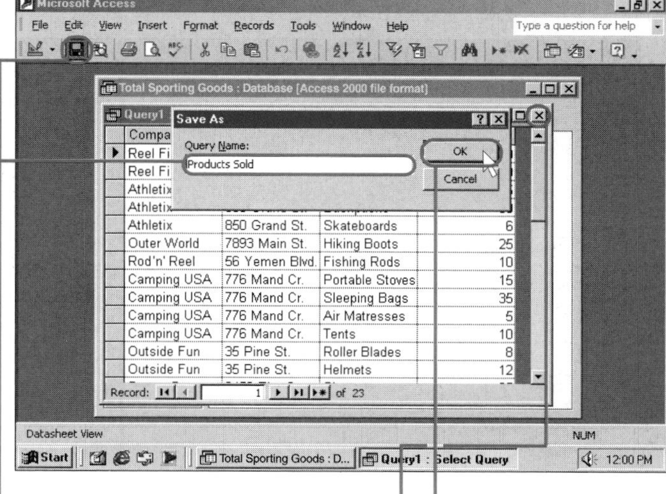

SAVE THE QUERY

1 Click 💾 to save your query so you can run the query again later.

■ The Save As dialog box appears.

2 Type a name for your query.

3 Click **OK** to save your query.

4 When you finish viewing the results of your query, click ☒ to close the query and return to the Database window.

CHANGE THE VIEW OF A QUERY

Access offers several ways that you can view a query. Each view allows you to perform different tasks.

CHANGE THE VIEW OF A QUERY

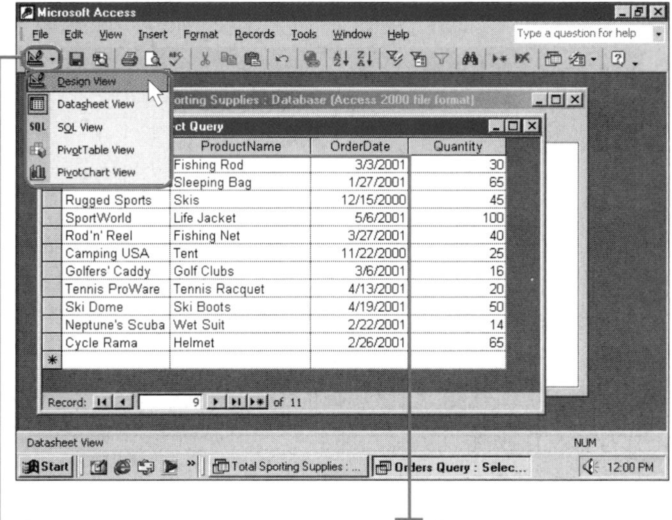

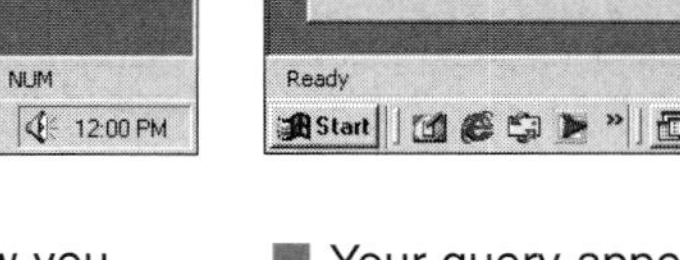

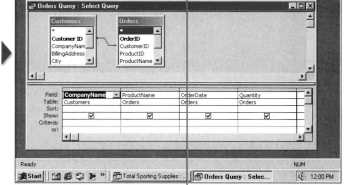

■ In this example, the query appears in the Datasheet view.

1 To change the view of your query, click ▾ in this area.

2 Click the view you want to use.

■ Your query appears in the view you selected.

■ In this example, the View button (✎) changes to (▦). You can click the View button to quickly switch between the Datasheet (▦) and Design (✎) views.

THE QUERY VIEWS

Design View

The Design view allows you to plan your query. You can use this view to specify the data you want to find.

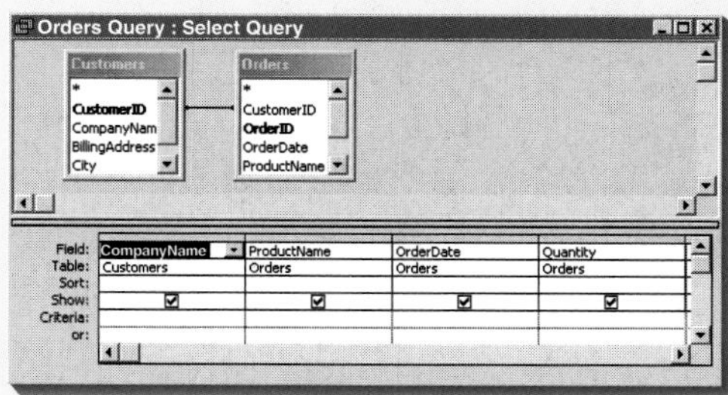

Datasheet View

The Datasheet view displays the results of your query. Each row shows the information for one record that meets the conditions you specified.

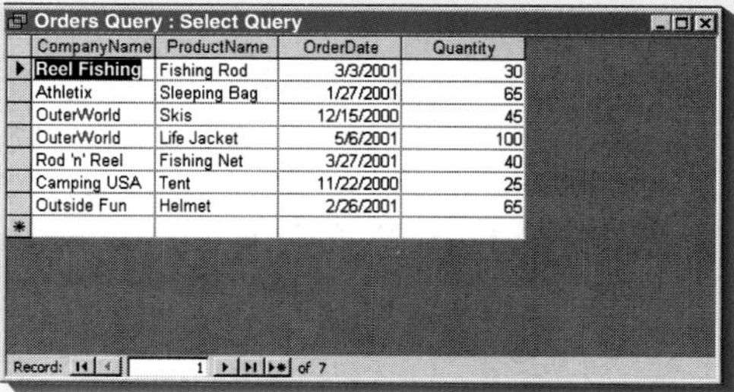

CompanyName	ProductName	OrderDate	Quantity
Reel Fishing	Fishing Rod	3/3/2001	30
Athletix	Sleeping Bag	1/27/2001	65
OuterWorld	Skis	12/15/2000	45
OuterWorld	Life Jacket	5/6/2001	100
Rod 'n' Reel	Fishing Net	3/27/2001	40
Camping USA	Tent	11/22/2000	25
Outside Fun	Helmet	2/26/2001	65

SQL View

SQL (Structured Query Language) is a computer language used to work with the information in a database. When you create a query, Access creates the SQL statements that describe your query. This view allows you to display the SQL statements for your query.

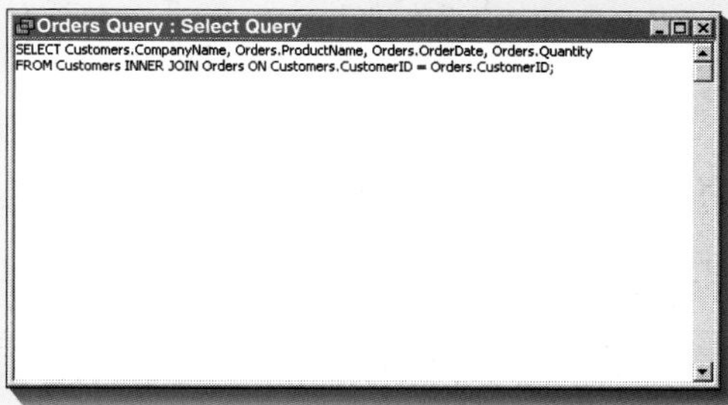

PivotTable View

The PivotTable view allows you to analyze and summarize the results of your query. The first time you display the results of your query in this view, you must specify the fields you want to display. For information on using the PivotTable view, see page 292.

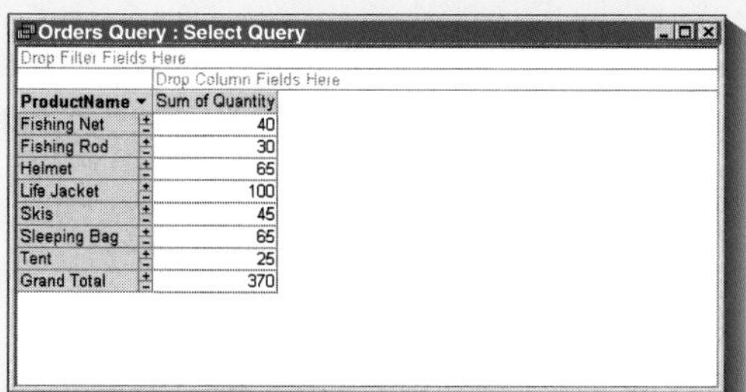

ProductName	Sum of Quantity
Fishing Net	40
Fishing Rod	30
Helmet	65
Life Jacket	100
Skis	45
Sleeping Bag	65
Tent	25
Grand Total	370

PivotChart View

The PivotChart view allows you to display a graphical summary of the results of your query. The first time you display the results of your query in this view, you must specify the fields you want to display. For information on using the PivotChart view, see page 296.

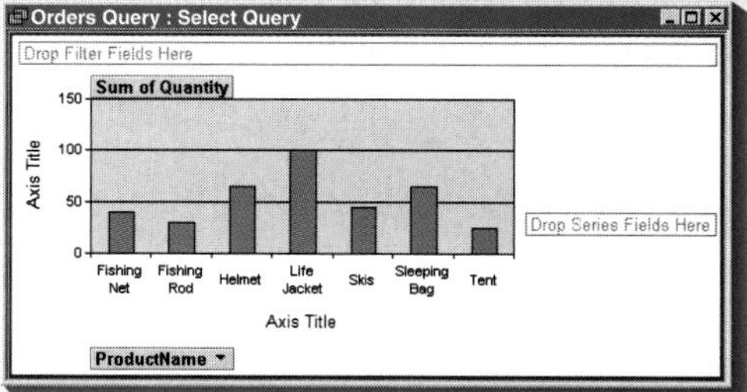

SORT QUERY RESULTS

You can sort the results of a query to better organize the results. This can help you quickly find information of interest.

There are two ways you can sort the results of a query.

Ascending
Sorts A to Z, 1 to 9

Descending
Sorts Z to A, 9 to 1

SORT QUERY RESULTS

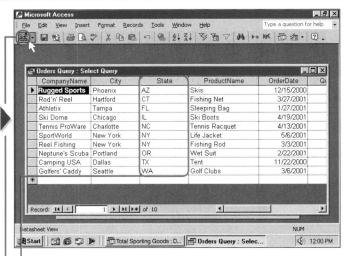

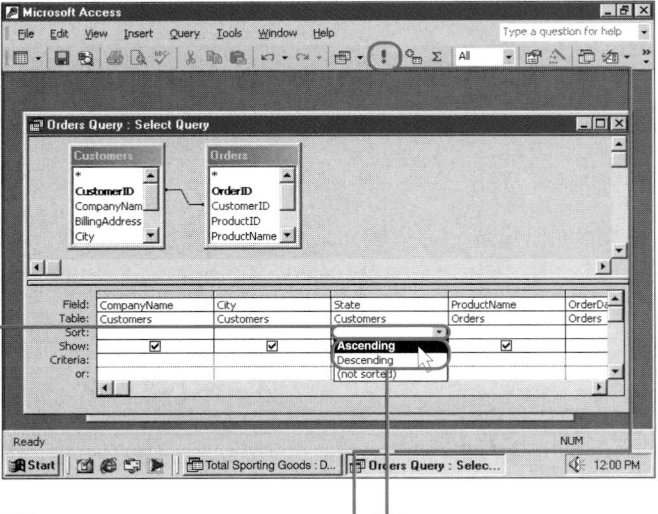

CompanyName	City	State	ProductName	OrderDate
Rugged Sports	Phoenix	AZ	Skis	12/15/2000
Rod'n' Reel	Hartford	CT	Fishing Net	3/27/2001
Athletix	Tampa	FL	Sleeping Bag	1/27/2001
Ski Dome	Chicago	IL	Ski Boots	4/19/2001
Tennis ProWare	Charlotte	NC	Tennis Racquet	4/13/2001
SportWorld	New York	NY	Life Jacket	5/6/2001
Reel Fishing	New York	NY	Fishing Rod	3/3/2001
Neptune's Scuba	Portland	OR	Wet Suit	2/22/2001
Camping USA	Dallas	TX	Tent	11/22/2000
Golfers' Caddy	Seattle	WA	Golf Clubs	3/6/2001

1 Click the **Sort** area for the field you want to use to sort the results of your query. An arrow (▾) appears.

2 Click the arrow (▾).

3 Click the way you want to sort the results.

4 Click ! to run the query.

■ The records appear in the order you specified. In this example, the records are sorted alphabetically by state.

■ To return to the Design view, click the Design view button.

■ To no longer use a field to sort the query results, repeat steps 1 to 3, selecting **(not sorted)** in step 3.

DELETE A FIELD

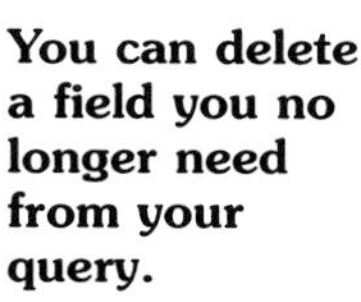

You can delete a field you no longer need from your query.

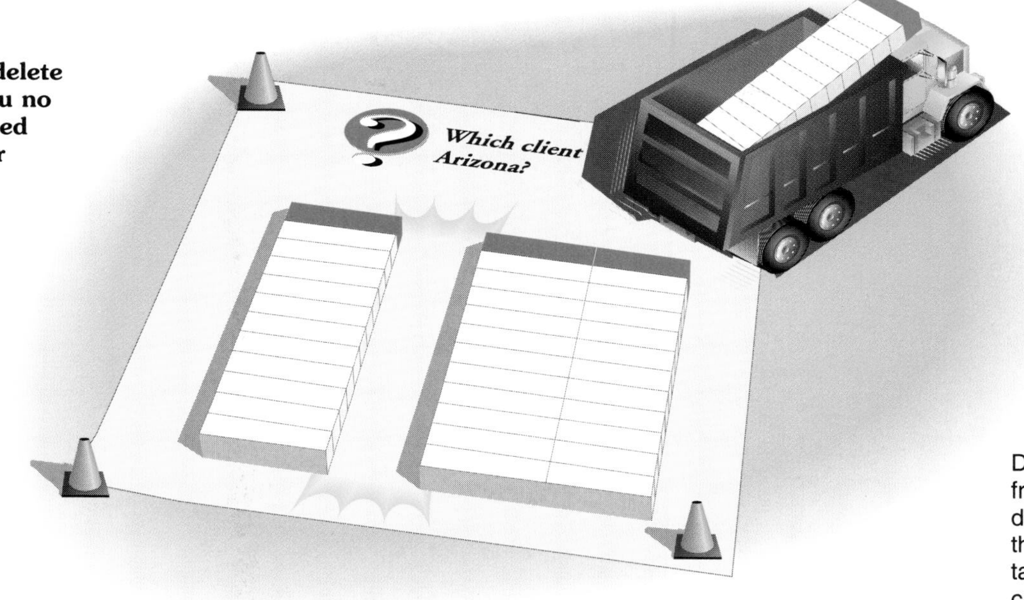

Deleting a field from a query does not delete the field from the table you used to create the query.

DELETE A FIELD

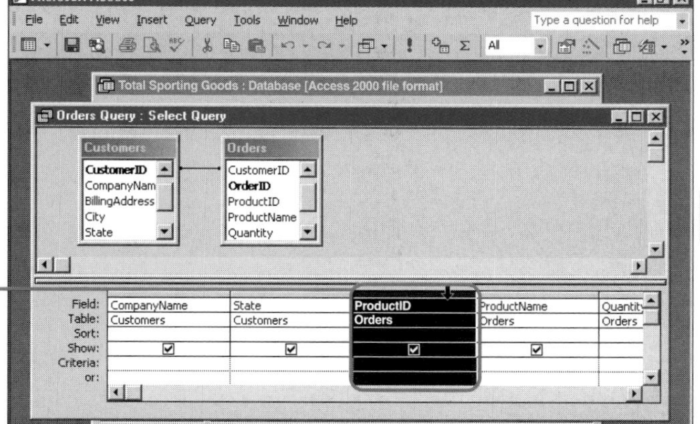

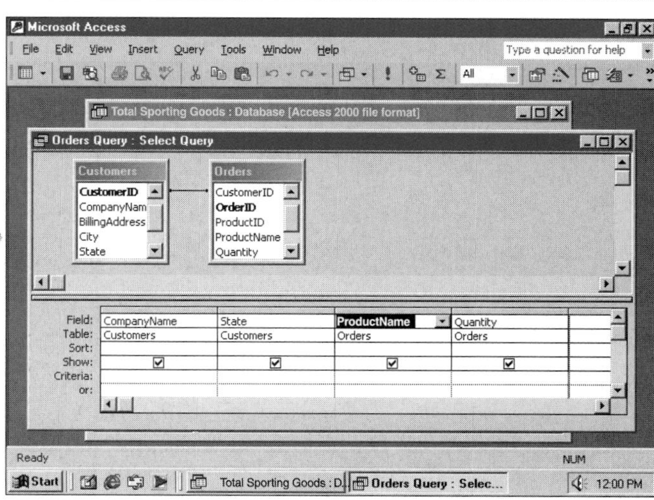

1 Position the mouse directly above the field you want to delete (changes to ⬇) and then click to select the field.

2 Press the Delete key.

■ The field disappears from your query.

USING CRITERIA

You can use criteria to find specific records in your database. Criteria are conditions that identify which records you want to find.

For example, you can use criteria to find customers who live in California.

Which customers live in California?
State =CA
Which students scored greater than 80% on their final grade?
Final grade >80%
Which recipes take less than 15 minutes to prepare?
Preparation Time <15 min

USING CRITERIA

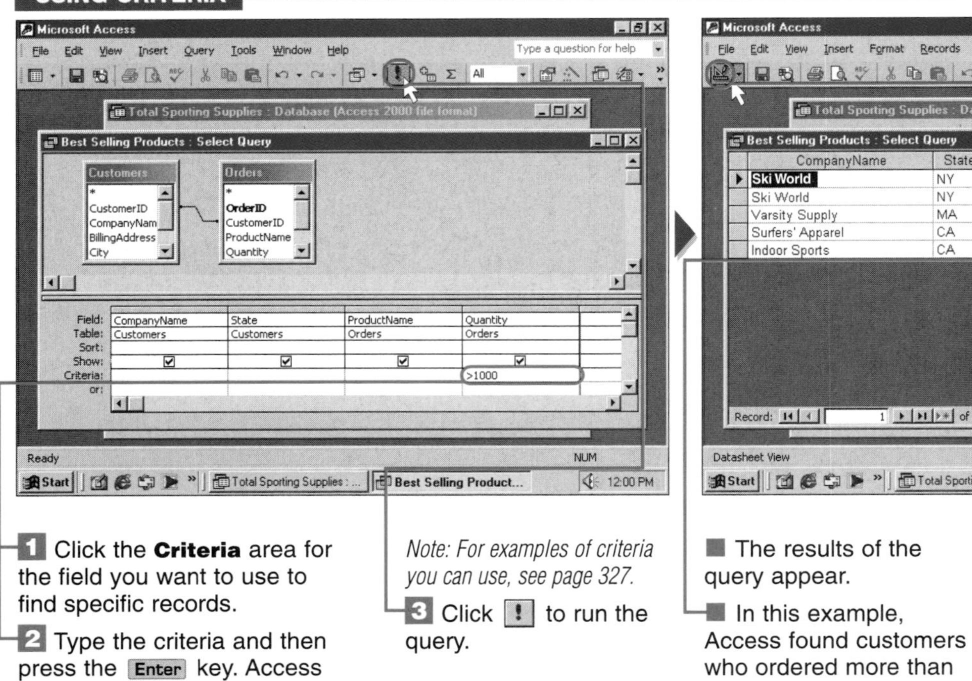

1 Click the **Criteria** area for the field you want to use to find specific records.

2 Type the criteria and then press the Enter key. Access may add quotation marks (" ") or number signs (#) to the criteria you type.

Note: For examples of criteria you can use, see page 327.

3 Click ! to run the query.

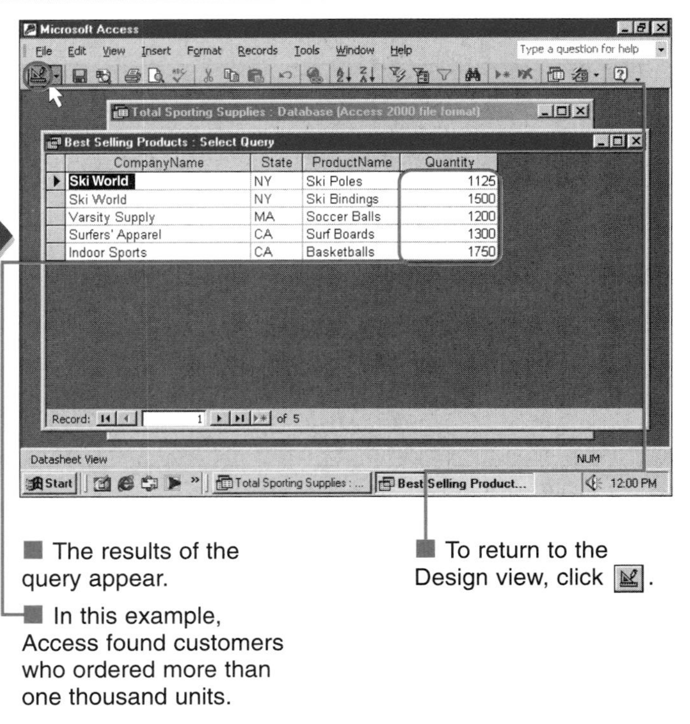

■ The results of the query appear.

■ In this example, Access found customers who ordered more than one thousand units.

■ To return to the Design view, click .

EXAMPLES OF CRITERIA

Here are examples of criteria that you can use to find records in your database.

Exact matches

=100	Finds the number 100.
=California	Finds California.
=5/9/2001	Finds the date 9-May-01.

Less than

<100	Finds numbers less than 100.
<N	Finds text starting with the letters A to M.
<5/9/2001	Finds dates before 9-May-01.

Less than or equal to

<=100	Finds numbers less than or equal to 100.
<=N	Finds the letter N and text starting with the letters A to M.
<=5/9/2001	Finds dates on and before 9-May-01.

Greater than

>100	Finds numbers greater than 100.
>N	Finds text starting with the letters N to Z.
>5/9/2001	Finds dates after 9-May-01.

Greater than or equal to

>=100	Finds numbers greater than or equal to 100.
>=N	Finds the letter N and text starting with the letters N to Z.
>=5/9/2001	Finds dates on and after 9-May-01.

Not equal to

<>100	Finds numbers not equal to 100.
<>California	Finds text not equal to California.
<>5/9/2001	Finds dates not on 9-May-01.

Empty fields

Is Null	Finds records that do not contain data in the field.
Is Not Null	Finds records that contain data in the field.

Last Name
Carroll
Lessels
Duncan
Thomas

Find list of items

In (100,101)	Finds the numbers 100 and 101.
In (California,CA)	Finds California and CA.
In (#5/9/2001#, #5/10/2001#)	Finds the dates 9-May-01 and 10-May-01.

Between...And...

Between 100 And 200	Finds numbers from 100 to 200.
Between A And D	Finds the letter D and text starting with the letters A to C.
Between 5/9/2001 And 5/15/2001	Finds dates on and between 9-May-01 and 15-May-01.

CREATE A REPORT

You can use the Report Wizard to create a professionally designed report that summarizes data from your database.

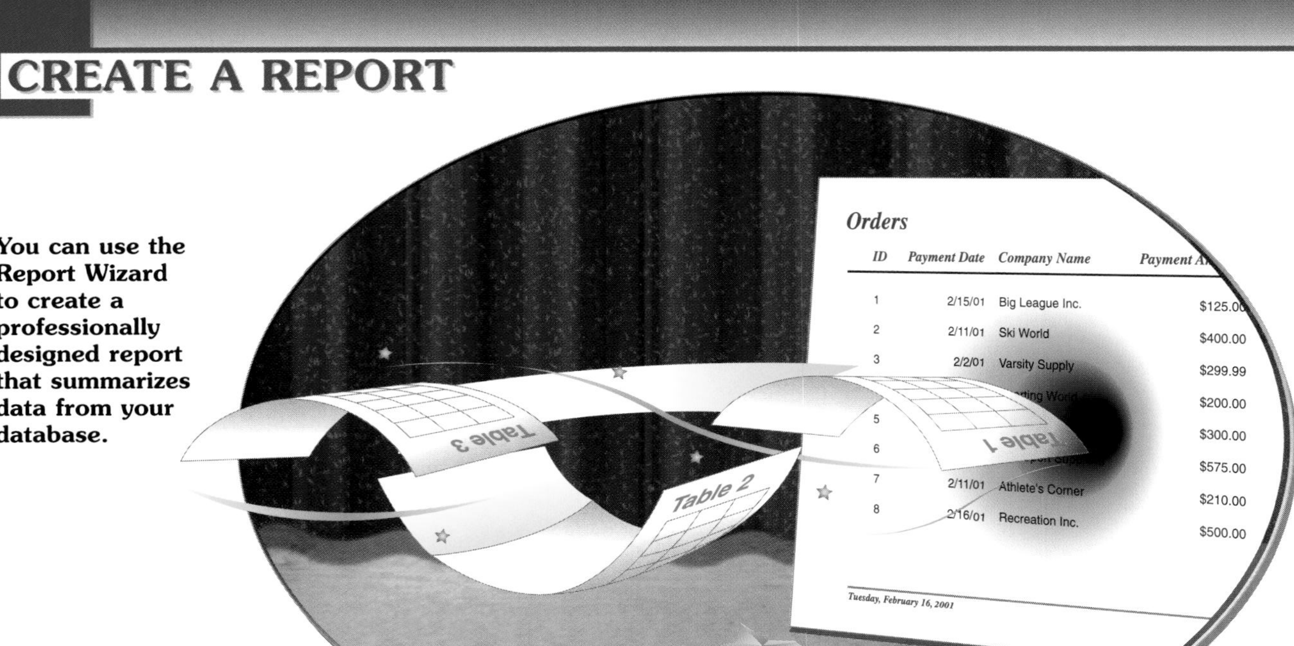

The Report Wizard asks you a series of questions and then creates a report based on your answers.

CREATE A REPORT

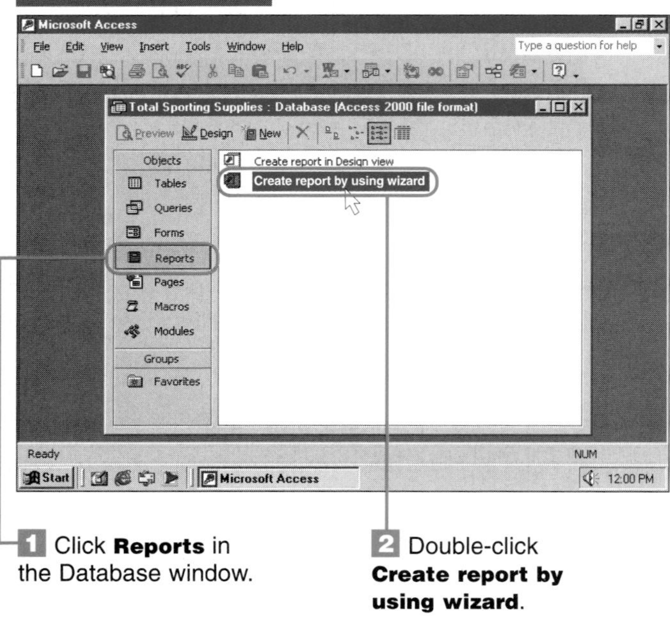

1 Click **Reports** in the Database window.

2 Double-click **Create report by using wizard**.

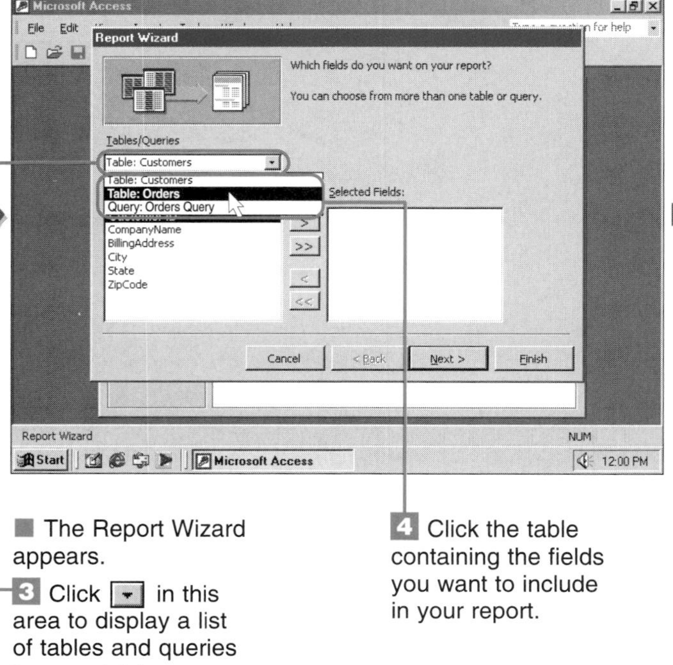

■ The Report Wizard appears.

3 Click ▾ in this area to display a list of tables and queries in your database.

4 Click the table containing the fields you want to include in your report.

Which tables in my database can I use to create a report?

You can use any table in your database to create a report. When creating a report that uses data from more than one table, the tables must be related. For information on relationships, see page 300.

Can I use a query to create a report?

Yes. A query gathers information from your database that meets certain criteria or conditions. For more information on queries, see pages 318 to 321. To use a query to create a report, perform steps **1** to **3** on page 328. In the list of tables and queries in your database, click the query you want to use. You can then perform steps **5** to **28** beginning on this page to finish creating the report.

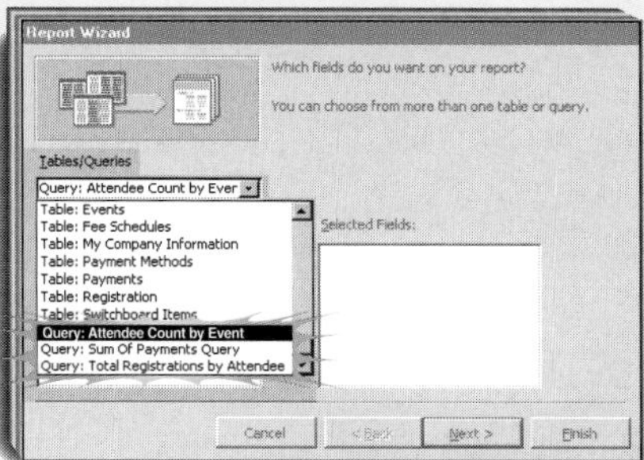

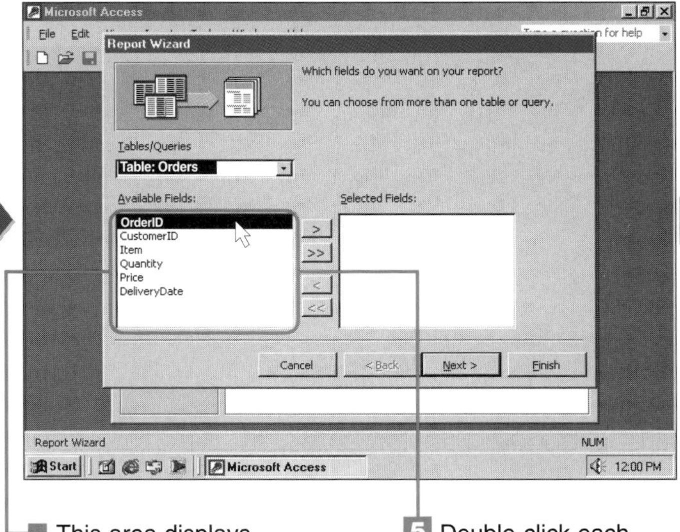

- This area displays the fields in the table you selected.

5 Double-click each field you want to include in your report.

Note: To add all the fields at once, click >> .

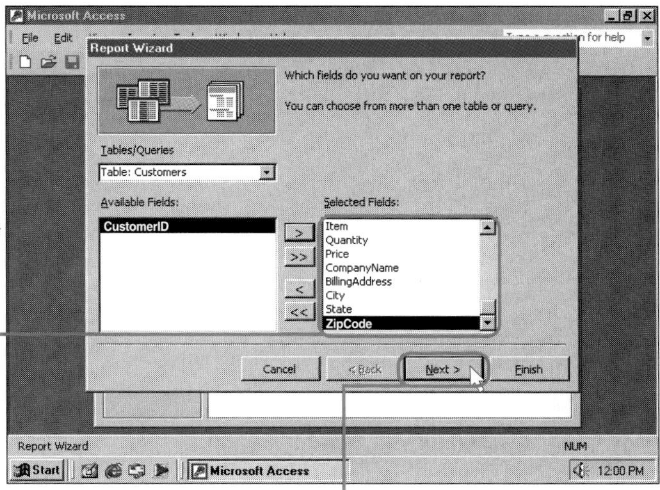

- Each field you select appears in this area.
- To remove a field you accidentally selected, double-click the field in this area.

Note: To remove all the fields at once, click << .

6 To add fields from other tables, repeat steps **3** to **5** for each table.

7 Click **Next** to continue.

CONTINUED

You can choose how you want to group data and sort records in your report.

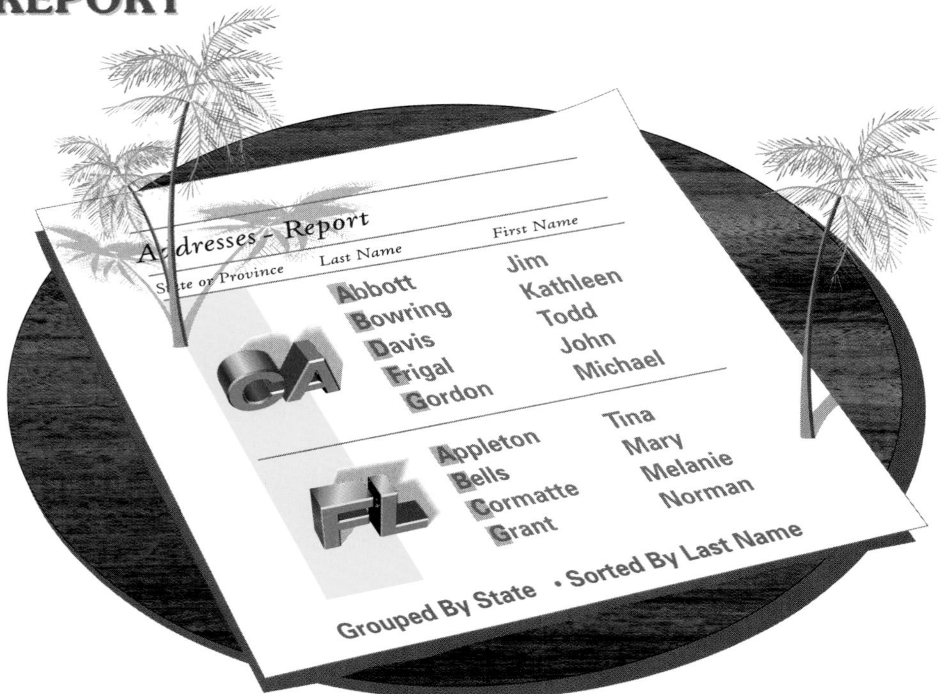

Addresses - Report
State or Province
Last Name
First Name
CA
Abbott
Bowring
Davis
Frigal
Gordon
Jim
Kathleen
Todd
John
Michael
FL
Appleton
Bells
Cormatte
Grant
Tina
Mary
Melanie
Norman
Grouped By State • Sorted By Last Name

CREATE A REPORT (CONTINUED)

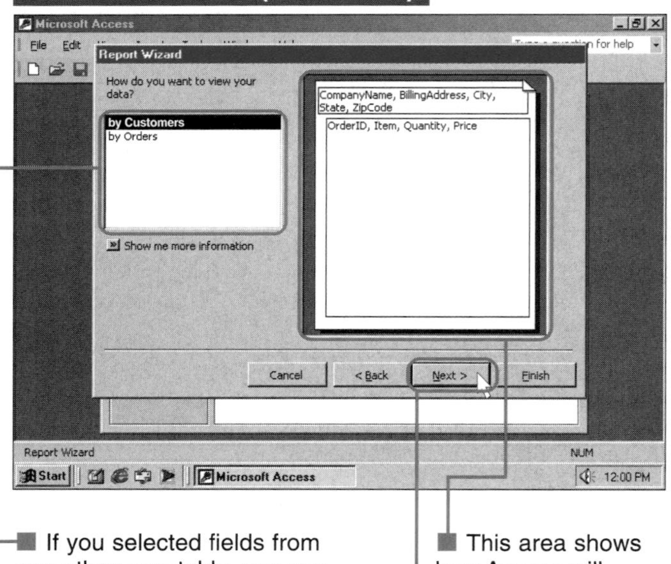

■ If you selected fields from more than one table, you can choose the table you want to use to group data in your report.

*Note: If this screen does not appear, skip to step **10**.*

8 Click the table you want to use to group data in your report.

■ This area shows how Access will group data in your report.

9 Click **Next** to continue.

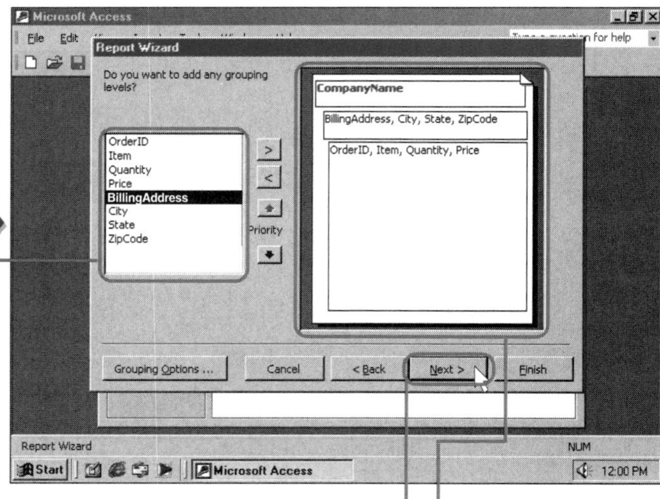

10 To use a specific field to group data in your report, double-click the field you want to use.

■ This area shows how Access will group data in your report.

11 Click **Next** to continue.

Why would I group data in my report?

You can group data to better organize and summarize the data that will appear in your report. Grouping data allows you to place related data together in the report. For example, you can group data by the State field to place all the customers from the same state together.

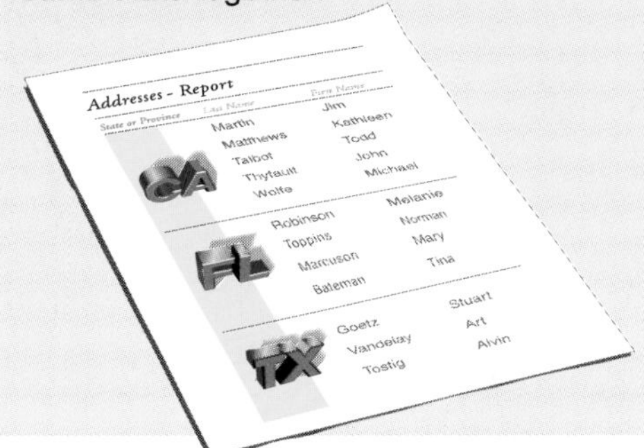

Why would I sort the records in my report?

You can sort the records in your report to better organize the data. For example, you can alphabetically sort records by the Last Name field to make it easier to find customers of interest. If the same last name appears more than once in the field, you can sort by a second field, such as First Name.

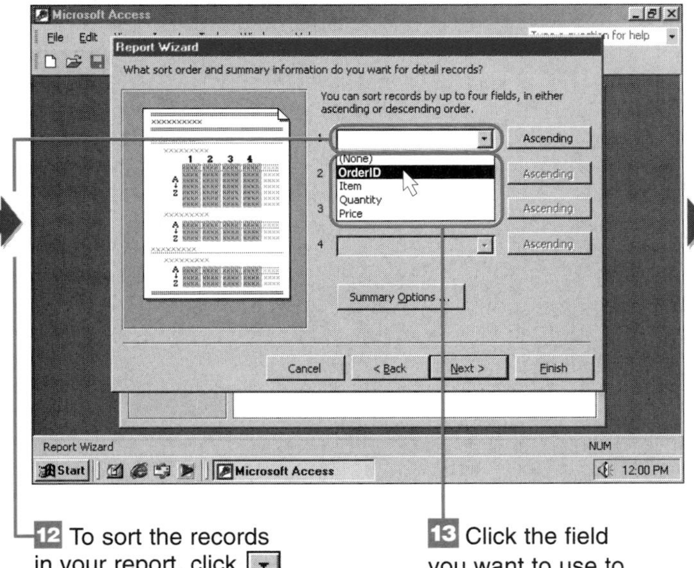

12 To sort the records in your report, click ▾ in this area.

13 Click the field you want to use to sort the records.

14 Click this button until it appears the way you want to sort the records.

Ascending - Sort A to Z, 1 to 9

Descending - Sort Z to A, 9 to 1

15 To sort by a second field, repeat steps 12 to 14 in this area.

CONTINUED

CREATE A REPORT

You can perform calculations in your report to summarize your data.

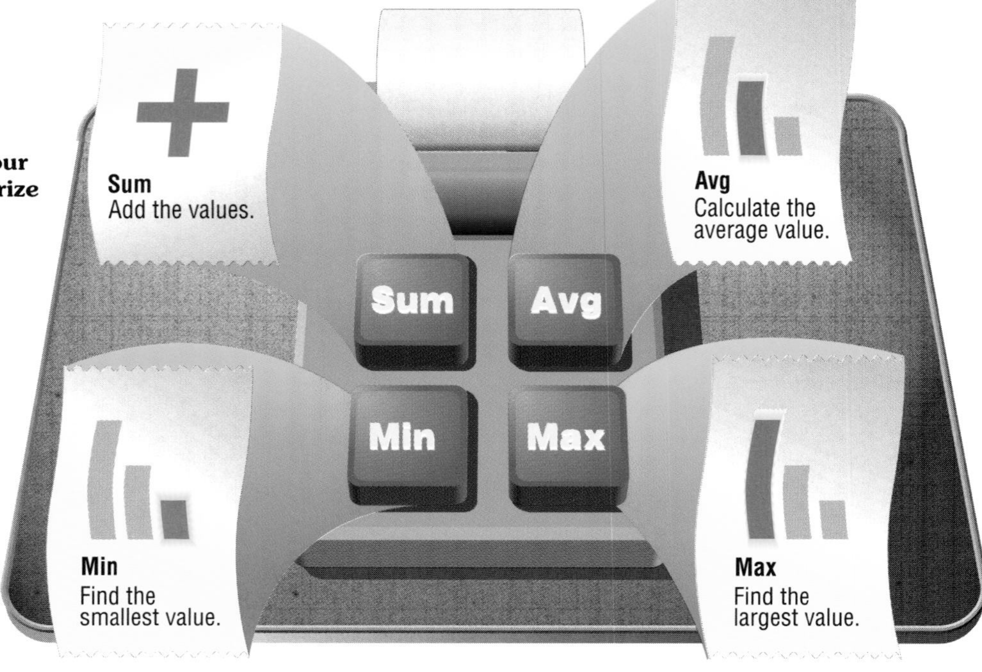

CREATE A REPORT (CONTINUED)

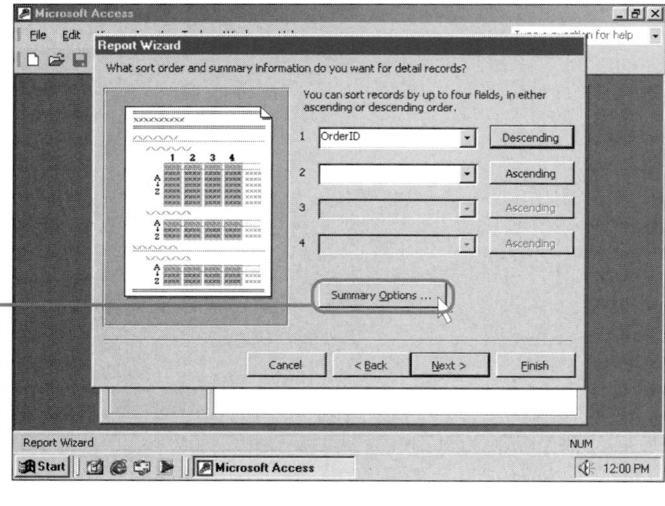

16 To perform calculations in your report, click **Summary Options**.

*Note: Summary Options may not be available for some reports. If Summary Options is not available, skip to step **21** to continue creating your report.*

■ The Summary Options dialog box appears.

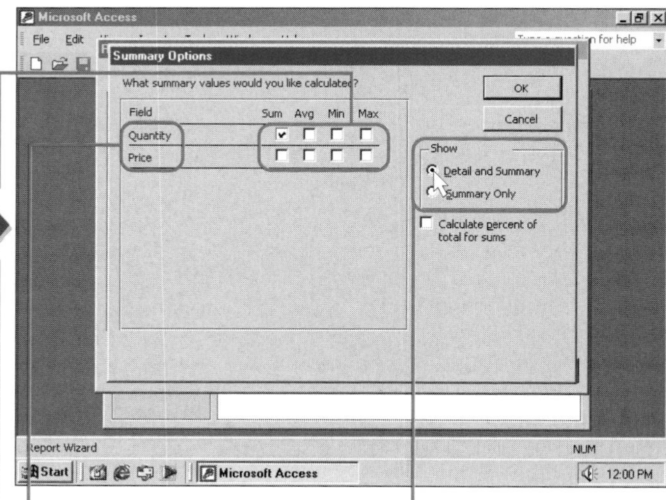

■ This area displays the fields you can perform calculations on.

17 Click the box (☐) for each calculation you want to perform (☐ changes to ☑).

18 Click an option to specify if you want to display all the records and the summary or just the summary (○ changes to ⊙). For more information, see the top of page 333.

When performing calculations in my report, what information can I include?

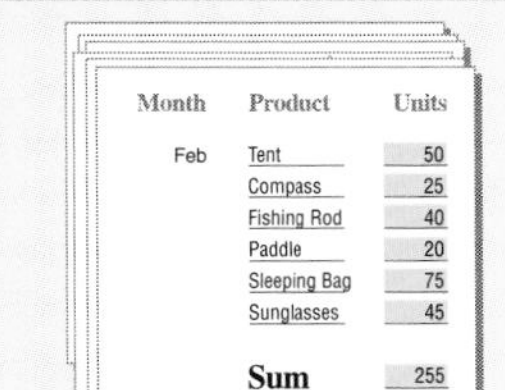

Detail and Summary

Display all the records and the summary. For example, show all orders and the total orders for each month.

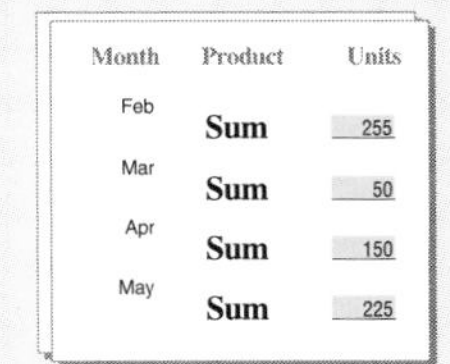

Summary Only

Display only the summary. For example, show only the total orders for each month.

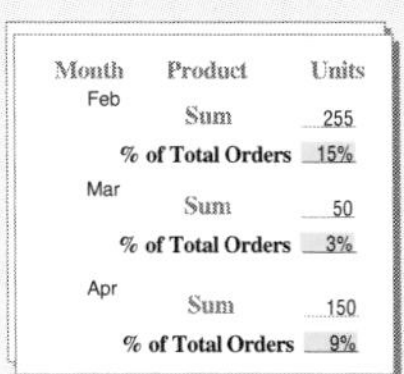

Calculate percent of total for sums

Display the percentage of the total that each group represents. For example, show the percentage of the total orders that each month represents.

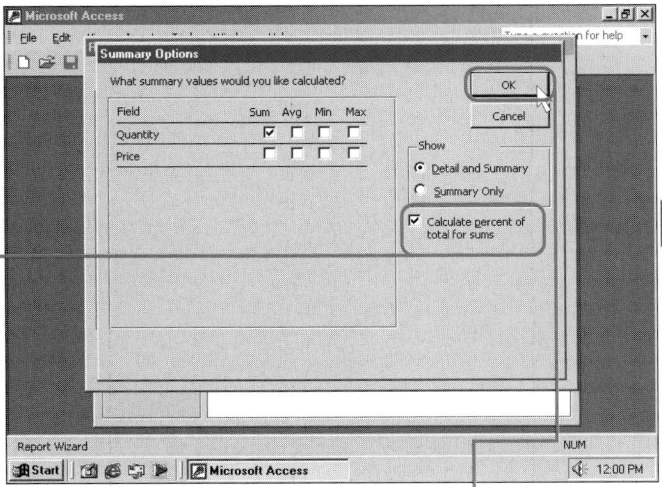

19 To calculate the percentage of the total that each group represents, click this option (☐ changes to ☑).

20 Click **OK.**

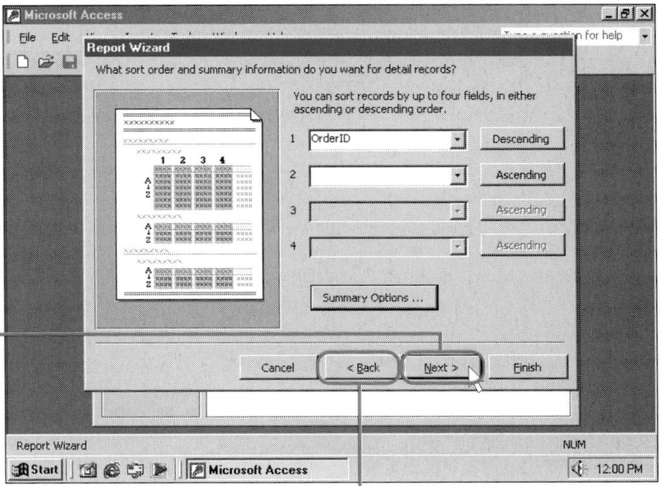

21 Click **Next** to continue.

■ You can click **Back** at any time to return to a previous step and change your answers.

CONTINUED

You can choose one of several different layouts for your report. The layout determines the arrangement of data in your report.

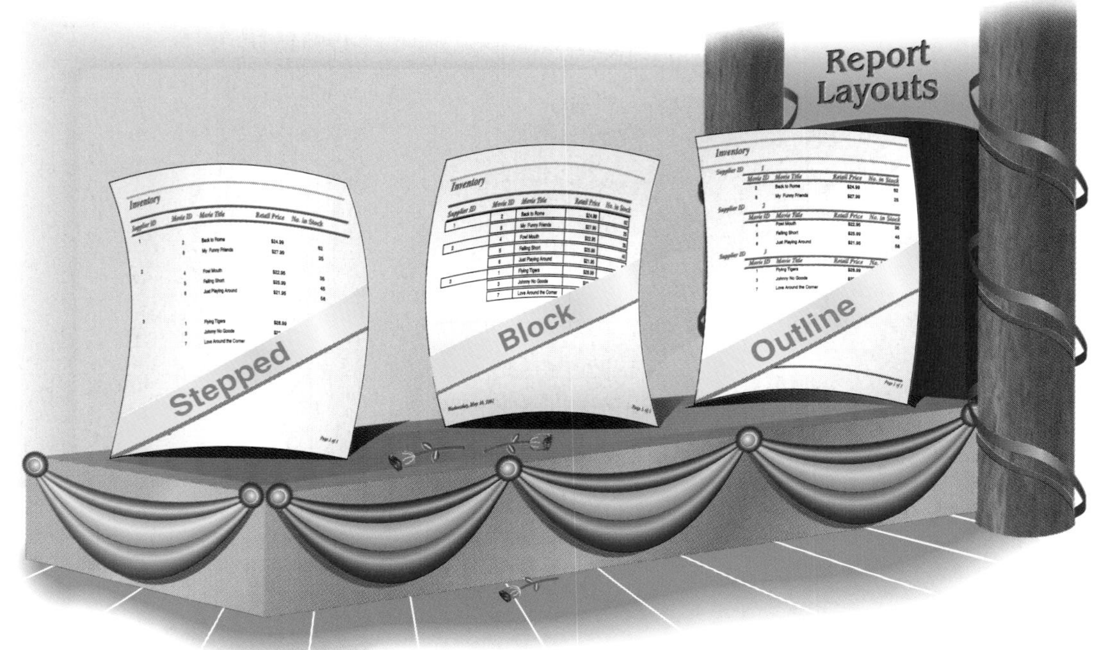

CREATE A REPORT (CONTINUED)

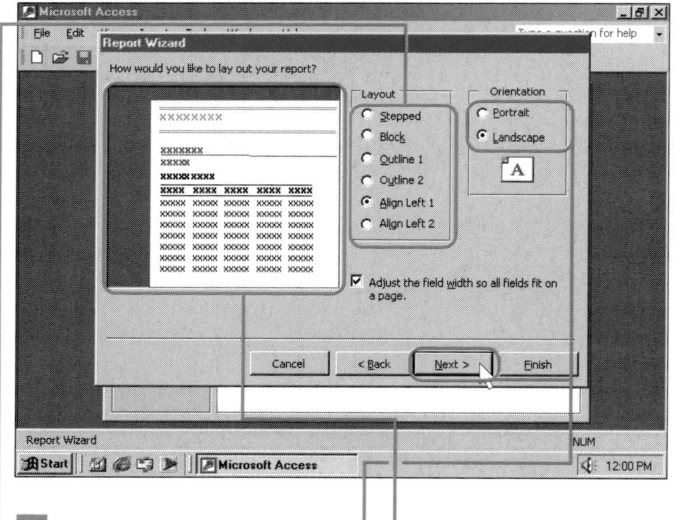

22 Click the layout you want to use for your report (○ changes to ⊙).

Note: The available layouts depend on the options you selected for your report.

■ This area displays a sample of the layout you selected.

23 Click the page orientation you want to use (○ changes to ⊙).

24 Click **Next** to continue.

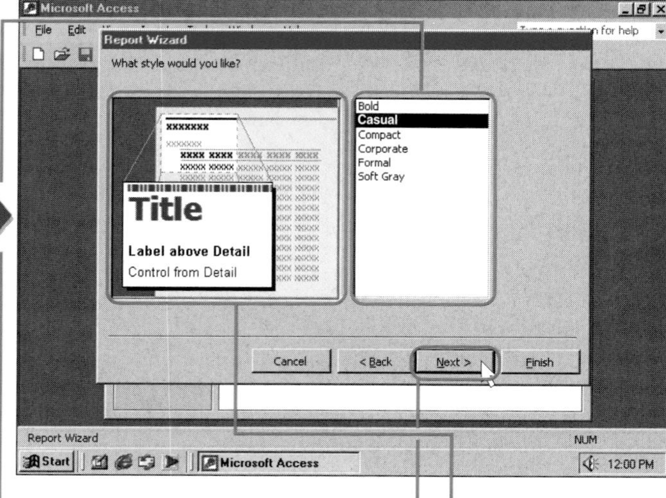

25 Click the style you want to use for your report.

■ This area displays a sample of the style you selected.

26 Click **Next** to continue.

Do I need to create a new report each time I change the data in my database?

No. Each time you open your report, Access will automatically gather the most current data from your database to create the report. This ensures that the report will always display the most up-to-date information. For information on opening a database object, see page 264.

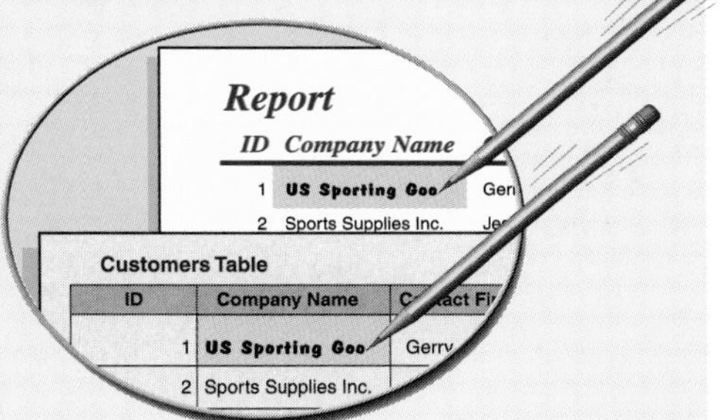

How do I delete a report from my database?

Each report you create appears in the Database window. If you no longer need a report, you can permanently delete the report from your database.

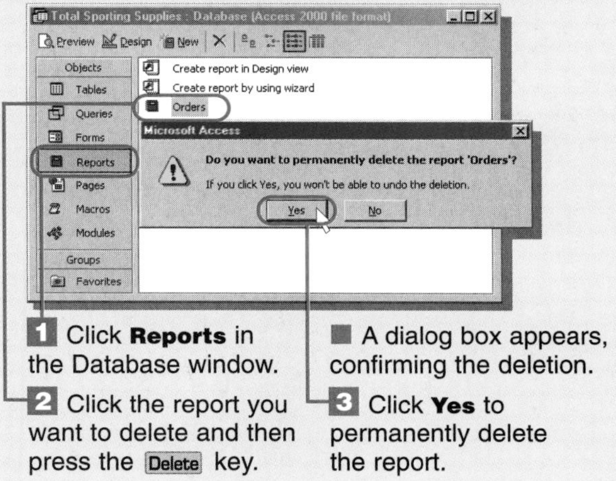

1 Click **Reports** in the Database window.

2 Click the report you want to delete and then press the Delete key.

■ A dialog box appears, confirming the deletion.

3 Click **Yes** to permanently delete the report.

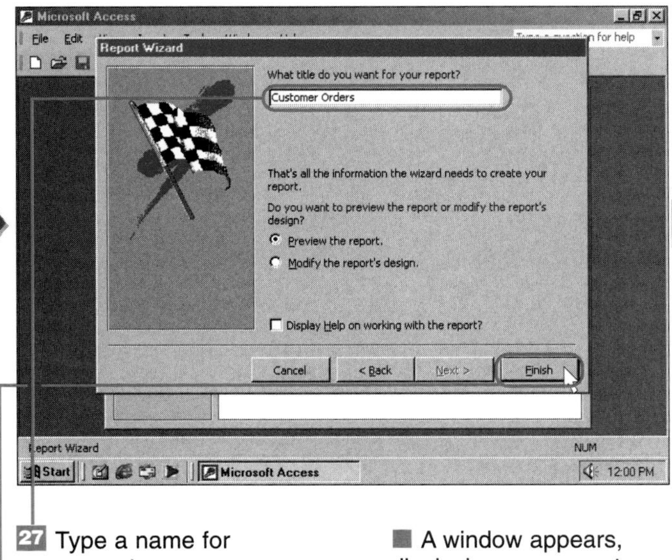

27 Type a name for your report.

28 Click **Finish** to create your report.

■ A window appears, displaying your report as it will look when printed.

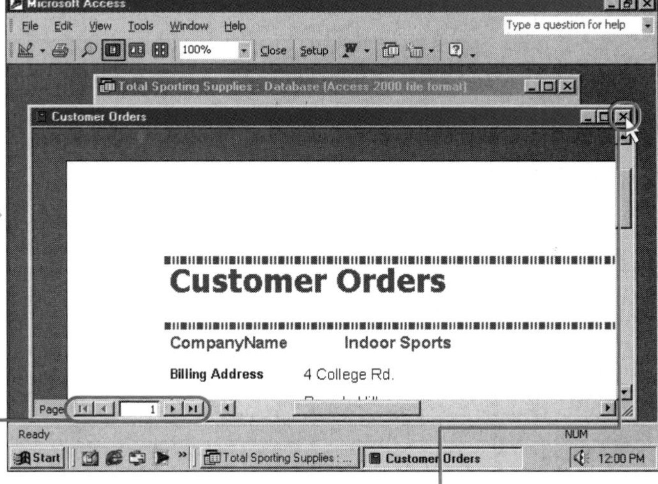

■ This area shows the number of the page displayed on your screen.

29 If your report contains more than one page, click one of these buttons to display another page.

- First page
- Previous page
- Next page
- Last page

30 When you finish viewing your report, click ✕ to close the report and return to the Database window.

PRINT A REPORT

You can produce a paper copy of the report displayed on your screen.

You can also use the method described below to print a table, form or query in your database.

Before printing your report, make sure your printer is turned on and contains paper.

PRINT A REPORT

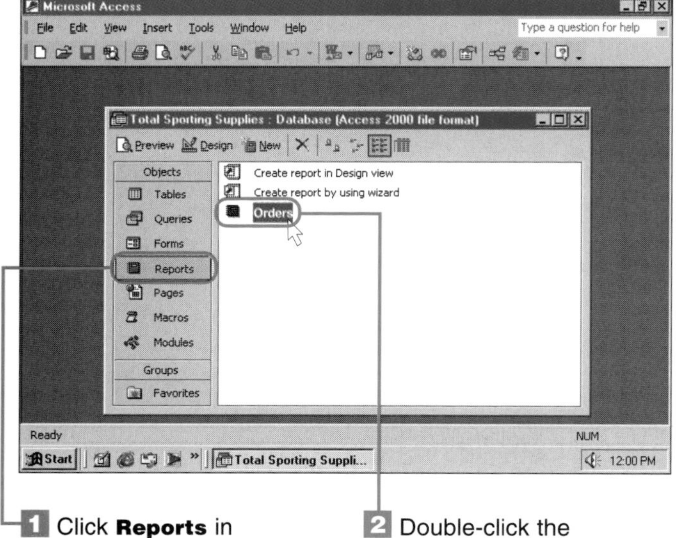

1 Click **Reports** in the Database window.

2 Double-click the report you want to print.

■ The report opens and appears on your screen.

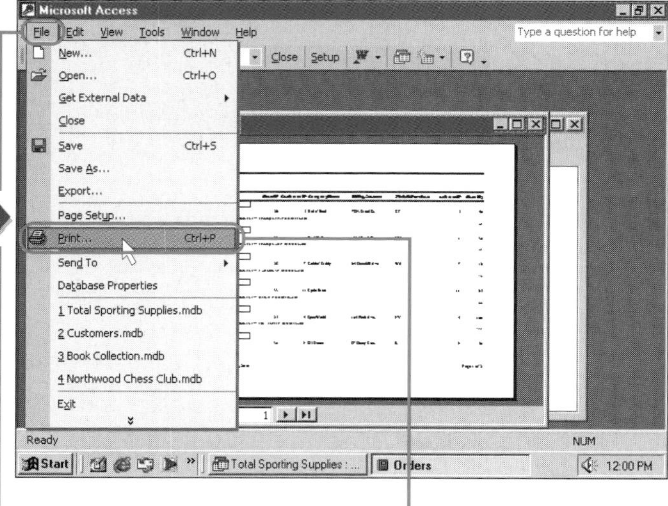

3 Click **File**.

4 Click **Print**.

■ The Print dialog box appears.

Which print option should I use?

All

Prints all the pages.

Pages

Prints the pages you specify.

How can I print multiple copies of a report?

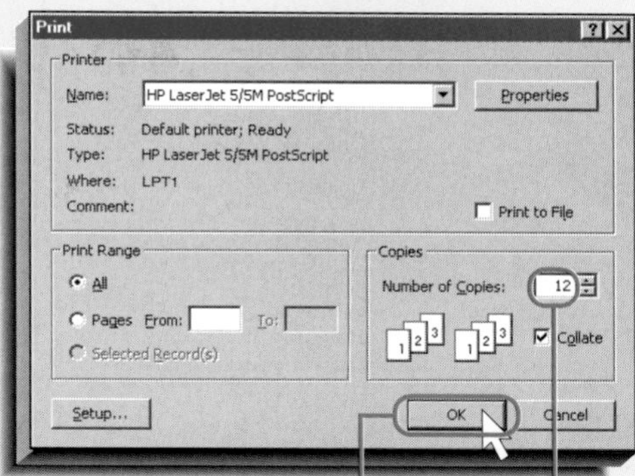

1 Perform steps 1 to 5 below to display the Print dialog box and specify the pages you want to print.

2 Double-click this area and type the number of copies you want to print.

3 Click **OK** to print multiple copies of the report.

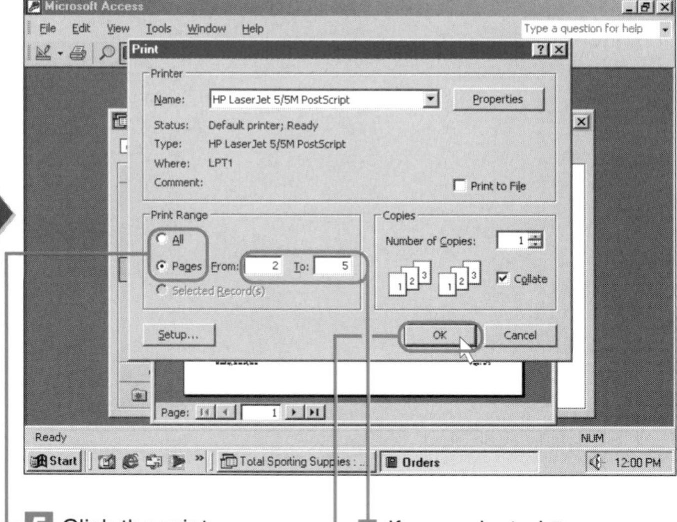

5 Click the print option you want to use (○ changes to ⊙).

Note: For information on the print options, see the top of this page.

■ If you selected **Pages** in step 5, type the number of the first page you want to print. Press the Tab key and then type the number of the last page you want to print.

6 Click **OK**.

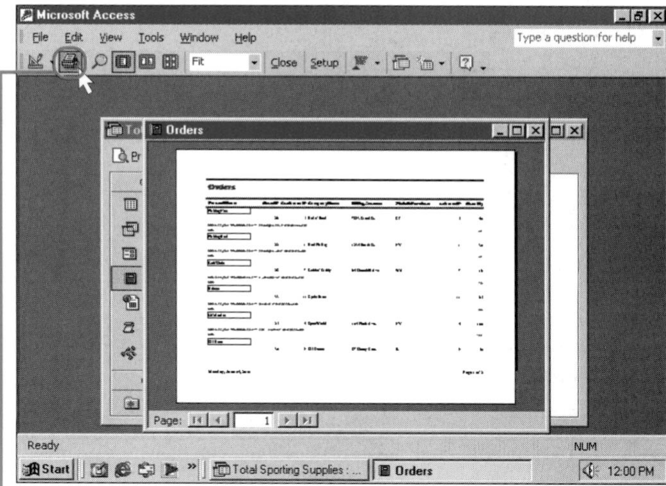

QUICKLY PRINT ENTIRE REPORT

1 Click the print button to quickly print the report displayed on your screen.

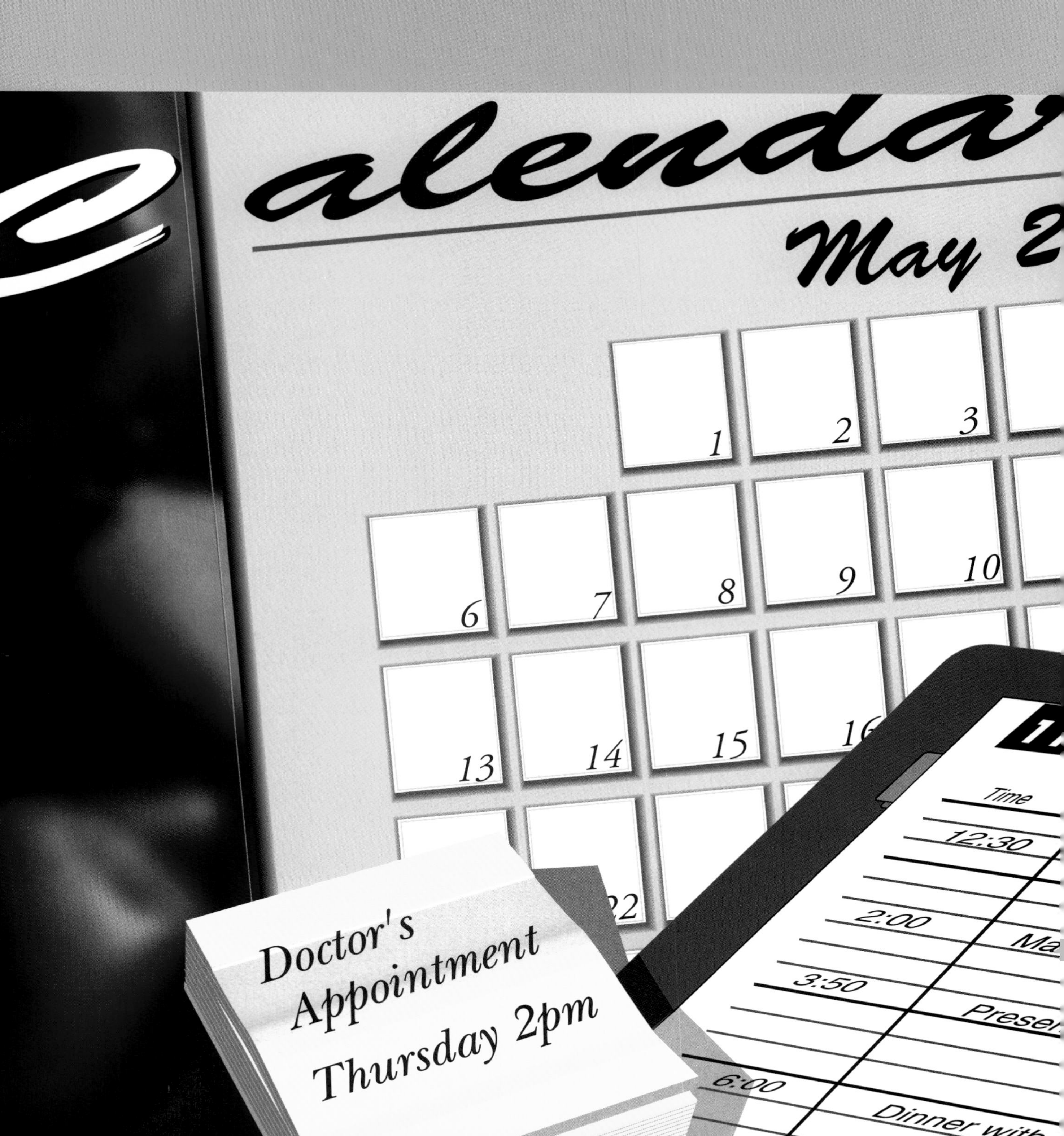
1
2
3
6
7
8
9
10
13
14
15
22
Doctor's Appointment Thursday 2pm
Time
12:30
2:00
3:50
6:00
Dinner with

Using Outlook

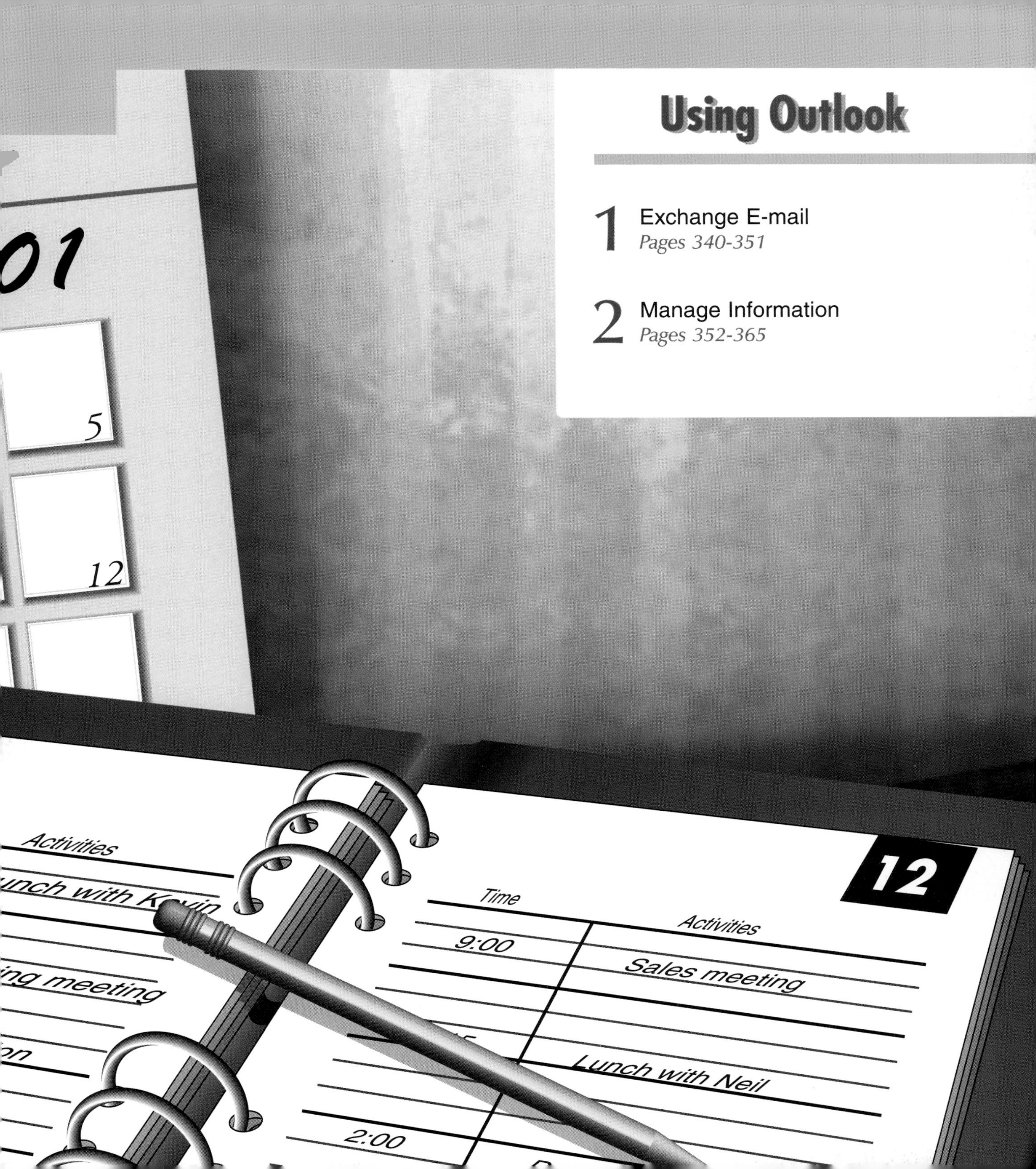

INTRODUCTION TO OUTLOOK

Outlook can help you manage your e-mail messages, appointments, contacts, tasks and notes.

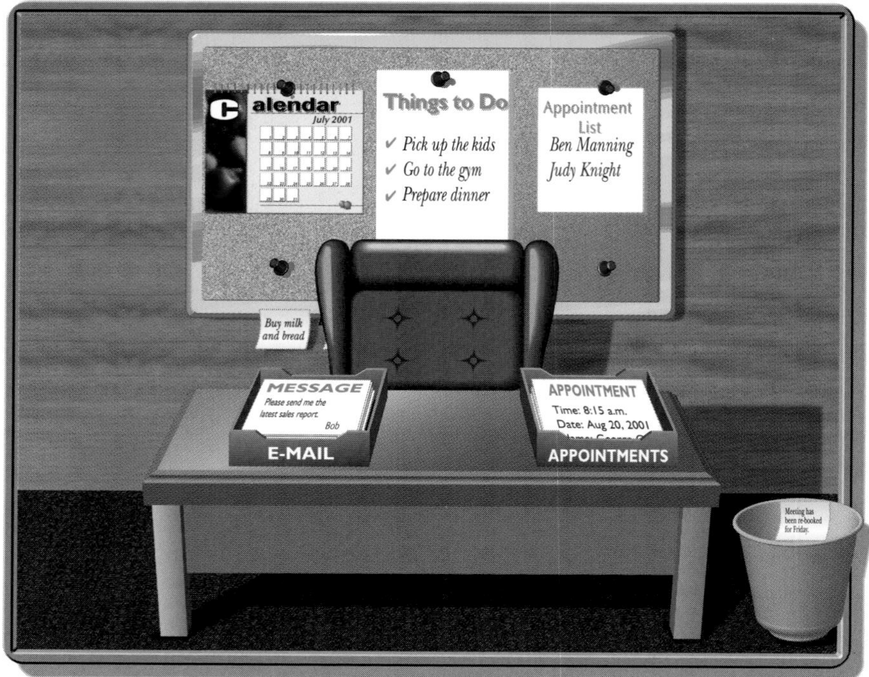

Exchange E-mail

You can use Outlook to exchange e-mail messages with friends, family members and colleagues. You can create a new message that you want to send or reply to a message you have received. Outlook provides several mail folders to help you organize your e-mail messages. You can quickly delete messages to prevent your folders from becoming too cluttered.

Manage Information

Outlook offers many features that allow you to manage information. You can keep track of your appointments, store information about your contacts and create a list of things to do. You can also create notes to store small pieces of information, such as reminders or ideas.

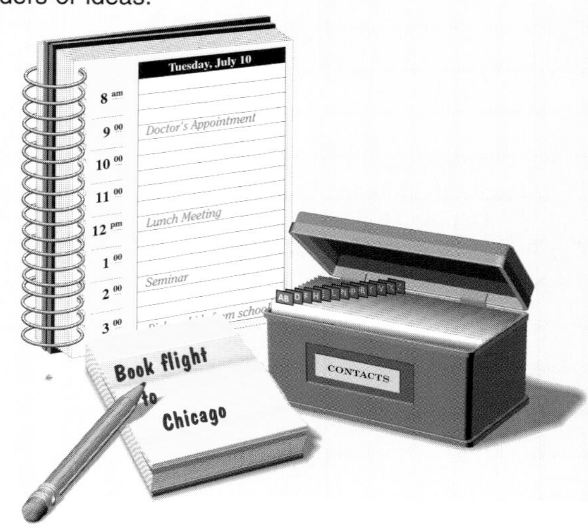

THE OUTLOOK WINDOW

The Outlook window displays several items to help you perform tasks efficiently.

Title Bar

Shows the name of the Outlook feature you are currently working with.

Menu Bar

Provides access to lists of commands available in Outlook and displays an area where you can type a question to get help information.

Toolbar

Contains buttons to help you select common commands, such as Print and Delete.

View Pane

Displays the Outlook feature you are currently working with.

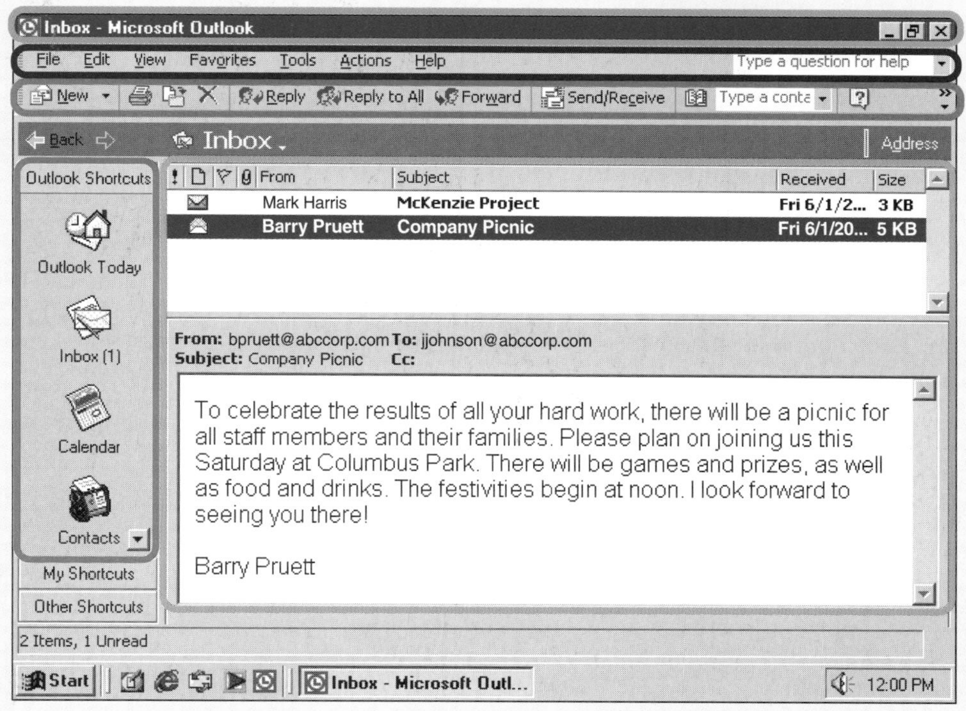

Outlook Bar

Provides access to the features included with Outlook. You can click ▼ in the Outlook Bar to browse through the features.

Outlook Today

Allows you to view a summary for the current day.

Inbox

Allows you to compose e-mail messages and stores messages you receive.

Calendar

Allows you to keep track of appointments.

Contacts

Contains an address book where you can store contact information.

Tasks

Allows you to create a list of things to do.

Notes

Allows you to create and store brief reminder notes.

Deleted Items

Stores items you delete.

READ MESSAGES

The Inbox stores the e-mail messages you receive. You can open a message to read the contents of the message.

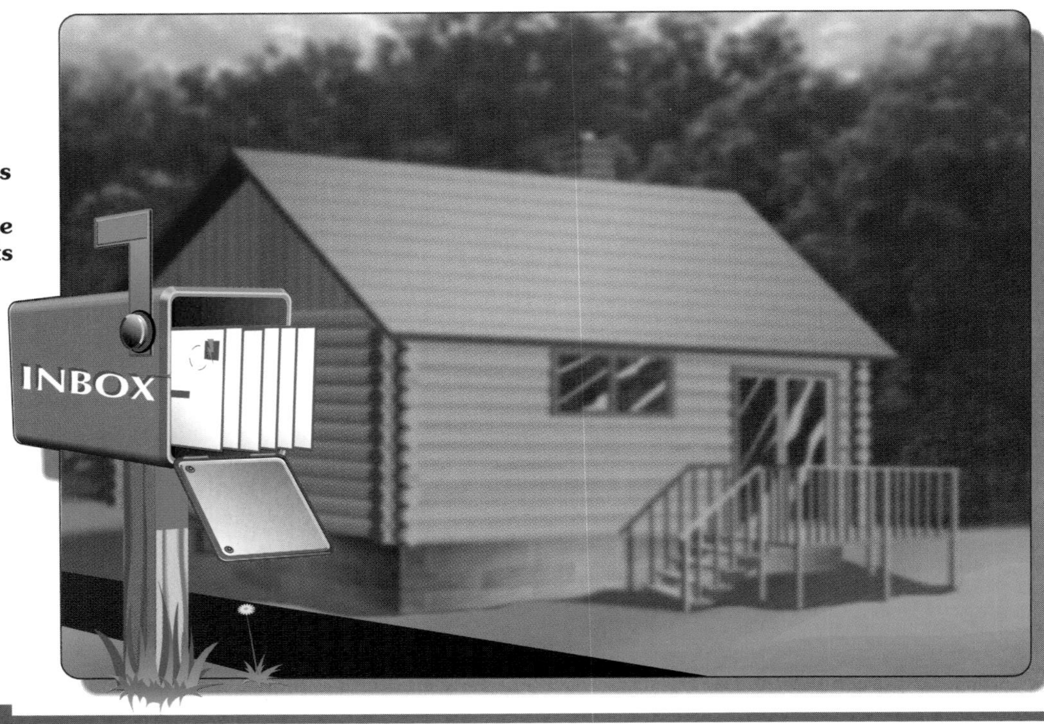

READ MESSAGES

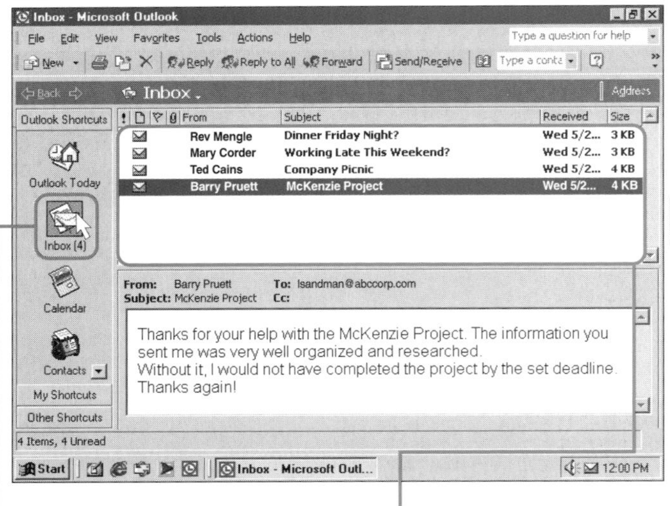

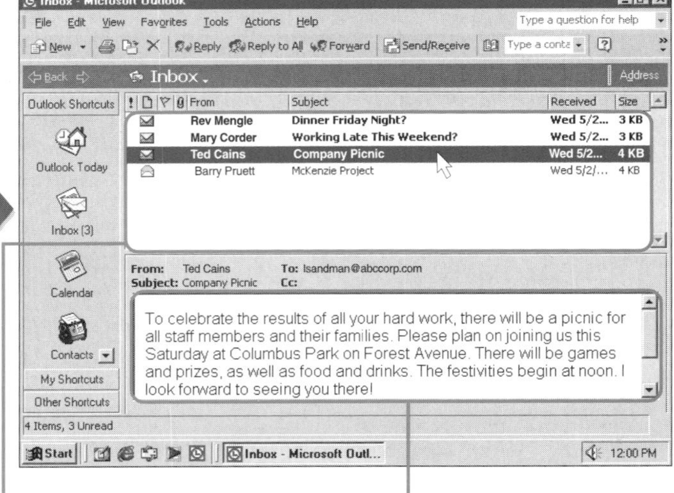

1 Click **Inbox** to view the messages you have received.

■ The number in brackets beside the Inbox icon indicates the number of messages you have not read.

■ This area displays your messages. Unread messages display a closed envelope ( ) and appear in **bold** type.

2 Click a message you want to read.

■ This area displays the contents of the message.

■ To view the contents of another message, click the message.

What are the mail folders Outlook uses to store my messages?

Drafts

Stores messages you have not yet completed.

Outbox

Temporarily stores messages that have not yet been sent.

Sent Items

Stores copies of messages you have sent.

How can I check for new messages?

To check for new messages, click the **Send/Receive** button. A dialog box may appear, asking for your password. Type the password for your e-mail account and then press the Enter key.

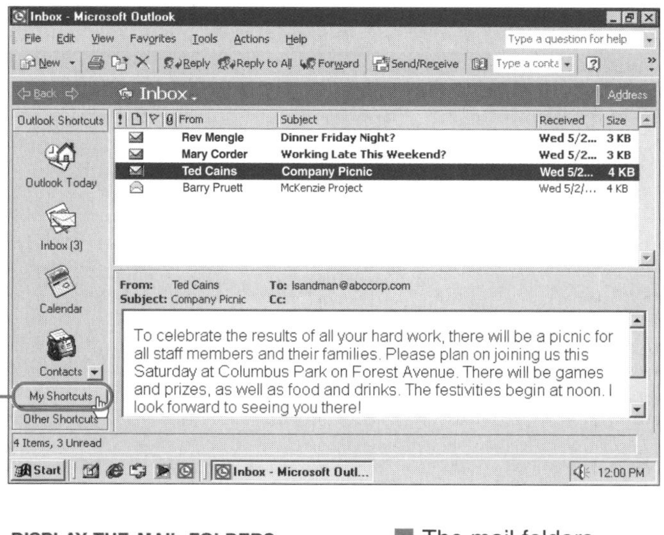

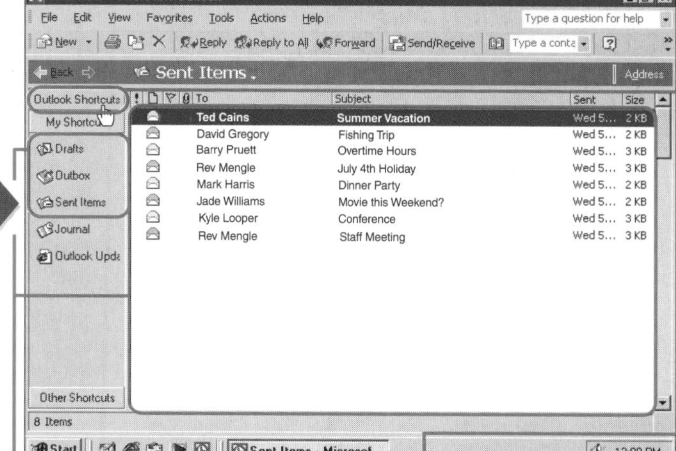

DISPLAY THE MAIL FOLDERS

1 To read the messages in other folders, click **My Shortcuts** to display the mail folders.

■ The mail folders appear.

2 Click the folder that contains the messages you want to read.

■ This area displays the messages in the folder you selected. To view the contents of a message, double-click the message.

3 To once again display the Inbox icon, click **Outlook Shortcuts**.

SEND A MESSAGE

You can send an e-mail message to express an idea or request information.

To practice sending a message, you can send a message to yourself.

SEND A MESSAGE

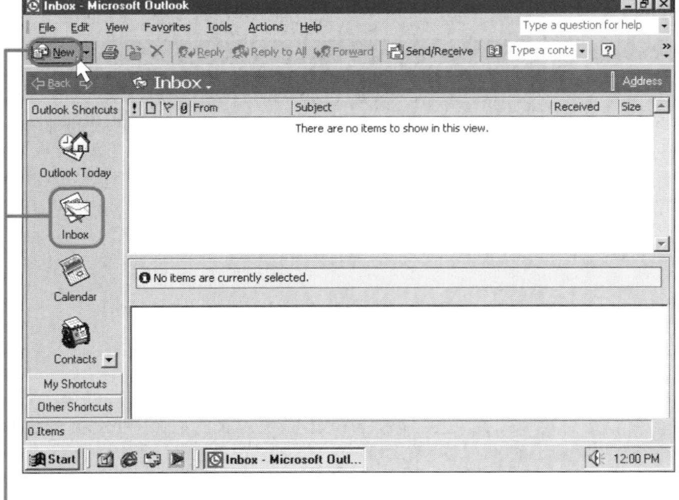

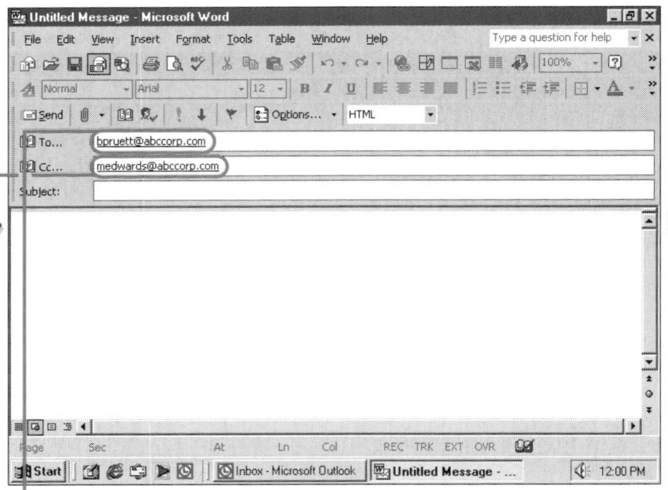

1 Click **Inbox**.

2 Click **New** to send a new message.

■ A window appears where you can compose the message.

3 Type the e-mail address of the person you want to receive the message.

4 To send a copy of the message to a person who is not directly involved but would be interested in the message, click this area and then type the e-mail address of the person.

*Note: To send the message or a copy of the message to more than one person in step **3** or **4**, separate each e-mail address with a semicolon (;).*

How can I express emotions in my e-mail messages?

You can use special characters, called smileys, to express emotions in e-mail messages. These characters resemble human faces if you turn them sideways.

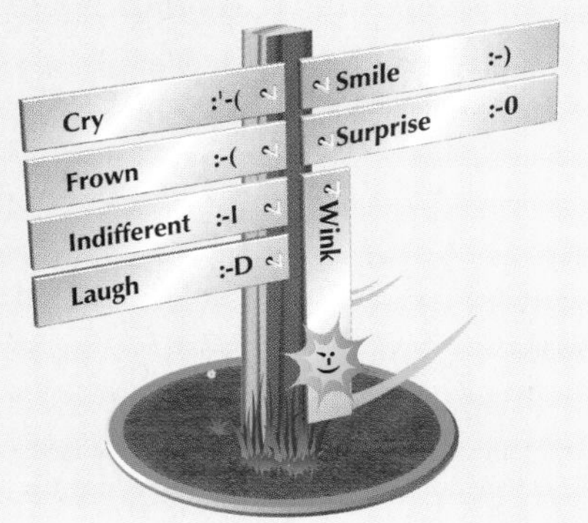

Why do red wavy underlines appear under words in my e-mail message?

Outlook automatically checks your message for spelling errors as you type. Misspelled words display a wavy red underline. Outlook will also automatically correct common spelling errors as you type, such as adn (and), recieve (receive) and teh (the).

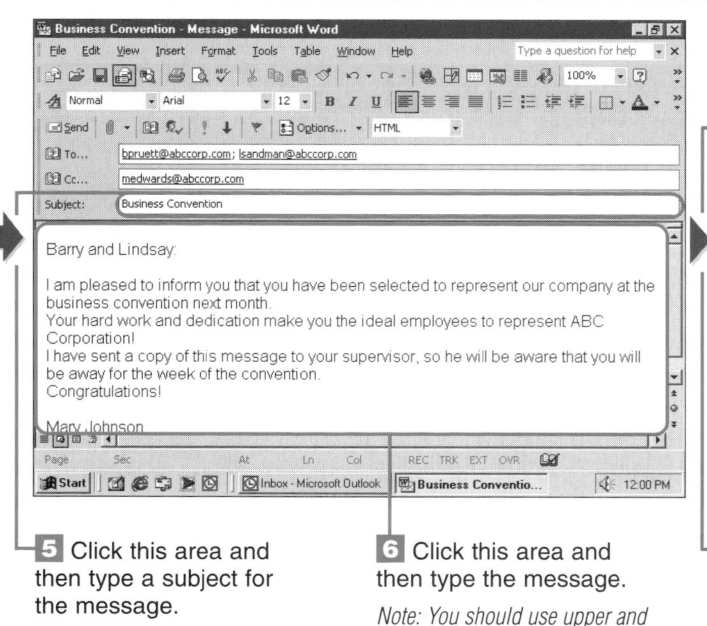

5 Click this area and then type a subject for the message.

6 Click this area and then type the message.

Note: You should use upper and lower case letters when typing the message. A message written all in CAPITAL LETTERS is annoying and difficult to read.

7 Click **Send** to send the message.

■ Outlook sends the message and stores a copy of the message in the Sent Items folder.

Note: To display the messages in the Sent Items folder, see page 343.

ATTACH A FILE TO A MESSAGE

You can attach a file to a message you are sending. Attaching a file is useful when you want to include additional information with a message.

You can attach many types of files to a message, including documents, pictures, videos and sounds. The computer receiving the message must have the necessary hardware and software installed to display or play the file you attach.

To:
Cc:
Subject:
Fishing Derby Winner
Congratulations on your achievement! I'm looking forward to seeing you at the awards ceremony! I've also included photos from the event in an attached file.

ATTACH A FILE TO A MESSAGE

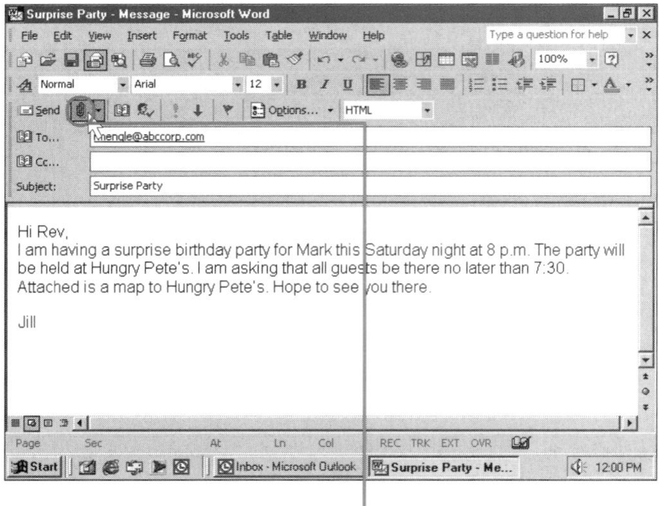

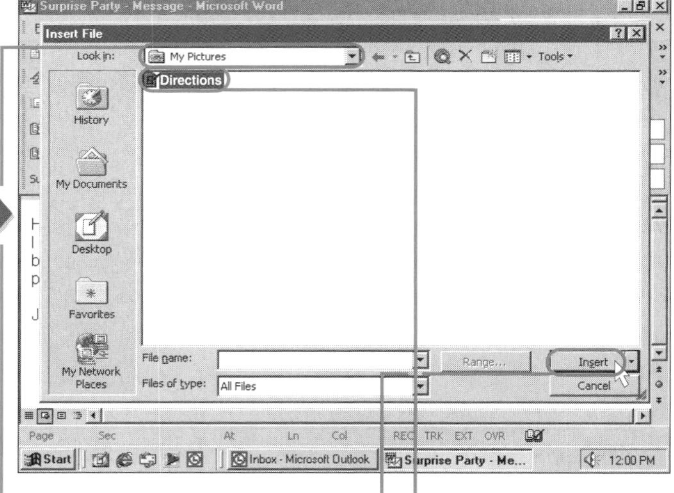

1 To create a message, perform steps 1 to 6 starting on page 344.

2 Click 📎 to attach a file to the message.

■ The Insert File dialog box appears.

■ This area shows the location of the displayed files. You can click this area to change the location.

3 Click the name of the file you want to attach to the message.

4 Click **Insert** to attach the file to the message.

Why did a dialog box appear saying the recipient may not be able to open the file I attached?

Some types of attached files, such as program files, may potentially contain viruses, which can damage the information on a recipient's computer. If the recipient of your message uses Outlook, their Outlook program will help protect their computer from viruses by blocking access to these types of files. If you still want to send the file, click **Yes** in the dialog box.

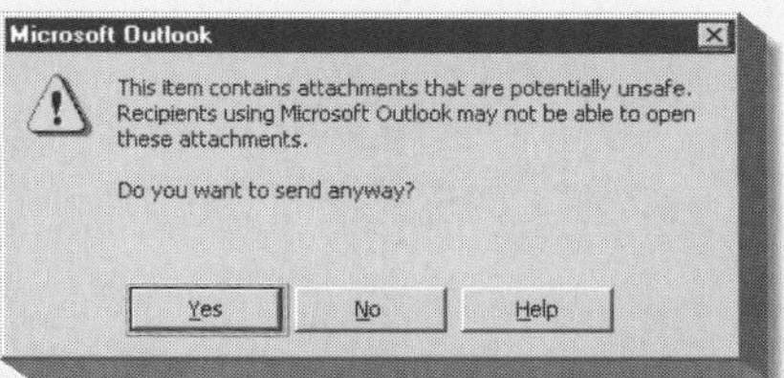

What should I consider before opening an attached file?

You should make sure the file is from a reliable source. Although Outlook blocks access to attached files that may contain viruses, you may also want to use an anti-virus program to check an attached file for a virus. Anti-virus programs, such as McAfee VirusScan or Norton AntiVirus, are available in computer stores and on the Internet.

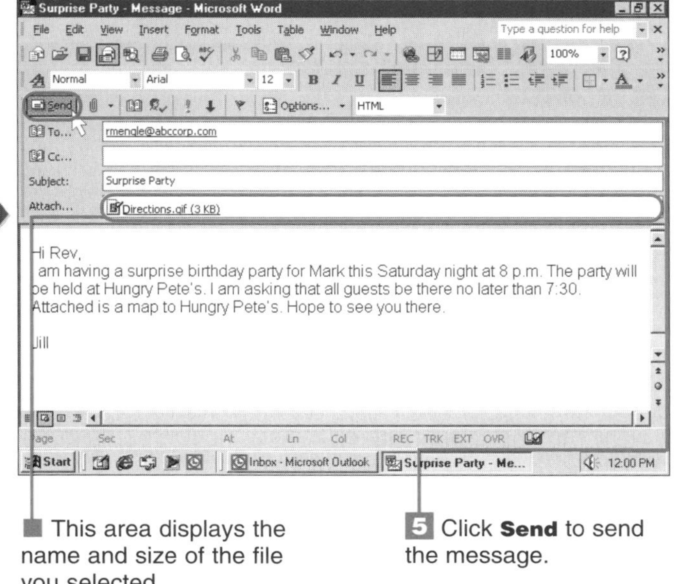

■ This area displays the name and size of the file you selected.

■ To attach additional files to the message, repeat steps 2 to 4 for each file you want to attach.

5 Click **Send** to send the message.

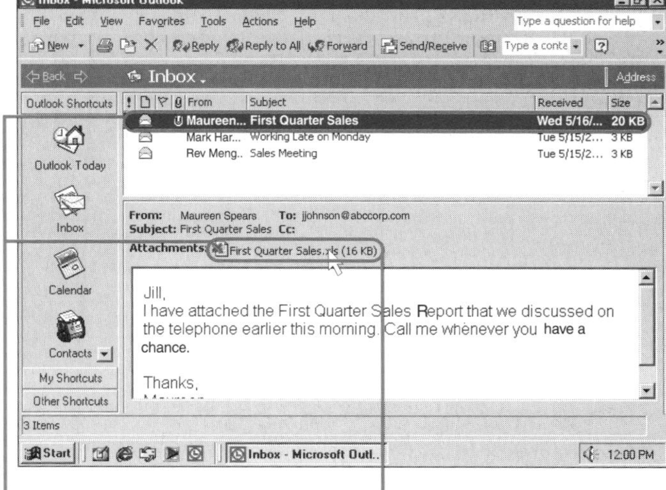

OPEN AN ATTACHED FILE

1 Click a message with an attached file. A message with an attached file displays a paper clip icon (📎).

■ This area displays the name(s) of the file(s) attached to the message.

2 To open an attached file, double-click the name of the file.

■ A dialog box may appear, asking if you want to open or save the file.

REPLY TO A MESSAGE

You can reply to a message to answer a question, express an opinion or supply additional information.

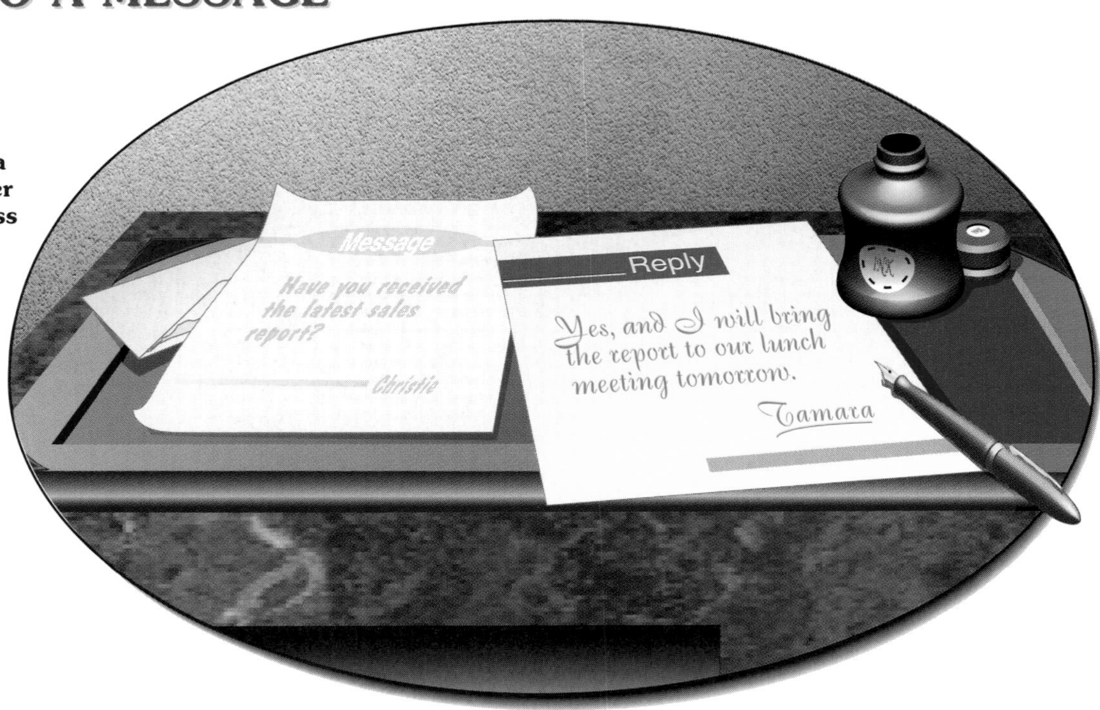

REPLY TO A MESSAGE

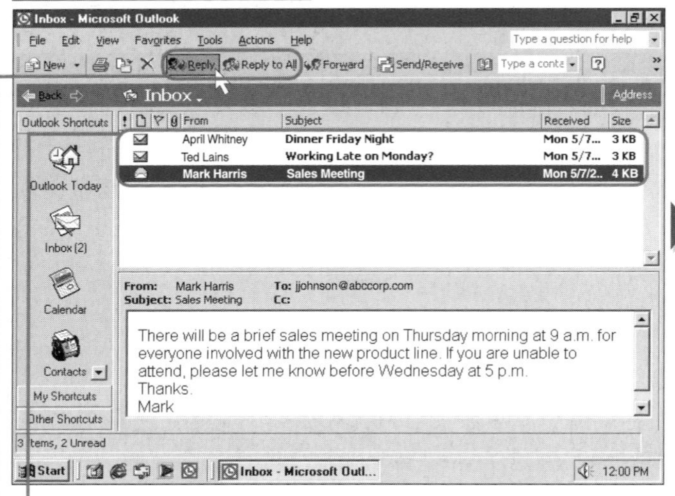

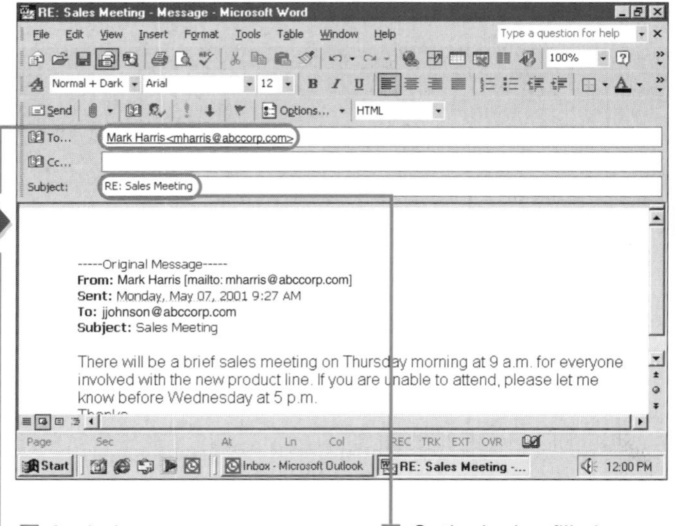

1 Click the message you want to reply to.

2 Click one of these buttons.

Reply - Send a reply to the author only.

Reply to All - Send a reply to the author and everyone who received the original message.

Note: If the button you want is not displayed, click ⁑ on the toolbar to display all the buttons.

■ A window appears for you to compose your reply.

■ Outlook fills in the e-mail address(es) for you.

■ Outlook also fills in the subject, starting the subject with **RE:**.

How can I save time when typing a message?

Abbreviations are commonly used to save time when typing messages.

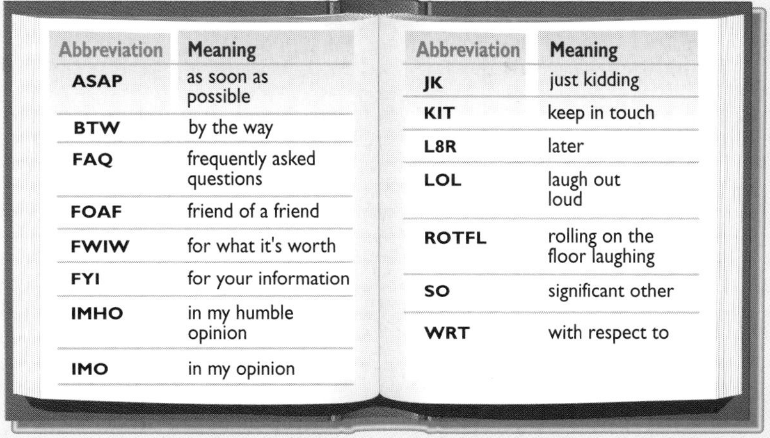

Abbreviation	Meaning
ASAP	as soon as possible
BTW	by the way
FAQ	frequently asked questions
FOAF	friend of a friend
FWIW	for what it's worth
FYI	for your information
IMHO	in my humble opinion
IMO	in my opinion

Abbreviation	Meaning
JK	just kidding
KIT	keep in touch
L8R	later
LOL	laugh out loud
ROTFL	rolling on the floor laughing
SO	significant other
WRT	with respect to

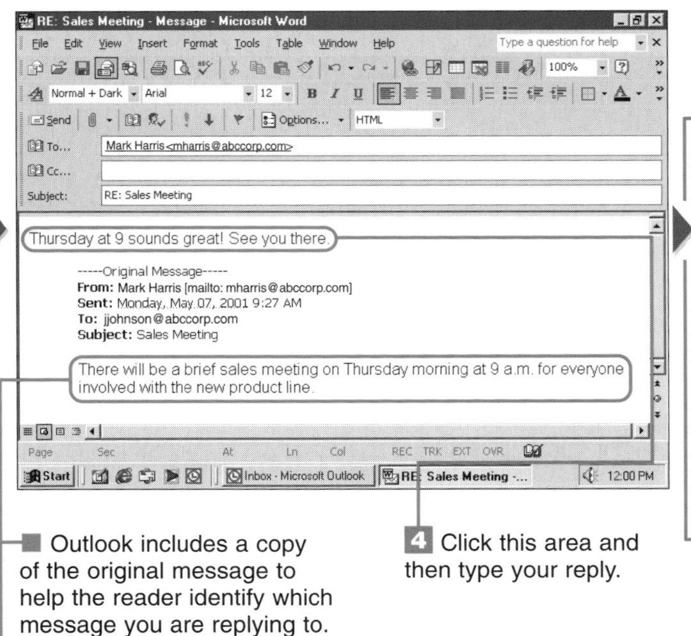

■ Outlook includes a copy of the original message to help the reader identify which message you are replying to.

3 To save the reader time, delete all parts of the original message that do not directly relate to your reply.

4 Click this area and then type your reply.

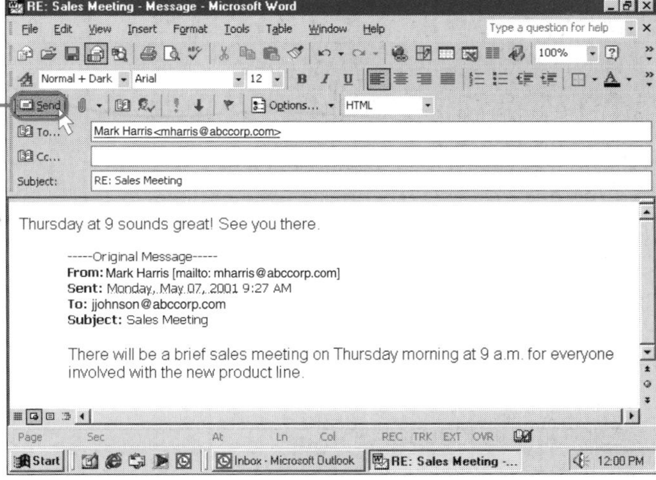

5 Click **Send** to send the reply.

■ Outlook sends the reply and stores a copy of the reply in the Sent Items folder.

Note: To display the messages in the Sent Items folder, see page 343.

FORWARD A MESSAGE

After reading a message, you can add comments and then forward the message to a friend, family member or colleague.

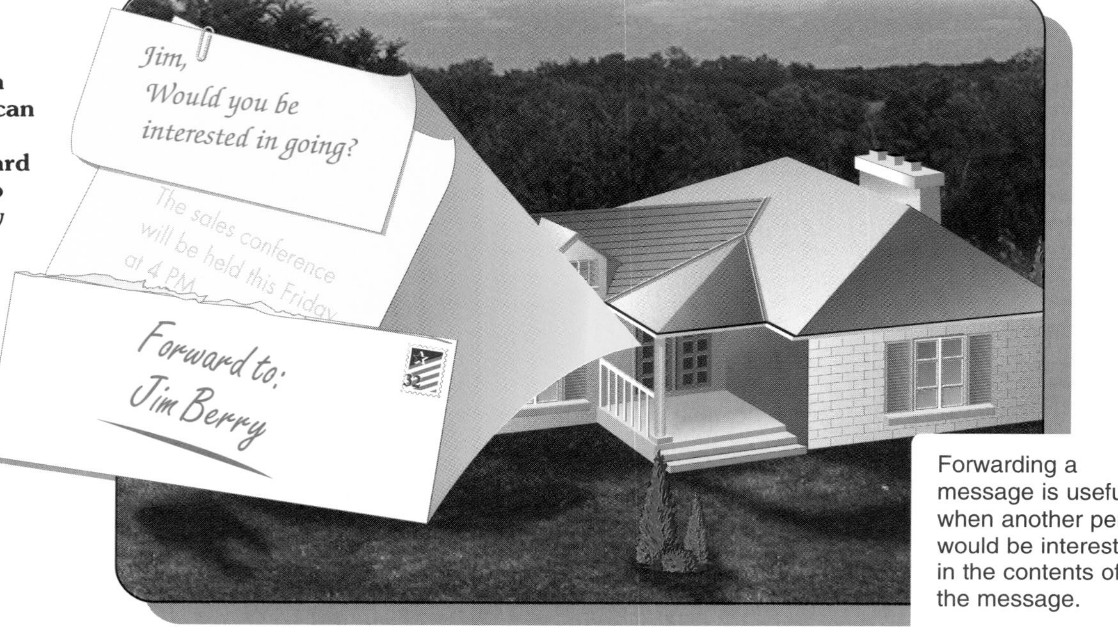

Forwarding a message is useful when another person would be interested in the contents of the message.

FORWARD A MESSAGE

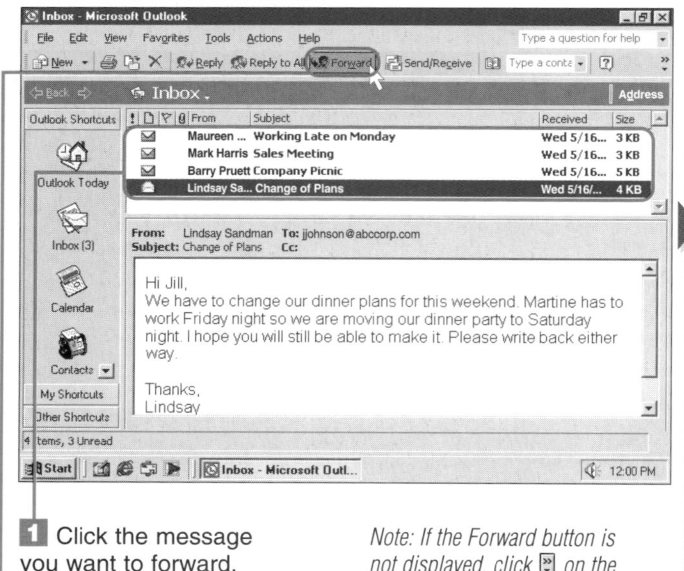

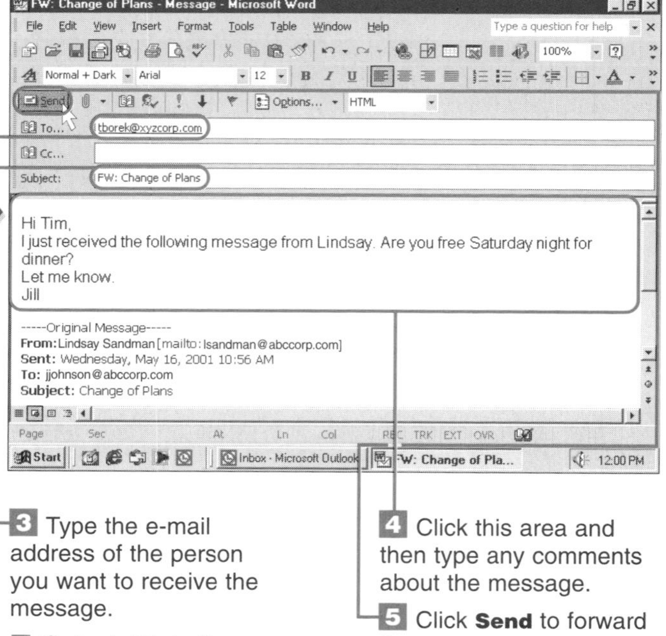

1 Click the message you want to forward.

2 Click **Forward**.

Note: If the Forward button is not displayed, click » on the toolbar to display all the buttons.

■ A window appears, displaying the contents of the message you are forwarding.

3 Type the e-mail address of the person you want to receive the message.

■ Outlook fills in the subject for you, starting the subject with **FW:**.

4 Click this area and then type any comments about the message.

5 Click **Send** to forward the message.

DELETE A MESSAGE

You can delete a message you no longer need. Deleting messages prevents your folders from becoming cluttered with messages.

DELETE A MESSAGE

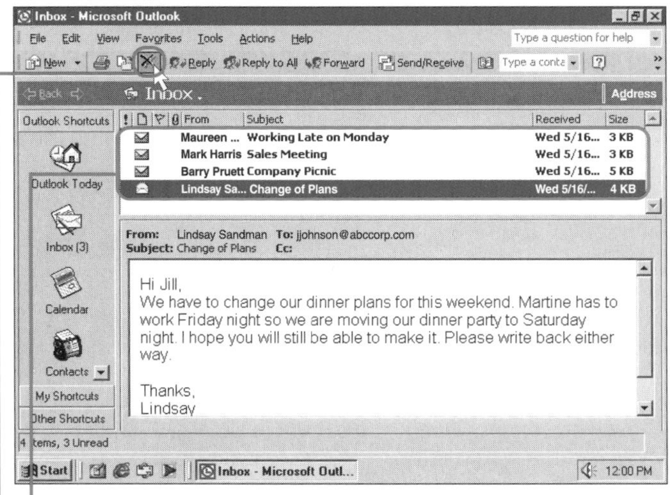

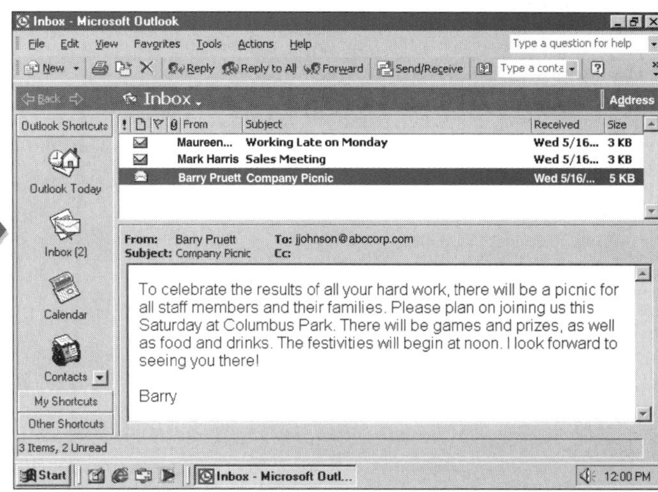

1 Click the message you want to delete.

2 Click ☒ to delete the message.

Note: If ☒ is not displayed, click » on the toolbar to display all the buttons.

■ The message disappears.

■ Outlook places the message in the Deleted Items folder. For information on the Deleted Items folder, see page 364.

You can use the Calendar to keep track of your appointments, such as business meetings and lunch dates.

Outlook uses the date and time set in your computer to determine today's date. To change the date and time set in your computer, refer to your Windows manual.

DISPLAY THE CALENDAR

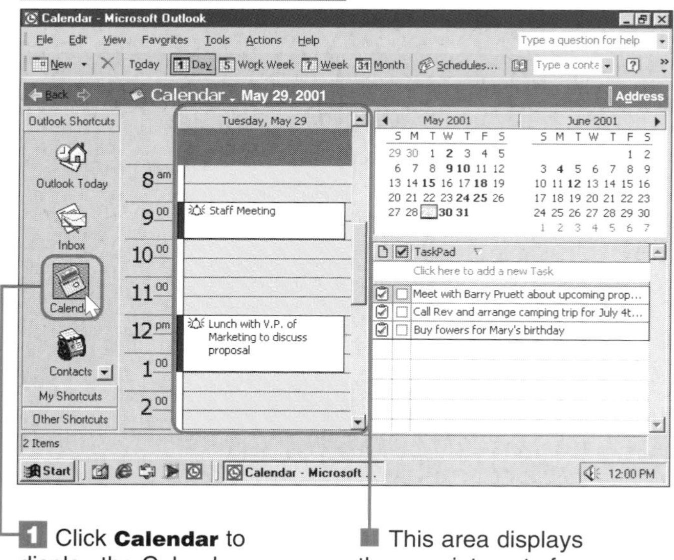

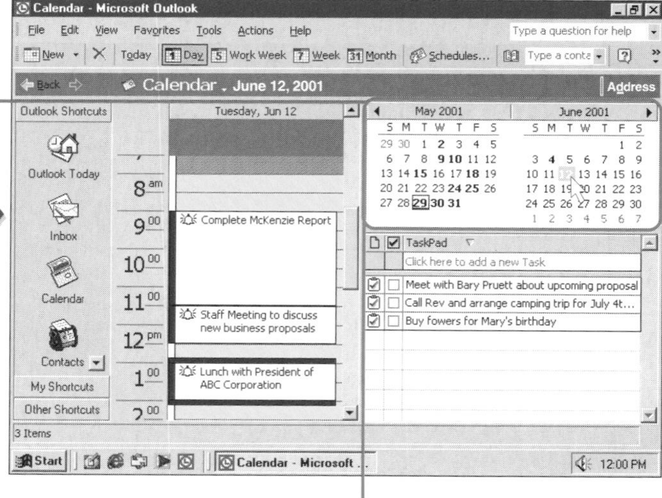

1 Click **Calendar** to display the Calendar.

■ This area displays the appointments for the current day.

Note: To add an appointment, see page 354.

■ This area displays the days in the current month and the next month. Days with appointments are shown in **bold**.

2 To display the appointments for another day, click the day. The day you select is highlighted.

■ The current day displays a red outline.

What ways can I view the Calendar?

You can change the view of the Calendar to display your appointments in one of the following views.

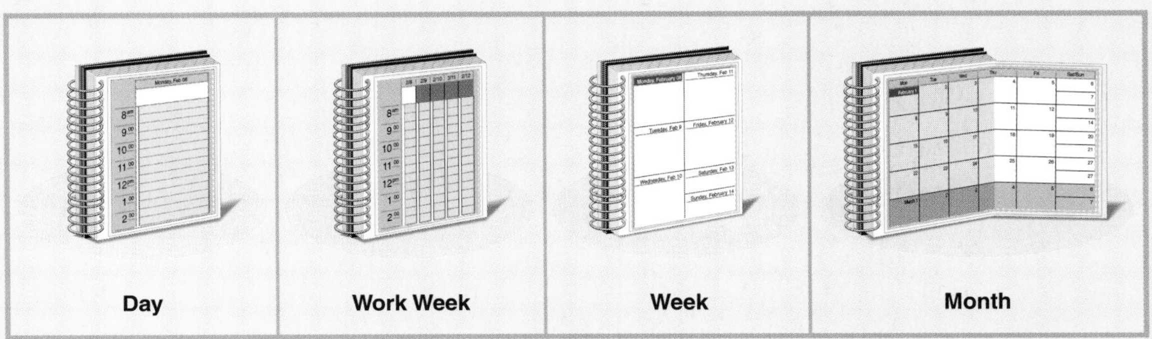

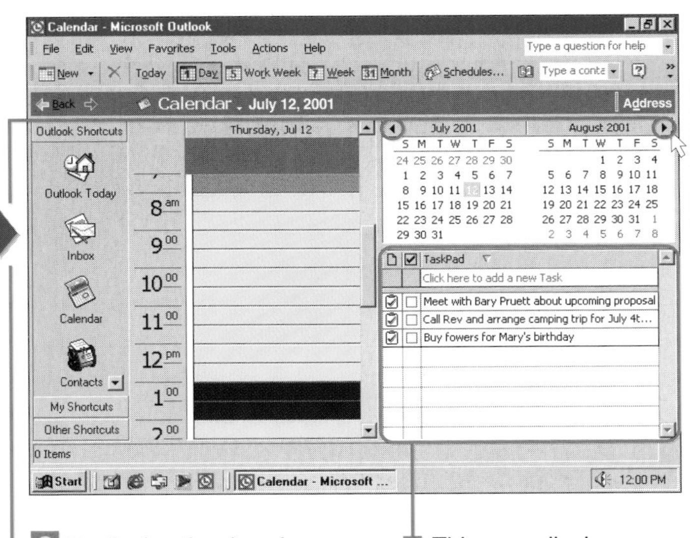

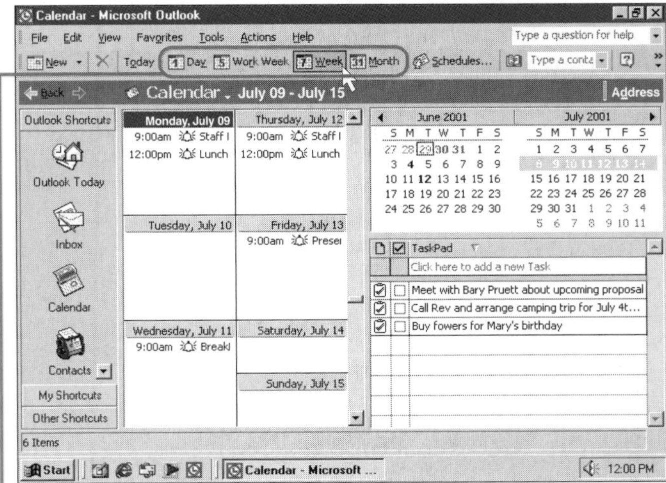

3 To display the days in another month, click one of the following options.

◀ Display previous month

▶ Display next month

■ This area displays your tasks. For information on tasks, see page 360.

CHANGE VIEW OF CALENDAR

1 Click the way you want to view the Calendar.

1 Day — Day

5 Work Week — Work Week

7 Week — Week

31 Month — Month

Note: If the button you want is not displayed, click » on the toolbar to display all the buttons.

CONTINUED

USING THE CALENDAR

You can add an appointment to the Calendar to remind you of an activity such as a seminar or doctor's appointment.

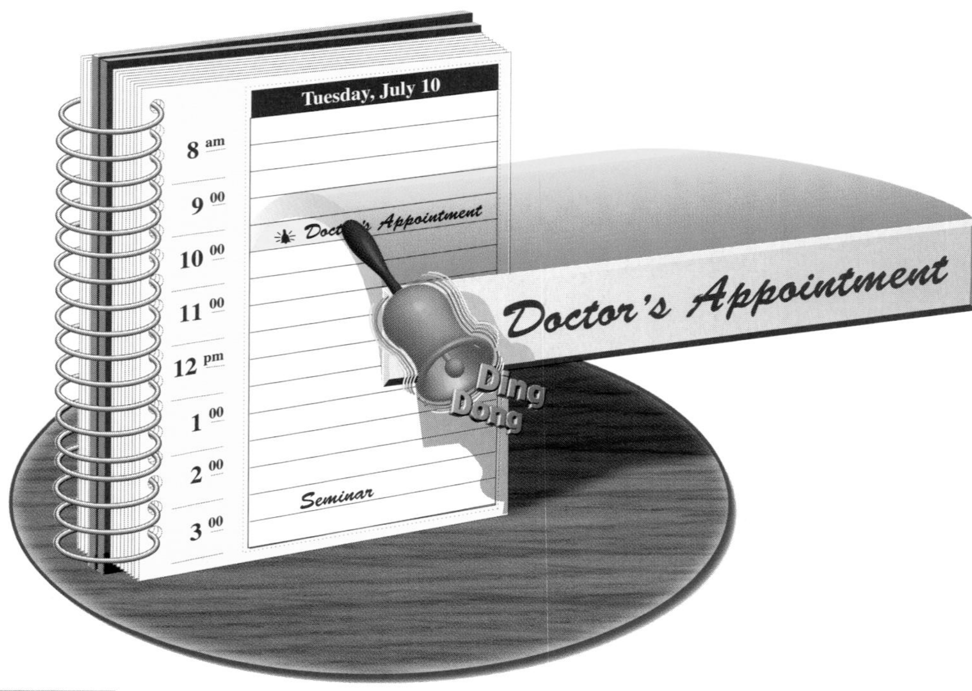

SCHEDULE AN APPOINTMENT

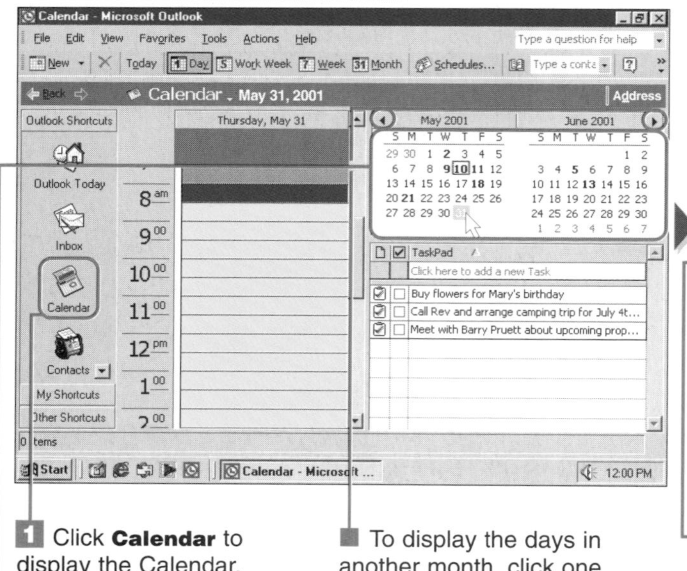

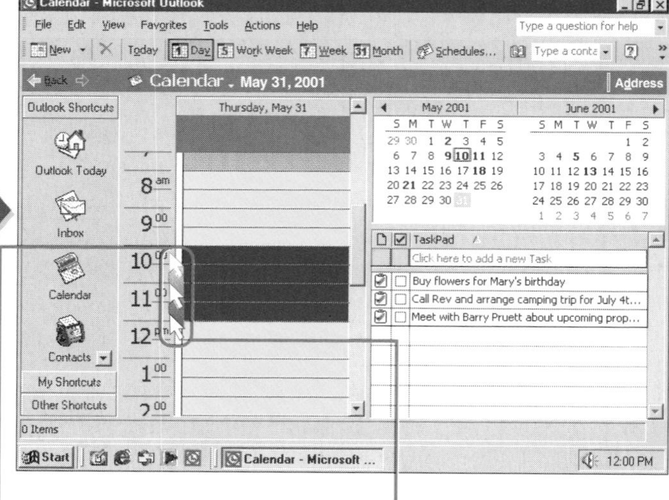

1 Click **Calendar** to display the Calendar.

2 Click the day you want to add an appointment to.

■ To display the days in another month, click one of the following options.

◀ Display previous month

▶ Display next month

3 Position the mouse over the starting time for the appointment.

4 Drag the mouse to select the amount of time you want to set aside for the appointment.

Will Outlook remind me of an appointment I have scheduled?

Outlook will play a brief sound and display the Reminder dialog box 15 minutes before a scheduled appointment.

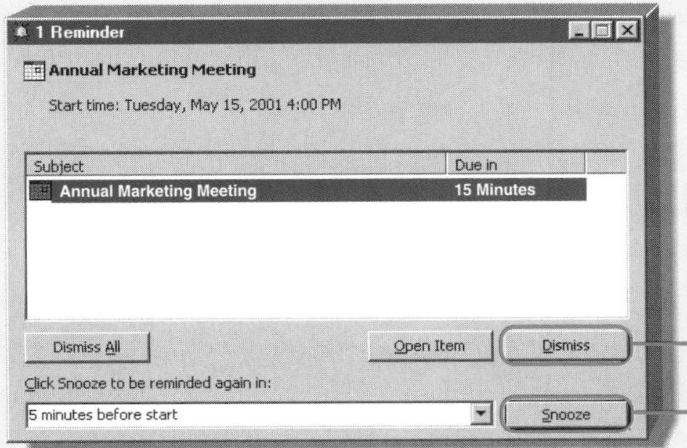

■ To close the Reminder dialog box, click one of the following options.

Dismiss - Close the reminder

Snooze - Remind again five minutes before the appointment

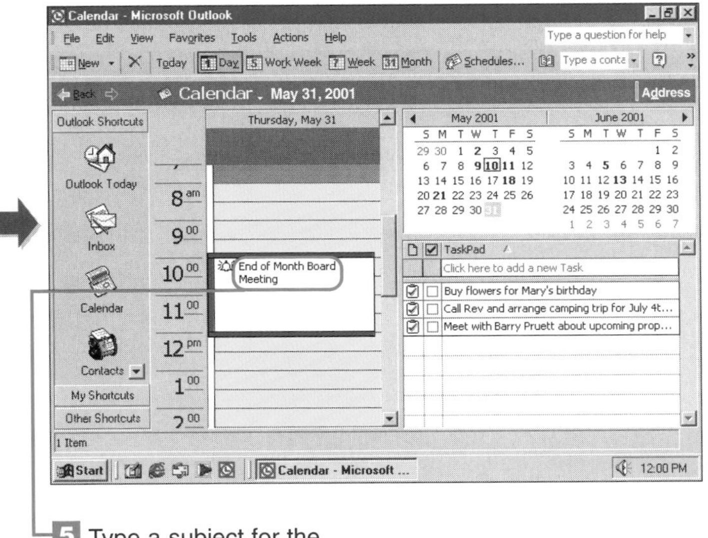

5 Type a subject for the appointment and then press the Enter key.

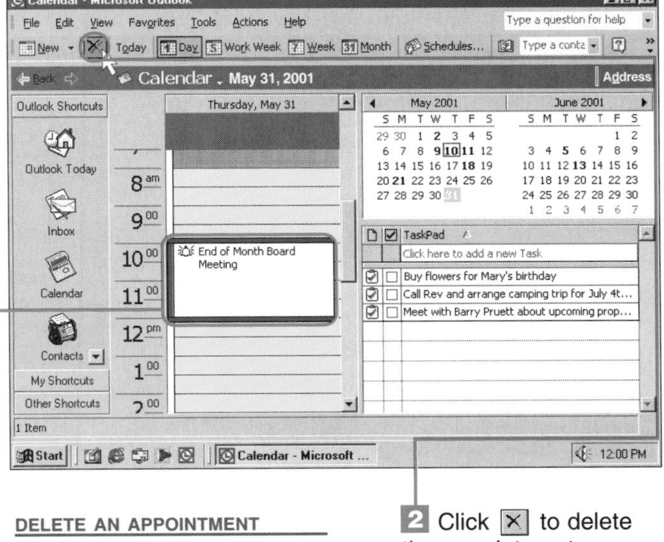

DELETE AN APPOINTMENT

1 To select the appointment you want to delete, click the left edge of the appointment (↖ changes to ✥).

2 Click ✕ to delete the appointment.

Note: If ✕ is not displayed, click » on the toolbar to display all the buttons.

Outlook allows you to keep detailed information about your friends, family members, colleagues and clients.

CREATE A NEW CONTACT

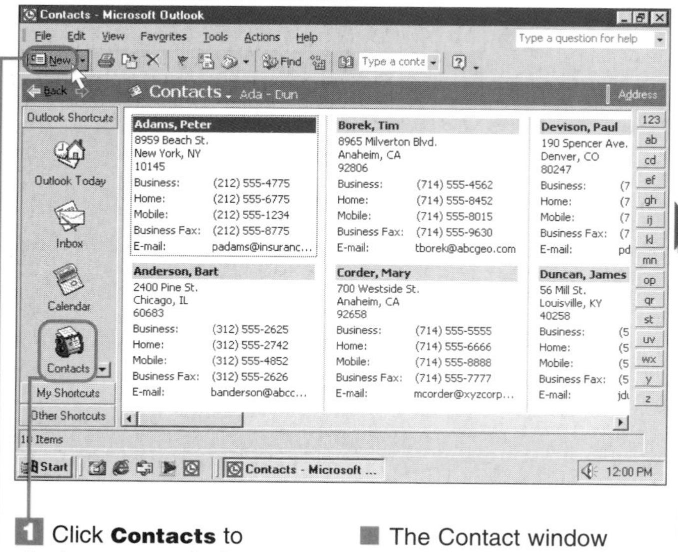

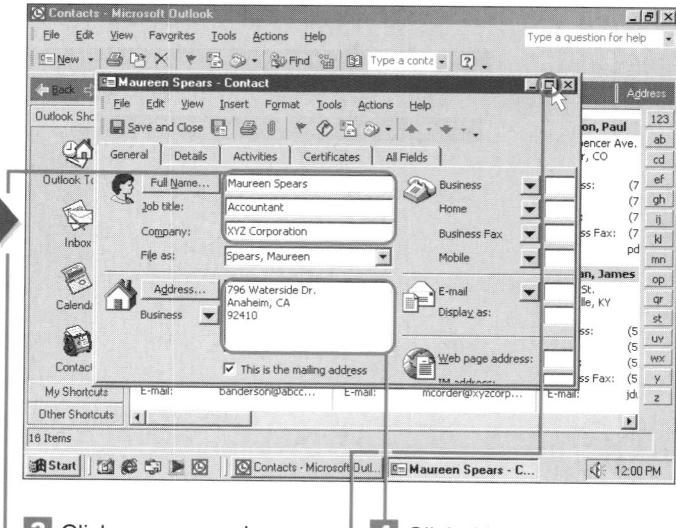

1 Click **Contacts** to display your contacts.

2 Click **New** to create a new contact.

■ The Contact window appears, displaying areas where you can enter information about a contact.

Note: You do not need to enter information in every area.

3 Click an area and type the contact's full name, job title and company name.

4 Click this area and type the contact's address.

5 To enlarge the window so you can clearly see all the areas in the window, click □.

Why did the Check Address dialog box appear after I entered an address?

If the address you entered is incomplete, Outlook displays the Check Address dialog box to help you complete the address.

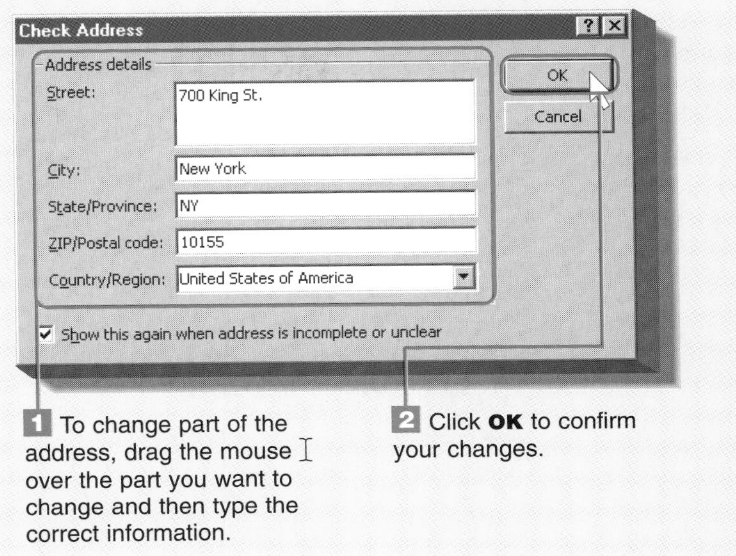

1 To change part of the address, drag the mouse over the part you want to change and then type the correct information.

2 Click **OK** to confirm your changes.

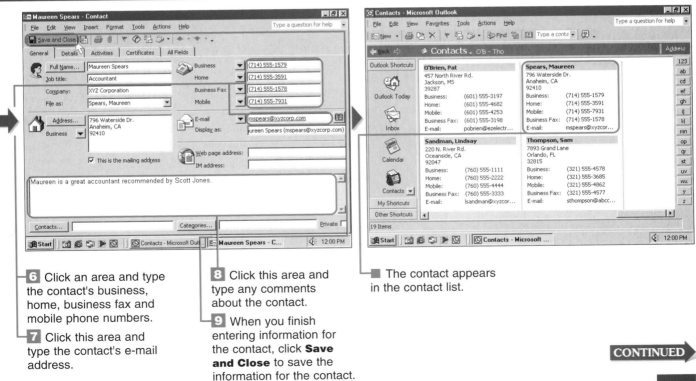

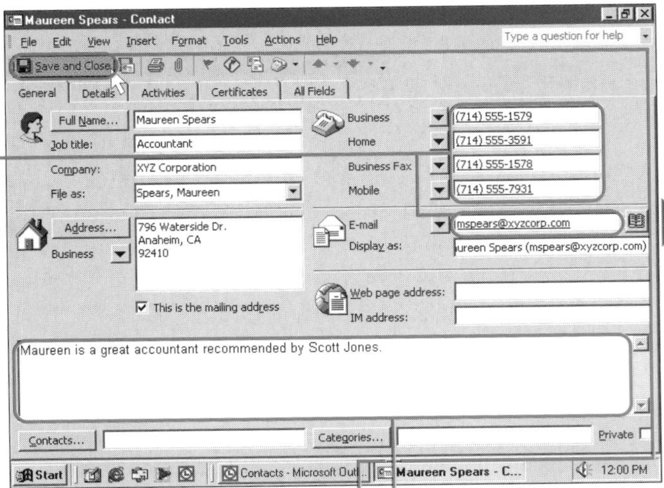

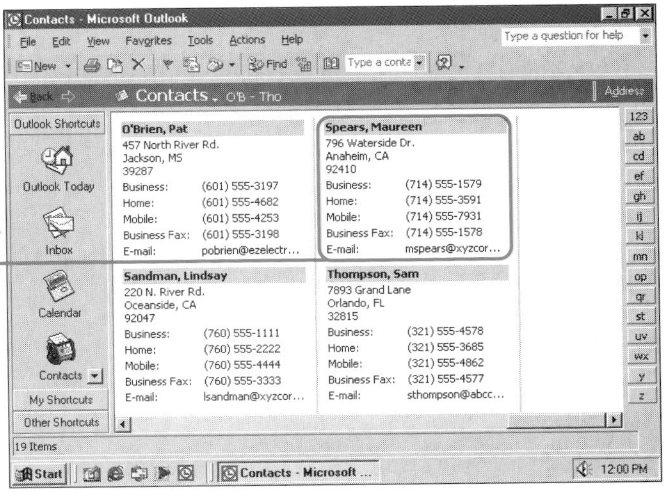

6 Click an area and type the contact's business, home, business fax and mobile phone numbers.

7 Click this area and type the contact's e-mail address.

8 Click this area and type any comments about the contact.

9 When you finish entering information for the contact, click **Save and Close** to save the information for the contact.

■ The contact appears in the contact list.

CONTINUED

USING CONTACTS

You can browse through your contacts to find the contact you want to work with. After you find the contact, you can remove the contact or update the information for the contact.

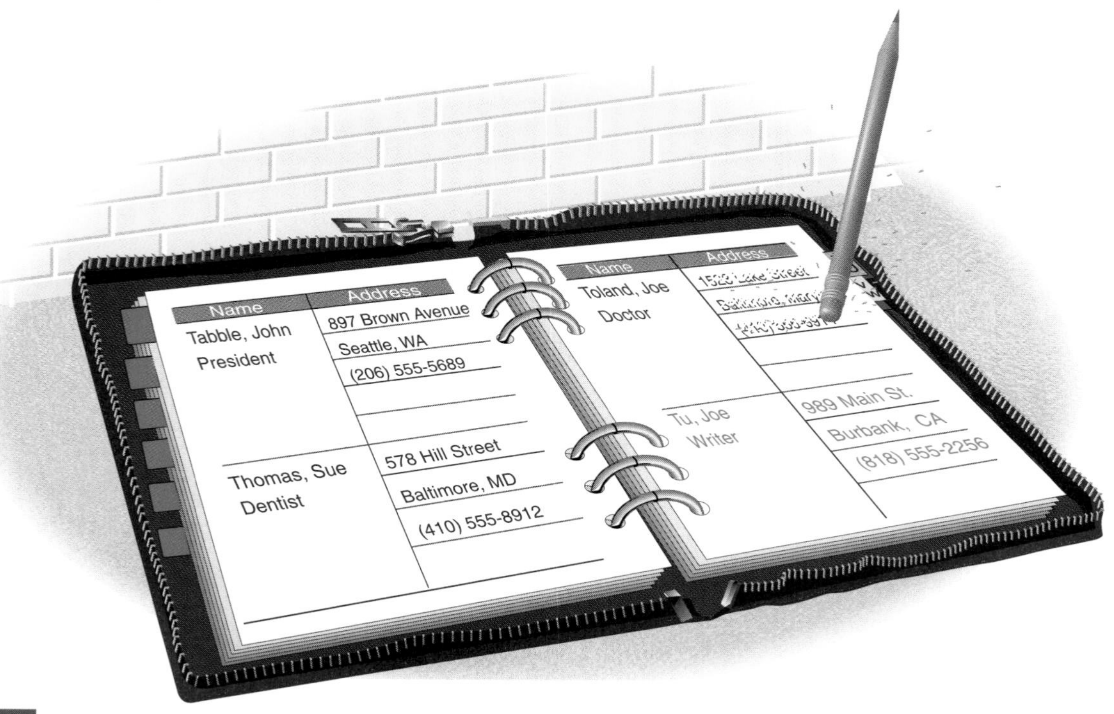

WORK WITH CONTACTS

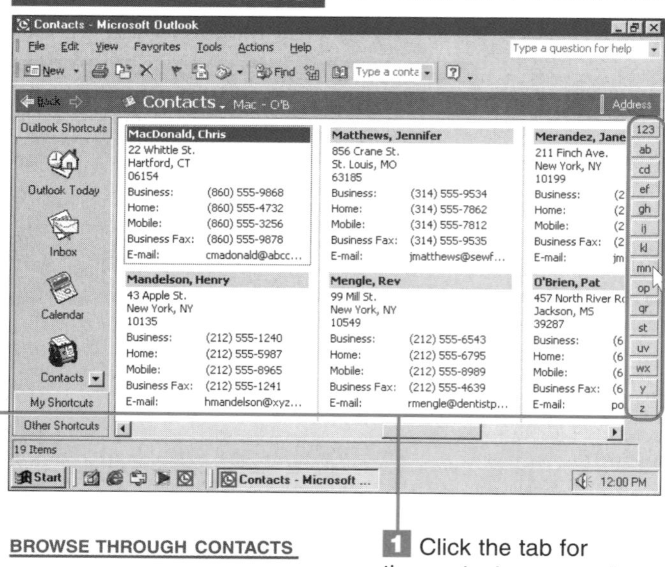

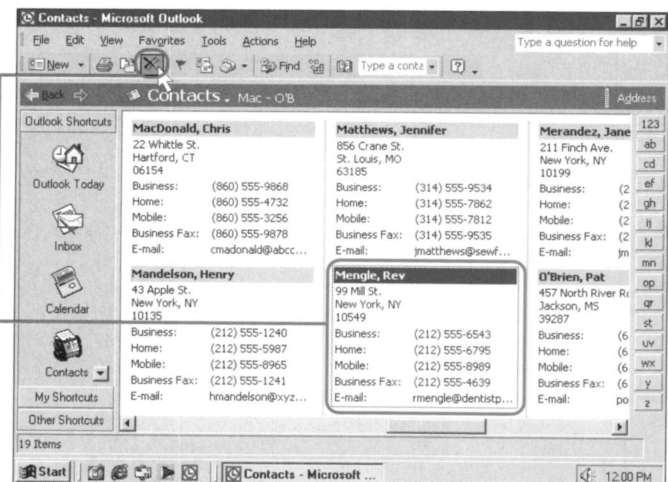

BROWSE THROUGH CONTACTS

■ These tabs allow you to browse through your contacts alphabetically.

1 Click the tab for the contacts you want to view.

■ Contacts beginning with the letter(s) you selected appear.

DELETE A CONTACT

1 Click the contact you want to delete.

2 Click ☒ to delete the contact.

■ The contact disappears from the list.

Can I display a map showing a contact's address?

While viewing the information for a contact, you can display a map for the contact's address.

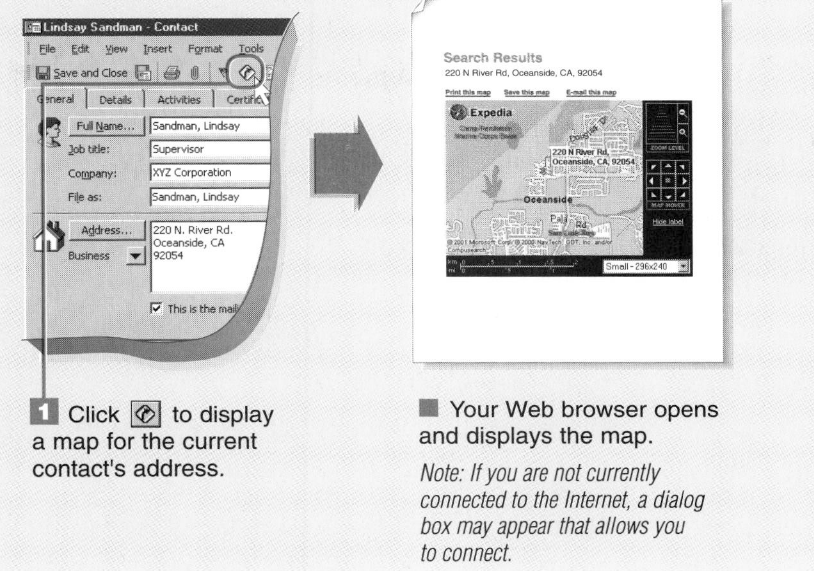

1 Click to display a map for the current contact's address.

■ Your Web browser opens and displays the map.

Note: If you are not currently connected to the Internet, a dialog box may appear that allows you to connect.

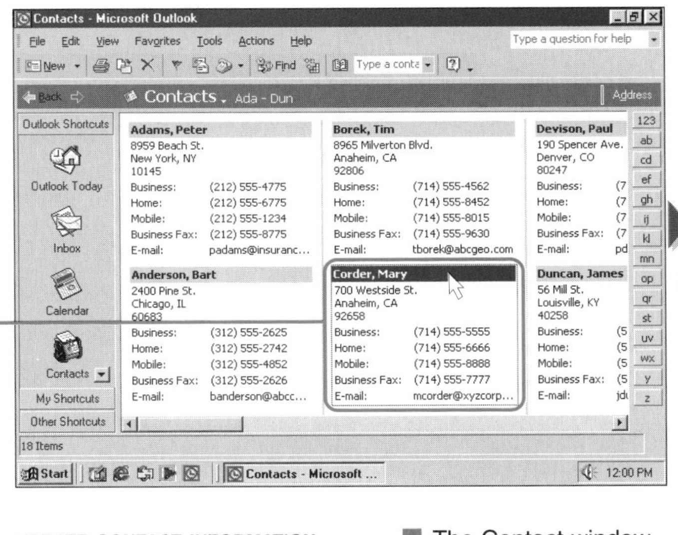

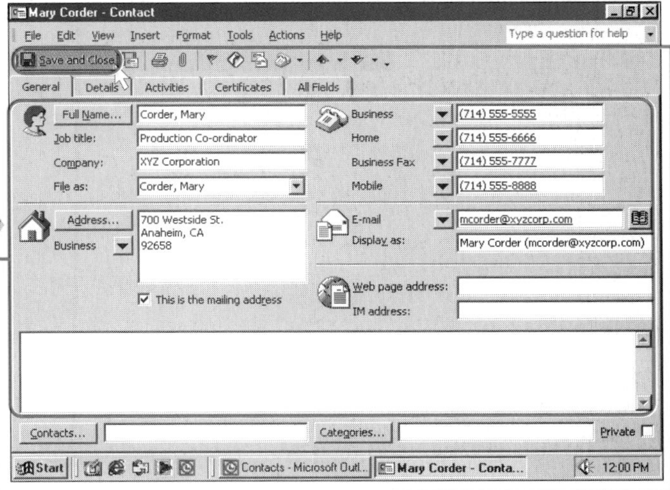

UPDATE CONTACT INFORMATION

1 To update the information for a contact, double-click the contact.

■ The Contact window appears, displaying the information for the contact.

2 Drag the mouse I over the information you want to change and then type the new information.

3 Click **Save and Close** to save your changes.

USING TASKS

You can create an electronic to-do list of personal and work-related tasks that you want to accomplish.

USING TASKS

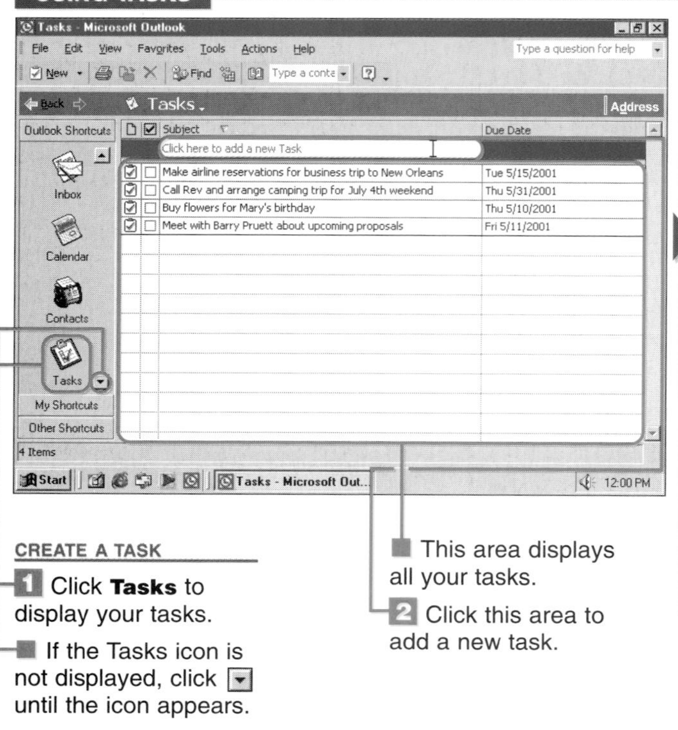

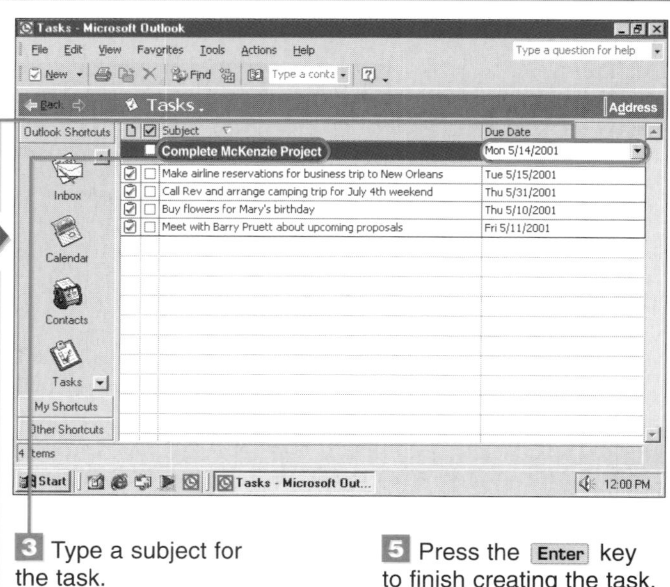

CREATE A TASK

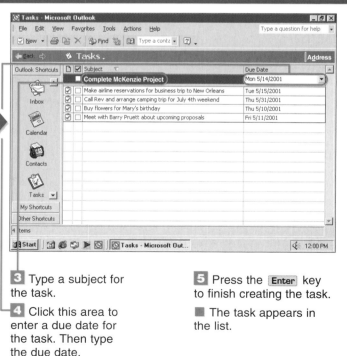

1 Click **Tasks** to display your tasks.

■ If the Tasks icon is not displayed, click ▼ until the icon appears.

■ This area displays all your tasks.

2 Click this area to add a new task.

3 Type a subject for the task.

4 Click this area to enter a due date for the task. Then type the due date.

5 Press the Enter key to finish creating the task.

■ The task appears in the list.

Is there a quick way to enter a due date for a task?

Yes. Instead of typing a date, you can type a brief description of the date, such as "Friday," "tomorrow," "next Thursday," "one month from now" or "Valentine's Day."

How can I quickly find a task in my task list?

You can sort the tasks in your task list by subject or due date to help you find tasks of interest.

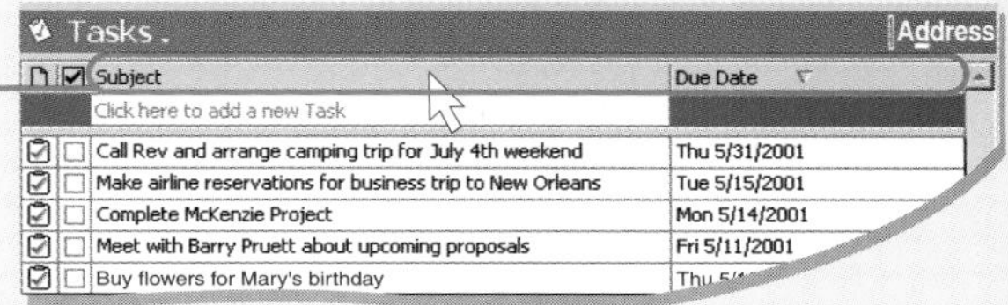

1 To sort your tasks, click the heading of the column you want to use to sort the tasks.

■ You can click the heading again to sort the tasks in the opposite order.

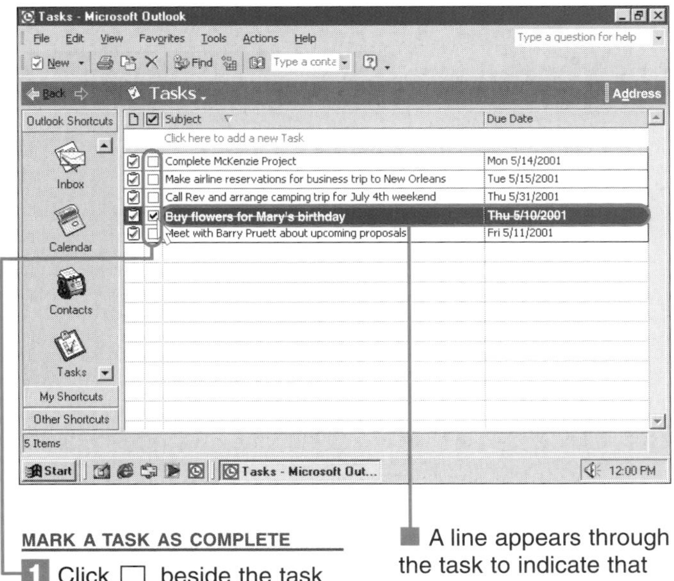

MARK A TASK AS COMPLETE

1 Click ☐ beside the task you want to mark as complete (☐ changes to ☑).

■ A line appears through the task to indicate that the task is complete.

*Note: To remove the line and once again display the task as incomplete, repeat step **1** (☑ changes to ☐).*

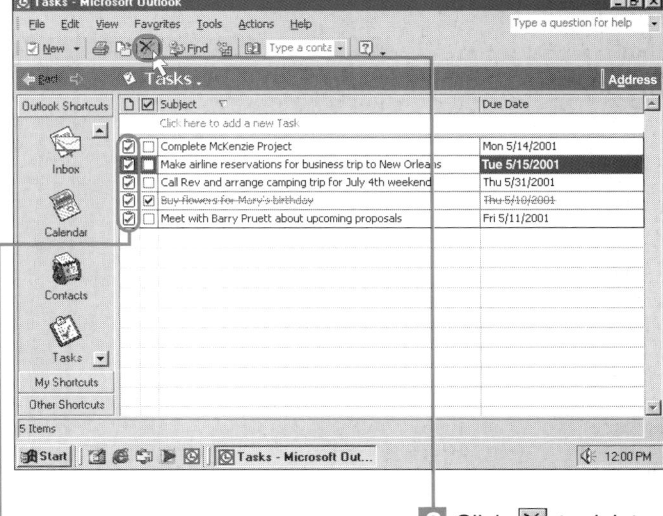

DELETE A TASK

1 Click the task icon beside the task you want to delete.

2 Click ☒ to delete the task.

■ The task disappears from the list.

USING NOTES

You can create electronic notes that are similar to paper sticky notes.

Notes are useful for storing small pieces of information such as reminders, questions, ideas and directions.

USING NOTES

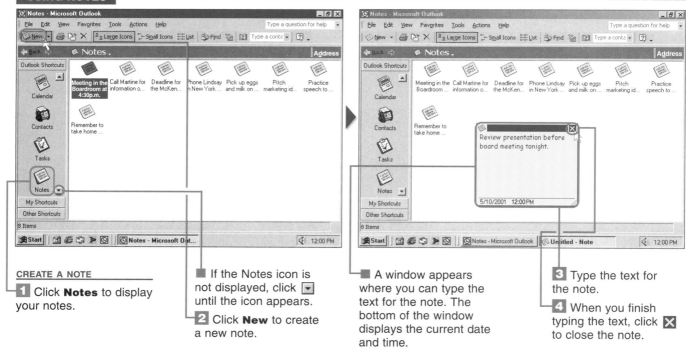

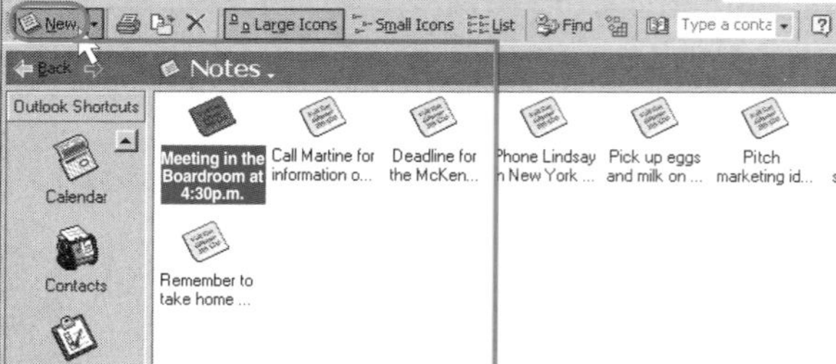

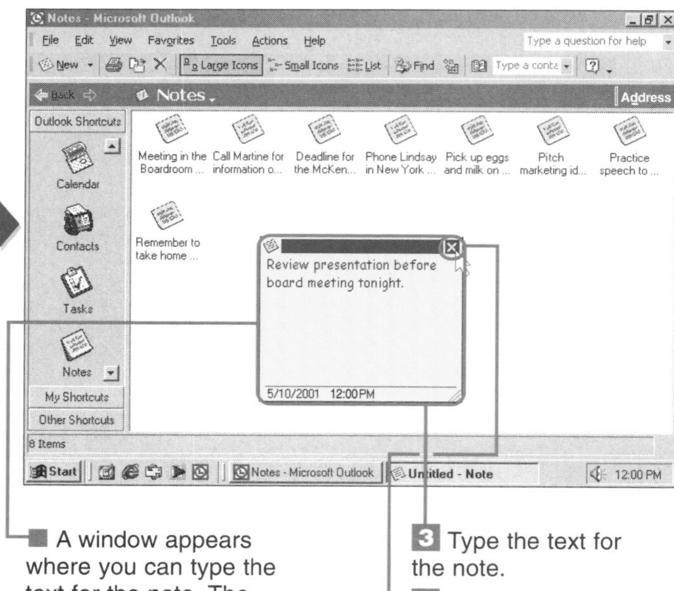

CREATE A NOTE

1 Click **Notes** to display your notes.

■ If the Notes icon is not displayed, click ▾ until the icon appears.

2 Click **New** to create a new note.

■ A window appears where you can type the text for the note. The bottom of the window displays the current date and time.

3 Type the text for the note.

4 When you finish typing the text, click ✕ to close the note.

How do I change the size of a note?

Position the mouse over the bottom right corner of the note (changes to) and then drag the corner until the note displays the size you want. Changing the size of a note is useful when the note is too small to display all the text in the note.

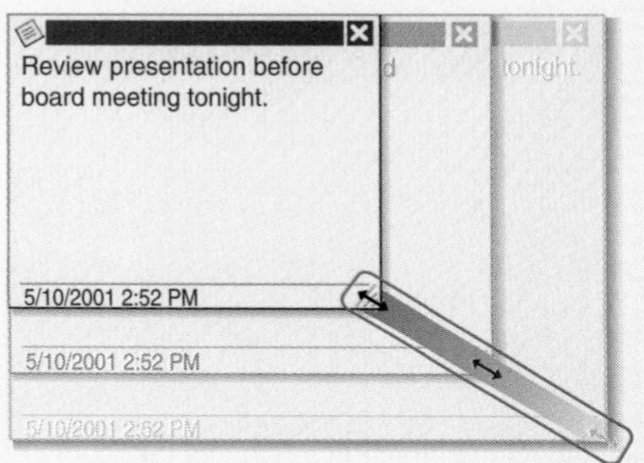

How do I delete a note?

To delete a note, click the icon for the note you want to delete and then press the Delete key. Outlook places the note in the Deleted Items folder. For information on the Deleted Items folder, see page 364.

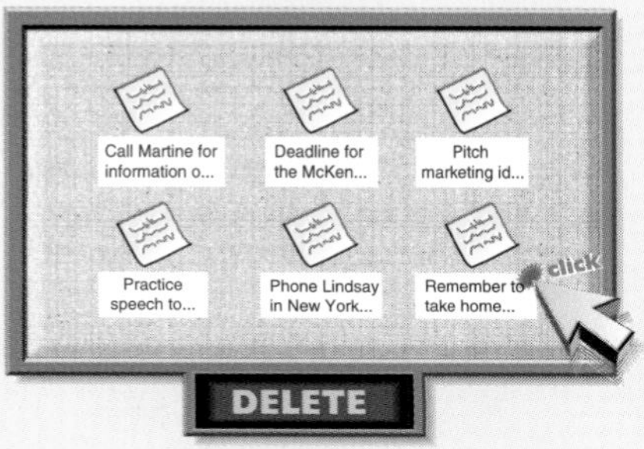

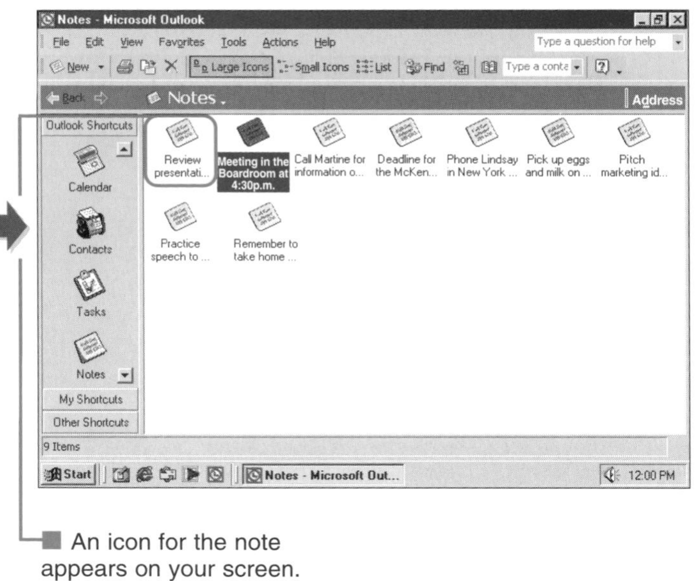

■ An icon for the note appears on your screen.

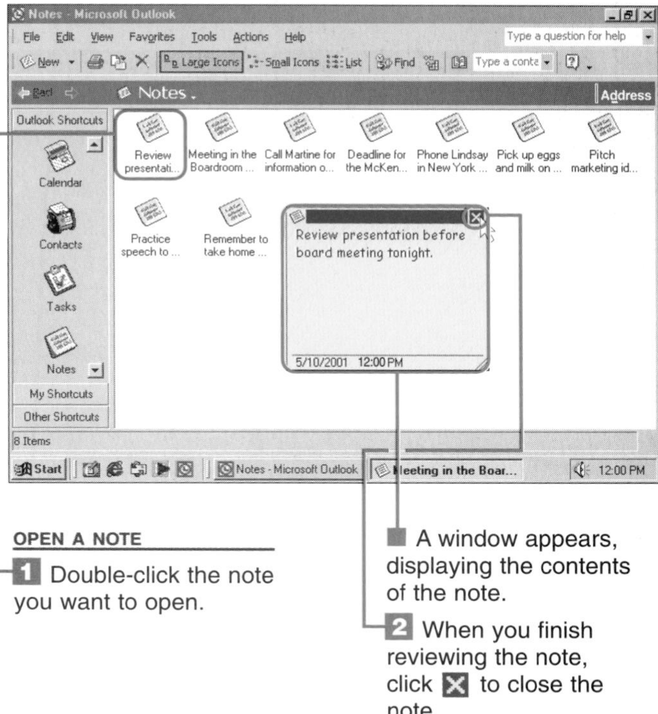

OPEN A NOTE

1 Double-click the note you want to open.

■ A window appears, displaying the contents of the note.

2 When you finish reviewing the note, click ☒ to close the note.

USING DELETED ITEMS

The Deleted Items folder stores items you have deleted in Outlook. You can recover an item you accidentally deleted.

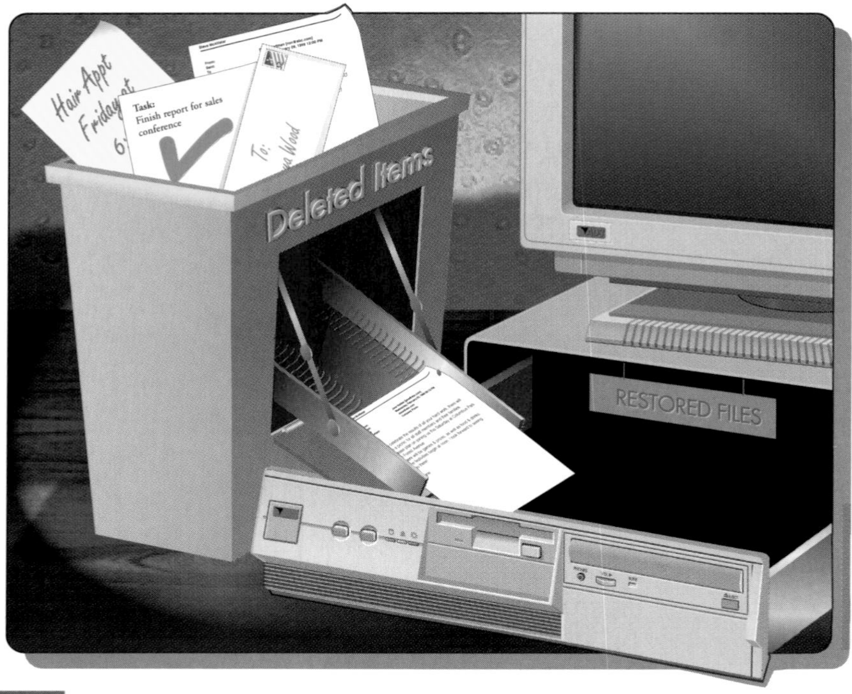

You can also empty the Deleted Items folder to permanently remove all the items from the folder.

You should regularly empty the folder to save space on your computer.

USING DELETED ITEMS

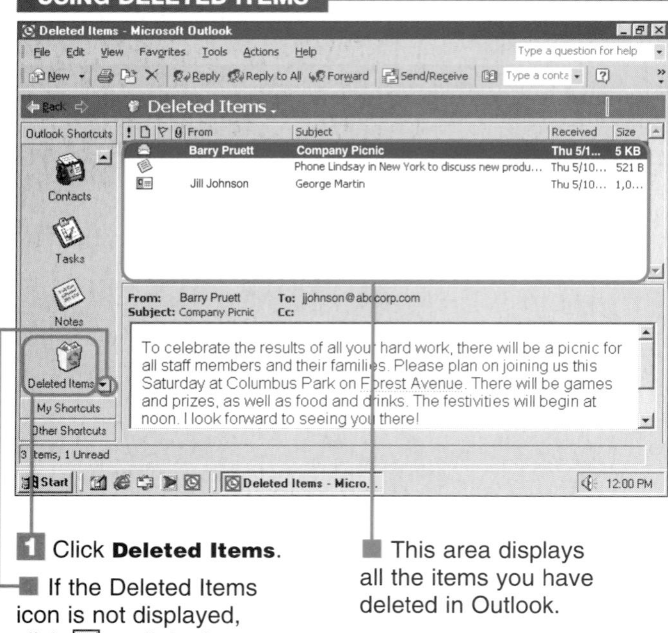

1 Click **Deleted Items**.

■ If the Deleted Items icon is not displayed, click ▼ until the icon appears.

■ This area displays all the items you have deleted in Outlook.

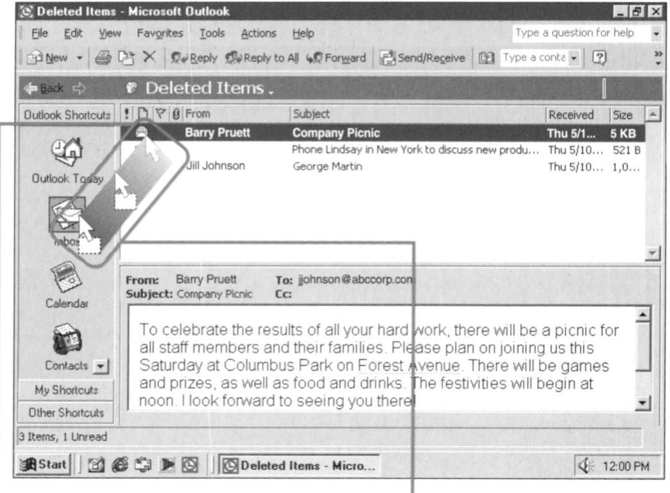

RECOVER A DELETED ITEM

1 Position the mouse over the item you want to recover.

2 Drag the item to a new location.

■ The item disappears from the list. Outlook places the item in the location you selected.

How can I identify the items in the Deleted Items folder?

A symbol appears beside each deleted item to help you identify the items.

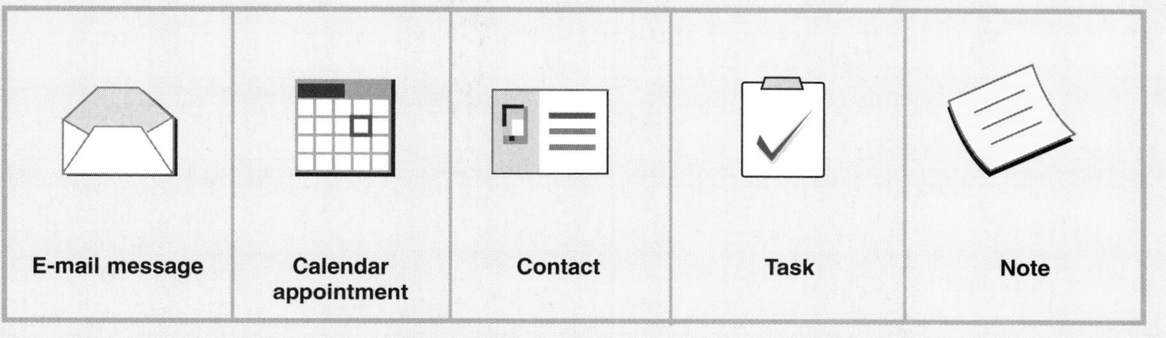

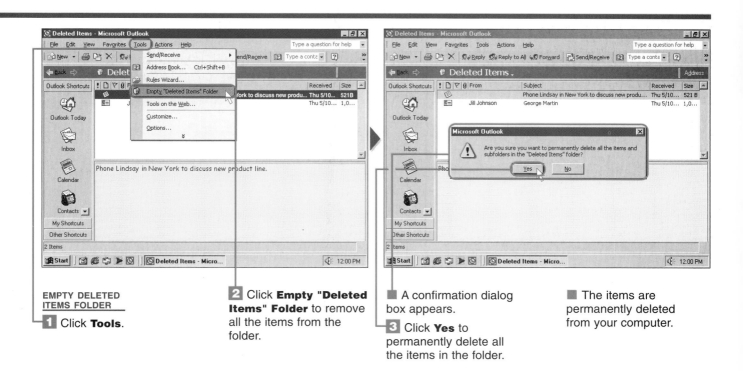

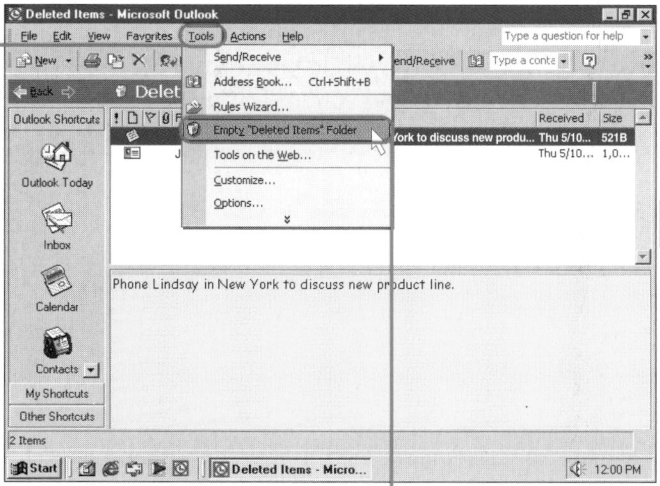

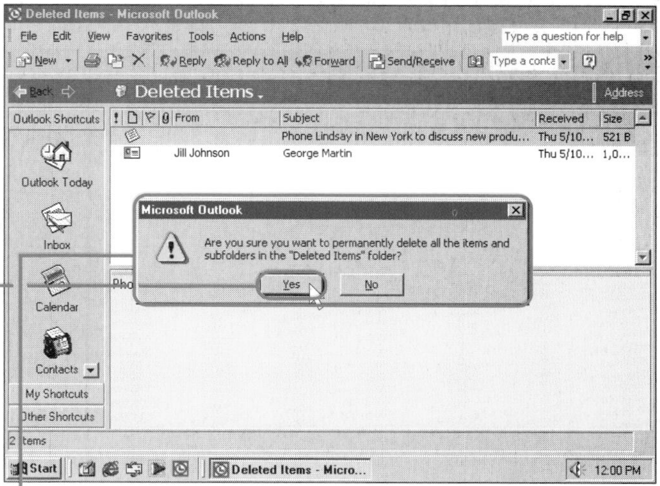

EMPTY DELETED ITEMS FOLDER

1 Click **Tools**.

2 Click **Empty "Deleted Items" Folder** to remove all the items from the folder.

■ A confirmation dialog box appears.

3 Click **Yes** to permanently delete all the items in the folder.

■ The items are permanently deleted from your computer.

Not Installed
Installed
Speech Recognition
Word
Excel
PowerPoint
Access
Outlook
Bass
Treble
On/Off

Using Speech Recognition
1 Using Speech Recognition
Pages 368-377
Bass Treble On/Off
Bass Treble On/Off

SET UP SPEECH RECOGNITION

Speech recognition allows you to use your voice to enter text and select commands in Office programs. Before you can use speech recognition, you must set up the feature on your computer.

Before you set up speech recognition, make sure your microphone and speakers are connected to your computer.

It will take you approximately 15 minutes to set up speech recognition on your computer.

SET UP SPEECH RECOGNITION

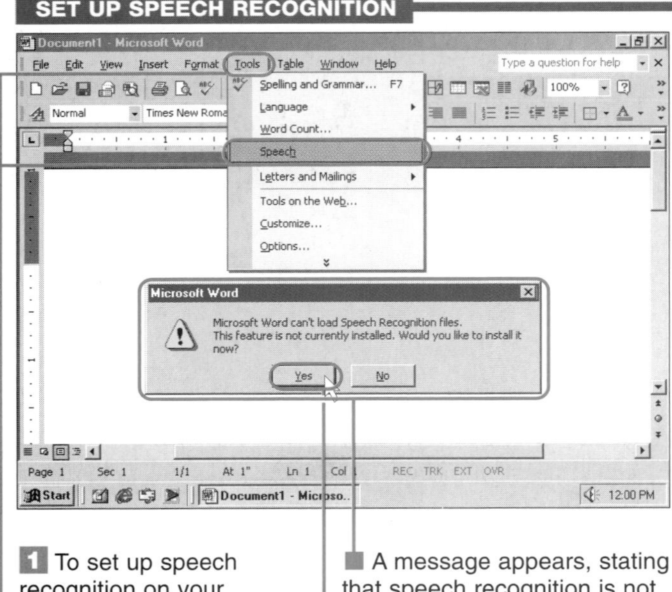

1 To set up speech recognition on your computer, start Microsoft Word. To start a program, see page 6.

2 Click **Tools**.

3 Click **Speech**.

■ A message appears, stating that speech recognition is not currently installed.

4 Insert the CD-ROM disc you used to install Office into your computer's CD-ROM drive.

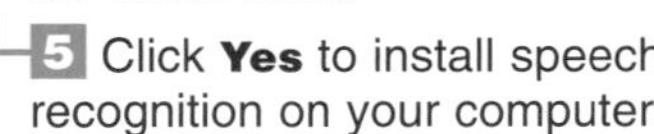

5 Click **Yes** to install speech recognition on your computer.

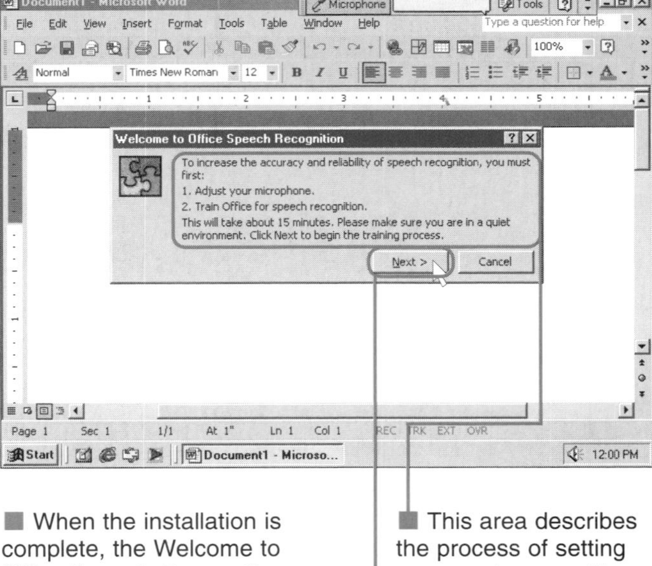

■ When the installation is complete, the Welcome to Office Speech Recognition dialog box appears.

■ This area describes the process of setting up speech recognition on your computer.

6 To begin setting up speech recognition, click **Next**.

Why does this dialog box appear when I try to set up speech recognition?

This dialog box appears if your computer does not meet the minimum hardware requirements needed to use speech recognition. You cannot set up speech recognition if your computer does not meet the minimum hardware requirements.

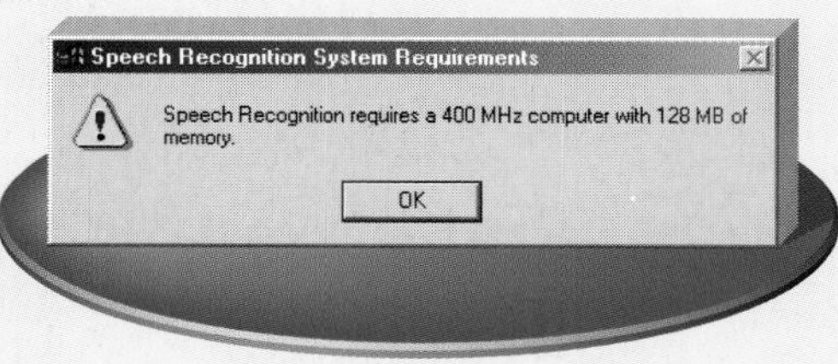

Do I need to set up speech recognition in each Office program?

No. Once you set up speech recognition in Word, it will be available in all of your Office programs.

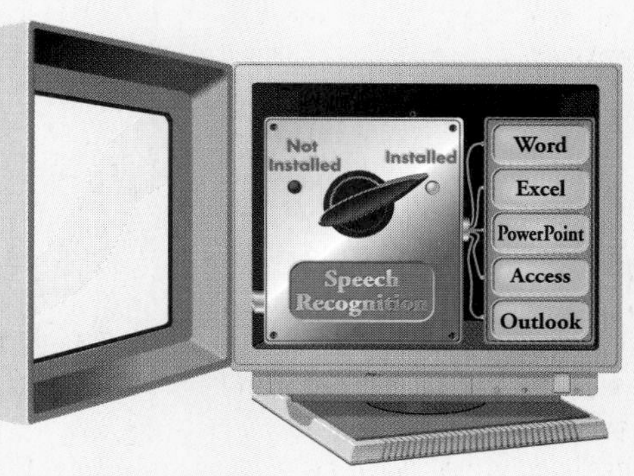

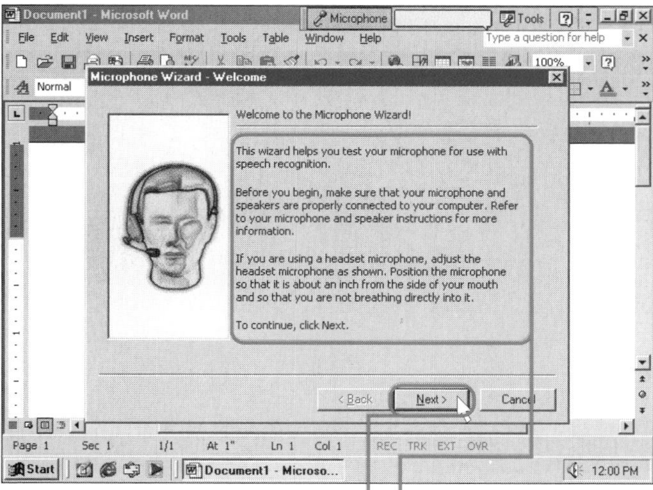

■ The Microphone Wizard appears. The wizard will help you adjust your microphone for use with speech recognition.

■ This area describes the wizard and provides instructions for adjusting a headset microphone.

7 To begin adjusting your microphone, click **Next**.

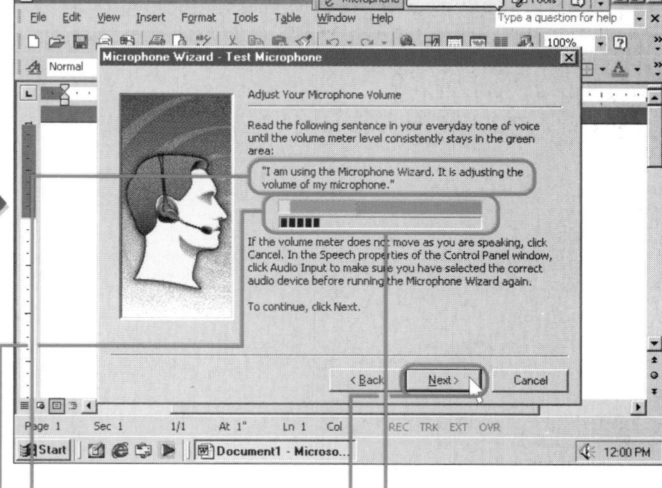

8 Read the text displayed in this area aloud to adjust the volume of your microphone.

■ This area displays a volume meter. As you read the text aloud, the volume meter indicates the volume of the microphone.

9 Repeat step 8 until the volume level of the microphone consistently appears in the green area of the volume meter.

10 Click **Next** to continue.

CONTINUED

SET UP SPEECH RECOGNITION

You can train speech recognition to recognize how you speak. The Microsoft Speech Recognition Training Wizard takes you step by step through the process of training speech recognition.

You can listen to a sample sentence to hear how you should speak during the training.

SET UP SPEECH RECOGNITION (CONTINUED)

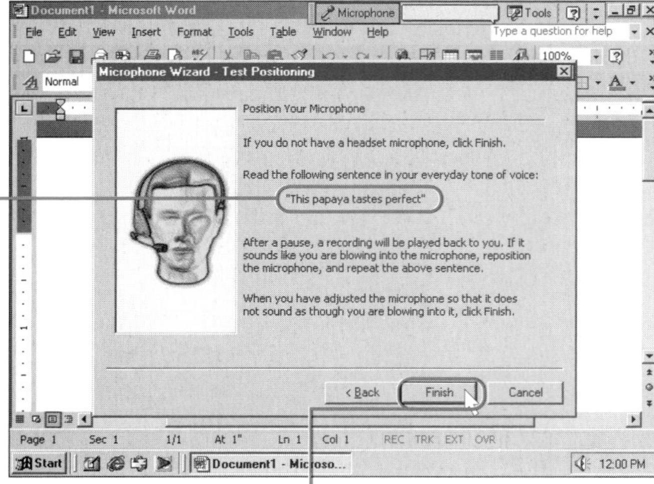

11 If you are using a headset microphone, read this text aloud to test the position of the microphone.

Note: If you are not using a headset microphone, skip to step 12.

■ After a few moments, your voice will be played back to you. If it sounds like you are blowing into the microphone, adjust the microphone's position and then repeat step **11**.

12 When you are finished positioning the microphone, click **Finish**.

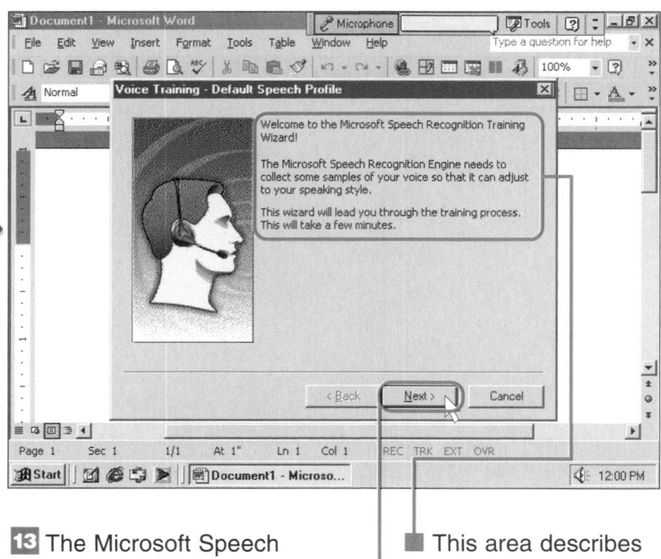

13 The Microsoft Speech Recognition Training Wizard appears. This wizard will help you train speech recognition to recognize how you speak.

■ This area describes the wizard.

14 To begin training speech recognition to recognize how you speak, click **Next**.

What type of microphone should I use with speech recognition?

You should use a headset microphone, since this type of microphone will remain in the correct position, even when you move your head. For best results, you should position the microphone approximately one inch from the side of your mouth so that you are not breathing directly into the microphone.

How should I speak during the training process?

You should speak in your everyday tone of voice, pronouncing words clearly and not pausing between words. You should also speak at a consistent speed.

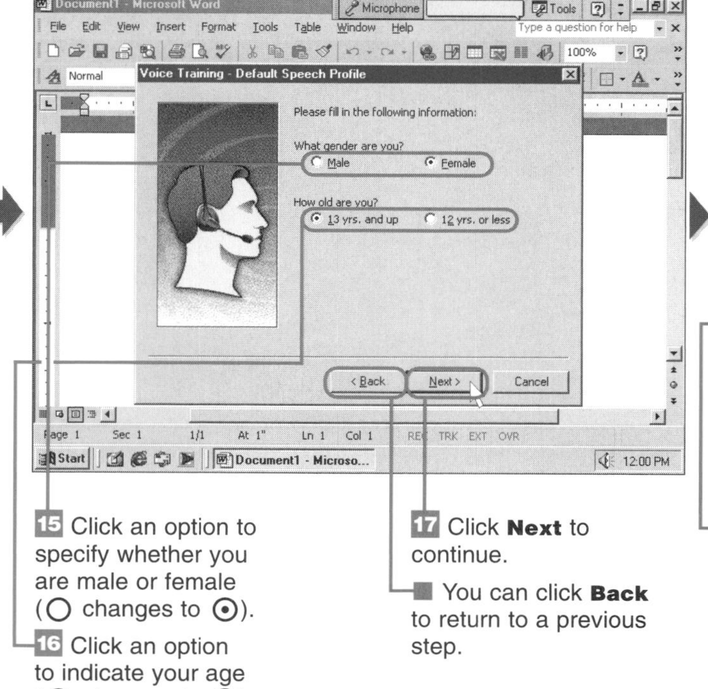

15 Click an option to specify whether you are male or female (○ changes to ⊙).

16 Click an option to indicate your age (○ changes to ⊙).

17 Click **Next** to continue.

■ You can click **Back** to return to a previous step.

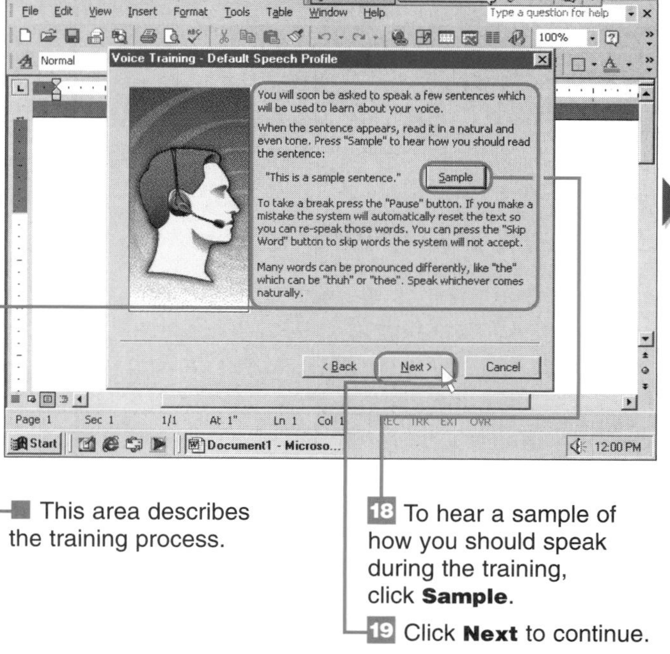

■ This area describes the training process.

18 To hear a sample of how you should speak during the training, click **Sample**.

19 Click **Next** to continue.

CONTINUED

The Microsoft Speech Recognition Training Wizard provides text you can read aloud to train speech recognition.

You should train speech recognition in a quiet area so that background noise does not interfere with the sound of your voice.

SET UP SPEECH RECOGNITION (CONTINUED)

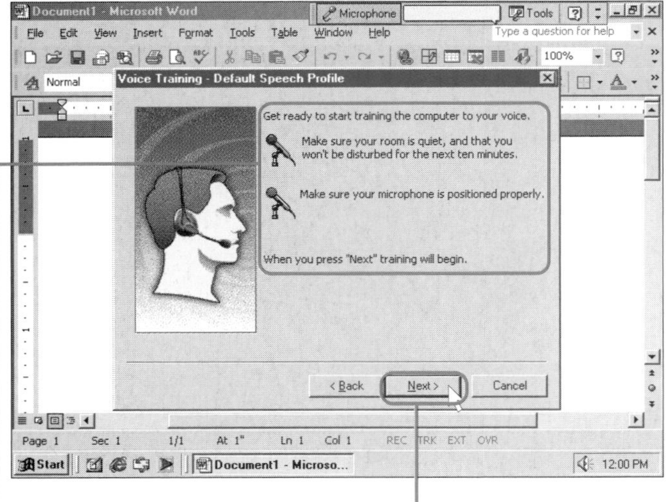

■ This area displays instructions about preparing for the training.

20 To begin the training, click **Next**.

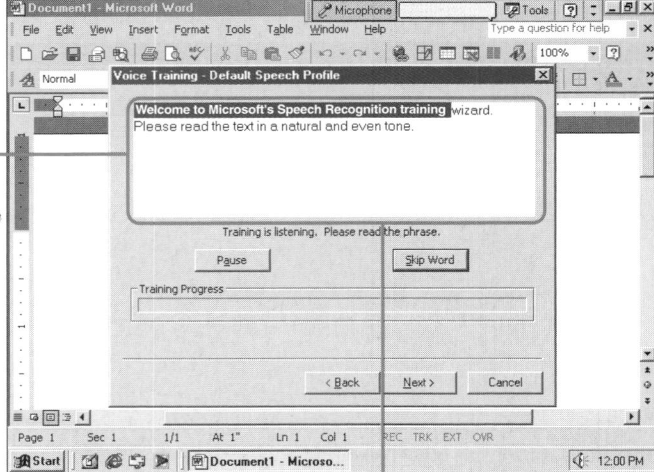

■ The wizard will display a series of screens containing sample text for you to read aloud.

21 Read the text displayed in this area of each screen aloud.

■ As you read aloud, the wizard highlights the words it recognizes.

■ If the wizard does not recognize a word, it stops highlighting text. If this happens, begin reading the text again, starting with the first word that is not highlighted.

I have repeated a word several times, but the wizard still does not recognize the word. What should I do?

If the wizard cannot recognize a word you say, you can click the **Skip Word** button to move on to the next word.

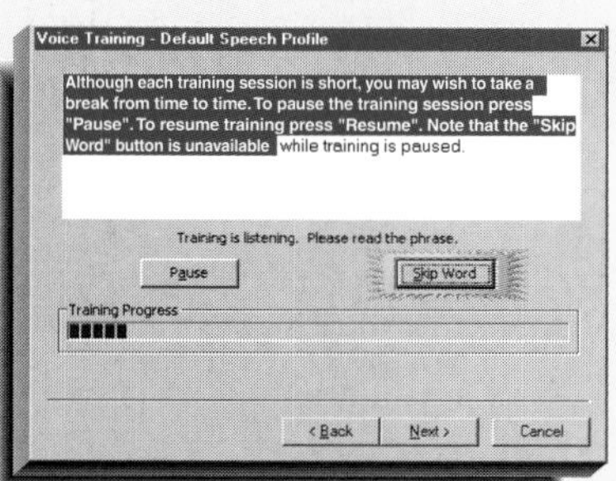

Can I perform more training?

The speech recognition feature provides additional training sessions you can perform to improve the accuracy of speech recognition.

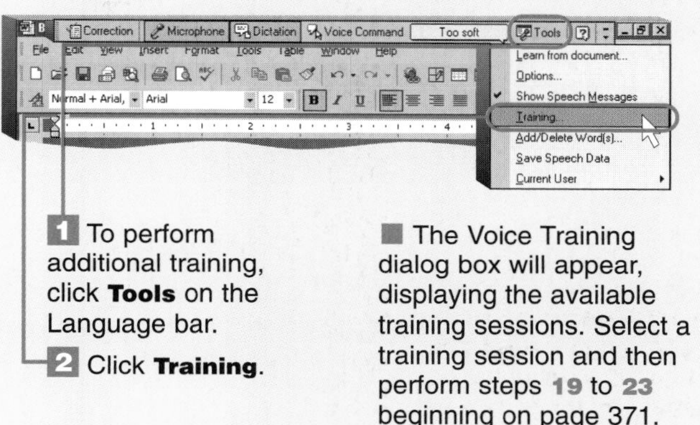

1 To perform additional training, click **Tools** on the Language bar.

2 Click **Training**.

■ The Voice Training dialog box will appear, displaying the available training sessions. Select a training session and then perform steps 19 to 23 beginning on page 371.

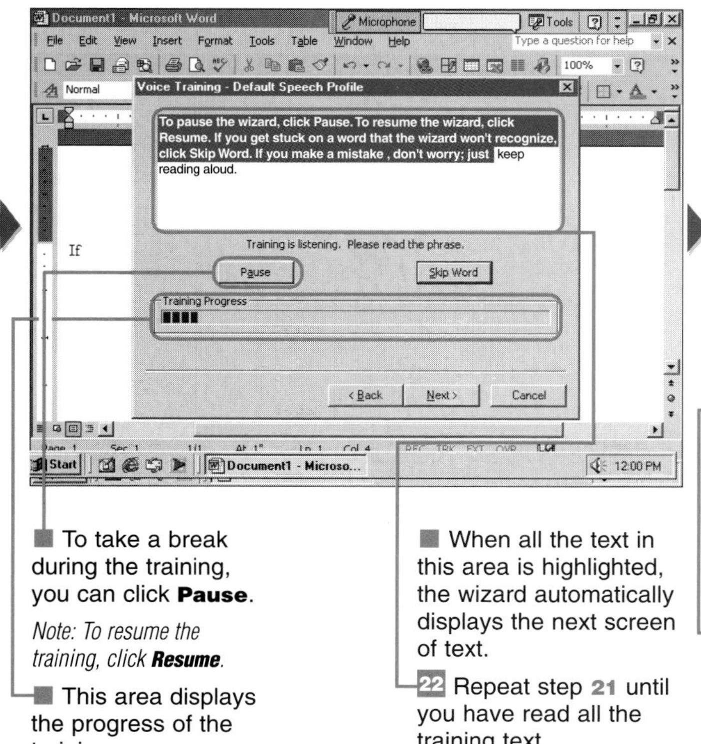

■ To take a break during the training, you can click **Pause**.

*Note: To resume the training, click **Resume**.*

■ This area displays the progress of the training.

■ When all the text in this area is highlighted, the wizard automatically displays the next screen of text.

22 Repeat step 21 until you have read all the training text.

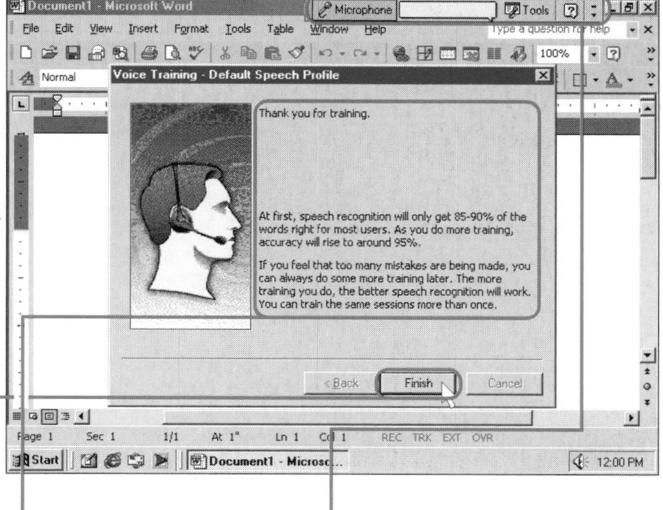

■ When the training is complete, this message appears.

23 Click **Finish** to close the Microsoft Speech Recognition Training Wizard.

■ This area displays the Language bar. The Language bar contains buttons you can use to perform tasks using speech recognition.

Note: A window will appear, displaying a video that introduces you to speech recognition. When the video is finished, you can click ☒ to close the window.

USING DICTATION MODE

Once you have set up speech recognition on your computer, you can use Dictation mode to enter text into an Office program using your voice.

Speech recognition is designed to be used along with your mouse and keyboard. You can use your voice to enter text into an Office program and then use your mouse and keyboard to edit the text you entered.

USING DICTATION MODE

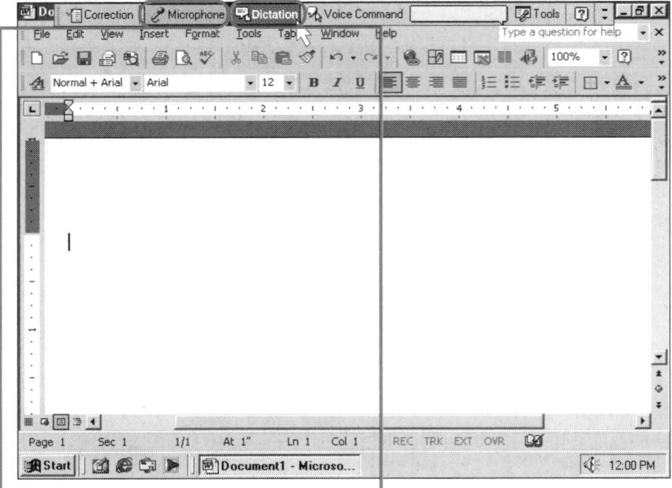

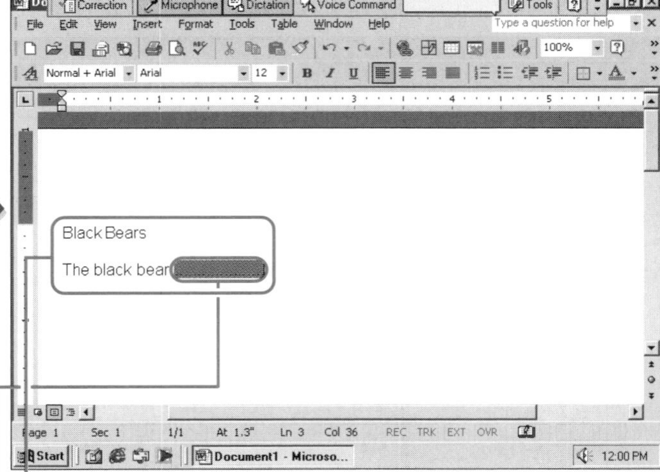

1 Start the Office program you want to enter text into using your voice. To start a program, see page 6.

2 If your microphone is turned off, click **Microphone** on the Language bar to turn the microphone on.

Note: When your microphone is turned on, the Dictation and Voice Command buttons appear on the Language bar.

3 Click **Dictation** to turn on Dictation mode.

4 Speak into your microphone to enter text into the Office program.

■ As you speak, a blue bar appears on the screen to indicate that the computer is processing your voice. You can continue to speak while the blue bar is displayed on the screen.

■ You should not use your mouse or keyboard while the blue bar is displayed on the screen.

What are some of the punctuation marks that I can enter using my voice?

To enter:	Say:
.	"Period"
,	"Comma"
:	"Colon"
;	"Semi-colon"
?	"Question mark"
!	"Exclamation point"
(	"Open parenthesis"
)	"Close parenthesis"
"	"Open quote"
"	"Close quote"
a new line	"New line"
a new paragraph	"New paragraph"

How should I speak when using speech recognition?

You should speak to your computer in your everyday tone of voice, pronouncing words clearly and not pausing between words. You should also speak at a consistent speed. If you speak too quickly or too slowly, the computer may not be able to recognize what you say.

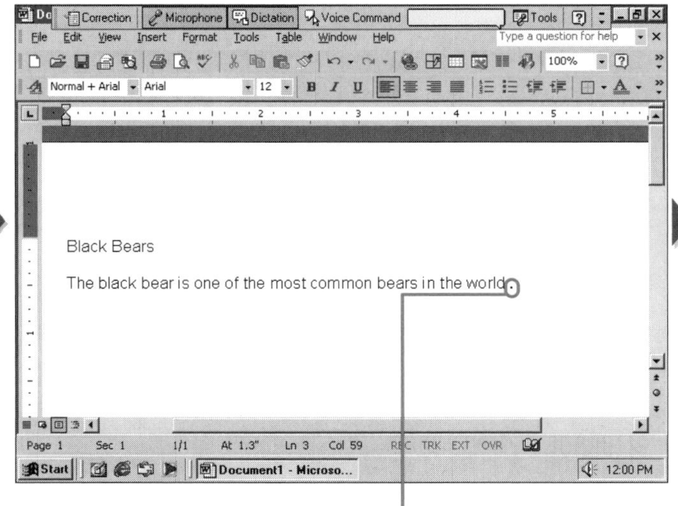

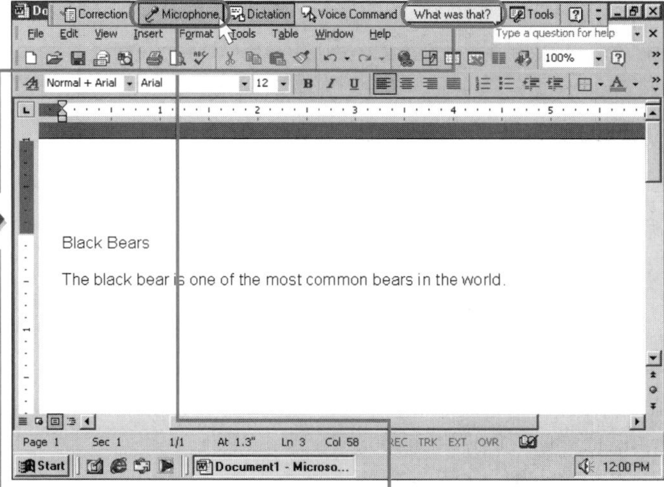

■ As the computer processes your voice, words appear on the screen.

5 To enter punctuation, say the name of the punctuation mark you want to enter.

Note: For a list of punctuation marks you can enter using your voice, see the top of this page.

■ As you enter text using your voice, this area may display one of the following messages to help you use Dictation mode.

Too soft - Speak louder

Too loud - Speak more quietly

Too fast - Speak more slowly

What was that? - Repeat your last words

6 When you finish entering text using your voice, click **Microphone** to turn your microphone off.

■ You can now edit the text you entered using your voice as you would edit any text.

USING VOICE COMMAND MODE

You can use Voice Command mode to select commands from menus and toolbars using your voice.

You can also use Voice Command mode to select options in dialog boxes.

USING VOICE COMMAND MODE

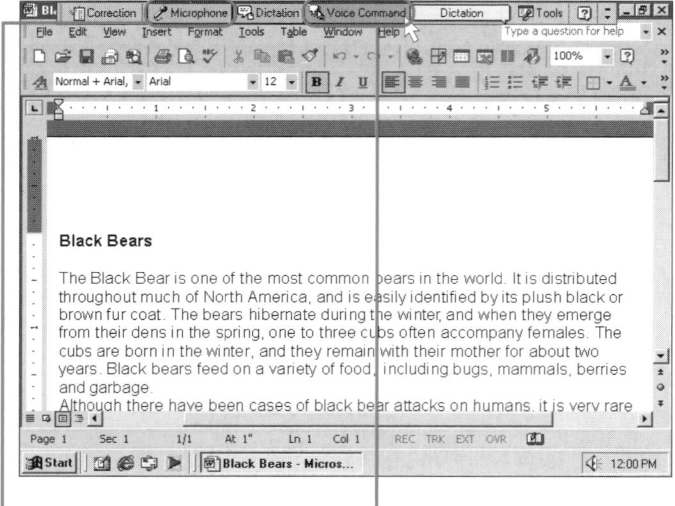

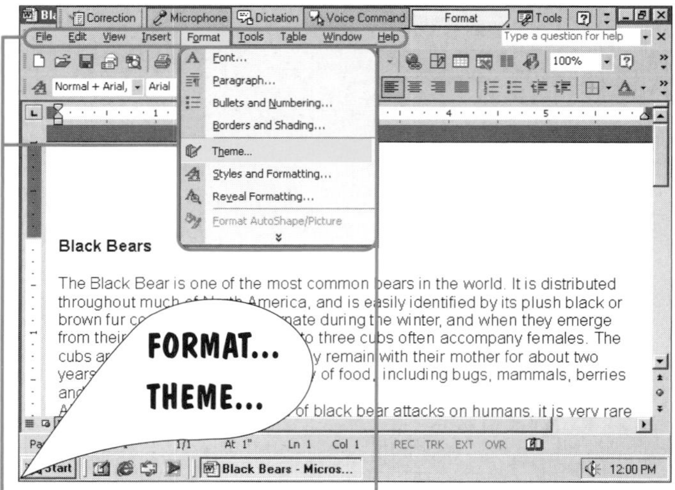

1 Start the Office program you want to enter commands into using your voice. To start a program, see page 6.

2 If your microphone is turned off, click **Microphone** on the Language bar to turn the microphone on.

Note: When your microphone is turned on, the Dictation and Voice Command buttons appear on the Language bar.

3 Click **Voice Command** to turn on Voice Command mode.

SELECT MENU COMMANDS

1 To select a command from a menu, say the name of the menu.

■ A short version of the menu appears, displaying the most commonly used commands.

Note: To expand the menu and display all the commands, say "expand."

2 To select a command from the menu, say the name of the command.

Can I use Voice Command mode to select an option in a task pane?

Yes. Task panes display links that allow you to perform common tasks. To select a link in a task pane using your voice, say the full name of the link. For more information on task panes, see page 12.

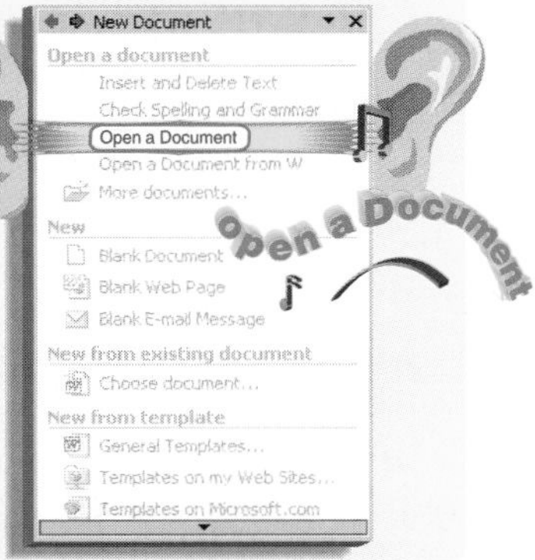

Can I use Voice Command mode to perform other tasks?

Yes. In addition to selecting commands, you can use Voice Command mode to perform the following tasks.

To:	Say:
Move up one line	"Up"
Move down one line	"Down"
Move left one character	"Left"
Move right one character	"Right"
Enter a tab	"Tab"
Enter a blank space	"Space"
Delete a character	"Backspace"

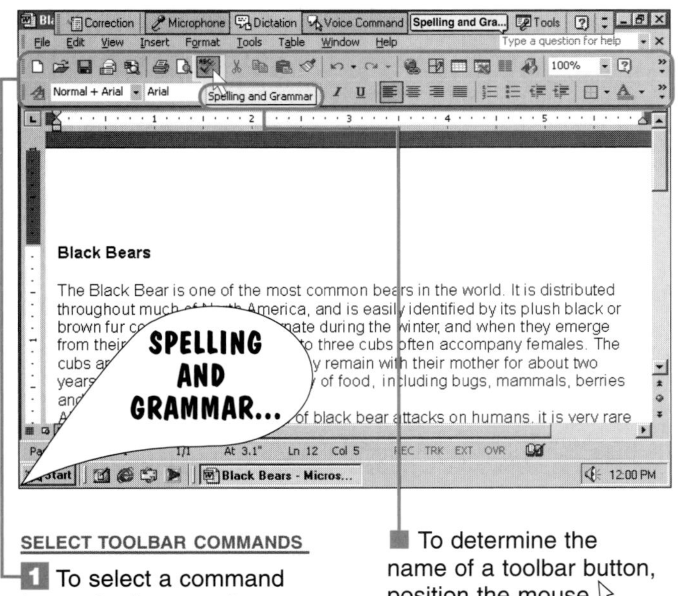

SELECT TOOLBAR COMMANDS

1 To select a command from a toolbar, say the name of the toolbar button.

■ To determine the name of a toolbar button, position the mouse over the button. After a few seconds, the name of the button appears in a yellow box.

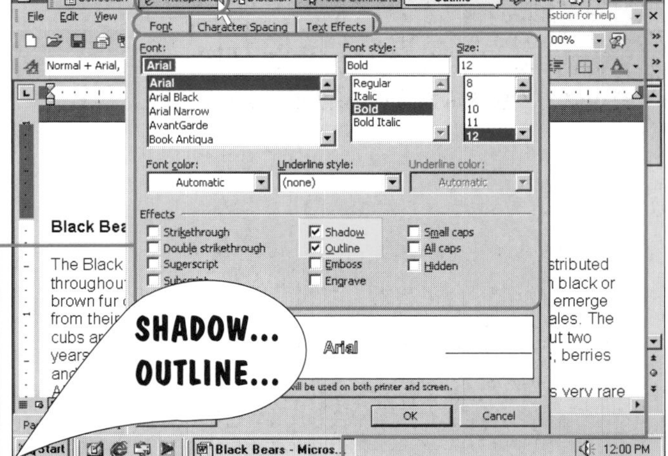

SELECT DIALOG BOX OPTIONS

■ A dialog box may appear when you select a menu or toolbar command.

1 To select an option in a dialog box, say the name of the option.

■ If the dialog box contains tabs, you can say the name of a tab to display the tab.

2 When you finish selecting commands using your voice, click **Microphone** to turn your microphone off.

Quarterly Review - Microsoft Internet Explorer
File Edit View Favorites Tools Help
Back Forward Stop Refresh Home Search Favorites History Mail Print
Address C:\WINDOWS\TEMP\Word\QuarterlyReview.htm
Go Links
ABC Incorporated
QUARTERLY REVIEW
Sales have risen to $140,000 for the first time in company history!
This is due to our new marketing plan and excellent customer relations.
We look forward to continuing our productivity throughout the year.
Revenue Chart
$150,000.00
$100,000.00
$50,000.00
$-
NET
REVENUE
January
February
March
PUSH
ABC Incorporated
QUARTERLY REVIEW
Sales have risen to $140,000 for the first time in company history! This is due to our new marketing plan and excellent customer relations. We look forward to continuing our productivity throughout the year.
Revenue Chart
$150,000.00
$100,000.00
$50,000.00
$-
NET
REVENUE
January

Microsoft Office and the Internet
1 Microsoft Office and the Internet
Pages 380-385

CREATE A HYPERLINK

You can create a hyperlink to connect a word or phrase in your file to another file on your computer, network, corporate intranet or the Internet.

An intranet is a small version of the Internet within a company or organization.

You can use the method shown below to create hyperlinks in Word, Excel and PowerPoint.

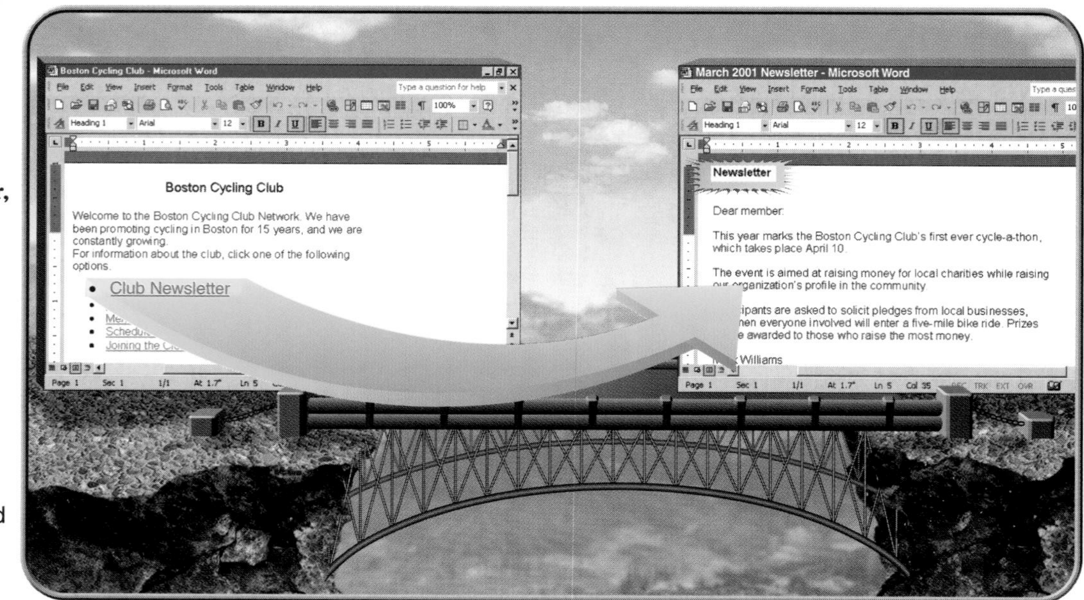

CREATE A HYPERLINK

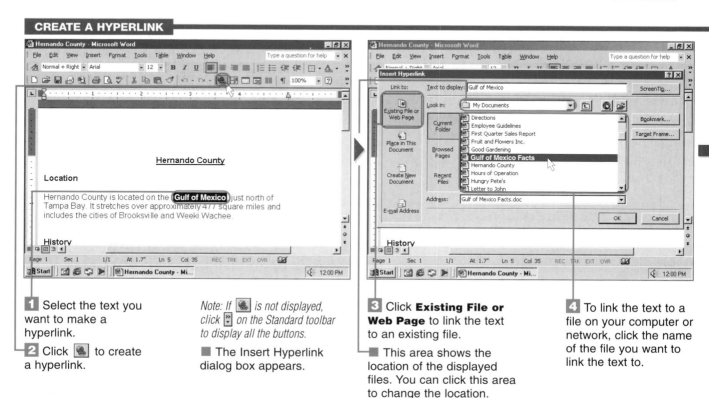

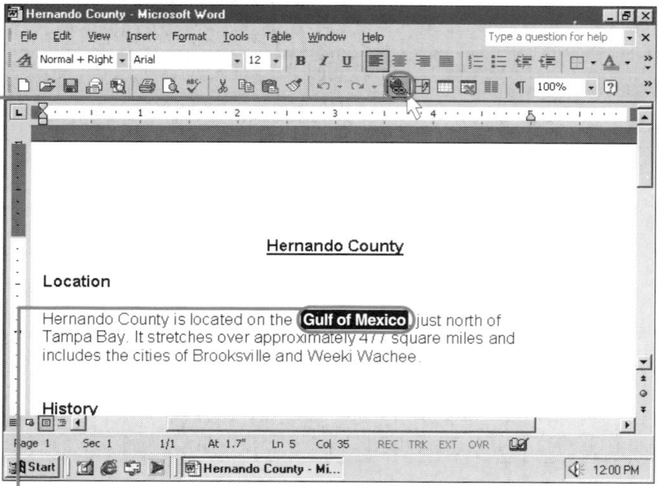

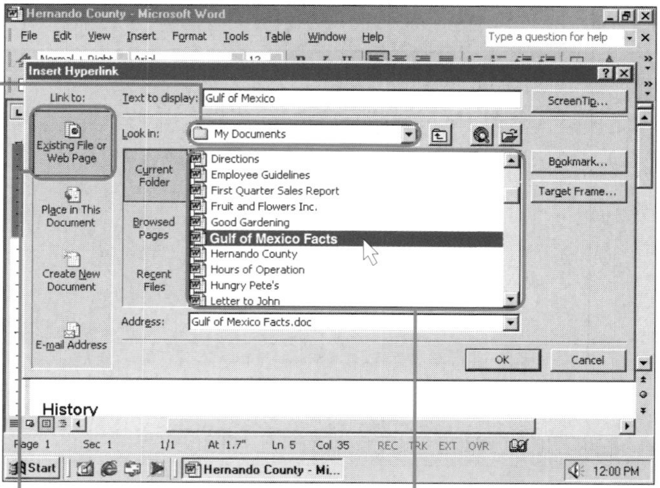

1 Select the text you want to make a hyperlink.

2 Click to create a hyperlink.

Note: If is not displayed, click on the Standard toolbar to display all the buttons.

■ The Insert Hyperlink dialog box appears.

3 Click **Existing File or Web Page** to link the text to an existing file.

■ This area shows the location of the displayed files. You can click this area to change the location.

4 To link the text to a file on your computer or network, click the name of the file you want to link the text to.

Can an Office program automatically create a hyperlink for me?

When you type the address of a file located on your network or the Internet, the Office program will automatically change the address to a hyperlink for you.

Why does nothing happen when I click a hyperlink on a PowerPoint slide?

If you click a hyperlink while viewing your presentation in the Normal or Slide Sorter view, the file or Web page connected to the hyperlink will not appear. You must display your presentation in the Slide Show view to display the file or Web page connected to a hyperlink. For information on displaying a presentation in the Slide Show view, see page 188.

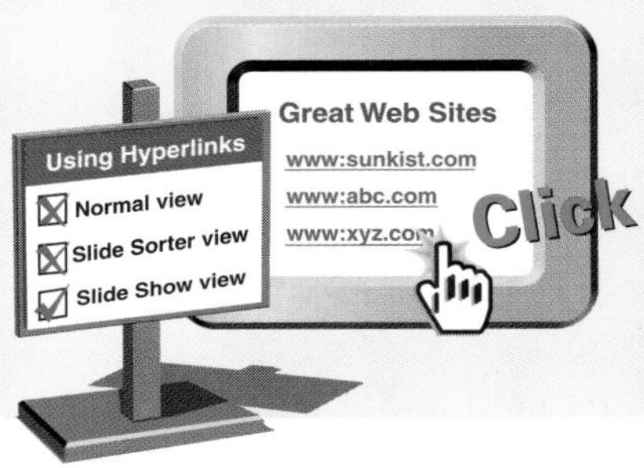

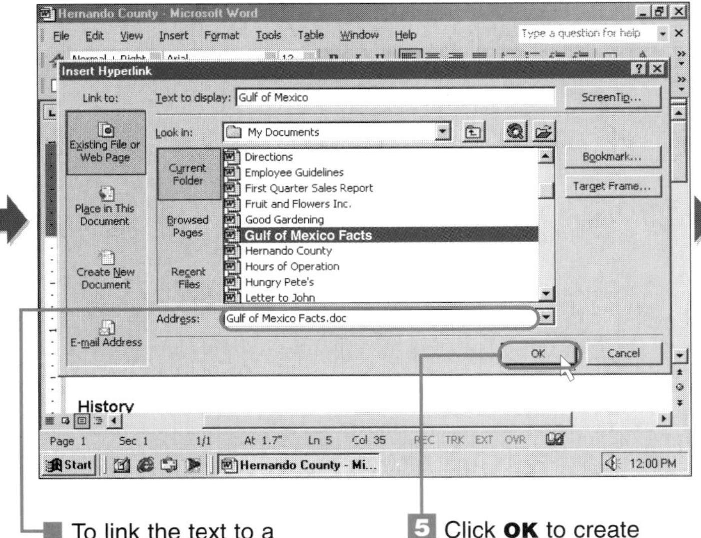

■ To link the text to a page on the Web, click this area and then type the address of the Web page.

5 Click **OK** to create the hyperlink.

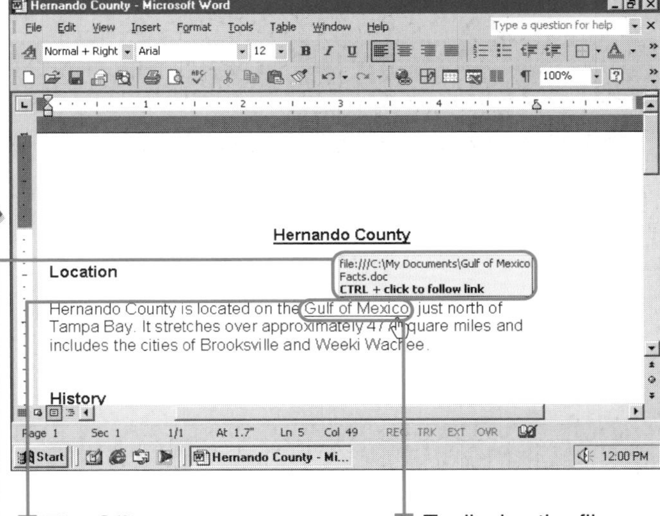

■ The Office program creates the hyperlink. Text hyperlinks appear underlined and in color.

■ When you position the mouse pointer over a hyperlink, a yellow box appears, indicating where the hyperlink will take you.

■ To display the file or Web page connected to the hyperlink, click the hyperlink.

Note: In Word, you must press and hold down the **Ctrl** *key before clicking the hyperlink.*

PREVIEW A FILE AS A WEB PAGE

You can preview how an Office file will look as a Web page. This allows you to see how the file will appear on the Internet or your company's intranet.

An intranet is a small version of the Internet within a company or organization.

You can use the method shown below to preview a file you created in Word, Excel or PowerPoint as a Web page.

PREVIEW A FILE AS A WEB PAGE

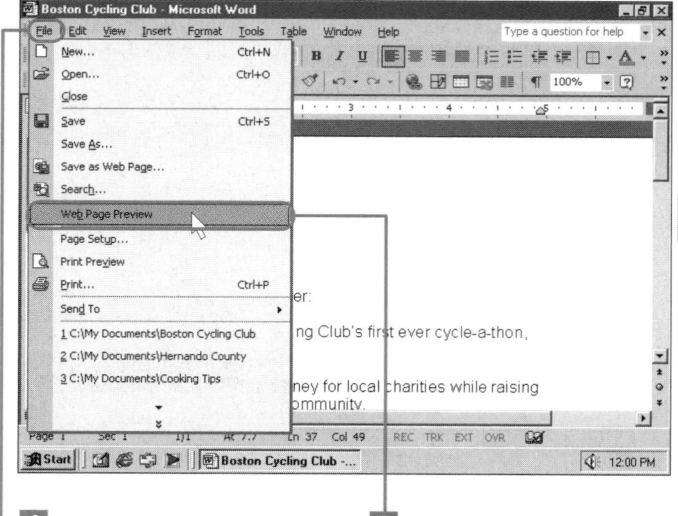

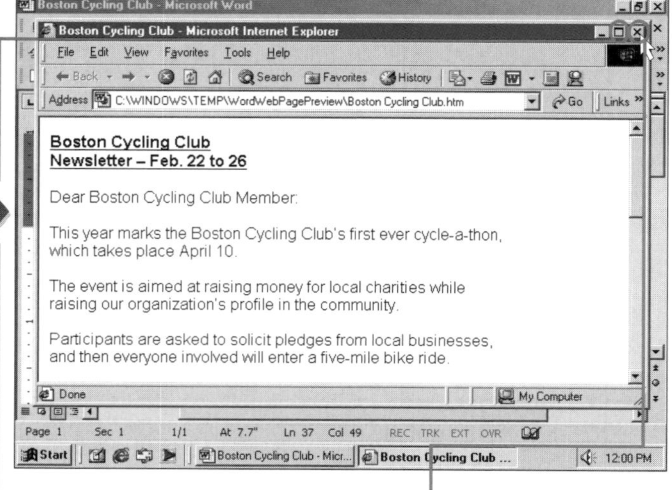

1 Display the file you want to preview as a Web page.

2 Click **File**.

3 Click **Web Page Preview** to preview your file as a Web page.

■ Your Web browser window opens, displaying the file as a Web page. In this example, a Word document is previewed as a Web page.

■ To maximize the Web browser window to fill your screen, click ☐.

4 When you finish reviewing the file as a Web page, click ☒ to close the Web browser.

Will my Web page look the same when displayed in different Web browsers?

No. Different Web browsers may display your Web page differently. There are many Web browsers used on the Web. The two most popular Web browsers are Microsoft Internet Explorer and Netscape Navigator.

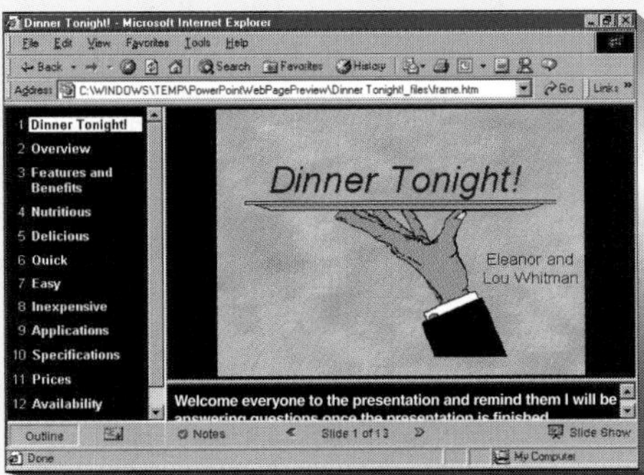

Microsoft Internet Explorer

Netscape Navigator

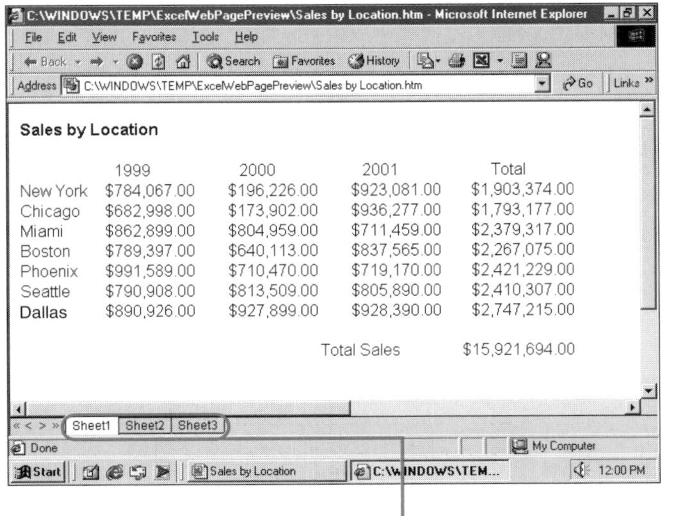

Sales by Location

	1999	2000	2001	Total
New York	$784,067.00	$196,226.00	$923,081.00	$1,903,374.00
Chicago	$682,998.00	$173,902.00	$936,277.00	$1,793,177.00
Miami	$862,899.00	$804,959.00	$711,459.00	$2,379,317.00
Boston	$789,397.00	$640,113.00	$837,565.00	$2,267,075.00
Phoenix	$991,589.00	$710,470.00	$719,170.00	$2,421,229.00
Seattle	$790,908.00	$813,509.00	$805,890.00	$2,410,307.00
Dallas	$890,926.00	$927,899.00	$928,390.00	$2,747,215.00
			Total Sales	$15,921,694.00

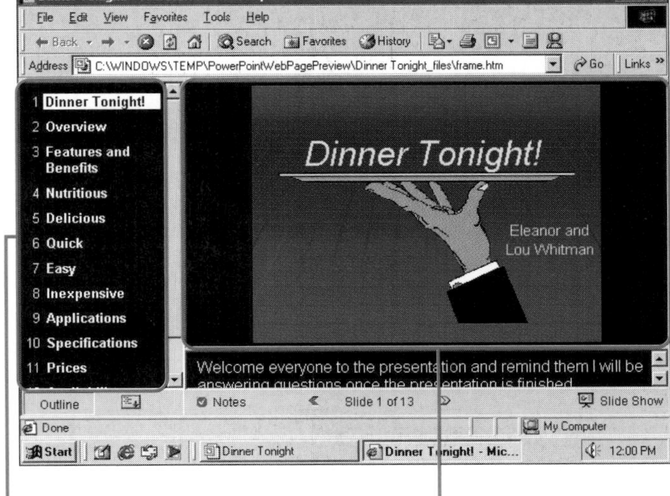

PREVIEW AN EXCEL WORKBOOK

■ When you preview an Excel workbook as a Web page, the gridlines that separate each cell do not appear.

■ If your workbook contains data in more than one worksheet, this area displays tabs for each worksheet. You can click a tab to display a different worksheet.

PREVIEW A POWERPOINT PRESENTATION

■ When you preview a PowerPoint presentation as a Web page, this area displays the title of each slide in your presentation. You can click a title to display a different slide.

■ This area displays the current slide.

SAVE A FILE AS A WEB PAGE

You can save an Office file as a Web page. This allows you to place the file on the Internet or your company's intranet.

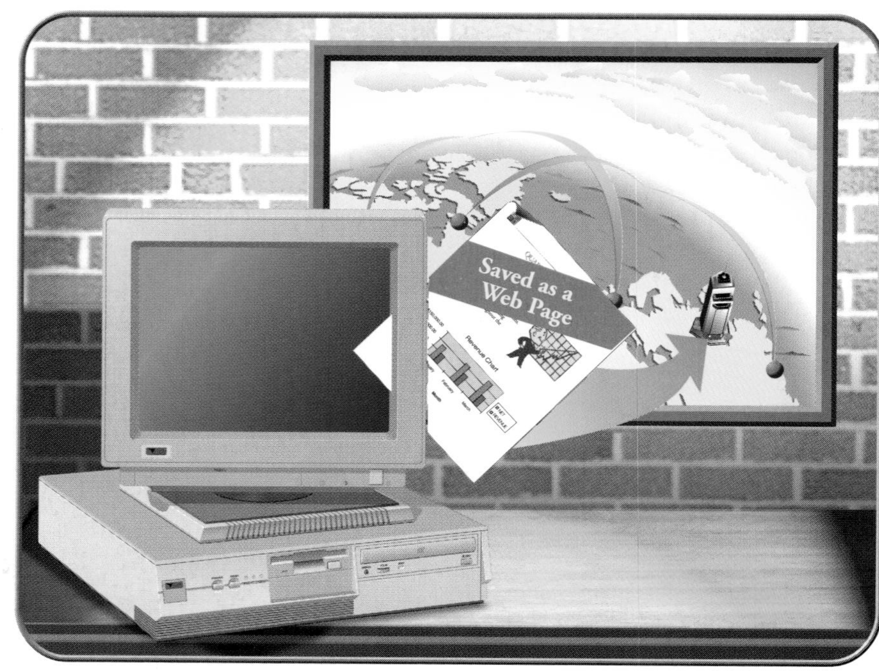

An intranet is a small version of the Internet within a company or organization.

You can use the method shown below to save a file you created in Word, Excel or PowerPoint as a Web page.

SAVE A FILE AS A WEB PAGE

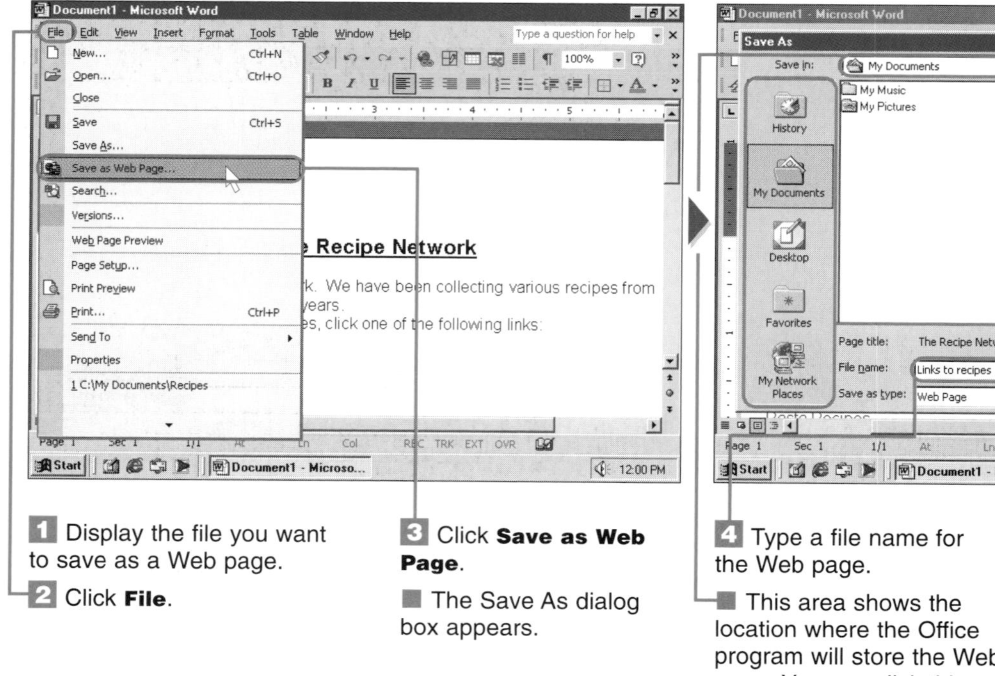

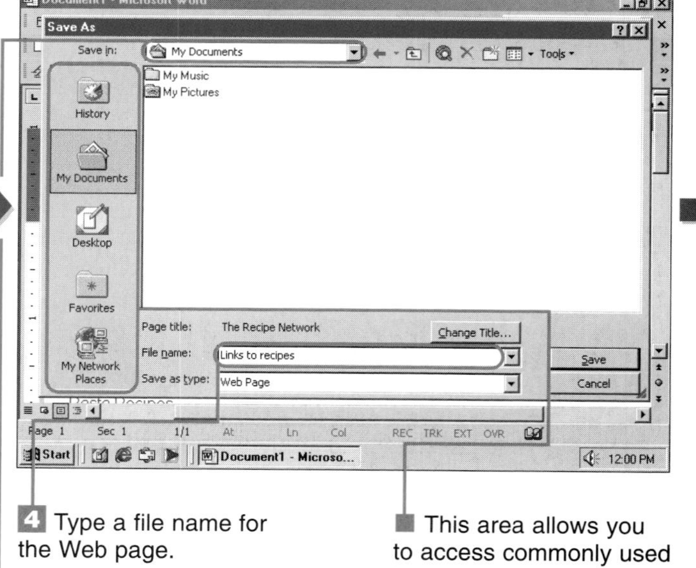

1 Display the file you want to save as a Web page.

2 Click **File**.

3 Click **Save as Web Page**.

■ The Save As dialog box appears.

4 Type a file name for the Web page.

■ This area shows the location where the Office program will store the Web page. You can click this area to change the location.

■ This area allows you to access commonly used locations. You can click a location to save the Web page in the location.

What is the difference between the file name and the title of a Web page?

The file name is the name you use to store the Web page on your computer. The title is the text that will appear at the top of the Web browser window when a person views your Web page.

How do I make my Web page available for other people to view?

After you save a file as a Web page, you can transfer the page to a computer that stores Web pages, called a Web server. Once the Web page is stored on a Web server, the page will be available for other people to view. For information on transferring a Web page to a Web server, contact your network administrator or Internet service provider.

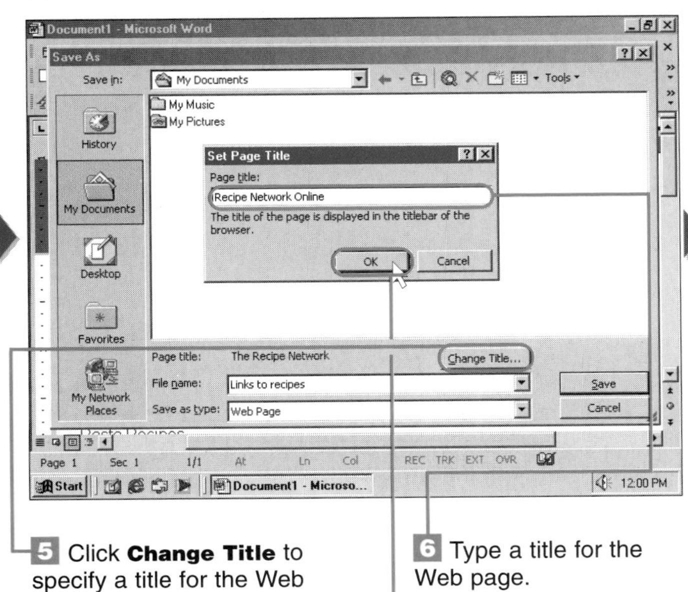

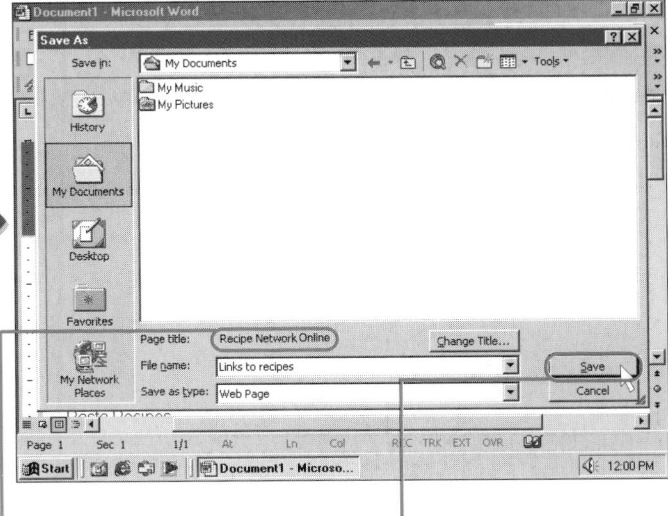

5 Click **Change Title** to specify a title for the Web page.

■ The Set Page Title dialog box appears.

Note: A default title may appear in the dialog box.

6 Type a title for the Web page.

7 Click **OK** to confirm the title.

■ This area displays the title you specified for the Web page.

8 Click **Save** to save the file as a Web page.

INDEX

Numbers & Symbols

A

B

C

E

G

H

I

N

O

Q

R

T

INDEX

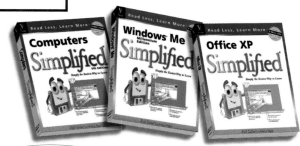

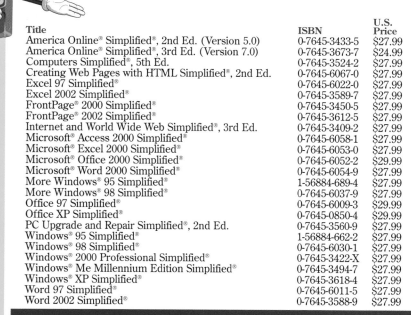

with these full-color Visual™ guides

The Fast and Easy Way to Learn

Discover how to use what you learn with "Teach Yourself" tips.

Title	ISBN	U.S. Price
Teach Yourself Access 97 VISUALLY™	0-7645-6026-3	$29.99
Teach Yourself FrontPage® 2000 VISUALLY™	0-7645-3451-3	$29.99
Teach Yourself HTML VISUALLY™	0-7645-3423-8	$29.99
Teach Yourself the Internet and World Wide Web VISUALLY™, 2nd Ed.	0-7645-3410-6	$29.99
Teach Yourself Microsoft® Access 2000 VISUALLY™	0-7645-6059-X	$29.99
Teach Yourself Microsoft® Excel 97 VISUALLY™	0-7645-6063-8	$29.99
Teach Yourself Microsoft® Excel 2000 VISUALLY™	0-7645-6056-5	$29.99
Teach Yourself Microsoft® Office 2000 VISUALLY™	0-7645-6051-4	$29.99
Teach Yourself Microsoft® PowerPoint® 97 VISUALLY™	0-7645-6062-X	$29.99
Teach Yourself Microsoft® PowerPoint® 2000 VISUALLY™	0-7645-6060-3	$29.99
Teach Yourself Microsoft® Word 2000 VISUALLY™	0-7645-6055-7	$29.99
Teach Yourself More Windows® 98 VISUALLY™	0-7645-6044-1	$29.99
Teach Yourself Office 97 VISUALLY™	0-7645-6018-2	$29.99
Teach Yourself Red Hat® Linux® VISUALLY™	0-7645-3430-0	$29.99
Teach Yourself VISUALLY™ Access 2002	0-7645-3591-9	$29.99
Teach Yourself VISUALLY™ Adobe® Acrobat® 5 PDF	0-7645-3667-2	$29.99
Teach Yourself VISUALLY™ Adobe® Photoshop® Elements	0-7645-3678-8	$29.99
Teach Yourself VISUALLY™ Adobe® Premiere® 6	0-7645-3664-8	$29.99
Teach Yourself VISUALLY™ Computers, 3rd Ed.	0-7645-3525-0	$29.99
Teach Yourself VISUALLY™ Digital Photography	0-7645-3565-X	$29.99
Teach Yourself VISUALLY™ Dreamweaver® 3	0-7645-3470-X	$29.99
Teach Yourself VISUALLY™ Dreamweaver® 4	0-7645-0851-2	$29.99
Teach Yourself VISUALLY™ E-commerce with FrontPage®	0-7645-3579-X	$29.99
Teach Yourself VISUALLY™ Excel 2002	0-7645-3594-3	$29.99
Teach Yourself VISUALLY™ Fireworks® 4	0-7645-3566-8	$29.99
Teach Yourself VISUALLY™ Flash™ 5	0-7645-3540-4	$29.99
Teach Yourself VISUALLY™ Flash™ MX	0-7645-3661-3	$29.99
Teach Yourself VISUALLY™ FrontPage® 2002	0-7645-3590-0	$29.99
Teach Yourself VISUALLY™ Illustrator® 10	0-7645-3654-0	$29.99
Teach Yourself VISUALLY™ iMac™	0-7645-3453-X	$29.99
Teach Yourself VISUALLY™ Investing Online	0-7645-3459-9	$29.99
Teach Yourself VISUALLY™ Macromedia® Web Collection	0-7645-3648-6	$29.99
Teach Yourself VISUALLY™ Networking, 2nd Ed.	0-7645-3534-X	$29.99
Teach Yourself VISUALLY™ Office XP	0-7645-0854-7	$29.99
Teach Yourself VISUALLY™ Photoshop® 6	0-7645-3513-7	$29.99
Teach Yourself VISUALLY™ Photoshop® 7	0-7645-3682-6	$29.99
Teach Yourself VISUALLY™ PowerPoint® 2002	0-7645-3660-5	$29.99
Teach Yourself VISUALLY™ Quicken® 2001	0-7645-3526-9	$29.99
Teach Yourself VISUALLY™ Windows® 2000 Server	0-7645-3428-9	$29.99
Teach Yourself VISUALLY™ Windows® Me Millennium Edition	0-7645-3495-5	$29.99
Teach Yourself VISUALLY™ Windows® XP	0-7645-3619-2	$29.99
Teach Yourself VISUALLY™ Word 2002	0-7645-3587-0	$29.99
Teach Yourself Windows® 95 VISUALLY™	0-7645-6001-8	$29.99
Teach Yourself Windows® 98 VISUALLY™	0-7645-6025-5	$29.99
Teach Yourself Windows® 2000 Professional VISUALLY™	0-7645-6040-9	$29.99
Teach Yourself Windows NT® 4 VISUALLY™	0-7645-6061-1	$29.99
Teach Yourself Word 97 VISUALLY™	0-7645-6032-8	$29.99

For visual learners who want to guide themselves through the basics of any technology topic. *Teach Yourself VISUALLY* **offers more expanded coverage than our best-selling** *Simplified* **series.**

The Visual™ series is available wherever books are sold, or call 1-800-762-2974. Outside the US, call 317-572-3993.